PSYCHOLOGY OF STEREOTYPES

PSYCHOLOGY OF EMOTIONS, MOTIVATIONS AND ACTIONS

Additional books in this series can be found on Nova's website under the Series tab.

Additional E-books in this series can be found on Nova's website under the E-books tab.

PSYCHOLOGY OF STEREOTYPES

ELEANOR L. SIMON
EDITOR

Nova Science Publishers, Inc.
New York

For permission to use material from this book please contact us:
Telephone 631-231-7269; Fax 631-231-8175
Web Site: http://www.novapublishers.com

NOTICE TO THE READER
The Publisher has taken reasonable care in the preparation of this book, but makes no expressed or implied warranty of any kind and assumes no responsibility for any errors or omissions. No liability is assumed for incidental or consequential damages in connection with or arising out of information contained in this book. The Publisher shall not be liable for any special, consequential, or exemplary damages resulting, in whole or in part, from the readers' use of, or reliance upon, this material. Any parts of this book based on government reports are so indicated and copyright is claimed for those parts to the extent applicable to compilations of such works.

Independent verification should be sought for any data, advice or recommendations contained in this book. In addition, no responsibility is assumed by the publisher for any injury and/or damage to persons or property arising from any methods, products, instructions, ideas or otherwise contained in this publication.

This publication is designed to provide accurate and authoritative information with regard to the subject matter covered herein. It is sold with the clear understanding that the Publisher is not engaged in rendering legal or any other professional services. If legal or any other expert assistance is required, the services of a competent person should be sought. FROM A DECLARATION OF PARTICIPANTS JOINTLY ADOPTED BY A COMMITTEE OF THE AMERICAN BAR ASSOCIATION AND A COMMITTEE OF PUBLISHERS.

Additional color graphics may be available in the e-book version of this book.

LIBRARY OF CONGRESS CATALOGING-IN-PUBLICATION DATA
Psychology of stereotypes / editor, Eleanor L. Simon.
p. cm.
Includes index.
ISBN 978-1-61761-463-7 (hbk.)
1. Stereotypes (Social psychology) I. Simon, Eleanor L.
BF323.S63P797 2010
303.3'85--dc22
2010029856

Published by Nova Science Publishers, Inc. † New York

CONTENTS

PREFACE

A stereotype is a commonly held public belief about specific social groups or types of individuals. This book presents current research in the study of stereotypes, including speech pathologists stereotyping stutterers; stereotype formation in children; the social neuroscience research applied to the study of stereotypes; Western societies' ageism stereotyping in the workforce; gender relationship portrayal in sport advertisements perpetuate sexist stereotyping; the psychological implications of stereotyping American Indians through the use of native-themed mascots, nicknames and logos; as well as when stereotypes become life-threatening.

Chapter 1 - Stuttering, a disorder of communication that disrupts the smooth, forward flow of speech, is often perceived negatively by fluent speakers. This chapter begins with a review of fluent speakers' attitudes toward stuttering and their perceptions of the effects of the disorder on the lives of people who stutter (PWS). A qualitative study is then presented which examines fluent speakers' beliefs about the ways in which PWS and fluent speakers may help each other to communicate more effectively. The results of this study suggest that while fluent speakers generally believe that they should treat PWS with patience and respect, there is some confusion regarding the ways in which these positive attitudes should manifest themselves as active behaviors. In addition, fluent speakers believe that PWS can facilitate communication by engaging in behaviors that reduce or eliminate stuttering. Many of these behaviors have been reported in the stuttering literature as adversely affecting the successful management of stuttering by PWS. The authors conclude the chapter with a discussion of how PWS may experience unintentional prejudice or discrimination from fluent speakers and how the public's perceptions may be altered to alleviate negative attitudes toward stuttering and individuals who stutter.

Chapter 2 - Why are some groups better off than others? Why are women more likely to take care of the children? How come Blacks generally achieve less educationally and economically? Stereotypes provide answers to these kinds of questions, albeit imperfectly, and help us provide meaning to the social world around us. Early stereotype researchers suggested that stereotypes help people explain and rationalize the position of groups in society (Lippman, 1922). While the influence of this observation has waxed and waned over the years, the explanatory power of stereotypes continues to be an important function of social stereotypes. The current chapter reviews research examining the role of stereotypes as explanatory and rationalization agents and the impact of stereotypes on intergroup behavior. The authors suggest that stereotypes serve explanatory and attributional functions at three interrelated levels of analysis: (a) individual level, wherein stereotypes are analyzed in terms of the attributional dimensions they imply (locus, stability, controllability); (b) intragroup level, in which stereotypes define and explain by combining stereotypic traits on dimensions of warmth and competence, which in turn predict unique patterns of emotions and behaviors; and (c) intergroup level, in which stereotypes explain the social order by providing compensatory or causally relevant traits in reference to other relevant groups. The resulting attributional signature of stereotypes influences attitudes and behaviors.

Chapter 3 - *Purpose.* Using an adaptation of the *Experimental Edition of the Public Opinion Survey of Human Attributes* (*POSHA-E*), investigators sought to compare public attitudes toward cluttering with those toward stuttering in four country samples, each in a different language. The *POSHA-E* was developed to measure public attitudes of stuttering but was modified to provide written definitions of cluttering and stuttering. *Method.* Convenience samples of 60 to 90 adult respondents from Turkey, Bulgaria, Russia, and the USA (302 total) rated *POSHA-E* items on 1-9 scales for cluttering and stuttering after reading the definitions. *Results.* Public attitudes toward cluttering and stuttering were similar for all respondents combined, but significant differences occurred. Attitude differences from country-to-country were greater than differences for cluttering versus stuttering. *Conclusions.* Positive and negative attitudes toward cluttering appear to be similar to those toward stuttering, and a cluttering stereotype appears likely.

Chapter 4 - This chapter explores the formation of stereotypes in children, particularly negative stereotypes that children hold about others. Theoretical views about stereotype formation in children are presented, and evidence from developmental studies on racism and ageism is summarized. Empirical research is also provided in an attempt to address unanswered questions about negative stereotype formation in children. Commonalities in the development of stereotypes will be drawn, with implications given about the course of stereotype development, and how children's reliance on stereotypes can be lessened.

Chapter 5 - The present chapter identifies, assesses, and examines the correlates of a previously understudied expression of contemporary prejudice— *Bayesian racism*, the belief that it is rational to discriminate against individuals based on stereotypes about their racial group. Individual differences in Bayesian racism are strongly related to intergroup prejudice and *negatively* correlated with indices of reliance on probabilities and logical thinking. Moreover, individuals who endorse Bayesian racism are unwilling to rely on base rates unfavorable to a high-status ingroup (i.e., Ivy League students). We relate the concept of Bayesian racism to existing theories of intergroup prejudice and outline future directions for research on the underpinnings of such beliefs.

Chapter 6 - According to a social cognitive perspective, stereotypes have been defined as cognitive structures that contain the perceiver's knowledge, beliefs, and expectations about social groups (Hamilton & Trolier, 1986). Perceivers regularly rely on stereotypes to simplify the complex social environment and quickly make sense of the social world. Because of the importance and pervasiveness of stereotypes in everyday life, these phenomena have been at the top of the interests of social psychological research. Traditionally, the nature and functions of stereotypes have been primarily investigated by using self-report measures (i.e., questionnaires) and more cognitive measures (mainly based on response latencies and accuracy) in order to infer the underlying cognitive mechanisms. However, responses in computerized tasks represent the final outcome of a large number of intervening cognitive processes, and variations in the response latencies may not often be attributed to a single specific process. Recently, the emergence of neuroscience has provided social psychology with new methods that can override this limitation. In particular, the event-related brain potential (ERP) technique can provide a direct, on line, continuous measure of processing between a stimulus and a response, giving direct access to the various stages of information processing between perception and behavior (Luck, 2005).

The main goal of this chapter is to introduce readers to recent social neuroscience research that has applied the ERP approach to the study of stereotypes and to show the major advances that it has produced in relation with the existing theories. We will first provide a brief overview of the recording, theory, and interpretation of the ERPs. Then, we will review studies that have used ERPs as useful tools to further investigate various aspects related to stereotyping:a) stereotype violation and confirmation; b) the influence of stereotype activation on behavioral processes, with specific attention given to the mechanisms involved in self-regulation; c) individual and situational differences in self-regulatory processes linked to the expression of stereotypes. In the chapter we will try to highlight how the integration of different methods, theories, and levels of analysis from both neuroscience and social psychology (i.e., the social neuroscience approach) can greatly facilitate a most comprehensive understanding of different important aspects of the human social mind.

Chapter 7 - Due to population ageing, Western societies' future economic growth may have to rely on the capacity of older workers in the labour market(Ilmainen, 2009). However, research suggests that stereotyping, age discrimination and negative manager attitudes may lead to early retirement and workforce losses(Furunes & Mykletun, 2007, 2010). Previous research indicates that there exist several stereotypes of how workers' capabilities change with age. To our knowledge this study is the first to profile managers' perceptions of age-related changes of the workforce and how these perceptions relate to both prevailing stereotypes of ageing workers and also to research outcomes describing older workers' adaption to the workplace. Whereas previous studies on stereotypes of older workers show an extensive list of negative characteristics, this study shows that managers perceive ageing as contributing to increased managerial and interpersonal skills, creative problem solving capacities, and work moral. On the negative side, age contributes to impaired learning capacities and basic functions. The findings of this study are closer to results of extensive research on older workers' capabilities and only partially in line with prevailing stereotypes of older workers. It is likely that managers working with older workers will develop conceptualisations of this part of the workforce that are closer to the characteristics demonstrated by research on actual behaviour, hence prevailing stereotypes of these workers may not be so general and persistent as argued by extant research.

Chapter 8 - The advertisementsof sportsare far from being able to reflect the changing realities of sports or physical activities in a country such as France. The purpose is to test the proposition that the gender relationships portrayed in specific sport advertisements perpetuate traditional and sexist stereotypes, are far from egalitarian shared social representations, and far from egalitarian social and professional activities.

Chapter 9 - The use of American Indian culture and imagery as mascots, nicknames, and logos in sport is a common societal practice that has been met with opposition from psychological research and from those interested in social justice and advocacy. Native-themed mascots, nicknames, and logos are considered harmful to American Indian communities because they misuse cultural symbols and sacred practices (e.g., eagle feathers, drums), perpetuate stereotypes of American Indians (e.g., noble savage, bloodthirsty savage, a historic race that only exists in past-tense status), and deny American Indians control over societal definitions of themselves. Additionally, this practice creates a racially hostile educational environment, and an estimated 115 organizations (e.g., American Psychological Association, American Counseling Association, Society of Indian Psychologists, National Association for the Advancement of Colored People) have produced resolutions calling for the immediate retirement of Native-themed mascots, nicknames, and logos. Because American Indians do not have control of these images, this process of racialized mascotery allows mainstream America to stereotype, undermine, and appropriate American Indian culture while systematically teaching the ideology of White supremacy. This manuscript describes ways that these stereotypic representations affect the psychological functioning of American Indians, and how this practice is harmful to both American Indian communities and to members of the mainstream culture. In sum, this manuscript provides an overview of psychological research and theory, discusses educational interventions and legislation aimed at curtailing this practice, and provides perspectives for the reader to have a greater understanding of the hegemonic and deleterious nature of racialized mascotery.

Chapter 10 – The authors examine the role of human motivation on stereotyping. People are motivated to carve the world into comprehensible segments (i.e., engage in categorization) that allow them to predict characteristics of new things or people. Categorization is a basic cognitive process that helps us structure our mental world to represent the physical world and relies on the similarity of unknown objects or people to previously created and stored categories. Objects can be grouped based on characteristics (e.g., red objects) or relational information (e.g., student). Our ability to classify new objects or people into known categories allows us to infer unknown features or behaviors and provides us with a known set of guidelines to use during interactions. For example, knowing someone is a student may lead us to ask about the individual's current classes. With objects, imperfect classification could lead to errors in prediction and interactions. Similarly, human stereotypes develop from this fundamental motivational drive for order, but can have deleterious consequences. The authors discuss the development of stereotypes and their application by children and adults. Even young children spontaneously categorize individuals on the basis of gender and ethnicity, and use group membership to infer individual possession of stereotypic traits. As children get older, their awareness of stereotypes includes an awareness of collectively endorsed stereotypes (McKown & Weinstein, 2003), and children use this stereotype knowledge to make sense of their social world as well.

Chapter 11 - The content of most stereotypes are not uniformly negative. African Americans are stereotyped as loud and aggressive, but also as musical and athletic. Asian Americans are stereotyped as being cold and aloof, but also as high in intelligence. People express more respect for men than women, but more liking for women than men. Thus, rather than uniform negativity, many stereotypes appear to be ambivalent, containing both positive and negative elements simultaneously. Ambivalent sexism and the stereotype content model have emerged to explain the ambivalence that is prevalent in intergroup attitudes. This chapter will review these theories and key findings in the field, as well as present applied data investigating stereotypes of men in nursing and stigma toward the wrongly convicted to illustrate how the ambivalence of intergroup attitudes can suggest support for stigmatized groups, while at the same time discriminating against them.

Chapter 12 - This chapter will discuss how epilepsy has been perceived throughout history and across different cultures. The chapter will highlight how historical conceptions of epilepsy and misrepresentation in the media have perpetuated current stereotypical perceptions of the disorder. Consequently, misconceptionsabout epilepsy serve to propagate discrimination and stigmatoward people with the condition. The myths that surround epilepsy will be explored emphasising how misconception, discrimination and stigma affect the quality of life of people with the condition. Myths, stigma and stereotypes can result in multiple interrelated psychosocial outcomes which can impede the cohesive integration of people with epilepsy in society. The impact of these factors on important psychosocial outcomes such as self esteem, depression, anxiety, employability, opportunities for social interaction and interpersonal relationships will be discussed.The chapter will explore these outcomes highlighting how society can be effective in engendering positive attitudes towards people with epilepsy. To conclude, educational interventions aimed at people with epilepsy, their families, employers, teachers and society at large will be considered along with future research suggestions with a view to reduce the impact of stigma and improve the social functioning of people with epilepsy.

Chapter 13 - In the last few decades, several studies, mostly performed in Western countries, have started to reveal the existence of various food and eating stereotypes. Interestingly, these studies imply that many people are still influenced by unfounded nutritional beliefs and practices regardless of the growing amount of scientific knowledge on nutrition and health. The aim of this chapter is to provide a brief overview of empirical research on food-related beliefs and stereotypes.

Firstly, the authors illustrate that consumer food choice and evaluation are influenced by various stereotypical beliefs about food. For example, people tend to categorize foods based on subjective beliefs (e.g., high-fat/low-fat, local/imported, branded/unbranded) and those beliefs further influence a consumer's food selections and food product evaluations (for example, a belief that local food products are more expensive than imports may prevent consumers from buying local products). We also discuss the nature of magical beliefs about food and health.

Secondly, we review consumption stereotypes, which are stereotypes based on what and how much people eat. Specifically, the authors focus on gender-based consumption stereotypes, in which femininity and masculinity are primarily associated with specific patterns of consumption. The authors discuss the nature of gender-based consumption stereotypes among the younger population in relation to social appeal and/or pressure. Young women often experience social pressure based on gender-based consumption stereotypes and form psychological barriers against consuming masculine foods and drinks. There is fear that these stereotypical attitudes among females result in several pathological eating behaviors.

Finally, the authors discuss the feasibility of introducing implicit attitude measures for the study of food-related stereotypes, partly based on our recent studies.

Chapter 14 - A large body of evidence has shown male superiority in performance of a mental rotation task, notably the MRT proposed by Vandenberg and Kuse (1978). The difference is considerable, males scoring as much as one standard deviation higher than females. Many reasons have been put forward for this underscoring by females: biological, cultural, strategic and motivational. Males are favoured by lateral specialisation, early familiarisation with spatial tasks and toys, use of holistic strategies, and an incremental theory of spatial abilities. Recently, gender stereotyping has been considered to be one of the factors affecting test accuracy, particularly for females. As a result of widely held stereotyping, females are thought to be less able than males in spatial tasks such as mental rotation. Awareness of this stereotype can intimidate females and increase theirexpectation of performing poorly, this indeed having negative affect on performance. Research examining these male/female differences and the underlying causes is reviewed and suggestions made for channels of future research.

Chapter 15 - According to the Centers for Disease Control (2005), approximately 15 percent of all new HIV/AIDS cases are among those aged 50 and older. The greatest increase in infection appears among older Black and Latino women who contract the virus through heterosexual contact. With the rapid growth of the older adult population in the next decade, it becomes critical that stereotypes regarding elderly sexuality are examined and dispelled. Older women are often subject to ageism; many health care providers fail to ask appropriate questions regarding their sexual health and remain unaware of unique age and gender specific risk factors. Stereotypes to be examined include beliefs that older women are asexual and have no need for HIV/AIDS education. Additional barriers to prevention include older women's lack of experience with condoms, culture specific factors including machismo, and stigma and discrimination toward older adults living with HIV/AIDS. This chapter will focus on knowledge and attitudes about HIV/AIDS among elderly women and health care providers, and will provide relevant clinical and public policy recommendations.

Chapter 16 - In this paper, the effects of few design parameters on human performancefor a common horizontal display/rotary control arrangement wereexamined. The results showed that the knob position, pointer type, and scale side and in particular the control position x scale side interaction significantly affectedhuman response time. Response time was found to decrease with increasing values of stereotype proportion and index of stereotype reversibility, andthe extents of decrease were different for the top and bottom controls. Based on the consideration of response time and stereotype characteristics, the optimum location for positioning a rotary control on a horizontal scale was found.

Chapter 17 - Stereotypes are conventionally understood to be generalizations about the behavior and characteristics of some group of people--based on race, nationality, ethnicity, religion, occupation, gender, and so on. Stereotypes can be negative, neutral, positive, or mixed. Some common stereotypes are that women are lousy drivers, Jews are cheap, Scots are thrifty, British people are snobs, and that Japanese are honest. The negative stereotype of the Japanese is that are also robotic and a bit fanatic. Stereotypes generally involve people characterizing some group on the basis of a limited experience with a relatively small number of representatives of that group. But in many cases, stereotypes are learned, from exposure to stereotypes found in the media and carried in jokes and other forms of humor.

In: Psychology of Stereotypes
Editor: Eleanor L. Simon

ISBN: 978-1-61761-463-7
©2011 Nova Science Publishers, Inc.

Chapter 1

Fluent Speakers' Advice for Communicating with People Who Stutter: The Concept of Mutual Help and its Effects on Successful Stuttering Management

Stephanie Hughes[*1], *Rodney Gabel*[2] *and Farzan Irani*[3]

Governors State University, Monee, Illinois, USA, s-hughes@govst.edu[1]
Bowling Green State University, rgabel@bgsu.edu[2]
Texas State University – San Marcos, firani@txstate.edu[3]

Abstract

Stuttering, a disorder of communication that disrupts the smooth, forward flow of speech, is often perceived negatively by fluent speakers. This chapter begins with a review of fluent speakers' attitudes toward stuttering and their perceptions of the effects of the disorder on the lives of people who stutter (PWS). A qualitative study is then presented which examines fluent speakers' beliefs about the ways in which PWS and fluent speakers may help each other to communicate more effectively. The results of this study suggest that while fluent speakers generally believe that they should treat PWS with patience and respect, there is some confusion regarding the ways in which these positive attitudes should manifest themselves as active behaviors. In addition, fluent speakers believe that PWS can facilitate communication by engaging in behaviors that reduce or eliminate stuttering. Many of these behaviors have been reported in the stuttering literature as adversely affecting the successful management of stuttering by PWS. The authors conclude the chapter with a discussion of how PWS may experience unintentional prejudice or discrimination from fluent speakers and how the public's perceptions may be altered to alleviate negative attitudes toward stuttering and individuals who stutter.

*Corresponding Author: Stephanie Hughes, Ph.D., CCC-SLP, Governors State University, s-hughes@govst.edu

AN INTRODUCTION TO FLUENT SPEECH, DISFLUENCY, AND STUTTERING

Verbal communication is generally effortless and requires little in the way of conscious thought, despite the complexity of speech production. Adults easily speak between 162-230 syllables per minute, (Guitar, 2006) a feat which requires the coordination, integration, and timing of several bodily systems, including respiration, phonation at the level of the larynx, and articulation (Perkins, Kent, & Curlee, 1991). A typical speaker (referred to throughout this chapter as a fluent speaker) generally produces smooth, free-flowing speech that has few pauses and is neither too fast nor too slow. But everyone, including fluent speakers, will experience disruptions in fluency, known as disfluencies, on occasion. For typical speakers these disfluencies often take the form of repeated phrases or whole words and interjections such as "um" or "uh." Unless they occur too frequently, these disfluencies are not distracting to speakers or their listeners, and are so commonplace that they may not be consciously noticed.

What behaviors differentiate fluent speakers from people who stutter (PWS)? While most individual speakers may ponder *what* to say, they rarely need to concentrate on the process of *how* to speak. PWS, on the other hand, generally know what they want to say but are impeded from doing so because of disruptions to the speech production mechanism. The speech of PWS is generally perceived as effortful and can be characterized not only by the more common types of general disfluencies, but also by those that are less common. (See Guitar, 2006, for a review of the types of disfluencies in addition to the ones provided here.) The type of disfluency associated most strongly with stuttering is arguably part-word repetitions, whereby a sound is repeated one or more times, as in "g-g-good morning," in which the "g" sound is repeated several times. In addition to part-word repetitions, stuttered speech can also include audible prolongations of a sound. "Sh—e wants to go to the park," in which the "sh" sound is extended, is an example of a prolongation. The most severe type of stuttered disfluency is known as a block, in which airflow or voice is stopped, resulting in a long, tense pause between the initial attempt to produce a sound its actual production. During blocks the tongue, lips, and jaw may appear frozen or have very little movement, accompanied by an absence of voice before the sound is eventually produced (e.g., "---I want to go home.").

While there are neurogenic and psychogenic forms of stuttering, most stuttering is developmental and starts in childhood between the ages of 2-5 years. Over 80% of children who begin to stutter will outgrow the condition, and children who receive intervention such as speech therapy can also recover from stuttering before adulthood (Yairi & Ambrose, 1999). Thus, the number of children with developmental stuttering who continue to stutter into adolescence and adulthood is relatively small, though individuals who stutter chronically account for 1% of the world's population (Bloodstein, 1995).

Stuttering manifests itself a bit differently in each individual who stutters. Some PWS may not experience blocks or prolongations at all, and PWS who experience part-word repetitions may differ in the number of times and the rapidity with which they repeat the sounds. The amount of muscular tension can also differ from person to person. In addition, though stuttering most directly manifests itself in recognizable patterns of disrupted speech, PWS differ in the ways in which they manage their disfluencies as compared to fluent speakers and even other individuals who stutter. As noted previously, fluent speakers tend not to react to their disfluencies. How often, for example, do we consciously note each time we repeat a word or say "um" in general conversation? But for PWS, the frequency and nature of their disfluencies are such that they are noticeable and can interfere with the forward flow of information from speaker to listener. As such disruptions are generally inconvenient and potentially embarrassing, PWS may develop compensatory strategies which are designed to help hide their stuttering or stutter less. Some of these strategies are avoidance behaviors (e.g., not speaking as much, substituting words that are easier to say for those that are problematic) and others are designed to help PWS "escape" from stuttering as they are speaking. An individual who stutters may, for example, snap his fingers, jerk his head back, or kick his leg in an attempt to stop stuttering during a conversation. The problem with such escape behaviors is that while finger-snapping, head-jerking, or leg-kicking may get PWS out of a moment of stuttering once or twice, stuttering is very adaptive to such novelties and will quickly reemerge. Individuals who stutter may continue to engage in these types of behaviors as a learned but ineffective habit. Thus, as compared to fluent speakers, PWS may develop secondary physical behaviors and thought processes that accompany their disfluencies. These secondary aspects may be even more disruptive to communication than stuttered speech.

Most PWS and many professionals who treat them have come to recognize that stuttering encompasses more than just speech disfluencies. Communication involves sharing one's thoughts and feelings in a wide range of settings and situations. As a result, the disruption of communication that stuttering causes may result in negative thoughts and emotions for PWS. Sheehan (1970) compared stuttering and its effects to an iceberg, in which the observable characteristics of stuttering, such as part-word repetitions, prolongations, blocks, and secondary physical behaviors, are only the tip of the iceberg. Just as the biggest part of an iceberg lies beneath the surface of the water, the most disruptive aspects of stuttering are internal and include the thoughts and emotions that stuttering engenders, such as sadness, fear, guilt, and anger. These emotions are "beneath the surface" and are not directly observable by others. While there is no cure for stuttering, speech therapy and other types of interventions that focus on the emotional and cognitive aspects of stuttering in addition to speech disfluencies may help to alleviate its severity and effects on PWS.

PERCEPTIONS OF PEOPLE WHO STUTTER

Having provided a brief overview of the ways in which both PWS and fluent speakers are affected by their disfluencies, we turn now to a discussion on the attitudes of fluent speakers toward stuttering and PWS. A large body of literature has been generated about the characteristics of PWS and the attitudes of listeners toward PWS. At one point in the past the concept of the "stuttering personality" was emphasized (Bender, 1939; Green, 1936), with most researchers of this period indicating that personality differences existed between PWS and fluent speakers (Bryngelson, 1937; Johnson, 1932; Solomon, 1938). Thus, the measurement of personality began to be emphasized as a clinical tool for speech therapists who treated PWS (Hawk, 1948), and a variety of personality tests such as the Rorschach test (Meltzer, 1944), the California Test of Personality (Perkins, 1947), and projection tests (Wilson, 1951) were administered to PWS. The results of these early research studies suggested that PWS possess more unstable or neurotic personalities as compared to the general population. Subsequent reviewers of this literature rejected the notion of the stuttering personality and indicated that PWS are not psychologically different from people who do not stutter (Andrews et al., 1983; Bloodstein, 1995; Prins, 1972; Sheehan, 1958; Van Riper, 1982). Currently researchers believe that developmental stuttering is not caused by a psychological condition, but rather by a number of reasons, including genetic, neurological, and environmental factors. Accordingly, research efforts have shifted away from psychological tests of personality and instead have focused on measuring listener perceptions of stuttering and PWS.

While it is not a cause of stuttering, it has been known for several decades that *anticipation* of negative listener reactions from listeners can exacerbate stuttering (Bloodstein, 1995). According to Charles Van Riper (1982, p. 148), one of the pioneers of stuttering therapy and himself a person who stuttered, "stuttering is apparently as much a disorder of communication as it is of speech; the [listener] is at least as important as the [person who stutters] in the interchange." As such, listener reactions to stuttering may affect PWS in a wide variety of contexts, including the formation of intimate and social relationships (Boberg & Boberg, 1990; Linn & Caruso, 1998; Shears & Jensema, 1969), educational experiences (Crowe & Walton, 1981; Dorsey & Guenther, 2000; Lass et al. 1992, 1994; Ruscello, Lass, Schmitt, & Pannbaker, 1994; Turnbaugh, Guitar, & Hoffman, 1981), and employment opportunities (Gabel, Blood, Tellis, & Althouse, 2004; Hurst & Cooper, 1983a,b). In the next sections we will examine various target populations' reactions to stuttering and the factors which may or may not influence perceptions of PWS.

ATTITUDES TOWARD PWS

A number of studies have found that between 50-75% of the general public has interacted with at least one person who stutters (e.g., Hughes, 2008; Schlagheck, Gabel, & Hughes, 2009). This is not surprising as developmental stuttering emerges in childhood, and as many as 5% of the population has stuttered at some point (Conture, 2001). For many people their relationships with PWS were familial or work-based; others knew a classmate at school who stuttered or had simply come across someone who stutters as a result of daily living, such as while running errands or attending a social event. Members of the general public in these studies who had never interacted with someone who stutters sometimes indicated that they had seen stuttering portrayed on television or elsewhere in the media. Thus, most fluent listeners seem to have some basis for their opinions on stuttering and their reactions to PWS. In addition, everyone, whether fluent speaker or person who stutters, will experience many disfluencies over the course of a lifetime. While PWS may have less common disfluencies that are accompanied by greater emotional and cognitive distress, fluent speakers have reported feelings of empathy toward PWS based on dread of disfluency during important situations like public speaking. To that extent fluent speakers may feel that they know what it is like to stutter, and may use their transient experiences of disfluency as their basis for judgments about stuttering and PWS.

Attitudes of speech therapists. Speech therapists, also known as speech-language pathologists, are the professionals who are most likely to treat PWS, so the bulk of the research literature has been derived from the work of researchers in that discipline. As professionals who are trained to treat communicative disorders, the attitudes of speech therapists to stuttering and PWS have important clinical implications. The first modern research study on this topic turned into a series of seminal studies that explored speech therapists' attitudes toward PWS. Yairi and Williams (1970) asked school-based speech therapists in the state of Iowa to complete an open-ended questionnaire. The respondents were asked to provide a written list of traits that could be used to describe elementary school-age boys who stutter. Participants most frequently provided a total of 26 traits to describe boys who stutter. Seventeen of these traits were judged by the researchers to be negative or undesirable, and only nine of the traits were judged to be positive or desirable. Most of these characteristics were related to personality traits rather than to physical or intelligence traits. The ten most cited traits were nervous, shy, withdrawn, tense, anxious, self-conscious, insecure, sensitive, quiet, and intelligent. As the therapists' years of clinical experience increased, so too did the median number of adjectives that they listed to describe boys who stutter. The provision of more adjectives was viewed as being indicative of a stronger, more stereotypical belief system about boys who stutter. In a similar study by Woods and Williams (1971) speech therapists were asked to write adjectives that described adult men who stutter. (Note that girls and women who stutter were omitted from this study because most PWS are male, especially in adolescence and adulthood.) Once again, the respondents provided mostly negative adjectives. The similarity of the adjectives used to describe both men and boys who stutter indicated that speech therapists may stereotype PWS regardless of individual differences. Thus, there may be a trend among clinicians to believe that "a stutterer is a stutterer is a stutterer" (Woods & Williams, 1971, p. 232).

The adjectives that the speech therapists provided to describe boys and men who stutter in the preceding studies were arranged as semantic differential scales by Woods and Williams (1976). These scales consisted of 25 paired items (e.g., open-guarded, friendly-unfriendly, fearful-fearless, etc.) which were administered to seven groups of respondents, including speech therapists in public school settings. Participants used these scales to rate each of four hypothetical people, including a typical eight-year-old male, a typical eight-year-old male who stutters, a typical adult male, and a typical adult male who stutters. The results of this study indicated that 95% of traits that were judged as negative were applied to males who stutter versus typical males who did not stutter. Significant differences in ratings were not found for the age of the hypothetical person who stutters (child versus adult) or for the participant group (e.g., speech therapists, students, teachers). These negative attitudes indicated the presence of a pervasive negative stereotype towards PWS by most groups of listeners, including speech therapists.

After the Woods and Williams (1976) study, semantic differential scales became a popular method to measure attitudes toward PWS. For example, Turnbaugh, Guitar, and Hoffman (1979) used semantic differential scales to measure the attitudes of speech therapists toward PWS based upon stuttering severity. The 36 therapists who served as participants were asked to rate a hypothetical "typical individual" who (a) was normally fluent, (b) stuttered mildly, (c) stuttered moderately, or (d) stuttered severely. The results of this study confirmed that speech therapists perceive PWS more negatively as compared to fluent speakers. There was an increase in negative attitudes toward PWS when responses toward the mild stuttering and severe stuttering conditions were compared. Only a weak negative correlation between speech therapists' years of experience and their ratings of PWS was found, leading the authors to conclude that there was not a linear relationship between speech therapists' experiences with PWS and their attitudes toward PWS.

Cooper and Cooper (1985) indicated that it is important to know what attitudes speech therapists hold about stuttering and PWS, as these attitudes will presumably influence therapeutic protocols and treatment outcomes. They examined the attitudes of 674 speech therapists toward stuttering, PWS, and related issues by administering the *Clinician's Attitudes Toward Stuttering* (CATS) *Inventory* to speech therapists who attended a workshop on stuttering over a ten-year period. The *CATS Inventory* asks 50 attitudinal questions about stuttering to which respondents indicate the strength of their agreement on a five-point scale which ranges from "strongly agree" to "strongly disagree." The authors found that over the ten-year time period there were some changes in speech therapists' attitudes toward the personality of PWS. For example, as compared to the sample gathered in 1973-1974, significantly fewer speech therapists agreed in 1983 that PWS have psychological problems and hold distorted perceptions of their own stuttering behavior and social relationships. Other attitudes toward the personality of PWS did not show a significant change over the course of the study. The majority of speech therapists continued to believe that stuttering, as compared to other speech disorders, is the most psychologically devastating. They also believed that there are personality traits that are representative of PWS, and that PWS have feelings of inferiority. Cooper and Cooper (1996) continued to administer the *CATS Inventory* to speech therapists until they had data that spanned two decades from 1983-1991. They found that attitudes among clinicians had not changed significantly across the two decades in regard to the personality of PWS.

Unlike other researchers of the time, Lass et al. (1989) did not use semantic differential scales or other quantitative methods to assess speech therapists' attitudes toward PWS. Instead, they asked speech therapists to write adjectives that described four hypothetical people who stutter, including a female child, male child, female adult, and male adult. The inclusion of females (i.e., a female child and female adult) was lacking in previous studies that had used this methodology (Woods & Williams, 1970; Yairi & Williams, 1971). The speech therapists provided a total of 529 adjectives to describe the four types of hypothetical PWS, of which 69.9% were negative in nature, 24.2% were positive, and 5.9% were neutral. Traits related to personality characteristics were most often listed, suggesting that many speech therapists have negative stereotypes of PWS. Lass and colleagues (1989) suggested that these negative stereotypes may be alleviated if speech therapists can learn to separate the person who stutters from his or her stuttering.

The attitudes of students in training to become speech therapists and audiologists have also been examined (St. Louis & Lass, 1981). In this study, 1,902 speech-language pathology and audiology students from among 33 universities completed the *CATS Inventory*. As a group, the speech-language pathology and audiology students appeared to believe that PWS have psychosocial problems and that counseling PWS and their parents is an important component of stuttering therapy. Students who had more clinical training also seemed to hold these views, a finding which the authors attributed more to social acculturation in the United States than a by-product of clinician training. Participants also seemed to feel that stuttering was one of the hardest disorders to treat and indicated that most speech therapists are neither competent nor comfortable when treating PWS. St. Louis and Lass (1981) suggested that more research is needed to examine the effects of specific types of training on student clinicians' attitudes toward PWS.

Horsley and FitzGibbon (1987) investigated the attitudes of speech therapists and student speech therapists with various degrees of training toward children who stutter (CWS). For comparison purposes, primary school student teachers and secondary school teachers also served as participants. Participants completed semantic differential scales (Woods & Williams, 1976) for eight hypothetical constructs that included stutterer/nonstutterer, pre-school/eight-year-old, and boy/girl variables. Ratings of CWS were consistently negative, and for all but five traits a statistically significant difference was found between ratings of CWS and children who do not stutter. Some participants reported knowing PWS, however, this variable did not appear to influence participants' ratings of CWS. This finding may have important implications for clinicians who treat PWS. The relationship between stereotypic beliefs and one's actions is not clear; however, stereotypes held by speech therapists may have an effect on the therapeutic interaction between clinicians and their clients who stutter, perhaps even to the extent that young CWS may learn to fulfill the clinician's negative expectations (Horsley & FitzGibon, 1987).

Schlagheck et al. (2009) used a mixed (quantitative and qualitative) approach to investigate over 150 communication disorders students' beliefs about stuttering and PWS. Responses to an open-ended and forced choice questionnaire were analyzed thematically and statistically on the basis of students' gender and familiarity with individuals who stutter. One aspect of the study was to investigate the total number of positive, neutral, and negative descriptions of PWS provided by the students. Schlagheck et al. concluded that while communication disorders students responded with stereotypically negative remarks regarding stuttering and PWS, those students who were familiar with someone who stutters reported significantly more positive descriptions of PWS, as did female students. These findings differ from those of other researchers who also investigated the effects of gender and familiarity with PWS (see subsections related to gender and familiarity later on in this chapter).

The preceding studies indicate that speech therapists and students consistently have held the same negative attitudes toward PWS for well over thirty years. It seems reasonable to assume that speech therapists who consider PWS to be psychologically different from typical speakers will interact with their clients in a less than desirable manner, but how the attitudes of therapists affect the client-clinician relationship remains unclear at this time. It does appear, however, that speech therapists report stereotypical beliefs about PWS that may not be very different from others professionals or laypersons, despite having been trained to treat communication disorders.

Attitudes of educators. Like speech therapists, the attitudes of educators toward stuttering and PWS have been examined for many decades. As the following discussion will indicate, educators generally report negative attitudes toward PWS. In one of the earliest studies of its kind, Emerick (1960) explored the relationship between elementary school teachers' ability to count or tally instances of stuttering and their attitudes toward stuttering. The *Iowa Scale of Attitude Toward Stuttering* was administered to 21 male and 127 female teachers. A speech stimulus consisting of a 3.5 minute audiotape recording of a male who stutters was made (the types and amount of disfluencies were not disclosed by the author). Participants were instructed to keep a count of the amount of stuttering they heard as the speech sample was played. The order in which participants completed the attitude scale or heard the speech sample varied. Statistical analysis of the data indicated a relationship between the amount of disfluencies noted by participants and their attitudes toward PWS. Participants who had a more tolerant attitude toward stuttering tended to observe more disfluencies. This trend applied most particularly to those teachers who had taken at least one course in speech pathology as compared to teachers with no formal training. Emerick (1960) suggested that training in speech pathology might result in more tolerant attitudes toward stuttering while at the same time decreasing tolerance for speech nonfluencies (e.g., typically occurring disfluencies that are not generally considered to be core stuttering behaviors). Emerick's conclusions do not appear to be supported given the large number of subsequent studies which have found that speech therapists do not hold more positive attitudes toward PWS than other groups of people.

More recent research has also explored teachers' attitudes toward stuttering. The attitudes of 100 elementary school teachers toward stuttering were examined by Crowe and Walton (1981). The teachers in this study completed the *Teacher Attitudes Toward Stuttering (TATS) Inventory* which consisted of 36 attitude-based statements and nine general information questions about stuttering. The *TATS Inventory* had not been validated at the time of the study. Participants also completed the *Alabama Stuttering Knowledge (ASK) Test*, which consists of 26 true/false statements about stuttering. A total of 33 speech-language pathologists rank-ordered, from zero to four, possible responses on the *TATS Inventory*, so that the most desirable teacher responses were given a value of four and least desirable were given a value of zero. The results indicated that teachers who had a greater knowledge of stuttering as measured on the *ASK Test* had more desirable attitudes toward stuttering. Teachers who indicated that they currently had a student who stuttered in their classroom had less desirable attitudes and scored lower on the *ASK Test* than did teachers who did not have a student who stuttered. These findings would seem to suggest that educators who teach students who stutter develop more negative attitudes toward stuttering and PWS as compared to educators who have not had a student who stutters in the classroom.

The research related to educators' attitudes toward PWS has not been limited to only elementary and secondary school teachers. Silverman (1990) examined whether 87 college professors from three universities held negative attitudes towards a hypothetical student who stutters. An 81-item semantic differential questionnaire (Silverman, 1985) was administered to participants, but data for only two of these items, competent-incompetent and intelligent-unintelligent, were reported. The results indicated that the vast majority of professors rated a student who stutters as being at the center or towards the more positive end of the Likert scale for these scale items. These results suggest that professors do not hold negative attitudes toward the intelligence or competence of students who stutter; however, a control group (i.e., instructions to rate "a typical student") was not implemented in this study.

Dorsey and Guenther (2000), citing the lack of control group in the Silverman (1990) study, conducted a survey in which 34 professors and 57 college students used a 7-point semantic differential scale to rate either an average college student or a college student who stutters on 20 personality traits. Four of the 20 traits (*guarded, perfectionist, reserved*, and *talkative*) were judged to be neutral traits by a separate group of college students and professors, and so participants' responses on these traits were not analyzed. The remaining items consisted of a number of positive traits (*open, intelligent, bold, calm, self-assured, competent*, and *bright*) and negative traits (*nervous, shy, self-conscious, passive, aggressive, dull, mediocre, reticent*, and *incompetent*). The results indicated that for all but one trait, aggressiveness, professors rated the hypothetical college student who stutters as possessing more negative traits than the hypothetical average college student. College students perceived the hypothetical college student who stutters to hold more negative personality traits for 13 items as compared to the hypothetical average college student. The college students felt that a student who stutters was more likely to be less aggressive, less incompetent, and more intelligent as compared to the average college student. Overall, the professors who participated in the study rated a college student who stutters more negatively than did the college students, though these ratings varied on individual items. Dorsey and Guenther (2000) suggested that although college students and professors may be reluctant to engage in interactions with students who stutter, increased interaction opportunities and educational programs about stuttering may help to change negative attitudes toward PWS.

A series of studies by Lass, Ruscello, and colleagues (Lass et al. 1992, 1994; Ruscello, Lass, Schmitt, & Pannbaker, 1994) asked elementary and secondary school teachers, school administrators, and special education teachers to provide adjectives that describe four hypothetical people who stutter, including a female child, male child, female adult, and male adult. Similar results were found for all groups of respondents. Elementary and secondary school teachers provided a total of 287 adjectives to describe PWS, of which 66.9% were negative in nature, 20.2% were positive, and 12.9% were neutral (Lass et. al., 1992). A replication of this study by Silverman and Marik (1993) found similar results. School administrators provided a total of 197 adjectives to describe PWS of which 72.6% were negative in nature, 19.8% were positive, and 7.6% were neutral (Lass et. al., 1994). Special educators provided a total of 241 adjectives to describe PWS of which 67.2% were negative in nature, 17.4% were positive, and 15.4% were neutral (Ruscello et. al., 1994). Thus, when asked to provide written descriptions of PWS, professionals involved in education are likely to provide adjectives that are primarily negative in tone, suggesting that educators, like speech therapists, may be more tolerant of PWS if they could separate stuttering from the person with the stuttering disorder (Lass et al., 1989).

Thus, with few exceptions (e.g., Silverman, 1990), it appears that educators and administrators in school and university settings hold negative attitudes toward PWS. Even when educators report knowing students who stutter (e.g., Crowe & Walton, 1981; Lass et al., 1992), the negative stereotype of PWS persists. It is not well understood how teachers' perceptions of PWS influence their behavior toward students who stutter in the classroom. More research is needed that provides a more in-depth exploration of teachers' attitudes toward PWS and correlates teachers' attitudes with their behavior toward students who stutter in their classrooms.

Attitudes of medical professionals. Parents who are concerned about stuttering in their child's speech often turn to the child's pediatrician for advice. Some physicians may take a "wait and see" approach that does not relate to current best practices in early childhood stuttering intervention (Yairi & Carrico, 1992). A comprehensive study was, therefore, conducted by Yairi and Carrico in which 439 pediatricians responded to a questionnaire that asked about their attitudes and practices toward young children who stutter. One item on the questionnaire asked the pediatricians to state whether preschool children who stutter are above normal, below normal, or are no different from normally-speaking children in terms of emotional stability, intelligence, and maturity. Fifty-six percent of pediatricians thought that there was no difference between preschoolers who stutter and those who do not in terms of emotional stability, but the remaining 44% felt that preschool children who stutter are below normal for emotional stability. Ten percent of pediatricians felt that preschoolers who stutter possess above normal intelligence, 1% below normal intelligence, and 56% of pediatricians felt that there was no difference in intelligence between preschoolers who stutter and those who do not. Finally, for maturity, 2% of pediatricians thought that preschoolers who stutter have above normal maturity, 24% below normal maturity, and 74% of pediatricians felt that there is no difference in maturity between preschoolers who stutter and those who do not. These results appear to indicate that the majority of physicians believe that there is no difference between preschoolers who stutter and those who do not on the traits of emotional stability, intelligence, and maturity.

Attitudes of employers and employment issues. Several researchers have examined perceptions of employability for PWS. These studies have examined the perceptions of rehabilitation counselors, employers, and students toward appropriate career choices for PWS. Most studies have indicated that respondents feel that PWS are less employable than are members of the general population and that PWS are better suited for some careers than others. The review of the following studies indicates that PWS are at risk for occupational stereotyping.

Hurst and Cooper (1983a) developed the *Alabama Rehabilitation Counselor's Attitudes Toward Stuttering (ARCATS) Inventory* to assess vocational rehabilitation counselors' attitudes toward and knowledge of stuttering. The *ARCATS Inventory* consists of 25 true-false statements that assess knowledge of stuttering and 15 statements that assess attitudes toward stuttering. One hundred fifty-two vocational rehabilitation counselors in the state of Alabama completed the *ARCATS Inventory*. Of these participants, 34.6% had never served PWS on a professional basis, but 50.8% had served between one and four PWS. The results of the study suggested that the participants believed that PWS have psychological problems and have certain identifiable personality traits. On a positive note, the rehabilitation counselors' responses suggested that stuttering is perceived as being amenable to therapy and that PWS are good candidates for vocational rehabilitation. Thus, vocational rehabilitation counselors may hold attitudes that are conducive to the rehabilitation of PWS (Hurst & Cooper, 1983a).

Hurst and Cooper (1983b) administered the *Employer Attitudes Toward Stuttering(EATS) Inventory* to 644 employers. The *EATS Inventory* did not undergo validity or reliability assessment prior to being used in the study. It consists of seven attitudinal statements about stuttering to which respondents indicate their agreement on a five-point scale that range from "strongly agree" to "strongly disagree." The employers who participated in the study had a variety of experience with interviewing and employing PWS. Thirty-six percent of employers had interviewed between one and three PWS, and 40% reported employing between one and three PWS. The results of the survey indicated that the majority of participants reported that stuttering interferes with employability, but does not necessarily impact job performance. Three out of five employers reported feeling uncomfortable when speaking with PWS, and the same amount of employers rejected the idea of affirmative action programs for PWS. These findings suggest that stuttering may handicap PWS for employability purposes.

Silverman and Paynter (1990) used an 81-item semantic differential questionnaire (Silverman, 1985) to assess 48 college students' perceptions of the occupational competency of PWS as compared to fluent speakers in the same occupations. Four groups of 12 students rated one of four hypothetical employees, including a factory worker, a factory worker who stutters, a lawyer, and a lawyer who stutters. Ratings of the factory workers indicated differences between the typical factory worker and factory worker who stutters on 16 items. Specifically, students judged the factory worker who stutters to be more afraid, insecure, tense, cowardly, and weak than the factory worker who does not stutter. In addition, the factory worker who stutters was perceived as being less talkative, sociable, coordinated, dominant, affluent, aggressive, and confident as compared to a typical factory worker. For the lawyer condition there were 34 items in which students perceived a difference based on stuttering. As compared to a typical lawyer, a lawyer who stutters was judged to be more afraid, confused, tense, discontented, frightened, lazy, dependent, uncomfortable, naïve, and disorganized, as well as being less intelligent, employable, competent, educated confident, talkative, mature, secure, natural, witty, stable, dominant, rich, sane, alert, and aggressive. These findings suggest that PWS may be perceived more negatively if they have careers in which communication is more highly valued.

In another study, Silverman and Bongey (1997) used a 20-item semantic differential questionnaire to assess nurses' attitudes toward physicians who stutter. Ten nurses received a questionnaire that asked them to rate "a physician" and ten nurses received the same questionnaire that asked them to rate "a physician who stutters." The nurses in the study rated a physician who stutters as being more afraid, tense, nervous, and aggravating in addition to being less mature, intelligent, secure, competent, confident, educated, and reputable than a physician who does not stutter. These results indicate that nurses, and perhaps others in the medical profession, hold negative stereotypes of professionals who stutter.

Gabel, Blood, Tellis, and Althouse (2004) used the *Vocational Advice Scale (VAS)* to investigate college students' perceptions of appropriate career choices for PWS. The *VAS* is a written questionnaire that asks respondents to indicate the degree (on a 5-point Likert-type scale) to which they would advise someone to train for 43 jobs. The *VAS* was administered to 385 university students. One group of students was asked to provide career advice to an adult male who stutters, and the other group of students was asked to give advice to an adult male who does not stutter. Statistical analysis indicated that 20 of 43 careers were judged to be significantly less advisable for an adult male who stutters than a typical adult male. Gabel et al. note that there appear to be some similarities among the careers that were judged as being less acceptable for PWS. Some careers (e.g., psychologist, physician, speech-language pathologist, etc.) may be perceived as requiring high levels of communicative competence or the ability to help others by speaking well. PWS may be limited in their career choices as a result of occupational stereotyping by fluent speakers.

A series of studies have further investigated the concept of occupational stereotyping. These studies administered Gabel et al.'s (2004) *Vocational Advice Scale* to teachers (Irani, Gabel, Hughes, Swartz, & Palasik, 2009) and speech-language pathologists (Swartz, Gabel, Hughes, & Irani, 2009). Participants' quantitative responses to the *VAS* items were supplemented by open-ended responses to a number of questions in which participants provided a rationale for their opinions. These open-ended responses were analyzed qualitatively (thematically) to develop a deeper understanding of occupational stereotyping of PWS. Irani et al. (2009) found that teachers had varying rationales for why certain careers were or were not suitable for PWS. Some teachers stated that PWS should pursue any career they want, regardless of their stuttering. Some teachers did not advise PWS to pursue a career (like astrology) because they felt that the career itself was unworthy of anyone. Still other teachers stated that PWS should not pursue careers in which they would be unhappy or endanger others because of their stuttering. Careers in law, public safety, and health care were among the 10 (of 43) careers that were significantly less likely to be recommended by teachers. Swartz et al. (2009) found that speech therapists were even less likely to occupationally stereotype PWS. Only two careers, speech-language pathologist and attorney were less likely to be recommended as viable careers for PWS. That PWS are encouraged not to become speech-language pathologists by speech therapists is ironic given that some of the pioneers of the field were themselves PWS.

Schlagheck et al. (2009) used a slightly different method to assess members of the general public's attitudes toward appropriate careers for PWS. A mixed method questionnaire consisting of qualitative open-ended items and quantitative forced-choice items was administered to approximately 150 people, many of whom were university students. Their responses indicated that over 80% of respondents believed that PWS have a hard time finding employment. Stuttering was perceived as affecting a person's employment only in careers that required a large amount of communication, like teaching or talking on the telephone. While many of the respondents wrote that PWS could pursue any career they wish, non-speaking jobs, like construction or working with computers, were considered advisable. The responses to the questionnaire did not vary according to respondents' familiarity with PWS.

The research tends to show that PWS are at risk for occupational stereotyping by employers and may be advised or expected to pursue careers that do not require a high degree of communicative competence or verbal expression. Furthermore, it seems likely that jobs that do not require a high level of communication will have less prestige than those that do not, and will pay less money. More research is needed regarding (a) the rationale behind employers' and laypersons' attitudes towards career suitability for PWS, (b) employers' actual hiring practices related to PWS, and (c) the effects of occupational stereotyping on quality of life issues for PWS.

Attitudes of laypersons. In addition to helping professionals and employers, some researchers have examined laypersons' attitudes toward PWS. College students and/or members of the general public have often served as participants in these studies. For the most part, researchers have tried to establish what laypersons know about stuttering and what they believe about PWS. Semantic differential scales have been utilized most often to address these questions, but other formats, such as interviews, have been used as well. The following studies are reviewed to demonstrate that laypersons' tend to have the same negative attitudes toward PWS as do other professionals who may interact with PWS.

White and Collins (1984) used semantic differential scales (Woods & Williams, 1976) to examine the origin of the stuttering personality stereotype. They hypothesized that student ratings of "a typical adult male stutterer" versus "a normally fluent adult male speaker who suddenly starts to stutter for a short period of time, after which he speaks fluently again" would be similar. The semantic differential scales were administered to 80 undergraduate students with 40 students in each condition. Student ratings of a typical adult male who stutters were indeed similar to those of a normally fluent male who stutters only temporarily. White and Collins proposed that listeners make inferences from their beliefs about the internal states of fluent speakers who exhibit disfluencies (i.e., fluent speakers who exhibit disfluencies do so because they are experiencing nervousness, shyness, etc.) and apply these inferences to PWS (e.g., individuals who stutter do so because they are nervous, shy, etc.). Thus, stereotypically negative judgments of PWS may be made out of uncertainty rather than derived from motivational factors (White & Collins, 1984).

Ham (1990) asked 536 people from Tallahassee, Florida, to provide their perceptions of people who stutter via semi-structured telephone interviews. These interviews were conducted by a total of 59 graduate and undergraduate students who each called 10 people randomly in the Tallahassee phone book. The age range of the participants varied from 11 to 85 years, and a wide variety of occupations were represented. Methodologically, some concerns exist regarding this study, particularly that the interviewers were described as "naïve" and did not seem to undergo training before conducting the interviews, and that the researcher was unable to verify the interviewees' responses, presumably because the interviews were not audio-recorded. Nevertheless, Ham found that participants' provided a broad range of responses when asked to define stuttering, state whether they have known a stutter or stuttered themselves, identify the sort of person they thought would be most likely to develop stuttering, and provide advice to a PWS to help their stuttering. The results of this study indicated that although many of the participants knew someone who stutters, there was confusion regarding the definition of stuttering. Forty percent of participants used circular reasoning to define stuttering (e.g., "Someone who stutters has a stutter in his speech"). Approximately 27% of respondents felt that stuttering was best defined as repetitions, but the term "repetition" was not used consistently among participants. Adding to this confusion over the definition of stuttering is that approximately 21% of participants said that they had stuttered in their past, and 12% of participants felt that they currently stuttered. This unusually high incidence/prevalence of stuttering would seem to suggest that laypersons consider stuttering to include disfluencies that are considered typical by speech therapists (e.g., revisions or repetitions of phrases), or that laypersons who infrequently use part-word repetitions, for example, consider themselves to stutter on such occasions. More than one-third of the participants indicated that they felt PWS are psychologically different from fluent speakers, and described PWS as being shy, frustrated, and anxious. Finally, in regard to the advice given to PWS, only 15% of the responses indicated that speech therapy might be beneficial. These results suggest that stuttering is not well understood by the general public.

This lack of understanding and the complexity of attitudes toward stuttering was acknowledged by Hulit and Wirtz (1994), who sought to determine how several variables impact attitudes toward PWS. They administered the *Stuttering Inventory* to 203 members of the general public, students in speech-language pathology classes, and professional staff at a school district. The *Stuttering Inventory* consists of 52 items that assess knowledge of and attitudes toward stuttering, and was constructed from a variety of existing survey instruments, including the *Clinician Attitudes Toward Stuttering Inventory*, the *Parental Attitudes Toward Stuttering Inventory*, and the *Alabama Stuttering Knowledge Test*. Attitude items on the *Stuttering Inventory* were represented by a Likert-type scale. The results indicated that gender, age, years of education, personally knowing a PWS, knowledge of stuttering, completing a stuttering course, and holding a certificate of clinical competence in speech-language pathology were not good predictors of attitudes toward stuttering. Hulit and Wirtz (1994) indicated that there was a narrow range in participants' attitude scores and suggested that the variables under investigation do not have an association with attitudes toward stuttering. Hulit and Wirtz further suggested that we are at a crossroad in attitude measurement, and provided a list of the problems that are inherent with survey research about stuttering. One of these problems is that there is not a universally accepted definition of stuttering. Researchers have typically assumed that stuttering has the same meaning for everyone when in fact it may not. Another issue is that the validity of the inventories used to measure attitudes toward stuttering has never been demonstrated; and indeed, it is very difficult to measure the validity of something as broad and inferential as an attitude. Finally, regardless of their methods, researchers have asked respondents to make judgments about people who stutter. The term stuttering may have negative implications, and certainly provides a signal to the respondent that the person that they are judging has a communication disorder. Hulit and Wirtz (1994, p. 258) suggest that "most people tend to react uniformly to "different" and "disordered" no matter their level of knowledge or degree of experience," which may explain why speech-language pathologists consistently report similar attitudes towards PWS as do the general public. Future research studies may investigate the actions of others toward PWS rather than conducting paper and pencil inventories.

The preceding studies indicate that members of the general public are confused about stuttering and hold negative attitudes toward PWS. It is unclear why such negative attitudes are so widely held by laypersons, but confusion regarding the definition of stuttering and its causes may help to contribute to the negative perceptions of PWS by this population.

VARIABLES THAT INFLUENCE ATTITUDES TOWARD PWS

In addition to examining the effects of group membership on perceptions of PWS, researchers have explored the effects of certain variables on listener reactions to stuttering and PWS. These studies have primarily relied upon laypersons as listeners. Some variables, such as making eye contact and disclosing stuttering, are within the control of PWS and appear to positively influence listener attitudes. Other variables, such as the listener's culture, the gender of the listener or the person who stutters, and the severity of the stuttering are largely beyond the control of PWS and have been found to negatively impact listeners' perceptions.

*Eye contact.*One variable that is under the control of PWS is the amount of eye contact they attempt to make with listeners. It is thought that appropriate eye contact is a part of effective communication and may influence listener perceptions of the speaker (Kamhi, 2003). Tatchell, van den Berg, and Lerman (1983) examined the effects of eye contact and fluency on listeners' perceptions of PWS. A videotape was shown to 127 college students in which one of four conditions was portrayed by an actor in conversation with another actor. These conditions were normal eye contact and normal fluency, normal eye contact and disfluency, low eye contact and normal fluency, and low eye contact and disfluency. Participants then completed semantic differential scales related to such variables such as trustworthiness, competence, and dynamism. The results indicated significant interaction effects for fluency and eye-contact. The authors suggested that increased eye contact by PWS can lead to improved listener attitudes toward PWS. A similar result was found by Atkins (1988) who used a 60-item semantic differential questionnaire to survey 133 college students regarding the personality traits of people who have good, minimal, and no eye contact. A hypothetical person who used minimal or no eye contact was rated less favorably on 70% of the scale items, suggesting that PWS may be perceived negatively if adequate eye contact is not maintained with listeners.

*Disclosure/acknowledgement of stuttering.*Disclosure of stuttering also seems to lead to increased positive perceptions of people who stutter. Silverman (1988) asked 46 college students who were enrolled in an introductory speech class to respond to an 81-item semantic differential questionnaire in which they rated either "a stutterer" or "a stutterer wearing a shirt on which is printed 'I stutter. So what!'" The person who wears a T-shirt that acknowledges the stuttering was rated more positively on 29 of the 81 traits; however, the trait "immature" was also associated with the T-shirt. A systematic replication of the study was conducted

(Silverman, Gazzolo, & Peterson, 1990) in which 54 employees at a shopping mall were surveyed using the same semantic differential scales. Similar results were found, suggesting that disclosure of stuttering may be one situation in which negative stereotypes of PWS can be reduced.

Collins and Blood (1990) examined the effects of stuttering severity and acknowledgement of stuttering as factors that may influence listeners' perceptions of PWS. The authors hypothesized that people who do not stutter will prefer to interact with PWS who acknowledge their stuttering, regardless of the stuttering severity, as compared to PWS who do not acknowledge their stuttering. Furthermore, acknowledgement of stuttering was proposed to alter listeners' perceptions of the intelligence, personality, and appearance of PWS. To test these hypotheses, 84 female college students who were not communication disorders majors served as participants. Participants were given a cover story in which they were told that they were going to work with one of two men who stutter for a class project about the effects of working with PWS. The participants were told that, in an effort to save time, they were going to watch brief interviews with the men who stuttered in order to determine with whom they would prefer to work. Participants then watched one of four videotapes that consisted of two 2-4 minute interviews with men who stuttered mildly or severely and who did or did not acknowledge their stuttering. After watching each interview, participants completed a survey that consisted of a 14-item semantic differential questionnaire (Burley & Rinaldi, 1986) and a written open-ended survey that asked participants to explain how they felt the speaker would interact with strangers and how he would act in a noisy environment. Participants were also asked to discuss how they would act around the speaker. Finally, after having watched both interviews, participants were asked to state which speaker they would prefer to work with and why. The results of the Collins and Blood (1990) study indicated that PWS, particularly those who stutter severely, were rated more favorably by participants when they acknowledged their stuttering. It is noteworthy that participant ratings were more negative for people who stuttered severely, regardless of whether or not they acknowledged their stuttering, as compared to those who stuttered mildly. This study suggests that helping clients who stutter to acknowledge their stuttering may facilitate improved interactions with others. Acknowledgement of stuttering by PWS may be a useful mechanism for facilitating attitude change; however, Collins and Blood (1990) stated that a limitation of the study is that mostly female participants rated male speakers. The findings may have been different had an equal number of male and female participants rated both male and female speakers who stutter.

A similar study (Healey, Gabel, Daniels, & Kawai, 2007) examined listeners' perceptions of videotaped samples of a male speaker who stuttered severely. Ninety laypersons were randomly assigned to one of three groups for a total of 30 participants in each group. In each of the three videos, the male speaker who stutters was asked the same question by the interviewer ("Can you tell me about a job you have had?"). In one video, the male speaker who stuttered disclosed that he stuttered at the beginning of his monologue. In another video, the disclosure came at the end of the monologue. The third video consisted of the monologue only, and no reference to the speaker's stuttering was made. To assess participants' reactions to each of these conditions, a six-item Likert-scale questionnaire was administered. These items included the following statements:

1) This person seems sincere.

2) This person is likeable.
3) This person is trustworthy.
4) This person is friendly.
5) This person shows character.
6) This person is emotionally well adjusted.

After completing the Likert scale, all participants were asked open-ended questions about their comfort level while listening to the speaker and whether disclosure of stuttering impacted their perceptions of the speaker. The quantitative data was analyzed using a multivariate analysis of variance, and the qualitative data was converted to percentages based on positive, negative, or neutral comments about the speaker. The results based on Likert scale data indicated that disclosing versus not disclosing stuttering did not result in an overall difference in listeners' ratings of the speaker. The time of disclosure was not significant on five of the six Likert scales, although listeners perceived the speaker who disclosed his stuttering at the end to be more friendly. The data from the open-ended questions indicated that the listeners felt comfortable listening to the PWS whether or not he disclosed his stuttering. Some participants who were in the disclosure groups seemed to perceive benefits to disclosing stuttering, particularly at the beginning of a speech, but the majority of participants in the non-disclosure group reported that disclosure of stuttering was not accompanied by any perceived benefits. The authors indicated that listeners may be comfortable with stuttering, regardless of its severity. More research is needed to determine whether society in general has become more accepting of PWS and stuttering.

The aforementioned studies appear to indicate that acknowledging or disclosing one's stuttering will help to ease communicative interactions between PWS and their listeners. It is not entirely clear as to why disclosure seems to have at least some positive affect on listeners' perceptions of PWS. It seems likely that disclosure of stuttering, like making eye contact, alleviates tension and confusion in the listener, but more research is needed that examines the thoughts and emotions of listeners as they interact with PWS.

Therapy and therapeutic techniques. Another variable that is under the control of PWS is whether to employ therapeutic techniques that may alleviate stuttering or help the person who stutters to stutter more easily. Two independent investigations were conducted by Manning, Burlison, and Thaxton (1999) to evaluate listener responses to stuttering modification techniques, in which PWS attempt not to eliminate stuttering, but to stutter more easily. Participants in the first study consisted of 24 employees of a food processing plant. They viewed two videotaped speech samples in counterbalanced order of a male speaker who simulated stuttering. In one sample, (the stuttering only video) the speaker simulated fluency breaks to a mild extent characterized by repetitions, sound prolongations, and blocks in which there was no voicing or airflow. In the other sample, the speaker repeated the content of the speech, but utilized a therapeutic technique called cancellations after fluency breaks. Cancellations involve finishing the stuttered word and then repeating that word more easily with less tension. Participants in the second study consisted of 50 volunteer listeners who were employees of a county school district. They also watched two videotaped speech samples of a man who simulated stuttering. One of these videos was the stuttering only video from the first study. The other video consisted of the same speaker applying pullouts. Pullouts allow PWS to decrease tension and stutter more easily while they are stuttering. After each video was presented, participants in both studies completed semantic differential scales

(Woods & Williams, 1976) and a 5-point handicap scale, in which listeners indicated how much they felt the speaker was handicapped by his condition. Participants in both studies then responded to open-ended questions that elicited their general reactions to the speaker, the degree to which they would interact socially with the speaker, and what it would be like to work with the speaker. The results of both studies indicated that participants felt that PWS who use pullouts or cancellations are more handicapped than PWS who do employ these techniques. Participants also responded less favorably to 42 of 50 semantic differential items when the speaker used therapy techniques. Responses to the open-ended questions revealed that participants in both studies provided the same types of generally negative reactions to the speaker who used therapy techniques. The specific nature of the comments was not provided by the authors; instead only a frequency count of positive and negative comments was documented. These results suggest that listeners react more negatively to stuttering modification techniques than stuttering only; however, the ability to generalize these results is limited because responses to only one speaker were gathered.

Gabel (2006) investigated university students' attitudes toward PWS based on stuttering severity and level of therapy involvement. Participants were given a 25-item semantic differential questionnaire (Woods & Williams, 1976) and were asked to rate one of four hypothetical conditions in which a man who stuttered severely or mildly chose or did not choose to attend therapy to improve his stuttering. The results indicated that participants reported more positive traits for the male who stutters mildly than the male who stutters severely. Attending therapy was also perceived more positively than not attending therapy to improve stuttering. There was no interaction between the stuttering and therapy variables, so that a person who stutters severely was not regarded more positively for attending therapy than someone who stutters mildly. Gabel (2006) suggested that most participants felt mildly positive or mildly negative toward PWS based on their semantic differential scores. This finding may indicate that participants feel mostly neutral or ambivalent toward PWS.

The Manning et al. (1999) and Gabel (2006) studies appear to indicate that although participants may perceive attending stuttering therapy to be beneficial, PWS who actually employ therapeutic techniques may be judged more negatively by their listeners. More information is needed about laypersons' perceptions of stuttering therapy and of therapeutic techniques in order to gain a better understanding of listeners' reactions to stuttering and how these reactions may help guide the therapy process.

Stuttering severity. The severity of stuttering has been examined by many researchers in order to determine whether the level of severity influences listeners' perceptions of PWS. For example, Turnbaugh, Guitar, and Hoffman (1979) used semantic differential scales (Woods & Williams, 1976) to measures speech therapists' attitudes toward PWS based upon stuttering severity. The 36 participants were asked to rate a hypothetical "typical individual" who was normally fluent, stuttered mildly, stuttered moderately, or stuttered severely. The results of this study confirmed that speech therapists perceive PWS more negatively than fluent speakers. There was also an increase in negative attitudes toward PWS when responses toward the mild stuttering and severe stuttering conditions were compared.

Susca and Healey (2001) investigated listeners' perceptions of simulated stuttering and fluency. A total of 60 individuals comprised of university staff, undergraduate students, and members of the general public served as participants. These participants did not have regular contact with or knowledge of someone who stutters. A speech sample (obtained while reading a standard piece of text called the Rainbow Passage) from a 27-year old male who stutters was digitized and was used as stimulus material. From this "core" sample containing 10% stuttered disfluencies, additional stimuli containing 0%, 5%, and 15% stuttered disfluencies were created using a computer program. An additional "treated" sample was developed, in which 0% disfluency was obtained by reducing pauses, eliminating extra glottal pulses, and eliminating sudden onsets and offsets from the core sample. A normal sample was developed that consisted of a 24-year-old male reading the Rainbow Passage with a normal rate and manner. Each participant was randomly assigned to one of the six conditions. After listening to the sample, participants were asked to verbally describe the speaker's speech. Participants then used a 7-point Likert scale that ranged from "strongly disagree to "strongly agree" to rate the perceptual features associated with the speaker. These scale items included: "This person is a competent speaker," "This person is a fluent speaker," "This person read the story easily," and "I felt comfortable listening to this person." Finally, three more open-ended questions were asked that included "What contributed to how comfortable you felt listening to this person?" "What were some of the features of his speech that caught your attention?" and "How easy or difficult was it to understand the story you just heard?" To interpret the data, the authors quantitized the qualitative data, and counted the number of participants' positive and negative comments. The results indicated that as the percentage of stuttered disfluencies increased, so too did the number of negative comments provided by the respondents. The Likert data suggested that as the speaker's disfluencies increased, the participants' comfort level decreased, and the speaker who stuttered was perceived as having less speech competency and fluency than the typical speaker.

In addition to the results obtained above, Susca and Healey (2002) also performed a phenomenological (qualitative) analysis of the 60 listeners' comments toward the speech stimuli based on different fluency levels. In phenomenological research, participants' comments are often grouped according to categories. Susca and Healey organized listener comments into three categories which included comments about the speaker, comments about the listener, and comments about the story (e.g., the Rainbow Passage). Speaker attributes included such theme clusters as speech production (e.g., rate, voice characteristics, articulation, flow, effort, naturalness); context (presentation style, context competence); and speaker identity (e.g., speaker characteristics, ideational issues, language expression). Listener attributes were comprised of those factors that influenced listener comfort, such as the effort required to listen to the speaker, content familiarity, the amount of attention required, and the listening context. Finally, story comprehension was influenced by the coherence, simplicity/complexity, and vocabulary of the story. These results indicated that listeners tend to hold more negative attitudes toward a speaker when increased stuttering is present in the speech sample; however, listeners also judge a person's speech on a variety of parameters other than stuttering. Furthermore, listener attributes as well as speaker attributes appear to be influential in perceptions of PWS, suggesting that therapeutic techniques should focus on helping clients who stutter be more effective communicators in addition to reducing the frequency of stuttering (Susca & Healey, 2002).

Panico, Healey, Brouwer, and Susca (2005) used a short Likert scale and open-ended questions to assess the degree to which stuttering severity influenced listeners' perceptions of PWS. The stimulus material was comprised of an adult male speaker who was videotaped while reading a passage with various levels of fluency (e.g., 0%, 5%, 10%, and 15% stuttering disfluency). An additional four audio samples were obtained from the videotapes. Sixty-four undergraduate students and members of the general community who had little familiarity with PWS were randomly assigned to one of the eight conditions. Participants then watched or listened to the stimulus and completed a questionnaire in which a Likert scale was used to indicate the degree to which participants agreed or disagreed with six statements that discussed the competence of the speaker, the effects of stuttering on the listener, and willingness to engage socially and professionally with the speaker. After completing this questionnaire, participants were asked to verbally provide their impressions of the speaker, to describe the speaker's speech, and to note anything about the speech that caught their attention. The results indicated that as the stuttering severity level increased, so too did the listeners' negative ratings and comments about the speech sample.

As previously discussed, Gabel (2006) investigated university students' attitudes toward PWS based on stuttering severity and level of therapy involvement. The results indicated that participants perceived a male who stutters mildly more positively than a male who stutters severely. Thus, it is apparent that those people who stutter severely are at a greater risk for being perceived negatively by listeners. The aforementioned studies indicate that as stuttering severity increases, so too does the amount of effort and concentration that the listener must spend while conversing with the individual who stutters. The listener's comfort level also seems to decrease when more stuttering is present. More research is needed to examine the perceptions of listeners as they engage in communication interactions with people who stutter mildly, moderately, and severely.

Cultural differences. One variable that has been shown to influence listeners' perceptions of PWS is the culture background of the listener. Bebout and Arthur (1992) investigated cross-cultural attitudes toward a variety of communication disorders, including stuttering. They compared the attitudes of foreign-born students with native North-American students. The participants' countries of origin included the United States, Canada, Hong Kong, Singapore, Malaysia, Taiwan, Southeast Asia, China, Japan, and Latin America. Participants responded to a 12-item questionnaire in which they were asked to provide their opinion to various statements on a 4-point scale which ranged from "probably no," "maybe no," "maybe yes," to "probably yes." The questionnaire items included statements that addressed the characteristics of PWS, such as intelligence and emotional stability; whether PWS should seek professional help from doctors or other helping professionals; effects of stuttering on the life of an individual who stutters, including social relationships and employment opportunities; and how other people should act toward PWS. Group comparisons indicated that non-native North Americans were more likely to think that people with communication disorders are emotionally disturbed. Participants from Asian countries, in particular, were also more likely to indicate that people with communication disorders could speak better if they tried harder. Bebout and Arthur (1992) concluded that it is important for speech-language pathologists to be aware of listeners' culturally-influenced beliefs and attitudes toward communication disorders in order to provide more effective treatment.

Cooper and Rustin (1985) utilized the *Clinician's Attitudes Toward Stuttering* (CATS) *Inventory* to assess cross-cultural attitudes toward stuttering and PWS. They administered the *CATS Inventory* to 371 American speech therapists from six states and 331 speech therapists from Great Britain. The results indicated that there were significant differences between British and American therapists in terms of appropriate treatment strategies and perceptions of attitudes toward PWS. British speech therapists were more likely to believe that PWS have psychological problems, but American therapists were more likely to believe that speech therapists should be more understanding of the feelings of their clients who stutter. American therapists were also more likely to believe that the general public has a more negative response toward stuttering as opposed to the British therapists. Cooper and Rustin (1985) indicated that the trend for both American and British speech therapists to attribute certain personality traits to PWS is troubling, as there is little data to support these beliefs.

More recently, St. Louis and colleagues (2010) investigated cultural stereotypes toward stuttering and another type of fluency disorder called cluttering. They found that people in Bulgaria, Russia, Turkey, and the United States express similar stereotypes toward both stuttering and cluttering, but that there are some cultural differences that emerge. Readers are encouraged to see Chapter 3 in this book for a more detailed account of this study.

Listener age. Many researchers have conducted studies using college students or adult members of the general public as participants, thus ensuring that data from participants with a moderately large age range has been obtained. One study (McGee, Kalinowski, & Stuart, 1996) explored high-school students' perceptions of PWS and found that they reported similarly negative reactions to PWS as did the general (adult) population. This research raises the question of at what age negative attitudes toward PWS begin to develop.

Ezrati-Vinacour, Platzky, and Yairi (2001) examined children's awareness of stuttering-like disfluencies. The research objectives were to identify at which age fluent children begin to recognize disfluencies, investigate whether specific types of disfluencies influence the age at which children become aware of stuttering, and determine if there is a relationship between children's attitudes toward stuttering-like disfluencies and their level of awareness. Eighty children ranging from ages three to seven years individually watched videotapes of two identical seal puppets that were positioned side by side. One puppet would say a six-word sentence using sound, syllable, and single-syllable-word repetitions for some of the sentences, and blocks and prolongations for the others. The other puppet would say these same sentences fluently. The order of fluent and nonfluent sentences was counterbalanced. After the child watched the puppets say a pair of sentences, the experimenter paused the tape and asked the child if both puppets talked in the same way. The child was also asked to point to the puppet on the screen that talked like him or her. After all six pairs of sentences were viewed, the child was asked to label the talking (e.g., "What do we call this kind of talking?"). The child was also asked if that kind of talking was good or not good. The child then viewed another pair of fluent-disfluent utterances from the puppets and was asked which puppet s/he would like to play with and why. The results indicated that children as young as age three can discriminate between fluent speech and stuttering-like disfluencies, but that awareness of stuttering continues to rise as children reach four and five years of age. The majority of five-year-olds can discriminate fluent from stuttered speech. Children had a greater awareness of disfluencies that were characterized by repetitions versus blocks or prolongations. The word "stuttering" was rarely used by children to label the stuttering-like disfluencies, but as children became older they were able to provide descriptions of stuttered speech. Children four-years and older almost unanimously agreed that the stuttered speech was "not good" and that they would prefer to have a fluent speaker for a friend. These findings suggest that the development of negative stereotypes may occur very early in a child's development, and that age-appropriate educational programs may be beneficial to prevent negative attitudes toward PWS and others with disabilities (Ezrati-Vinacour et al., 2001). It is still unclear as to why children perceive disfluent speech to be bad, and which variables influence this perception. It does seem likely that the negative attitudes demonstrated by children toward PWS are maintained throughout the life span and are hard to ameliorate.

Davis, Howell, and Cooke (2007) interviewed 400 fluent school children between the ages of about 8-15 years old. These students were classmates of children who stutter who were being treated for stuttering at a clinic with which the researchers were associated. Individual children were asked to look at the roster of students and to identify three children they liked most and three children they liked the least. They were also requested to give the names of three children who best fit certain traits, like being shy, assertive, cooperative, a bully, or a victim of bullies. The results indicated that children who stutter ranked lowest in social status, meaning that children who stutter were found to be less popular and more likely to be rejected by peers. Children who stuttered were also more likely to be perceived as the victim of bullying and less likely to be perceived as leaders.

Evans, Healey, Kawai, and Rowland (2008) also investigated children's perceptions of stuttering. The 64 middle school children who participated in the study watched a video recording of a young adolescent who stuttered with varying degrees of severity. They administered a survey in which the students indicated their agreement with 11 Likert scale items. These items addressed affective, behavioral, and cognitive factors, such as the comfort level of students who watched the video, the speech characteristics of the adolescent in the video, and how the extent to which students felt that the adolescent who stutters would fit in at school. While it was encouraging that the frequency of stuttering did not influence whether the students themselves were willing to have a friend who stutters, they did believe that adolescents who stutter more severely would have a harder time fitting in at school and making friends with others.

Gender. Like cultural differences, gender differences may also account for some listener perceptions. Burley and Rinaldi (1986) asked ten male and ten female naïve listeners who ranged in age from 15-35 years to rate recorded speech samples of both male and female PWS on a variety of traits using previously existing semantic differential scales. The authors found that there were significant differences between the male and female listener ratings, with males tending to rate the speech samples of PWS more negatively than the females. The sex of the PWS did not have an effect on the ratings by the male or female listeners. Patterson and Pring (1991) replicated this study but included a control group of fluent speech samples for the 20 male and 20 female naïve listeners. The results indicated that male and female listeners did not provide significantly different ratings. In both the Burley and Rinaldi (1986) and the Patterson and Pring (1991) studies, there was not a gender difference observed when respondents rated both male and female stuttered speech samples. These findings suggest that the gender of PWS and their fluent listeners may be irrelevant in the formation and maintenance of negative attitudes toward PWS.

Silverman (1982) investigated the perceptions of 160 speech therapists and 176 university students regarding eight hypothetical individuals ("a girl," "a girl who stutters," "a boy," "a boy who stutters," "a woman," "a woman who stutters," "a man," and "a man who stutters"). The primary purpose of this study was to determine if perceptions of girls and women who stutter are different than the negative stereotype that has been reported for boys and men who stutter. A 47-scale semantic differential questionnaire (Silverman & Zimmer, 1979) was administered to participants, with each participant completing the scales for only one of the eight hypothetical individuals. The results indicated that speech therapists view females who stutter as being significantly different on a variety of personality traits as compared to females in general and males who stutter. The speech therapists seemed to have a stronger negative stereotype for a female who stutters than for a male who stutters, a finding that conflicts with that of Ragsdale and Ashby (1982). The university students who participated in the study appeared to have a stronger stereotype for males than for females who stutter, suggesting that different groups of people (e.g., professionals versus laypersons) may hold different perceptions of PWS depending on the gender of the PWS (Silverman, 1982).

Social distance. Perhaps one of the only variables that is somewhat beyond the control of PWS that has been found to positively influence attitudes toward PWS is the degree of social distance between PWS and their listeners. It has been theorized (Allport, 1954) that under certain circumstances, a reduction in prejudice (and negative stereotypes) can occur from increased intergroup contact. This theory has been tested by a several researchers with mixed results.

Fowlie and Cooper (1978) administered semantic differential scales (Woods & Williams, 1976) to the mothers of 34 stuttering and 34 nonstuttering male children who were between the ages of 6-11 years. The results indicated that mothers of children who stutter tended to describe their child as being significantly more anxious, introverted, fearful, sensitive, withdrawn, and insecure as compared to mothers who described their child who did not stutter. Fowlie and Cooper's research raises important questions about the temperament of children who stutter, but raises the equally important question of whether individuals hold stereotypical beliefs about stuttering that they apply to family members who stutter.

Doody, Kalinowski, Armson, and Stuart (1993) surveyed a total of 106 members of the general public in three small, rural communities in Newfoundland, Canada. The authors asked participants to complete a 25-item semantic differential questionnaire (Woods & Williams, 1976) in order to investigate attitudes toward adult males who stutter as compared to adult males who do not stutter. Eighty-five percent of the respondents knew at least one person who stutters and 39% reported a familial relationship with someone who stutters. Statistical analysis indicated that there were not significant differences between members of the three rural communities or between respondents with a family member who stutters versus those who did not have a family member who stutters. People who stutter were perceived as being significantly different from people who do not stutter on 20 of the 25 scale items and were perceived as being more guarded, nervous, shy, self-conscious, tense, sensitive, anxious, withdrawn, quiet, avoiding, fearful, passive, afraid, introverted, insecure, emotional, self-derogatory and inflexible. The five items that were not significantly different included such traits as being friendly, cooperative, pleasant, intelligent and perfectionistic. Thus, the rural communities under investigation had mostly negative attitudes toward a hypothetical adult male who stutters as compared to a hypothetical typical normal adult male speaker. These results are surprising because the majority of respondents in the close-knit communities under investigation knew PWS or had a familial relationship with someone who stutters. Doody et al. (1993) suggested that the negative stereotype of PWS might persist under these conditions because the stuttering behavior (e.g., tension, struggle) is particularly salient, or because PWS may actually have significantly different character traits as compared to fluent speakers. Doody et al. suggest that future research "should examine the strength, genesis, and possible clinical implications of an existing and pervasive negative stereotype" (p. 371) with an emphasis on examining ways in which the negative stereotype can be changed.

Klassen (2001, 2002) conducted a series of studies to determine whether different groups of people may interpret and understand stuttering differently. In the first study, (2001), 114 friends and colleagues of PWS were given a written questionnaire. The first part of the questionnaire assessed participants' attitudes toward PWS in general and consisted of semantic differential scales (Woods & Williams, 1976), portions of the *CATS Inventory* (Cooper 1975), and the *Parental Attitudes Toward Stuttering Inventory* (Crowe & Cooper, 1977). The second part of the questionnaire assessed participants' attitudes toward one PWS in particular with whom they were familiar. The participants in this study reported having less stereotypical beliefs about PWS in general as compared to previously reported results (e.g., Hulit & Wirtz, 1994). These results indicated that the increased social closeness of some people to PWS had a positive effect on their attitudes toward PWS in general.

Using a similar methodology, Klassen (2002) identified six PWS and surveyed their close acquaintances (including friends, family, teachers, fellow students, and colleagues) to see if these significant others held the same negative stereotypes toward PWS that have been pervasive throughout the stuttering literature. The six PWS were also surveyed for comparison purposes. The 175 participants completed a two-part questionnaire. The first part asked participants to rate PWS in general, and utilized six semantic differential items as taken from the Woods and Williams (1976) scales. The second part asked participants to list the name of a PWS that they knew personally (e.g., one of the six PWS with whom they were acquainted). The results indicated that the people who were personally acquainted with at least one person who stutters rated PWS more favorably on personality dimensions than has been reported for members of the general public (Hulit & Wirtz, 1994). In addition, the people who stutter who also served as participants in this study rated their speech as being more abnormal than did their acquaintances. These findings suggest that different groups of people may hold different attitudes toward PWS depending on their level of social distance. As a whole, the Klassen (2001, 2002) studies suggest that ongoing contact with someone who stutters may lead to increased positive attitudes toward PWS; conversely, people who have little or no contact with someone who stutters may be more likely to hold negative stereotypes about PWS.

Gabel, Tellis, and Althouse (2004) also investigated the effects of familiarity on perceptions of PWS. College students who had varying degrees of familiarity with PWS completed a 25-item semantic differential questionnaire (Woods & Williams, 1976). Unlike the findings of Klassen (2001, 2002), no significant differences were found based on level of familiarity with PWS. Gabel et al. (2004) suggested that future studies should investigate both the quality and the quantity of relationships that participants have with individuals who stutter, as the nature of the relationship and the number of PWS that one knows may influence one's attitudes toward PWS.

Hughes (2008) also surveyed college students to address the affects of familiarity with PWS. A written, open-ended survey was administered to approximately 150 university students and the resulting data were analyzed both qualitatively and quantitatively to determine (a) the descriptions of PWS students provided when not constrained by pre-determined items on semantic differential scales; (b) the rationale for these descriptions; and (c) whether such factors as gender and familiarity with PWS influenced the types of descriptions associated with PWS. Thematic analysis of the data suggested that individuals may hold simultaneously positive and negative attitudes toward PWS regardless of their gender or familiarity with stuttering. The respondents indicated that PWS can be shy, frustrated, and anxious individuals who are nonetheless "normal" or "just like everyone else." Many of these descriptions of PWS were based on actual observations of (or assumptions about) how society in general reacts to stuttering. PWS were perceived as being less intelligent and capable by others due to their stuttering and the negative impressions that stuttering seems to convey. These societal reactions were generally viewed as causing PWS to develop negative personality traits such as avoidance, shyness, and anxiety, though sometimes PWS were perceived as being particularly kind, caring, or compassionate because they are misunderstood or even persecuted, and do not want to do so to others. Hughes, Gabel, Irani, and Schlagheck (2010) postulate that fluent speakers appear to perceive PWS as being likeable individuals who are poorcommunicators, a combination of perceived high-warmth and low-competence that elicits pity and passive harmfrom listeners according to social psychologists (Cuddy, Fiske, & Glick, 2008).

While it is not entirely clear to what extent such factors as listener familiarity with stuttering influences attitudes toward PWS, it is well understood that attitudes toward PWS tend to become more negative as the severity of stuttering increases. Listeners' responses to stuttering also tend to be consistently negative regardless of their age or whether they have professional or personal relationships with PWS. More research is needed to determine how attitudes toward stuttering and toward PWS in general are formed and the extent to which these negative attitudes can be changed.

ATTEMPTS TO AMELIORATE NEGATIVE ATTITUDES

A small number of researchers have examined factors which might change listeners' attitudes toward PWS. For example, McGee, Kalinowski, and Stuart (1996) examined whether watching a videotape about stuttering would change the negative perceptions of high school students toward a hypothetical male high school student who stutters. Thirty-six high school students completed semantic differential scales for either a hypothetical "normal high school male" or a "high school male who stutters." Analysis of these data indicated that the high school students held strong negative stereotypes of a high school male who stutters. These stereotypes remained unchanged after participants watched the video "Voices to Remember" in which stuttering by adults was depicted by an 11-year-old female narrator. The results of this study suggest that watching the video "Voices to Remember" in and of itself was not enough to change viewers' attitudes about PWS. It may also be that the video simply enhanced the negative stereotypes that the participants already possessed.

Snyder (2001) investigated how attitudes toward PWS may be changed as a result of learning about stuttering via videotapes. Twenty-one graduate students in a speech-language pathology program were administered the *CATS Inventory* prior to and after watching an emotionally-charged video that documented the life of a young girl who stutters. Another group of thirty-four graduate speech therapy students completed the *CATS Inventory* prior to and after watching a videotape that demonstrated immediate amelioration of stuttering via therapeutic techniques. A comparison of the two conditions indicated that few, if any, changes, in participants' attitudes toward stuttering and PWS resulted from viewing the videotapes. Snyder indicated that it may be more beneficial to measure listeners' psychophysiological responses to stuttering rather than to continue to administer paper and pencil questionnaires to measure attitudes towards PWS.

Guntupalli et al. (2006) addressed this issue in a study examined the psychophysiological responses of fluent speakers to PWS. The fifteen fluent speakers, including university students and other laypersons, watched one-minute video samples of PWS and fluent speakers. Data about participants' emotional and physiological reactions were gathered via measurements of heart rate and skin conductance. Participants tended to have a slower heart rate when listening to PWS, indicating that listeners pay more attention to the speech of PWS than that of fluent speakers. Increased skin conductance was also noted as participants watched the videos of PWS, suggesting that listeners experience unpleasant emotional arousal when listening to PWS. Such findings complement the work of Susca and Healey (2001, 2002) who found that such factors as listener comfort and the mental effort required to understand the disrupted speech of PWS influences fluent speakers' perceptions of stuttering and PWS. The Guntupalli et al. study did not pair heart rate and skin conductance measures with participants' self-reports about their experiences while watching PWS speak. Future research could combine psychophysiological and self-report data in order to provide a more complete understanding of how survey-based responses of fluent speakers correlate with more direct measures of their reactions to PWS.

Given that proximity to stuttered speech can cause cognitive, affective, and even physical discomfort for fluent listeners, it is perhaps unsurprising that negative attitudes toward stuttering and PWS cannot be easily ameliorated. At the present time little is known about the ways in which fluent speakers behave when interacting with PWS. In the next section we describe the results of a study we conducted to obtain more information about the ways in which fluent speakers believe they can facilitate effective interactions with PWS, and we describe the implications of these findings relative to quality of life issues for PWS.

STUDY: FLUENT SPEAKERS' PERCEPTIONS OF MUTUAL HELP WHEN INTERACTING WITH PWS

Introduction

Wendell Johnson, a well-known pioneer in the field of stuttering therapy and research, conducted a survey of the reactions of PWS to stuttering in front of various types of listeners. Johnson (1934) found that for PWS, stuttering in front of a close friend or family member was perceived as less embarrassing than stuttering in front of strangers. Johnson concluded that listener reactions influence PWS in a variety of ways, including general comfort and stuttering severity, and that listeners should make PWS feel as comfortable as possible by:

> acting and speaking [so that the person who stutters] will feel secure in one's presence, will feel that he is being accepted as an individual, and will feel that he has nothing to lose by stuttering. Classroom teachers, speech clinicians, parents and society in general should apply this knowledge at every opportunity. (44)

This statement suggests that there are appropriate and beneficial communication strategies that all listeners should employ in their interactions with PWS; however, few if any researchers have provided specific details about these strategies or evidence for their effectiveness.

Some guidelines have been put forth regarding how to interact with PWS. The Stuttering Foundation, a non-profit organization dedicated to people who stutter, has made a pamphlet

(2008) widely available to the general public in which tips for speaking with someone who stutters are provided. This six-item list suggests that fluent listeners:

1) Avoid giving PWS advice like slowing down, relaxing, or taking a breath.
2) Let PWS know that listeners care about the content of the message rather than the way the message is delivered.
3) Make normal eye contact and wait patiently for PWS to finish speaking.
4) Avoid filling in words for PWS.
5) Be patient when interacting with PWS on the telephone, as this situation is usually difficult for them.
6) Maintain a relaxed rate and natural tone of speech.

It is unclear to what extent the general public knows of and adheres to these guidelines. The documented life experiences of PWS suggest that these guidelines are not always followed by fluent speakers (Daniels, 2007; Hughes, 2007). But the extent to which fluent speakers require support from PWS is also unclear. If the general public could provide guidelines for PWS in conversation with their fluent listeners, what would these guidelines be? And, perhaps more importantly, what implications do the beliefs of fluent speakers in this regard hold for the quality of interactions between PWS and their listeners?

Method

Design

To begin to answer these questions a qualitative research design was implemented. Qualitative methodologies are becoming increasingly common in stuttering research in terms of understanding the experiences of PWS (Corcoran & Stewart, 1998; Klompas & Ross, 2004; Petrunik & Shearing, 1983; Whaley& Parker, 2000) and analyzing recovery from stuttering (Finn & Felsenfeld, 2004; Huber et al., 2004; Plexico, Manning, & DiLollo, 2005). A standard definition of qualitative research has been provided by Creswell (1998, p. 15):

> Qualitative research is an inquiry process of understanding based on distinct methodological traditions of inquiry that explore a social or human problem. The researcher builds a complex, holistic picture, analyzes words, reports detailed views of informants, and conducts the study in a natural setting.

The concept of qualitative research is founded on a constructivist paradigm. In this mode of thought, qualitative research is beneficial when attempting to interpret "a world in which reality is socially constructed, complex, and ever changing" (Glesne, 1999, p. 5). Thus, qualitative researchers wish to explore, in detail, how participants in a study perceive or experience a particular phenomenon, such as stuttering and PWS. To gain a deeper understanding of the research topic, qualitative researchers ask questions that begin with *how* or *what* to assess the deeper meaning of the phenomenon under investigation (Creswell, 1998). Qualitative research methods were necessary for this study in order to conduct an in-depth exploration of fluent speakers' beliefs about interactions with PWS.

Participants

University students served as research participants in the present study for several reasons. College students are a convenient population from which to gather data, and they have often been included in studies that have examined attitudes toward PWS (Bebout & Arthur, 1992; Collins & Blood, 1990; Dorsey & Guenther, 2000; Gabel et al., 2004; Panico et al., 2005; Tatchell et al., 1983 Silverman, E., 1982; Silverman, F.H., 1988; Silverman & Paynter, 1990; Susca & Healey, 2001, 2002; White & Collins, 1984). Only a few of these studies have given participants the opportunity to justify their responses (e.g., Collins & Blood, 1990; Panico et al., 2005; Susca & Healey, 2001, 2002), and so the use of college student participants was deemed appropriate in order to gain information that could help to develop an understanding of why students in previous studies have reported generally negative attitudes toward PWS in quantitatively-driven studies. Furthermore, of those studies that have used multiple groups of participants, such as speech-language pathologists, teachers, college students, and members of the general public, (e.g., Dorsey & Guenther, 2000; Horsley & FitzGibbon, 1987; Kalinowski, Armson, Stuart, & Lerman, 1993; Panico et al., 2005; Susca & Healey, 2001, 2002), only a few of these studies have reported minor differences among groups of participants (e.g., Dorsey & Guenther, 2000). Thus, the attitudes reported in the literature appear to be consistent among most groups of participants, indicating that attitudes toward PWS tend to be universal rather than a byproduct of one's profession or group membership. It was presumed that the responses of college students to the written survey and interview questions would be similar enough to those of speech therapists, teachers, and members of the general public that surveying college students would be sufficient to answer the research questions.

The number of participants in qualitative research studies can vary. As many as ten participants have been suggested as an ideal number of participants for interviews in qualitative research studies (Creswell, 1998); however, there is no pre-determined number of interviewees that is needed. The only other qualitative study that has examined listener attitudes toward stuttering (Susca & Healey, 2002) involved 60 interviewees who were asked simple questions about a stuttered speech sample that required only a brief response. Glesne (1999) suggests that a breadth of understanding on a given topic can be achieved by involving a greater number of research participants in a qualitative study. Thus, a relatively large sample of 150 university students participated in the present study in order to gain a breadth of understanding regarding students' attitudes toward stuttering and PWS.

In order to participate in the present study, participants were required to be at least 18 years of age, have no history of stuttering, not be a communication disorders major, and be enrolled as a student at a mid-sized Midwestern university. Of the 580 surveys distributed to students, 207 were returned for a response rate of 35.8%. Six participants (1%) reported that they currently or previously identified as a person who stutters and were excluded from the data set. Despite attempts to recruit from equal numbers of men and women, there were fewer male than female respondents. Of the 201 students who returned a survey and met the criteria to participate in the study, 153 (76.1%) were women and 48 (23.9%) were men. The disparity between men and women respondents was lessened somewhat by excluding from the data set 51 surveys from women received during the later stages of data collection. Thus, for data analysis purposes, the final sample size was 150 participants consisting of 102 women (68%) and 48 men (32%). These gender differences may be accounted for in part by the lower ratio of males (44.3%) to females (55.7%) at the university. In addition, more women than men volunteered to take the survey (58.6% versus 41.4%), and women were more likely to return the completed survey than men (45% response rate versus 20%). Two men and 16 women also completed an oral interview. Women who returned the written survey were also more likely than men to volunteer to be interviewed (67% versus 55%). Finally, Dillman (2007) suggests that women are simply more likely to complete survey studies.

The average age of the participants was 22.5 years (SD = 6.18) with an age range of 18-58 years. Reports of academic standing indicated that 42% of participants were freshmen or sophomores, 34% were juniors or seniors, 22.7% were graduate students, and 1.3% were nontraditional students. Information about the ethnicities of participants was also obtained. The majority of participants were white/Caucasian (82%), but other ethnicities included black/African-American (10%), Hispanic (3.3%) and Asian/Pacific-Islander (3.3%). A small number of participants (1.3%) declined to give their ethnicity. With the exception of Native American/American Indian students, no ethnic group was underrepresented in the data set as compared to the larger University population.

Participants reported a variety of academic majors. The majority of participants (54%, n = 81) were in the College of Education and Human Development which included such diverse majors as rehabilitation counseling, interior design, tourism, and human movement/leisure studies in addition to education. Other participants were from the College of Arts and Sciences (22%, n = 33), the College of Business Administration (10%, n = 15), the College of Health and Human Services (7%, n = 11), and the College of Technology (5%, n = 7). Three participants (2%) reported that they were undecided as to their major.

Participants varied in terms of their familiarity with PWS and ranged from knowing no one who stutters to knowing nine PWS (M = 1.42, SD = 1.51). One participant reported knowing a total of 36 PWS and was removed as an outlier. Thirty-seven participants (24.7%) reported not knowing anyone who stutters. The remaining 112 participants reported knowing a combined total of 265 PWS. The relationships they had with these PWS included casual acquaintances, teammates, fellow church-goers, classmates, and family members.

Instrumentation

Written survey. A written survey was developed for use in this study. This survey consisted of two parts. The first part of the survey was a demographic questionnaire (adapted from Gabel et al., 2004), which asked participants to provide such information as their age, gender, ethnicity, and academic major. Participants were also asked to indicate whether they consider themselves to be a person who stutters (either currently or in the past), and if they ever had a class that discussed communication problems. In addition, participants were asked if they know someone who stutters, and if so, how well they know that person. The second part of the survey consisted of two open-ended questions. The first question was simply, "What is a good way to act around someone who stutters?" The second question was similar and asked, "What can people who stutter do to help their listeners?" These questions were designed to assess perceived sources of communication breakdowns and barriers to effective communication between fluent speakers and PWS. They were also meant to allude to ways in which fluent speakers believe people in general should behave toward PWS, and how PWS themselves can also help to facilitate effective communication with their listeners.

Interviews. Participants who completed the written survey were given the opportunity to indicate whether they would be willing to participate in an oral interview with the researcher. If they were willing to be interviewed, participants provided their name and e-mail address on the written survey. Participants were contacted via e-mail to set up an interview time if the participant's written responses were ambiguous or required more clarification, or if the responses seemed particularly insightful or useful when interpreting the data. Follow-up interviews with these participants served the purpose of obtaining additional information that helped to illuminate themes or clarify general trends among participants' responses.

Interview questions in general were participant-specific, e.g., "I noticed that you said that 'special precautions' should be taken when interacting with people who stutter. Could you elaborate on some of these precautions?" Other questions were participant-specific but also asked for elaboration on trends among participants' responses in general, e.g., "You, like many other participants, wrote that one should 'act normally' around people who stutter. Can you give me some examples of how to act normally?" Open-ended questions and probes were used to obtain information from participants.

The written survey data and the interviews were conducted concurrently. As soon as a survey was received the first author read it to determine if that participant's responses warranted an interview based on the criteria as previously described. If so, attempts to schedule an interview with the participant were made. Interviews were scheduled for 30 minutes but most required 20 minutes or less to complete. Each interview was audio-recorded and transcribed verbatim. Information from the interviews was used to make inferences when analyzing the survey data. There was not a specific number of interviews that were required, as the number of interviews depended upon participants' written survey responses and the availability of participants to complete the interview. Instead, interviews were conducted until data saturation was obtained, which occurred after the 18th interview, or 12% of the total sample.

Procedures

*Pilot study.*A short pilot study was completed to examine the effectiveness of the survey questions. The questionnaire was administered to 28 students in an introductory communication disorders course. The students were offered a small amount of extra credit to complete the questionnaire and provide a critique of its format, grammar, and overall ease of use. A review of these data suggested that most students provided thoughtful answers and did not feel that the questionnaire needed to be changed from its original format. While reading students' responses to the questions it became apparent that, on occasion, some students provided answers that were vague or confusing, while other students provided responses that seemed particularly well articulated and insightful. As a result of this finding, conducting interviews with participants was considered appropriate to gain a more thorough understanding of the thought processes of students as they contemplate stuttering and PWS.

Data collection. The first author visited a total of 38 classrooms on the university campus to recruit participants. The purpose of the study and participants' responsibilities for both the written survey and interview were explained using a standard script. The exclusionary criteria were also discussed at this time. It was emphasized that even students who did not know someone who stutters could participate in the study, as the inclusion of participants with different levels of familiarity with stuttering was necessary to provide a broader perspective from which to analyze and interpret the data. Students who volunteered to participate received a written survey and consent form. As an incentive to participate, a form to enter into a drawing to win an iPod Shuffle™ was also included with the survey. Students who took a survey were asked to place their name and e-mail address on a sign-up sheet so that response rate data could be obtained and friendly reminders to complete the survey could be sent via e-mail at weekly intervals. Also included on the survey was a separate page that asked if participants would be interested in participating in a follow-up interview about stuttering and PWS. The purpose of these interviews was to clarify written survey responses, so only 18 participants were interviewed. The interviews occurred concurrently with analysis of the written data.

Instructor permission to visit each classroom was obtained via e-mail prior to recruiting participants. Identifying these instructors was largely a matter of convenience, e.g., the first author's personal or professional acquaintance with the instructors; however, to achieve the target sample of 150 students of various ages and majors, instructors unknown to the researcher were also contacted. An attempt was made to recruit students of various ages and majors. Thus recruiting took place in several sections of an introductory public speaking course that was required for all majors. These classes were attended mostly by freshmen and sophomores, but also some juniors and seniors. Other participants were recruited from 300-400 level courses attended primarily by juniors and sophomores of a particular major (e.g., biology, sociology, English), and from graduate level courses. In some cases, disproportionate numbers of men or women attended courses for upper-level undergraduate and graduate courses. For example, in education classes women far outnumbered men, but in technology classes there were more men than women. Every attempt was made to recruit equal numbers of men and women by visiting similar numbers of classrooms that were heavily skewed in terms of gender.

*Data analysis.*Participants' written responses to the survey questions were typed into a Word document and interview responses were transcribed verbatim during ongoing data collection. The general format for analysis of qualitative research as proposed by Maxwell (2005) was used to analyze all data. In the first step in the analysis process, the authors read over the data and took notes regarding initial impressions. Preliminary ideas about the nature of participants' attitudes and how their responses could be categorized and organized were developed. This process, called coding, was used to develop relationships among participants' statements that allowed for comparisons of the data. Once the codes were established the data were arranged into themes, which allowed the authors to present the broader issues that were representative of participant's individual responses (Maxwell, 2005).

*Credibility.*Qualitative researchers do not employ control groups, randomized sampling of participants, or other methods that are designed to account for extraneous variables or other threats to validity (Maxwell, 2005). Thus, there is a need to establish that the qualitative methods and the conclusions drawn by qualitative researchers are credible and do not stem from the researchers' own biases. In qualitative research, the term validity is used to refer to the "correctness or credibility of a description, conclusion, explanation, interpretation, or other sort of account" (Maxwell, 2005, p. 106). The validity of the research process and the conclusions drawn from the data in this study were addressed in a variety of ways. A methodological journal was kept as a log of how the study progressed and the rationale that was used to help make certain decisions and interpret the data. The journal was reviewed by others who were not directly involved in the study to verify that there was a lack of researcher bias throughout the study. Another way that researcher bias was minimized was through the use of bracketing. Bracketing occurs when a researcher is interviewed about the topic under investigation so that his or her opinions and potential biases can be acknowledged before the researcher interacts with participants and analyzes the data. The first author, therefore, completed the written survey and was interviewed about stuttering and PWS by a peer who had knowledge of stuttering and PWS, but who was not affiliated with the study itself.

In addition to bracketing and journaling, a number of other validation procedures as described by Crewsell (1998) were employed to ensure that the data and the authors' conclusions were credible. The types of validation procedures that were used in this study included triangulation, providing detailed descriptions of the research process and the participants, and peer review. Triangulation involves the "use of multiple and different sources, methods, investigators, and theories to...shed light on a theme or perspective" (Creswell, 1998, p. 202). Obtaining data from a variety of sources, including the written surveys and oral interviews served as the basis for triangulation in the present study. Providing detailed descriptions of the participants and the research process allows readers of the study to make inferences regarding how well the outcomes of the study would transfer to similar participants and settings (Creswell, 1998). This study incorporated these procedures to ensure that the themes and conclusions that were derived from the data were trustworthy and as free from the authors' personal biases as possible. Additionally, two reviewers provided constructive criticism and took on a "devil's advocate" role, as they were not directly involved in the research process and had no stake in the study's outcome. One reviewer had extensive theoretical knowledge of stuttering and the other had qualitative research expertise.

Reliability.Measures of inter-rater reliability were obtained to help ensure that the results were reliable as well as credible. A subset of the larger data pool (approximately 25% of the responses for each survey question or 38 participants' responses for each question) was randomly selected for analysis by the authors. Once the codes for each question were agreed upon, responses were coded by the first and third authors, and as well as a graduate student who was trained in qualitative data analysis. This process allowed the authors to statistically analyze the extent to which the statements made by participants were perceived as thematically similar by the authors. Measures of intra-rater reliability were obtained when the primary researcher re-coded the data subset approximately two weeks after the group coding session. Percent agreement and Cohen's Kappa were used to establish inter- and intra-rater reliability. These measures were obtained via the use of the Program for Reliability Assessment with Multiple Coders (PRAM Version 4.5), available online through Skymeg Software. Percent agreement for each survey questionranged from 91% - 92% for inter-rater measures and 95% - 98% for intra-rater measures. Cohen's Kappa was also determined, as it is a more robust measure than percent agreement because it accounts for agreements that may occur by chance (Sim & Wright, 2005). Cohen's Kappa coefficients ranged from .88 - .89 for inter-rater measures and .93 - .97 for intra-rater measures. Cohen's Kappa coefficients that fall between .81-1.00 indicate almost perfect agreement (Landis & Koch, 1977).

Results

Data from the two survey questions were analyzed separately, and the results for each are presented below. While the results of qualitative research do not generally employ descriptive statistics as part of their analysis, an exception was made in this case due to the large number of participants in this study as compared to the much smaller numbers of participants that are usually to be found in qualitative research.

Question 1: What is a Good way to Act around Someone who Stutters?

The participants provided examples of acceptable and unacceptable listener reactions to stuttering and explained why these behaviors were or were not recommended for fluent speakers as they interact with PWS. The 149 participants who responded to the survey question provided a total of 472 statements (M = 3.17; SD = 1.50). These statements accounted for four major themes:

1) Behaviors that could not be readily observed, such as having patience or acting normally, referred to as intangible behaviors. These statements accounted for 59.1% of the total statements made by participants (n = 279, M = 1.87, SD = 1.05).

2) Observable behaviors such as eye contact or finishing words for PWS. Observable behaviors statements accounted for 16.10% of participants' statements (n = 76, M = .51, SD = .84).

3) Explanations that consisted of participants' beliefs about the emotional reactions of PWS to the behaviors of fluent speakers. Emotional reactions statements accounted for 12.1% of the participants' statements (n = 57, M = .38, SD = .55).

4) Explanations that focused on the humanity or normality of PWS. Normality of PWS statements accounted for 11.2% of the participants' statements (n = 53, M = .36, SD = .63).

In addition, miscellaneous statements not associated with any theme accounted for 1.3% of the total statements (n = 6, M = .04, SD = .20).

*Intangible behaviors.*Nearly 60% of participants indicated that people should employ behaviors which are unlikely to be directly observable by PWS during conversations with fluent listeners. Over one third (n = 97, 34.8%) of these statements indicated that listeners should act normally or naturally around PWS, or that PWS should be treated like anyone else. Examples of these statements are, "I think it is good to just act normal," and "A good way to act would be the same way as you act with other people." Other types of intangible behaviors consisted of being patient with a conversational partner who stutters (n = 48, 17.2%). For example, "You would just have to be more patient," and "It's my understanding that it takes someone who stutters longer to express their statements/thoughts. To this extent, listeners should act and be patient." It was not clear whether participants who reported needing patience to speak with PWS considered this to be a burden or limitation of interacting with PWS. Participants also made statements about ignoring the stuttering or focusing instead on the speaker's message rather than his or her stuttering (n = 21, 7.5%). One participant wrote, "I think a good way to act is to act as though the person doesn't have a stutter." Similarly, another participant stated, "I think that a good way to act is to ignore the stutter and focus on what the person is saying."

In addition to acting normally, being patient, and ignoring stuttering, the remaining *intangible behaviors*statements (n = 113, 40.5%) provided miscellaneous types of non-observable behaviors for fluent speakers who interact with PWS. These statements were typically positive but non-specific, such as "Care and be legitimate," "Give respect," and act in a way that is "not judgmental!" These results suggest that because the majority of the responses to this survey question were found to consist of intangible behaviors, it may be difficult for researchers, and indeed, PWS, to gauge listeners' reactions to stuttering via the use of direct observation techniques. Furthermore, it is very possible that such listener behaviors as acting normally, being patient, or ignoring stuttering would manifest themselves differently among various fluent listeners during actual conversations with PWS.

Observable behaviors. In direct contrast to intangible behaviors, 16% of the participants' statements indicated that there are specific behaviors that fluent listeners should employ when interacting with PWS. These behaviors would be observable by PWS and could be directly measured in research studies. In general, participants' statements were not clustered around specific sub-themes and were seemingly random. For example, which one participant suggested that "the listener, when speaking, could also speak more slowly and pause often," another participant recommended that "if [PWS] are nervous, maybe take them to a safe place where they are more comfortable." There were, however, some participant trends in terms of reporting such behaviors as making eye contact, not laughing at PWS, asking/not asking for clarification when the listener does not understand, and finishing/not finishing words for PWS.

The four statements related to eye contact unanimously indicated that fluent speakers should make increased or good eye contact with PWS. Refraining from laughing at PWS was also advocated by nine participants, e.g., "Don't stare or laugh or make fun." Unlike eye contact and not laughing at PWS, participants reported mixed beliefs regarding the acceptability of asking PWS for clarification or finishing words for PWS. For example, of the eight participants who mentioned asking PWS to repeat themselves, four indicated that it was acceptable to ask for clarification, e.g., "If you didn't catch something they said, ask them to repeat it. If you didn't hear what a person with normal speech said you would ask them to repeat it, so why treat someone who stutters any different?" The other four participants indicated that it would be best *not* to ask PWS to repeat themselves, e.g., "It may be more respectful not to ask questions like 'Can you repeat that?' or 'I don't understand.'" Similarly, 13 participants reported that one should not finish words or sentences for PWS, but 5 participants suggested that listeners could "try to fill in gaps or sentences for them," "suggest synonyms of the words, so that [PWS] would choose the words more easily," and "ask questions that needed a shorter response." These responses indicate that as a group, participants felt some confusion over certain behaviors, such as whether one should ask PWS to repeat themselves and whether to fill in words or otherwise "help" PWS with their speech.

It is interesting to note that only one participant reported that it would be acceptable to discuss one's role as a listener with the person who stutters:

"I think if I was with somebody with whom I needed to interact on a prolonged basis, and if I became close enough friends with them, I would try to ask them if I could do anything to make them more comfortable talking to me. I would ask them to coach me so that I could be a part of their environment in which they feel comfortable."

Thus, it is possible that the participants in this study generally did not believe that it is acceptable to discuss stuttering with PWS, or that participants had never considered such a possibility. The small number of reported observable behaviors as compared to intangible behaviors also indicates that participants may believe that it is more important to have a good attitude toward PWS than to verbally express or overtly demonstrate these positive attitudes to PWS.

Emotional reactions. Approximately 12% of the total number of statements consisted of participants' perceptions about the emotions that PWS experience because of fluent listeners' behaviors. Participants reported that PWS experience negative emotions when listeners act inappropriately, or that PWS are spared from negative emotions when listeners act appropriately. Thus, participants appeared to believe that fluent listeners often act as the emotional caretakers of PWS. For example, one participant wrote, "People who stutter should be treated with respect,and therefore I should be cognizant of their needswithout violating them or making them feel different." Similarly, other participants stated, "Don't treat them different or you could hurt their self-esteem," and "Just treat them normal so they don't feel like they are some sort of a freak." Listeners were also perceived as impacting the independence of PWS: "It is best to remain patientand let [PWS] finish their words. It is their idea, their thoughts, and finishing their words takes away that autonomy a little." Other statements that were representative of this theme included, "Be understanding and don't make them feel ignorant or disabled," and "I'd imagine they'd feel awkward enough. They don't need me to add to it." One participant even wrote that listener responses to stuttering could "promote, in some meager way, [PWS] overcoming their condition." In general, these statements indicate that the participants in this study assigned much importance to listeners' reactions to stuttering and perceived that listeners have the potential to positively or negatively affect the lives of PWS.

*Normality of PWS.*Approximately 11% of the total statements made by participants indicated that PWS are no different from anyone else. PWS were perceived as human beings who are normal with the exception of a communication problem that they cannot control and did not ask for. Examples of these statements included: "Act normal. They are just like you and I," and "[Act] like you would around someone who doesn't stutter. Just because someone stutters, it doesn't make them any less intelligent or any less of a person." These statements suggest that participants believe that PWS, though sometimes challenged by their stuttering, are essentially the same as anyone else and should be treated as such.

Question 2: What can People who Stutter do to Help their Listeners?

For this question participants provided a list of ways in which PWS can help to facilitate conversations with PWS and their fluent listeners. The 145 participants who responded to the survey question provided a total of 316 statements (M = 2.18; SD = 1.08). These statements accounted for five major themes:

1) Strategies for more effective communication or increased intelligibility, referred to as communication strategies. These statements accounted for 44.3% of the total statements made by participants (n = 140, M = .96, SD = .97).
2) Self-advocating behaviors, including acknowledging one's stuttering and educating others about stuttering. Advocacy statements accounted for 21.2% of participants' statements (n = 67, M = .46, SD = .87).
3) Advice to PWS to control their emotions or to tolerate the negative behaviors of fluent listeners. Emotional control statements accounted for 20.9% of the participants' statements (n = 66, M = .46, SD = .77).
4) The belief that PWS can do nothing to help fluent listeners, or expressions of uncertainty related to what, if anything, could be done. Uncertainty/nothing

statements accounted for 7.6% of the participants' statements (n = 24, M = .17, SD = .43).

5) The belief that fluent listeners, rather than PWS, are responsible for ensuring that the communicative interaction goes smoothly. Listener responsibility statements accounted for 6.3% of the total statements (n = 20, M = .14, SD = .42).

Communication strategies. Nearly 40% of participants indicated that PWS should employ strategies that would make them more effective communicators. More effective communication appeared to be related to less stuttering. Furthermore, reduced stuttering appeared to be associated with more intelligible speech. For example, one participant wrote, "A way that people who stutter can help their listeners is by talking slower, because that way the listener can make out what the person is trying to say instead of trying to guess what the person said." Similarly, another participant wrote that listeners would appreciate it if "people who stutter can try to speak slowly and think about what they are trying to say before they actually began a conversation."

Talking more slowly and thinking before speaking were not the only suggestions offered by participants. Other examples of strategies that were perceived to lead to more effective communication included talking less, avoiding problematic words, and using gestures or writing. For example, one participant wrote, "I think that people who stutter can help their listeners by expressing their thoughts completely yet briefly. If possible, it might help if they are able to compound their thoughts. This would help a listener know what the person who stutters is saying." Another participant stated, "I know that with some people who stutter they have a problem with certain letters. My advice would be to try and avoid words with these particular letters." The use of gestures was also mentioned: "I think that they can use gestures so that the listener knows what they are saying." Similarly, one participant stated that PWS could "talk with their hands and move around so that people don't just focus on the stuttering." The use of writing was also suggested in addition to the use of gestures: "I think that if it's an emergency situation that requires immediate attention, a stuttering person could write down a few words like, 'Call 911 now, woman heart attack!' or act out or point to something really quickly to show whoever they are trying to tell." One participant suggested that PWS "could carry a pen and note pad around to write things down for the people who can't understand them at all."

Only thirteen participants (9%) indicated that PWS could seek some form of treatment for their stuttering. These participants stated that PWS could visit a "speech pathologist," "speech therapist," or a "speech coach" in order to speak more clearly. Participants also mentioned that PWS could try to use therapeutic devices, e.g., "I've heard of an experimental device that, when inserted in the ear, eliminates the problem of stuttering completely." People who stutter were also advised to "take public speaking classes," presumably as a way to gain more experiences with speaking in public. Thus, very few participants appeared to believe that PWS may benefit from the services of a speech therapist. These results support Ham's (1990) finding that members of the general public had a decreased awareness of the availability of speech therapy services for PWS.

In general, participants' statements suggest that PWS should employ whatever strategies are necessary to avoid stuttering, thus increasing their intelligibility for listeners. The use of gestures to distract listeners from stuttering, not talking as much, and avoiding certain sounds or words are all examples of classic avoidance behaviors that are frequently employed by

PWS but are ultimately unhelpful (Guitar, 2006). Likewise, the advice of participants to "slow down" and "think before you speak," have been found to be equally unhelpful and frustrating for PWS (Guitar, 2006; Manning, 2001). Thus, there appears to be a discrepancy between participants' desire for people who stutter to demonstrate increased fluency and intelligibility versus the therapeutic techniques that PWS may employ that do not focus solely on increased fluency. Therapy goals such as open and honest stuttering without avoidance behaviors (e.g., Van Riper, 1982), may not be perceived as helpful by participants and may explain why research participants in other studies have not demonstrated increased positive regard for individuals who utilize such therapeutic techniques (Manning et al, 1999). The limited number of participants who believed that speech therapy services are of use to PWS is also of concern.

*Advocacy.*Approximately 21% of the participants' statements indicated that PWS should engage in advocacy behaviors such as acknowledging one's stuttering and educating others about stuttering. For example:

> "[PWS] maybe should inform their listener that they have a stuttering problem, and if the listener doesn't understand what stuttering is, explain it to them.Once the listener is informed it will be easier for them to communicate with a person who stutters and to be patient."

Similarly, another participant wrote,

> "I think people who stutter can help their listeners by explaining if they have any special needs or by being willing to answer their listeners' questions about stuttering."

As empowering and beneficial as it may be for PWS to express that they stutter and educate others, participants appeared to consider the benefits of acknowledgement only from the perspective of fluent listeners. From this viewpoint, acknowledging one's stuttering is seen as helpful because it eliminates the element of surprise that some participants experience when speaking with someone who stutters. For example, one participant stated, "Possibly [PWS] could warn the listeners of their stuttering problem before the conversation starts.I think this will help because the listener will not be surprised when they stutter." The word "warning," significant because it connotes the presence of imminent danger, was also used by another participant in a similar context. Likewise, one participant suggested that PWS should interact with young children to "minimalize the shock" that these children may otherwise experience as they grow up and are exposed to someone who stutters for the first time. Thus, stuttering appears to be perceived by some participants as a disconcerting experience for which forewarning is appreciated. This finding would appear to confirm that listeners are more comfortable with PWS when stuttering is acknowledged (e.g., Collins & Blood, 1990; Healey et al., 2007).

Other suggestions included the use of humor in addition to acknowledging one's stuttering:

> "Perhaps break the ice with something like, 'I stutter. You smell funny. We all have our issues.'Honestly, I would think that acknowledging the proverbial elephant in the room can be a good thing.Maybe [the person who stutters could] communicate to the listener things that will enhance communication."

Examples of advocacy described by participants also included simply being oneself, e.g., "Be yourself. Express who you are just as anyone else would. This should dispel some of the myths/preconceived notions about those who stutter." In addition to being one's self, continuing to talk despite one's stuttering was reported, e.g., "Just be yourself. Say something if it is on your mind." One participant simply wrote "Talk!" Thus, participants reported that PWS can advocate for themselves in diverse ways, some of which are perceived as having direct benefits for listeners.

Emotional control. Approximately 21% of the total number of statements consisted of participants' beliefs that PWS should exert effort to control their emotional reactions to (1) their own stuttering, (2) the often negative or frustrating reactions of listeners, or (3) both their own and listeners' emotional reactions. Forty statements indicated that PWS should work to control their own emotions. For example, one participant reported that PWS should try "not be so insecure when they speak to people." Likewise, another participant stated that PWS should "appear confident, because [listeners] are less likely to feel awkward and judged if someone is confident or unashamed of a disability." These types of statements appear to indicate that PWS are perceived as being shy, insecure, or unconfident, and that these characteristics can negatively impact the interactions of PWS and fluent speakers. Similarly, PWS were perceived as being excitable, anxious, or frustrated because of their stuttering. For example, "People who stutter can just stay calm and try not to get so frustrated," and "Try not to get frustrated as they speak so as to make it worse." Presumably, participants' descriptions of PWS as frustrated, anxious, or shy as reported on the second survey question appear to correspond with participants' beliefs that these negative characteristics are apparent in conversations with PWS.

Some statements (n = 21) indicated that PWS should try to control their emotional reactions to the sometimes unhelpful behaviors of listeners. Listeners were perceived as being frustrating, often because they cannot comprehend the message of PWS. For example, one participant wrote, "Be patient with someone who has trouble understanding [the person who stutters] because that could encourage more interaction." Similarly, another participant advised, "Do not get frustrated or upset if [listeners] don't understand what is being said at first." In addition to being patient with fluent listeners, a relatively small number of statements (n=5) advised that both PWS and listeners need to work on controlling their emotions so that the conversation goes smoothly. For example, "Both listeners and people who stutter need to not become frustrated if they are not connecting, and [they should] be willing to talk it out, as this also happens when talking to lots of other people whether they stutter or not." Thus, participants tended to perceive listeners as being one source of frustration and other negative emotions for PWS. They suggested that PWS may help their fluent listeners by being patient with them as listeners struggle to comprehend PWS in conversational interactions.

Uncertainty/nothing can be done. Approximately 8% of the total statements made by participants indicated that participants were unsure of what PWS could do to help their fluent listeners or felt that nothing could be done in this respect. For example, one participant wrote, "I'm not really sure if there is anything they can do, although I really don't know much about it. I've never known a person who stutters." Similarly, another participant stated, "I'm not sure exactly.I don't know if there are strategies to it or if it is just trying to say the words fast and clear." Other examples included such statements as, "I think that not much can be done," and "I really don't know. Nothing, I guess." These statements indicate that some participants may not have thought about this question or were not willing or able to provide suggestions or advice for PWS on this topic.

Listener responsibility. Approximately 6% of the total statements made by participants indicated that listeners, not PWS, should take responsibility for ensuring the effectiveness of conversational interactions between fluent speakers and PWS. Patience on the part of the listener was reported, e.g., "Listeners should be more patient, but a stutterer can't help someone be a better listener. Listeners should do this themselves." Other statements regarding the importance of listener patience included, "I just think the listeners need to be patient and pay attention," and "Based on my experiences it is more incumbent on the listener to be patient and ask for clarification if [they are] confused or unsure." In addition to having patience, one participant reported, "I think it is up to the listeners themselves to give people who stutter a chance to speak.[Listeners should be] open to take the time to allow people who stutter to express their feelings without putting pressure on them to speak faster or clearer." Thus, although the majority of participants indicated that PWS could take steps to help their listeners during conversations, a small number of participants felt that listeners themselves should take this responsibility.

Discussion

The purpose of this study was to ask fluent speakers to consider the ways in which PWS and their fluent listeners could most effectively interact. The results generally indicate that most fluent speakers believe that people should not be impatient, inattentive, or otherwise act negatively toward someone because he or she stutters. These intangible behaviors are not particularly behaviors at all—instead they appear to be a cognitive reminder to check the emotional impulses which may suggest that stuttering is frustrating to listen to, and that listeners may disengage emotionally and mentally from stuttering due to its disruptive effects on communication. There did not appear to be any overtly negative reactions to stuttering in the responses of participants in this study, and so it appears that cognitively, most fluent speakers recognize that they should respect PWS. Most of the directly observable behaviors recommended by participants indicated that fluent speakers are less sure about how to act toward PWS. Fewer participants reported observable behaviors such as making eye contact, not laughing at PWS, finishing or not finishing words or sentences for PWS, and asking or not asking PWS to repeat themselves. There was some disagreement among participants as a whole regarding whether listeners should ask PWS to repeat themselves or whether it is acceptable to finish words or sentences for PWS. Thus, although participants appeared believe that treating PWS like anyone else and with patience and respect were appropriate behaviors for fluent listeners, there was some confusion regarding the ways in which these behaviors should manifest themselves in more tangible, observable ways. This confusion is perhaps magnified by the belief of the fluent speakers in this study that their actions as listeners can have a great effect on PWS, whether positively or negatively.

Participants provided many types of suggestions for the ways in which PWS may help their fluent listeners. The most common of these suggestions was for PWS to engage in any behaviors that would alleviate or eliminate stuttering. Thus, common suggestions included avoiding problem sounds and words, writing instead of persevering through instances of severe stuttering, using gestures as a means of making one's point or distracting the listener from the stuttering, and simply speaking less. These avoidance behaviors were regarded as having a beneficial effect for listeners because they would decrease stuttering and therefore increase the intelligibility of individuals who stutter. Other suggestions included organizing one's thoughts before speaking and talking slower. Despite participants' reports that PWS should attempt to reduce or eliminate their stuttering, less than 10% of participants' statements indicated that speech therapy was a viable form of remediation for stuttering. Given fluent speakers' dislike of therapeutic techniques PWS can use to manage their stuttering, (Gabel, 2006; Manning et al., 1999), it seems as though the general public does not view speech therapy as a particularly effective way for PWS to cope with their stuttering. Thus, PWS who attend speech therapy or use therapeutic techniques may have difficulty in some respects as they try to manage both their stuttering and cope with reactions from fluent speakers.

Participants also reported that PWS should try to control their often negative emotional responses toward their stuttering. Such advice generally consisted of remaining calm and not becoming frustrated. These suggestions may indicate that PWS tend to be perceived as frustrated, excited, or anxious about their stuttering because these characteristics are perceived by listeners during conversations with PWS. Other participants indicated that PWS should have patience and be understanding toward their listeners, many of whom will have difficulty comprehending the message of the person who stutters and will ask him or her to repeat this message frequently. Fewer participants reported that it is the responsibility of PWS and their listeners to be patient with each other and ensure that the interaction is a smooth one. Similarly, a small number of participants indicated that it is not the responsibility of the person who stutters to help the listener; rather, it is the reverse. These participants felt that listeners should be more patient with PWS.

Other suggestions by participants indicated that PWS should be advocates for themselves and educate others about stuttering. A commonly suggested form of advocacy, acknowledging or disclosing that one stutters, was perceived as being helpful to listeners because they would then be better equipped emotionally to interact with that person who stutters. Some participants reported that PWS should use humor, be themselves, or not stop talking just because they stutter. Participants also reported that it is helpful for PWS to willingly discuss their stuttering with listeners, to educate listeners as to the causes of stuttering, and to provide listeners with suggestions regarding how the individual who stutters would like to be treated. This advice would seem to correspond well with the therapeutic approach to coping with stuttering that is advocated by many speech therapists.

To a great extent, the responses of fluent listeners to the survey questions are unable to be judged as correct or incorrect, or perhaps more appropriately, helpful or harmful to facilitating communication between fluent speakers and PWS. Few if any researchers have investigated the extent to which PWS benefit or do not benefit from the behaviors of fluent listeners, whether on a psychological or fluency level. The advice to PWS provided in this study does indicate that fluent speakers view stuttering as a rather debilitating disorder which impairs communication between fluent individuals and PWS. Very few of the study's participants declined to answer the survey questions or indicated that they were unsure of how PWS and fluent speakers could communicate more effectively. This finding may suggest that fluent speakers believe they should take on a helping role when interacting with PWS, but that PWS should also do what they can to minimize stuttering or to make their listeners feel at ease. Thus, fluent speakers and PWS seem to be required to engage in mutually supportive behaviors which further communication. Given the negative aspects of avoiding stuttering or trying not to stutter, however, some of the advice that fluent speakers give to PWS seems to have little benefit, ultimately, for PWS as they try to manage their stuttering and live their lives.

While there are a variety of ways to conceptualize the behaviors of the larger population to a stereotyped minority group, Cuddy, Fiske, and Glick's (2008) consideration of active facilitation and passive harm may be especially relevant to our discussion of PWS and fluent speakers. The stuttering literature suggests that fluent speakers consistently label PWS as friendly and cooperative but also less employable, assertive, and outgoing due to their communication difficulties. This high-warmth/low-competence combination may lead to pity from fluent speakers. Cuddy et al. indicate that groups of people who are pitied receive both active facilitation and passive harm. For PWS active facilitation could come in the form of advice from fluent speakers, such as to slow down, relax, and take a deep breath. Or fluent speakers may attempt to speak for PWS. Passive harm may involve behaviors like avoiding interactions with PWS, failure to employ PWS, or minimizing or not giving PWS opportunities to speak on the supposition that PWS prefer not to express themselves if it means that they will stutter in front of others. Few studies have examined interactions between PWS and fluent speakers in non-hypothetical contexts. Until such studies are implemented, it is unclear to what extent these suppositions are correct. The studies that have identified issues of concern for PWS in their daily lives, however, do suggest that the actions of fluent speakers can greatly impact quality of life for PWS (Corcoran & Stewart, 1998; Klompas & Ross, 2004; Whaley& Parker, 2000).

CHAPTER SUMMARY

This chapter started with an overview of stuttering and those factors which separate people who stutter from typically fluent speakers. A review of the stuttering literature suggested that attitudes toward people who stutter are nearly universally similar. Helping professionals as well as members of the general public seem to view people who stutter as likeable individuals who are somewhat less competent than other individuals in society. To further examine this point, a qualitative study was conducted in which fluent university students were asked to write about how people who stutter and fluent speakers could communicate more effectively. The overall tone of the responses was positive and indicated that fluent speakers believe that it is important to treat PWS with kindness and to engage in behaviors which might make communication easier for both PWS and fluent speakers. Further examination of the responses seem to confirm Cuddy et al.'s (2008) model of social competence, in which individuals who are perceived as having high-warmth but low-competence are pitied and can be subject to paternalism. People who stutter may encounter advice which is contrary to their own efforts to manage their stuttering. It is probable that individuals who stutter may spend copious amounts of time and mental energy as they attempt to manage their stuttering as well as the overt and covert behaviors of fluent speakers. More research on this topic from both a qualitative and experimental perspective is needed to better understand how the cognitive, attitudinal, and behavioral reactions of fluent speakers toward stuttering affect people who stutter.

REFERENCES

Allport, G.W. (1954). *The nature of prejudice.* Reading, MA: Addison Wesley.

Andrews, G., Craig, A., Feyer, A., Hoddinott, S., Howie, P., & Neilson, M. (1983). *Stuttering: A review of research findings and theories circa 1982.* Journal of Speech and Hearing Disorders, 48, 226-246.

Atkins, C.P. (1988). *Perceptions of speakers with minimal eye contact: implications for stutterers.* Journal of Fluency Disorders, 13, 439-436.

Bebout, L., & Arthur, B. (1992). *Cross-cultural attitudes toward speech disorders.* Journal of Speech and Hearing Research, 35, 45-52.

Bender, J.F. (1939). *The personality structure of stuttering.* Oxford: Pitman.

Bloodstein, O. (1995). *A handbook on stuttering (5th ed.).* San Diego, CA: Singular.

Boberg, J.M., & Boberg, E. (1990). *The other side of the block: The stutterer's spouse.* Journal of Fluency Disorders, 15, 1-75.

Bryngelson, B. (1937). *Psychological problems in stuttering.* Mental Hygiene, 21, 631-639.

Burley, P.M., & Rinaldi, W. (1986). *Effects of sex of listener and of stutterer on ratings of stuttering speakers.* Journal of Fluency Disorders, 17, 329-333.

Collins, C.R., & Blood, G.W. (1990). *Acknowledgment and severity of stuttering as factors influencing nonstutterers' perceptions of stutterers.* Journal of Speech and Hearing Disorders, 55, 75-81.

Conture, E.G., (2001). *Stuttering: Its nature, diagnosis, and treatment.* Needham Heights, MA: Allyn and Bacon.

Cooper, E.B., & Cooper, C.S. (1985). *Clinician attitudes toward stuttering: A decade of change (1973-1983).* Journal of Fluency Disorders, 10, 19-33.

Cooper, E.B., & Cooper, C.S. (1996). *Clinician attitudes toward stuttering: Two decades of change.* Journal of Fluency Disorders, 21, 119-135.

Corcoran, J.A., & Stewart, M. (1998). *Stories of stuttering: A qualitative analysis of interview narratives.* Journal of Fluency Disorders, 23, 247-264.

Creswell, J.W. (1998). *Qualitative inquiry and research design: Choosing among five traditions.* Thousand Oaks, CA: Sage.

Crowe, T.A., & Cooper, E.B. (1977). *Parental attitudes toward and knowledge of stuttering.* Journal of Communication Disorders, 10, 343-357.

Crowe, T.A., & Walton, J.H. (1981). *Teacher attitudes toward stuttering.* Journal of Fluency Disorders, 6, 163-174.

Cuddy, A.J.C., Fiske, S.T., & Glick, P. (2008). *Warmth and competence as universal dimensions of social perception: The stereotype content model and the BIAS map.* Advances in Experimental Social Psychology, 40, 61-150.

Daniels, D.E. (2007). *Recounting the school experiences of adults who stutter: A qualitative analysis.* Unpublished doctoral dissertation, Bowling Green State University.

Davis, S., Howell, P., & Cooke, F. (2007). *Sociodynamic relationships between children who stutter and their non-stuttering classmates.* Journal of Child Psychology and Psychiatry, 43, 939-947.

Dillman, D.A. (2007). *Mail and internet surveys: the tailored design method.* Hoboken, N.J.: Wiley.

Doody, I., Kalinowski, J., Armson, J., & Stuart, A. (1993). *Stereotypes of stutterers and nonstutterers in three rural communities in Newfoundland.* Journal of Fluency Disorders, 18, 363-373.

Dorsey, M., & Guenther, R.K. (2000). *Attitudes of professors and students toward college students who stutter.* Journal of Fluency Disorders, 25, 77-83.

Emerick, L.L. (1960). *Extensional definition and attitude toward stuttering.* Journal of Speech and Hearing Research, 3, 181-186.

Ezrati-Vinacour, R., Platzky, R., & Yairi, E. (2001). *The young child's awareness of stuttering-like disfluency.* Journal of Speech, Language, and Hearing Research, 44, 368-380.

Evans, D., Healey, E.C., Kawai, Norimune, & Rowland, S. (2008). *Middle school students' perceptions of a peer who stutters.* Journal of Fluency Disorders, 33, 203-219.

Finn, P., & Felsenfeld, S. (2004). *Recovery from stuttering: The contributions of the qualitative research approach.* Advances in Speech-Language Pathology, 6, 159-166.

Fowlie, G.M., & Cooper, E.B. (1978). *Traits attributed to stuttering and nonstuttering children by their mothers.* Journal of Fluency Disorders, 3, 233-246.

Gabel, R.M. (2006). *Effects of stuttering severity and therapy involvement on attitudes towards people who stutter.* Journal of Fluency Disorders, 31, 216-227.

Gabel, R.M., Blood, G.W., Tellis, G.M., & Althouse, M.T. (2004). *Measuring role entrapment of people who stutter.* Journal of Fluency Disorders, 29, 27-49.

Glesne, C. (1999). *Becoming qualitative researchers: An introduction (2nd ed.).* New York: Longman.

Green, J.S. (1936). *The stutter-type personality and stuttering.* New York State Journal of Medicine, 36, 757-765.

Guitar, B. (2006). *Stuttering: An integrated approach to its nature and treatment.* Baltimore: Lippincott Williams & Wilkins.

Guntupalli, V.K., Kalinowski, J., Nanjundeswaran, C., Saltuklaroglu, T., & Everhart, D.E. (2006). *Psychophysiological responses of adults who do not stutter while listening to stuttering.* International Journal of Psychophysiology, 62, 1-8.

Ham, R.E. (1990). *What is stuttering: Variations and stereotypes.* Journal of Fluency Disorders, 15, 259-273.

Hawk, S. S. (1948). *Personality measurement in speech correction.* Journal of Speech and Hearing Disorders, 13, 307-312.

Healey, E.C., Gabel, R.M., Daniels, D.E., & Kawai, N. (2007). *The effects of self-disclosure and non self-disclosure of stuttering on listeners' perceptions of a person who stutters.* Journal of Fluency Disorders, 32, 51-69.

Horsley, I.A., & FitzGibbon, C.T. (1987). *Stuttering children: Investigation of a stereotype.* British Journal of Disorders of Communication, 22, 19-35.

Huber, A., Packman, A., Quine, S., Onslow, M., & Simpson, J. (2004). *Improving our clinical interventions for stuttering: Can evidence from qualitative research contribute?* Advances in Speech-Language Pathology, 6, 174-181.

Hughes, C.D. (2007). *An investigation of family relationships for people who stutter.* Unpublished master's thesis, Bowling Green State University.

Hughes, S. (2008). *Exploring attitudes toward people who stutter: A mixed methods approach.* Unpublished doctoral dissertation, Bowling Green State University.

Hughes, S., Gabel, R., Irani, F., & Schlagheck, A. (in press). *University students' explanations for their descriptions of people who stutter: An exploratory mixed model study.* Journal of Fluency Disorders.

Hulit, L.M., & Wirtz, L. (1994). *The association of attitudes toward stuttering with selected variables.* Journal of fluency disorders, 19, 247-267.

Hurst, M.A., & Cooper, E.B. (1983a). *Vocational rehabilitation counselors' attitudes toward stuttering.* Journal of Fluency Disorders, 8, 13-27.

Hurst, M.A., & Cooper, E.B. (1983b). *Employer attitudes toward stuttering.* Journal of Fluency Disorders, 8, 1-12.

Irani, F., Gabel, R., Hughes, S., Swartz, E.R., & Palasik, S.T. (2009*). Role entrapment of people who stutter reported by K-12 teachers.* Contemporary Issues in Communication Science and Disorders, 36, 48-56.

Johnson, W. (1932). *The influence of stuttering on the personality.* University of Iowa Studies: Child Welfare, 5, 140.

Johnson, W. (1934). *Stutterers' attitudes toward stuttering.* Journal of Abnormal and Social Psychology, 29, 32-44.

Kalinowski, J., Armson, J., Stuart, A., & Lerman, J.W. (1993). *Speech clinicians' and the general public's perceptions of self and stutterers.* Journal of Speech-Language Pathology and Audiology, 17, 79-85.

Kalinowski, J., Stuart, A., & Armson, J. (1996). *Perceptions of stutterers and nonstutterers during speaking and nonspeaking situations.* American Journal of Speech-Language Pathology, 5, 61-67.

Kamhi, A.G. (2003). *Two paradoxes in stuttering treatment.* Journal of Fluency Disorders, 28, 187-196.

Klassen, T.R. (2001). *Perceptions of people who stutter: Re-assessing the negative stereotype.* Perceptual and Motor Skills, 92, 551-559.

Klassen, T.R. (2002). *Social distance and the negative stereotype of people who stutter.* Journal of Speech-Language Pathology and Audiology, 26, 90-99.

Landis, J.R., & Koch, G.G. (1977). *The measurement of observer agreement for categorical data.* Biometrics, 33, 159-174.

Lass, N.J., Ruscello, D.M., Pannbacker, M., Schmitt, J.F., Everly-Myers, D.S. (1989). *Speech-language pathologists' perceptions of child and adult female and male stutterers.* Journal of Fluency Disorders, 14, 127-134.

Lass, N.J., Ruscello, D.M., Pannbacker, M., Schmitt, J.F., Kiser, A.M., Mussa, A.M., et al. (1994). *School administrators' perceptions of people who stutter.* Language, Speech, and Hearing Services in Schools, 25, 90-93.

Lass, N.J., Ruscello, D.M., Schmitt, J.F., Pannbacker, M.D., Orlando, M.B., Dead, K.A., et al. (1992). *Teachers' perceptions of stutterers.* Language, Speech, and Hearing Services in Schools, 23, 78-81.

Linn, G.W., & Caruso, A.J. (1998). *Perspectives on the effects of stuttering on the formation and maintenance of intimate relationships.* Journal of Rehabilitation, 64, 12-15.

Manning, W.H. (2001). *Clinical decision making in fluency disorders (2nd ed.).* Vancouver, Canada: Singular.

Manning, W.H., Burlison, A.E., & Thaxton, D. (1999). *Listener response to stuttering modification techniques.* Journal of Fluency Disorders, 24, 267-280.

Maxwell, J.A. (2005). *Qualitative research design: An interactive approach. (2nd ed.).* Thousand Oaks, CA: Sage Publications.

McGee, L., Kalinowski, J., & Stuart, A. (1996). *Effect of a videotape documentary on high school students' perceptions of a high school male who stutters.* Journal of Speech-Language Pathology and Audiology, 20, 240-246.

Meltzer, H. (1944). *Personality differences between stuttering and non-stuttering children as indicated by the Rorschach test.* Journal of Psychology, 17, 39-59.

Panico, J., Healey, E.C., Brouwer, K., & Susca, M. (2005). *Listener perceptions of stuttering across two presentation modes: A quantitative and qualitative approach.* Journal of Fluency Disorders, 30, 65-85.

Patterson, J., & Pring, T. (1991). *Listener attitudes to stuttering speakers: No evidence for a gender difference.* Journal of Fluency Disorders, 16, 201-205.

Perkins, D.W. (1947). *An item by item compilation and comparison of the scores of 75 young stutterers on the California Test of Personality.* Speech Monographs, 14, 211 (Abstract).

Perkins, W.H., Kent, R.D., & Curlee, R.F. (1991). *A theory of neuropsycholinguistic function in stuttering.* Journal of Speech and Hearing Research, 34, 734-752.

Petrunik, M., & Shearing, C.D. (1983). *Fragile facades: Stuttering and the strategic manipulation of awareness.* Social Problems, 31, 125-138.

Plexico, L., Manning, W.H., & DiLollo, A. (2005). *A phenomenological understanding of successful stuttering management.* Journal of Fluency Disorders, 30, 1-22.

Prins, D. (1972). *Personality, stuttering severity, and age.* Journal of Speech and Hearing Research, 15, 148-154.

Ragsdale, J.D., & Ashby, J.K. (1982). *Speech-language pathologists' connotations of stuttering.* Journal of Speech and Hearing Research, 25, 75-80.

Ruscello, D.M., Lass, N.J., Schmitt, J.F., & Pannbacker, M.D. (1994). *Special educators' perceptions of stutterers.* Journal of Fluency Disorders, 19, 125-132.

Schlagheck, A., Gabel, R., & Hughes, S. (2009). *A mixed method study of stereotypes of people who stutter.* Contemporary Issues in Communication Science and Disorders, 43, 45-60.

Shears, L.M., & Jensema, C.J. (1969). *Social acceptability of anomalous persons.* Exceptional Child, 36, 91-96.

Sheehan, J. (1958). *Projective studies of stuttering.* Journal of Speech Disorders, 23, 18-25.

Sheehan, J.G. (1970). *Stuttering*: Research and therapy. New York: Harper and Row.

Silverman, E. (1982). *Speech-language clinicians' and university students' impressions of women and girls who stutter.* Journal of Fluency Disorders, 7, 469-478.

Silverman, E. & Zimmer (1979). *Women who stutter: Personality and speech characteristics.* Journal of Speech and Hearing Research, 22, 553-564.

Silverman, F.H. (1985). *Research design and evaluation in speech-language pathology and audiology (2nd edition).* Englewood Cliffs, NJ: Prentice Hall.

Silverman, F.H. (1988). *Impact of a T-shirt message on stutterer stereotypes.* Journal of Fluency Disorders, 13, 279-281.

Silverman, F.H. (1990). *Are professors likely to report having "beliefs" about the intelligence and competence of students who stutter?* Journal of Fluency Disorders, 15, 319-321.

Silverman, F.H., & Bongey, T.A. (1997). *Nurses' attitudes toward physicians who stutter.* Journal of Fluency Disorders, 22, 61-62.

Silverman, F.H., Gazzolo, M., & Peterson, Y. (1990). *Impact of a T-shirt message on stutterer stereotypes: A systematic replication.* Journal of Fluency Disorders, 15, 35-37.

Silverman, F.H., & Marik, J.H. (1993). *"Teachers' perceptions of stutterers": A replication.* Language, Speech, and Hearing Services in Schools, 24, 108.

Silverman, F.H., & Paynter, K.K. (1990). *Impact of stuttering on perception of occupational competence.* Journal of Fluency Disorders, 15, 87-91.

Sim, J., & Wright, C.C. (2005). *The Kappa statistic in reliability studies: Use, interpretation, and sample size requirements.* Physical Therapy, 85, 257-268.

Solomon, M. (1938). *The psychology of stuttering.* Journal of Speech Disorders, 3, 59-61.

St. Louis, K.O., & Lass, N.J. (1981). *A survey of communicative disorders students' attitudes toward stuttering.* Journal of Fluency Disorders, 6, 49-79.

St. Louis, K.O., Filatova, Y., Coskun, M., et. al. (2010). *Public attitudes toward cluttering and stuttering in four countries.* In E. L. Simon (Ed.) Psychology of Stereotypes. Hauppauge, NY: Nova Science Publishers.

Susca, M., & Healey, E.C. (2001). *Perceptions of stimulated stuttering and fluency.* Journal of Speech, Language, and Hearing Research, 44, 61-72.

Susca, M., & Healey, E.C. (2002). *Listener perceptions along a fluency-disfluency continuum: A phenomenological analysis.* Journal of Fluency Disorders, 27, 135-161.

Swartz, E., Gabel, R., Hughes, S., & Irani, F. (2009). *Speech-language pathologists' responses on surveys on vocational stereotyping (role entrapment) regarding people who stutter.* Contemporary Issues in Communication Science and Disorders, 36, 157-165.

Tatchell, R.H., van den Berg, S., & Lerman, J.W. (1983). *Fluency and eye contact as factors influencing observers' perceptions of stutterers.* Journal of Fluency Disorders, 8, 221-231.

Turnbaugh, K., Guitar, B., & Hoffman, P. (1979). *Speech clinicians' attribution of personality traits as a function of stuttering severity.* Journal of Speech and Hearing Research, 22, 37-45.

Turnbaugh, K., Guitar, B., & Hoffman, P. (1981*). The attribution of personality traits: The stutterer and nonstutterers.* Journal of Speech and Hearing Research, 24, 288-291.

Van Riper, C. (1982). *The Nature of Stuttering (2nd ed.).* Englewood Cliffs, NJ: Prentice-Hall.

Whaley, B.B., & Parker, R.G. (2000). *Expressing the experience of communicative disability: Metaphors of persons who stutter.* Communication Reports, 13, 115-125.

White, P.A., & Collins, S.R.C. (1984). *Stereotype formation by inference: A possible explanation for the "stutterer" stereotype.* Journal of Speech and Hearing Research, 27, 567-570.

Wilson, D. M. (1951). *A study of the personalities of stuttering children and their parents as revealed through projection tests.* Speech Monographs, 19, 133 (Abstract).

Woods, C.L., & Williams, D.E. (1971). *Speech clinicians' conceptions of boys and men who stutter.* Journal of Speech and Hearing Disorders, 36, 225-234.

Woods, C.L., & Williams, D.E. (1976). *Traits attributed to stuttering and normally fluent males.* Journal of Speech and Hearing Research, 19, 267-278.

Yairi, E., & Ambrose, N. (1999). *Early childhood stuttering I: Persistency and recovery rates.* Journal of Speech, Language, and Hearing Research, 42, 1097-1112.

Yairi, E., & Carrico, D.M. (1992). *Early childhood stuttering: Pediatricians' attitudes and practices*. American Journal of Speech-Language Pathology, 1, 51-62.

Yairi, E., & Williams, D.E. (1970). *Speech clinicians' stereotypes of elementary-school boys who stutter*. Journal of Communication Disorders, 3, 161-170.

In: Psychology of Stereotypes
Editor: Eleanor L. Simon

ISBN: 978-1-61761-463-7
©2011 Nova Science Publishers, Inc.

Chapter 2

STEREOTYPES AS ATTRIBUTIONS

Mark J. Brandt and Christine Reyna
DePaulUniversity, Chicago, Illinois, USA

ABSTRACT

Why are some groups better off than others? Why are women more likely to take care of the children? How come Blacks generally achieve less educationally and economically? Stereotypes provide answers to these kinds of questions, albeit imperfectly, and help us provide meaning to the social world around us. Early stereotype researchers suggested that stereotypes help people explain and rationalize the position of groups in society (Lippman, 1922). While the influence of this observation has waxed and waned over the years, the explanatory power of stereotypes continues to be an important function of social stereotypes. The current chapter reviews research examining the role of stereotypes as explanatory and rationalization agents and the impact of stereotypes on intergroup behavior. We suggest that stereotypes serve explanatory and attributional functions at three interrelated levels of analysis: (a) individual level, wherein stereotypes are analyzed in terms of the attributional dimensions they imply (locus, stability, controllability); (b) intragroup level, in which stereotypes define and explain by combining stereotypic traits on dimensions of warmth and competence, which in turn predict unique patterns of emotions and behaviors; and (c) intergroup level, in which stereotypes explain the social order by providing compensary or causally relevant traits in reference to other relevant groups. The resulting attributional signature of stereotypes influences attitudes and behaviors.

INTRODUCTION

Why are some groups better off than others? Why are women more likely to take care of the children, and men more likely to hold positions of power? How come racial minorities generally achieve less educationally and economically compared to Whites? The answers to these questions are not easy. Evaluating and addressing underlying causes of intergroup disparities and outcomes is a necessary but daunting task, sincemany of these disparities and status differences in society have ambiguous, multidimensional, or unknown causes. Despite this, when it comes to making decisions about policies that impact groups differently, or programs designed to ameliorate group differences, the pressure on policy- and decision-makers to make causal judgments about disparate group outcomes is tremendous. This pressure can compel people to consider any information that can disambiguate possible underlying causes of group outcomes, even if that information if derived from stereotypes. Understanding the strategies that people use to disambiguate possible underlying causes of group outcomes, especially strategies that can lead to or justify erroneous conclusions, is especially urgent if we ever hope to alleviate and eliminate social group disparities.

One source of readilyavailable information about the causes of behaviors or outcomes in individuals and groups is cultural stereotypes. Along with information about *what* a group is and does, stereotypes also provide information about *why* group members arein their present state (see also Hamilton, 1979; Wittenbrink, Gist, & Hilton, 1997;Yzerbyt, Rocher, & Schandron, 1997). For example, the stereotype that "Blacks are lazy" is not just a disparaging description of Blacks, but an explanation for why Blacks might continue to struggle economically. Implicit in stereotypes are attributions for the behaviors and outcomes of the stereotyped groups (e.g., "not working hard to succeed"), and this causal information is often used to justify our social worlds(the lazy do not deserve assistance) (Allport, 1954; Lippman, 1922). So while stereotypes are largely descriptive, attributions are cause-and-effect explanations of why a specific individual or group behaved in a certain manner. These resulting causal beliefs can influence or guide emotional, behavioral and system justifying responses to the stereotyped group.

The authors of this chapter posit that analyzing group behavior and outcomes through the combined use of stereotype and attribution perspectives informs us more adequately about these group dynamics. This chapter will first explore when perceivers might rely on stereotypes to guide attributional judgments. It then will explore the ways in which stereotypes can guide attributions. Specifically, we advance the specific thesis that stereotypes can serve attributional functions at three interrelated levels of analysis (see Figure 1) and that stereotypes at all three levels help to explain and justify social structures. The three levels, described below, are (a) the individual level; (b) the intragroup level, called here *intragroup stereotype packages*; and (c) the intergroup level, the broadest analysis, called here *intergroup stereotype packages*.

Each of these three approaches emphasizes different attributional processes associated with stereotypesthat combine to help us make sense out of our social world.By conceptualizing stereotypes at these three levels of analysis, it is possible to see the unique functions of stereotypic traits when perceived in the context of dimensions of causality, other traits, or other groups.These three approaches will be explored using three models that have specifically examined the attributional consequences of stereotypes: the attributional model of stereotypes (Reyna, 2000; 2008), the stereotype content model (Cuddy, Fiske, & Glick, 2008; Fiske, Cuddy, Glick, & Xiu, 2002), and research on complementary stereotypes (Jost & Kay, 2005; Kay & Jost, 2003;Kay, Jost, Mandisodza, Sherman, Petrocelli, & Johnson, 2007).

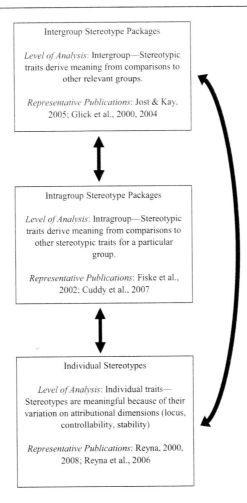

Figure 1. Conceptual Model of Intergroup, Intragroup, and Individual Attributional Stereotypes.

AN OVERVIEW OF STEREOTYPES AND ATTRIBUTIONS

Before we can begin to understand how stereotypes guide attributional judgments, we must first understand the definition and function of stereotypes. In this chapter, *stereotypes* are defined as broad generalizations made about a group of people (Fiske, 1998; Reyna, 2000; Tajfel, 1981, 1982). Stereotypes are primarily cognitive in nature (Fiske, 1998) and can reflect positive (e.g., "Asians are good at math") or negative (e.g., "welfare recipients are lazy") beliefs about a group (cf. Glick & Fiske, 2001a). They can also include physical descriptions ("Asians are short"), traits ("gays are effeminate"), behaviors ("Mexicans like to get drunk"), attitudes ("Whites are racist"), or life outcomes or circumstances ("Blacks go to ghetto schools") of the stereotyped group.

But what makes a stereotype a stereotype is that the belief in question is applied broadly to a group of people and is often assumed of group members based solely on their group membership. Because these beliefs are overgeneralizations applied to large groups of people, they are often inaccurate, leading some to conclude that a stereotype is "...a fixed impression, which conforms very little to the facts it pretends to represent...." (Katz & Braly, 1935, p. 181; however, see Lee, Jussim, & McCauley, 1995, for a discussion of stereotype accuracy). Nevertheless, people rely on stereotypes to explain and predict the behavior of others,except under ideal informational or motivational circumstances (Kunda & Spencer, 2003).

Attributions, on the other hand, are beliefs about the causes of a person's or a group's behavior, attitudes, outcomes, and location within a social structure (Andersen, Krull, & Weiner, 1996; Gilbert, 1998; Kelley, 1973; Reyna, 2008; Weiner, 1980). The need to explain and anticipate our social worlds has led many attribution theorists to conclude that people engage in attributional searches pervasively and automatically, especially following negative, unfamiliar, unexpected, or personally relevant events (Weiner, 1980; Weiner, Perry, & Magnusson, 1988; Wong & Weiner, 1981).

WHEN STEREOTYPES GUIDE ATTRIBUTIONS

The idea that stereotypes are used to explain group behaviors and outcomes has a long history in social psychology. In the early part of the 20th century, scholars were beginning to identify stereotypes as a tool for explaining the social situation of groups (Allport, 1954; Katz & Braly, 1935) and for rationalizing group outcomes (Lippman, 1922). Others suggested that stereotypes help to justify ingroup favoritism and outgroup derogation (Sherif, Harvey, White, Hood, & Sherif, 1954/1961; Tajfel, 1981, 1982). More recently, the rationalizing function of stereotypes has garnered increased theoretical and empirical attention (Crandall & Eshleman, 2003; Cuddy, Fiske, & Glick, 2007; Fiske, Cuddy, Glick, & Xu, 2002; Jost & Banaji, 1994; McGarty, Yzerbyt, & Spears, 2002; Reyna, 2008) in an attempt to understand the broader functions of stereotype content (Cuddy, et al., 2007; Fiske et al., 2002; McGarty, Yzerbyt, & Spears, 2002; Reyna, 2008), as well as persistent societal inequity aided by stereotypes (Jost & Banaji, 1994; Reyna, Henry, Korfmacher, & Tucker, 2006).

For example, the stereotypes that the poor are poor because they are lazy, and the rich are rich because they are hard-working both explain and justify economic disparities. Similarly, stereotypes suggesting that women are good at raising children because they are nurturing and communal, and men are better suited for the workplace because they are analytical and assertive have kept gender roles relatively intact (Eagly & Steffen, 1984; Hoffman & Hurst, 1990).

In general, people are more likely to rely on attributional stereotypes when three conditions are present: (1) there is a "stereotype eliciting event," i.e., a behavior or outcome that corresponds to or cues a particular stereotype (e.g., a girl doing poorly on a math test); (2) there is an impetus to make a causal ascription, as is often the case when making sense of negative or atypical outcomes; (3) for informational, cognitive, or motivational reasons, the stereotype provides the "best explanatory fit" with the perceiver's short-term attributional goals and/or chronic worldview.

Stereotype-eliciting events. Any event that primes a stereotype (e.g. Bargh, Chen, & Burrows, 1996; Blair & Banaji, 1996; Devine, 1989) or otherwise makes a stereotype more salient can strengthen the use of stereotypes as attributions. This event could be an unusual or unexpected occurrence--like a woman getting the top score in a math class--or it could be an event that caters to expectations, like an Asian getting the top score in a math class. The event could grab attention--like a news exposé on welfare mothers exploiting social services--or it could be subtle--like the news exposé that disproportionately airs images of *Black* welfare mothers. Also, a stereotype-eliciting event does not have to represent a discrete moment in time, but can be an ongoing situation or behavior. For example, the knowledge that certain ethnic minority groups are more likely to be unemployed or to hold lower-paying jobs may make certain stereotypes regarding those group members' work ethic or capabilities chronically accessible in memory. In sum, a stereotype-eliciting event could be any type of event that primes or makes a stereotype more available when judging others or the self. Once a stereotype is invoked, all the implications of that stereotype are simultaneously activated, including the causal implications that are packaged in the stereotype. Thus, when a stereotype gets activated, the causal explanations that stereotype implies are activated as well.

Impetus to make attributional judgments. As already discussed, negative, unfamiliar or unexpected events are especially likely to elicit attributional reasoning (e.g. Weiner, Perry, & Magnusson, 1988; Wong & Weiner, 1981). Because intergroup interactions are often perceived negatively (Mallett, Wilson, & Gilbert, 2008; Shelton & Richeson, 2005) occur less frequently, and often involve unfamiliar judgments (e.g., judgments about an outgroup) than intragroup interactions, and because there appears to be a strong motive to justify intergroup arrangements (Jost & Banaji, 1994; Jost, Banaji, & Nosek, 2004; Kay, Gaucher, Peach, Laurin, Friesen, Zanna et al, 2009), the urge to make attributionally laden judgments in intergroup contexts may be especially strong.

Informational, cognitive, and motivational factors that prioritize stereotypes. Motivational and psychological factors can exacerbate the use of stereotypes as attributions, or increase the effectiveness of stereotypes as justifications. Individual differences in how one sees the world and the theories one holds about the origins of group differences can make one rely more on stereotypes when making attributional judgments. For example, those who are prejudiced or who otherwise hold negative intergroup attitudes may be especially likely to rely on stereotypes when evaluating others (e.g. Sherman, Stroessner, Conrey, & Azam, 2005).

Another personal factor is how cohesive and consistent one perceives the qualities of a group. Groups that are perceived in more essentialist terms (that they share innate qualities that define them as a group, such as race or gender) may be associated with stereotypes that are seen as carrying greater explanatory power. This perceived underlying "essence" provides an explanation for the perceiver that ties together the behaviors and attitudes of otherwise disparate target group members. When a person believes that a group's outcome (e.g. widespread unemployment) stems from something about the group identity (e.g. African-American), people will be more likely to search for an underlying stereotyped essence (e.g. being lazy or less capable) to explain this outcome (Yzerbyt, Rocher, & Schadron, 1997). This kind of reasoning increases the likelihood of dispositional attributions for group members' behaviors and helps to validate existing social arrangements (Yzerbyt & Rogier, 2001). That is, attributing group differences to underlying dispositional causes, especially to causes that are seen as essential qualities that distinguish a group from other groups, validates that group's position relative to other groups.

A person's values and worldviews can also lead people to make use of the attributional information provided by stereotypes, especially if the stereotype fits with or validates the worldview (e.g. Overbeck, et al., 2004; Reyna et al., 2006; Skitka et al., 2002). For example, if a person endorses a system justifying ideology or worldview (e.g. Jost & Hunyady, 2005;

also called hierarchy enhancing myths, Sidanius & Pratto, 1999) such as "hard work leads to success," he or she may be more likely to utilize the attributional stereotype of "lazy" because it allows one to explain widespread group disadvantage within the context of their beliefs. Similarly, a person who endorses the system justifying ideology of meritocracy may be more prone to attribute the positive outcomes of power and success to the stereotypes of intelligence or high ability (e.g., for Whites or the rich).

Similarly, conservatives, who are more tolerant of social inequities if they are seen as deserved, are more likely to use the attributional information provided by stereotypes to determine whether a group is deserving of public assistance (Reyna et al., 2006; see also Brandt, 2010; Farwell & Weiner, 2000; Skitka & Tetlock, 1993). Group-based stereotypes provide an ideologically consistent and efficient method for determining a group's deservingness. For example, conservatives are more likely to endorse stereotypes that paint Black Americans as responsible and deserving of their lower-status (e.g. lazy, don't work hard), which then predict opposition to affirmative action for Blacks (Reyna et al., 2006). These results suggest that conservatives determine their support or opposition to group-based policy by assessing the responsibility of the beneficiary group—a judgment that is easily informed and justified through the use of the attributional information conveyed through stereotypes.

In summary, because interactions with unfamiliar groups often trigger stereotypes automatically, place attributional demands on the perceiver (the need to explain and understand negative and/or unfamiliar social outcomes), and are often intertwined with a variety of ongoing motivations (such as prejudice or chronic worldviews), stereotypes will likely inform attributions made about other groups and their members. Once activated, stereotypes can serve attributional functions by conveying specific attributional information (individual level stereotypes), combining with other traits to paint a nuanced attributional picture (intragroup stereotype packages), and comparing and contrasting relevant societal groups (intergroup stereotype packages). The multidimensional and fluid nature of attributional stereotypes takes place at these three interrelated and mutually reinforcing levels of analysis.   In the sections that follow, the three interrelated levels of analysis in understanding how stereotypes serve attributional functions are discussed in turn.

INDIVIDUAL LEVEL STEREOTYPES

Analysis at the individual level focuses on the specific attributional content implied by individual stereotypes and most directly links stereotypes with this content. The attributional model of stereotypes (Reyna, 2000, 2008) follows from some of the basic observations of attribution theory. As with other traits, stereotypes convey specific attributional information that influences emotional reactions and behavioral intentions directed towards the stereotyped group. Specifically, the causes inferred by stereotypes can be classified in terms of their stability, locus (internal vs. external) and controllability, consistent with Weiner's attribution theory (Weiner, 1980, 1995, 2006). However, the attributional model of stereotypes asserts that, by definition, all stereotypes provide information about stable group qualities. While the content of stereotypes may vary across time (Garcia-Marques, Santos, & Mackie, 2006) due in part to changes in culture or intergroup relations (Duckitt, 1992), the traits implied bystereotypes (aggressive, industrious) at any given point in time are considered stable within that group for that cultural context. This stability helps make stereotypes particularly effective at explaining and justifying social conditions.

Some evidence for the underlying stability of stereotypes comes from research that shows that, when targets were successful on stereotype-consistent tasks, the success was attributed to internal-*stable* causes, such as ability (Swim & Sanna, 1996). However, when a target was successful at a stereotype-inconsistent task, success was attributed to extreme effort, an internal but *unstable* cause (see also Jackson et al., 1993). The stable qualities suggested by stereotypes may cause perceivers and targets alike to view the stereotyped behavior as chronic and thus difficult to extinguish (Anderson et al, 1996), which, as will be discussed later, can have profound consequences for the targets of the stereotype.

Stereotypes can also imply internal or external causes for a group's outcome. The majority of stereotypes implies qualities that are internal to group members (e.g. smart, nice, lazy, aggressive; see, e.g., the Ultimate Attribution Error, Hewstone, 1990; Pettigrew, 1979); however, it is possible for stereotypes to imply external forces surrounding a group. For example, some people may believe that African-Americans have lower educational achievement because inner-city school districts lack necessary funding, qualified and motivated teachers, and the safety and security for African-American students to receive the quality education they deserve—all external causes to African-Americans. However, while this may be true in some cases, many African-Americans do not attend run-down and dangerous inner-city schools. In this case, the generalization that African-Americans have lower educational achievement because they attend inner-city schools is a stereotype that implies external causes for a negative outcome, regardless of the actual validity of the attribution for any particular African-American.

Finally, stereotypes can convey controllable or uncontrollable causes. Continuing with the example from above, some people may stereotype African-Americans as lacking effort, which suggests a controllable cause of lower academic achievement. Others may stereotype African-Americans as lacking intelligence, which suggests an uncontrollable cause (assuming one believes that intelligence is innate). Stereotypes are more likely to vary on the controllability dimension than on the other two dimensions, and it is the controllability dimension that has received much of the empirical attention when it comes to dissecting the consequences of attributional stereotypes (Henry & Reyna, 2007; Henry, Reyna, & Weiner, 2004; Reyna et al, 2006; Reyna, Brandt, Viki, 2009; Reyna, Brandt, Viki, & Hughs, 2010).

It should also be noted that, although most groups are associated with a variety of stereotypes (see intragroup stereotypes), the attributional model of stereotypes asserts that when it comes to making causal judgments about groups, certain stereotypes or stereotype-clusters will emerge as more germane to the judgment, and thus will take precedence in the attributional process. For example, although there are many stereotypes about women, stereotypes related to logic and mathematical ability will exert more influence on attributions about women in math. Thus, when examining the social and personal consequences of attributional stereotypes, one must be mindful of the degree of relevance between the stereotype, the causal judgment, and the outcome. The stereotypes that best explain the outcomes of a group will likely be deemed the most relevant for making a causal judgment about a group and/or the best suited for justifying the existing social structure.

SOCIAL CONSEQUENCES OF INDIVIDUAL STEREOTYPES

Given these unique properties of stereotypes, the attributional model of stereotypes proposes that the attributions conveyed through stereotypes always represent one of three patterns:Stereotypes can communicate causes that are (a) internal/controllable/stable (I/C) by the stereotyped person (e.g., being lazy, hardworking, nurturing, aggressive); (b) internal/uncontrollable/stable (I/UC) by the stereotyped person (e.g., being intelligent, stupid, weak, shy); and (c) external/uncontrollable/stable (E/UC) by the stereotyped person (e.g., being the victim of discrimination or the beneficiary of special favors).Because stability is uniform, the attributional signatures of stereotypes will be referred to by the first two qualities (I/C; I/UC; E/UC). Furthermore, because external attributions are by definition uncontrollable (Heider, 1958; Weiner, 1985), there is no external/controllable/stable pattern.Each attributional signature is associated with specific psychological, emotional and behavioral consequences for both social and self-perception following either desirable or undesirable outcomes or events (see Figure 2). This section outlines some of the social and personal consequences of each of the three attributional signatures of stereotypes.

Internal/Controllable (I/C) stereotypes. Some of the most potent stereotypes imply internal, controllable causes for life outcomes (top path, Figure 2). For example, the stereotypes that, "Blacks are lazy," "Irish are alcoholics," "Immigrants don't want to learn the language of their host countries," and so on, have profound implications for how these groups are treated by others. I/C stereotypes may depict an internal, chronic behavior pattern, but more informative is that this undesirable pattern is under the volitional control of the stereotyped individuals. The stereotype that certain groups are "lazy" implies that these people do not have to be lazy, but they *choose* to be. This choice is frowned upon as a violation of societal norms, and the stereotyped individual described as lazy is thus often met with disdain, condemnation, punishment, and denial of help or benefits (Brandt, 2010; Darley & Zanna, 1982; Fincham & Jaspers, 1980; Henry & Reyna, 2007; Reyna & Weiner, 2001; Rudolph, Roesch, Greitemeer, & Weiner, 2004; Weiner, 1993; Weiner, Graham, & Reyna, 1997; Weiner & Kukla, 1970; Weiner, Perry, & Magnusson, 1988). For example, people undergoing home mortgage foreclosure for controllable reasons are likely to face more anger, less sympathy, and less help than people undergoing foreclosure for uncontrollable reasons (Brandt, 2010). Similarly, students who fail an exam because they did not put in the effort are less likely to receive assistance from teachers and in fact may be punished (Reyna & Weiner, 2001).

The controllability implied by group stereotypes also influences emotional and behavioral reactions. For example, groups stereotyped with negative, controllable qualities are denied assistance and civil rights(Henry & Reyna, 2007; Hoeken & Hustinx, 2007; Reyna et al., 2006, 2009), so if African-Americans are stereotyped as lacking effort, they are denied assistance, such as affirmative action (Reyna et al., 2006) and perceivers endorse punitive public policies that disproportionately target African-Americans (Reyna et al., 2009). The denial of assistance often matches the stereotyped domain.For example, gay men and lesbianwomen are stereotyped as not upholding family values and are thus not given the opportunity to express family values via legally recognized same-sex marriage (Haider-Markel & Joslyn,

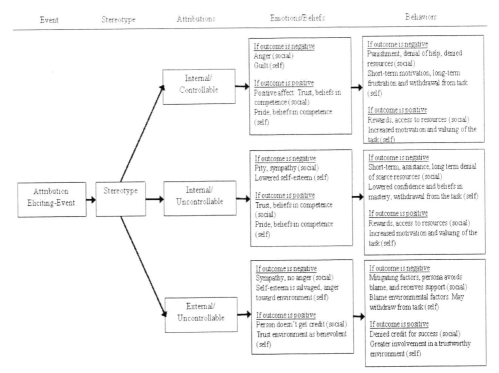

Figure 2. Individual Stereotypes: The Attributional Model of Stereotypes.
2008; Henry & Reyna, 2007; Wood & Bartkowski, 2004).

Similarly, those who stereotype Middle Eastern Muslims as violating American values are more likely to support harsh immigration policies that disproportionately target Muslims (Henry & Reyna, 2007). The power of controllability attributions in group stereotypes can also explain differential support for policies that help the poor. People are more likely to support policies that are framed as "government assistance to the poor" compared to identical policies described as "welfare policies" (Henry, Reyna, & Weiner, 2004). The cause of this differential support for the same basic policy is due to the stereotypes of these two recipient groups (poor vs. welfare). On the one hand, people described as "poor" are often stereotyped as those who work hard but have fallen on hard times through no fault of their own (i.e., uncontrollable causes of poverty). These beliefs are more likely to elicit sympathy and support. Welfare recipients, on the other hand, are stereotyped as lazy and opportunistic (i.e., controllable causes of poverty), which leads to anger and a denial of support (Henry & Reyna, 2007; Henry, Reyna, & Weiner, 2004).

Controllability stereotypes are evident in a variety of domains. People generally stereotyped as aggressive are also perceived as more aggressive drivers (traveling faster, more likely at fault in an accident; Davies & Patel, 2005). Women stereotyped as promiscuous are judged as less traumatized by, and more responsible for, sexual harassment (Ferguson, Berlin, Noles, Johnson, Reed, & Spicer, 2005). Even more dramatically, controllability stereotypes can even lead to perceptions of a group as less human (Reyna et al., 2010).

When the stereotype implies that people are in control of positive outcomes, these people are held responsible for outcomes; but the emotional reactions toward them are positive--such as trust, gratitude, beliefs in competence, and so forth--and they are more apt to receive rewards and recognition (Weiner, 1985, 1993).One notable example of the relationship between positive stereotypes and positive reactions to stereotyped group members is that of FarEast Asians (e.g., the Chinese or Japanese).One salient stereotype of these Asian groups is that they are hard-working.In fact, these groups are considered a "model minority" in the United States because, despite discrimination, they worked hard to get ahead in society and have largely succeeded (Kitano & Sue, 1973; Sue & Kitano, 1973).This interpretation of the Asian experience is based more on the stereotypes that Asians are hardworking than it is on other Asian stereotypes (such as Asians being passive, or Asians being communal).Thus, a stereotype that communicates positive, controllable characteristics can have a very strong impact on the attributional beliefs surrounding the behaviors of those group members, just as negative stereotypes can.

Internal/Uncontrollable (I/UC) Stereotypes. The stereotypes "Women are illogical," "Blacks are genetically less intelligent," and "White men can't jump" all are examples of stereotypes that are both internal and often uncontrollable. Stereotypes that imply internal, uncontrollable causes, especially for negative outcomes (e.g., lack of innate ability, possessing traits that are deemed "genetically determined" like femininity or physical weakness), can be a double-edged sword (middle path, Figure 2). On the one hand, these stereotypes suggest that members of the stereotyped group are not responsible or in control of their outcomes, which can result in greater sympathy and assistance (Brandt, 2010; Reyna & Weiner, 2001; Weiner, 1993). We tend to feel sorry for the girl failing the math exam because of perceived low aptitude, or the Asian youth whom we think is not successful in sports because of low physical prowess. This sympathy will likely increase helping behaviors in the short term, like transferring the girl to a lower-level class or letting the Asian athlete play a less-challenging position on the team (Graham, 1991). However, targets of I/UC stereotypes will likely eventually be neglected and denied opportunities (e.g., relevant to math or sports) if their inability is deemed inalterable, which is suggested by the stable nature of stereotypes (Blaine, Crocker, & Major, 1995). For example, while the Asian athlete may be allowed to play in a less-challenging position, eventually he or she may be excluded from participation altogether, getting chronically benched or being removed from the team, especially if it is perceived that he or she cannot improve or contribute to the success of the team.

Many, if not most, I/UC stereotypes imply a biological origin of traits or behaviors, which can have a variety of consequences, depending on the implications of the trait. For example, beliefs that sexual orientation is biologically determined (people are born gay, or not) absolve gay men and lesbian women from responsibility for their marginalized status. This belief can increase support for gay rights (Haider-Markel & Joslyn, 2008; Wood & Bartkowski, 2004). In more hostile intergroup contexts, such as race relations, traits that are deemed innate or organic can be used to justify excluding and marginalizing the group. For example, the belief that status disparities between races is rooted in biological differences (e.g., in ability or civility) results in lower support for equality and less interest in interacting with members of other races (Williams & Eberhardt, 2008).

On the other hand, positive outcomes that are attributed to I/UC stereotypes inspire trust and beliefs in long-term competence, as well as rewards and access to recourses. For example, despite negligible empirical differences between boys and girls in math and math-related fields (Hyde & Mertz, 2009), stereotypes suggesting that males have higher math ability than females persist (Ambady, Shih, Kim, & Pittinsky, 2001; Farenga & Joyce, 1999; Nosek, Banaji, & Greenwald, 2002). Such stereotypes may explain why males, relative to females, are given more attention in math and science classes and encouraged to pursue higher education and careers in math and science, compared to females (Hill, Corbett, & St. Rose, 2010). Conversely, because females are stereotyped as lacking ability and competence in math and related fields, they are denied opportunities in these domains. Regardless of the frame, internal/uncontrollable stereotypes about mathematical ability result in encouragement and opportunities for men, but neglect and denial of opportunities for women.

External/Uncontrollable (E/UC) Stereotypes. The attributional model of stereotypes also suggests that generalizations about external, uncontrollable causes can constitute stereotypes (bottom path, Figure 2). The suggestions that people of color are disadvantaged because they attended "ghetto schools," White Americans are in positions of power because of White privilege, or Mexicans face exploitation in the American labor market are all examples of E/UC stereotypes and constitute broad generalizations about a group that explain the situation of the group through external causes. While these stereotypes may contain some truth (cf. Lee, Jussim, & McCauley, 1995), as some people of color do attend inner-city schools, some White Americans only have power due to privilege, and some Mexicans are exploited, not all members of these groups are subject to the same external and uncontrollable forces. These stereotypes suggest that responsibility for both positive and negative outcomes are attributed to external forces (Farwell & Weiner, 2000), so the targets of these stereotypes are neither blamed for failure, nor credited for success.

In the case of negative outcomes (e.g., poverty, low achievement, incarceration), stereotypes that imply external causes, such as disadvantage, oppression, or exploitation, can work to absolve the group from responsibility. Indeed, research on group-based beliefs that imply external causes of misfortune, such as systemic or historical discrimination, shows that the stereotyped group is more likely to be perceived positively (Stewart, Latu, Kawakami, & Myers, 2010; Vescio, Sechrist, & Paolucci, 2003) and receive help via reparation policies (Banfield, Blatz, & Ross, 2010; Starzyk & Ross, 2008) and government aid (Henry, Reyna, & Weiner, 2004). Also consistent with the attributional model of stereotypes, the relationship between external/uncontrollable stereotypes and support for policies that help the group are mediated by feelings of sympathy for the stereotyped group (Starzyk & Ross, 2008, Wetherell & Reyna, 2010). In addition to emotional reactions and helping behavior, external/uncontrollable stereotypes also discourage prejudicial reactions towards the target group. For example, people who endorse external/uncontrollable stereotypes are more likely to feel compunction when they act in a prejudicial manner that goes against their values, compared to people who do not endorse these stereotypes (Gill & Andreychik, 2007). This research, overall, suggests that the external/uncontrollable causal attributions implied by stereotypes can influence intergroup emotions and behaviors consistent with past attributional theorizing.

Regarding positive outcomes, success attributed to external/uncontrollable causes may lead to perceptions of incompetence (e.g. success *only* due to affirmative action; Heilman, 1996; Resendez, 2002), and can be used to perpetuate the status quo by denying a low-status group credit for accomplishments. These external/uncontrollable stereotypes may be more likely in domains in which a group is negatively stereotyped (see O'Brien, Kinias, & Major, 2008), such as minorities succeeding in white-collar jobs or women succeeding in math. This is perhaps in response to the dominant cultural interpretation of the group's traits or behavior, such as thinking that the group in question needs help to succeed. However, these stereotypes can also work against the dominant group, such as the perception of success due simply to group-based privilege (e.g. Case, 2007).

SELF CONSEQUENCES

Stereotypes are powerful social cognitions, in part, because they can be internalized and can impact the thoughts, behaviors, and attitudesof the stereotyped group's members (Bonnot & Croizet, 2007; Levy, 2009; Puhl, Moss-Racusin, & Schwartz, 2007; Steele, 1997). Internalizing stereotypes that imply controllable attributions for positive outcomes may lead an individual to have feelings of accomplishment and increased confidence in the successful domain (Weiner, 1985), while those that imply controllable attributions for negative outcomes may lead an individual to feel guilty and thus attempt to change the outcome in the future (e.g. Dweck, 1975).

When a person fails and the stereotype implies internal/uncontrollable attributions,the ensuing psychological and motivational results can be debilitating. The individual may feel ashamed, incompetent (Weiner, 1985) and helpless (Anderson et al., 1994), which can result in diminished motivation and persistence in the stereotyped domain (Crocker & Major, 1989; Crocker, Major, & Steele, 1998). Positive outcomes associated with internal/uncontrollable attributions (high natural ability) should be associated with positive feelings and persistence in the domain. External/uncontrollable attributions for positive outcomes do not allow an individual to take credit for a success; however, for negative outcomes, external/uncontrollable attributions allow individuals to sidestep the guilt and shame that can come from internal attributions. For example, attributing failure due to discrimination (external/uncontrollable) can relieve an individual from responsibility and thus bolster the individual's self-esteem (Crocker & Major, 1989; Kaiser & Miller, 2001).

Stereotype Threat. Stereotype threat research focuses "on the immediate situational threat that derives from the broad dissemination of negative stereotypes about one's group—the threat of possibly being judged and treated stereotypically, or of possibly self-fulfilling such a stereotype" (Steele & Aronson, 1995, p. 798; see also, Steele, 1997). In general this research focuses on the application of a general stereotype about a group (e.g. women, African-Americans) and observes its effects on subsequent performance, such as a standardized math or verbal test (for reviews see Schmader, Johns, & Forbes, 2008; Shapiro & Neuberg, 2007; Wheeler & Petty, 2001). Research on stereotype threat suggests the attributional power of stereotypes on the stereotyped individual and provides the most comprehensive support for the self-related consequences predicted by the attributional model of stereotypes. Importantly, stereotype threat has been implicated in the lower academic achievement of low-status groups (Cohen, Garcia, Apfel, & Master, 2006; Walton & Spencer, 2009), providing one explanation for the achievement gap.

The attributional model of stereotypessuggests that one way stereotypes can impact performance is through the attributional content of the activated stereotypes (Reyna, 2000). Stereotype threat may suggest internal qualities that alter the attributions made by people in the threatened group. As discussed above, many stereotypes (though not all) imply internal qualities, so reminding a group of its stereotype may increase the availability of internal explanations of poor performance. Several studies provide support for this prediction.When under stereotype threat, women attributed computer failure to internal reasons like their own ability, while men used external reasons, such as poor equipment (Koch, Muller, & Sieyerding, 2008).Importantly, these initial threats and subsequent attributions can influence future behavior as well.For example, when women allegedly failed on a task assessing math ability, they, more than men, attributed this failure to internal ability (Kiefer & Shih, 2006).These internal ability attributions mediated the relationship between gender and choice of future task (a measure of persistence).

More direct evidence for the role of attributional stereotypes in stereotype threat research can be found in research that manipulates the attributional content of the activated stereotype, rather than stereotypes of women/men/Blacks/Whites/etc. generally. Two studies in particular take this approach.First, Dar-Nimrod and Heine (2006) activated the content of stereotypes and found that women performed best on a math test in experimental conditions of "no gender differences in math" and "gender differences due to external causes (teachers' bias, different mothering techniques for males and females)" compared to conditions of "standard stereotype threat (gender is made salient)" or "gender differences due to genetics."These results suggest that stereotypes that imply an external attribution that absolves participants from responsibility for differences in math achievement(e.g., women are discriminated against) are as effective in preserving women's math performance as knowing that there are no gender differences. On the other hand, stereotypes that implied internal/uncontrollable explanations (genetic differences) may make participants feel as if improvement was impossible. A second study, for example, found that women performed better on a math exam following a threat with an effort (controllable) based stereotype compared to conditions with no threat or a threat with an ability (uncontrollable) based stereotype (Thoman, White, Ymawaki, & Koishi, 2008). Taken as a whole, these studies suggest that the attributional content of stereotypes may provide an explanation for stereotype threat effects.

PERPETUATION OF STEREOTYPES: THE ROLE OF STABILITY IN SELF-DIRECTED STEREOTYPES

The attributional content of stereotypes and their impact on self views can be complicated by the assumed stability of stereotyped traits.. For example, while failure due to internal/controllable forces can serve to motivate people to change their behavior (Dweck, 1975), even in stereotype threat conditions (Dar-Nimrod & Heine, 2006; Thoman et al., 2008), repeated failure on a task by a stereotyped group member may cause group members to continually question their strategies. Although this could eventually lead to the optimal strategy (e.g., greater effort; better tactics), if attempts at success are embedded within an environment of hostility and discrimination—as is likely the case for many groups targeted by negative/internal/controllable stereotypes—"success" may never be achieved. This could cause the stereotyped individual to ultimately turn the responsibility and blame inward, threatening the individual's self-worth and persistence on the task (Crocker & Major, 1989; Crocker, Major, & Steele, 1998).

Even when examining stereotypes that impact perceptions of the self, stereotypes can be seen as bolstering the status quo. Negative stereotypes about women and math ability will likely decrease as people see more women succeeding in math-related domains; however, the attributions supplied by stereotype threat (e.g. Dar-Nimrod & Heine, 2006) reduce women's chances of succeeding in these domains, which further perpetuates the stereotypes. Similarly, as disadvantaged groups internalize the stability implied by a negative stereotype, they may withdraw from a task and suffer from a threatened self-worth. In both of these cases, rather than challenging a stereotype, the members of the stereotyped group may unwittingly confirm the stereotype if they are not seen succeeding in these domains. Stereotypes are then viewed as descriptive, perhaps containing more than a kernel of truth, which allows stereotypes to more efficiently justify and rationalize the social system. These stereotypes provide ready explanations for high status groups to judge low status groups and serve as an internalized barrier for the advancement of disadvantaged groups.

SUMMARY OF INDIVIDUAL LEVEL STEREOTYPES

The attributional model of stereotypes (Reyna, 2000, 2008) provides a lens for understanding the attributional implications of individual stereotypes. The level of the individual stereotypes provides a finer-grained analysis of the causal components of stereotypes, which allows social scientists to make specific predictions regarding the perception of stereotyped groups and the perception of the self in reference to membership in a stereotyped group. This perspective also allows us to make specific predictions regarding novel stereotypes that may emerge with changes in intergroup relations and contact, or cultural shifts in beliefs about certain groups within a society. Attributional stereotypes not only provide explanations for group or personal outcomes, but they can be used to justify how we treat members of stereotyped groups. As we will see, this perspective is a necessary accompaniment to both the intra- and intergroup levels of stereotype analysis, especially in the context of how packages of stereotypes can be used to explain a group's actions and position within society.

INTRAGROUP STEREOTYPE PACKAGES

The prior section discussed the attributional content and consequences of stereotypes at the level of individual stereotypes, but we know that the stereotypes we hold about groups often contain a variety of interlinked traits and ideas that serve to inform us about the nature of the group. In this chapter, the multitude of interrelated traits used to stereotype a particular group will be referred to as intragroup stereotype packages, which can explain and provide causal information about a group's outcomes or circumstances. Stereotypes at this level of analysis help us make sense of the interlinked traits and ideas connected to a group. While intragroup stereotype packages can be influenced by a group's relation to other groups (*inter*group stereotypes), the particular packages created by stereotypic traits have unique effects on the attitudes and behaviors directed towards a particular group. The type of traits that make up these intragroup stereotype packages can provide explanations and attributions for a group's outcomes and position in society.

Previous research has examined how stereotypic traits within groups can impact perceptions of a group by influencing the activation and meaning of individual traits on the perception of the group as a whole (Kunda & Thagard, 1996; Richards & Hewstone, 2001). For example, Brewer and colleagues (1981) found that participants differentiated between three distinct groups of older adults—the "grandmotherly," "elder statesmen," and "senior citizen" types. By considering the traits associated with these three subgroups of the elderly, participants' stereotypes of the elderly more generally were diluted (see also, e.g., Mauer, Park, & Rothbart, 1995; Park et al., 1992), suggesting that the stereotypes within the superordinate elderly group were influenced by the different stereotypes of the elderly subgroups. Others have examined how multiple stereotypic traits can influence the activation or the use of a stereotype to interpret behavior depending on the goals and motivations of the situation (e.g. Kunda & Thagard, 1996). These lines of research, however, do not examine the attributional implications of intragroup stereotypes.

WARMTH AND COMPETENCE IN THE STEREOTYPE CONTENT MODEL (SCM)

One prominent model of intragroup stereotypes that has directly examined attributional consequences of interrelated stereotypes is the stereotype content model, or SCM (Fiske, Cuddy, Glick, & Xu, 2002; Cuddy et al., 2008), which is the focus of this section. The SCM starts with the premise that judgments of warmth (e.g., sociable, helpful, happy) and competence (e.g., competent, skillful, able) are fundamental dimensions of social judgment (Asch, 1946; Rosenberg, Nelson, & Vivekananthan, 1968; Tordorov, Mandisodza, Goren, & Hall, 2005; Williams & Bargh, 2008).Stereotypes are also expected to vary on these two fundamental dimensions. Research in the United States (Fiske, Cuddy, Glick, & Xu, 2002) and across cultures (Cuddy, Fiske, Kwan, Glick, Demoulin, Leyens et al., 2009)has used multidimensional scaling to statistically tease apart the underlying dimensions of a variety of stereotypic traits. This technique allows the researchers to see if a number of disparate traits actually share any kinds of underlying qualities. Using multidimensional scaling, these researchers have found that judgments of warmth and competence underlie stereotyped perceptions of groups in America and throughout the world (Fiske et al., 2002; Cuddy et al., 2007, 2009). The combination of stereotypes on these two dimensions serves to explain the group's position in society as well as drive emotions and behaviors directed towards the group.

As a theory that sits between both individual and intergroup level stereotypes, the SCM most obviously blursthese distinctions. As will be reviewed below, the content of the intragroup stereotype packages outlined by the SCM are informed by intergroup relations and predict emotions and behaviors via their attributional implications. Nonetheless, the SCM provides a unique perspective on intragroup stereotypes as attributions that explain and justify social relations. This perspective highlights how the specific meaning and function of stereotypes change as they are interpreted within the context of other stereotypes about the same group. Before examining the nature of these intragroup stereotype packages it is first necessary to understand why some groups are stereotyped with high vs. low competence and high vs. low warmth.Whether a group is stereotyped with warmth or competence traits depends on specific intergroup relations in society.

Stereotypes that imply traits of warmth explain the competition and threat posed by a social group (Fiske et al. 2002). If a group is stereotyped with traits such as cold or immoral, it suggests that that the group has conflicting goals and interests with one's own group. This general prediction—that a group's perceived threat influences its level of stereotyped warmth—has been demonstrated with correlational research showing that perceived threat is positively related to stereotypic conceptions of warmth (Fiske et al, 2002; Cuddy, Fiske, & Glick, 2007). Experimental evidence has demonstrated the causal influence of goal compatibility on warmth stereotypes by manipulating the threat posed by a hypothetical immigrant group (Caprariell, Cuddy, & Fiske, 2009). A hypothetical group which was described as threatening to another groups' economic well-being—by taking power and resources—was stereotyped as less warm than a group not described as threatening. Although this suggests an intergroup process (see next section), the evaluation of warmth has important intragroup ramifications.

Competence stereotypes explain the social power and status of a group (Fiske, Cuddy, Glick, & Xu, 2002). High-status groups control and provide resources in a society. In order to be in such a position, they must be capable and intelligent (competence stereotypes). Low-status groups do not control resources and are often stereotyped as less competent and able. Beliefs in competence or incompetence provide both explanations and justifications for a group's status. Again, this prediction is supported by correlational (Fiske, Cuddy, Glick, & Xu, 2002; Cuddy, Fiske, & Glick, 2007; Cuddy et al., 2009) and experimental evidence (Caprariell, Cuddy, & Fiske, 2009). Participants who read about a high status hypothetical immigrant group were more likely to perceive the group as competent compared to participants who read about a low status group. Thus, competence stereotypes can provide a clear explanation for the status of social groups.

Four Combinations of Warmth and Competence

Most relevant to the idea of intragroup stereotype packages, the dimensions of warmth and competence create mixtures of intragroup stereotypes with unique emotional and behavioral consequences.Four clusters of stereotypes are created by variation on the two dimensions (warmth and competence) and serve to explain the motivations, circumstances, and ensuing responsibility of the stereotyped group. Like the attributional model of stereotypes, each cluster of stereotypes in the SCM is expected to result in different emotional and behavioral reactions (Fiske et al., 2002; Cuddy et al., 2007; see Figure 3). The dimension of warmth is associated with good intentions and predicts active helping or harming behavior, such as direct aid to those in need (active helping) or legalized segregation (active harm). The dimension of competence is associated with responsibility and predicts passive helping or harming behavior, such as interaction with a group to serve self- and group-interests (passive helping) or behavior that is dismissive or ignoring (passive harm).

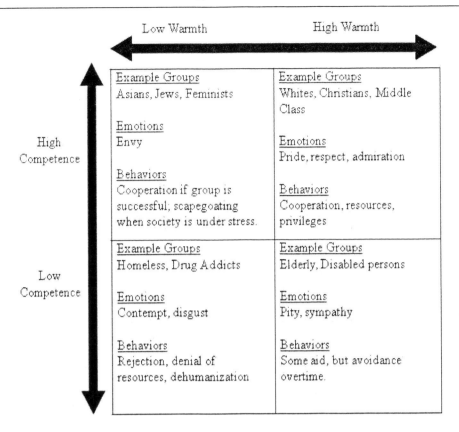

Figure 3. Intragroup Stereotypes: The Stereotype Content Model.

The four combinations of the two dimensions elicit four distinct emotional and behavioral reactions based upon the intentions, goals, and attributions implied by the stereotype packages (Cuddy et al., 2008). These are as follows: (a) low competence/low warmth, (b) low competence/high warmth, (c) high competence/low warmth, and (d) high competence/high warmth.

Low competence/low warmth. Those stereotyped in this manner (e.g. homeless, drug addicts) receive contempt because the lack of warmth suggests bad intentions and thus responsibility for their position (Harris & Fiske, 2005; Weiner, et al., 1988; Weiner, 2006). This package of stereotypes signals controllability and responsibility for negative outcomes. Groups which elicit contempt are rejected and ignored, but also actively expelled, harmed, and dehumanized (Harris & Fiske, 2005).

Low competence/high warmth. Groups stereotyped with these traits receive pity because groups in this position—such as elderly people or disabled people—are often perceived as having negative outcomes (e.g., low-status) that they cannot control due to their lower competence (Weiner, 1985). Pity elicits behaviors that aim to actively help the group, such as through economic aid, but that also may lead to social distance or avoidance, which is more generally the case, in an effort to disassociate oneself from an unfortunate other.

High competence/low warmth. Groups that are described with high competence/low warmth stereotype packages (e.g. Asians, Jews, feminists) elicit envy because the group is perceived as responsible for success yet competitive with one's own group. Positive outcomes for others that deprive oneself of status or resources are met with envy (Parrott & Smith,

1993), which prompts behaviors that elicit cooperation with the envied group simply because the group is successful. However, when society is under stress, this envy may lead to scapegoating (Glick, 2005), such as what occurred with the Jews in Nazi Germany.

High competence/high warmth. These group stereotypes lead to admiration because the group is perceived as both responsible and deserving of success. These groups are often ingroups (or at least groups whose success has positive implications for the self or one's group), or referent (i.e. dominant) groups in the society, such as Christians, or the middle class. Groups that elicit admiration are actively and passively aided, such as via increased contact and cooperation with the particular group and its goals.

THE MEANING AND CONSEQUENCES OF INTRAGROUP STEREOTYPES

The SCM demonstrates how the meaning of stereotypic traits within groups (i.e., intragroup stereotype packages) can change as a function of the other stereotypic traits that are also relevant to those groups. In other words, the effects of a warmth stereotype can be countered by the effects of a competence stereotype combined with it. For example, both low- and high-status groups are stereotyped with warmth-related traits, but these traits take on different meanings and provoke different outcomes when paired with traits suggesting low or high competence. Groups with high competence/high warmth stereotypes, such as Whites, are privileged in society, receiving more cooperation and opportunity for advancement than do low-status groups. However, groups with low competence/high warmth stereotypes, such as disabled persons, receive pity. This pity can be beneficial, but it also represents a sort of paternalism that can marginalize the stereotyped group (Glick & Fiske, 2001b). Thus, while Whites and disabled people are both stereotyped as warm, the behaviors and emotions directed towards these groups differ because of the added meaning provided by the competence stereotypes.

These interactions between the dimensions of warmth and competence not only help us explain the causes of a group's situation, but also help us to understand the many variations of prejudice and discrimination, especially among groups that may be stereotyped with both positive and negative traitssimultaneously (Clausell & Fiske, 2005; Glick & Fiske, 2001a; Lin, Kwan, Cheung, & Fiske, 2005). For example, stereotypes of the elderly as warm but not competent helps to explain perceptions and treatment of the elderly (Cuddy, Norton, & Fiske, 2005). Warmth stereotypes suggest that the elderly should be treated with benevolence, as they are not a threat and have good intentions. Low competence stereotypes, on the other hand, suggest that the elderly are not in control of their low status, but they also suggest that the elderly may not have much to offer in the way of status, power, and resources. The combination of these two stereotype dimensions help to explain why Americans generally think well of the elderly, but at the same time often distance themselves by putting the elderly in nursing and retirement homes away from the general, and younger, population.

The unique combinations of intragroup stereotypes may also help to explain the variety of reactions towards gay men. Research utilizing warmth and competence stereotypes consistently finds that gay men are stereotyped neutrally (Fiske et al., 2002), which is in contrast with a variety of evidence documenting the negative impressions and treatment of gay men (Brandt & Reyna, 2010; Haider-Markel & Joslyn, 2008; Henry & Reyna, 2007;

Herek, 2000, 2002). The solution to this empirical puzzle appears to lie in the various subgroups associated with gay men and the content of their intragroup stereotypes, such that different subgroups of gay men face different forms of stereotypes (Clausell & Fiske, 2005). Feminine-typed subgroups (e.g. flamboyant) are stereotyped similarly to women (warm, but not competent) and masculine-typed subgroups (e.g. activist, artistic) are stereotyped similarly to men (competent, but not warm). Moreover, two subgroups (cross-dressers, leather/biker) are stereotyped as low on both dimensions, which is suggestive of dehumanization (Harris & Fiske, 2005). This research suggests that prejudice and discrimination towards gay men may differ systematically depending on the specific stereotype combinations associated with a particular subgroup of gay men. It may be that the most dehumanizing and contemptuous prejudice is directed towards subgroups stereotyped as low in both warmth and competence, while helpful behavior may be offered to groups stereotyped as having a mixture of warmth and competence.

SUMMARY OF INTRAGROUP LEVEL STEREOTYPES

Stereotypes often exist in conjunction with multiple traits and their meaning, and consequences can be influenced by their interactions with one another. Intragroup stereotypes that vary on dimensions of warmth and competence combine to produce distinct stereotype packages that explain the prestige and benevolence of the stereotyped group. These packages suggest, for example, that high-status dominant groups deserve admiration and status because they are both smart and kind, while ultra-low-status groups deserve derision because they are incompetent and antisocial. Moreover, the specific combination of warmth and competence stereotypes predict specific emotional and behavior patterns, suggesting that the attributions and intentions implied by the stereotype packages influence consequential intergroup behavior. Research on intragroup stereotype packages thus allows us to understand the nature of intergroup relations when stereotypes combine within groups.

INTERGROUP STEREOTYPE PACKAGES

Intergroup stereotype packages consist of the stereotypesof comparative groups in society (e.g. Men and Women, Blacks and Whites). The stereotypes at this level derive their meaning and explanatory power from the relationship of one group's stereotypes to another's, and are used to explain the status differences between the comparative groups (Kay et al, 2007). Analyses at the level of intergroup stereotype packages comprise the broadest level of analysis.

COMPLEMENTARY STEREOTYPES OF RELATED GROUPS

Just as stereotypes do not exist in a vacuum, neither do the groups that stereotypes describe. Often, we judge one group in reference to other groups that are considered related to it or opposite of it, due to the close relevance of other people, groups, and social situations surrounding the judgment (e.g. Ho, Sanbonmatsu, & Akimoto, 2002). This is especially the case for comparative groups in society, such as men and women, Blacks and Whites, rich and poor, low-status and high-status. These groups areoften stereotyped in paired, complementary ways that justify one group's position in society as compared to the other (e.g., Kay et al., 2007). For example, high-status groups are generally stereotyped with traits that explain and justify their high status (competence, assertiveness), while low-status groups are stereotyped with traits that explain and justify their low status (unintelligent. indolent), or are status-irrelevant but positive (happy) (Eagly & Steffen, 1984; Hoffman & Hurst, 1990; Mullen, Brown, & Smith, 1992).

These forms of intergroup stereotype packages have been termed complementary stereotypes by some (Jost & Kay, 2005) because the stereotype traits are often reflections of one another, and make the most attributional sense within the context of the other relevant groups and stereotypes. Not all of these stereotypes are negative, and in fact, sometimes positive or socially-valued qualities serve to perpetuate existing social arrangements. For example, the stereotype that women are communal (a trait viewed positively) justifies women's over-representation in low-paying or low-status "service" occupations, such as child care, nursing, and hospitality.

DIFFERENT FORMS OF COMPLEMENTARY INTERGROUP STEREOTYPE PACKAGES

Intergroup stereotype packages can take several forms. Two such forms that have attributional implications are (a) status- relevant stereotypes for a high-status group, coupled with a status-irrelevant (but positive) stereotype for the low-status group; and (b) status-relevant stereotypes for the high-status group, paired with status-relevant stereotypes for the low-status group. A third form, status-irrelevant for both groups, contains fewer attributional messages, yet still functions to make stereotypes more believable and justifiable. Each form is described below.

Status-relevant for high-status group/status irreleveant for low-status group. Status-relevant/status irrelevant stereotype packages provide attributions for the position of the high-status group (e.g. competent, hard working), but status irrelevant and positive stereotypes for the low-status group (e.g. happy). In order to obtain a sense of systemic justice and fairness, perceivers trade the objective group success of the high status for beliefs that those in lower status are content. These combinations of stereotypes help to justify the social system by providing attributionally positive reasons for the high-status group's success and by also providing perceivers with a positive view of the low-status group. The positive stereotype compensates for the negative position of the lower class, while the attributionally relevant stereotype explains the better position of the higher class. For example, students at a high status university are more likely to be stereotyped with traits that serve to explain the university's status, such as "smart" and "intelligent." Students at a rival, but lower-status, university, however, are more likely to be stereotyped with traits that are positive, but irrelevant to the school's status (Jost, Pelham, & Carvallo, 2002).

Status-relevant for high status/status-relevant for low status. Here, intergroup stereotype packages are used to explain and justify current status disparities with little regard as to whether or not any "cosmic scales of justice" are in balance between those who have and have not. Rather, the justice implied by these stereotypes is one of deservingness. The stereotypes associated with the low-status group may be objectively positive, as in the case of women being more communal and nurturing (Eagly & Mladinic, 1989), but can also be negative, as in the case of stereotyping Blacks or Latinos as "lazy" (Kay, Czaplinski, & Jost, 2009; Kay, Jost, & Young, 2005). Therefore, the high-status group is imbued with an implicit sense of entitlement that is denied the low-status group based on the stereotypical perception of the latter.

Status-irrelevant for both groups. Finally, the last form of complementary stereotypes does not provide causal information regarding the status of the stereotyped groups, but it provides information regarding their overall moral standing—what groups lack in equality of resources, they make up for through the fabric of their character, thus bringing the "scales back into balance." These kinds of compensatory stereotypes—positive versus negative (but status irrelevant)—can serve to legitimize the system, though not through the attributional implications of the stereotypes. For example, exposure to stereotypes that the poor are honest and the rich are dishonest increases perceptions of the social system as just and fair (Kay & Jost, 2003). These studies suggest that endorsement, or even exposure, to stereotypes that suggest low-status groups are not perceived wholly negatively and high-status groups are not perceived wholly positively may make stereotypes that justify disparities more believable and palatable, such as by diminishing the perception that justifications are rooted in prejudice. This allows the perceiver to view the entire social system as more just and fair, such that every group in society enjoys benefits and suffers costs. For the purpose of this chapter, research findings regarding intergroup stereotype packages will be limited to stereotypes that convey attributional information.

RESEARCH FINDINGS IN INTERGROUP STEREOTYPE PACKAGES

One well-researched example of intergroup stereotype packages concerns the complementary nature of gender stereotypes. Women are typically stereotyped with traits that convey a communal, interpersonal orientation; while men are stereotyped with traits implying independence, assertiveness, and a competitive drive (e.g. Eagly, 1987; Eagly & Steffen, 1984). These stereotypes can explain the social positions of men and women. Communal traits are often associated with the jobs and social roles attributed to women, such as childcare, while competitive traits are often associated with the jobs and social roles associated with men, such as positions of leadership or competitive industries like business (Eagly & Karau, 2002). Thus, women stay at home to raise children because they are communal and nurturing, while men succeed at and belong in business because they are assertive (Eagly & Steffen, 1984; Hoffman & Hurst, 1990). The gendered division of labor is perceived as acceptable because the stereotypes of men and women can provide underlying causes (in this case, traits) that rationalize the differing social roles of men and women. If men were stereotyped with more communal traits and women with more competitive traits, it is unlikely that people would perceive current gender inequality as acceptable (cf. Diekman & Eagly, 2000).

Several lines of evidence support the justifying function of complementary intergroup stereotype packages. Across several cultures, larger perceived status differences are predictive of greater endorsement of complementary stereotypes (Jost, Kivetz, Rubini, Guermandi, & Musso, 2005). This research suggests that when there is a greater need to justify the system—such as when there are greater differences between low- and high-status groups—people endorse stereotypes that explain the existing social arrangements. Moreover, experimental evidence also suggests that just the exposure to intergroup stereotype packages can serve to increase the perceived legitimacy of the system. Participants who were exposed to complementary gender stereotypes were generally more likely to view the system as just (Jost & Kay, 2005).

One feature of intergroup stereotype packages that serves to make them especially powerful at explaining intergroup situations is that across several cultures (Jost et al., 2005; Overbeck, Jost, Mosso, &Flizik, 2004), both high- and low-status groups endorse intergroup stereotype packages that explain the extant hierarchy (Haines & Jost, 2000; Jost & Burgess, 2000; Jost, Pelham & Carvallo, 2002). Moreover, endorsement of system-justifying intergroup stereotype packages results in less ingroup attachment for low-status groups (Jost et al., 2002). It could also be possible that the stereotypes play a palliative role (Jost & Hunyady, 2002), such that endorsement of intergroup compensatory stereotypes by low-status group members serves to assuage frustration, anger, and negative affect more broadly for their lower social status. Overall, these results suggest that intergroup stereotype packages help to explain the hierarchy of the social world and cause people, even those hurt the most by the current system, to view the system as just and fair.

Intergroup stereotypes have consequences beyond the abstract support of justice and system legitimacy. For example, complementary gender beliefs are expressed in ambivalent prejudices, such as ambivalent sexism against both men and women (Glick et al., 2000, 2004; Glick & Fiske, 1996, 2001a). Ambivalent sexist beliefs, especially benevolent sexism, suggest that women are dependent on men and should follow traditional gender norms. Men, however, are perceived as assertive, powerful, and in control of resources in society. These beliefs append onto the stereotypes of men and women as agentic and communal, respectively. The societal endorsement of ambivalent sexist beliefs limits the advancement of women and justifies harmful actions taken by the high-status group. For example, greater gender inequality within a country, as measured by the United Nations Gender Empowerment Measure and Gender Development Index, is related to greater ambivalent sexism (Glick et al., 2000, 2004). These results suggest that stereotypes and beliefs about the proper and complementary roles of men and women hinder the advancement of women at a societal level.

Benevolent sexism also predicts greater hostility towards women. For example, benevolent sexism specifically has been related to less positive attitudes toward rape victims (Chapleau, Oswald, & Russell, 2007; Sakalli-Ururlu, Yalcin, & Glick, 2007), the perceived legitimacy of wife abuse (Glick & Sakalli-Ugurlu, Ferreira, & Aguiar de Souza, 2002), and discrimination in the public sector (Cikara, Lee, Ficke, & Glick, 2009). Moreover, women who are perceived to violate the norms set by the stereotypes face increased blame for negative events (e.g. abuse; Capezza & Arriaga, 2008).Nontraditional women who were described as being abused were perceived as less warm and were blamed more for the abuse than were traditional women. That is, the women who violated traditional stereotypes of women by acting assertive, like the stereotypic behavior of men, were perceived as cold and thus *deserving* of abuse. Complementary gender beliefs can even lead women to see a system of male dominance as legitimate (Moya, Glick, Exposito, de Lemus, & Hart, 2007). Overall, these results suggest that complementary stereotypes—especially gender stereotypes—lead to attitudes and behaviors that are harmful to the low-status group.

Stereotypes that explain the causes of a social system are also bound to change as the social system changes (Doosje, Haslam, Spears, Oakes, & Koomen, 1998; Doosje & Haslam, 2005; Haslam, Turner, Oakes, McGarty, & Hayes, 1992; Haslam, Turner, Oakes, Reynolds, & Doosje, 2002; Stott, Hutchinson, & Drury, 2001). Changes in the social system will change the nature of intergroup stereotype packages in order to explain evolving group relationships, intentions, and behaviors. Changes in the perceived distribution of men and women into traditional gender roles over time predicts the stereotypical attributes assigned to men and women, such that the stereotypes of men and women seem to converge overtime due to changes in social roles (Diekman & Eagly, 2000). Stereotypes of high-status groups can also change as the social system changes in order to serve the goals of subservient social groups (Reynolds, Oakes, Haslam, Nolan, & Dolnik, 2000). Specifically, in open social systems where status is perceived to be legitimate, complementary stereotypes, where both low- and high-status groups endorse stereotypes that legitimize the social system, are more common. When status is illegitimate (a closed system), the high-status group is attributed unfavorable stereotypes, and the low-status group is attributed stereotypes that could foreshadow collective action, such as the overthrow of a despotic government's high-status group. Unfavorable stereotypes of the high-status group mediate intentions for collective action, suggesting that the stereotypes of the group have failed to sufficiently explain the group's high-status position (see also Stott & Drury, 2004). As this research demonstrates, stereotypes serve to explain and justify the evolving state of intergroup relations.

SUMMARY OF INTERGROUP STEREOTYPE PACKAGES

One manifestation of stereotypes as attributions takes place at the intergroup level where stereotypes help people explain their social world by providing explanations for the positions of low- and high-status groups in reference to one another. These intergroup stereotype packages often provide complementary traits that help to justify the social system and even disparage low- status groups. Understanding stereotypes at this level of analysis allows for a comparative understanding of groups that takes context into account when deriving causal meaning from stereotypes. This contextual understanding is especially interesting when the context changes, such as the increase of women in typically male occupations (Diekman & Eagly, 2000), or the dynamic changes in mobility within a system (Reynolds et al., 2000; Stott & Drury, 2004). In a social world where very little exists in isolation from the surrounding system, intergroup stereotype packages helpus understand and justifyintergroup arrangements in dynamic and interconnected environments.

INTERCONNECTIONS BETWEEN INDIVIDUAL, INTRAGROUP, AND INTERGROUP LEVELS OF ANALYSIS

This chapter reviewed three major perspectives in the study of stereotypes and attributions that explain how stereotypes provide causal explanations at three levels of analysis, each with three distinct purposes. All three levels have the same underlying goal of explicating how stereotypes provide explanation and understanding of the social world. However, like the tools in a toolbox, stereotypes at all three levels of analysis can also work together to efficiently explain and justify our complex social environment.

The level of individual stereotypes provides a tool for understanding specific emotional and behavior reactions to groups based on judgment-relevant stereotypes by outlining the common attributional signatures of stereotypes (Reyna, 2008). This perspective allows us to both understand the underlying attributional meaning conveyed in a variety of diverse group-based stereotypes (positive or negative), and to predict emotional and behavioral reactions to groups depending on these attributional patterns. In addition, this perspective provides a means for understanding the self-perceptions and behaviors of group members in reaction to reminders of their group membership and associated stereotypes. Although, in this chapter, this model was primarily used in the context of individual-level stereotypes, the attributional meaning of individual stereotypes can interact with one another to better inform attributional judgments in an intragroup manner. For example, the stereotypes "poor" and "lazy" create a different attributional signature (undeserving) than the stereotypes "rich" and "lazy," which would be more associated with being privileged. Similarly, stereotypes that imply deservingness can be used to justify group-based inequality and other intergroup arrangements (e.g., Henry et al., 2004; Reyna et al., 2006, 2009).

Intragroup stereotype packages help us understand the unique meaning of stereotypic traits when combined with other traits. These stereotype packages are extremely diverse across groups and cultures, but many appear to vary on dimensions of warmth and competence (Cuddy et al., 2008). The four quadrants created by combining these two dimensions elicit four unique combinations of stereotypes that drive emotional and behavioral expressions toward the stereotyped group. This perspective can provide insight into the unique prejudices some groups face by explicating the meaning of a stereotype within the context of other stereotypes and aspects of the intergroup situation (Cuddy et al., 2008; Lin et al., 2005).

Although the emphasis in this chapter was on how the dimensions of warmth and competence interact to create unique attributions and their associated consequences, this perspective can also inform both individual-level and intergroup-level understanding of the role of stereotypes and attributions. On an individual level, both warmth and competence can be independent categories that guide attributional consequences. For example, stereotypes associated with high competence will produce very different outcomes for job candidates than stereotypes associated with low competence. The SCM is also rooted in intergroup dynamics. Judgments of warmth are directly tied to intergroup relations, and judgments of competence are often made in terms of one group's relation to other groups (e.g., status, power). Thus, while this model provides insight into the attributional functions of intragroup stereotypes, this model also has utility across levels of analysis.

At the intergroup level, stereotypes provide explanations by comparing relevant groups to one another. Intergroup stereotype packages can provide perceivers with a sense of justice (e.g. Jost & Kay, 2005) or an explanation for extant social hierarchies and other status differentials (Eagly & Steffen, 1984; Hoffman & Hurst, 1990; Kay et al., 2005). These packages offer explanations for a group's position in reference to another relevant group in the social system, and reflect the dynamic nature of intergroup relationships and perceptions (Reynolds et al., 2000). Once again, intergroup comparisons can inform both individual level stereotypes and their attributions as well as intragroup stereotype packages. For example, how one group fares in one set of circumstances has attributional ramifications when compared to other groups' outcomes in similar circumstances. In one study, participants who were exposed to successful individuals or the successes of Asian-Americans as a group negatively stereotyped African-Americans and Mexican-Americans (Ho, Sanbonmatsu, & Akimoto, 2002). Being exposed to the success of either an individual or a group caused participants to see more opportunity for advancement in America, which in turn, led participants to see the disadvantaged groups (African- or Mexican-Americans) as responsible for their social position. Symbolic racism theorists have taken advantage of this effect and use the idea that other groups facing discrimination have successfully pulled themselves out of poverty as a potential rationalization that Blacks are to blame, at least somewhat, for their continued hardship (Henry & Sears, 2002). Thus, intergroup comparisons can inform individual level stereotypes (e.g., "Blacks are lazy"). As was previously discussed in terms of the SCM, intergroup dynamics give meaning to intragroup stereotype packages by providing a larger context from which to derive attributional meaning, such as status differences.

CONCLUSION

The research reviewed in this chapter suggests that stereotypes can help us find meaning and understanding in our complex social world through various routes and at various levels of analysis. Whether we are thinking about groups in comparison to other groups, a group in comparison to itself, or just individual stereotypes, stereotypes provide us with prepackaged information that can help us disambiguate the complex, multidimensional underpinnings of a group's qualities, behaviors, or life outcomes. However, the attributional clarity stereotypes provide may come at a steep social cost. Stereotypes rarely contain the truth we might desire when we embark on an attributional search, or accurately reveal the forces that drive widespread social inequities. Instead, we must be mindful that the stereotypes that we use to help us make sense of the world likely play a role in perpetuating the very social arrangements that we struggle to understand.

REFERENCES

Allport, G. W. (1954). *The nature of prejudice.* Reading, MA: Addison-Wesley.

Ambady, N., Shih, M., Kim, A., & Pittinsky, T. (2001). *Stereotype susceptibility in children: Effects of identity activation on quantitative performance.* Psychological Science, 12, 385–90.

Anderson, C. A., Krull, D. S., & Weiner, B. (1996). *Explanations: Processes and consequences.* In A. W. Kruglanksi & E. T. Higgins (Eds.) Social psychology: Handbook of basic principles (pp. 271-296). New York: Guilford Press.

Asch, S. E. (1946). *Forming impressions of personality.* Journal of Abnormal and Social Psychology, 41, 258-290.

Banfield, J. C., Blatz, C., & Ross, M. (2010). *Do conservatives abandon their opposition to government reparations when redress is targeted at members of their own group?* Poster presented at the annual meeting of the Society for Personality and Social Psychology (Las Vegas, NV).

Bargh, J. A., Chen, M., & Burrows, L. (1996). *Automaticity of social behavior: Direct effects of trait construct and stereotype activation on action.* Journal of Personality and Social Psychology, 71, 230–244.

Blaine, B., Crocker, J., & Major, B. (1995). *The unintended negative consequences of sympathy for the stigmatized.* Journal of Applied Social Psychology, 25, 889-905.

Blair, I. V., & Banaji, M. R. (1996). *Automatic and controlled processes in stereotype priming.* Journal of Personality and Social Psychology, 70, 1142–1163.

Bonnot, V., & Croizet, J. C. (2007). *Stereotype internalization and women's math performance: The role of interference in working memory.* Journal of Experimental Social Psychology, 43, 857–866.

Brandt, M. (2010). *Onset and offset controllability, ideology, and home foreclosures.* Manuscript submitted for publication.

Brandt, M., & Reyna, C. (2010). *The role of prejudice and the need for closure in religious fundamentalism.* Personality and Social Psychology Bulletin, 36, 715-725.

Brewer, M. B., Dull, V., & Lui, L. (1981). *Perceptions of the elderly: Stereotypes as prototypes.* Journal of Personality and Social Psychology, 41, 656-670.

Capezza, N., M., & Arriaga, X. (2008). *Why do people blame victims of abuse? The role of stereotypes of women on perceptions of blame.* Sex Roles, 59, 839-850.

Caprariello, P. A., Cuddy, A. J. C., & Fiske, S. T. (2009). *Social structure shapes cultural stereotypes and emotions: A causal test of the stereotype content model.* Groups Processes and Intergroup Relations, 12, 147-155.

Case, K. A. (2007). *Raising male privilege awareness and reducing sexism: An evaluation of diversity courses.* Psychology of Women Quarterly, 31(4), 426–435.

Clausell, E., & Fiske, S. T. (2005). *When do subgroup parts add up to the stereotypic whole? Mixed stereotype content for gay male subgroups explains overall ratings.* Social Cognition, 23(2), 161–181.

Chapleau, K. M., Oswald, D. L., & Russell, B. L. (2007). *How ambivalent sexism toward women and men support rape myth acceptance.* Sex Roles, 57, 131–136.

Cikara, M., Lee, T. L., Fiske, S. T., & Glick, P. (2009). *Ambivalent Sexism at Home and at Work: How Attitudes Toward Women in Relationships Foster Exclusion in the Public Sphere.* In J. T. Jost, A. C. Kay, & H. Thorisdottir (Eds.) Social and Psychological Bases of Ideology and System Justification (pp. 444-462). New York: Oxford University Press.

Cohen, G. L., Garcia, J., Apfel, N., & Master, A. (2006*). Reducing the racial achievement gap: A social-psychological intervention.* Science, 313(5791), 1307.

Crandall, C. S., & Eshleman, A. (2003). *A justification-suppression model of the expression and experience of prejudice.* Psychological Bulletin, 129(3), 414–446.

Crocker, J., & Major, B. (1989*). Social stigma and self-esteem: The self-protective properties of stigma.* Psychological review, 96(4), 608–630.

Crocker, J., Major, B., & Steele, C. (1998). *Social stigma.* In D. T. Gilbert, S. T. Fiske, & L. Gardner (Eds.) The handbook of social psychology (pp. 504-553). New York: McGraw-Hill.

Cuddy, A. J., C., Fiske, S. T., & Glick, P. (2007). *The BIAS map: Behaviors form intergroup affect and stereotypes.* Journal of Personality and Social Psychology, 92, 631-648.

Cuddy, A. J. C., Fiske, S. T., & Glick, P. (2008). *Warmth and competence as universal dimensions of social perception: The stereotype content model and the BIAS map.* Advances in Experimental Social Psychology, 40, 61-149.

Cuddy, A. J. C., Fiske, S. T., Kwan, V. S. Y., Glick, P., Demoulin, S., Leyens, J-P., et al. (2009). *Stereotype content model across cultures: Towards universal similarities and some differences.* British Journal of Social Psychology, 48, 1-33.

Cuddy, A. J., Norton, M. I., & Fiske, S. T. (2005). *This Old Stereotype: The Pervasiveness and Persistence of the Elderly Stereotype.* Journal of Social Issues, 61, 267–285.

Darley, J. M., & Zanna, M. P. (1982). *Making moral judgments.* American Scientist, 70(5), 515–521.

Dar-Nimrod, I., & Heine, S. J. (2006). *Exposure to scientific theories affects women's math performance.* Science, 314, 435.

Davies, G. M., & Patel, D. (2005). *The influence of car and driver stereotypes on attributions of vehicle speed, position on the road and culpability in a road accident scenario.* Legal and Criminological Psychology, 10, 45-62.

Devine, P. G. (1989). *Stereotypes and prejudice: Their automatic and controlled components.* Journal of personality and social psychology, 56(1), 5–18.

Duckitt, J. H. (1992). *Psychology and prejudice: A historical analysis and integrative framework.* American Psychologist, 47, 1182–1193.

Diekman, A. B., & Eagly, A. H. (2000*). Stereotypes as dynamic constructs: Women and men of the past, present, and future.* Personality and Social Psychology Bulletin, 26, 1171-1188.

Doosje, B., & Haslam, S. A. (2005). *What have they done for us lately? The dynamics of reciprocity in intergroup contexts.* Journal of Applied Social Psychology, 35, 508-535.

Doosje, B., Haslam, S. A., Spears, R., Oakes, P. J., & Koomen, W. (1998). *The effect of comparative context on central tendency and variability judgments and the evaluation of group characteristics.* European Journal of Social Psychology, 28, 173-184.

Dweck, C. S. (1975). *The role of expectations and attributions in the alleviation of learned helplessness.* Journal of Personality and Social Psychology, 31(4), 674–685.

Eagly, A. H. (1987 *Sex differences in social behavior: A social-role interpretation.* Hillsdale, NJ: Lawrence Erlbaum Associates.

Eagly, A. H., & Karau, S. J. (2002). *Role congruity theory of prejudice toward female leaders.* Psychological Review, 109, 573–598.

Eagly, A. H., & Mladinic, A. (1989). *Gender stereotypes and attitudes toward women and men.* Personality and Social Psychology Bulletin, 15, 543-558.

Eagly, A. H., & Steffen, V. J. (1984). *Gender stereotypes stem from the distribution of women and men into social roles.* Journal of Personality and Social Psychology, 46, 735–754.

Farenga, S. J., & Joyce, B. A. (1999). *Intentions of young students to enroll in science courses in the future: An examination of gender differences.* Science Education, 83(1), 55–76.

Farwell, L., & Weiner, B. (2000*). Bleeding hearts and the heartless: Popular perceptions of liberal and conservative ideologies.* Personality and Social Psychology Bulletin, 26, 845.

Ferguson, T., Berlin, J., Noles, E., Johnson, J., Reed, W., & Spicer, C. V. (2005). *Variation in the application of the 'promiscuous female' stereotype and the nature of the application domain: Influences on sexual harassment judgments after exposure to the Jerry Springer Show.* Sex Roles, 52, 477-487.

Fincham, F. D., and Jaspers, J. M. (1980). *Attribution of responsibility: From man the scientist to man as lawyer.* Advances in Experimental Social Psychology, 13, 82–139.

Fiske, S. T. (1998). *Stereotyping, prejudice, and discrimination.* In D. T. Gilbert, S. T. Fiske, and L. Gardner (Eds.) The handbook of social psychology (pp. 357-411). New York: McGraw-Hill.

Fiske, S. T., Cuddy, A. J. C., Glick, P., & Xu, J. (2002). *A model of (often mixed) stereotype content: Competence and warmth respectively follow from perceived status and competition.* Journal of Personality and Social Psychology, 82, 878-902.

Garcia-Marques, L., Santos, A. S. C., & Mackie, D. M. (2006). *Stereotypes: Static abstractions or dynamic knowledge structures?* Journal of Personality and Social Psychology, 91, 814-831.

Gilbert, D. T. (1998). *Ordinary personology.* In D. T. Gilbert, S. T. Fiske, & L. Gardner (Eds.) The handbook of social psychology (pp. 89-150). New York: McGraw-Hill.

Gill, M. J., & Andreychik, M. R. (2007). *Explanation and intergroup emotion: Social explanations as a foundation of prejudice-related compunction.* Groups Processes and Intergroup Relations, 10, 87-106.

Glick, P. (2005). *Choice of scapegoats.* In J. F. Dovidio, P. Glick, & L. A. Rudman (Eds) On the nature of prejudice. Fifty years after Allport (244-261). Malden MA: Blackwell Publishing.

Glick, P., & Fiske, S. T. (1996). *The Ambivalent Sexism Inventory: Differentiating hostile and benevolent sexism.* Journal of Personality and Social Psychology, 70, 491–512.

Glick, P., & Fiske, S. T. (2001a). *An ambivalent alliance: Hostile and benevolent sexism as complementary justifications for gender inequality.* American Psychologist, 56, 109-118.

Glick, P., & Fiske, S. T. (2001b). *Ambivalent stereotypes as legitimizing ideologies: Differentiating paternalistic and envious prejudice.* In J. T. Jost & B. Major (Eds.) The psychology of legitimacy: Emerging perspectives on ideology, justice, and intergroup relations (pp. 278–306). New York: Cambridge University Press.

Glick, P., Fiske, S. T., Mladinic, A., Saiz, J. L., Abrams, D., Masser, B. et al. (2000). *Beyond prejudice as simple antipathy: Hostile and benevolent sexism across cultures.* Journal of Personality and Social Psychology, 79, 763-775.

Glick, Lameiras, Fiske, Eckes, Masser, Volpato et al. (2004). *Bad but bold: Ambivalent attitudes toward men predict gender inequality in 16 nations.* Journal of Personality and Social Psychology, 86, 713-728.

Glick, P., Sakalli-Ugurlu, N., Ferreira, M. C., & Aguiar de Souza, M. (2002*). Ambivalent sexism and attitudes toward wife abuse in Turkey and Brazil.* Psychology of Women Quarterly, 26(4), 292–297.

Graham, S. (1991). *A review of attribution theory in achievement contexts.* Educational Psychology Review, 3, 5-39.

Haider-Markel, D. P., & Joslyn, M. R. (2008). *Beliefs about the origins of homosexuality and support for gay rights: An empirical test of attribution theory.* Public Opinion Quarterly, 72, 291-310.

Haines, E.L., & Jost, J.T. (2000). *Placating the powerless: Effects of legitimate and illegitimate explanation on affect, memory, and stereotyping.* Social Justice Research, 13, 219-236.

Hamilton, D. L. (1979). *A cognitive-attributional analysis of stereotyping.* Advances in Experimental Social Psychology, 12, 53-84.

Harris, L. T., & Fiske, S. T. (2005). *Dehumanizing the lowest of the low: Neuroimaging responses to extreme out-groups.* Psychological Science, 17, 847-853.

Haslam, S. A., Turner, J. C., Oakes, P. J., McGarty, C., & Hayes, B. K. (1992). *Context-dependent variation in social stereotyping 1: The effects of intergroup relations as mediated by social change and frame of reference.* European Journal of Social Psychology, 22, 3-20.

Haslam, S. A., Turner, J. C., Oakes, P., Reynolds, K., & Doosje, B. (2002). *From personal pictures in the head to collective tools in the world: How shared stereotypes allow groups to represent and change social reality.* In C. McGarty, V. Y. Yzerbyt, & R. Spears (Eds.), Stereotypes as explanation: The formation of meaningful beliefs about social groups. Cambridge: Cambridge University Press.

Heider, F. (1958). *The psychology of interpersonal relations.* Hoboken, NJ: John Wiley & Sons.

Heilman, M. E. (1996). *Affirmative action's contradictory consequences.* Journal of Social Issues, 52, 105-109.

Henry, P. J., & Reyna, C. (2007). *Value judgments: The impact of perceived value violations on American political attitudes.* Political Psychology, 28, 273-298.

Henry, P. J., Reyna, C., & Weiner, B. (2004). *Hate welfare but help the poor: How the attributional content of stereotypes explains the paradox of reactions to the destitute in America.* Journal of Applied Social Psychology, 34, 34-58.

Henry, P. J., & Sears, D. O. (2002). *The Symbolic Racism 2000 Scale.* Political Psychology, 23, 253–283.

Herek, G. M. (2000). *The psychology of sexual prejudice.* Current Directions in Psychological Science, 9(1), 19-22.

Herek, G. M. (2002). *Gender gaps in public opinion about lesbians and gay men.* Public Opinion Quarterly, 66(1), 40-66.

Hewstone, M. (1990). *The" ultimate attribution error"? A review of the literature on intergroup causal attribution.* European Journal of Social Psychology, 20, 311–335.

Hill, C., Corbett, C. & St. Rose, A. (2010). *Why so few? Women in science, technology, engineering, and mathematics.* Washington DC: American Association of University Women.

Ho, E. A., Sanbonmatsu, D. M., & Akimoto, S. A. (2002). *The effects of comparative status on social stereotypes: How the perceived success of some persons affects the stereotypes of others.* Social Cognition, 20, 36-57.

Hoeken, H., & Hustinx, L. (2007). *The impact of exemplars on responsibility stereotypes in fundraising letters.* Communication Research, 34, 596-617.

Hoffman, C., & Hurst, N. (1990). *Gender stereotypes: Perception or rationalization?* Journal of Personality and Social Psychology, 58, 197-208.

Hyde, J. S., & Mertz, J. E. (2009). *Gender, culture, and mathematics performance.* In Proceedings of the National Academy of Science, 106, 8801-8807.

Jackson, L. A. Sullivan, L. A., & Hodge, C.N. (1993). *Stereotype effects on attributions, predictions, and evaluations: No two social judgments are quite alike.* Journal of Personality and Social Psychology, 65, 69-84.

Jost, J. T., & Banaji, M. R. (1994). *The role of stereotyping in system-justification and the production of false consciousness.* British Journal of Social Psychology, 33, 1-27.

Jost, J.T., & Burgess, D. (2000). *Attitudinal ambivalence and the conflict between group and system justification motives in low status groups.* Personality and Social Psychology Bulletin, 26, 293-305.

Jost, J. T., Banaji, M. R., & Nosek, B. A. (2004). *A Decade of System Justification Theory: Accumulated Evidence of Conscious and Unconscious Bolstering of the Status Quo.* Political Psychology, 25, 881–919.

Jost, J. T., & Hunyady, O. (2005). *Antecedents and Consequences of System-Justifying* Ideologies. Current Directions in Psychological Science, 14, 260–265.

Jost, J. T. & Hunyady, O. (2002). *The psychology of system justification and the palliative function of ideology.* European Review of Social Psychology, 13, 111-153.

Jost, J. T., & Kay, A. C. (2005). *Exposure to benevolent sexism and complementary gender stereotypes: Consequences for specific and diffuse forms of system justification.* Journal of Personality and Social Psychology, 88, 498-509.

Jost, J. T., Kivetz, Y., Rubini, M., Guermandi, G., & Mosso, C. (2005). *System-justifying functiosn of complementary region and ethnic stereotypes: Cross-national evidence.* Social Justice Research, 18, 305-333.

Jost, J.T., Pelham, B.W., &Carvallo, M. (2002). *Non-conscious forms of system justification: Cognitive, affective, and behavioral preferences for higher status groups.* Journal of Experimental Social Psychology, 38, 586-602.

Kaiser, C. R., & Miller, C. T. (2001). *Reacting to impending discrimination: Compensation for prejudice and attributions to discrimination.* Personality Social Psychology Bulletin, 27, 1357-1367.

Katz, D., & Braly, K. W. (1935). *Racial prejudice and racial stereotypes.* Journal of Abnormal and Social Psychology, 30, 175-193.

Kay, A.C., Czáplinski, S., & Jost, J.T. (2009). *Left-right ideological differences in system justification following exposure to complementary versus noncomplementary stereotype exemplars.*European Journal of Social Psychology, 39, 290-298.

Kay, A. C., Gaucher, D., Peach, J. M., Laurin, K., Friesen, J., Zanna, M. P., & Spencer, S. J. (2009). *Inequality, discrimination, and the power of the status quo: Direct evidence for a motivation to see the way things are as the way they should be.* Journal of personality and social psychology, 97, 421–434.

Kay, A. C. & Jost, J. T. (2003). *Complementary justice: Effects of "poor but happy" and "poor but honest" stereotype exemplars on system justification and implicit activation of the justice motive.* Journal of Personality and Social Psychology, 85, 823-837.

Kay, A. C., Jost, J.T., Mandisodza, A.N., Sherman, S.J., Petrocelli, J.V., & Johnson, A.L. (2007). *Panglossian ideology in the service of system justification: How complementary stereotypes help us to rationalize inequality.*Advances in Experimental Social Psychology, 39, 305-358.

Kay, A. C., Jost, J. T., & Young, S. (2005). *Victim derogation and victim enhancement as alternate routes to system justification.* Psychological Science, 16, 240-246.

Kelley, H. H. (1973). *The processes of causal attribution.* American psychologist, 28, 107–128.

Kiefer, A., & Shih, M. (2006). *Gender Differences in Persistence and Attributions in Stereotype Relevant Contexts.* Sex Roles, 54, 859-868.

Kitano, H. H., & Sue, S. (1973). *The model minorities.* Journal of Social Issues, 29, 1–9.

Koch, S., Muller, S., & Sieverding, M. (2008). *Women and computers. Effects of stereotype threat on attribution of failure.* Computers and Education, 51, 1795-1803.

Kunda, Z., & Spencer, S. J. (2003). *When do stereotypes come to mind and when do they color judgment? A goal-based theoretical framework for stereotype activation and application.* Psychological Bulletin, 129, 522–544.

Kunda, Z., & Thagard, P. (1996). *Forming impressions from stereotypes, traits, and behaviors: A parallel-constraint-satisfaction theory.* Psychological Review, 103, 284–308.

Lee, Y-T, Jussim, L., & McCauley, C. R. (Eds.) (1995). *Stereotype accuracy: Toward appreciating group differences.* Washington DC: American Psychological Association.

Levy, B. (2009). *Stereotype embodiment: A psychosocial approach to aging.* Current Direction in Psychological Science, 18, 332-336.

Lin, M. H., Kwan, V. S., Cheung, A., & Fiske, S. T. (2005). *Stereotype content model explains prejudice for an envied outgroup: Scale of anti-Asian American stereotypes.* Personality and Social Psychology Bulletin, 31, 34.

Lippman, W. (1922). *Public opinion.* New York: Harcourt, Brace and Company.

Mallett, R. K., Wilson, T. D., & Gilbert, D. T. (2008). *Expect the unexpected: Failure to anticipate similarities leads to an intergroup forecasting error.* Journal of personality and social psychology, 94, 265–277.

Mauer, K. L., Park, B., & Rothbart, M. (1995). *Subtyping versus subgrouping processes in stereotype representation.* Journal of Personality and Social Psychology, 69, 812-824.

McGarty, C., Yzerbyt, V. Y., & Spears, R. (Eds.) (2002). *Stereotypes as explanations.* Cambridge: Cambridge University Press.

Moya, M., Glick, P., Exposito, F., de Lemus, S., & Hart, J. (2007). *It's for Your Own Good: Benevolent Sexism and Women's Reactions to Protectively Justified Restrictions.* Personality and Social Psychology Bulletin, 33, 1421-1434.

Mullen, B., Brown, R., & Smith, C. (1992). *Ingroup bias as a function of salience, relevance, and status: An integration.* European Journal of Social Psychology, 22, 103-122.

Nosek, B. A., Banaji, M. R., & Greenwald, A. G. (2002b). *Math = male, me = female, therefore math ≠ me.* Journal of Personality and Social Psychology, 83, 44–59.

O'Brien, L. T., Kinias, Z., & Major, B. (2008). *How status and stereotypes impact attributions to discrimination: The stereotype-asymmetry hypothesis.* Journal of Experimental Social Psychology, 44, 405-412.

Overbekc, J. R., Jost, J. T., Mosso, C. O., & Flizik, A. (2004). *Resistant versus acquiescent responses to ingroup inferiority as a function of social dominance orientation in the USA and Italy.* Group Processes and Intergroup Relations, 7, 35-54.

Park, B., Ryan, C. S., & Judd, C. M. (1992). *Role of meaningful subgroups in explaining differences in perceived variability for in-groups and outgroups.* Journal of Personality and Social Psychology, 63, 553-567.

Parrott, G. W., & Smith, R. H. (1993). *Distinguishing the experiences of envy and jealousy.* Journal of Personality and Social Psychology, 64, 906-920.

Pettigrew, T. F. (1979). *The ultimate attribution error: Extending Allport's cognitive analysis of prejudice.* Personality and Social Psychology Bulletin, 5, 461-476.

Puhl, R. M., Moss-Racusin, C. A., & Schwartz, M. B. (2007). *Internalization of Weight Bias: Implications for Binge Eating and Emotional Well-being&ast.* Obesity, 15, 19–23.

Resendez, M. G. (2002). *The stigmatizing effects of affirmative action: An examination of moderating variables.* Journal of Applied Social Psychology, 32, 185-206.

Reyna, C. (2000). *Lazy, dumb, or industrious: When stereotypes convey attribution information in the classroom.* Educational Psychology Review, 12, 85-110.

Reyna, C. (2008*). Ian is intelligent but Leshaun is lazy: How status, cultural beliefs, and the preference for internal judgments may perpetuate attributional stereotypes in the classroom.* European Journal of Psychology of Education, 23, 439-458.

Reyna, C., Brandt, M., & Viki, G. T. (2009*). Blame it on hip-hop: Anti-rap attitudes as a proxy for prejudice.* Group Processes and Intergroup Relations, 12, 360-380.

Reyna, C., Brandt, M., Viki, G. T., & Hughs, E. (2010). *Falling from grace: Value violations can lead to the dehumanization of the ingroup.* Manuscript submitted for publication.

Reyna, C., Henry, P. J., Korfmacher, W., & Tucker, A. (2006). *Examining the principles in principled conservatism: The role of responsibility stereotypes as cues for deservingness in racial policy decisions.* Journal of Personality and Social Psychology, 90, 109-128.

Reyna, C., & Weiner, B. (2001*). Justice and utility in the classroom: An attributional analysis of the goals of teachers' punishment and intervention strategies.* Journal of Educational Psychology, 93, 309-319.

Reynolds, K. J., Oakes, P. J., Haslam, S. A., Nolan, M., & Dolnik, L. (2000*). Responses to powerlessness: Stereotypes as an instrument of social conflict.* Group Dynamics: Theory, Research and Practice, 4, 275-290.

Richards, Z., & Hewstone, M. (2001). *Subtyping and subgrouping: Processes for the prevention and promotion of stereotype change.* Personality and Social Psychology Review, 5, 52-73.

Rosenberg, S., Nelson, C., & Vivekananthan, P. S. (1968). *A multidimensional approach to the structure of personality impressions.* Journal of Personality and Social Psychology, 9, 283-294.

Rudolph, U., Roesch, S. C., Greitemeyer, T., & Weiner, B. (2004). *A meta-analytic review of help giving and aggression from an attributional perspective: Contribution to a general theory of motivation.* Cognition and Emotion, 18, 815-848.

Sakallı-Uğurlu, N., Yalçın, Z. S., & Glick, P. (2007). *Ambivalent sexism, belief in a just world, and empathy as predictors of Turkish students' attitudes toward rape victims.* Sex Roles, 57, 889–895.

Schmader, T., Johns, M., & Forbes, C. (2008). *An integrated process model of stereotype threat effects on performance.* Psychological Review, 115, 336–356.

Shapiro, J. R., & Neuberg, S. L. (2007). *From stereotype threat to stereotype threats: Implications of a multi-threat framework for causes, moderators, mediators, consequences, and interventions.* Personality and Social Psychology Review, 11, 107-130.

Shelton, J. N., & Richeson, J. A. (2006). *Interracial interactions: A relational approach.* Advances in experimental social psychology, 38, 121-181.

Sherif, M., Harvey, O. J., Jack White, B., Hood, W. R., & Sherif, C. W. (1961*). Intergroup conflict and cooperation: the Robbers Cave experiment.* Classics in the history of psychology. Retrieved August 28, 2007, from http://psychclassics.yorku.ca/Sherif/

Sherman, J. W., Stroessner, S. J., Conrey, F. R., & Azam, O. A. (2005). *Prejudice and Stereotype Maintenance Processes: Attention, Attribution, and Individuation.* Journal of Personality and Social Psychology, 89, 607-622.

Sidanius, J., & Pratto, F. (1999). *Social dominance: An intergroup theory of social hierarchy and oppression.* New York: Cambridge University Press.

Skitka, L. J., Mullen, E., Griffin, T., Hutchinson, S., & Chamberlin, B. (2002*). Dispositions, scripts, or motivated correction?: Understanding ideological differences in explanations for social problems.* Journal of Personality and Social Psychology, 83, 470-487.

Skitka, L. J., & Tetlock, P. E. (1993). *Providing public assistance: Cognitive and motivational processes underlying liberal and conservative policy preferences.* Journal of Personality and Social Psychology, 65, 1205–1223.

Starzyk, K. B., & Ross, M. (2008). *A tarnished silver lining: Victim suffering and support for reparations.* Personality and Social Psychology Bulletin, 34, 366-380.

Steele, C. M. (1997). *A threat in the air: How stereotypes shape intellectual identity and performance.* American Psychologist, 52, 613-629.

Steele, C. M., & Aronson, J. (1995). *Stereotype threat and the intellectual test performance of African Americans.* Journal of Personality and Social Psychology, 69, 797-811.

Stewart, T. L., Latu, I. M., Kawakami, K., & Myers, A. C. (2010). *Consider the situation: Reducing automatic stereotyping through Situational Attribution Training.* Journal of Experimental Social Psychology, 46, 221–225.

Stott, C., & Drury, J. (2004). *The importance of social structure and social interaction in stereotype consensus and content: Is the whole greater than the sum of its parts?* European Journal of Social Psychology, 34, 11-23.

Stott, C., Hutchison, P., & Drury, J. (2001). *'Hooligans' abroad? Inter-group dynamics, social identity and participation in collective 'disorder' at the 1998 World Cup finals.* British Journal of Social Psychology, 40, 359-384.

Sue, S., & Kitano, H. H. (1973). *Stereotypes as a measure of success.* Journal of Social Issues, 29, 83–98.

Swim, J. K., & Sanna, L. J. (1996). *He's skilled, she's lucky: A meta-analysis of observers' attributions for women's and men's successes and failures.* Personality and Social Psychology Bulletin, 22, 507.

Tajfel, H. (1981). *Social stereotypes and social groups.* In J. C. Turner & H. Giles (Eds.) Intergroup behavior (pp. 144-167). Chicago: The University of Chicago Press.

Tajfel, H. (1982). *Social psychology of intergroup relations.* Annual review of psychology, 33, 1–39.

Thoman, D. B., White, P. H., Yamawaki, N., & Koishi, H. (2008). *Variations of gender-math stereotype content affect women's vulnerability to stereotype threat.* Sex Roles, 58, 702-712.

Todorov, A., Mandisodza, A. N., Goren, A., & Hall, C. C. (2005). *Inferences of competence from faces predict election outcomes.* Science, 308, 1623-1626.

Vescio, T. K., Sechrist, G. B., & Paolucci, M. P. (2003). *Perspective taking and prejudice reduction: the mediational role of empathy arousal and situational attributions.* European Journal of Social Psychology, 33, 455-472.

Walton, G. M., & Spencer, S. J. (2009). *Latent ability: Grades and test scores systematically underestimate the intellectual ability of negatively stereotyped students.* Psychological Science, 20, 1132-1139.

Weiner, B (1980). *A cognitive (attribution)-emotion-action model of motivated behavior: An analysis of judgments of help-giving.* Journal of Personality and Social Psychology, 39, 186-200.

Weiner, B. (1985). *An attributional theory of achievement motivation and emotion.* Psychological Review, 92, 548-573.

Weiner, B. (1993). *A sin versus sickness: A theory of perceived responsibility and social motivation.* American Psychologist, 48, 957-965.

Weiner, B. (2006). *Social motivation, justice, and the moral emotions.* Mahwah, NJ: Lawrence Erlbaum Associates.

Weiner, B., Graham, S., & Reyna, C. (1997). *An attributional examination of retributive versus utilitarian philosophies of punishment.* Social Justice Research, 10, 431-452.

Weiner, B., & Kukla, A. (1970). *An attributional analysis of achievement motivation.* Journal of Personality and Social Psychology, 15, 1-20.

Weiner, B., Perry, R. P., Magnusson, J. (1988). *An attributional analysis of reactions to stigma.* Journal of Personality and Social Psychology, 55, 738-748.

Wetherell, G. & Reyna, C. (2010). *Political Orientation and Healthcare Support: Stereotypes and Attributions Explain Differences.* Talk given at Midwestern Psychological Association Conference, Chicago, Illinois.

Wheeler, S. C., & Petty, R. E. (2001). *The effects of stereotype activation on behavior: A review of possible mechanisms.* Psychological Bulletin, 127, 797-826.

Williams, L. E., & Bargh, J. A. (2008*). Experiencing physical warmth promotes interpersonal warmth.* Science, 322, 606-607.

Williams, M. J., & Eberhardt, J. L. (2008*). Biological conceptions of race and the motivation to cross racial boundaries.* Journal of Personality and Social Psychology, 94, 1033-1047.

Wittenbrink, B., Gist, P. L., & Hilton, J. L. (1997). *Structural properties of stereotypic knowledge and their influences on the construal of social situations.* Journal of Personality and Social Psychology, 72, 526–543.

Wong, P. T., & Weiner, B. (1981). *When people ask" why" questions, and the heuristics of attributional search.* Journal of Personality and Social Psychology, 40, 650–663.

Wood, P. B., & Bartkowski, J. P. (2004). *Attribution Style and Public Policy Attitudes Toward Gay Rights.* Social Science Quarterly, 85, 58-74.

Yzerbyt, V. Y., Rocher, S., & Schadron, G. (1997). *Stereotypes as explanations: A subjective essentialistic view of group perception.* In Spears, R., Oakes, P. J., Ellemers, N., & Haslam, S. A. (Eds.), The social psychology of stereotyping and group life (pp. 20-50). Oxford: Blackwell.

Yzerbyt, V. Y., & Rogier, A. (2001). *Blame it on the group: Entitativity, subjective essentialism and social attribution.* In J. Jost and B. Major (Eds.), The psychology of legitimacy: Emerging perspectives on ideology, justice, and intergroup relations. New York: Cambridge University Press.

In: Psychology of Stereotypes
Editor: Eleanor L. Simon

ISBN: 978-1-61761-463-7
©2011 Nova Science Publishers, Inc.

Chapter 3

PUBLIC ATTITUDES TOWARD CLUTTERING AND STUTTERING IN FOUR COUNTRIES**

Kenneth O. St. Louis[1], Yulia Filatova[2], Mehmet Coşkun[3],
Seyhun Topbaş[4], Sertan Özdemir[4], Dobrinka Georgieva[5],
Elise McCaffrey[6] and Reshella D. George[7]*
West Virginia University, Morgantown, West Virginia, USA[1]
Moscow State Pedagogical University, Moscow, Russia[2]
Private Practice, Marmaris, Turkey[3]
Anadolu University, Eskisehir, Turkey[4]
SouthWest University, Blagoevgrad, Bulgaria[5]
Portland State University, Portland, Oregon, USA[6]
James Madison University, Harrisonburg, Virginia, USA[7]

ABSTRACT

Purpose. Using an adaptation of the *Experimental Edition of the Public Opinion Survey of Human Attributes* (*POSHA-E*), investigators sought to compare public attitudes toward cluttering with those toward stuttering in four country samples, each in a different language. The *POSHA-E* was developed to measure public attitudes of stuttering but was modified to provide written definitions of cluttering and stuttering. *Method.* Convenience samples of 60 to 90 adult respondents from Turkey, Bulgaria, Russia, and the USA (302 total) rated *POSHA-E* items on 1-9 scales for cluttering and stuttering after reading the definitions. *Results.* Public attitudes toward cluttering and stuttering were similar for all respondents combined, but significant differences occurred. Attitude differences from country-to-country were greater than differences for cluttering versus stuttering. *Conclusions.* Positive and negative attitudes toward cluttering appear to be similar to those toward stuttering, and a cluttering stereotype appears likely.

---

*Address correspondence to: Kenneth O. St. Louis, Ph.D., Department of Speech Pathology and Audiology, 805 Allen Hall, PO Box 6122, West Virginia University, Morgantown, WV 26506-6122, Phone: 304-293-2946, FAX: 304-293-2905, Email: kstlouis@wvu.edu

KeyWords: Cluttering, Stuttering, Attitudes, Stereotype, Turkey, Bulgaria, Russia, USA, International, Translation

INTRODUCTION

Speech-language pathologists and their medically-oriented predecessors (e.g., phoniatrists) have described behaviors, reactions, personalities, and temperaments of people who clutter for more than a century. Historical and anecdotal reports suggest that people who clutter are untidy, careless, hurried, compulsive, and so on (Lewis,1907; Luchsinger & Arnold, 1965; Weiss, 1964). In spite of the volume of these published reports, studies of public attitudes toward clutterers are rare. Halevy, Egoz, & Ezrati-Vinacour (2010) compared two groups of female students: one group that heard a male speaker read fluently and another that heard the same speaker reading while cluttering. Participants were asked, for example, if they would want to date the person they heard reading. Those who heard the fluent speaker were more likely to say "yes" than those who heard the clutterer. In a study of public opinions about the differential sensitivity of person-first versus direct terminology, St. Louis (1999) reported more positive ratings for "clutterer" and "person who clutters" than "stutterer" and "person who stutters." There were, however, no significant differences between the person-first versus direct label in either pair. In that study, a definition of cluttering was not provided, and it was noted that several respondent-written comments interpreted "cluttering" as being messy or untidy rather than as a communication disorder.

In sharp contrast to the lack of information about public attitudes toward cluttering, numerous studies have documented that the public holds predictable and often negative attitudes toward people who stutter (e.g., Blood, 1999; Cooper & Cooper, 1996; Craig, Tran, & Craig, 2003; Doody, Kalinowsky, Armson, & Stuart, 1993; Hughes, Gabel, & Irani, 2010; Klassen, 2002; St. Louis, Andrade, Georgieva, & Troudt, 2005). These and many other studies have demonstrated that a "stuttering stereotype" exists which, among other characteristics, assumes that stutterers are shy, nervous, introverted, and are likely to manifest psychological problems.

MacKinnon, Hall, and MacIntyre (2007) sought to explore the reasons for the formation of such a robust stereotype. Using a process known as "anchoring-adjustment,"Tversky & Kahneman (1974) hypothesized that nonstutterers would rate a ficticious male with temporary stuttering more negatively than a male chronic stutterer. That, in fact, is what they found, especially for the very attributes that characterize the stuttering stereotype, i.e., the temporary stutterer was judged to be more afraid, fearful, nervous, tense, anxious, introverted, and unpleasant than the chronic stutterer. The anchoring-adjustment process is a quick but incomplete way that people make decisions. In this case, respondents presumably thought first of their own instances of temporary disfluency that probably occurred during periods of stress (White & Collins, 1984). Remembering their own discomfort, they assumed high emotions for the temporary stutterer. But,realizing that the chronic stutterer would be different, they *incorrectly* assumed that he had adapted to the emotions and, hence, rated him lower.

The current study is one of a series of pilot studies designed to develop a measure of public opinion or attitudes toward stuttering internationally (St. Louis, 2005; St. Louis et al., 2005). To date, the results of these pilot studies have confirmed the stuttering stereotype in a wide variety of sample populations around the world. The prototype questionnaire used in these studies is known as the *Public Opinion Survey of Human Attributes* (*POSHA*), and adaptations of three experimental versions (*POSHA-E*) have been used. Early *POSHA-E*s have been shown to be unaffected by the order of presentation of items, robust with regard to different rating procedures and scales, demonstrating satisfactory test-retest reliability, and showing satisfactory construct validity (St. Louis, Lubker, Yaruss, Adkins, & Pill, 2008; St. Louis, Lubker, Yaruss, & Aliveto, 2009; St. Louis, Reichel, Yaruss, & Lubker, 2009).

Given the absence of empirical information on public attitudes toward cluttering, the current study asked the following research questions: (a) What are attitudes (perceptions, beliefs, knowledge and reactions) of the general public toward cluttering? (b) To what extent do public attitudes toward cluttering differ from those toward stuttering and other human attributes? (c) To what extent dofour different cultures and languages affect attitudes toward cluttering?

METHOD

Questionnaire and Ratings

Experimental versions of the *POSHA-E* contained the following components: instructions, a general component comparing stuttering to eight other "anchor" attributes, hypothesized to evoke ratings ranging from positive to neutral to negative in approximately the following rank order: intelligent, multilingual, good talker, left handed, old, overweight, wheelchair use, and mental illness (St. Louis et al., 2008). For stuttering and all of the other attributes, prompts asked respondents to rate their "overall impression," degree to which they would "want to have," "amount known," and categories of "people known" (including themselves). Next, a detailed component asked respondents to rate their reactions to—and opinions about—stuttering, and, in some studies, one or two other attributes (St. Louis, 2005). The final component asked for demographic information such as residence, birthplace, occupation, marital status, educational level, languages known, and physical or mental health.The *POSHA-E*was adapted for the current study by including cluttering in the general section and adding a detailed section on cluttering to an existing detailed section for stuttering. The questionnaire began with written lay definitions of cluttering and stuttering, since earlier research had confirmed that many people view cluttering as an organizational problem (i.e., "messy")—not a fluency disorder (St. Louis, 1999). The ensuing lay definition for cluttering was adapted from an earlier version used in surveys of speech-language pathologists and teachers (Georgieva, 1998; Georgieva, 2001; St. Louis & Hinzman, 1986; St. Louis & Rustin, 1992). A parallel lay definition for stuttering was developed for this study.

> "Cluttering is a speech problem in which a person's speech is either too fast, too jerky, or both. Most people who clutter seem to run their words or sentences together, and they often have many more fillers, hesitations, revisions, or other breaks in their speech than normal speakers do. Their speech sounds 'cluttered' as though they do not have a clear idea of what they want to say, and they are often not aware that they have a speech problem."

"Stuttering is a speech problem in which a speaker typically repeats or prolongs (draws out) parts of words, or gets stuck or blocked on words. Sometimes stuttering consists of strategies that try to reduce or avoid repeating, prolonging, or blocking. Stuttering is often associated with psychological stress or unpleasant feelings. Finally, the person who stutters often experiences a loss of voluntary control in saying certain words."

The cluttering and stuttering versions of all questionnaire items were parallel, changing only the word "stutter/stuttering/stutterer" to "clutter/cluttering/clutterer." Half of the respondents rated cluttering items first, and half rated stuttering items first. The biographical section was essentially unchanged from other research using the *POSHA-E* (St. Louis, 2005). The general item asking "people known" asked respondents to indicate choices (including themselves) for "cluttering" or "stuttering." Respondents could check both to indicate "cluttering-stuttering." The revised questionnaire also asked if respondents were speech-language clinicians or students and whether they had any experience in speech therapy or self-help for cluttering or stuttering.

For most *POSHA-E* items, respondents circled numbers from 1-9, or "?" (for no opinion or unsure). For all items, t tests for independent samples were run to test for significance of differences. Bonferroni corrections for statistically significant differences were applied to correct alpha levels for multiple pair-wise comparisons (Maxwell & Satake, 1997). The average number of items in a subset of items with the same or similar prompt was approximately 12, so the normal alpha level of $p < .05$ was divided by 12 ($p < .0042$ [.05/12]). The alpha level of $p < .01$ was similarly adjusted to $p < .00083$ (.01/12). After tabulating the ratings, from which statistical analyses were carried out, a formula converted mean 1-9 scores to a -100 to +100 scale, where -100 = 1 (the lowest rating), 0 = 5 (the neutral rating), and +100 = 9 (the highest rating) for tabular and graphic comparisons.

The original English version of the questionnaire, distributed in West Virginia and several other mid-Atlantic states in the USA to 60 respondents (St. Louis & McCaffrey, 2005), was translated to Turkish, Russian, and Bulgarian by authors and their assistants. It was then copied and distributed to conveniencesamples in and around Mugla, Turkey, Moscow, Russia, and the cities of Blagoevgrad and Sofia, Bulgaria. It should be noted that the research was carried out with additional questions designed to measure public awareness of both cluttering and stuttering (St. Louis, Filatova,Coşkun, Topbaş, Özdemir, Georgieva, McCaffrey, & George, in press), the data of which are not included in this report.

RESULTS

Respondents

There were 302 respondents total, 60 from the USA, 90 from Turkey, 85 from Russia, and 67 from Bulgaria. Table 1 provides a summary of selected demographic data for the four samples. Systematic demographic data, except for age and sex, was unavailable for the Bulgarian sample, since the demographic section was overlooked during the translation phase and hence, not included. Various demographic variables were estimated from either limited data provided by respondents or from distributors in Bulgaria. The mean ages ranged from 26 to 33 years. For the three samples wherein information was available, 12 to15 years of schooling had been completed; 18 to 56% were married, and 15% to 48% were current students. None of the respondents answered "yes" to the question, "Are you a speech-language pathologist?" Additional demographic data and interpretation thereof is provided in the companion study (St. Louiset al., in press)

Table 1. Demographic data from respondents in four adult samples in four countries.

	USA	Turkey	Russia	Bulgaria
Number of respondents	60	90	85	67
Sex (%M / %F)	17% / 83%	48% / 52%	15% / 85%	21% / 79%*
Mean age (Years)	26.4	31.2	30.8	33.4 yr*
Education (Total years)	13.5	12.4	15.4	Unavailable
Marital status (%)				
Single	77%	37%	73%	Unavailable
Married	18%	56%	27%	Unavailable
Native language (%)	100% English	100% Turkish	98% Russian	100% Bulgarian*
Race	98% Caucasian	60% Turk; 40% No Response**	89% Slavic	Unavailable
Religion	91% Christian	>90% Islam***	86% Christian or Orthodox	>75% Orthodox*
Occupation (%)				
Professional	30%	32%	23%	Unavailable
Service	38%	16%	11%	Unavailable
Clerical	2%	0%	1%	Unavailable
Labor	2%	10%	0%	Unavailable
Student	20%	15%	48%	Unavailable
Other	0%	26%	16%	Unavailable
Self-identification of a fluency disorder				
Clutterer (%)	1.7%	8.9%	1.2%	0%*
Stutterer (%)	3.5%	5.6%	0%	3.0%*
Clutterer-stutterer (%)	1.7%	2.2%	0%	0%*
Total	6.9%	16.7%	1.2%	3.0%
Past speech therapy (%)	3.3%	1.1%	1.2%	3.0%
Past self help (%)	0%	1.1%	1.2%	0%

*Estimates for Bulgaria from limited data available or from sixth author.

**Ethnicity was not included on the questionnaire due to the sensitivity of the topic in Turkey.

***Religion was not included on the questionnaire, but Turkey is approximately 98% Muslim (Miller, 2010).

Differences in Summary Data

The Appendix provides a list of all means and results of statistical tests. Means for each item are shown for the four countries: USA, Turkey, Russia, and Bulgaria. The labels and ensuing discussion imply that the differences are due primarily to differences in geography and culture, which is influenced by education, religion, social norms, and so on. Yet, it is important to point out that each sample responded to questionnaires in different languages, i.e., English, Turkish, Russian, and Bulgarian. It is possible, therefore, that observed differences could be influenced not only by geography and culture; they could also be influenced by translations from English to the other three languages. For the sake of simplicity in presentation, the different languages will not be used in the descriptions of results, although the different languages and accuracy of translations are recognized as important factors differentiating each group.

Comparison of Cluttering and Stuttering to Anchor Attributes

Figures 1, 2, and 3 compare the four samples on ratings associated with the general component. This component compares stuttering and cluttering with a variety of other human attributes. The graphic profiles for overall impression (Figure 1) among the four groups are much more similar than different. Nevertheless, small but significant differences did occur. The statistical comparisons, summarized in the Appendix, indicate that Bulgarian respondents rated cluttering significantly more positively than the American, Turkish, and Russian samples. The same was true for stuttering except that the Bulgarians were not significantly different from the Russians. None of the comparisons between cluttering and stuttering for any of the four groups, or all groups combined, were significantly different between cluttering and stuttering. Otherwise, the Bulgarian sample had significantly higher scores for intelligence than the other three samples. The USA sample was significantly lower than the Russian and Bulgarian samples for ratings of multilingualism. The Russian sample was significantly lower than the other three for overall impressions of mental illness.

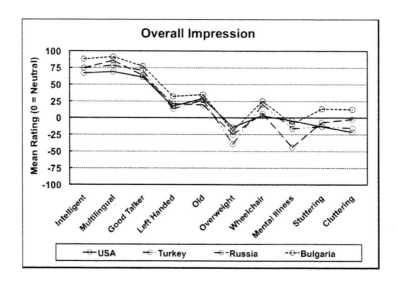

Figure 1. Mean ratings of respondents from four countries for overall impression of ten human attributes.

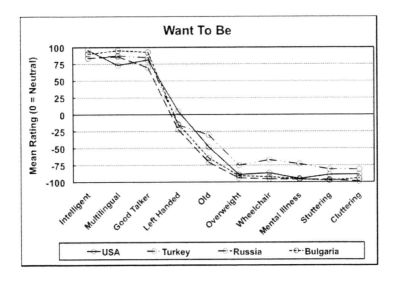

Figure 2. Mean ratings of respondents from four countries for wanting to be or have ten human attributes.

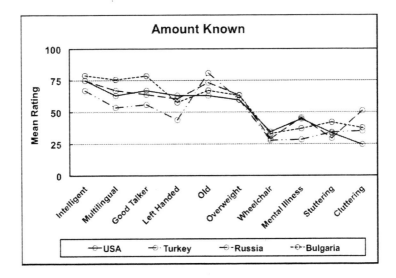

Figure 3. Mean ratings of respondents from four countries for amount known about ten human attributes.

"Wanting to be" or "wanting to have" the various disorder ratings are seen in Figure 2. The most salient fact is that all groups rejected wanting either cluttering or stuttering as much or nearly as much as they rejected being overweight, needing to use a wheelchair, or being mentally ill. Cluttering was no different from stuttering for any of the groups. Russians and Bulgarians were least likely to want to have either fluency disorder, followed by Americans, and then Turks (significantly more positive than the Russians and Bulgarians for cluttering and the Russians for stuttering). Americans, too, were less negative than the Russians for stuttering. Beyond these comparisons, a number of other pairs were significantly different.

For example, similar to the fluency disorders, the Turkish means were the least negative for old, overweight, wheelchair use, and mental illness; these were significantly higher than the Russian means, which were least positive. The Americans had the highest ratings (almost exactly neutral) for left handedness, but they were least positive about wanting to be multilingual, significantly lower than the Bulgarians who most wanted to be multilingual. This finding is not surprising given the fact that only 2.3% of West Virginians know another language besides English (US Census Bureau, 2006).

The combined sample was not significantly different on cluttering versus stuttering ratings on "amount known" even though, compared to stuttering, the Russian sample rated cluttering higher and the American sample rated it lower (Figure 3). This yielded significant differences between these two samples. Differences between Russia and either Turkey or Bulgaria were also significant for cluttering. The remainder of comparisons for "amount known" was significant mainly for the highest versus lowest mean ratings. For example, the Turks (lowest) and Bulgarians (highest) differed on multilingualism and good talking. Also, the Turkish sample (lowest) was different from the American sample (highest) for left handedness. These two comparisons reversed for old age, where the Turks reported knowing the most, and the Americans knowing the least. The country comparisons for mental illness, though lower overall, were similar to the comparisons for left handedness.

Comparisons of Attitudes on Cluttering Versus Stuttering

Beginning in the second section of the Appendix, means for cluttering and stuttering for each of the four country samples and all subjects combined are listed. These are followed by statistical comparisons between the two fluency disorders for each category and also statistical comparisons between all pair-wise country comparisons for cluttering.

The last row at the bottom of the Appendix shows the percentages of statistically significant cluttering versus stuttering comparisons for each country and percentages of significant pair-wise country comparisons for cluttering only. It can be seen that of the 84 t test comparisons for cluttering versus stuttering, 2(2%) were significant for the Bulgarian sample, 4 (5%) for the Turkish sample, 19 (23%) for the American sample, 26 (31%) for the Russian sample, and 25 (30%) for all respondents combined. These represent only 15% of the four country comparisons, indicating that similarities between ratings for cluttering and stuttering dramatically outweighed differences. By contrast, the percentage of pair-wise comparisons for cluttering only between countries ranged from 20 to 57% of the total for countries (or 38% of all comparisons), suggesting that differences were relatively greater among the countries than between the two fluency disorders. This finding will be apparent in the following series of graphs showing all respondents combined for cluttering and stuttering means, and then for cluttering and stuttering in each country.

Sources of Knowledge. Figure 4 shows ratings of sources of knowledge of cluttering or stuttering for all respondents combined. Significant differences occurred for the following sources: others who cluttered/stuttered, school teachers, professionals (doctors, nurses, or other specialists), electronic media (television, radio, and film), and print media (magazines, newspapers, and books). No differences were observed for information from the respondents themselves, their family and friends, famous clutterers/stutterers, or the Internet. Figure 5 compares means for each country for cluttering and stuttering. It can be seen that the Russian and American respondents' means are lowest for cluttering—and visibly different from stuttering—for eight of the nine sources of information. Seven of nine differences were significant for the Russian sample; six of nine were significant for the American sample. Turkish ratings were highest for seven of the nine, but were only significant between stuttering and cluttering for "my own personal experience." Concerning pair-wise country comparisons for cluttering, Turks were often significantly different from Russians and/or Americans, Russians were different from Bulgarians in eight of nine comparisons, and Americans were not significantly different from Russians on any knowledge source comparisons.

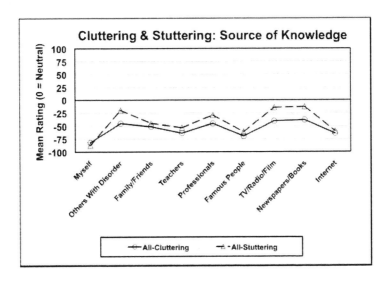

Figure 4. Mean ratings of all respondents on sources of knowledge about cluttering and stuttering.

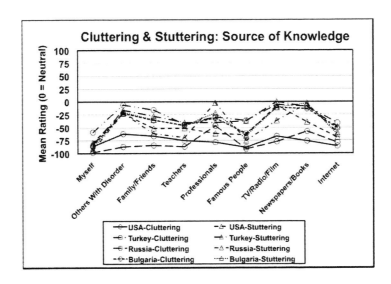

Figure 5. Mean ratings of respondents from four countries on sources of knowledge about cluttering and stuttering.

Cause. Fifteen items related to cause. Figure 6 for all respondents combined shows gaps between differences that were significant for injuries or accidents, psychological factors, emotionally traumatic experiences, pressure or tension at home, trying to talk or think too fast, and acts of God. "Physical makeup or body function" was also significantly different, although the difference is not apparent on the graph. Brain functioning, viruses or diseases, parents' overreacting to their children's speech, learning or habits, imitation, problems learning one's language, and ghosts, demons or spirits were not significantly different suspected causes for cluttering versus stuttering. Figure 7 shows that cluttering ratings were typically lower than stuttering ratings, sometimes only by a small amount, for the USA, Russia, and Bulgaria samples. Lower cluttering ratings did not appear to be the case for the

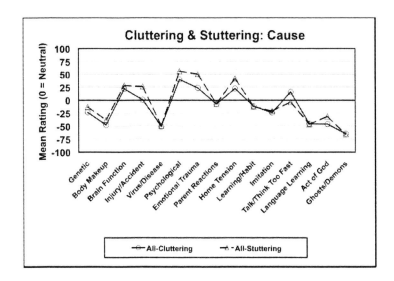

Figure 6. Mean ratings of all respondents on causes of cluttering and stuttering.

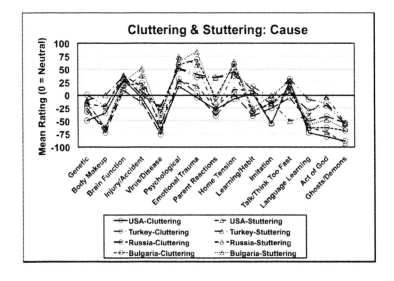

Figure 7. Mean ratings of respondents from four countries on causes of cluttering and stuttering.

Turkey sample.Russian and American respondents often had the lowest causal ratings for cluttering, indicating more uncertainty about cause than for stuttering. Again, by contrast, the Turkish respondents often had the highest ratings. Differences between the two disorders were significant in 6/15 comparisons for Russians versus 1/15 for Turks, Bulgarians, and Americans, respectively. For pair-wise cluttering comparisons, the Turkish sample was most often significantly different from the others, especially the Russian and American samples. This was not the case for "ghosts, demons, and spirits," however.The Americans were significantly different from the Turks and Russians.

Sources of Help. The profiles of sources of help for the two fluency disorders appear very similar in Figure 8. In 7/8 cases, the sources are slightly higher for stuttering than cluttering and statistically significant for the person himself/herself, a medical doctor or pediatrician, and for a speech therapist or clinician. In Figure 9, Russian means were highest or lowest in 5/9 items, most visibly different for rejecting physical or occupational therapy as viable sources of help for either disorder. Significantly different ratings between cluttering and stuttering occurred twice for Russians and once for Americans. The American sample was significantly higher than the other three samples for "other people who clutter/stutter" as a source of help. Although just neutral, it suggests that self-help for either disorder is more likely considered by the general public to be an option in the USA than in Russia, Bulgaria, or Turkey. Russians and Americans were most and least likely, respectively, to recommend a psychologist, psychiatrist, or counselor for cluttering, yielding significant differences.

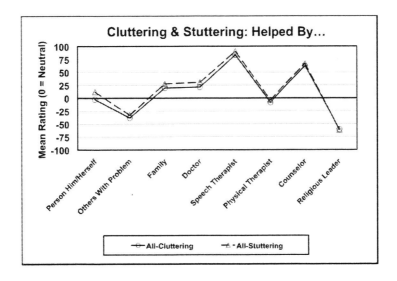

Figure 8. Mean ratings of all respondents on sources of help for cluttering and stuttering.

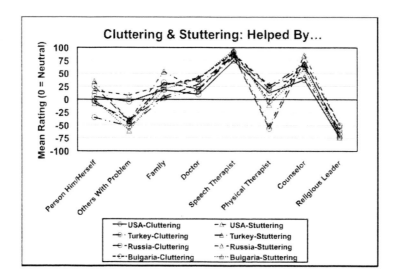

Figure 9. Mean ratings of respondents from four countries on sources of help for cluttering and stuttering.

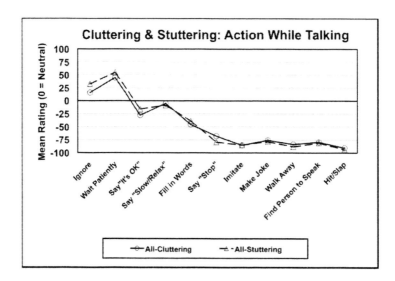

Figure 10. Mean ratings of all respondents on reported actions while talking with a clutterer and a stutterer.

Reported Actions. The *POSHA-E* asked respondents to rate various reactions when talking with a person who stutters or clutters. Figure 10 for all respondents shows very similar profiles for the two fluency disorders. Nevertheless, stuttering was rated significantly higher for ignoring the speech disorder and telling the speaker it is "OK" to clutter/stutter. Cluttering was significantly higher for telling the speaker to "stop cluttering/stuttering," occurring in all four samples (see below). None of the other 11 items was significantly different overall.

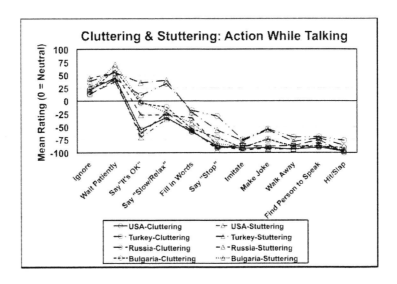

Figure 11. Mean ratings of respondents from four countries on reported actions while talking with a clutterer and a stutterer.

Within country comparisons, Figure 11 shows a significant difference between cluttering and stuttering for the American sample on ignoring the problem and saying "It's OK, " Similar significant differences were observed for the Turks saying "It's OK" and saying "Stop cluttering/stuttering." For 9/11 items, the Turkish respondents rated the actions highest; therefore, most of the significant pair-wise comparisons for cluttering favored the Turkish samples over one, two, or three of the other samples.

Reported Feelings. Again, hypothetically confronted with speaking to a person who clutters or stutters, the *POSHA-E* asked respondents for ratings of 10 emotional reactions. The profiles for cluttering and stuttering are nearly identical in Figure 12. None of the cluttering versus stuttering comparisons for all respondents was statistically significant. Curiosity and pity were scored higher than the other feelings; annoyance/anger and fear were scored the lowest. Figure 13 reveals that the country samples were quite different, but relief and surprise were significantly lower for cluttering versus stuttering in the American sample, and surprise was significantly higher for cluttering in the Russian sample.

The Turkish sample had the highest scores for both disorders in 5/10 comparisons: feeling comfortable, relief, curiosity, pity, and fear. They also had the lowest ratings for frustration. Thus, pair-wise cluttering comparisons showed Turks being significantly different from one, two, or three of the other groups for 6/10 items. Bulgarians differed significantly from Russians and Americans for frustration and from Americans for impatience.

Concern About Cluttering/Stuttering in Others. Figure 14 again portrays virtually parallel profiles for cluttering and stuttering for all of the respondents combined, with no significant differences. Figure 15 indicates that, whereas no country sample cluttering-stuttering comparisons were statistically significant, country samples did diverge on some of the items. Turkish respondents rated the highest mean concern if their neighbor, doctor, or religious leader cluttered or stuttered, with a trend for higher rating for cluttering. Russian and Bulgarian respondents rated the highest concern for the remainder of the nine items: child's friend, child's teacher, spouse, son, daughter, and self. Americans were least concerned on

5/9 items, especially for client's friend. Unlike the Turkish data, these showed trends of cluttering being lower than stuttering.Pair-wise contrasts for cluttering were significant between Americans and Russians versus Turks and Bulgarians relative to concern about a neighbor cluttering. Turks' ratings were significantly higher than the other three groups regarding concern about one's religious leader who cluttered, and Americans' mean ratings were significantly lower than the other three with respect to concern about a child's friend cluttering.

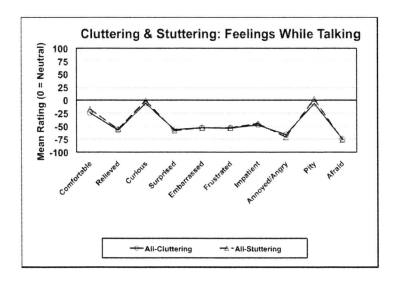

Figure 12. Mean ratings of all respondents on reported feelings while talking with a clutterer and a stutterer.

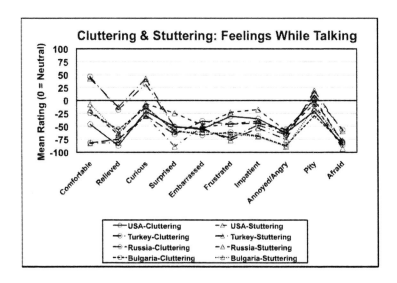

Figure13. Mean ratings of respondents from four countries on reported feelings while talking with a clutterer and a stutterer.

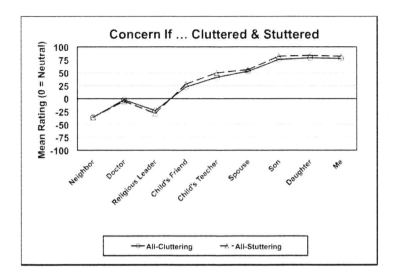

Figure 14. Mean ratings of all respondents on concern about various individuals cluttering and stuttering.

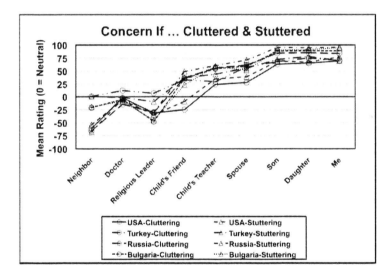

Figure 15. Mean ratings of respondents from four countries on concern about various individuals cluttering and stuttering.

Abilities and Characteristics. The last series of items are shown in the Appendix under the prompt "People who clutter/stutter…." To foster easy comparisons, they are divided in the ensuing discussion in terms of (a) what people with the disorder *can* do, (b) what they *should* do, or (c) how they *might be described*.

Figure 16 shows uniformly high ratings for clutterers or stutterers being able to function effectively in social situations, getting jobs, doing well in school or at work, raising a family, and leading a normal life. Ratings were somewhat lower for doing any job they want but were

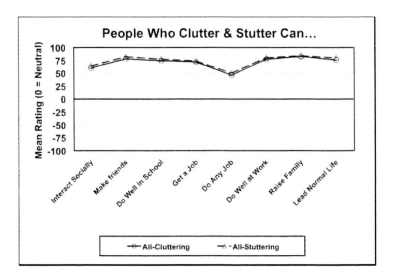

Figure 16. Mean ratings of all respondents on abilities of people who clutter and stutter in social, school, and work related settings.

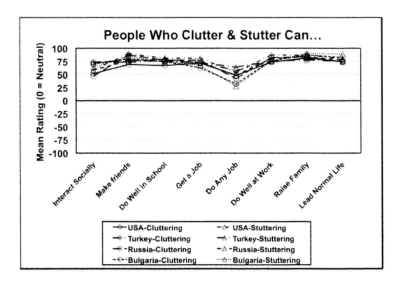

Figure 17. Mean ratings of respondents from four countries on abilities of people who clutter and stutter in social, school, and work related settings.

still positive. No cluttering-stuttering comparisons were significant for the country samples either (Figure 17). Cluttering pair-wise contrasts were significant only for being able to interact with people socially and to make friends. For social interactions, Turks had higher ratings than Americans and Russians, and Russians had lower ratings than Bulgarians. For making friends, Russians believed clutterers would be more able to do so than Americans and Turks would.

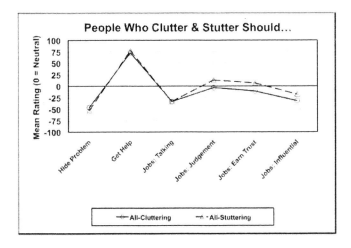

Figure 18. Mean ratings of all respondents on what people who clutter and stutter should do relative to dealing with their problem and working.

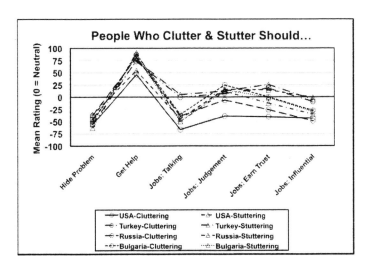

Figure 19. Mean ratings of respondents from four countries on what people who clutter and stutter should do relative to dealing with their problem and working.

Clutterers were judged to have significantly lower ratings than stutterers for holding jobs that required good judgment, required earning people's trust, or were influential jobs (Figure 18). For these items, as well as having jobs that require lots of talking, only the USA sample rated stuttering items higher than cluttering items (Figure 19). The Turkish sample rated both disorders highest in 3/6 items. Pair-wise cluttering comparisons were significant between the USA, Russia, or Turkey versus one, two, or three of the other countries in 5/6 items, and between Bulgaria and the other countries in 4/6 items.

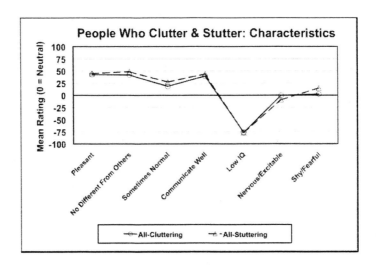

Figure 20. Mean ratings of all respondents on characteristics of people who clutter and stutter.

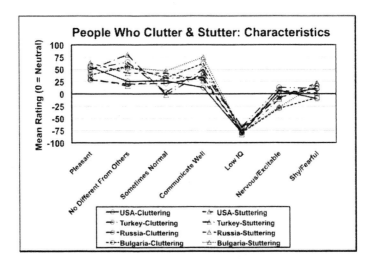

Figure 21. Mean ratings of respondents from four countries on characteristics of people who clutter and stutter

The seven descriptive items from combined respondents shown in Figure 20 were not significantly different between cluttering and stuttering. None of the differences for any of the four country samples were significant either (Figure 21). Nevertheless, pair-wise cluttering samples were significant for Turks versus Russians on clutterers being pleasant to be around and versus Russians and Americans on clutterers seeming to be no different from anyone else. Bulgarians differed from Americans and Russians on ratings of clutterers' ability to communicate effectively, and from Turks on clutterers being nervous or excitable. There were no differences on a clutterer's ability to sometimes speak without cluttering.

DISCUSSION

This study sought to compare the opinions or attitudes of "people on the street" toward people who clutter. It did so by comparing attitudes toward cluttering with stuttering on all items and with other anchors on a few items. The study also sought to identify differences among four widely diverse geographic/language groups.

Attitudes toward Cluttering and Stuttering

Inspection of Figures 4, 6, 8, 10, 12, 14, 16, 18, and 20 unambiguously gives the impression that attitudes toward cluttering are very similar—and in some cases almost identical—to attitudes toward stuttering. For that reason, the first two research questions—"What are public attitudes toward cluttering?" and "How do these attitudes differ from those toward stuttering?"—can be discussed together. Whatever the attitudes toward stuttering that have been shown to exist in numerous investigations, they also appear to be present for the much less known fluency disorder, cluttering. It would be tempting to assume that respondents were responding to the same hypothetical disorder, regardless of the differences in the definitions provided. The *POSHA-E* framework, however, provides for comparison of these two fluency disorders with eight other anchor attributes, ranging from positive to neutral to negative. The bottom row of the Appendix shows that combined mean ratings for cluttering were significantly different from mean stuttering ratings on 25 items or 30% of the total. Significant differences, discussed below, were especially apparent for sources of knowledge (5 of 9 comparisons), cause (7/15), abilities and characteristics relating to "should" (3/6), and sources of help (3/8). Given these results and the additional 51 country-specific significant differences between the two disorders (15% of the total), it is justifiable to conclude that participants responded to two *different* fluency disorders, however accurately or inaccurately they may have done so.

What are the attitudes the general public holds toward cluttering compared to stuttering? Cluttering was viewed as negatively as mental illness, a diagnosis that has been shown to carry a great deal of stigma (Sartorius, 1998). Knowledge of cluttering is rated among the four lowest attributes (Figure 3). Most respondents rated their personal experience with cluttering virtually nonexistent and for other sources of knowledge, less than for stuttering, significantly so from others who clutter, teachers, television/radio/films, and magazines/ newspapers/books (Figure 4). Psychological and related factors such as emotional trauma and tension in the home were generally the highest suspected causes for cluttering, but all were significantly lower than those factors for stuttering (Figure 6). Physical makeup or body function and talking and thinking too fast were also possible causes receiving positive mean scores for cluttering. Speech therapists and mental health professionals were ranked first and second as those who should help clutterers (Figure 8), while the clutterer's doctor and family were ranked third and fourth as sources of help. Respondents indicated that they would be likely to wait patiently as a person cluttered and would be likely to try to ignore it, but not as likely as with a person who stuttered (Figure 10). Telling a clutterer to "Slow down" or "Relax" was next most likely. Most of the other items in Figure 10, e.g., telling the person to "Stop cluttering" or making a joke about the cluttering, are considered to be unhelpful things to do. Although they were rated low, the ratings were slightly to significantly more likely than those for stuttering. Curiosity and pity tied for the most common feelings reported for cluttering, being slightly less than neutral (Figure 12). Feeling comfortable was the next ranking item, and annoyance/anger and fear were the lowest ranked feelings. As with stuttering, respondents would be most concerned if a son, daughter, or they, themselves, cluttered, followed by a spouse, their child's teacher, and their child's friend (Figure 14). They would be slightly more concerned if their doctor or religious leader cluttered than stuttered. Clutterers are viewed to be able—and about equally so—to make friends, socialize, do well in school or at work, raise a family, or lead normal lives (Figure 16). Ratings for being able to do any job they wanted were slightly lower. The public believes clutterers should definitely get help, but probably not try to hide their cluttering (Figure 18). The mean ratings for having jobs that require talking, good judgment, earning people's trust, or described as influential were all below neutral for clutterers, three of them significantly *lower* than for stutterers. Clutterers were seen to generally be pleasant, no different from others, able sometimes to speak without cluttering, and able to communicate effectively, but not as high as the social/school/work ratings seen in the previous figure (Figure 20). By contrast, clutterers were scored lower (close to neutral) in terms of being nervous/excitable or shy/fearful.

Ratings for stuttering were indicative of a stuttering stereotype, e.g., failure to reject the notion that stutterers are nervous and excitable, that they are shy and fearful, or that the cause of stuttering is psychological. This finding, confirmed in numerous other pilot investigations using the *POSHA-E* (St. Louis, 2005), indicate that the results for stuttering in the four samples in this study were typical of other convenience and probability samples as shown in Figure 22. The Figureshows the mean stuttering data for the four samples in this investigation compared to mean stuttering ratings from more than 2000 respondents in 38 samples from 12 countries, five continents, and eight languages (St. Louis, 2008).

Is there a similar cluttering stereotype? Respondents' overall impressions of cluttering in all four countries were relatively neutral; yet, by contrast, respondents rated "wanting to" clutter even lower than "wanting to" have mental illness, use a wheelchair, or be overweight. Most respondents accepted the idea that cluttering has a psychological cause and rejected the idea that its cause is genetic, views that are not consistent with the facts (e.g., St. Louis, Myers, Bakker, & Raphael, 2007; Weiss, 1964). Moreover, failure to completely reject the idea that cluttering is caused by a virus or disease; an "act of God"; or ghosts, demons, and spirits suggests parallel stigmatizing attitudes for cluttering and stuttering in these samples. Similarly, negative ratings for beliefs that clutterers should work in jobs that require considerable talking (or other responsible positions) and views that clutterers might well be nervous or excitable, or shy and fearful, together reinforce a cluttering stereotype that is very similar to the well-known stuttering stereotype.

The question emerges, "What is the origin of a cluttering stereotype?" MacKinnon and his colleagues carried out a study with some important similarities to this one (MacKinnon et al., 2007). They asked respondents to rate both a hypothetical temporary stutterer and a hypothetical chronic stutterer, with order of ratings counterbalanced. Most of the characteristics of the stuttering stereotype were significantly higher in the temporary stutterer, and all of them named emotions or items with clear emotional overtones.

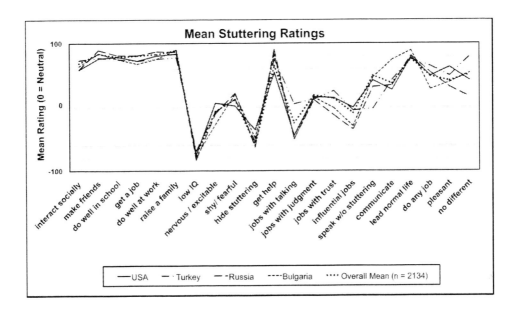

Figure 22. Mean ratings of respondents from four countries compared to the mean of 2134 respondents from previous investigations on various characteristics and expectations for people who stutter.

Given conventional wisdom about cluttering versus stuttering (e.g., Weiss, 1964; St. Louis et al., 2007), we assumed that respondents would rate cluttering less negatively than stuttering, but that was not the case. Perhaps the anchoring-adjustment process was active in that mean cluttering ratings were as negative as they were, but it did not appear to elevate the cluttering ratings to a more negative level than those observed for stuttering. If the predictions of MacKinnon and his associates would have obtained, ratings of clutterers being nervous or excitable and shy or fearful would have been significantly higher than they were for stutterers. The opposite would have occurred for being pleasant and a few other positive characteristics. Instead, clutterers were rated higher, but nonsignificantly so, for nervousness and excitability than stutterers, and the reverse for shyness and fear. These differences seem plausible and consistent with our understanding of the rapid rate of speech for clutterers and the likelihood of emotional reactions in stuttering (St. Louis & Myers, 1997).

Another possibility for the strength and item-specific negativity of the respondents' views on cluttering is that, lacking knowledge, experience, or opinions about cluttering, they simply substituted their views of stuttering. If so, this might explain the surprising similarity of attitudes toward the two disorders. The aforementioned significant differences, however, do not support this hypothesis.

Country/Language Differences in Attitudes toward Cluttering

Given the similarities observed between cluttering and stuttering from all respondents combined, inspection of profiles in Figures 1, 2, 3, 5, 7, 9, 11, 13, 15, 17, 19, and 21 clearly suggests that country differences far outweighed overall differences for cluttering and stuttering. Forty-six percent of the pair-wise comparisons between the four country/language groups were statistically significant, compared to 15% of those for cluttering versus stuttering (Appendix).

As noted in the Results section, different profiles of results emerged for different items or groups of items considering relative mean ratings for the four samples across the four country/language groups. Following are some examples.

Overall, Russian and American respondents in this study were more similar in many attitudes than any other pairs or triads among the four groups. Both rated several sources of knowledge considerably less for cluttering than for stuttering, and these were no doubt responsible for the overall significant differences for all respondents combined. Russian and American respondents were also the most similar in rejecting unhelpful reactions or advice for the clutterer, such as filling in words, walking away, hitting or slapping, and so on. Even so, there were some important differences. Russians reported knowing the most about cluttering; Americans, the least. Russians, too, rated getting help from the clutterer himself/herself the highest of the four samples, as well as, help from the clutterer's family. The Americans were most likely to believe that clutterers could be helped by other clutterers, or, by extension, to be open to a cluttering self-help movement. Americans were least likely to assign a genetic cause to cluttering, which is not consistent with conventional wisdom. Americans were also least likely to attribute the cause to an act of God or ghost, demons, or spirits, which is consistent with mainstream thought about etiology (Van Riper, 1971; Weiss, 1964).

Turkish respondents appeared to be the most opinionated for some items, but this might be interpreted as being the most "open" to cluttering or stuttering. For example, Turkish ratings were highest for most of the behavior reactions, such as offering advice that may or may not be welcome or making a joke. Turks were also the most pitying, most afraid, and most concerned about cluttering neighbors, doctors, or religious leaders than the other three groups. By contrast, they were also the most comfortable around clutterers, most optimistic about clutterers having jobs that required a lot of talking, and least rejecting of wanting to be a clutterer.

Bulgarian respondents varied considerably, depending on specific questionnaire items. For example, they were least likely to report feeling embarrassment, impatience, annoyance or anger, or pity when talking with a clutterer, but their ratings for feeling comfortable, relieved, surprised, frustrated, or afraid were close to the overall means. Bulgarian respondents also rated clutterers being sometimes able to speak without cluttering and communicating effectively highest of the four samples, and they found clutterers to be the least nervous or excitable and shy or fearful. They had the highest concern if they or a son or daughter cluttered, but the least concern if a religious leader cluttered.

Overall, to the extent that the four samples surveyed here represent a valid range of beliefs, reactions, and expectations about cluttering worldwide, these views are more similar than different. Nevertheless, a presumably complex combination of effects derived from different geographic areas of origin; different cultures that include religion, vocations, education, and socio-political factors; different languages; and separate translations from English to three different languages did affect the results of this study. Comparing these effects to those between cluttering and stuttering alone, these effects were greater than the differences determined by differences between the two fluency disorders.

CONCLUDING STATEMENTS

This study indicates that cluttering and stuttering definitions can be translated to different languages and evoke similar results from convenience samples of adults responding to surveys in those same languages. The reactions or beliefs about clutterers are similar regardless of whether the name of the disorder is familiar or non-familiar, and whether it has a long history of use or has been a long-used or familiar term, as in English (St. Louis et al., in press). Even though differences among four country samples were greater than differences between cluttering and stuttering, mean ratings were more similar than different. Whereas the public appears to recognize these as two distinct disorders, attitudes toward cluttering may best be explained by a concept of "fluency disorders" that posits, correctly or incorrectly, almost identical views of the effects of cluttering and stuttering on a hypothetical individual.

We suggest that future research should measure public attitudes without introducing the term or concept of stuttering, per se. Such research would be helpful in determining the extent to which considerations, thoughts, or memories of stuttering affect attitudes toward cluttering. Future research to compare further attitudes toward cluttering with other attributes besides stuttering would also be helpful to estimate the relative negativity of cluttering in society. Views of specialists in fluency disorders, and of clutterers themselves, would also be useful in identifying optimal standards against which any future efforts to change attitudes might be gauged.

ACKNOWLEDGMENTS

The authors acknowledge the assistance of the following persons in translations, distribution of questionnaires, and tabulating or analyzing results: USA—Dorinda Horter; Turkey—Bariş Dincer; Russia—Alexander Olenin; and Bulgaria—Irina Jakimova and Miglena Simonska.

REFERENCES

Blood, G. W. (1999). *The stigma of stuttering: Centuries of negative perceptions and stereotypes.* Paper presented at the Annual Convention of the American Speech-Language-Hearing Association, San Francisco, CA.

Cooper, E. B., & Cooper, C. S. (1996). *Clinician attitudes toward stuttering: Two decades of change.* Journal of Fluency Disorders, 21, 119-135.

Craig, A., Tran, C., & Craig, M. (2003). *Stereotypes towards stuttering for those who have never had direct contact with people who stutter: A randomized and stratified study.*Perceptual and Motor Skills, 97, 235-245.

Doody, I., Kalinowski, J., Armson, J., Stuart, A. (1993). *Stereotypes of stutterer's and nonstutterer's in three rural communities in Newfoundland.*Journal of Fluency Disorders, 18, 363-373.

Georgieva, D. (1998). *Professional awareness of cluttering: A comparative study.* Paper presented at the 24th Congress of the International Association of Logopedics and Phoniatrics, Amsterdam, The Netherlands.

Georgieva, D. (2001*). Professional awareness of cluttering: A comparative study (Part two). In H. G. Bosshardt, J. S. Yaruss, & H. F. M. Peters (Eds.). Fluency disorders: Theory, research, treatment and self-help.* Proceedings of the Third World Congress on Fluency Disorders in Nyborg, Denmark, International Fluency Association (pp. 630-635). Nijmegen, The Netherlands: Nijmegen University Press.

Halevy, M., Egoz, T. & Ezrati-Vinacour, R. (2010). *Will you date a person with cluttered speech?*In K. Bakker & L. J. Raphael (eds.) Proceedings of the First World Conference on Cluttering. (pp. 147-152). International Cluttering Association. Retrieved Ausust 2, 2010 from <http://associations. missouristate.edu/ICA/>.

Hughes, S, Gabel, R., & Irani, F. (2010). *Fluent speakers' advice for communicating with people who stutter: The concept of mutual help and its effects on successful stuttering management.* In E. L. Simon (Ed.) Psychology of Stereotypes. Hauppauge, NY: Nova Science Publishers.

Klassen, T. R. (2002). *Social distance and the negative stereotype of people who stutter.*Journal of Speech-Language Pathology and Audiology, 26, 90-99.

Lewis, G. A. (1907). *Home cure for stammering.* Detroit, MI: Winn & Hammond.

Luchsinger, R., & Arnold, G. E. (1965). *Voice-speech-language: Clinical communicology: Its physiology and pathology.*Belmont, CA: Wadsworth.

MacKinnon, S. P., Hall, S., & MacIntyre, P. D. (2007). *Origins of the stuttering stereotype: Stereotype formation through anchoring-adjustment.* Journal of Fluency Disorders, 32, 297-309.

Maxwell, D. L., & Satake, E. (1997). *Research and statistical methods in communication disorders.* Baltimore, MD: Williams & Wilkins.

Miller, T.(Ed). (2009, October).*Mapping the global muslim population: A report on the size and distribution of the world's Muslim population.* Pew Research Center.Retrieved August 2, 2010 from <http://pewforum.org/newassets/images/reports/Muslimpopulation /Muslimpopulation.pdf>.

Sartorius, N. (1998). *Stigma: What can psychiatrists do about it?*The Lancet, 352, 1058-1059.

St. Louis, K. O. (1999*). Person-first labeling and stuttering.* Journal of Fluency Disorders, 24, 1-24.

St. Louis, K. O. (2005). *A global project to measure public attitudes of stuttering.*The Asha Leader, 10, 12-13; 22.

St. Louis, K. O. (2008). *Public opinion toward stuttering: Similarities and differences around the world.* Plenary address presented at the 12th meeting of the International Clinical Phonetics and Linguistics Association. Istanbul, Turkey.

St. Louis, K. O., Andrade, C. R. F., Georgieva, D., & Troudt, F. O. (2005). *Experience and personal report about an international cooperation research—Brazil, Bulgaria and*

*Turkey—Attitudes toward stuttering.*Pró-Fono Revista de Atualização Cientifica, 17, 413-416.

St. Louis, K. O., & Hinzman, A. R. (1986). *Studies of cluttering: Perceptions of speech-language pathologists and educators of cluttering.* Journal of Fluency Disorders, 11, 131-149.

St. Louis, K. O., Filatova, Y., Coşkun, M., Topbaş, S., Özdemir, S., Georgieva, D., McCaffrey, E., & George, R. D. (in press).*Identification of cluttering and stuttering by the public in four countries.* International Journal of Speech-Language Pathology.

St. Louis, K. O., Lubker, B. B., Yaruss, J. S., & Aliveto, E. F. (2009). *Development of a prototype questionnaire to survey public attitudes toward stuttering: Reliability of the second prototype.* Contemporary Issues in Communication Sciences and Disorders, 36, 101-107.

St. Louis, K. O., Lubker, B. B., Yaruss, J. S., Adkins, T. A., & Pill, J. C. (2008). *Development of a prototype questionnaire to survey public attitudes toward stuttering: Principles and methodologies in the first prototype.* The Internet Journal of Epidemiology, 5(2). <http://www.ispub.com/ostia/index.php?xmlFilePath=journals/ije/vol5n2/stuttering.xml>

St. Louis, K. O., & McCaffrey, E. (2005). *Public awareness of cluttering and stuttering: Preliminary results.* Poster presented at the Annual Convention of the American Speech-Language-Hearing Association. San Diego, CA, November, 2005.

St. Louis, K. O. & Myers, F. L. (1997). *Management of cluttering and related fluency disorders.* Chapter in R. F. Curlee and G. M. Siegel (Eds). Nature and Treatment of Stuttering: New Directions. (pp. 313-332). New York: Allyn & Bacon.

St. Louis, K. O., Myers, F. L., Bakker, K. & Raphael, L. J. (2007). *Understanding and treating cluttering.* In Conture, E. & Curlee, R. (Ed.), Stuttering and related disorders of fluency (pp. 297-325). New York: Thieme.

St. Louis, K. O., Reichel, I., Yaruss, J. S., & Lubker, B. B. (2009). *Construct and concurrent validity of a prototype questionnaire to survey public attitudes toward stuttering.* Journal of Fluency Disorders, 34, 11-28.

St. Louis, K. O., & Rustin, L. (1992). *Professional awareness of cluttering.* In F. L. Myers & K. O. St. Louis (Eds.) Cluttering: A clinical perspective (pp. 23-35). Kibworth, Great Britain: Far Communications. (Reissued in 1996 by Singular, San Diego, CA.)

Tversky, A., & Kahneman, D. (1974). *Judgment under uncertainty: Heuristics and biases.* Science, 185, 1124-1130.

U.S. Census Bureau (2006) American Community Survey: Fact Sheet, West Virginia. Retrieved August 2, 2010 from <http://factfinder.census.gov/servlet/ACSSAFFFacts ?_event=Search&geo_id=&_geoContext=&_street=&_county=&_cityTown=&_state=04 000US54&_zip=&_lang=en&_sse=on&pctxt=fph&pgsl=010>

Weiss, D. (1964). *Cluttering.* Englewood Cliffs, NJ: Prentice-Hall.

White, P. A., & Collins, S. R. (1984). *Stereotype by inference: A possible explanation for the "stutterer" stereotype.* Journal of Speech and Hearing Research, 27, 567-570.

Van Riper, C. (1971). *The nature of stuttering.* Englewood Cliffs, NJ: Prentice-Hall.

Appendix. (1) Column 1: questionnaire items for anchor attributes, cluttering, and stuttering (but wording for stuttering is not shown in second part of the table); (2) Columns 2-6 [top part of table—left]: means for each general anchor attribute item, converted to numbers from -100 to +100, with 0 = neutral (exception: "Amount known" items converted from 0 to 100); (3) Columns 2-6 [remainder of table]: means for each item for cluttering; (4) Columns 7-11 [remainder of table]: means for each item for stuttering in the general and detailed components, converted to numbers from -100 to +100, with 0 = neutral; and (5) significance of t-tests for independent samples run (a) Columns 17-22 [top part of table—right] between parallel items for anchor attributes in the general component and all samples combined, (b) Column 12-16 [remainder of table] between parallel items for cluttering and stuttering in the general component and detailed component and all samples combined, (c) Columns 17-22 [remainder of table]: between all pair-wise comparisons for cluttering among the four country samples. The Bonferroni correction was applied to alpha levels by dividing the significance levels of p < .05 (*) and p < .01 (**) by 12 (the average number of items in each prompt). Abbreviations in the table are as follows: US = USA, TR = Turkey, RU = Russia, BG = Bulgaria, and NS = nonsignificant.

Questionnaire Item	Means for Anchor Attributes															T-tests: Pair-wise Comparisons for Anchor Attributes					
	US	TR	RU	BG	All											US v. TR	US v. RU	US v. BG	TR v. RU	TR v. BG	RU v. BG
Column: 1	2	3	4	5	6	7	8	9	10	11	12	13	14	15	16	17	18	19	20	21	22
(From General Component)																					
My overall impression of a person who…																					
is intelligent	67	75	75	88	76	—	—	—	—	—	—	—	—	—	—	NS	NS	**	NS	*	*
is multilingual	69	79	86	91	81	—	—	—	—	—	—	—	—	—	—	NS	**	**	NS	NS	NS
is a good talker	61	71	64	77	68	—	—	—	—	—	—	—	—	—	—	NS	NS	NS	NS	NS	NS
is left handed	17	13	21	32	21	—	—	—	—	—	—	—	—	—	—	NS	NS	NS	NS	NS	NS
is old	29	27	20	35	26	—	—	—	—	—	—	—	—	—	—	NS	NS	NS	NS	NS	NS
is overweight	-14	-39	-25	-20	-27	—	—	—	—	—	—	—	—	—	—	NS	NS	NS	NS	NS	NS
uses a wheelchair	3	20	6	25	15	—	—	—	—	—	—	—	—	—	—	NS	NS	NS	NS	NS	NS
is mentally ill	-5	-16	-44	-10	-20	—	—	—	—	—	—	—	—	—	—	NS	**	NS	**	NS	*
has a stuttering disorder	-13	-13	-7	13	-4	—	—	—	—	—	—	—	—	—	—	NS	NS	**	NS	**	*

Questionnaire Item	Means for Anchor Attributes																T-tests: Pair-wise Comparisons for Anchor Attributes					
	US	TR	RU	BG	All												US v. TR	US v. RU	US v. BG	TR v. RU	TR v. BG	RU v. BG
Column: 1	2	3	4	5	6	7	8	9	10	11	12	13	14	15	16	17	18	19	20	21	22
has a cluttering disorder	-21	-15	-2	13	-5	—	—	—	—	—	—	—	—	—	—	NS	NS	**	NS	**	NS
(From General Component)																					
I would want to be a person who…																					
is intelligent	96	83	84	90	87	—	—	—	—	—	—	—	—	—	—	NS	NS	NS	NS	NS	NS
is multilingual		87	86	95	86	—	—	—	—	—	—	—	—	—	—	NS	NS	**	NS	*	NS
is a good talker	81	85	70	93	80	—	—	—	—	—	—	—	—	—	—	NS	NS	**	**	**	**
is left handed	5	-16	-23	-14	-12	—	—	—	—	—	—	—	—	—	—	NS	*	NS	**	NS	NS
is old	-48	-30	-71	-64	-53	—	—	—	—	—	—	—	—	—	—	NS	*	NS	**	NS	NS
is overweight	-89	-75	-94	-91	-86	—	—	—	—	—	—	—	—	—	—	NS	*	NS	**	NS	NS
uses a wheelchair	-86	-67	-95	-92	-84	—	—	—	—	—	—	—	—	—	—	NS	*	NS	**	*	NS
is mentally ill	-95	-73	-96	-96	-88	—	—	—	—	—	—	—	—	—	—	NS	NS	NS	**	**	NS
has a stuttering disorder	-89	-81	-96	-98	-91	—	—	—	—	—	—	—	—	—	—	NS	**	NS	**	**	NS
has a cluttering disorder	-89	-81	-99	-94	-91	—	—	—	—	—	—	—	—	—	—	NS	**	NS	**	NS	NS
The amount I know about people who…																					
are intelligent	75	67	75	79	74	—	—	—	—	—	—	—	—	—	—	NS	NS	NS	NS	NS	NS
are multilingual	63	54	67	76	63	—	—	—	—	—	—	—	—	—	—	NS	NS	**	**	**	NS
are good talkers	67	56	64	79	66	—	—	—	—	—	—	—	—	—	—	*	NS	*	NS	**	**
are left handed	63	44	60	58	55	—	—	—	—	—	—	—	—	—	—	**	NS	NS	**	NS	NS
are old	63	81	73	67	72	—	—	—	—	—	—	—	—	—	—	**	NS	NS	NS	NS	NS
are overweight	60	60	63	63	62	—	—	—	—	—	—	—	—	—	—	NS	NS	NS	NS	NS	NS
use wheelchairs	35	28	29	33	31	—	—	—	—	—	—	—	—	—	—	NS	NS	NS	NS	NS	NS
are mentally ill	45	28	46	37	39	—	—	—	—	—	—	—	—	—	—	**	NS	NS	**	NS	NS
have stuttering disorders	34	34	29	42	34	—	—	—	—	—	—	—	—	—	—	NS	NS	NS	NS	NS	*
have cluttering disorders	24	35	51	38	38	—	—	—	—	—	—	—	—	—	—	NS	**	NS	**	NS	*

Appendix (Continued)

	Means for Cluttering					Means for Stuttering					T-tests: Cluttering vs. Stuttering					T-tests: Pair-wise Comparisons for Cluttering					
	US	TR	RU	BG	All	—	—	—	—	—	—	—	—	—	—	US v. TR	US v. RU	US v. BG	TR v. RU	TR v. BG	RU v. BG
(Repeated from General Section)																					
My overall impression of a person who…has a cluttering~ disorder	-21	-15	-2	13	-5	-13	-13	-7	13	-4	—	NS	NS	NS	NS	NS	NS	**	NS	**	NS
I would want to be a person who…has a cluttering~ disorder	-89	-81	-99	-94	-91	-89	-81	-96	-98	-91	NS	NS	NS	NS	NS	NS	**	NS	**	NS	NS
The amount I know about people who…have cluttering~ disorders	24	35	51	38	38	34	34	29	42	34	NS	NS	**	NS	NS	NS	**	NS	**	NS	*
(From Cluttering and Stuttering Items in Detailed Component)																					
My knowledge about cluttering~ comes from…																					
my own personal experience	-87	-59	-98	-85	-82	-80	-83	-95	-91	-88	NS	*	NS	NS	NS	*	NS	NS	**	NS	*
my experience with other people who clutter~	-62	-6	-87	-22	-45	-23	-16	-22	-20	-20	*	NS	**	**	**	**	NS	*	**	NS	**
my family or friends	-67	-16	-84	-36	-51	-51	-28	-62	-35	-45	NS	NS	**	NS	NS	**	NS	NS	**	NS	**
my school teachers	-75	-44	-87	-45	-64	-51	-40	-70	-46	-53	**	NS	*	*	NS	*	NS	NS	**	NS	**
doctors, nurses, or other specialists	-79	-30	-47	-32	-45	-62	-40	-2	-22	-29	NS	NS	**	**	*	**	**	**	NS	NS	NS
famous people who clutter	-89	-36	-92	-62	-70	-65	-37	-76	-66	-61	*	NS	NS	NS	NS	**	NS	**	**	NS	**
television, radio, or films	-67	-6	-78	-11	-41	-8	0	-36	-11	-15	**	NS	**	**	**	**	NS	**	**	NS	**
magazines, newspapers, or books	-76	-9	-58	-14	-39	-39	-10	-4	-3	-13	**	NS	**	**	**	**	NS	**	**	NS	**
the Internet	-86	-41	-79	-51	-64	-69	-48	-60	-64	-60	*	NS	*	NS	NS	**	NS	**	**	NS	*

I believe cluttering~ is caused by…	Means for Cluttering					Means for Stuttering					T-tests: Cluttering vs. Stuttering					T-tests: Pair-wise Comparisons for Cluttering					
	US	TR	RU	BG	All	—	—	—	—	—	—	—	—	—	—	US v. TR	US v. RU	US v. BG	TR v. RU	TR v. BG	RU v. BG
genetic inheritance	-49	1	-25	-32	-23	-17	-9	-12	-15	-13	*	NS	NS	NS	NS	**	NS	NS	NS	NS	NS
physical make-up or body function	-34	-21	-72	-65	-48	-22	0	-67	-62	-38	NS	NS	NS	NS	**	NS	**	NS	**	**	NS
brain functioning	30	31	9	19	22	39	37	13	27	29	NS	NS	NS	NS	NS	NS	NS	NS	NS	NS	NS
a physical injury or accident	-5	7	-14	23	1	16	0	38	51	26	NS	NS	**	*	**	NS	NS	NS	NS	NS	NS
a virus or disease	-67	-22	-76	-34	-50	-56	-23	-68	-43	-49	NS	NS	NS	NS	NS	**	NS	NS	**	NS	**
psychological factors	18	52	31	58	40	28	52	74	65	56	NS	NS	**	NS	**	**	NS	**	NS	NS	*
an emotionally traumatic experience	-5	34	4	69	24	18	41	59	84	51	NS	NS	**	NS	**	**	NS	**	*	*	**
parents overreacting to their children's speech	-27	35	-40	-4	-7	-24	34	-30	-12	-7	NS	NS	NS	NS	NS	**	NS	NS	**	**	*
pressure or tension at home	-7	38	3	60	23	11	45	46	65	42	NS	NS	**	NS	**	**	NS	**	**	NS	**
learning or habits	4	17	-40	-31	-12	9	9	-35	-25	-12	NS	NS	NS	NS	NS	NS	**	NS	**	**	NS
imitating other people	-55	-6	-25	-14	-24	-54	-17	-15	0	-21	NS	NS	NS	NS	NS	**	NS	*	NS	**	NS
trying to talk too fast or think too fast	28	32	-5	12	16	18	5	-50	27	-4	NS	*	**	NS	**	NS	*	NS	**	NS	NS
problems from learning one's language	-72	-8	-50	-63	-45	-62	-30	-40	-58	-46	NS	NS	NS	NS	NS	**	**	NS	**	**	NS
an act of God	-80	-15	-41	-63	-46	-71	-20	-3	-48	-31	NS	NS	**	NS	*	**	**	NS	NS	**	NS
ghosts, demons, or spirits	-88	-56	-53	-68	-64	-92	-56	-54	-65	-66	NS	NS	NS	NS	NS	*	**	NS	NS	NS	NS

Appendix (Continued)

	Means for Cluttering					Means for Stuttering					T-tests: Cluttering vs. Stuttering					T-tests: Pair-wise Comparisons for Cluttering					
	US	TR	RU	BG	All	—	—	—	—	—	—	—	—	—	—	US v. TR	US v. RU	US v. BG	TR v. RU	TR v. BG	RU v. BG
I believe cluttering~ should be helped by...																					
the person who clutters~ himself/herself	6	-35	25	-3	-2	17	-8	35	-1	12	NS	NS	NS	NS	*	*					
other people who clutter~	-4	-52	-43	-47	-38	8	-38	-41	-60	-33	NS	NS	NS	NS	NS	**	NS	*	**	NS	NS
the family of the person who clutters	19	2	33	27	20	28	5	54	20	28	NS	NS	**	NS	NS	NS	*	NS	*	NS	NS
a medical doctor or pediatrician	10	19	20	39	21	42	29	17	40	30	*	NS	NS	NS	*	NS	NS	NS	NS	NS	NS
a speech therapist or clinician	75	82	85	92	83	88	86	93	96	90	NS	NS	NS	NS	**	NS	NS	NS	NS	NS	NS
a physical or occupational therapist	13	21	-56	-3	-8	28	25	-51	-10	-4	NS	NS	NS	NS	NS	NS	**	NS	**	NS	**
a psychologist, psychiatrist, or counselor	38	64	74	67	62	44	69	86	59	67	NS	NS	*	NS	NS	NS	**	NS	**	NS	NS
a religious leader	-73	-60	-50	-66	-61	-58	-69	-49	-73	-62	NS	NS	NS	NS	NS	NS	NS	NS	NS	NS	NS
If I were talking with a person who clutters~, I would...																					
ignore the cluttering~	22	12	14	18	16	44	38	28	20	33	*	*	NS	NS	**	NS	NS	NS	NS	NS	NS
wait patiently during his/her cluttering~	45	43	37	60	45	55	55	43	71	55	NS	NS	NS	NS	NS	NS	NS	NS	NS	NS	NS
tell the person it is okay to clutter~	-56	11	-64	-4	-28	-27	35	-71	-1	-16	**	*	NS	NS	*	**	NS	**	**	NS	**
tell the person to "slow down" or "relax"	-32	33	-23	-12	-5	-27	40	-35	-23	-9	NS	NS	NS	NS	NS	**	NS	NS	**	**	NS
fill in the person's words	-60	-18	-58	-54	-46	-33	-22	-56	-42	-39	NS	NS	NS	NS	NS	**	NS	NS	**	*	NS
tell the person to stop cluttering~	-87	-29	-91	-71	-68	-87	-56	-94	-83	-79	NS	*	NS	NS	**	**	NS	NS	**	**	*

	Means for Cluttering					Means for Stuttering					T-tests: Cluttering vs. Stuttering					T-tests: Pair-wise Comparisons for Cluttering					
	US	TR	RU	BG	All	US	TR	RU	BG	All	US	TR	RU	BG	All	US v. TR	US v. RU	US v. BG	TR v. RU	TR v. BG	RU v. BG
imitate the person's cluttering	-92	-75	-87	-91	-85	-95	-77	-82	-89	-85	NS	NS	NS	NS	NS	NS	NS	NS	NS	NS	NS
make a joke about cluttering~	-90	-54	-88	-74	-76	-92	-56	-93	-75	-78	NS	NS	NS	NS	NS	**	NS	NS	**	NS	NS
walk away from the person	-94	-70	-87	-88	-84	-93	-79	-93	-89	-88	NS	NS	NS	NS	NS	*	NS	NS	NS	NS	NS
find somebody else to speak for the person	-90	-70	-76	-88	-79	-87	-72	-81	-88	-81	NS	NS	NS	NS	NS	*	NS	NS	NS	NS	NS
hit or slap the person	-97	-77	-100	-91	-91	-97	-86	-97	-95	-94	NS	NS	NS	NS	NS	**	NS	NS	**	NS	*
If I were talking with a person who clutters~, I would feel...																					
comfortable or relaxed	-46	46	-82	-24	-24	-18	43	-83	-7	-17	NS	NS	NS	NS	NS	**	**	NS	**	**	**
relieved	-87	-18	-75	-56	-58	-67	-13	-81	-63	-56	*	NS	NS	NS	NS	**	NS	**	**	**	NS
curious to know more about cluttering~	-21	31	-29	-14	-6	-6	42	-30	-11	-1	NS	NS	NS	NS	NS	**	NS	NS	**	**	NS
surprised	-51	-51	-65	-58	-57	-25	-51	-89	-61	-59	*	NS	**	NS	NS	NS	NS	NS	NS	NS	NS
embarrassed	-55	-56	-40	-67	-53	-47	-53	-52	-61	-53	NS	NS	NS	NS	NS	NS	NS	NS	NS	NS	NS
frustrated	-30	-73	-46	-61	-54	-23	-77	-45	-65	-53	NS	NS	NS	NS	NS	**	NS	NS	*	NS	NS
impatient	-35	-47	-44	-69	-48	-17	-53	-40	-70	-45	NS	NS	NS	NS	NS	NS	NS	*	NS	NS	NS
annoyed or angry	-62	-66	-56	-87	-66	-59	-75	-64	-89	-71	NS	NS	NS	NS	NS	NS	NS	*	NS	NS	**
pity for the person	-21	11	1	-29	-6	-6	19	4	-15	3	NS	NS	NS	NS	NS	NS	NS	NS	NS	*	NS
afraid the cluttering~ might affect or hurt me	-85	-57	-80	-82	-75	-93	-59	-79	-77	-76	NS	NS	NS	NS	NS	*	NS	NS	NS	NS	NS
If the following people cluttered~, I would be concerned.																					
my neighbor	-61	1	-66	-21	-36	-54	1	-68	-20	-36	NS	NS	NS	NS	NS	**	NS	**	**	NS	**
my doctor	-2	12	-14	-5	-2	-6	-1	-5	-9	-5	NS	NS	NS	NS	NS	NS	NS	NS	NS	NS	NS
my religious leader	-31	7	-30	-48	-23	-34	-10	-30	-45	-28	NS	NS	NS	NS	NS	*	NS	NS	**	**	NS
my child's friend	-25	33	37	36	22	-9	37	49	23	28	NS	NS	NS	NS	NS	**	**	**	NS	NS	NS

Appendix (Continued)

	Means for Cluttering					Means for Stuttering					T-tests: Cluttering vs. Stuttering					T-tests: Pair-wise Comparisons for Cluttering					
	US	TR	RU	BG	All	—	—	—	—	—	—	—	—	—	—	US v. TR	US v. RU	US v. BG	TR v. RU	TR v. BG	RU v. BG
my child's teacher	24	30	56	55	41	35	44	60	58	50	NS	NS	NS	NS	NS	NS	NS	NS	NS	NS	NS
my husband or wife	28	58	61	59	53	39	56	71	52	56	NS	NS	NS	NS	NS	NS	*	NS	NS	NS	NS
my son	63	68	84	88	76	69	72	95	90	82	NS	NS	NS	NS	NS	NS	NS	NS	NS	NS	NS
my daughter	65	75	85	89	79	67	78	94	91	83	NS	NS	NS	NS	NS	NS	NS	*	NS	NS	NS
me	69	70	84	89	78	77	70	96	94	82	NS	NS	NS	NS	NS	NS	NS	NS	NS	NS	NS
People who clutter~...																					
can interact with people socially	52	73	47	70	60	58	73	59	64	64	NS	NS	NS	NS	NS	*	NS	NS	**	NS	*
can make friends	69	74	87	80	78	76	77	90	84	82	NS	NS	NS	NS	NS	NS	*	NS	*	NS	NS
can do well in school	67	76	78	75	74	79	75	81	75	78	NS	NS	NS	NS	NS	NS	NS	NS	NS	NS	NS
can get a job	72	73	77	63	72	72	72	81	68	74	NS	NS	NS	NS	NS	NS	NS	NS	NS	NS	NS
can do any job they want to do	48	57	42	33	46	49	64	54	28	50	NS	NS	NS	NS	NS	NS	NS	NS	NS	NS	NS
can do well at work	74	75	82	76	77	81	76	87	75	80	NS	NS	NS	NS	NS	NS	NS	NS	NS	NS	NS
can raise a family	81	80	84	88	83	84	78	87	90	84	NS	NS	NS	NS	NS	NS	NS	NS	NS	NS	NS
can lead normal lives	75	76	74	83	76	78	75	80	89	80	NS	NS	NS	NS	NS	NS	NS	NS	NS	NS	NS
should try to hide their cluttering~	-56	-45	-37	-50	-46	-36	-55	-63	-49	-53	NS	NS	NS	NS	NS	NS	NS	NS	NS	NS	NS
should get help for their problem	46	73	81	87	73	54	75	90	83	77	NS	NS	NS	NS	NS	*	**	**	NS	NS	NS
should work in jobs that require lots of talking	-67	-1	-39	-36	-34	-45	5	-50	-50	-33	*	NS	NS	NS	NS	**	**	*	**	*	NS
should work in jobs that require good judgment	-39	7	-6	24	-3	16	12	11	15	13	**	NS	NS	NS	**	**	NS	**	NS	NS	*
should work in jobs that require earning people's trust	-41	18	-26	0	-11	14	25	-13	-1	7	**	NS	NS	NS	**	**	NS	*	**	NS	NS
should work in influential jobs	-44	-9	-49	-28	-32	-1	-5	-35	-30	-18	**	NS	NS	NS	**	*	NS	NS	**	NS	NS

	Means for Cluttering					Means for Stuttering					T-tests: Cluttering vs. Stuttering					T-tests: Pair-wise Comparisons for Cluttering					
	US	TR	RU	BG	All											US v. TR	US v. RU	US v. BG	TR v. RU	TR v. BG	RU v. BG
are pleasant to be around	55	50	28	38	43	63	49	31	39	45	NS	NS	NS	NS	NS	NS	NS	NS	*	NS	NS
seem no different from anybody else	25	64	20	56	42	42	80	16	54	48	NS	NS	NS	NS	NS	**	NS	NS	**	NS	**
can sometimes speak without cluttering~	26	3	21	32	18	42	-2	31	46	27	NS	NS	NS	NS	NS	NS	NS	NS	NS	NS	NS
can communicate effectively	13	49	33	62	39	27	43	34	74	43	NS	NS	NS	NS	NS	**	NS	**	NS	NS	*
have lower-than-average intelligence	-80	-67	-80	-80	-76	-75	-69	-83	-79	-77	NS	NS	NS	NS	NS	NS	NS	NS	NS	NS	NS
are nervous or excitable	7	13	-1	-30	0	6	-7	-11	-27	-9	NS	NS	NS	NS	NS	NS	NS	NS	NS	**	NS
are shy or fearful	-10	10	10	-8	2	2	12	22	20	15	NS	NS	NS	NS	NS	NS	NS	NS	NS	NS	NS
Percent Cluttering / Stuttering Items Statistically Significant	—	—	—	—	—	—	—	—	—	—	23	5	31	2	30	57	20	37	56	21	39

~   Questionnaire items for the detailed components are shown in the cluttering version only. "Cluttering" and "clutter" were written as "stuttering" or "stutter," respectively, in the stuttering version.

*   T-test is significant at the alpha level of $p < .05$ (using Bonferroni correction [$.00083 < p < .0042$]).

**   T-test is significant at the alpha level of $p < .01$ (using Bonferroni correction [$p < .00083$]).

NS   T-test is nonsignificant ($p > .05$) (using Bonferroni correction [$p > .0042$]).

In: Psychology of Stereotypes
Editor: Eleanor L. Simon

ISBN: 978-1-61761-463-7
©2011 Nova Science Publishers, Inc.

Chapter 4

THE FORMATION OF STEREOTYPES IN CHILDREN: EVIDENCE FROM AGE AND RACE STUDIES

Denise Davidson[*], *Vanessa R. Raschke, and Sandra B. Vanegas*
Loyola University, Chicago, Illinois, USA

ABSTRACT

This chapter explores the formation of stereotypes in children, particularly negative stereotypes that children hold about others. Theoretical views about stereotype formation in children are presented, and evidence from developmental studies on racism and ageism is summarized. Empirical research is also provided in an attempt to address unanswered questions about negative stereotype formation in children. Commonalities in the development of stereotypes will be drawn, with implications given about the course of stereotype development, and how children's reliance on stereotypes can be lessened.

INTRODUCTION

As psychological research has demonstrated, the use of stereotypes is ubiquitous. Of interest, then, is how these stereotypes begin, how they develop, and how their course of development may be altered. Previous studies have shown that children form stereotypes on the basis of race, gender and age, and that these stereotypes can be quite negative (e.g., Averhart & Bigler, 1997; Davidson, Luo, & Fulton, 2007; Davidson, Cameron, & Jergovic, 1995; Levy, 2000; Theimer, Killen, & Stangor, 2001; Williams & Davidson, 2009). Of particular interest in the present research is how negative stereotypes begin and how they might be eliminated. Although the focus will be on empirical research exploring children's negative racial and age stereotypes, parallels will be made to research on other stereotypes. Commonalities in the development of these stereotypes will be drawn, with implications

---

[*] Address correspondence to Denise Davidson, Department of Psychology, Loyola University Chicago, 1032 W. Sheridan Rd., Chicago, Il. 60660. E-mail: ddavids@luc.edu.

given about the course of stereotype development, and how children's and other individuals' reliance on stereotypes can be lessened.

STEREOTYPE DEVELOPMENT AND PREJUDICE IN CHILDREN: AN OVERVIEW

In a seminal discussion on stereotype development in children, Gordon Allport (1954/1979) began by asking, "How is prejudice learned?" Common mechanisms of learning were cited, including paired association, reinforcement, observation, and imitation. In particular, Allport emphasized the transfer of information from parents to children, including their words, beliefs and emotions, through learning and conformity. He also described how a child-rearing environment that promotes hatred provides ample opportunity for children to acquire negative stereotypes.However, Allport (1979) wrote that prejudice was "not merely a matter of specific parental teaching...blind imitation, or mirroring the culture" (p. 318). He also suggested that emotional and cognitive stages of development could affect children's beliefs about others.

More recent research supports Allport's suggestion that stereotypes and their development is more complicated than a simple transmission between parent and child. Before discussing this research, however, several key concepts need to be defined. Although stereotypes are often seen as traits or behavioral dispositionsthat are believed to be shared by members of a social group (e.g., LePalley, Reimers, Calvini, Spears, Beesley, & Murphy, 2010), they are not necessarily the same as negative stereotypes toward others that are often expressed as prejudice. Stereotypes can be positive, negative or a combination thereof. Additionally, recent research on stereotype formation suggests the need to look beyond the individual's views about others, and instead focus on majority and minority group membership of both the perceiver and the target, and in-group and out-group preferences and biases (e.g., Cameron, Alvarez, Ruble, & Fuligni, 2001; Nesdale, 2004). To illustrate, early studies on children's stereotypes focused almost exclusively on majority (e.g., European American) children's in-group preferences—their liking of themselves and others like them, and their out-group biases, or their dislike of others different from them. This led to the argument that stereotype formation might simply reflect in-group preferences and out-group biases. The problem, however, is that majority and minority group membership may affect these preferences. As recent research has shown, minority group children (e.g., African-Americans) sometimes show the opposite effect: an in-group bias and an out-group preference (Williams & Davidson, 2009). Thus, theories that have been posited to explain stereotype development in children need to take into account not just how stereotypes are formed, but how one's majority and minority group membership may affect one's expression of stereotypes.

THEORETICAL VIEWS AND MODELS OF STEREOTYPE DEVELOPMENT

Two theories of stereotype formation, the sociocognitive theory (SOCT) and the social identity theory, later replaced by the more recent self categorization theory (SCT), have generated considerable psychological research. A third theory, the developmental intergroup theory (DIT) of stereotyping and prejudice has also been posited, with the goal of examining stereotype formation specifically in children(Bigler, 1998; Bigler & Liben, 2008).

Proposed by Aboud (1988), the sociocognitive theory (SOCT) argues that a child's response to others depends on his or her level of development in relation to two overlapping developmental processes. Initially, the child is dominated by affective processes associated with attachment to the familiar or known and a fear of the unknown. At this stage of development, the child's preferences are often based on physical attributes (e.g., body size, skin color) that are similar between the child and others. With the advent of more sophisticated thinking, such as concrete operational thinking around 7 years of age, or formal operational thinking in adolescence (Piaget, 1954/1986), children's preferences and biases toward others are based more on an understanding about the individual and characteristics unique to the individual. That is, the child's increasingly sophisticated ways of thinking allow him or her to pay attention to characteristics about the individual and to judge the individual accordingly. Subsequently, Aboud (1988) argued that in-group preferences and out-group prejudices increase up to about age 7, with a systematic decline in group-based biases past the age of 9. Nevertheless, most children will express some preference for their own group throughout childhood and adolescence.

In line with SOCT, preoperational children, or children younger than 7 or so, often focus their attention on perceptually salient dimensions of their world, which often results in young children's attention to perceptually salient features about others, such as race. With age, children's understanding of concrete operational concepts results in a better understanding of ethnic flexibility and ethnic constancy, or the understanding that ethnic groups share both similarities and differences, and that certain features about ethnicity remain the same, regardless of superficial transformationssuch as changes in hair coloring or clothing (e.g., Doyle & Aboud, 1995; Doyle, Beaudet, & Aboud, 1988).

In contrast to the SOCT view, self-categorization theory (SCT) suggests that because ethnic preferences reflect primarily motivational rather than cognitive considerations, ethnic preferences are not expected to decline during middle childhood as a result of cognitive acquisitions (e.g., Nesdale, 2000; Turner, Hogg, Oakes, Reicher, & Wetherall, 1987). Consistent with this theory, research has shown that in-group preferences either remain the same between ages 7 to 12 (e.g., Asher & Allen, 1969; Nesdale, 1999; Weiland & Coughlin, 1979), or actually increase during these years (e.g., Rice, Ruiz, & Padilla, 1974). Additionally, some have suggested that any reported decline in in-group preferences by majoritygroup children after age 7 simply reflects a social desirability response (see Nesdale, 2000, for a review).According to SCT, "although prejudice is unlikely to occur in children younger than 6 or 7 years of age because their cognitive abilities would not have achieved the requisite level of development, its emergence thereafter would be dependent on their unique social situation" (Nesdale, 2004, p. 233). Children who do display ethnic prejudice, according to SCT, pass through four sequential developmental phases: undifferentiated, ethnic awareness, ethnic preference, and ethnic prejudice. According to Nesdale (2004), the hallmark of this four-stage model of development is ethnic self-identification leading to an in-group focus rather than an out-group bias.

Consistent with this view are the findings from ethnic preference studies that have shown that when given a forced choice between in-group and out-group stimulus figures (e.g., dolls, pictures, drawings), majority group children almost always indicate a preference for the in-group figures (see Nesdale, 2001, for a review). In fact, Nesdale (2004) argued that it is precisely during the period of middle childhood, from age 7 and beyond, that "prejudice actually crystallizes and emerges in those children who come to hold such attitudes" (p. 229). That is to say, prejudice does not emerge in all children as a matter of course.

Additionally, some have suggested that it is a combination of cognitive and social factors, as well as a combination of individual and environmental factors, that affect children's reliance on stereotypes. According to Bigler and her colleagues' developmental intergroup theory of stereotype and prejudice formation (DIT), four basic principles underlie the formation of children's stereotypes. This includes the principle that social groups that are marked by perceptually salient attributes are much more likely to become the target of intergroup bias than social groups that are not marked by perceptually salient attributes. Likewise, social groups that are used in a functional manner—separating children in a classroom by gender—may render more intergroup bias. Membership into a group, particularly a minority group, may also affect the formation of stereotypes. This is true even when the majority and minority groups are artificial groups created for a study. For example, Brown and Bigler (2002) asked children in a classroom to wear either a red or yellow t-shirt, with the preponderance of children being asked to wear a red one (the majority group). Brown and Bigler found that children who were in the minority group (the yellow t-shirt group) preferred other minority group members as playmates, they rated their own minority group less favorably than the majority group, and they wanted to change color groups more readily than majority-group (red t-shirt) children. Similar results were also demonstrated by Patterson and Bigler (2007).

In addition to perceptual salience and functional use, DIT states that linkages or associations between certain traits and behaviors to a particular group often leads to stereotype formation in children. In fact, such links can be explicit or implicit, as Bigler (1998) suggests in the following example: suppose that a child is told "African-Americans are good at basketball" providing an explicit link, whereas a child might observe that three out of four basketball players in the NBA are African-American, providing an implicit link. Empirical research largely supports such use of explicit and implicit links in children to form stereotypes (see, e.g., Bem, 1983 or Fishbein, 1996). Finally, Bigler (1998) points out that it is the interaction of multiple factorsthat affects stereotype development. In fact, she argues that any combination of two of the three factors –perceptual salience, functional use, and linkages– is quite likely to produce intergroup stereotyping and bias.

In addition to these theoretical views of stereotype formation, some have posited more general models to explain stereotype formation, including the pure abstraction model and the pure exemplar model of stereotypes. Historically, the pure abstraction model of stereotypes was seen as synonymous with the notion that stereotypes are a type of schema, with prototypical properties and expectancies. According to this view, when a target individual is encountered, he or she is automatically categorized by the perceiver, with all relevant stereotypes pertaining to that particular category or group subsequently activated (e.g., Hamilton, Sherman, & Ruvolo, 1990; see also Sherman, Gawronski, Gonsalkorale, Hugenberg, Allen, & Groom, 2008, for a related discussion). In contrast, the pure exemplar model of stereotypes views the content of stereotypes as flexible and constantly changing because perception is dependent upon whatever exemplars are activated at that time (Smith &Zaraté, 1992). It has been suggested that at low levels of experience, social perceptions are exemplar-based and at high levels of experience, social perceptions are more abstraction-based (e.g., Fiske, 2000; Fiske, Neuberg, Beattie, & Milberg, 1987). For example, with more experience with individuals from a group, subcategories of these groups can be formed, making individuals more distinct and removed from the stereotyped group. This is consistent with the continuum model used to describe the range of ways people form impressions of others. According to the continuum model, the processes people use to form impressions of others is dependent upon what information is readily available and the perceiver's level of motivation to seek out that information or counter information (Fiske, 2000). A central premise of this model is that perceivers prefer categorization over individuation, although information fit, perceived relevance and the motivation on the part of the perceiver also play important roles in forming impressions.

Although research assessing models of stereotype formation have been primarily with adult participants, at least some research with children has shown that they may be applicable to children as well. For example, Memon, Holliday, and Hill (2006) established what they referred to as "pre-event stereotypes' in 5-year-old children. To do so, they read stories to the children about a man who was described in positive, negative or neutral terms. The man then visited the children's classroom, and children were asked questions about the man following his visit. Children's views of the man, their answers to their questions about the man, and their use of misinformation provided after his visit, were consistent with the type of pre-event stereotype that had been established before he visited. This was particularly true for the group hearing positive information about the man, as they were much more likely to accept positive information about him than the other groups. However, recollection measures revealed that negative misinformation was better recalled than positive misinformation (Memon et al).

THE STUDY OF CHILDREN'S STEREOTYPES: AN OVERVIEW

Regardless of theoretical or model orientation about the origins of stereotype formation, all agree that children's expression of negative stereotypes and prejudice is less sophisticated and often more tentative than that of adults. Because children lack the emotional and verbal sophistication of adults, children's prejudice usually does not take the form of anger or overt hostility, but instead may be experienced by the child as fear, sadness, or disapproval (e.g., Aboud, 2003). When overt methods of expressions are exhibited by children they may consist of avoidance, social exclusion, or name-calling and fighting.

Subsequently, research methods have been designed to capture children's often unique expression of stereotypes and prejudice. Indeed, many have noted the failure of past methods to adequately demonstrate the depth of children's stereotypes, and how majority- and minority-group membershipof the children themselves may affect these stereotypes. For example, many have criticized the doll preference technique first introduced by Clark and Clark (1939/1950), whereby children are required to choose a preferred doll from ethnically-different dolls or other representations of persons such as puppets, drawings or photographs. As Nesdale (2000) notes, these methods do not allow for an assessment of a child's feelings toward in-group and out-group members, nor do they provide an assessment of the intensity of liking or disliking by the child. In contrast, more recent methods of assessing children's stereotypes about others have focused not only on the stereotypes themselves, but the impact these stereotypes have on children's processing of information about others, from examining how information that is consistent or inconsistent with stereotypes is recalled (e.g., Averhart & Bigler, 1997; Davidson et al., 2007; Williams & Davidson, 2009), toexamining how primes that are consistent or inconsistent with children's stereotypes affects both their memory and judgments about others(Bigler, 1998; Bigler & Liben, 2008).

Past research presents conflicting ideas about how children's stereotypes may affect their memory for, and judgment of, others (see, Ruble & Stangor, 1986; Stangor & McMillan, 1992, for reviews). On the one hand, a memory advantage for stereotype-consistent information has been found across a range of studies. For example, Averhart and Bigler (1997) found that 7-year-old African-American children displayed better memory for stereotype-consistent information than stereotype-inconsistent information about other African-American children. Similar results have been found with older children (Williams & Davidson, 2009). Likewise, studies of children in middle grade school (between 8 and 10 years of age) have found better memory for stereotype-consistent information than stereotype-inconsistent information (see Stangor & McMillan, 1992, for a review). It has been suggested that stereotype-consistent information is easier to recall because it can be easily integrated into one's schema or stereotype for a particular group.

Indeed, in children 7 and younger, children will sometimes distort the information they remember so that it matches stereotypes. Cordua, McGraw, and Drabman (1979) found that when 5- and 6-year-olds were shown a male physician and a female nurse they were 100% accurate in their recall of whether a man or woman was the doctor and was the nurse. However, when shown a female physician and a male nurse, over 50% said they had seen the reverse. Likewise, Davidson et al., (1995) found that when an elderly person was described as healthy and active, children between 6 and 7 years of age recalled the information in its opposite form—the elderly person was recalled as inactive and unhealthy. However, such distortions are not common in children older than age 7 (Stangor & McMillan, 1992).

On the other hand, information that is inconsistent with stereotypes may be well recalled precisely because it is unique and unexpected, and therefore may receive deeper processing when encountered (see Ruble & Stangor, 1986; Srull, 1981; Stangor & McMillan, 1992, for discussions). The match between the participant and the target may also impact these results. Nesdale (2000) explored whether age-related changes in beliefs about in-group and out-group members affected children's memories about others, their affection toward others, and their causal attributions about positive and negative behaviors believed to be enacted by others. In his study, 8-, 10- and 12-year-old majority-group children (Anglo-Australian) remembered a story about an Australian and a Vietnamese boy, each of whom displayed equal numbers of stereotype-consistent and stereotype-inconsistent traits and behaviors. Overall, Anglo-Australian children remembered more about the character like them (i.e., in-group character) than about the character dissimilar to them, and such memory increased with age. Interestingly, the overall effect was due in part to the fact that children remembered more stereotype-inconsistent information about the in-group character than stereotype-consistent information.

Nevertheless, children's memory for stereotype-consistent and stereotype-inconsistent information about others may not match up with their ratings of others. In Nesdale's (2000) study, children preferred the in-group character until about 10 years of age, thereafter the effects were less pronounced or children preferred the out-group character. Likewise, older children did not necessarily make positive attributions about the in-group character. For example, when presented with negative information that was inconsistent with stereotypes, older children believed that the in-group character, in particular, behaved this way due to negative personal characteristics and not due to external causes. These results suggest that negative behavior exhibited by an in-group member may be perceived even more negatively than negative behavior exhibited by an out-group person, although one has to be cautious with this interpretation as minority-group children's memory and beliefs were not assessed in Nesdale's study. As discussed below, being a member of a minority group may affect one's attributions in a way that is different from that seen in members of the majority.

NEGATIVE STEREOTYPES AND RACISM IN CHILDREN

The development of racial stereotypes is very complex, involving environmental, cognitive and biological features (e.g., Aboud, 2003; Bigler & Liben, 1993; Liben & Bigler, 2002). For example, despite desegregation efforts and increased racial tolerance, studies show that individuals still adopt stereotyped attitudes toward, and beliefs about, African-Americans (e.g., Hall, 2001; Jones, 1997; Russell, Wilson, & Hall, 1993).Although previous research has focused on interracial stereotypes, several researchers have explored intra-racial stereotypes, such as those related to skin tone or skin color (e.g., Averhart & Bigler, 1997; Harvey, LaBeach, Pridgen, & Gocial, 2005; Keith & Herring, 1991; Maddox & Gray, 2002; Porter, 1991; Wade & Bielitz, 2005).

DEVELOPMENTAL STUDIES ON INTERRACIAL STEREOTYPES

In terms of interracial views, developmental studies have explored how children view individuals of other races, and how they view their own race. For example, in African-American children, the focus has often been on how they view both their own race and other races. Beginning with some of the earliest studies conducted in this area, it has been found that African-American children often possess a pro-white bias in their beliefs.Perhaps the most famous of these studies was carried out by Clark and Clark (1939/1950) who asked African-American children to choose between a Black and a White doll. It was found that African-American preschoolers preferred the White dolls, a phenomenon that has come to be called the "White bias." Although more recent studies have confirmed Clarks' findings (Justice, Lindsey, & Morrow, 1999; Spencer & Markstrom-Adams, 1990), other have not (see Aboud, 1987, for a review of this literature). It has been suggested that minority group children's views of race may be more complicated, and often opposite of, the majority group.Specifically, the results of previous studies suggest that minority children often reject their in-group in favor of the culturally dominant out-group (e.g., Averhart & Bigler, 1997; Justice et al., 1999; Spencer & Markstom-Adams, 1990).

The cultural makeup of the United States provides many opportunities to explore multiple facets of racial awareness and stereotype understanding. Given the heterogeneity of many communities, children are exposed to environments that may foster stereotype development. When young children between 6 and 10 years of age were questioned about present day situations that elicit differential treatment based on appearances, minority children (i.e., African-American, Latino, and Asian American) demonstrated greater perception of racial stereotypes at an earlier age than children in the majority group (i.e., White). Although minority children report knowing of racial stereotypes, their understanding may be limited at earlier ages. Between 6 and 9 years of age, minority children explain racism in descriptive terms, usually along one dimension, such as explaining how specific groups dislike one another (McKown, 2004). However, by 9 to 10 years of age, children report a more in-depth understanding of racism, discussing the causal mechanisms of prejudice and discrimination. Descriptions of racism at this age include specific incidents of oppression, indicating a piecing together of specific beliefs about racial groups and their manifestations in children's daily experiences. By 10 years of age, some minority groups may have experienced varying levels of racism. For example, African-American and Latino-American children display a greater awareness of racism and are more likely to report racism than White and Asian-American children (McKown & Weinstein, 2003). Thus, even though minority children across racial groups are aware of racial stereotypes, they may not all experience racism to the same degree.

An important factor to consider when evaluating racial stereotypes in the United States is the immigrant status of most racial groups. For example, Pfeifer and colleagues examined children's beliefs about ethnic groups in first and second generation immigrant children (i.e., Chinese, Dominican, and Russian) and third and fourth generation non-immigrant children (i.e. White, African-American; Pfeifer, Ruble, Bachman, Alvarez, Cameron, & Fuligni, 2007). Children were asked to rate how characteristic positive and negative attributes were for five ethnic groups (i.e., Chinese, Dominican, Russian, White, and African-American), and how well they identified with their own ethnic group. Immigrant children exhibited greater intergroup bias (i.e., reporting more positive and less negative traits towards their own ethnic group) than non-immigrant White and African-American children. However, levels of intergroup bias varied by children's ethnic identity ratings. Immigrant children, who identified themselves as more American than ethnic, reported less intergroup bias than immigrant children who identified as more ethnic than American. In this case, young children's national identity had the potential to neutralize racial stereotypes.

The development and understanding of racial stereotypes in other countries show similar patterns as the United States. Racial stereotypes in Canada are prominent among the Native Canadians, who are often described as poor, ignorant and unfriendly. When presented with positive and negative characteristics of Euro-Canadians and Native Canadians, children between 7- and 10-years of age from both ethnic groups recalled more stereotype-relevant information than stereotype-irrelevant information (Corenblum, 2003). This parallels African-American children's recall of stereotype-relevant information found in the United States (e.g. Williams & Davidson, 2009). Furthermore, Native Canadian children recalled more positive descriptions of Euro-Canadians and more negative descriptions of Native Canadians (Corenblum, 2003). This contrasts Euro-Canadian children's group serving biases when recalling more positive information for the in-group (Euro-Canadian) and more negative information for the out-group (Native Canadian). For Native Canadians, the negative stereotypes associated with their ethnic group appeared to prevail above in-group preferences. This indicates that Native Canadian children had adopted these negative beliefs for their own ethnic group to some degree.

The previous findings have supported the prominence of racial stereotypes of groups within a specific country. Perceived stereotypes across countries may also provide valuable clues as to how children acquire beliefs about racial groups having minimal contact. A preliminary study evaluated how 6-year-olds across five different nations (i.e., Azerbaijan, Britain, Georgia, Russia, and Ukraine) perceived their own and other ethnic groups on numerous positive and negative traits, such as lazy, happy, and dishonest (Bennett, Barrett, Karakozov, Kipiani, Lyons, Pavlenko, Riazanova, 2004). Children across all nations applied a greater number of positive traits to their in-group as expected, however, contrary to expectations, children applied more negative traits only to out-groups that presented a direct conflict to their own ethnic group. For example, Azeri children applied more negative traits to Russians than other ethnic groups and Ukrainians applied more negative traits to Georgians than other ethnic groups. This indicates that 6-year-olds have some understanding of existing alliances and conflicts present for their ethnic group. Although children may possess strong in-group preferences, this is not always coupled with a prejudice or bias against all out-groups, supporting previous findings of Brewer (1999) and Aboud (2003).

Negative Stereotyping within Racial Groups

In addition to interracial stereotyping, intra-racial stereotyping can also occur. In particular, skin tone appears to be a source of discrimination among African-Americans today just as it was historically (e.g., Blair, Judd, Sadler, & Jenkins, 2002; Robinson & Wade, 1995; Russell et al., 1993; Wade & Bielitz, 2005). For example, during slavery and the post-slavery era, lighter-complexioned African-Americans were extended greater privileges and rights than their darker-complexioned peers (Russell et al., 1993).Russell et al. defined this intraracial discrimination on the sole basis of skin color and features as the "color complex." However, while the impact that racial and skin tone stereotypeshas on various aspects of adult African-American life has been well documented in empirical studies, there has not been a strong impetus toward examining the development of skin tone stereotypes in African-American children.

In fact, Averhart and Bigler (1997) noted that they found only three contemporary (i.e., post 1950) studies on skin tone attitudes among African-American children.These included a study by Baugher (1973), who found that African-American preschoolers evaluated lighter-complexioned stimulus figures more positively than darker-complexioned figures; a study by Anderson and Cromwell (1977), who found that African-American adolescents held both positive attitudes toward their race and negative stereotypes about darker-complexioned African-Americans; and a study by Porter (1991), who showed that African-American children between 6 and 13 years of age preferred lighter skin tones over darker skin tones.

These studies were supplemented by their own research. In 1997, Averhart and Bigler assessed the effects of self-perceived skin color on 5- and 7-year-old African-American children's stereotypes about skin color. They found that children's self-ratings of skin tone and their interracial stereotypes were both related to negative intra-racial views.Specifically, African-American children who showed a bias against their own race (i.e., held more interracial stereotyped views) were more likely to hold a bias against darker-complexioned individuals (i.e., held more intra-racial stereotypes).Children who reported their own skin tone to be lighter than that rated by the experimenter also gave more stereotyped responses on the interracial and intra-racial measures. That is, these children rated African-Americans as a group, and rated darker-complexioned African-Americans more negatively than their peers who rated themselves darker complexioned or whose ratings more closely matched that of the experimenter. In contrast, African-American children with more favorable views of their own race were less likely to hold a bias against darker skin tones (Averhart & Bigler, 1997).

A recent study by Williams and Davidson (2009) with slightly older, 7- and 9-year-old children, replicated Averhart and Bigler's (1997) findings. Williams and Davidson found that African-American children, overall, exhibited more negative views toward other African-Americans, labeling pictures of African-American children with negative adjectives more often than pictures of European-American children. African-American children who displayed negative views about other African-American children were also more likely to display more negative views about darker skin tones.

Children's memory for stereotype-consistent and stereotype-inconsistent information was also examined in the Williams and Davidson (2009) study. Nine-year-olds showed a significant recall advantage for stereotype-consistent stories, and 7- to 9-year-old children who were found to be highly stereotyped recalled more stereotype-consistent information than less stereotyped children. Thus, Williams and Davidson showed that stereotypes in children can impact other cognitive processes such as memory.

In light of the above-mentioned findings, developmental research suggests that not only do interracial and intra-racial stereotyping exist in children, but that this stereotyping may lead to negative views within the children themselves. Therefore, the need to eliminate such beliefs is an important step for future research.

NEGATIVE STEREOTYPES AND AGEISM IN CHILDREN

In addition to negative racial stereotypes, negative stereotypes about the elderly have been found in younger and older children. Interestingly, in assessing children's stereotypes about the elderly, in-group and out-group membership is no longer of importance given that children cannot, obviously, belong to the group of older adults. Thus, assessing children's views about older adults can reveal stereotypes that are not affected by in-group and out-group status.

Indeed, some of the most negative views of individuals stem from children's attitudes toward older adults. Research has shown that children of all ages, and from many backgrounds, hold at least some negative concepts about older adults (e.g., Davidson et al., 1995; Falchikov, 1990; Isaacs & Bearison, 1986; Jantz, Seefeldt, Galper, & Serock, 1980; Larkin Friedlander, Newman, & Goff, 2004; Newman, Faux, & Larimer, 1997; Seefeldt, 1989).In fact, some of the earliest stereotypes seen in children are their stereotypes for older individuals, as children as young as three years of age have been shown to have negative attitudes about older adults (e.g., Jantz et al., 1980; Seefeldt, Jantz, Galper, & Serock, 1977). These stereotypes about older adults, or ageism, refers to the subtle negative and persistent attitudes generally associated with aging adults, encompassing characteristics such as senility, passivity, inactivity, incompetence, and dependency (Ansello, 1978; Levy, 1996; Montepare & Zebrowitz, 2002).

In line with theoretical views of aging, research has shown that children are more likely to pay attention to physical appearances in older adults than personality traits (e.g., Mitchell, Wilson, Revicki & Parker, 1985; Seefeldt et al., 1977). Due to maturational limitations, children may relyon perceptual features that distinguish older adults from others, without knowledge that these features may simply be the result of the normal aging process (Perry & Bussey, 1984). As noted previously, for young children, salient physical characteristics may be more readily used because of their inability to process more complex information about others.

Unfortunately, physical characteristics such as drooping eyes and stooped posture can lead to negative inferences concerning the general emotional well-being of an individual (e.g., sad or depressed). This is not to say that age stereotypes based on personality or psychological traits do not exist in children. Other age stereotypes may consist of traits such as grouchiness, fatigue, passivity, slower processing, senility, and impaired mental abilities (e.g., Cuddy, Norton, & Fiske, 2005). Past research has shown that at least some of these traits are generalized across older adults by children (Davidson et al., 1995; 2007; Jantz et al., 1980; Seefeldt, 1989).

It may be, however, that in some societies (American) these views are more prevalent than in other societies that view aging in a more positive light. For example, it is often assumed that Asian societies revere and value the elderly, although few studies have empirically assessed this belief, particularly in children. Nevertheless, some support for this assumption was obtained by Seefeldt and Ahn (1990), who found that Korean children rated their elders as more friendly and good than American children.Likewise, Asian families have been shown to spend more time with their elderly family members, as their care may be the sole responsibility of the family.For example, research has found that older adults in the People's Republic of China are more likely to be cared for by their own families than by outside care, even when ill (Davis, Martinson, Gan, Jin, Liang, Davis & Lin, 1995).

Traditional beliefs about family responsibilities in these cultures may afford children more opportunities to interact with their grandparents, who may be living in their home, than that afforded American children who often live separate from their grandparents and other older family members.In a large study comparing 3,286 Taiwanese, European American, African-American and Mexican American families, it was found that Taiwanese grandparents spent significantly more time with their grandchildren than their American counterparts (Strom, Strom, Wang, Shen, Griswold, Chan, Yang, 1999).Unfortunately, children's view about their time spent with their grandparents was not assessed. Thus, it is not clear how Taiwanese children felt about their grandparents, and the time they spent together, nor is it known how these children view older adults in general.

Although recent studies have explored differences in Eastern and Western children's self-concept (e.g., Wang, 2001; Wang, 2006), only one study that we know of has compared Eastern (People's Republic of China) and Western (United States) children's stereotype of older adults (Davidson et al., 2007). In Davidson et al.'s research, artist-drawn line illustrations were presentedto American and Chinese children. While previous studies have often assessed children's stereotypes of others by comparing different younger and older adults, in the Davidson et al. (2007) study, drawings of American and Chinese adults were shown across four ages:approximately 25, 35, 65 and 80 years of age. Thus, children saw pictures of the same adult at four ages. In doing so, it was possible to assess how stable children believed these characteristics to be because children were rating the same person as a young adult and as an older adult. Of particular interest was whether children would believe that positive characteristics described about young adults remained positive as these adults became older. Additionally, children's memory for the adult, and information presented about that adult, was also assessed in their research.

Although 10-year-old American children were more negative about older adults than other children, 6- and 10-year-old children in both the People's Republic of China and the United States expressed negative views of older adults (Davidson et al., 2007). However, these negative views, or age stereotypes, were more readily found when the task required a comparison between younger and older adults, even when that comparison was for the same person as a younger and older person. Although children were more positive in their views of the adults following the presentation of positive information, children did not necessarily see these characteristics as being stable, especially if they ran counter to stereotype. This was particularly true for the 6-year-old children. Studies such as this provide evidence that negative age stereotypes may exist the world over. However, questions about the formation of these stereotypes remain.

NEW DATA ON NEGATIVE STEREOTYPES AND AGEISM IN CHILDREN

Past research on children's stereotypes toward older adults has left at least some questions unanswered. Answers to these questions are needed because they may provide clues to how these stereotypes form in the first place and how they may be lessened in children. Firstly, it is not clear how much a priori information about younger (child) and older (elderly) characters affect children's subsequent liking of the characters. Importantly, by looking at children's ratings immediately following the presentation of individuating information, and their ratings again a day later, it can be determined whether children's ratings matched the information given about the characters or whether it matched stereotypes of those individuals regardless of the information presented. In other words, it is possible to assess how individuating information might override children's stereotypes toward others. For example, positive information provided about specific older individuals might override general, negative stereotypes about them.This prediction is supported by previous research (Hoe & Davidson, 2002), that found that primes about specific individuals (e.g., grandparent primes) promoted positive responses in children on attitude scales.

In the present research, children's liking of male and female child and elderly characters was assessed. Previous research with adults has shown that women are judged to be elderly at a younger age than men, and that physical signs of aging are generally more accepted for men than women (e.g., Deutsch, Zalenski, & Clark, 1986; Harris, 1994). However, in terms of psychological traits, older women are often seen in a more positive light than older men (e.g., Hoe & Davidson, 2002; Jelenec & Steffens, 2002; Laditka, Fischer, Laditka, & Segal, 2004; Zandi, Mirle, & Jarvis, 1990). Such a finding has been dubbed the "Grandmother Effect" (Hoe & Davidson, 2002).

Also of interest in this research was how younger and older children would recall information that was consistent or inconsistent with age stereotypes. Past research has suggested that children are more likely to recall information that is consistent with stereotypes, although this research asked children to recall information about other children and, therefore, could have been affected by children's in-group and out-group status (e.g., Averhart & Bigler, 1997; Williams & Davidson, 2009). Additionally, given that past research is equivocal about whether stereotypes become more or less pronounced with age, "liking" ratings and memory was assessed across two age groups, 4- to 5-year-old children and 10- to 11-year-old children, in the present study. Information about behavioral traits (active and inactive) and information about psychological traits (positive and negative traits such as nice versus mean) were given to the children because some have suggested that children's stereotypes about older adults focuses on behavioral limitations and not psychological ones. Additionally the assignment of such traits may differ across older men and older women (Hoe & Davidson, 2002; Mitchell, et al, 1985).

METHOD

Participants

Participants were 128 American children, 64 children were 4 to5years of age (*M* age = 4.6) and 64 children were 10 to11years of age(*M* age = 10.7). In each age group, half the children were male and half were female. Approximately 65% of the sample was European American, 25% wasAfrican-American, and about 10% was Mexican American or Asian American. Children completed the ratings and memory tasks twice, immediately after information about the characters was presented and 24 hours later.

Materials and Procedure

Children were tested individually in a quiet room of their school. Children were randomly assigned to one of four conditions: a behavioral-active, a behavioral-inactive condition, a psychological-positive ora psychological-negative trait condition. For example, children in the behavioral-inactive condition were shown pictures and heard brief descriptions about a child or an older adult whose behavior was characterized by inactive behaviors (e.g., watching TV), whereas children in the behavioral-active condition saw pictures and heard a description about a child or older adult that was active (e.g., likes to ride a bicycle). The positive and negative psychological conditions were constructed in a similar way, with children hearing either positive "psychological" characteristics, e.g., friendly, likes to share, or their opposites. In order to communicate this information, each child was shown a set of four pictures, taken from popular press periodicals, of a character (a boy, a girl, an older man and an older woman) and each character and their actions were described in the pictures. This methodology allowed for an assessment of how children's stereotypes of the young and old might affect their ratings, as well as how information congruent and incongruent with stereotypes might affect their ratings across immediate and 24 hour delays. Children were asked to rate the characters on 5-point rating scales, with 1 representing "not liked at all" to 5 representing "liked very much."

Results and Discussion

Ratings of Liking Across Child and Elderly Characters. Younger and older children's mean ratings for the child and elderly characters are shown in Table 1. A mixed-model analysis of variance was conducted on this data, with between-subjects variables Age of Participant (4-5; 10-11), Condition (Positive Psychological, Negative Psychological, Active Behavioral, Inactive Behavioral), and Delay (Immediate, 24-Hours), and within-subjects variable Age of Character (Child, Elderly). No significant differences were found in the ratings of male and female child characters, and no significant differences were found between male and female elderly characters, $t(127) \leq -1.33$, ns., therefore this variable was collapsed to form the 2-level Age of Character (Child, Elderly) variable. This analysis resulted in a significant three-way interaction: Character x Condition x Age, $F(9, 336) = 1.95$, $p < .04$, partial $\eta^2 = .05$, as well as several two-way interactions: Character x Age of Participant, $F(3, 336) = 3.52$, $p < .02$, partial $\eta^2 = .03$, and Condition x Delay, $F(3, 112) = 3.00$, $p < .03$, partial $\eta^2 = .07$. The Condition x Delay x Age of Participant approached significance, $F(3, 112) = 2.51$, $p < .06$, partial $\eta^2 = .06$. Main effects of Character (Child, Elderly), $F(1, 336) = 3.08$, $p < .05$, partial $\eta^2 = .03$, and Condition (Positive Psychological, Negative Psychological, Active Behavioral, Inactive Behavioral), $F(3, 336) = 3.26$, $p < .02$, partial $\eta^2 = .03$, were also found.

Table 1. Children's Ratings of Child and Elderly Characters Following Positive or Negative Psychological or Behavioral Trait Information.

Age of Participants		Age of Target Character
4- to 5-Year-Olds	Child Characters	Elderly Characters
Positive Psychological	4.09 (1.16)	4.16 (.81)
Negative Psychological	2.14 (1.26)	2.58 (1.22)
Active Behavioral	4.03 (1.11)	3.67 (1.06)
Inactive Behavioral	3.41 (1.31)	3.31 (1.30)
10- to 11-Year-Olds	Child Characters	Elderly Characters
Positive Psychological	3.88 (.85)	4.11 (.75)
Negative Psychological	3.36 (.97)	2.75 (.85)
Active Behavioral	3.88 (.81)	3.65 (.77)
Inactive Behavioral	3.69 (.75)	2.98 (.74)

Note. Standard deviations are in parentheses.

Memory for Child and Elderly Characters Across Conditions. In order to explore the significant interactions, pairwise t-tests were conducted, with familywise error rate controlled for by using Holm's sequential Bonferroni approach. Concerning the three-way interaction, the main interest was how the age of the characters affected younger and older children's "liking" ratings across the psychological and behavioral conditions. In the Positive Psychological condition, younger and older children's ratings were generally very positive, and did not differ between child and elderly characters, ($M = 4.09$, $SD = 1.16$; $M = 4.16$, $SD = .82$, child and elderly characters, respectively), nor did the ratings differ between the younger and older children, $t(7) \leq -.28$, ns. Thus, child and elderly characters described with positive psychological characteristics were liked by all children. The patterns changed, however, for younger and older children in the other conditions and across characters. For the Negative Psychological and the Inactive Behavioral conditions, 4- and 5-year-old children's ratings did not differ between child and elderly characters, and were lower than in the other conditions, $t(15) \leq .84$, ns (see Table 1). In the Active condition, 4- and 5-year-old children's ratings differed significantly between child and elderly characters, $t(15) = 2.86$, $p< .05$, with their liking of active elderly characters less than their liking of active child characters, see Table 1.

For 10- and 11-year-old children, their ratings of older adults were significantly lower than their ratings of the child characters in both the Negative Psychological and the Inactive Behavioral conditions, see Table 1, $t(15) \geq 2.96$, $p\leq .01$. In the Active condition, 10- and 11-year-old children's ratings were not significantly different across child and elderly characters, $t(15) = .81$, ns, see Table 1.

In terms of the significant Condition x Delay X Age of Participants interaction, the ratings of the characters in the positive Psychological Condition decreased by the second day, as the characters were not as well liked on the second day as the first across all children, ($M = 4.45$, $SD = .73$; $M = 3.68$, $SD = .81$, immediate and 24-hour delays, respectively), $t(30)$ 3.41, $p< .002$. In the Negative Psychological condition the ratings stayed about the same on the second day for all children, ($M = 2.67$, $SD = .96$). The behavioral conditions produced somewhat different results, as the results appeared to be dependent upon the age of the child, as well as how the character was described. Four- to 5-year-old children's ratings of active characters increased by the second day ($M = 3.62$, $SD = .88$ $M = 3.97$, $SD = .98$, immediate and 24-hour delays, respectively), $t(15)$ 3.33, $p< .01$, and decreased for the inactive characters by the second day, ($M = 3.54$, $SD = .77$ $M = 3.28$, $SD = .54$, immediate and 24-hour delays, respectively), $t(15)$ 2.96, $p< .01$. For the older children, the opposite was found, with active character ratings decreasing ($M = 4.13$, $M = 3.41$, immediate and 24-hour delays), and inactive character ratings increasing on the second day, ($M = 3.53$, $M = 3.13$, immediate and 24-hour delays).

Thus, for psychological characteristics, the ratings of the characters were either not as positive or not as negative on the second day as on the first. This was true across younger and older children. For behavioral characteristics, a similar pattern was found for the older children with more positive ratings on one day giving way to lower ratings the next and vice versa for low ratings on day one. In contrast, younger children's ratings became more positive or negative in line with the initial descriptions.

The results of the mixed-model ANOVA conducted on the memory data revealed only three significant findings: a Condition (Positive Psychological, Negative Psychological, Active Behavioral, Inactive Behavioral) x Delay interaction, $F(3, 112) = 9.10$, $p < .0001$, partial $\eta^2 = .10$, and main effects of Condition, $F(3, 112) = 16.41$, $p < .0001$, partial $\eta^2 = .08$ and Age of Participants, $F(1, 112) = 7.49$, $p < .01$, partial $\eta^2 = .06$. Using the Bonferroni approach, follow-up t-tests revealed that memory was better in the positive psychological and active behavioral conditions on the first day ($M = 2.90$, $SD = .15$; $M = 3.30$, $SD = .61$, positive psychological and active behavioral conditions, respectively) than on the second ($M = 2.39$, $SD = .57$; $M = 2.20$, $SD = .76$, positive psychological and active behavioral conditions, respectively), whereas no significant differences were found in the recall of information in the negative psychological and inactive behavioral conditions at immediate or 24-hour delays, $t(62) =1.03$, ns. Overall, more information was recalled in the active behavioral condition ($M = 2.75$, $SD = .88$) than in the inactive behavioral condition ($M = 2.29$, $SD = .76$), $t(62) = 2.20$, *p*< .03. As expected, older children recalled more information (*M* = 2.78, *SD* = .51) than younger children (*M* = 2.36, *SD* = .84), *t*(12) = -3.49, *p*< .001.

The results of this study provide evidence that positive information about older adults, at least positive information about the psychological traits of older adults, may result in positive views of these older adults in children. That is, neither 4-year-olds nor 10-year-olds rated older adult targets differently from child targets in the positive psychological trait condition. Children's positive ratings of older adults following positive information may have occurred because providing positive information about an older adult may result in the child seeing the individual as belonging to a subcategory removed from the stereotyped group.Recent findings in the adult literature on stereotypes support this assumption, as these studies have shown that adults are less likely to use stereotyped judgments about others when the person is seen as distinct from the stereotype (Fiske, 2000).These results are also compatible with past findings suggesting that using a "grandparent prime" can increase children's positive ratings of older adults (Hoe & Davidson, 2002). However, while past studies have shown differences in children's ratings of older men and women (e.g., Hoe & Davidson, 2002; Jelenec & Steffens, 2002; Laditka et al., 2004; Zandi et al., 1990), no gender differences were found in the present research.

The present results suggest that children's view of older adults is not always negative. That is, it is not accurate to say that children's views of older adults always reflect negative stereotypes.Nevertheless, active older adults were not as well liked as active children, and older adults described in a negative manner were sometimes seen as more negative than children described with the same negative adjectives. Thus, the presentation of negative information can be particularly damaging to children's views of older adults, while presenting positive information can help decrease these views at least over the course of a day. It may be that promoting children's use of individual trait information, particularly counter-stereotypic trait information, may encourage children to rely less on stereotypes, at least when judging individuals. The present results also suggest that children may recall more positive than negative information, and that the presentation of positive information may be particularly important for decreasing children's reliance on stereotypes. Such results suggest the need to examine all facets of stereotype use in order to precisely identify the situations in which they will be used, and the situations in which they may affect memory and judgment of others.

CONCLUSION

The results of the present research, as well as past studies, have shown that numerous factors appear to promote stereotyping, suggesting that the opposite of these factors may reduce stereotypes and their formation in both children and adults. Mental busyness and distraction are associated with greater use of activated stereotypes (e.g., Gilbert & Hixon, 1991; Macrae, Hewstone, & Griffiths, 1993), and similarly, when a judgment situation is especially difficult or demanding, or when an overabundance of information is available, individuals may rely on simplifying strategies and stereotype-based heuristics as a way of coping (e.g., Bodenhausen, Macrae, & Sherman, 1999). Some have suggested that stereotyping is often the default strategy, and that it is only superseded by individuating strategies when there is sufficient motivation and attentional capacity to do so (Bodenhausen et al., 1999). Indeed, it has been suggested that those with firmly established stereotypes are less likely to seek out individuating information regardless of other factors (Trope & Thompson, 1997).

As noted earlier, Allport (1979) assumed that if children learn to become prejudiced through observation and reinforcement, they can learn to become less prejudiced through similar mechanisms. Unfortunately, studies have found that children's exposure to positive role models and respectful attitudes do not always result in a positive change (Cole et al., 2003; Persson & Musher-Eizenman, 2003). As Aboud (2005) has noted, "Psychologists now realize that to change an already-existing attitude requires overcoming a stubborn obstacle, namely, the tendency to dismiss contradictory attitudes and attend only to evidence confirming the existing attitude" (p. 315). In fact, parents of minority children often recognize the prejudice their children may one day face and often reveal that they try and prepare their children for it, beginning at an early age (see, e.g., Graves, 1996). Nevertheless, research has suggested that presenting positive information about others may at least be helpful in lessening the effects of negative stereotypes in children.

REFERENCES

Aboud, F. E. (1987). *The development of ethnic self-identification and attitudes*. In J. S. Phinney, & M. J. Rotheram (Eds.), Children's ethnic socialization: Pluralism and development (pp. 32-55). Newbury Park, CA: Sage Publications.

Aboud, F. E. (1988*). Children and prejudice*. NY: Basil Blackwell.

Aboud, F. E. (2003). *The formation of in-group favoritism and out-group prejudice in young children: Are they distinct attitudes?* Developmental Psychology, 39, 48-60.

Aboud, F. E. (2005).*The development of prejudice in childhood and adolescence*. In J. F. Dovidio, P. Glick, & L. A. Rudman (Eds)., On the nature of prejudice: Fifty years after Allport (pp. 310-326). Malden, MA: Blackwell Publishing.

Allport, G. W. (1954/1979*). The nature of prejudice*. Cambridge, MA: MIT Press Books.

Anderson, C., & Cromwell, R. L. (1977). *"Black is beautiful" and the color preferences of Afro-American youth*. The Journal of Negro Education, 46, 76-88.

Ansello, E. F. (1978). *Ageism- The subtle stereotype*. Childhood Education, 54, 118-122.

Asher, S. R., & Allen, V. L. (1969). *Racial preference and social comparison processes*. Journal of Social Issues, 25, 157-167.

Averhart, C. J., & Bigler, R. S. (1997). *Shades of meaning: Skin tone, racial attitudes and constructive memory in African-American children*. Journal of Experimental Child Psychology, 67, 363-388.

Baugher, R. (1973). *The skin color gradient as a factor in the racial awareness and racial attitudes of preschool children*. Unpublished Master's thesis. California State University, Fresno.

Bem, S. L. (1983). *Gender schema theory and its implications for child development: Raising gender-aschematic children in a gender-schematic society*. Signs, 8, 598-616.

Bennett, M., Barrett, M., Karakozov, R., Kipiani, G., Lyons, E., Pavlenko, V., & Riazanova, T. (2004). *Young children's evaluations of the ingroup and of outgroups: A multi-national study*. Social Development, 13, 124-141.

Bigler, R. S. (1998). *The development of social stereotyping in children*. Paper presented at the Annual Meeting of the American Educational Research Association, San Diego, CA.

Bigler, R. S., & Liben, L. S. (1993*). A cognitive-developmental approach to racial stereotyping and reconstructive memory in Euro-American children*. Child Development, 63, 351-365.

Bigler, R. S., & Liben, L. S. (2008). *A developmental intergroup theory of social stereotypes and prejudice*. In R. V. Kail (Ed.), Advances in child development and behavior, 34, (pp. 39-89). San Diego, CA: Elsevier Academic Press.

Blair, I. V., Judd, C. M., Sadler, M. S., & Jenkins, C. (2002). *The role of Afrocentric facial features in criminal sentencing*. Journal of Personality and Social Psychology, 83, 5-25.

Bodenhausen, G. V., Macrae, C. N., & Sherman, J. W. (1999). *On the dialectics of discrimination*. In S. Chaiken & Y. Trope (Eds.),Dual-process theories in social psychology (pp. 271-290). New York, NY: Guilford Press.

Brewer, M.B. (1999). *The psychology of prejudice: Ingroup love or outgroup hate?* Journal of Social Issues, 55, 429-444.

Brown, C. S., & Bigler, R. S. (2002*). Effects of minority status in the classroom on children's intergroup attitudes*. Journal of Experimental Child Psychology, 83, 77-110.

Cameron, J. A., Alvarez, J. M., Ruble, D. N., & Fuligni, A. J. (2001). *Children's lay theories about ingroups and outgroups: Reconceptualizing research on prejudice*. Personality and Social Psychology Review, 5, 118-128.

Clark, K. B., & Clark, M. P. (1939). *The development of consciousness of self and the emergence of racial identity in Negro preschool school-children*. Journal of Social Psychology, 10, 591-599.

Clark, K. B., & Clark, M. P. (1950). *Emotional factors in racial identification and preference in Negro children*. Journal of Negro Education, 19, 341-350.

Cole, C., Arafat, C., Tidhar, C., Tafesh, W., Fox, N., Killen, M., Ardila-Rey, A., Leavitt, L.,Lesser, G., Richman, B., & Yung, F. (2003). *The educational impact of Rechov Sumsum/Shara'a Simsim: A Sesame Street television series to promote respect and understanding among children living in Israel, the west Bank and Gaza*. International Journal of Behavioral Development, 27, 409-422.

Cordua, G. D., McGraw, K. O., & Drabman, R. S. (1979). *Doctor or nurse: Children's perceptions of sex-typed occupations*. Child Development, 50, 590-593.

Corenblum, B. (2003). *What children remember about ingroup and outgroup peers: Effects of stereotypes on children's processing of information about group members*. Journal of Experimental Child Psychology, 86, 32-66.

Cuddy, A. J. C., Norton, M. I., & Fiske, S. T. (2005). *This old stereotype: The pervasiveness and persistence of the elderly stereotype*. Journal of Social Issues, 61, 267-285.

Davidson, D., Cameron, P., & Jergovic, D. (1995*). The effects of children's stereotypes on their memory for elderly individuals*. Merrill-Palmer Quarterly, 41, 70-90.

Davidson, D., Luo, Z., & Fulton, B. R. (2007). *Stereotyped views of older adults in children from the People's Republic of China and from the United States*. Journal of Intergenerational Relations, 5(4), 6-24.

Davis, A. J., Martinson, I., Gan, L., Jin, Q., Liang, Y., Davis, D. B., & Lin, J. (1995). *Home care for the urban chronically ill elderly in the People's Republic of China*. International Journal of Aging and Human Development, 41, 345-358.

Deutsch, F. M., Zalenski, C. M., & Clark, M. E. (1986). *Is there a double standard for aging?* Journal of Applied Social Psychology, 16, 771-785.

Doyle, A., & Aboud, F. E. (1995). *A longitudinal study of White children's racial prejudice as a social cognitive development.* Merrill-Palmer Quarterly, 41, 209-228.

Doyle, A. B., Beaudet, J., & Aboud, F. E. (1988). *Developmental patterns in the flexibility of children's ethnic attitudes.* Journal of Cross-Cultural Psychology, 19, 3-18.

Falchikov, N. (1990). *Youthful ideas about old age: An analysis of children's drawings.*International Journal of Aging and Human Development, 31, 79-99.

Fishbein, H. D. (1996). *Peer prejudice and discrimination.* Boulder, CO: Westview Press.

Fiske, S. T. (2000). *Stereotyping, prejudice, and discrimination at the seam between the centuries: Evolution, culture, mind and brain.* European Journal of Social Psychology, 30, 299-322.

Fiske, S. T., Neuberg, S. L., Beattie, A. E., & Milberg, S. J. (1987). *Category-based and attribute-based reactions to others: Some informational conditions of stereotyping and individuating processes.* Journal of Experimental Social Psychology, 23, 399-427.

Gilbert, D. T., & Hixon, J. G. (1991). *The trouble of thinking: Activation and application of stereotypic beliefs.* Journal of Personality and Social Psychology, 60, 509-517.

Graves, S. B. (1996). *Diversity on television.* In T. MacBeth (Ed.), Tuning in to young viewers (pp. 61-86). Thousand Oaks, CA: Sage.

Hall, R. E. (2001). *The ball curve: Calculated racism and the stereotype of African-Americanmen.* Journal of Black Studies, 32, 104-119.

Hamilton, D. L., Sherman, S. J., & Ruvolo, C. M. (1990). *Stereotype-based expectancies: Effects on information processing and social behavior.*Journal of Social Issues, 46, 35-60.

Harris, M. B. (1994). *Growing old gracefully: Age concealment and gender.* Journal of Gerontology, 49, 149-158.

Harvey, R. D., LaBeach, N., Pridgen, E., & Gocial, T. M. (2005). *The intragroup stigmatization of skin tone among Black Americans.* Journal of Black Psychology, 31, 237-253.

Hoe, S., & Davidson, D. (2002). *The effects of priming on children's attitudes toward older individuals.* The International Journal of Aging and Human Development, 55, 341-366.

Isaacs, L. W., & Bearison, D. J. (1986). *The development of children's prejudice against the aged.* International Journal of Aging and Human Development, 23(3), 175-195.

Jantz, R. K., Seefeldt, C., Galper, A., & Serock, K. (1980). *The CATE: Children's attitudes toward the elderly.* Test manual. College Park, MD: University of Maryland. (ERIC Document Reproduction Service No. PSO 12399).

Jelenec, P., & Steffens, M. C. (2002). *Implicit attitudes toward elderly women and men.* Current Research in Social Psychology, 7, 275-293.

Jones, J. M. (1997). *Prejudice and racism* (2nd edition). NY: McGraw-Hill.

Justice, E., Lindsey, L., & Morrow, S. (1999*). The relation of self-perceptions to achievement among African-American preschoolers.* Journal of Black Psychology, 25, 48-60.

Keith, V. M., & Herring, C. (1991). *Skin tone and stratification in the Black community.*American Journal of Sociology, 97, 760-778.

Laditka, S. B., Fischer, M., Laditka, J. N., & Segal, D. R. (2004). *Attitudes about aging and gender among young, middle age, and older college-based students.* Educational Gerontology, 30, 403-421.

Larkin, E., Friedlander, D., Newman, S., & Goff, R. (2004). *Intergenerational relationships: Conversations on practice and research across cultures.* New York, NY: Haworth Press.

Le Palley, M. E., Reimers, S. J., Calvini, G., Spears, R., Beesley, T., & Murphy, R.A. (2010). *Stereotype formation: Biased by association.* Journal of Experimental Psychology: General, 139, 138-161.

Levy, B. (2000). *Improving memory in old age through implicit self-stereotyping.* Journal of Personality and Social Psychology, 71, 1092-1107.

Liben, L. S., & Bigler, R. S. (2002). *The developmental course of gender differentiation: Conceptualizing, measuring, and evaluating constructs and pathways.* Monographs of the Society for Research in Child Development, 67, Boston, MA: Blackwell Publishing.

Macrae, C. N., Hewstone, M., & Griffiths, R. J. (1993). *Processing load and memory for stereotype-based information.* European Journal of Social Psychology, 23, 77-87.

Maddox, K. B., & Gray, S. A. (2002). *Cognitive representations of Black Americans: Re-exploring the role of skin tone.* Personality and Social Psychology Bulletin, 28, 250-259.

McKown, C. (2004). *Age and ethnic variation in children's thinking about the nature of racism.* Applied Developmental Psychology, 25, 597-617.

McKown, C., & Weinstein, R.S. (2003). *The development and consequences of stereotype consciousness in middle childhood.* Child Development, 74, 498-515.

Memon, A., Holliday, R., & Hill, C. (2006). *Pre-event stereotypes and misinformation effects in young children.* Memory, 14, 104-114.

Mitchell, J., Wilson, K., Revicki, D., & Parker, L. (1985). *Children's perceptions of aging: A multidimensional approach to differences by age, sex, and race.* The Gerontologist, 25, 182-187.

Montepare, J. M., & Zebrowitz, L. A. (2002). *A social developmental view of ageism.* In T. D. Nelson (Ed.), Ageism: Stereotyping and prejudice against older persons (p. 77-125). Cambridge, MA: MIT Press.

Nesdale, D. (1999). *Social identity and ethnic prejudice in children.* In P. Martin & W. Nobel (Eds.), Psychology and society (pp. 92-110). Brisbane: Australian Academic Press.

Nesdale, D. (2000). *Developmental changes in children's ethnic preferences and social cognitions.* Journal of Applied Developmental Psychology, 20, 501-519.

Nesdale, D. (2001). *Development of prejudice in children.* In M. Augoustinos & K. Reynolds (Eds.), Understanding prejudice, racism and social conflict (pp. 57-72). London: Sage Publications.

Nesdale, D. (2004). *Social identity processes and children's ethnic prejudice.* In M. Bennett & F. Sani (Eds.), The development of the social self (pp. 219-245). NY: Psychology Press.

Newman, S., Faux, R. & Larimer, B. (1997). *Children's views on aging: Their attitudes and values.* The Gerontologist, 37(3), 412-417.

Patterson, M. M., & Bigler, R. S. (2007). *Effects of physical atypicality on children's social identities and intergroup attitudes.* International Journal of Behavioral Development, 31, 433-444.

Perry, D. G., & Bussey, K. (1984). *Social development.* Englewood Cliffs, NJ: Prentice-Hall.

Persson, A., & Musher-Eizenman, D.R. (2003). *The impact of a prejudice-prevention television program on young children's ideas about race.* Early Childhood Research Quarterly, 18, 530-546.

Piaget, J. (1954/1986). *The construction of reality in the child.* New York, NY: Ballatine Books.

Pfeifer, J.H., Ruble, D.N., Bachman, M.A., Alvarez, J.M., Cameron, J.A., & Fuligni, A.J. (2007). *Social identities and intergroup bias in immigrant and nonimmigrant children.* Developmental Psychology, 43, 496-507.

Porter, C. P. (1991). *Social reasons for skin tone preferences of Black school-age children.* American Journal of Orthopsychiatry, 61, 149-154.

Rice, A. S., Ruiz, R. A., Padilla, A. M. (1974). *Person perception, self-identity, and ethnic groupn preference in Anglo, Black and Chicano preschool and third grade children.* Journal of Cross-Cultural Psychology, 5, 100-108.

Robinson, T. L., & Wade, J. V. (1995). *African-American adolescents and skin color.* Journal of Black Psychology, 256-274.

Ruble, D. N., & Stangor, C. (1986). *Stalking the elusive schema: Insights from developmental and social-psychological analyses of gender schemas.* Social Cognition, 4, 227-261.

Russell, K., Wilson, M., & Hall, R. (1993). *The color complex: The politics of skin color among African-Americans.* New York, NY: Harcourt, Brace & Jovanovish.

Seefeldt, C. (1989). *Intergenerational programs--Impact on attitudes.* Journal of Children in Contemporary Society, 20, 185-194.

Seefeldt, C., & Ahn, U. R. (1990). *Korean children's attitudes toward the elderly.* International Journal of Comparative Sociology, 29, 264-269.

Seefeldt, C., Jantz, R. K., Galper, A., & Serock, K. (1977). *Using pictures to explore children's attitudes toward the elderly.* The Gerontologist, 17, 506-512.

Sherman, J. W., Gawronski, B., Gonsalkorale, K., Hugenberg, K., Allen, T. J., & Groom, C. J. (2008). *The self-regulation of automatic associations and behavioral impulses.* Psychological Review, 115, 314-335.

Smith, E. R., & Zaraté, M. A. (1992). *Exemplar-based models of social judgment.* Psychological Review, 99, 3-21.

Spencer, M. B., & Markstrom-Adams, C. (1990). *Identity processes among racial and ethnic minority children in America.* Child Development, 61, 290-310.

Srull, T. K. (1981). *Person memory: Some tests of associative storage and retrieval models.* Journal of Experimental Psychology: Human Learning & Memory, 7, 440-463.

Stangor, C., & McMillan, D. (1992). *Memory for expectancy-congruent and expectancy-incongruent information: A review of the social and social developmental literatures.* Psychological Bulletin, 111, 42-61.

Strom, R. D., Strom, S. K., Wang, C., Shen, Y., Griswold, D., Chan, H., Yang, C. (1999). *Grandparents in the United States and the People's Republic of China: A comparison of generations and cultures. International* Journal of Aging and Human Development, 49, 279-317.

Theimer, C. E., Killen, M. & Stangor, C. (2001). *Young children's evaluations of exclusion in gender-stereotypic peer contexts.* Developmental Psychology, 37, 18-27.

Trope, Y., & Thompson, E. P. (1997). *Looking for truth in all the wrong places: Asymmetric search of individuating information about stereotyped group members.* Journal of Personality and Social Psychology, 73, 229-241.

Turner, J. C., Hogg, M. A., Oakes, P. J., Reicher, S.D., & Wetherell, M. S. (1987). *Rediscovering the social group: A self-categorization theory.* Oxford: Basil Blackwell.

Wade, T. J., & Bielitz, S. (2005). *The differential effect of skin color on attractiveness, personality evaluations, and perceived life success of African-Americans.* Journal of Black Psychology, 31, 215-236.

Wang, Q. (2001). *Culture effects on adults' earliest childhood recollection and self-description: Implications for the relation between memory and self.* Journal of Personality and Social Psychology, 81, 220-233.

Wang, Q. (2006). *Relations of maternal style and child self-concept to autobiographical memories in Chinese, Chinese Immigrant, and European American 3-year-olds.* Child Development, 77, 1794-1809.

Weiland, A., & Coughlin, R. (1979). *Self-identification and preferences. A comparison of White and Mexican-American first and third graders.* Journal of Cross Cultural Psychology, 10, 356-365.

Williams, T. L., & Davidson, D. (2009). *Interracial and intra-racial stereotypes and constructive memory in 7- and 9-year-old African-American children.* Journal of Applied Developmental Psychology, 30, 366-377.

Zandi, T., Mirle, J., & Jarvis, P. (1990). *Children's attitudes toward older individuals: A comparison of two ethnic groups.* International Journal of Aging and Human Development, 30, 161-174.

In: Psychology of Stereotypes
Editor: Eleanor L. Simon

ISBN: 978-1-61761-463-7
©2011 Nova Science Publishers, Inc.

Chapter 5

BAYESIAN RACISM: A MODERN EXPRESSION OF CONTEMPORARY PREJUDICE

Eric Luis Uhlmann[*1] *and Victoria L. Brescoll*[2]
[1]Northwestern University
[2]Yale University

ABSTRACT

The present chapter identifies, assesses, and examines the correlates of a previously understudied expression of contemporary prejudice— *Bayesian racism*, the belief that it is rational to discriminate against individuals based on stereotypes about their racial group. Individual differences in Bayesian racism are strongly related to intergroup prejudice and *negatively* correlated with indices of reliance on probabilities and logical thinking. Moreover, individuals who endorse Bayesian racism are unwilling to rely on base rates unfavorable to a high-status ingroup (i.e., Ivy League students). We relate the concept of Bayesian racism to existing theories of intergroup prejudice and outline future directions for research on the underpinnings of such beliefs.

Keywords: Bayesian racism, Bayesian prejudice, stereotyping, rationality, attitudes

Taxi drivers, storekeepers, and women who clutch their purse or cross the street [are] amateur statisticians acting on impressionistic but not unreasonable generalizations of the sort we all make in other contexts every day. Such people are unlikely to be intimidated by accusations of prejudice. For them, the charges are meaningless, because the prejudice is warranted. In this context, a bigot is simply a sociologist without credentials.
-- Dinesh D'Souza, The End of Racism (p. 268)

Opinions similar to those espoused by D'Souza are echoed not only by other political pundits (e.g., Malkin, 2004) but also by many laypeople (Khan & Lambert, 2001) and

---

* CONTACT: Eric Luis Uhlmann, Ford Motor Company Center for Global Citizenship, Kellogg School of Management, Northwestern University, Donald P. Jacobs Center, 2001 Sheridan Road, Evanston, IL 60208-2001, Tel: (203)-687-9269, E-mail: e-uhlmann@northwestern.edu

intellectuals from a variety of academic fields (e.g., Arkes & Tetlock, 2004; Fox, 1992; Levin, 1997; McCauley, Jussim, & Lee, 1995; Phelps, 1972; Wilson, 2002). Such commentators argue that people engage in stereotype-based discrimination out of a desire to make accurate judgments, rather than because of irrational prejudices (for rejoinders, see Armour, 1997; Banaji & Bhaskar, 2000; Glaser, 2001, 2006; Stangor, 1995). Indeed, the purported accuracy of stereotype-based judgments is among the last socially acceptable justifications for explicitly discriminating against members of racial minorities.

Are people who endorse stereotype-based discrimination naïve statisticians, as D'Souza (1995) argues, or do other motives underlie such judgments? The research reviewed here suggests the belief that it is rational to discriminate against individuals based on stereotypes about their racial group is primarily an expression of prejudice, not a personal conviction in the usefulness of base rates. The utility of using base rates to discriminate against others serves as a justification for prejudiced beliefs and judgments. Indeed, such beliefs represent a significant manifestation of contemporary prejudice that we term *Bayesian racism*.

THEORETICAL UNDERPINNINGS OF BAYESIAN RACISM

A wealth of prior theoretical and empirical work is consistent with the concept of Bayesian racism. Relevant research has examined the rationalization of prejudice and inequality, the construct of symbolic racism, and the effects of the motive to make accurate judgments on stereotyping.

The Motivated Rationalization of Prejudice

A number of theories of intergroup attitudes suggest that prejudice is expressed in increasingly subtle, rationalizable ways (Crandall & Eshleman, 2003; Gaertner& Dovidio, 1986; Snyder, Kleck, Strenta, & Mentzer, 1979). One key moderator of the expression of prejudice is attributional ambiguity— the extent to which there are multiple plausible explanations for the judgment or behavior (Jones & Davis, 1965; Kelley, 1971). Consistent with this, people avoid contact with and are less likely to come to the aid of members of stigmatized groups, but mainly in ambiguous situations in which such behavior is not clearly attributable to prejudice (Gaertner & Dovidio, 1986). In one classic study, college students were asked to choose between two seating areas. In the first area, their potential seating partner was physically disabled, and in the second he was not. The experimenters further manipulated whether the same or different movies were playing in the two areas. Participants overwhelmingly chose not to sit with a disabled student, but only when they could justify their decision as stemming from a desire to see a different movie (Snyder et al., 1979).

Such justifications are aided and abetted by basic psychological processesinvolving motivated reasoning (Ditto & Lopez, 1992; Dunning & Cohen, 1992;Haidt, 2001; Kunda, 1990; Kunda & Spencer, 2003; Lord, Ross, & Lepper, 1979; Pyszczynski& Greenberg, 1987). Numerous empirical studies demonstrate that people are adept at shifting seemingly objective standards in order to reach desired conclusions (Dunning & Cohen, 1992;Kunda, 1987; Simon, Snow, & Read, 2004). For example, judgmental standards are shifted to rationalize favoritism toward applicants from groups stereotypically suited for the job (Hodson, Dovidio, & Gaertner, 2002;Norton, Vandello, & Darley, 2004; Uhlmann & Cohen, 2005). In one study, male participants told that a male applicant for the job of police chief had a formal education, but lacked "street" experience, subsequently rated a formal education as crucial to the job of police chief. However, when he had considerable street experience but lacked a formal education, the importance of a formal education was downplayed. No such favoritism was displayed toward female applicants for police chief (Uhlmann & Cohen, 2005).

More complex ideologies and beliefs systems are also employed as rationalizations for intergroup bias and inequality (Jost, Banaji, & Nosek, 2004; Sidanius & Pratto, 1999). For example, one way in which the desire to uphold hierarchical social arrangements is expressed is through legitimizing ideologies such as the Protestant work ethic. Consistent with this hypothesis, endorsement of the Protestant ethic mediates the relationship between anti-egalitarian values and opposition to affirmative action (Sidanius & Pratto, 1999). These findings suggest that an appeal to base rates similarly injects attributional ambiguity into group-based preferences, making it unclear whether prejudice or a reasonable reliance on statistical probabilities is at work.

Symbolic Racism

Theories of symbolic or modern racism propose that in the post-civil rights era, a new, politicized form of prejudice has risen to replace blatant forms of racism (Kinder & Sears, 1981; McConahey, 1986). Symbolic racism is conceptualized as a blend of anti-Black affect and traditional American values such as individual merit (Sears & Henry, 2003). Example items from scales of symbolic racism include"It's really a matter of people not trying hard enough; if Blacks would only try harder they could be just as well-off as Whites," and "Irish, Italian, Jewish and many other minorities overcame prejudice and worked their way up.Blacks should do the same." Measures based on these andother similar questions explain unique variance in attitudes toward affirmative action (Kinder & Sears, 1981; McConahey, 1986) and racial discrimination in some studies (Beal, O'Neal, Ong, & Ruscher, 2000; McConahay, 1983;Nail, Harton, & Decker, 2003) suggesting that symbolic racism is tapping into a psychological construct that other more traditional scales measuring racial prejudice are not.

Both symbolic racismand Bayesian racism suggest that prejudice can be couched in terms of more socially acceptable values such as individualism and the rational use of base rates.At the same time, there are major differences between the concepts of symbolic and Bayesian racism. First and foremost, symbolic racism is conceptualized as an "emergent" form of racism that draws on anti-Black affect and traditional values but it is reducible to neither (Kinder & Sears, 1981; Sears & Henry, 2003). Traditional values such as individual merit are a causally potent contributor to symbolic racism, such that a commitment to these values predisposes one to endorse symbolic racism. Consistent with this, symbolic racism is positively correlated with conservatism and other traditional values (Kinder & Sears, 1981; Sears & Henry, 2003).

In contrast, we argue that in the case of Bayesian racism, the utility of statistical probabilities serves as an excuse for the expression of prejudice. Just as the desire to see a different movie provides an excuse for avoiding contact with a member of a stigmatized group (Snyder, et al., 1979), base rates provide a ready excuse for the expression of prejudice. From our theoretical perspective, a personal conviction in the usefulness of probabilities does not predispose individuals to endorse Bayesian racism. If so, individuals who endorse the use of statistical probabilities more generally should *not* be any more likely to endorse Bayesian racism. Symbolic and Bayesian racism therefore represent qualitatively distinct sets of beliefs with different theoretical underpinnings.

Effects of the Accuracy Motive on Stereotyping

There are additional empirical reasons to suspect that individuals who engage in stereotype-based discrimination are not simply seeking to enhance the accuracy of their judgments. Indeed, motivating people to make accurate judgments systematically *decreases*, rather than increases, reliance on social stereotypes (Bogart, Ryan, & Stefanov, 1999; Fiske & Neuberg, 1990; Moreno & Bodenhausen, 1999; Neuberg & Fiske, 1987; Rudman, 1998). This is the case regardless of whether participants are directly instructed to be accurate (Neuberg & Fiske, 1987) or motivated to be accurate by being told that the amount of money they earn will depend in part on the target person's performance (Neuberg & Fiske, 1987; Rudman, 1998). This is consistent with the idea that social perceivers look beyond stereotypes and at individuating information about a person when motivated to think carefully and be accurate (Fiske & Neuberg, 1990). The relationship between the motivation to be accurate and social stereotyping is therefore directly opposite to that predicted by some defenders of stereotyping.

REVIEW OF EMPIRICAL FINDINGS

This led us to hypothesize that prejudice, rather than a reliance on base rates, underlies the belief that it is appropriate to discriminate against individuals based on stereotypes of their racial group (Uhlmann, Brescoll, & Machery, in press).In this case, the value of using statistical probabilities serves as a justification for prejudiced beliefs and judgments.Approval of stereotype-based discrimination therefore represents an important expression of contemporary prejudice that we term Bayesian racism. Our first study assessed the correlations between individual differences in Bayesian racism and established measures of prejudice and a reliance on statistical probabilities. Our second study examined whether individuals who endorsed Bayesian racism were willing to use base rates unfavorable to a high-status ingroup, and further assessed the empirical relationship between symbolic and Bayesian racism.

In our first study, a sample of White adultlaypersons completed the following questionnaires:

Bayesian Racism Scale (BRS). Participants completed an individual differences measure of Bayesian racism based on larger pools of items developed byUhlmann and Banaji (2001),McDell, Uhlmann, Omoregie, and Banaji (2006), and Uhlmann et al. (in press). The Bayesian racism items were as follows: "When the only thing you know about someone is their race, it makes sense to use your knowledge of their racial group to form an impression of them," "If your personal safety is at stake, it's sensible to avoid members of ethnic groups known to behave more aggressively," "If you want to make accurate predictions, you should use information about a person's ethnic group when deciding if they will perform well," "Law enforcement officers should pay particular attention to those social groups more heavily involved in crime, even if this means focusing on members of particular ethnic groups," "Law enforcement officers should act as if members of all racial groups are equally likely to commit crimes" (reverse scored), and "It is always wrong to avoid someone because members of their racial group are more likely to commit violent crimes" (reverse scored).

Social Dominance Orientation. The Sidanius and Pratto (1999) SDO scale assesses support for hierarchical relationships between social groups (e.g., "It's really not a big problem if some people have more of a chance in life than others,""Some groups of people are simply not the equals of others").Social dominance is considered a type of intergroup prejudice (Sidanius & Pratto, 1999).

Biological attributions for race differences in crime. Participants indicated their agreement with the statement "Blacks commit more violent crimes than Whites because they are biologically more aggressive."

Racist joke. Participants were presented with a joke implying Black Americans are intellectually inferior to animals and indicated whether they found the joke amusing (Talbot, 2003). The joke read: "A Black guy walks into a bar with a huge, beautiful parrot on his shoulder. The bartender says: 'Wow, that's amazing, where did you get that?' And the parrot says: 'Africa.'"

Racial affect. Participants reported their attitudes towards White Americans, Black Americans, Hispanic Americans, and Arab Americans on feeling thermometer scales (i.e., "How warmly (or coldly) do you feel toward the following groups?") using a scale from 0 (extremely cold) to 100 (extremely warm).

Attitudes towards statistics. The Wise (1985) measure assesses the value respondents place on statistical probabilities (e.g., "By relying on statistical probabilities, we can make our judgments much more accurate").

Rationality scale. The rationality subscale of the Rational-Experiential inventory assesses the degree of logical thought participants put into their judgments (Epstein, Pacini, Denes-Raj, & Heier, 1996). Representative rationality items are "I enjoy thinking in abstract terms" and "Knowing the answer without having to understand the reasoning behind it is good enough for me (reverse coded)."

Table 1 displays the correlations between the key measures. As seen in the Table, endorsement of Bayesian racism was positively correlated with Social Dominance Orientation ($r = .55$), attributing race differences in crime to genetic factors($r = .53$), and finding the racist joke amusing ($r = .41$). Bayesian racism was unrelated to attitudes towards Whites ($r = -.02$)but was associated with negative feelings towards Blacks ($r = -.45$), Hispanics ($r = -.46$) and Arabs ($r = -.49$).

Figure 1 displays feelings towards Black, Hispanic and Arab Americans relative to White Americans among participants above and below the median on Bayesian racism. As seen in the Figure, participants high in Bayesian racism reported significantly more favorable feelings towards Whites than all three minority groups. Participants low in Bayesian racism reported significantly less ethnocentric attitudes.

Table 1. Means, Standard Deviations, and Correlations

Variable	Mean	SD	1	2	3	4	5	6	7	8	9
1. Bayesian Racism	3.18	.96									
2. Social Dominance Orientation	3.12	1.53	.55**								
3. Crime differences genetic	2.13	1.35	.53**	.55**							
4. Racist joke funny	3.46	2.15	.41**	.22*	.29**						
5. Attitude towards Whites	87.10	16.85	-.02	.01	.06	.02					
6. Attitude towards Blacks	69.12	22.76	-.45**	-.33**	-.38**	-.30**	.34**				
7. Attitude towards Hispanics	64.82	24.80	-.46**	-.26**	-.35**	-.35**	.26**	.66**			
8. Attitudes toward Arabs	57.52	27.46	-.49**	-.28**	-.23*	-.27**	.18†	.54**	.62**		
9. Attitudes towards Statistics	4.31	.82	-.19*	-.07	-.10	.11	-.11	.01	.03	.10	
REI Rationality Subscale		4.98	1.01	-.26**			-.22*	-.32**	-.13	-.09	.19†	.12†

Note. N = 109.

†p<.10, *p < .05, **p < .01

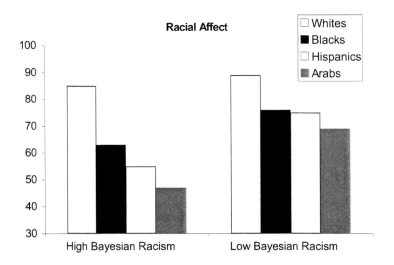

Figure 1. Attitudes towards Whites, Blacks, Hispanics, and Arabs among participants high and low in Bayesian racism. Higher numbers indicate more positive attitudes towards members of each racial group.

Remarkably, Bayesian racism was significantly *negatively* correlated with the value participants placed on the use of statistical probabilities (*r* = -.19). In other words, participants who believed it appropriate to apply base rates about racial groups to individual group members were actually significantly *less* likely to endorse the use of probabilities more generally. Similarly, Bayesian racism was significantly negatively related to the tendency to think logically about one's judgments (*r* = -.26).

In sum, the belief that it is appropriate to discriminate against individuals based on stereotypes about their racial group– what we have termed Bayesian racism– is positively correlated with indices of prejudice and negatively associated with the tendency to rely on statistical probabilities and think logically. Whether a person endorses using base rates about Black Americans has surprisingly little to do with their feelings about base rates, and a lot to do with their feelings toward Black people.

Our first study revealed that individual differences in Bayesian racism were negatively related to the tendency to rely on statistical probabilities. Our second study examined whether participants who endorsed Bayesian racism would be willing to use a base rate unfavorable to a high-status ingroup. Specifically we examined whether undergraduates at an Ivy League institution would endorse "Bayesian" discrimination against Ivy League students.

Of further interest was the empirical relationship between Bayesian racism and symbolic racism. Although these two sets of beliefs are conceptually distinct, they may or may not be highly correlated. Participants therefore also completed the Modern Racism Scale (MRS; McConahay, Hardee, & Batts, 1981), one of the most widely used individual differences measure of symbolic racism in psychology.

A sample of White undergraduates at an Ivy League university completed the Bayesian Racism Scale, the MRS, and responded to a scenario dealing with the job and graduate school applications of Ivy League students. The scenario noted that Ivy League universities are documented to have more grade inflation than non-Ivy League schools (Rosovsky & Hartley, 2002). Participants were then asked whether, given this fact, graduate schools and potential employers should take into consideration grade inflation at Ivy League universities when considering applicants from such schools.

Most participants disagreed with adjusting for grade inflation at Ivy League universities when considering applicants from such schools. More importantly, responses to the grade inflation scenario did not vary by Bayesian racism scores ($r = .02$), or by MRS scores ($r = .07$). Participants who endorsed Bayesian racism significantly opposed corrections for grade inflation in the Ivy League. In other words, participants who endorsed Bayesian racism—the belief that it is rational to use base rates to discriminate against racial minorities—were unwilling to use a base rate promoting discrimination against a high-status ingroup.

MRS scores were positively correlated with Bayesian racism ($r = .27$). Thus, as suggested by our theorizing regarding the underpinnings of Bayesian racism, symbolic and Bayesian racism are related but not redundant.

THE NATURE OF BAYESIAN RACISM

The research reviewed here identifies, assesses, and examines the correlates of a previously understudied expression of contemporary prejudice – Bayesian racism—the belief that it is rational to discriminate against individuals based on stereotypes about their racial group. Bayesian racism is strongly correlated with intergroup prejudice and negatively related to indices of reliance on probabilities. Moreover, individuals high in Bayesian racism did not endorse the use of base rates unfavorable to a high-status ingroup. Specifically, Ivy League students who endorsed Bayesian racism rejected adjusting for grade inflation at Ivy League universities when evaluating the applicants from such schools. Below we relate these findings to major theories of contemporary prejudice and outline future directions for research on Bayesian racism.

Relationship to Existing Theories of Prejudice

The concepts of symbolic and Bayesian racism share the theoretical premise that prejudice is often justified using more socially acceptable values such as individualism and the rational use of probabilities. More generally, measures of symbolic and Bayesian racism both assess beliefs unsympathetic toward the plight of African-Americans. It is therefore not surprising that our second study revealed a significant correlation between Bayesian racism and symbolic racism ($r = .27$), as did an additional supplemental data collection ($r = .37$).

But at the same time, symbolic racism is conceptualized as a *blend* of anti-Black effect and traditional American values, such that a commitment to values such as individualism predisposes one to endorse symbolic racism (Sears & Henry, 2003). In contrast, we argue that in the case of Bayesian racism, the utility of statistical base rates serves as an excuse for the expression of prejudice. Individuals who view statistical probabilities as particularly useful are not any more likely to endorse Bayesian racism.

Partly for this reason, Bayesian racism is not subject to some of the interpretational ambiguities that may apply to symbolic racism. Critics have argued that because measures of symbolic racism are designed to assess a blend of anti-Black affect and traditional American values, individuals who endorse such values (e.g., politically conservatives) may be falsely categorized as racists (Sniderman &Tetlock, 1986; for a defense of the symbolic racism construct, see Sears & Henry, 2005).

In contrast, traditional values do not represent potential confounding variables when it comes to Bayesian racism. Individuals who endorse stereotype-based discrimination couch their arguments in terms of the rational use of probabilities, not traditional values. Moreover, while symbolic racism measures and conservative values are positively correlated, Bayesian racism and attitudes towards the use of statistical probabilities are negatively correlated– precisely the wrong direction for an ostensive confounding variable. Thus, one is on shaky empirical ground arguing that individuals who endorse Bayesian racism are merely rational actors engaging in the logical use of statistical probabilities.

Rather than an offshoot of symbolic racism theory, Bayesian racism is consistent with the expression of prejudice under conditions of attributional ambiguity (Crandall & Eshleman, 2003; Gaertner & Dovidio, 1986; Snyder et al., 1979) and ideological rationalizations for discrimination and inequality (Jost & Banaji, 1994; Jost et al., 2004; Sidanius & Pratto, 1999). As blatant forms of racism have gradually declined, prejudice is expressed in increasingly indirect ways. For example, White Americans are less willing to help Black people than White people, but only when such acts can be attributed to causes other than race(Gaertner & Dovidio, 1977, 1986). White Americans may similarly express their prejudices to a greater extent when bias can be justified as the rational use of probabilities.

Future Directions

The research reviewed here represents an initial inquiry into the nature of Bayesian racism and leaves a number of important questions unanswered. One remaining goal is to account for the variability in Bayesian racism scores that is not explained by our indices of intergroup prejudice and reliance on probabilities. Prejudice that goes unreported on questionnaire measures may account for some of this residual variance. In other words, Bayesian racism may stem in part from prejudices participants are unwilling to admit to others (Jones & Sigall, 1971) or perhaps even to themselves (Banaji & Bhaskar, 2000). At the same time, there may be alternative measures of base rate use that do correlate positively with Bayesian racism scores.

Another important avenue for future research is how Bayesian racism develops across the lifespan. Biases against racial outgroups are observed as early as age three (Aboud, 1988; Augoustinos& Rosewarne, 2001; Baron & Banaji, 2006; Olson, Banaji, Dweck, & Spelke, 2006; Olson, Dunham, Dweck, Spelke, & Banaji, 2008). Thus, group-based prejudices develop earlier in life than opinions on the utility of base rates. This suggests the use of statistical information to discriminate often serves to justify pre-existing prejudices.

There may also be subgroups of individuals who endorse Bayesian racism because they genuinely do favor the use of base rates more generally. For example, graduate training in statistics may lead to greater endorsement of Bayesian racism items without any increase in negative feelings towards racial minorities.

Another remaining issue is what psychological factors drive endorsement or rejection of Bayesian racism among individuals who bear the brunt of stereotype-based discrimination.We were unable to answer this question due to the limited availability of Black participants in our samples.One might expect, for example, that a bias in favor of their ingroup would lead Black Americans to reject Bayesian racism.However, work on the rationalization of social hierarchies finds that members of low status groups frequently endorse beliefs that run counter to the interest of their group (Jost, 2001; Jost, Pelham, Sheldon, & Sullivan, 2003; Sidanius & Pratto, 1999). This raises the possibility that Bayesian racism is also common among Blacks, Hispanics, and others who are frequently the target of stereotype-based discrimination.

There are also reasons to anticipate cultural and subcultural differences in Bayesian racism. Membersof cultures with a history of collective punishment may be more willing todiscriminate against individuals based on group stereotypes. Also, high SES individuals aremore likely than low SES individuals to exhibit cognitive dissonance (Snibbe & Markus, 2005), which suggests they may feelespecially motivated to rationalize their prejudices by appealing to base rates.Finally, in cultures torn by intergroup violence and overt hatred, Bayesian racism may not be a central aspect of intergroup relations.

CONCLUSION

The present chapter draws on empirical findings and theories of intergroup attitudes in identifying an understudied expression of contemporary prejudice. Bayesian racism correlates highly with established measures of prejudice and it is either unrelated or negatively related to a reliance on more neutral probabilities.In other words, individuals who endorse "rational racism" (i.e., Bayesian racist attitudes) are far more consistently racist than they are rational.These findings call into question the popular belief that people who use stereotypes are rational actors engaging in a logical use of base rates.

REFERENCES

Aboud, F. E. (1988). *Children and prejudice*. New York: Basil Blackwell.

Arkes, H. R., & Tetlock, P. E. (2004). Attributions of implicit prejudice, or "Would Jesse Jackson 'fail' the Implicit Association Test?" *Psychological Inquiry, 15*, 257-279.

Armour, J.D. (1997). *Negrophobia and reasonable racism: The hidden costs of being black in America*. New York, NY: New York University Press.

Augoustinos, M., & Rosewarne, D. L. (2001). Stereotype knowledge and prejudice in children. *British Journal of Developmental Psychology, 19*, 143 – 156.

Banaji, M.R., & Bhaskar, R. (2000).Implicit stereotypes and memory: The bounded rationality of social beliefs.In D.L. Schacter, & E. Scarry (Eds.). *Memory, brain, and belief.* (pp. 139-175). Cambridge, MA: Harvard University Press.

Baron, A.S. & Banaji, M.R. (2006).The development of implicit attitudes: Evidence of race evaluations from ages 6, 10 & adulthood.*Psychological Science, 17,* 53-58.

Beal, D.J., O'Neal, E.C., Ong, J., & Ruscher, J.B. (2000). The ways and means of interracial aggression: Modern racists' use of covert retaliation. *Personality and Social Psychology Bulletin, 26,* 1225-1238.

Bogart, L.M., Ryan, C.S., &Stefanov, M. (1999). Effects of stereotypes and outcome dependency on the processing of information about group members. *Group Processes & Intergroup Relations, 2*, 31-50.

Crandall, C.S.& Eshleman, A. (2003). A justification-suppression model of the expression and experience of prejudice. *Psychological Bulletin, 129*, 414-446.

Devine, P.G. (1989). Stereotypes and prejudice: Their automatic and controlled components. *Journal of Personality and Social Psychology, 56,* 5-18.

Ditto, P. H., & Lopez, D. F. (1992). Motivated skepticism: The use of differential decision criteria for preferred and nonpreferred conclusions. *Journal of Personality and Social Psychology, 63*, 568-584.

D'Souza, D. (1995). *The end of racism*. New York, NY: Free Press.

Dunning, D., & Cohen, G.L. (1992). Egocentric definitions of traits and abilities in social judgment. *Journal of Personality and Social Psychology, 63,* 341-355.

Epstein, S., Pacini, R., Denes-Raj, V., & Heier, H. (1996). Individual differences in intuitive-experiential and analytical-rational thinking styles. *Journal of Personality and Social Psychology, 71*, 390-405.

Fiske, S. T. & Neuberg, S. L. (1990). A continuum of impression formation, from category-based to individuating processes: Influences of information and motivation on attention and interpretation. In M. P. Zanna (Ed.), *Advances in experimental social psychology*(Vol. 23, pp. 1—74). New York: Academic Press.

Fox, R. (1992). Prejudice and the unfinished mind: A new look at an old failing. *Psychological Inquiry, 3*, 137-152.

Gaertner, S. L., & Dovidio, J. F. (1977). The subtlety of white racism, arousal and helping behavior. *Journal of Personality and Social Psychology, 35,* 691-707.

Gaertner, S. L., & Dovidio, J. F. (1986). The aversive form of racism. In J. F. Dovidio & S. L. Gaertner (Eds.), *Prejudice, discrimination, and racism* (pp. 61-89). Orlando, FL: Academic Press.

Glaser, J. (2001). The fallacy inherent in racial profiling. In D. Hazen, T. Hausman, T. Straus, & M. Chihara (Eds.), *After 9/11: Solutions for a Saner World.* San Francisco, CA: Alternet.org.

Glaser, J. (2006). The efficacy and effect of racial profiling: A mathematical simulation approach. *Journal of Policy Analysis and Management, 25,* 395-416.

Haidt, J. (2001). The emotional dog and its rational tail: A social intuitionist approach to moral judgment. *Psychological Review, 108,* 814-834.

Hodson, G., Dovidio, J.F., & Gaertner, S.L. (2002). Processes in racial discrimination: Differential weighting of conflicting information. *Personality and Social Psychology Bulletin, 28,* 460-471.

Jones, E. E., & Davis, K. E.(1965).From acts to dispositions:The attribution process in person perception.In L. Berkowitz (Ed.), *Advances in experimental social psychology:Vol. 2.* (pp. 219-266).New York:Academic Press.

Jones, E. E., & Sigall, H. (1971). The bogus pipeline: A new paradigm for measuring affect andattitude. *Psychological Bulletin, 76,* 349-364.

Jost, J. (2001). Outgroup favoritism and the theory of system justification: A paradigm for investigating the effects of socio-economic success on stereotype content. In G. Moskowitz (Ed.), *Cognitive social psychology: The princeton symposium on the legacy and future of social cognition.* Hillsdale, NJ: Erlbaum.

Jost, J. T., & Banaji, M. R. (1994). The role of stereotyping in system-justification and the production of false consciousness. *British Journal of Social Psychology, 33,* 1-27.

Jost, J.T., Banaji, M.R., & Nosek, B.A. (2004). A decade of system justification theory:accumulated evidence of conscious and unconscious bolstering of the status quo. *Political Psychology, 25,* 881-919.

Jost, J. T., Pelham, B. W., Sheldon, O., & Sullivan, B. N. (2003). Social inequality and the reduction of ideological dissonance on behalf of the system: Evidence of enhanced system justification among the disadvantaged. *European Journal of Social Psychology, 33,* 13-36, 2003

Kelley, H. H.(1971).*Attribution in social interaction.*Morristown, NJ:General Learning Press.

Khan, S.R., & Lambert, A.J. (2001). Perceptions of rational discrimination: When do people attempt to justify race-based prejudice? *Basic and Applied Social Psychology; 23,* 42-54.

Kinder, D., & Sears, D. O. (1981). Prejudice and politics: Symbolic racism versus racial threats to the good Life. *Journal of Personality and Social Psychology, 40,* 414-431.

Kunda, Z. (1987). Motivated inference: Self-serving generation and evaluation of causal theories.*Journal of Personality and Social Psychology, 53,* 37-54.

Kunda, Z. (1990). The case for motivated reasoning. *Psychological Bulletin, 108,* 480-498.

Kunda, Z., & Spencer, S.J. (2003). When do stereotypes come to mind and when do they color judgment? A goal-based theoretical framework for stereotype activation and application. *Psychological Bulletin, 129,* 522-544.

Levin, M. (1997). *Why race matters: Race differences and what they mean.*Westport, CT: Praeger Publishers.

Lord., C. G., Ross, L., & Lepper, M. R. (1979). Biased assimilation and attitude polarization: The effects of prior theories on subsequently considered evidence. *Journal of Personality and Social Psychology, 37,* 2098-2109.

Malkin, M. (2004). *In defense of internment: The case for "racial profiling" in World War I.* New York: Regnery Publishing.

McCauley, C.R., Jussim, L.J., & Lee, Y. (1995). Stereotype accuracy: Toward appreciating group differences. In Y. Lee, L.J. Jussim & C.R.McCauley (Eds.). *Stereotype accuracy: Toward appreciating group differences.* Washington, DC: American Psychological Association.

McConahay, J. B. (1983). Modern racism and modern discrimination: The effects of race, racial attitudes, and context on simulated hiring decisions. *Personality and Social Psychology Bulletin, 9,* 551-558.

McConahay, J.B. (1986). Modern racism, ambivalence, and the Modern Racism Scale. In J.F. Dovidio & S. Gaertner (Eds.), *Prejudice, discrimination, & racism* (pp. 91-125). San Diego, CA: Academic Press.

McConahay, J. B., Hardee, B. B., & Batts, V. (1981). Has racism declined in America? It depends on who is asking and what is being asked. *Journal of Conflict Resolution, 25,* 563-579.

McDell, J., Uhlmann, E.L., Omoregie, H., & Banaji, M.R. (2006).*The psychological correlates of Bayesian racism.*Poster presented at the Society of Personality and Social Psychology. Palm Springs, CA.

Moreno, K.N., & Bodenhausen, G.V. (1999). Resisting stereotype change: The role of motivation and attentional capacity in defending social beliefs. *Group Processes & Intergroup Relations, 2,* 5-16.

Nail, P.R., Harton, H.C., & Decker, B.P. (2003). Political orientation and modern versus aversive racism: Tests of Dovidio and Gaertner's (1998) integrated model. *Journal of Personality and Social Psychology, 84,* 754-770.

Neuberg, S.L., & Fiske, S.T. (1987). Motivational influences on impression formation: Outcome dependency, accuracy-driven attention, and individuating processes. *Journal of Personality and Social Psychology, 53,* 431-444.

Norton, M.I., Vandello, J.A., & Darley, J.M. (2004). Casuistry and social category bias. *Journal of Personality and Social Psychology, 87,* 817-831.

Olson, K. R., Banaji, M. R., S., Dweck, C., & Spelke, E. (2006). Children's bias against unlucky people and groups. *Psychological Science, 17,* 845-846.

Olson, K., Dunham, Y., Dweck, C. S., Spelke, E. S., & Banaji, M. R. (2008).Judgments of the lucky across development and culture. *Journal of Personality and Social Psychology, 94,* 757-776.

Phelps, E. (1972). The statistical theory of racism and sexism. *American Economic Review, 62,* 659-661.

Pyszczynski, T., & Greenberg, J. (1987). Toward an integration of cognitive and motivational perspectives on social inference: A biased hypothesis-testing model. In L. Berkowitz (Ed.), *Advances in experimental social psychology,* Vol. 20. (pp. 297-340). San Diego, CA: Academic Press.

Rosovsky, H., & Hartley, M. (2002). *Evaluation and the academy: Are we doing the right thing?* Cambridge, MA: American Academy of Arts and Sciences.

Rudman, L. A. (1998). Self-promotion as a risk factor for women: The costs and benefits of counterstereotypical impression management. *Journal of Personality and Social Psychology, 74*, 629-645.

Sears, D. O., & Henry, P. J. (2003). The origins of symbolic racism. *Journal of Personality and Social Psychology*, 85, 259-275.

Sears, D. O, & Henry, P. J. (2005). Over thirty years later: A contemporary look at symbolic racism and its critics. *Advances in Experimental Social Psychology, 37*, 95-150.

Sidanius, J., & Pratto, F. (1999). *Social dominance: An intergroup theory of social hierarchy and oppression.* New York, NY: Cambridge University Press.

Simon, D., Snow, C.J., & Read, S.J. (2004). The redux of cognitive consistency theories: Evidence judgments by constraint satisfaction. *Journal of Personality and Social Psychology, 86*, 814-837.

Snibbe, A. & Markus, H.R. (2005). You can't always get what you want: Educational attainment, agency, and choice. *Journal of Personality and Social Psychology, 88*, 703-720.

Sniderman, P.M., &Tetlock, P.E. (1986). Symbolic racism: Problems of political motive attribution. *Journal of Social Issues, 42*, 129-150.

Snyder, M. L., Kleck, R. E., Strenta, A., & Mentzer, S. J. (1979). Avoidance of the handicapped: An attributional ambiguity analysis.*Journal of Personality and Social Psychology, 37*, 2297-2306.

Stangor, C. (1995). Content and application inaccuracy in social stereotyping.In Y. Lee, L.J. Jussim & C.R. McCauley (Eds.). *Stereotype accuracy: Toward appreciating group differences.* Washington, DC: American Psychological Association.

Talbot, C. (2003). *Reactions to racism: Effects of relationship, responsibility, and racial attitudes.* Unpublished thesis, School of Psychological Science, La Trobe University, Bundoora Campus Victoria, Australia.

Uhlmann, E.L., & Banaji, M.R. (2001). *The correlates of Bayesian racism.* Unpublished raw data.

Uhlmann, E.L., Brescoll, V.L., & Machery, E. (in press). The motives underlying stereotype-based discrimination against members of stigmatized groups. *Social Justice Research.*

Uhlmann, E.L., & Cohen, G.L. (2005). Constructed criteria:Redefining merit to justify discrimination. *Psychological Science, 16*, 474-480.

Wilson, J.Q. (2002). Crime. In Thernstrom, A., & Thernstrom, S. (Eds.) *Beyond the color line: New perspectives on race and ethnicity in America.* New York, NY: Manhattan Institute.

Wise, S. L. (1985). The development and validation of a scale measuring attitudes toward statistics. *Educational and Psychological Measurement, 45*, 401-405.

In: Psychology of Stereotypes
Editor: Eleanor L. Simon

ISBN: 978-1-61761-463-7
©2011 Nova Science Publishers, Inc.

Chapter 6

STEREOTYPES ON THE BRAIN: USING EVENT-RELATED BRAIN POTENTIALS TO INVESTIGATE STEREOTYPING

Silvia Tomelleri and Luigi Castelli

Dipartimento di Psicologia dello Sviluppo e della Socializzazione, University of Padova, Padova, Italy

ABSTRACT

According to a social cognitive perspective, stereotypes have been defined as cognitive structures that contain the perceiver's knowledge, beliefs, and expectations about social groups (Hamilton & Trolier, 1986). Perceivers regularly rely on stereotypes to simplify the complex social environment and quickly make sense of the social world. Because of the importance and pervasiveness of stereotypes in everyday life, these phenomena have been at the top of the interests of social psychological research. Traditionally, the nature and functions of stereotypes have been primarily investigated by using self-report measures (i.e., questionnaires) and more cognitive measures (mainly based on response latencies and accuracy) in order to infer the underlying cognitive mechanisms. However, responses in computerized tasks represent the final outcome of a large number of intervening cognitive processes, and variations in the response latencies may not often be attributed to a single specific process. Recently, the emergence of neuroscience has provided social psychology with new methods that can override this limitation. In particular, the event-related brain potential (ERP) technique can provide a direct, on line, continuous measure of processing between a stimulus and a response, giving direct access to the various stages of information processing between perception and behavior (Luck, 2005).

The main goal of this chapter is to introduce readers to recent social neuroscience research that has applied the ERP approach to the study of stereotypes and to show the major advances that it has produced in relation with the existing theories. We will first provide a brief overview of the recording, theory, and interpretation of the ERPs. Then, we will review studies that have used ERPs as useful tools to further investigate various aspects related to stereotyping:a) stereotype violation and confirmation; b) the influence of stereotype activation on behavioral processes, with specific attention given to the mechanisms involved in self-regulation; c) individual and situational differences in self-regulatory processes linked to the expression of stereotypes. In the chapter we will try to highlight how the integration of different methods, theories, and levels of analysis from both neuroscience and social psychology (i.e., the social neuroscience approach) can greatly facilitate a most comprehensive understanding of different important aspects of the human social mind.

WHAT ARE STEREOTYPES?

Try to briefly think about each of the following categories of people: African Americans, women, elderly, and painters. What comes to your mind? Probably, you would quickly and easily generate quite a detailed view of what these groups of people look like in terms of physical features as well as personality traits, attitudes, beliefs, and social roles that characterize them. For instance, you may imagine African Americans with dark skin and very curly hair, or you may think about them as athletic and musical. You may further see women as dependent, emotional, and with capacities for humanistic disciplines and for taking care of others; elderly as wise and harmless; and painters as nonconformist and creative.

The mental representations you generate for each of the aforementioned groups, on the basis of your knowledge and past experiences, have been traditionally conceptualized in social psychology as stereotypes. More specifically, stereotypes have been defined as cognitive structures that contain the perceiver's knowledge, beliefs, and expectations about social groups (Hamilton & Trolier, 1986, p. 133). Differently said, stereotypes are images that pop up in our mind once we think about social groups (Lippmann, 1922). Importantly, these mental representations are not limited to relevant ethnic, gender, age or occupational groups, but they apply to whatever social grouping is salient to the perceiver and may refer to a prototypical instance of people from a social group as well as to a group as a whole (see Hamilton & Sherman, 1994 for a review). To sum up, stereotypes are mental representations that contain knowledge of what a social group or their group members are like (or should be like). Importantly, as such, stereotypes may act as general expectancies that guide the processing of information (i.e., the way people perceive, process, store, and retrieve information) and influence judgments and behaviors toward social groups (Mackie, Hamilton, Susskind, & Rosselli, 1996; Stangor & Schaller, 1996). In other words, stereotypes influence how we think about, judge, attend to, feel, remember, and act toward others.

It is important to note that stereotyping (i.e., the use of stereotypic knowledge to mentally represent others) is an ordinary, functional, and adaptive process we can hardly do without (van Knippenberg & Dijksterhuis, 2000). Indeed, given the cognitive limitations of perceivers in a complex and demanding social environment, people regularly rely on stereotypes in order to ease the burden of the overwhelming social information and to quickly and easily understand the social world by forming articulated representations of others in a manner that is efficient in terms of mental energy and time (Allport, 1954; Brewer, 1988; Fiske & Neuberg, 1990; Gibert & Hixon, 1991; Macrae & Bodehausen, 2000; Macrae, Milne, & Bodenhausen, 1994). In spite of these benefits, the use of stereotypes in social judgment carries important social costs. Indeed, the mental representation of people belonging to outgroups is often characterized by the presence of negative traits, which may lead stereotyped people to experience prejudice, discrimination, and several forms of inequalities and disadvantages in different social domains (Fiske, 1998). For this reason, in Western societies the use of stereotypes to form impressions about others is often normatively sanctioned and considered as an inappropriate way to deal with members of stigmatized groups (Crandall, Eshleman, & O'Brien, 2002). Despite these normative concerns, a consistent body of research has shown that stereotypes are still pervasive and resistant to change since they continue to linger at an automatic level, without conscious intent and awareness (e.g., Dovidio & Gaertner, 2000).

Stereotyping indeed can be manifested at two different levels: automatic and controlled (Devine, 1989). On the controlled level, stereotyping is the outcome of conscious and intentional processes that, as said, are however often inhibited due to the pressure of the normative rules that have developed in Western societies in the last decades. On the less controlled side, instead, stereotyping is sustained by the automatic activation of stereotypes. Even if they are not personally endorsed, stereotypes are shared and widespread within societies and represent a form of over-learned knowledge due to the repeated exposure to cultural images, media portraits, and so on (e.g., Devine, 1989; Weisbuch, Pauker, & Ambady, 2009). In other words, even people who consciously reject the use of stereotypes to describe others, and do not personally endorse them, are nevertheless likely to automatically activate stereotypical mental associations about social groups once exposed to group members (Brewer, 1988; Devine, 1989; Fiske & Neuberg, 1990; Wittenbrink, Judd, & Park, 1997). This, in turn, may then impact on several spontaneous behaviors (McConnell & Leibold, 2001). It is however important to mention that in contrast to this "inevitability of stereotype activation" view, several researchers have demonstrated that there are meaningful individual and situational differences in stereotype activation and use (Blair, 2002; Castelli & Tomelleri, 2008; Gilbert & Hixon, 1991; Lepore & Brown, 1997; Macrae, Bodenhausen, Milne, Thorn, & Castelli, 1997; Spencer, Fein, Wolfe, & Dunn, 1998; Wittenbrink, Judd, & Park, 2001). For instance, egalitarian people who do not endorse stereotypic beliefs, and are motivated to expunge them from their social behaviors, also develop more efficient (automatic) self-regulatory processes that rapidly suppress stereotype activation (e.g., Moskowitz, Gollwitzer, Wasel, & Shaal, 1999; Moskowitz, Salomon, & Taylor, 2000).

STEREOTYPES: METHODOLOGICAL ISSUES

Because of the pervasiveness and the impact that stereotyping exerts in shaping interpersonal and intergroup relations in everyday life, this phenomenon has been always at the forefront of social psychological research. Traditionally, stereotypes have been investigated through the use of self-report measures (e.g., adjectives checklists or rating scales), such as the Modern Racism Scale (McConahay, 1986) or the Subtle and Blatant Prejudice Scale (Pettigrew & Meertens, 1995). More recently, new methods derived from cognitive psychology have been developed. These measurement techniques, commonly called in the psychophysiology field of research by the general term "behavioral measures", are mainly based on computerized tasks, like priming procedures, which assess response latencies and errors (e.g., Fazio, Jackson, Dunton, & Williams, 1995; Macrae, Bodenhausen, & Milne, 1995). They allowed a more fine-grained understanding of the automatic and less controlled cognitive mechanisms underlying stereotype activation and use, thus circumventing social desirability concerns associated to verbal reports. All these methods have been very useful in understanding the nature and functions of stereotypes. However, some key aspects of the psychology of stereotyping have received less attention than others and some major questions concerning these phenomena and the cognitive processes underlying them remain still to be answered. The reason for these gaps is, at least partially, to be found in the difficulties and limitations intrinsic to the research methodology that has been primarily used to investigate this topic. The use of stereotypes is a complex multistage process that involves and integrates various aspects of the information processing, like attention, perception and cognition, that may take place in a very rapid temporal succession, and that behavioral measures are unable to separately pick up. Behavioral measures represent indeed the final outcome of all these intervening processes, occurring from stimulus presentation to behavioral expression, but variation in response latencies or error rates may not be attributed to a single specific process.

Importantly, this limit has recently led scientists to expand their approach and to complement the existing behavioral measures with methods commonly used in the related areas of cognitive neuroscience and psychophysiology. The emergence of neuroscience has indeed provided social psychology with new techniques, like the functional brain imaging techniques (e.g., functional magnetic resonance imaging, fMRI; or event-related brain potentials, ERPs), able to override the above-mentioned methodological limitation giving new insights in the investigation of crucial aspects of social behavior. Besides providing new tools to better understand long-standing key questions of social cognition, the integration of theories and methods of cognitive neuroscience to the social psychology perspective is now expanding classic theories and models. Moreover, this integration between disciplines is beneficial to derive novel hypotheses about important social processes, especially those that were relatively unexplored, due to methodological limitations, like self-regulatory mechanisms in the expression of stereotypes and prejudice.

This chapter will particularly focus on the application of the event-related brain potentials (i.e., ERPs) as a prominent approach to understand the processes underlying stereotype activation and use. After providing a brief overview of ERP recording, theory, and interpretation (for a more detailed view see Bartholow & Amodio, 2009; Luck, 2005), highlighting the major advantages that this technique offers relative to traditional behavioral measures, we specifically examine recent social neuroscience studies in which ERPs have been profitably used to further address several questions revolving around stereotyping.

UNDERSTANDING ERPS: AN OVERVIEW

What Are ERPs?

Physiologically, ERPs are summated post-synaptic potentials from a large group of synchronously firing neurons primarily in the cerebral cortex (Coles & Rugg, 1995; Fabiani, Gratton, & Federmeier, 2007). ERPs index the electrical brain activity that occurs in preparation for or in response to discrete events, such as stimulus presentation or a response. Most importantly from a conceptual point of view, ERPs are considered as neural manifestations of specific psychological operations associated to the event of interest for the researcher.

Measuring, Recording, and Deriving ERPs

ERPs can be recorded non-invasively from the surface of the scalp with an array of electrodes, made of highly conductive materials, which are placed at various scalp locations and connected to amplifiers that magnify the weak electrical signals of the neurons in a way that can be measured. Note that in order to obtain an ERP, at least two electrodes are needed for measuring the difference in voltage. Usually, the electrodes are fixed in a stretch nylon cap, which can be worn by participants, and they are placed on the scalp according to the International 10-20 System (Jasper, 1958) to permit and facilitate between-experiment and between-laboratory comparisons.

A signal filtering and averaging analysis, which is composed by several steps (see Luck 2005; Fabiani et al., 2007 for a more detailed view), is used to discriminate and extract the very small ERPs (i.e., signal) from the much higher amplitude background EEG (i.e., noise). Importantly, considering a large numbers of trials, any brain activity that is unrelated to the event of interest (i.e., not time-locked) is assumed to vary randomly across samples and thus will average to zero. Instead, any brain activity that is consistently related to an event (i.e., time-locked) will remain in the average rendering the event related potentials visible and quantifiable. The resulting ERP waveform is a time-by-voltage function that is composed of several positive and negative deflections. Those deflections are called peaks, waves or components and are labeled with P or N, to indicate the positive or negative trend of the function, and with a number to indicate the typical timing of the peak (e.g., P600 is a positive going component that usually has its maximum peak at 600 ms after the onset of the event of interest). In other cases, these deflections are named according to the psychological processes that are known to represent (e.g., error-related negativity, ERN, is a negative going component that occurs when making an error). Further, each ERP component has its own characteristic distribution in the scalp (e.g., frontal, occipital).

Interpreting ERP Components

The importance of the ERPs to study social psychological processes comes from the specific association of each ERP component with a distinct mental operation. Indeed, the sequence of the ongoing waves following the presentation of a target stimulus reflects closely each step in sensory, cognitive and motor processes of the information processing chain. In other words, the sequence of ERP components reflects the flow of the information processing through the brain.

There are three important aspects that characterize each ERP component and that furnish important information to researchers: amplitude, latency, and scalp spatial distribution. The amplitude of a component (in microvolts; μV) is thought to reflect the extent to which the specific psychological process associated to the component has been engaged. There are mainly two different modes to calculate the amplitude of a component depending upon the specific question being asked and the component that is examined. One possibility is to score the amplitude by determining the peak amplitude of the ERP component of interest (i.e., peak-to-peak measure), commonly defined as the minimum or maximum voltage within a predefined time window in which that component emerges. Alternatively, amplitude can be computed as the average voltage within that time window. The latency of a component (in milliseconds, ms) is known to reflect the point in time by which a process has been completed and corresponds to the point in time at which the component reaches its peak value (Rugg & Coles, 1995). Further, the scalp spatial distribution of a component (i.e., topography) is used to estimate the neuroanatomical source of the process associated to it.

It is important to note that, despite of the excellent temporal resolution offered by the ERP technique (i.e., in the order of a millisecond), spatial information is poor and this makes it difficult to clearly determine the functional locus of the neural activity. However, in recent years several steps forward have been made in the assessment of the neural sources of ERPs by using scalp recoding from a dense array of electrodes combined with interpolated mapping and complex source analysis algorithms (e.g., Brain Electrical Source Analysis procedure; BESA).

ERPs Advantages to Study Stereotyping

There are several unique advantages that make the ERP technique well suited to study stereotyping. One of major advantages is that event-related brain potentials can provide a direct, on line, continuous measure of processing between the presentation of a stimulus and a response, giving direct access to the various stages of information processing between perception and behavior, making also possible to determine which stage (or stages) is affected by a specific experimental manipulation (Luck, 2005). Indeed, as multidimensional measures of processing, ERPs represent a powerful tool in order to directly and non-invasively assess brain activity and to unpack the stereotyping process providing separate information for each one of its multiple underpinning cognitive sub-processes. Moreover, ERPs can provide an excellent temporal resolution that, combined with their ongoing measurement starting from the onset of a stimulus presentation, permit to assess operations occurring very early in processing and to pick up social cognitive processes assumed to unfold very quickly. Furthermore, the ERP approach allows keeping track of the time course of stereotype activation and use providing new insights about both the more automatic and controlled aspects of these processes.

Another valuable advantage of using ERPs concerns the possibility to measure the information processing even in the absence of participants' overt response. Further, even in cases in which experimental tasks required the generation of a response from participants, ERPs (e.g., P300 latency) can furnish information that, in contrast with traditional behavioral methods, can more purely index cognitive processes independently of motor operations related to response preparation and execution (e.g., Ito & Cacioppo, 2007; Kutas, McCarthy, & Donchin, 1977).

Taken as a whole, ERPs can chart the neural correlates of stereotyping and can reveal important information on several critical aspects of this core process that otherwise would be impossible to assess. ERPs overcome some of the previously mentioned limitations of self-reports and behavioral measures, and their use can thus be profitably integrated with those more traditional measures.

With this background in mind, we next consider specific studies that have relied on ERPs to better understand stereotyping. In reviewing the major advances that this recent social neuroscience work has produced, we particularly focus on three main key aspects of stereotyping on which the next section is divided: a) stereotype violation and confirmation; b) the influence of stereotype activation on behavioral processes, with a specific attention to the mechanisms involved in self-regulation; c) individual and situational differences in the self-regulatory processes linked to the expression of stereotypes.

ERPs Application to Study Stereotyping

Neural Correlates of Stereotype Violation and Confirmation

As previously mentioned, stereotypes may act as expectancies that, once formed,influence subsequent information processing (usually in a confirmatory and self-perpetuating manner), as well as judgments and behavior (Hamilton & Sherman, 1994). What happens when perceivers encounter individuals or events that clearly do not conform to stereotype-based expectations?

Recent ERP research has investigated this question by examining the neural correlates of stereotype-based expectancies in cases of violation and confirmation. In one early interesting study, Osterhout, Bersick, and McLaughlin (1997) asked participants to read sentences containing reflexive pronouns whose antecedent nouns were either congruent or incongruent with the definitional male or female (e.g., uncle, actress) or stereotypically male or female roles (e.g., electrician, aerobics instructor), while ERPs were recorded. In other words, sentences that either violated or confirmed the definitional male or female noun-pronoun agreement were presented to participants (e.g., "The man prepared *herself/himself* for the interview"). More important to the aim of this chapter, the authors monitored ERPs in response to sentences that were congruent with gender-based occupational stereotypes (i.e., confirming the male/female stereotype-based expectancies; e.g., "The doctor prepared *himself* for the operation") versus stereotype-incongruent (i.e., disconfirming the male/female stereotype-based expectations; e.g., "The doctor prepared *herself* for the operation"), with regard to the antecedent noun and the reflexive pronoun. The authors reasoned that readers should react to the incongruence between the subject and pronoun when they refer to a different gender (e.g., uncle-her), but also to stereotype-inconsistent sentences (e.g., doctor-her) if stereotypes are automatically activated. The grammatical violations, as well as the violation of stereotype-based expectancies, were expected to impact onto the ERP response, as indexed by the P300-P600 complex components (also labeled more generically as the late positive potential or LPP).

To sum up, this research was designed to answer to the following questions: can violations of gender-based occupational stereotypesbe indexed by ERP responses? If yes, do grammatical and stereotype-based violations differ?

Results showed that both definitionally and stereotypically incongruent sentences produced a similar brain response in terms of a larger positive going ERP component starting at about 500 ms (i.e., P600) than did non-violation sentences. Importantly, this effect occurred even when participants overtly judged grammatical and syntactic aspects of the sentences as being correct. These findings permit to draw several clear-cut important observations.First, ERPseffectively assess violations of gender-based occupational stereotypesthat produce a clear and measurable ERP response. Indeed, violations of gender-based stereotypes produce distinct larger amplitude P600 as compared tostereotype confirming sentences. Second, the qualitative nature of this ERP effect provides a basis for making hypotheses about mental representations and their underlying processes in cases of stereotype-based expectancy violations. Indeed, the P600 effect elicited by violations of the noun-pronoun agreement represents an anomaly effect, showing that disconfirming stereotype-based expectancies are perceived and processed as an error and proving initial evidence of a relationship between ERPs amplitude and the processing of anomalous (i.e., unexpected) social information. Third, the persistence of the positive ongoing ERP response (i.e., P600) to stereotype violation, independently of participants' acceptability judgment of the grammatical and syntactical aspects of the sentence, indicates that ERPs reveal sensivity to gender stereotypes even when participants overtly acknowledge that the sentence is formally correct. More importantly, even when perceivers view gender stereotypical occupational roles as possible they still perceive them as an anomaly at a more automatic level. This last finding seems indeed to show an automatic activation of gender-based stereotypes, highlighting that ERPs are helpful tools to reveal automatic judgment processes.

These results, beyond furnishing new important insights, nicely support the existing literature at least in relation to two different aspects. First, Osterhout and colleagues (1997) provided evidence about the automaticity of stereotype activation in line with a consistent body of literature, which relied on reaction time-based tasks (e.g., Banaji & Greenwald, 1994, 1995; Banaji & Hardin, 1996; Bargh, 1994; Devine, 1989). For instance, Banaji and Hardin (1996) found that when a pronoun was presented immediately after a priming word indicating a gender-stereotypical role (e.g., *secretary, doctor*), subsequent responses were faster to pronouns that were congruent rather than incongruent with the gender stereotype activated by the priming word. Further, this was true both when the task required gender-related judgments (i.e., is the pronoun male or female?) and gender irrelevant judgments (i.e., is the word a pronoun or not?). These results demonstrate the spontaneous activation of gender stereotypes related to occupational roles in accordance with the above-mentioned ERPs study (Osterhout et al., 1997). Second, the ERP findings indicate that gender-based stereotype violations are processed as anomalies (Osterhout et al., 1997). This piece of evidence can be considered as a necessary first step to subsequent explanatory processes predicting that when perceivers are exposed to individuals who unambiguously disconfirm stereotypes, they may be skilled to find out ways to view such cases as exceptions to a generally valid rule. Indeed, facing this disconfirming information as an anomaly, people can easily resolve such inconsistencies keeping intact their original stereotypical views. This further indicates how stereotypes are remarkably resistant to change (for reviews, see Hewstone, 1994; Fiske, 1998).

In a recent study, conceptually similar to Osterhout and colleagues' work (1997), Bartholow and his collaborators (Bartholow, Fabiani, Gratton, & Bettencout, 2001) established behavioral expectations by having participants read paragraphs describing a target person, that were pre-tested to strongly convey an intended trait inference, and asking them to form an impression about this person. Following each paragraph, sentences depicting behaviors performed by the target person were presented one word at the time, while ERPs were recorded. Importantly, those sentences either described an expectancy consistent, an expectancy violating, or an expectancy irrelevant behavior in relation to the initial description of the target person. In line with earlier ERPs research, expectancy discrepant behaviors elicited a larger amplitude positive wave than did expectancy confirming behaviors. Further, the time course of this effect was similar to that obtained by Osterhout and colleagues (1997), showing that differences in positivity due to expectancies violation began at about 300 to 400 ms, peaked at around 500 to 600 ms, and then finally disappeared around 800 ms post-stimulus. It is further interesting to note that while expectancy relevant behaviors elicited a positivity in the ERP (both when violating and confirming the established impression about the target person), the expectancy irrelevant behaviors produced instead a negativity in the ERPs. In other words, beyond corroborating previous findings by Osterhout et al. (1997), this study further suggests that perceivers differently engage in the initial stages of the social information processing depending on whether information is related to an already existing impression or not. Moreover, this result can account for the frequent recall advantage for expectancy-relevant violating information (e.g., Stangor & McMillan, 1992), by showing that differences in this early engagement in information processing, indexed by the ERP positivity, are likely to involve different working memory operations that influence later consolidation in long-term memory producing such a recall advantage.

More recently, based on these research findings, Bartholow et al. (Bartholow, Dickter, & Sestir, 2006; Experiment 1) investigated the P300-P600 ERP positivity as a neural correlate of stereotype violation in a different procedure, namely in a stereotype priming paradigm (see Dovidio, Evans, & Tyler, 1986). Importantly, before performing the priming task, an equal number of participants was randomly assigned to consume either an alcoholic beverage dose or a placebo. Alcohol assumption is indeed known to deplete control related resources and to specifically impair control resources associated with inhibition (e.g., Easdon & Vogel-Sprott, 2000). After this beverage consumption, ERPs, as well as reaction time measures, were recorded while participants responded to trait words that were stereotype consistent, stereotype inconsistent or irrelevant with regard to racial stereotypes. Immediately before the trait word, either a Black or a White face was briefly primed. Replicating previous works using a similar paradigm, results showed faster reaction times to stereotype consistent than stereotype inconsistent words (Dovidio et al., 1986; Dovidio, Kawakami, Johnson, Johnson, & Howard, 1997). Moreover, ERP results demonstrated that stereotype violating words (e.g., *musical* following a White face prime) elicited a larger (i.e., amplitude) and slower (i.e., latency) P300 ERP component compared to stereotype consistent words. This research replicated previous work (Osterhout et al., 1997; Bartholow et al., 2001), and extended it by showing that stereotype violating information is more difficult to be processed as indicated by the P300 latency data, which is a pure index of cognitive operations that is not dependent on response related motor processes (whereas RTs are deeply affected). Importantly, none of these indicators of stereotype violation (i.e., RTs and P300 amplitude and latency) was affected by alcohol intoxication supporting again the view about the automatic activation of stereotypes.

In another recent paper, gender-based stereotype violations have been investigated by recording ERPs from a rather different intriguing perspective as compared to the previously reviewed papers (Lattner & Friederici, 2003). The authors indeed investigated whether contextual information conveyed by the speaker's voice leads to the creation of gender stereotypical expectations and whether violating those expectations would lead to a distinct ERP. It is worth noting that in everyday verbal communications the listener can extract several social cues about the speaker from his/her voice (e.g., gender and age) that may activate stereotypes in a similar way as physical features do. Lattner and Friederici (2003) recorded ERPs while presenting auditory sentences that could be either stereotypically male or female self-referenced utterances. In the stereotype confirming conditions, speakers pronounced sentences whose content was stereotypically consistent with the gender of speaker (e.g., a male voice who says "I like to play soccer"). In the stereotype violating conditions, stereotypically male statements were instead produced by female speakers, and vice versa (e.g., a male voice who says "I like to wear lipstick"). Results showed that sentences in which the final word violated the listeners' stereotypical expectations, compared with sentences that contained a matching words, elicited a larger ERP late positivity (i.e., P600 component). These findings reveal that the information conveyed by a speaker's voice has a clear impact on the content processing paralleling what found by Osterthout et al. (1997) for reflexive pronouns that either matched or mismatched gender-based occupational stereotypes.

To sum up, as underlined thorough the review, the use of ERP technique in the domains of stereotype violation and confirmation supports and integrates earlier studies by furnishing fundamental new insights useful to better understand the nature of stereotyping and its underlying processes in relation to classical theoretical models.

THE INFLUENCE OF STEREOTYPE ACTIVATION ON BEHAVIORAL PROCESSES, WITH A SPECIFIC ATTENTION TO THE MECHANISMS INVOLVED IN SELF-REGULATION

As previously mentioned, it is now well-established that stereotypic notions can automatically break into perceiver's thoughts once exposed to social group members independently of whether they are desired or not. Stereotypes are indeed so pervasive and widespread within a cultureso that to become over-learned and to be automatically triggered even by people with sincere egalitarian beliefs who do not subscribe them (Devine, 1989). Low-prejudiced people holding egalitarian beliefs may indeed often face uncomfortable conflict situations between these automatically activated tendencies toward stereotypic thinking and their personal egalitarian values that mark stereotype use as inappropriate (e.g., Plant & Devine, 1998). In other words, egalitarian people may be strongly motivated to effortfully override the expression of stereotypes,in line with their personal beliefs, resulting in a self-regulatory challenge.

In the social cognition literature, several models have been proposed seeking to account for the regulation of automatically activated biased tendencies (e.g., Bodenhausen & Macrae, 1998; Devine, 1989; Monteith, 1993). Importantly, these models revolved around the central assumption that control mechanisms are deployed only following people awareness of a failure or a potential failure to control stereotyping. Hence, without conscious reflection about a biased response or a potential bias, regulatory strategies cannot be engaged to prevent for future failure. Despite the advances produced by these models in the understanding of behavior regulation, some aspects of the processes through which people may detect and override automatically activated stereotype-based tendencies remain still unclear. In particular, these traditional models have not addressed the possibility that regulatory processes may detect and override biased responses in a single, rapidly unfolding step. The traditional tools of socio-cognitive psychology (e.g., computerized reaction-time tasks) are indeed poorly equipped for measuring cognitive processes that occur very rapidly and very early in processing. This gap can however be addressed by employing the ERP technique and by further applying general neurocognitive models of control and behavioral regulation (e.g., Botvinick, Braver, Barch, Carter, & Cohen, 2001). In an initial successful application of this approach, Amodio, Harmon-Jones, Devine, Curtin, Hartely, and Covert (2004) examined the processes underlying behavioral regulation in the context of stereotyping. In particular, they sought to dissociate the process of conflict monitoring from the implementation of control to unintentional biased responses. This point can indeed be crucial in order to further determine whether a failure to override automatic stereotype activation may be due to the inability to detect the undesired influence of stereotypes or to a failure to implement control, even when the unwanted influences of stereotypes are detected.

Applying the neural model of cognitive control proposed by Botvinik et al. (2001), Amodio and his colleagues (2004) suggested that the self-regulation of responses to stereotyped targets is supported by two separate neural systems that work in concert to produce a behavior. The first mechanism is the *conflict-detection* system, which monitors ongoing responses and it is sensitive to competition between different response tendencies. This initial process is constantly active, it operates without conscious awareness (Nieuwenhuis, Ridderinkhhof, Blom, Band, & Kok, 2001) and it is supported by the activity of the dorsal region of the anterior cingulate cortex (i.e., dACC) that is reflected by the error-related negativity (ERN; a response-locked component peaking around 50-80 ms post error response) and the N200, a stimulus-locked component of the ERP. Once a conflict is detected, the second *regulatory* system comes into play in the deliberate effort to implement the intended response while inhibiting the unwanted tendency. This second system is supported by the activity of the dorsolateral prefrontal cortex (i.e., dlPFC) that is often associated with the Negative Slow Wave component (i.e., NSW) of the ERP. In order to understand whether the failure to override the unwanted influence of stereotypes is due to a failure in the conflict detection system or to the regulatory functions, Amodio et al. (2004) asked participants to complete a sequential priming task specifically called Weapon Identification Task (WIT; Payne, 2001) while EEG, as well as reaction time and accuracy measures, were recorded. In this task, participants are required to quickly and accurately classify guns and tools that are preceded by briefly presented Black and White male prime faces. Amodio et al. (2004) further told participants that the erroneous classification of tools as guns after the presentation of Black faces would be indicative of racial prejudice in terms of an inappropriate use of Black stereotypes, which typically associate violence and danger to Black people (Devine & Elliot, 1995). Previous work (Payne, 2001) demonstrated that Black faces facilitated the correct categorization of guns. In addiction, when forced to respond very quickly, participants are more likely to miscategorize tools as guns following Back faces than White faces. This pattern of results suggests that a correct response on Black-tool trials should require greater control relative to Black-gun trials, due to the influence of racial stereotypes.

To examine the role of conflict detection associated with stereotype-based tendencies, Amodio et al. (2004) compared the ERN amplitude, as a neural index of the conflict detection system, on trials that should required greater response control (i.e., Black-tool trials) with trials in which such control should not be active or at least less required (i.e., Black-gun trials). Findings supported the predictions, showing larger ERNs on Black-tool trials than in Black-gun trials, indicating a stronger response conflict and a greater need for control.

Moreover, although prevalent responses across participants showed a pattern of automatic race bias, participants with a larger ERN were those with a higher level of control during the task, in terms of greater accuracy and slower response times following errors.

Overall, these findings indicate that stereotype-biased responses may occur despite the activation of neural systems that detect the need for control. In other words, the failure to control stereotype-biased tendencies seems to be related to problems specifically linked to the regulatory system. Importantly, these results extended traditional models of cognitive control by showing that: a) conflict detection processes are activated at very early stages of response implementation; b) bias detection in controlling undesired automatically activated tendencies does not necessarily operate under conscious deliberation but can also function below awareness as indicated by the ERN component.

In a recent similar study, Bartholow et al. (2006; Experiment 2) used ERPs to examine more directly the role of regulatory mechanisms of cognitive control in the inhibition of stereotype-biased responses. More specifically, the study aimed at investigating how a temporary impairment of regulatory control by alcohol intoxication would affect the expression of such a bias and the neural processes relevant to its control (i.e., conflict detection system and regulatory system). Participants were randomly assigned to consume a beverage containing a dose of alcohol or a placebodose before performing the so-called Go-stop task (Logan, 1994). Alcohol consumption specifically impairs control resources associated with inhibitory processes while it has no influence on the activation and implementation of responses (e.g., Easdon & Vogel-Sprott, 2000; Fillmore & Vogel-Sprott, 1999, 2000).

The Go-stop priming task was specifically designed and adapted to separately assess, relying on ERPs, the inhibition and expression of stereotype-based tendencies. The task required participants to respond as quickly as possible to targets words, which were either stereotype-consistent or stereotype-inconsistent trait words, after the presentation of White and Black man faces (i.e., primes). Importantly, a visual cue following the presentation of each target word signaled participants to respond (i.e., go-signal; 75% of the trials) or to withhold their responses (i.e., stop-signal; 25% of the trials). Previous research indicated that once stereotypes are activated, stereotype-consistent relatively to stereotype-inconsistent responses are facilitated (e.g., Dovidio et al., 1986; 1997; Perdue, Dovidio, Gutman, & Tyler, 1990). Based on these findings the authors predicted that a more effortful inhibitory control should be expected to withhold responses on stereotype-consistent trials than on stereotype-incongruent trials (i.e., larger N2 amplitude). Furthermore, the stereotype-consistent trials should be particularly difficult to be managed by alcohol-intoxicated participants. To test their predictions, Bartholow et al. (2006) considered the amplitude of two ERP components: the N200, associated with the conflict detection system, and the Negative Slow Wave that indexed the activity in the regulatory control system. Results showed that NSW was overall larger for participants in the placebo condition (vs. intoxicated subjects)especially in the stereotype-consistent stop trials. These findings indicated that the inhibition of the predominant stereotype-congruent response required the engagement of greater regulatory control resources than the inhibition of stereotype-inconsistent responses. Furthermore, this process was found to be significantly impaired by alcohol consumption. Similarly, the N200 component was larger in response to the stereotype-consistent stop trials relative to the stereotype-inconsistent stop trials. Importantly, no differences in the N200 amplitude emerged across beverage groups to indicate that the conflict monitoring system is not impaired by alcohol intoxication. The different pattern of results observed for the NSW and the N200 supported the idea that alcohol causes the selective impairment in the regulatory system processes while it has no impact on conflict monitoring functions and, more important, that the control of stereotype biased responses involved multiple dissociable mechanisms.

These findings extend Amodio et al.'s research (2004) demonstrating that the neural detection of stereotype-based expressions does not ensure unbiased responses. Indeed, even though the need to suppress stereotype-biased tendencies has been detected by the conflict monitoring system of cognitive control, the successful inhibition of stereotype-based responses can only be obtained if the subsequent regulatory system is intact.

In another recent study, Correll, Urland and Ito (2006) examined the mechanisms underlying the behavior regulation of stereotype-biased responses by measuring individual responses in a particularly externally valid experimental paradigm, namely the shooter task (Correll, Park, Judd, & Wittenbrink, 2002). In this paradigm participants view pictures of Black and White man holding handguns or harmless objects (e.g., wallets, cell phones) and are asked to decide, as quickly and as accurately as possible, "to shoot" armed targets and "not shoot" unarmed targets. With the aim of examining whether behavior regulation processes may differ for Black and White targets in the decision to shoot, Correll et al. (2006) recorded ERPs, as well as traditional behavioral measures, while participants performed the shooting task. The authors considered the N200 ERP component that, as previously mentioned, has been linked with the ACC activity and the detection of conflict (Nieuwenhuis, Yeung, Van Den Wildenberg, & Ridderinkhof, 2003, Van Veen & Carter, 2002). In line with previous work (Correll et al., 2002), participants were faster and more accurate "to shoot" armed Blacks relative to Whites. Furthermore, they were faster and more accurate to "not shoot" unarmed White as compared with Black targets. More importantly, the N200 ERP component was larger to White than Black targets indicating differences in conflict monitoring processes as a function of target race, even though race was task irrelevant. For a combination of different reasons such as the experimental design and task instructions, "shoot" tends to be the dominant response in this task. Coherently to this, participants were faster and more accurate in "shoot" than to "not shoot" decisions. Coupled with the prevalent stereotype that depicts Black people as more violent than White people, the authors reasoned that deciding whether to shoot an unarmed White man should elicit greater conflict than making the same decision about unarmed Black man. This prediction was supported by Correll et al.'s findings (2006) in terms of larger N200s to unarmed White relative to unarmed Black targets. Furthermore, results showed that the difference in conflict monitoring depending on targets' race predicts subsequent behavior in terms of a biased response on reaction times. Differently said, participants with a larger race difference in the N200 were those who also showed larger differences on the reaction time measure. Of great importance, the authors also found that the N200 effect mediated the relation between stereotype endorsement (assessed with a self-report questionnaire) and biased response latencies. In other words, participants who more strongly associated Black vs. White people with violence, aggression, and danger were those who showed more stereotype-biased behaviors. Importantly, this effect was accounted for by stronger neural signal of conflict monitoring detection associated to White compared to Black people, indexed by the N200 ERP component.

Taken together, these findings unpack the sub-processes involved in response control providing important new insights on the specific neural underpinnings of stereotype-based expression and its cognitive control. Furthermore, more in general, these data indicate that to fully account for the observation of a stereotype-based behavior it is important to consider both stereotype activation mechanisms as well as the role played by cognitive control.

INDIVIDUAL AND SITUATIONAL DIFFERENCES IN SELF-REGULATORY PROCESSES LINKED TO THE EXPRESSION OF STEREOTYPES

The research reviewed in the previous section demonstrated that conflict monitoring is one of the key mechanisms involved in the regulation of stereotyping. A step further within this framework has been made by trying to identify the individual differencesrelated to this process and, more specifically, to clarify why some egalitarian individuals are more effective than others (with equally egalitarian beliefs) to provide unbiased responses (e.g., Devine, Plant, Amodio, Harmon-Jones, & Vance, 2002). In other words, among truly egalitarians some people appear to be good at regulating biased responses, whereas others turn out to be poor regulators. Recently, Amodio, Devine, and Harmon-Jones (2008) addressed this issue hypothesizing that the variability in regulating stereotyped expressions among low-prejudice people may stem from a different sensivity in their conflict monitoring systems. More specifically, Amodio et al. (2008) predicted that the neural systems of poor regulators, relative to good regulators, might be less sensitive to detect the conflict between the automatically activated stereotype-based tendencies and the egalitarian intentions.

Past work suggested that individual differences in stereotype and prejudice control may correspond to differences in the internal vs. external motivation to respond without prejudice (Amodio, Harmon-Jones, & Devine, 2003; Devine et al., 2002). According to Plant and Devine (1998), who developed a questionnaire to measure these differences among individuals, people internally motivated to control biased expressions are those who desire to act in an egalitarian manner because of their personal, internal beliefs and values, independently on external incentives or sanctions related to societal norms. Instead, people who are externally motivated to respond without prejudice are those who deliberately act in an egalitarian manner to avoid social disapproval and for social normative reasons despite they have not fully internalized the egalitarian principles. To test their predictions, Amodio et al. (2008) recruited participants with the following three different profiles based on their scores on the Internal and External Motivation to Respond Without Prejudice scale (i.e., IMS/EMS; Plant & Devine, 1998): 1-2) low-prejudice participants characterized by high internal motivation (and low external motivation) to respond without prejudice (i.e., high IMS/low EMS group; good regulators) versus those with a combination of high internal and high external motivation (i.e., high IMS/high EMS group; poor regulators); 3) high-prejudiced participants characterized by low internal motivation to respond without prejudice (i.e., non regulators). All participants were asked to perform the Weapon Identification Task (WIT; Payne, 2001) while ERPs were recorded. We first specifically focus on the data concerning the first two types of profiles by comparing good vs. poor regulators to then look at the non-regulator individuals. Results showed that both good and poor regulators displayed equivalent and significant level of automatic stereotyping on their behavior in the WIT. Further, both groups reported explicit positive attitudes toward Black people assessed with the Attitude Toward Blacks (ATB) scale (Brigham, 1993). More importantly, high IMS/low

EMS participants (i.e., good regulators) were more effective to control their responses, in terms of a better capacity to inhibit stereotype-biased expressions on the WIT than did those with high IMS/high EMS (i.e., poor regulators). Consistently with the authors' expectation, this effect corresponded to differences in the conflict monitoring activity, as indexed by a larger ERN component, indicating greater conflict monitoring control, for high IMS/low EMS participants vs. high IMS/high EMS individuals when responses required stereotype inhibition (i.e., Black-tool trials). In addiction, the ERN activity did not differ between these two groups of participants on trials that did not required the control of automatic stereotypes (i.e., Black-gun trials). In other words, these data suggest that poor regulators are less effective than good regulators at inhibiting biased responses because their conflict monitoring system is less sensitive in detecting the conflict between the automatic activation of stereotypes and egalitarian tendencies during response implementation. Finally, data from the third group of high-prejudice participants, who were not motivated to respond without prejudice (i.e., non-regulators), coherently with their profile, showed high levels of stereotype-biased responses as well as low levels of conflict monitoring activity.

To sum up, these data importantly demonstrated that differences in the sensitivity in the neural conflict monitoring mechanisms, which may operate at an unconscious level, can enlighten why some egalitarians are better than others to respond without prejudice bringing an important new insight in the social psychology literature.

In a similar line of research, Amodio, Kubota, Harmon-Jones, and Devine (2006) directly investigated the neural basis of behavior regulation according to internal vs. external cues. As said before, several studies suggested that different motivation may underlie unbiased responses. Individuals may indeed be more internally or externally motivated to avoid biased expressions (e.g., Dunton & Fazio, 1997; Plant & Devine, 1998). It remains however still to be addressed whether behavioral regulation according to internal motivations to respond without prejudice may rely on different underlying mechanisms as compared to regulation according to external motivation to respond without prejudice.

Seeking to address this issue, Amodio et al. (2006) considered recent neuroscience studies showing that empathy and mentalizing, abilities that implicate concern about others in order to take their perspectives, are supported by activity of the medial prefrontal cortex (i.e., mPFC) and of the rostral region of the anterior cingulate cortex (i.e., rACC) (see Amodio & Frith 2006 for a review). Based on these findings, and on previous work by Amodio et al. (2004), Amodio et al. (2006) hypothesized that internal vs. external forms of control involved different mechanisms supported by distinct neurocognitive structures. More in details, the authors predicted that the activations of the mPFC and rACC might be important for externally driven forms of regulation, that are influenced by the presence of others and by normative pressures, while the dACC regions, linked to the conflict monitoring system, should be more important for internally driven motivations regardless of the presence or absence of others. To test their predictions, the authors recorded ERPs while participants completed the Weapon Identification Task either in a private (i.e., while performing the task alone) or in a public situation (i.e., while being observed via video monitor by an experimenter looking for signs of prejudiced responses). Importantly, participants were selected on the basis of their scores on the Plant & Devine's scales (1998) such as to be low-prejudice individuals who reported to be either high or low in sensitivity to external normative pressures to respond without prejudice.

In order to assess the activation of the rACC/mPFC, Amodio et al. (2006) considered the error-positivity component of the ERP (i.e., P_e), that is a positive voltage wave peaking around 100-200 ms following a response error, just after the ERN, known to reflect the activity of these specific structures of the brain (Herrmann, Rommler, Ehlis, Heidrich, & Fallgatter, 2004; Kiehl, Liddle, & Hopfinger, 2001; van Veen & Carter, 2002). Similarly to the ERN, the P_e has been linked with behavioral control but whereas the ERN is independent of conscious awareness the P_e is associated with the conscious perception of unintended responses (Nieuwenhuis et al., 2001). According to the authors' predictions, the activity of theP_e should be recruited for regulating stereotype-biased responses only among highly externally motivated participants who respond in the public situation. As in Amodio et al. (2004), findings showed that, for all participants and across conditions, larger ERNs amplitudes were associated with stereotype inhibition attempts and greater response control, indicating that the ERN, linked to the dACC activity, reflects an internal cue to engage control among low-prejudice participants. Importantly, the P_e component was more strongly associated with response control only among participants who were highly sensitive to external pressures to respond without prejudice (i.e., externally motivated) and performed the task in a public condition.

Overall, these findings demonstrated for the first time that internally and externally motivated forms of prejudice control originate from separate neural underlying mechanisms that are respectively sustained by the activity of the dACC and the rACC/mPFC regions of the brain. Moreover, these data suggested that the externally motivated form of control involved a supplementary step and thus a more complex set of processes, relatively to the internally motivated form of control, which probably may account for the decreased efficiency of this form of regulatory mechanism according to external cues.

Overall, the studies reviewed in this section extended previous findings by showing that both dispositional individual differences in motivation to respond without prejudice and the social situation in which individuals find themselves significantly influence the regulatory processes underlying the expression of stereotypes, making new important steps further to the aim of understanding the automatic and controlled aspects of stereotyping.

CONCLUSIONS

The main goal of this chapter was to provide readers an overview on recent research that has profitably applied the ERP technique to answer longstanding questions revolving around stereotyping. We hope that the work reviewed here has convincingly demonstrated the potential value of the ERP approach, especially when employed in combination with traditional behavioral methods, to shed new light on basic mechanisms involved in stereotyping and, more in general, to extend social psychological theories. Given the excellent temporal resolution, the ongoing measurement property, as well as the versatility of the ERP, this technique uniquely permits us to test hypotheses otherwise impossible to assess by only relying on behavioral measures. ERPs can indeed pick up both automatic and controlled processes, occurring even very early and unfolding very quickly in the brain, thus providing an exclusive opportunity to unpack processes into their multiple underlying sub-components.

In this review we have particularly focused on three different core aspects of stereotyping, trying to underline the major advances that the use of ERPs has produced. When applied to investigate stereotype violation and confirmation, the ERP approach has supported the existent literature by showing that stereotypes can be automatically activated and, further, that information disconfirming stereotype-based beliefs is perceived as an anomaly that is indeed more difficult to be processed, as compared to stereotype-confirming information. ERPs have also been used to investigate aspects of self-regulation in relation to the expression of stereotypes. This line of research has interestingly permitted us to better clarify the mechanisms underlying regulatory cognitive control by further showing that such processes may be engaged without conscious awareness, in addition to the more deliberative mode of control investigated in previous studies relying only on behavioral methods. In addition, recent ERPs studies have made a step further by examining the important role played by individual and situational differences in self-regulatory processes associated with the expression of stereotypes.

Overall, we believe that the ERP technique, corroborated with more traditional behavioral measures based on cognitive performances, and self-reports, can significantly facilitate a further illumination of the basic aspects of social cognition and behavior. Moreover, we hope that this review has provided several examples of how the integration of different methodologies, theories and levels of analysis from neuroscience and social psychology, resulting in the social neuroscience approach, can greatly make possible a more comprehensive understanding of the human mind and of human social behavior.

REFERENCES

Allport, G.W. (1954). *The nature of prejudice*. Oxford: Addison-Wesley.

Amodio, D. M., & Frith, C. D. (2006). Meeting of minds: the medial frontal cortex and social cognition.*Nature Reviews Neuroscience*, 7, 268-277.

Amodio, D. M., Harmon-Jones, E., & Devine, P. G. (2003).Individual differences in the activation and control of affective race bias as assessed by startle-eyeblink responses and self-report.*Journal of Personality and Social Psychology*, 84, 738-753.

Amodio, D. M., Devine, P. G., & Harmon-Jones, E. (2008). Individual differences in the regulation of intergroup bias: The role of conflict monitoring and neural signals for control.*Journal of Personality and Social Psychology*, 94, 60-74.

Amodio, D. M., Harmon-Jones, E., Devine, P. G., Curtin, J. J., Hartley, S. L., & Covert, A. E. (2004). Neural signals for the detection of unintentional race bias.*Psychological Science*, 15, 88-93.

Amodio, D. M., Kubota, J. T., Harmon-Jones, E., & Devine, P. G. (2006). Alternative mechanisms for regulating racial responses according to internal vs. external cues. Social *Cognitive and Affective Neuroscience*, 1, 26-36.

Banaji, M. R., & Greenwald, A. G. (1994). Implicit stereotyping and prejudice. In M. P. Zanna & J. M. Olson (Eds.), *The psychology of prejudice: The Ontario Symposium* (Volume 7, pp. 55-76). Hillsdale, NJ: Erlbaum.

Banaji, M. R., & Greenwald, A. G. (1995*)*. Implicit gender stereotyping in judgments of fame. *Journal of Personality and Social Psychology*, 68, 181-198.

Banaji, M. R., & Hardin, C. D. (1996). Automatic stereotyping. *Psychological Science*, 7, 136-141.

Bargh, J. A. (1994). The four horsemen of automaticity: Awareness, intention, efficiency, and control in social cognition. In R. S. Wyer, Jr., & T. K. Srull (Eds.), *Handbook of social cognition* (2nd ed.) (pp. 1-40). Hillsdale, NJ: Lawrence Erlbaum Associates.

Bartholow, B. D., & Amodio, D. M. (2009). Using event-related brain potentials in social psychological research: A brief review and tutorial. In E. Harmon-Jones & J. S. Beer (Eds.), *Methods in social neuroscience* (pp. 198-232). New York: Guilford Press.

Bartholow, B. D., Dickter, C. L., & Sestir, M. A. (2006). Stereotype activation and control of race bias: Cognitive control of inhibition and its impairment by alcohol. *Journal of Personality and Social Psychology*, 90, 272-287.

Bartholow, B. D., Fabiani, M., Gratton, G., & Bettencourt, B. A. (2001). A psychophysiological analysis of cognitive processing of and affective responses to social expectancy violations. *Psychological Science*, 12, 197-204.

Blair, I. V. (2002*)*. The malleability of automatic stereotypes and prejudice. *Personality and Social Psychology Review*, 6, 242-261.

Bodenhausen, G. V., & Macrae, C. N. (1998). Stereotype activation and inhibition. In R. Wyer, Jr. (Ed.), *Stereotype activation and inhibition* (pp. 1-52). Mahwah, NJ: Erlbaum.

Botvinick, M. M., Braver, T. S., Barch, D. M., Carter, C. S., & Cohen, J. D. (2001). Conflict monitoring and cognitive control.*Psychological Review*, 108, 624-652.

Brewer, M. B. (1988). A dual process model of impression formation. In R. S. Wyer, Jr. e T. K. Srull (Eds.), *Advances in social cognition* (Vol. 1, pp. 1-36). Hillsdale, NJ: Lawrence Erlbaum Associates.

Brigham, J. C. (1993). College students' racial attitudes. *Journal of Applied Social Psychology*, 23, 1933-1967.

Castelli, L., & Tomelleri, S. (2008). Contextual effects on prejudiced attitudes: When the presence of others leads to more egalitarian responses.*Journal of Experimental Social Psychology,*44, 679-686.

Coles, M. G. H., & Rugg, M. D. (1995). Event-related brain potentials: An introduction. In M. D. Rugg & M. G. H. Coles (Eds.), *Electrophysiology of mind: Event-related brain potentials and cognition* (pp. 1-26). New York: Oxford University Press.

Correll, J., Park, B., Judd, C. M., & Wittenbrink, B. (2002). The police officer's dilemma: Using ethnicity to disambiguate potentially threatening individuals. *Journal of Personality and Social Psychology*, 83, 1314-1329.

Correll, J., Urland, G. R., & Ito, T. A. (2006). Event-related potentials and the decision to shoot: The role of threat perception and cognitive control. *Journal of Experimental Social Psychology*, 42, 120-128.

Crandall, C. S., Eshleman, A., & O'Brien, L. (2002). Social norms and the expression and suppression of prejudice: The struggle for internalization. *Journal of Personality and Social Psychology*, 82, 359-378.

Devine, P. G. (1989). Stereotypes and prejudice: Their automatic and controlled components.*Journal of Personality and Social Psychology*, 56, 5-18.

Devine, P. G., & Elliot, A. J. (1995). Are racial stereotypes really fading? The Princeton Trilogy revisited. *Personality and Social Psychology Bulletin*, 21, 1139-1150.

Devine, P. G., Plant, E. A., Amodio, D. M., Harmon-Jones, E., & Vance, S. L. (2002). The regulation of explicit and implicit race bias: The role of motivations to respond without prejudice.*Journal of Personality and Social Psychology*, 82, 835-848.

Dovidio, J. F., & Gaertner, S. L. (2000). Aversive racism and selection decisions: 1989 and 1999.*Psychological Science*, 11, 315-319.

Dovidio, J. F., Evans, N., & Tyler, R. B. (1986). Racial stereotypes: The contents of their cognitive representations.*Journal of Experimental Social Psychology*, 22, 22-37.

Dovidio, J. F., Kawakami, K., Johnson, C., Johnson, B., & Howard, A. (1997). On the nature of prejudice: Automatic and controlled processes.*Journal of Experimental Social Psychology*, 33, 510-540.

Dunton, B. C., & Fazio, R. H. (1997). An individual difference measure of motivation to control prejudiced reactions.*Personality and Social Psychology Bulletin*, 23, 316-326.

Easdon, C. M., & Vogel-Sprott, M. (2000). Alcohol and behavioral control: Impaired response inhibition and flexibility in social drinkers. *Experimental and Clinical Psychopharmacology*, 8, 387-394.

Fabiani, M., Gratton, G., & Federmeier, K. (2007). Event related brain potentials. In J. T. Cacioppo, L. G. Tassinary, & G. G. Berntson (Eds.), *Handbook of psychophysiology* (3rd ed., pp. 85-119). New York: Cambridge University Press.

Fazio, R. H., Jackson, J. R., Dunton, B. C. & Williams, C. J. (1995). Variability in automatic activation as an unobtrusive measure of racial attitudes: A bona fide pipeline?*Journal of Personality and Social Psychology*, 69, 1013-1027.

Fillmore, M. T., & Vogel-Sprott, M. (1999). An alcohol model of impaired inhibitory control and its treatment in humans.*Experimental and Clinical Psychopharmacology*, 7, 49-55.

Fillmore, M. T., & Vogel-Sprott, M. (2000). Response inhibition under alcohol: Effects of cognitive and motivational control.*Journal of Studies on Alcohol*, 61, 239-246.

Fiske, S. T. (1998). Stereotyping, prejudice, and discrimination. In D. T. Gilbert, S. T. Fiske, & G. Lindzey (Eds.), *The handbook of social psychology* (Vol. 2, 4th ed., pp. 367-411). New York: McGraw-Hill.

Fiske, S. T., & Neuberg, S. L. (1990). A continuum of impression formation, from category-based to individuating process: Influences of information and motivation on attention and interpretation.*Advances in Experimental Social Psychology*, 23, 1-73.

Gilbert, D. T., & Hixon, J. G. (1991).The trouble of thinking: Activation and application of stereotypic beliefs.*Journal of Personality and Social Psychology*, 60, 509-517.

Hamilton D. L., & Sherman J. W. (1994). Stereotypes. In R. S. Wyer & T. K. Srull (Eds.), *Handbook of social cognition* (2nd ed., Vol. 2, pp. 1-68). Hillsdale, NJ: Erlbaum.

Hamilton, D. L., & Trolier, T. K. (1986). Stereotypes and stereotyping: An overview of the cognitive approach. In J. F. Dovidio & S. L. Gaertner (Eds.),*Prejudice, discrimination, and racism*(pp. 127-163). Orlando, FL: Academic Press.

Herrmann, M.J., Rommler, J., Ehlis, A.C., Heidrich, A., & Fallgatter, A.J. (2004*).* Source localization (LORETA) of the error-related-negativity (ERN/Ne) and positivity (Pe).*Cognitive Brain Research*, 20, 294-299.

Hewstone, M. (1994). Revising and change of stereotypic beliefs: In search of the elusive subtyping model. In W. Stroebe & M. Hewstone (Eds.), *European review of social psychology* (Vol. 5, pp. 69-109). Chichester, UK: Wiley.

Ito, T. A., & Cacioppo, J. T. (2007). Attitudes as mental and neural states of readiness: Using physiological measures to study implicit attitudes. In B. Wittenbrink & N. Schwarz (Eds.),

Implicit measures of attitudes (pp. 125-158). New York: Guilford Press.

Jasper, H. H. (1958). The ten-twenty electrode system of the International Federation. *Electroencephalography and Clinical Neurophysiology*, 10, 371-375.

Kiehl, K. A., Liddle, P. F., & Hopfinger, J. B. (2001). Error processing and the rostral anterior cingulate: an event-related fMRI study.*Psychophysiology*, 37, 216-223.

Kutas, M., McCarthy, G., & Donchin, E. (1977). Augmenting mental chronometry: The P300 as a measure of stimulus evaluation time.*Science*, 197, 792-795.

Lattner, S., & Friederici, A. D. (2003). Talker's voice and gender stereotype in human auditory sentence processing - evidence from event-related brain potentials. *NeuroscienceLetters*, 339, 191-194.

Lepore, L., & Brown, R. (1997). Category and stereotype activation: Is prejudice inevitable?*Journal of Personality and Social Psychology*, 72, 275-287.

Lippmann, W. (1922). *Public opinion*. New York: Harcourt, Brace, Jovanovitch.

Logan, G. D. (1994). On the ability to inhibit thought and action: A user's guide to the stop-signal paradigm. In D. Dagenbach & T. H. Carr (Eds.), *Inhibitory processes in attention, memory, and language* (pp. 189-240). San Diego, CA: Academic Press.

Luck, S. J. (2005). *An Introduction to the Event-related potential technique*. Cambridge: MIT Press.

Mackie, D. M., Hamilton, D. L., Susskind, J., & Rosselli, F. (1996). Social psychological foundations of stereotype formation.In C. N. Macrae, C. Stangor, & M. Hewstone (Eds.), *Stereotypes and Stereotyping* (pp. 41-78). New York: Guilford.

Macrae, C. N., & Bodenhausen, G. V. (2000*)*. Social cognition: Thinking categorically about others.*Annual Review of Psychology*, 51, 93-120.

Macrae, C. N., Bodenhausen, G. V., & Milne, A. B. (1995). The dissection of selection in person perception: Inhibitory processes in social stereotyping.*Journal of Personality and Social Psychology,* 69, pp. 397-407.

Macrae, C. N., Bodenhausen, G. V., Milne, A. B., Thorn, T. M. J., & Castelli, L. (1997). On the activation of social stereotypes: The moderating role of processing objectives.*Journal of Experimental Social Psychology*, 33, 471-489.

Macrae, C. N., Milne, A. B., & Bodenhausen, G. V. (1994). Stereotypes as energy-saving devices: A peek inside the cognitive toolbox. *Journal of Personality and Social Psychology*, 66, 77-87.

McConahay, J. B. (1986). Modern racism, ambivalence, and the modern racism scale. In J. F. Dovidio & S. L. Gaertner (Eds.), *Prejudice, discrimination and racism* (pp. 91-126). New York: Academic Press.

McConnell, A. R., & Leibold, J. M. (2001). Relations among the Implicit Association Test, discriminatory behavior, and explicit measure of racial attitudes. *Journal of Experimental Social Psychology*, 37, 435-442.

Monteith, M. (1993). Self-regulation of prejudiced responses: Implications for progress in prejudice-reduction efforts.*Journal of Personality and Social Psychology*, 65, 469-485.

Moskowitz, G. B., Salomon, A. R., & Taylor, C. M. (2000). Preconsciously controlling stereotyping: Implicitly activated egalitarian goals prevent the activation of stereotypes.*Social Cognition*, 18, 151-177.

Moskowitz, G. B., Gollwitzer, P. M., Wasel, W., & Schaal, B. (1999*)*. Preconscious control of stereotype activation through chronic egalitarian goals.*Journal of Personality and Social Psychology,* 77, 167-184

Nieuwenhuis, S., Ridderinkhof, K. R., Blom, J., Band, G. P. H., & Kok, A. (2001). Error-related brain potentials are differently related to awareness of response errors: Evidence from an antisaccade task.*Psychophysiology*, 38, 752-760.

Nieuwenhuis, S., Yeung, N., van den Wildenberg, W., & Ridderinkhof, K. R. (2003). Electrophysiological correlates of anterior cingulated function in a go/no-go task; Effects of response conflict and trial type frequency. *Cognitive, Affective, and Behavioral Neuroscience*, 3, 17-26.

Osterhout, L., Bersick, M., & McLaughlin, J. (1997). Brain potentials reflect violations of gender stereotypes. *Memory & Cognition*, 25, 273-285.

Payne, B. K. (2001). Prejudice and perception: The role of automatic and controlled processes in misperceiving a weapon. *Journal of Personality and Social Psychology*, 81, 181-192.

Perdue, C. W., Dovidio, J. F., Gurtman, M. B., & Tyler, R. B. (1990). Us and them: Social categorization and the process of intergroup bias.*Journal of Personality and Social Psychology*, 59, 475-486.

Pettigrew, T. F., & Meertens, R. W. (1995). Subtle and blatant prejudice in western Europe. *European Journal of Social Psychology*, 25, 57-75.

Plant, E. A., & Devine, P. G. (1998). Internal and external motivation to respond without prejudice.*Journal of Personality and Social Psychology*, 75, 811-832.

Rugg, M. D., & Coles, M. G. H. (1995). *Electrophysiology of mind: Event-related brain potentials and cognition.*New York: Oxford University Press.

Spencer, S. J., Fein, S., Wolfe, C. T., Fong, C., & Dunn, M. A. (1998). Automatic activation of stereotypes: The role of self-image threat.*Personality and Social Psychology Bulletin*, 24, 1139-1152.

Stangor, C., & McMillan, D. (1992). Memory for expectancy-congruent and expectancy-incongruent information: A review of the social and social developmental literatures. *Psychological Bulletin*, 111, 42-61.

Stangor, C., & Schaller, M. (1996). Stereotypes as individual and collective representations. In C. N. Macrae, C. Stangor, & M. Hewstone (Eds.), *Stereotypes and Stereotyping* (pp. 3-40). New York: Guilford.

van Knippenberg, A., & Dijksterhuis, A. (2000). Social categorization and stereotyping: A functional perspective. *European Review of Social Psychology*, 11, 105-144.

van Veen, V., & Carter, C. S. (2002). The timing of action-monitoring processes in the anterior cingulate cortex. *Journal of Cognitive Neuroscience*, 14, 593-602.

Weisbuch, M., Pauker, K., & Ambady, N. (2009). The subtle transmission of race bias via televised nonverbal behavior.*Science*, 326, 1711-1714.

Wittenbrink, B., Judd, C. M., & Park, B. (2001). Spontaneous prejudice in context: Variability in automatically activated attitudes.*Journal of Personality and Social Psychology*, 81, 815-827.

In: Psychology of Stereotypes
Editor: Eleanor L. Simon

ISBN: 978-1-61761-463-7
©2011 Nova Science Publishers, Inc.

Chapter 7

DO MANAGERS' PERCEPTIONS COINCIDE WITH ESTABLISHED STEREOTYPING OF OLDER WORKERS' CAPABILITIES?**

Trude Furunes and Reidar J. Mykletun*
University of Stavanger, Norway

ABSTRACT

Due to population ageing, Western societies' future economic growth may have to rely on the capacity of older workers in the labour market(Ilmainen, 2009). However, research suggests that stereotyping, age discrimination and negative manager attitudes may lead to early retirement and workforce losses(Furunes & Mykletun, 2007, 2010). Previous research indicates that there exist several stereotypes of how workers' capabilities change with age. To our knowledge this study is the first to profile managers' perceptions of age-related changes of the workforce and how these perceptions relate to both prevailing stereotypes of ageing workers and also to research outcomes describing older workers' adaption to the workplace. Whereas previous studies on stereotypes of older workers show an extensive list of negative characteristics, this study shows that managers perceive ageing as contributing to increased managerial and interpersonal skills, creative problem solving capacities, and work moral. On the negative side, age contributes to impaired learning capacities and basic functions. The findings of this study are closer to results of extensive research on older workers' capabilities and only partially in line with prevailing stereotypes of older workers. It is likely that managers working with older workers will develop conceptualisations of this part of the workforce that are closer to the characteristics demonstrated by research on actual behaviour, hence prevailing stereotypes of these workers may not be so general and persistent as argued by extant research.

Keywords: stereotyping, manager perceptions, ageing, older workers

---

** Peer reviewed by Dr. Christina Björklund, PhD, Karolinska Institute, Sweden.

* Correspondence address: Trude Furunes,University of Stavanger, Norway, e-mail: trude.furunes@uis.no, Phone: +47 53 81 37 62

INTRODUCTION

As a consequence of decreasing birth rates and increasing life expectancy, the developed world is experiencing a demographic change that will lead to a steep increase in the relative proportion of the elderly in the society(OECD, 2007). If retirement ages remain stable within Europe, the number of workers retiring will exceed the number of labour-market entrants from year 2015. This development will affect the dependency ratio, i.e. the number of workers per inactive person, and accordingly put substantial pressure on public finances. Due to this scenario, several European countries have considered retention of older workers in the labour market as important (Schalk, et al., 2010). Nevertheless, previous research suggests that stereotypes and negative manager attitudes about older people are barriers to recruitment (Davies, Matthews, & Wong, 1991; Furunes & Mykletun, 2005), employment and retention of older workers (Kaeter, 1995; Magd, 2003). Age bias in the workplace can lead to ageist discourse, expressed ageist attitudes, and discriminatory attitudes based on age (McCann & Giles, 2002),along with severe recommendations for poor performance(Rupp, Vodanovich, & Credé, 2006).Perceived ageist behaviour and negative treatment have also shown to be associated with lowered self-efficacy, decreased performance, and cardiovascular stress among older employees (Levy, 1996, 2000; Levy, Ashman, & Dior, 1999), as well as decreased job satisfaction, organisational commitment and job involvement (Orpen, 1995). Negative stereotypes about older workers have been identified in several studies (e.g. Chiu, Chan, Snape, & Redman, 2001; Furunes & Mykletun, 2007), nevertheless Furunes and Mykletun (2005, 2007) suggest that managers' attitudes towards older workers are more nuanced. In a meta-analytic review, Kite, Stockdale, Whitley, and Johnson(2005) state that although views about ageing are multidimensional, containing both positive and negative elements, attitudes towards older adults were found to be systematically more negative than towards younger adults. To our knowledge few studies have surveyed the degree to which managers' perceptions of older workers coincide with traditional stereotypes of elderly persons. This study aimed at giving a more nuanced view and wider range of perceptions of older workers' capacities.

STEREOTYPING, DISCRIMINATION AND AGEISM

In order to understand the phenomenon, it is important to explore the link between stereotypes and discriminating acts. Stereotypes are defined as widely shared intergroup attitudes that take form from the wider socio-historical context in which they exist (Hogg, 2006). Stereotypes reflect generalizations and "...are in the interest of simplifying the demands on thinking and feeling and promoting adaptation. By automatic categorization into social groups, such as age, the perceiver, it is assumed, is able to reorient cognitive resources and attention to nonroutine tasks" (Levy & Banaji, 2002, pp. 64-65). This means that stereotypes are ready-made impressions that free the perceivers from having to carefully process new information (Madon, Guyll, Hilbert, Kyriakatos, & Vogel, 2006). Stereotypes are often used in a negative or prejudicial sense and are frequently used to justify certain discriminatory behaviours (Aronson, Wilson, & Akert, 2007). Such automatic categorisation with negative consequences for older individuals was first defined by Butler (1969), who named it 'ageism', also known as age discrimination. However, age was not a recognised part of the social psychology discussion of stereotypes and prejudice until the 1980's, after which it was regarded a social category worthy of attention for study (Levy & Banaji, 2002).

Levy and Banaji (2002, p. 50) define ageism as "an alteration in feeling, belief, or behaviour in response to an individual's or group's perceived chronological age." Ageism can be implicit, thus "operate without conscious awareness, control, or intention to harm" (2002, p. 50). This means that it is not malevolent in its intention, but might become so in its consequences. There are few research explanations to the development of implicit social cognition, however it is suggested that conscious thought (explicit) concerning a specific topic might become automatic (implicit) through chronic activation (Bargh, Chen, & Burrows, 1996). This may imply that "once age stereotypes are acquired; they are likely to be automatically triggered by the presence of an elderly person" (Levy & Banaji, 2002, p. 64).

According to Levy and Banaji, implicit ageism is somewhat unique, as there are no hate groups targeting older people, like there are hate groups towards religious, racial or ethnic groups. There are also few social sanctions against expressions of negative attitudes towards elderly; rather widespread occurrences of socially acceptable negative expressions towards elderly have been documented (Williams & Giles, 1998, in Levy & Banaji, 2002). Negative attitudes, stereotypes and thoughts about age are prevalent in public spheres, and are easily accepted by children. Several studies have shown that the automatic categorization of individuals into social groups occurs effortlessly regarding age, race and gender (Banaji & Hardin, 1996). Schalk et al. (2010) use the term *social age* when referring to attitudes, expectations and norms about appropriate behaviour, lifestyle and characteristics for people at different ages.

Implicit attitudes contrast explicit attitudes, with the implicit attitude showing more negativity towards elderly individuals than found by the explicit measure. Furthermore, implicit age bias does not vary across respondents' age. This implies that both younger and older individuals have positive implicit attitudes towards the young and negative implicit attitudes towards the old. This finding stands against other implicit attitudes (e.g. religion, race and gender), where group membership is found to play a role. According to Levy and Banaji (2002, p. 67), "the elderly is the only group that shows as strong negative implicit attitudes towards their own group as to the out-group (the young)". They thereby suggest that this is because the psychologically permeable nature of the boundary between age groups may allow oneself to dissociate from the group, hence allowing no benefit from group membership. They hereby suggest that conscious attitudes are more sensitive to group membership than unconscious attitudes, such as automatic stereotypes. Another interesting finding by the same researchers is that elderly individuals with high self-esteem "implicitly preferred young to old age and implicitly identified as young rather than old" (Levy & Banaji, 2002, p. 56).

Along the same lines, Perdue and Gurtman (1990) found that "cognitively categorizing a person as 'old' may create a subset of predominantly negative constructs which are more accessible and more likely to be employed in evaluating that person – and this will tend to perpetuate ageism from the beginning of the social perception process" (Perdue & Gurtman, 1990, p. 213). Levy (1996) found that older individuals' perceptions could be affected by implicit self-stereotypes. In one of her studies, she found that older participants exposed to positive age stereotypes prior to their memory test performed better than those exposed to negative age stereotypes. This may imply that negative age stereotypes act as self-fulfilling prophecies(Merton, 1957), hence have an automatic self-stereotyping effect. Levy and Banaji (2002) claim that as "implicit self-stereotypes of aging operate without awareness, the process may be particularly harmful. Just as younger individuals who are not aware of the impact of implicit age stereotypes are unlikely to correct for resulting discriminatory behaviour, older individuals are unlikely to recognise outcomes they experience as being due to implicit age stereotypes" (Levy & Banaji, 2002, p. 61). Hence, it is particularly interesting to know more about the perceptions managers hold about older workers. Although Furunes & Mykletun's (2005) research suggests that older managers find their own ageing experience help them to understand their older employees, the empirical evidence indicates that it is hard for any manager to avoid being a victim of age-related stereotypes (Levy & Banaji, 2002).

DIMENSIONS OF STEREOTYPES

Research has identified two critical dimensions of stereotypes; *warmth* and *competence* (Figure 1). Closer investigations have shown that some stereotypical images, such as the elderly stereotype, are of mixed nature, where the stigmatised out-group is stereotyped as high on one dimension and low on the other. Cuddy, Norton, and Fiske (2005) argue that, groups that are viewed as competitive in the labour market (e.g. Asian and Jews in America) are stereotyped as lacking warmth; compared to groups that are rated less competitive (e.g. disabled people or housewives). The competence dimension can be predicted from a group's perceived status relative to other groups in society, thus rich high-status people are viewed more competent than poor low-status people. This stereotype content model describes how groups are sorted and how a group's position is related to the type of prejudice its members may suffer. The prediction of where a group will be in this map is related to its perceived social structural relationships with other groups. On the competence dimension a group's position is judged from its perceived status in society relative to other groups (i.e. rich people are competent and poor people are incompetent). According to Cuddy et al. (2005), these combinations of stereotype dimensions carry at least four emotions: Contempt, Pity, Envy and Admiration. *Envy* is directed at competitive, high status groups (high competence, low warmth), and involves feelings of inferiority(see Smith, Parrott, Ozer, & Moniz, 1994). *Pity* is directed at non-competitive, low-status groups (low competence, high warmth), often downwards at people with non-controllable stigmas (e.g. physical disability, old age).
Admiration goes to dominant social reference groups (high competence, high warmth), whereas *contempt* (low competence, low warmth) is directed towards groups with negative stigmas for which they are responsible, such as poverty due to chronic gambling. When it comes to elderly people, findings point in two different directions (Cuddy, et al., 2005). Pity is directed towards the elderly individual, whereas 'elderly people' are seen as a collective group that recalls admiration. In their study, elderly people were perceived to have low status and being non-competitive, and Cuddy et al. (2005) suggest that these stereotypes are pan-cultural and persistent.

		Warmth	
		High	Low
Competence	High	ADMIRATION (in-groups and social reference groups, whose positive outcomes reflect on the self)	ENVY (high status, competitive groups that are viewed threateningly capable and untrustworthy)
	Low	PITY (low status, non-competitive groups)	CONTEMPT (low status groups that have negative stigmas for which they are responsible)

Figure 1. Stereotype Content Model (based on Cuddy, et al., 2005).

Furthermore, they propose that at least four mechanisms have probably lowered the status of older people in the industrial societies. First, medical progress has increased life expectancy and the size of the elderly population, however as people do not work longer, this implies that increasing numbers of older people are removed from high-status positions into retirement. Second, experience is overshadowed by technical skills and older workers are made redundant. Third, younger people are more mobile and lose ties with older relatives. Since they do not socialise with older people, their stereotypes of older people are not challenged and their attitudes towards elderly are built on second-hand information. Fourth, elderly persons' status as sage storytellers is challenged by the increasing literacy. Along these societal changes, older people's competitiveness has decreased, "thus creating the warm, incompetent elderly stereotype" (Cuddy et al., 2005, p. 274).

The elderly stereotype is persistent and pervasive; hence Cuddy et al. propose, "elderly people who disconfirm stereotypes of their incompetence may be denigrated on warmth" (2005, p. 274). In a controlled experiment, they found that the negative component of the elderly stereotype (incompetence) is more resistant to change than the positive (warmth). It is also suggested that elderly who behave in a manner consistent with the expectation (incompetent) gain warmth; implying that if an elderly person confirms the negative stereotype (e.g. is less effective than a younger colleague) he or she is perceived as warmer, however not less competent than the average elderly.

Elderly are also rated warmer and friendlier, as well as less ambitious, less responsible and less intellectually competent. Age stereotypes are also found to outweigh the gender stereotypes, and older people are perceived more feminine and less masculine than younger people, regardless of their gender. Complex out-group stereotypes are perceived more harmful than negative beliefs, as they carry emotional prejudice in terms of envy, pity, admiration or contempt (Cuddy et al., 2005).

STEREOTYPES VERSUS RESEARCH EVIDENCE ON AGE-RELATED CHANGES IN WORKFORCE CAPACITIES

Stereotypes of elderly individuals in general and older workers in particular, contain collective perceptions on how individuals develop with age. Kaeter (1995), reports the most common stereotypes concerning older workers to be: older workers cost more, older workers have higher absentee rates, older people cannot learn new skills, and older workers are less productive. Other examples of myths and stereotypes include that older workers have more outdated training, less physical capabilities, greater resistance to change, less opportunity for self-development (Davies, et al., 1991), and that creative potential declines in old age(Levy & Langer, 1999). These stereotypes are seen as age limits in recruitment (Davies, et al., 1991; Furunes & Mykletun, 2005), and may be a result of the common belief that job performance decreases with age (Rupp, et al., 2006). In general, these stereotypes are in line with Cuddy et al.'s (2005) notion about lower competence for older people.

However, to a large degree, stereotypes of older workers are contradicted by research. Job performance shows no consistent average decline with increasing age (Davies, et al., 1991; Davies, Taylor, & Dorn, 1992; Griffiths, 1997; McEvoy & Cascio, 1989; Rodes, 1983; Salthouse, Hambrick, Lukas, & Dell, 1996; Waldman & Avolio, 1986; Warr, 1994, 1996), and within-age-group differences have been found to exceed between-age-group differences (Davies, et al., 1992). Older workers demonstrate greater inter-individual variability in performance than do their younger colleagues, as well as greater intra-individual differences in abilities (Hansson, DeKoekkoek, Neece, & Patterson, 1997) . Referring to their meta-analysis study, Ng and Feldman (2008) support previous findings that, overall, there are small, if any, relationships between age and core work tasks, creativity and performance in training programs. However, for noncore tasks, their results show that older workers demonstrate greater levels of citizenship and safety-related behaviors, engage in less counterproductive behavior, demonstrate better emotional control and less aggression, as well as less on-the-job substance use, tardiness and voluntary absence. The findings indicate that older workers are as motivated as younger workers and they may engage in discretionary behaviors to compensate for any loss in core technical performance. These findings are, however, based on those who remain at work, and hence are able and willing to attain appropriate standards, while other under-performing workers of any age may be weeded out over time.

Creativity can be defined as "the ability to transcend traditional ways of thinking by generating ideas, methods, and forms that are meaningful and new to others" (Levy & Langer, 1999, p. 45). The research is inconsistent on whether creativity develops or declines over time. The peak and decline model (Lindauer, in Levy & Langer, 1999) apply a combination of psychometric and productivity tests results to suggest that creativity starts to decline in one's 30s. Contrary to this, Levy and Langer suggest that a life span development model describes creativity better than the peak and decline model proposed by Lindauer. The life span model divides creativity from productivity and suggests that creativity develops over the life course, and also changes in content and style (Levy & Langer, 1999). In either case, creativity differs between individuals due to differences in personality and social interaction patterns. Social norms can limit creativity, thus those who remain creative in later life have possibly learnt to reject these norms. Openness to new ideas promotes creativity, and people that are able to question surroundings and have a tolerance for uncertainty seem to be more creative. Uncertainty leads to choice that again fosters mindfulness and further creativity. It is suggested that stereotyping may contribute to the decline in creative productivity with age, hence creating a self-fulfilling prophecy (Levy & Langer, 1999).

As summarised by Griffiths (2007) and Ilmarinen (2001), one must realize that sensory information processing, cognitive processing of information between the senses and memory, and the motor system that enact functional decisions, all start to decline in early adulthood. Warr (1994, 1996) found that in some situations reduced speed of information processing may lead to poorer performance on tasks that require rapid cognitive processing of older people, who also might seem to be slower in acquiring new skills and knowledge (Warr, 1994). This coupled with a lack of skills updating opportunities through training, might increase the effect of age-impairment in jobs where the content is changing rapidly (Warr, 1996). But older workers' capacities show decline only in job activities dominated by continuous, paced data processing, rapid learning, and heavy lifting, but impairments in these activities are likely to be counteracted by mastery knowledge in skilled manual and cognitive work due to tenure and experience. Other job activities are age-enhanced, age-counteracted, or age-neutral (Warr, 1996).

Age-related decline in intellectual functioning is least for verbal cognitive functioning and, on average, is insignificant within the time span of a normal working career (Mortensen, 2007; Schaie, 2005). Verbal memory peaks at midlife (ages 40–60 years), as also do vocabulary, inductive reasoning and spatial orientation (Willis & Schaie, 1999). Experience may interact with performance and compensate for a decline in age-related functioning, depending upon the quality and variability of these experiences(Salthouse, 1997; Salthouse & Maurer, 1996; Warr, 1996).The overall development of expertise where the acquired knowledge is the base for new skills permits more appropriate responses to new situations. Moreover, older people learn to compensate for reduced cognitive ability through building other day-to-day tactics(Warr, 1996). Use of adaptive strategies like selection, optimization and compensation may be effective to counteract loss of functional capacities (Baltes, Staudinger, & Lindenberger, 1999). Experienced workers often feel that they have more possibilities to choose work methods than their younger peers (Ilmarinen & Rantanen, 1999). Due to experience, older workers may accommodate their behaviour to avoid situations that can reveal defects, either through selecting tasks they know they can handle, through their knowledge of the organisation gaining access to others that may assist, or through career progress to positions from where they can delegate problematic tasks. Finally, experience may be used to cope with age challenges in the work place by cognitive compilation, which intends that new information can effortlessly be 'compiled' into existing categories (Warr, 1996). In line with this, Birdi, Pennington, and Zapf (1997) argue that, in computer-based work, age differences do exist, but only for more advanced cognitive functions and these differences can be partly compensated for by experience in carrying out such tasks. It is found that other activities and task performances benefit from accumulated experience; therefore older employees are likely to be more effective on these activities. Taking the above research into consideration, the low competence stereotype identified by Cuddy et al. (2005) receives only scant support.

Some research has also addressed the relationship between workers' emotional outcomes and work in relation to age and found that older workers thrive well. Thus, increasing age predict high levels of vigor(Van den Broeck, Vansteenkiste, De Witte, & Lens, 2008), and age relates positively to well-being at work (Doering, Rhodes, & Schuster, 1983). Positive work-related attitudes increase with increasing age Rhodes (1983) while job boredom declines linearly with increasing age (Birdi, Warr, & Oswald, 1995). Job satisfaction is positively related to age (Spector, 2007; Wright & Hamilton, 1978), see also a meta-analysis of 19 studies by Brush, Moch, and Pooyan(1987). Furthermore, older adults are generally more satisfied with their financial situation compared to younger adults as they have less debt and a greater number of assets(Hansen, Slagsvold, & Moum, 2008). This concurs with the idea that "money buys happiness" (Blanchflower & Oswald, 2004). A recent large-scale cross-sectional study by Blanchflower & Oswald (2008) clearly demonstrates U-shaped relationships between age and psychological well-being for Americans and Europeans, based on data from the General Social Surveys, 1972–2006, and the Eurobarometer, 1976–2002, respectively. The lowest level of well-being occurred in the 45 to 55 year age range, the curve flattening out for the highest age groups. The findings were robust for cohort effects, and an inverted U-shaped relationship also applied to mental distress, as measured by the General Health Questionnaire (GHQ-N6), which peaked at 44 to 45 years of age. It is likely that work satisfaction plays a role in total life satisfaction and vice versa, supporting the U-shape hypothesis. The above studies support Cuddy et al.'s (2005) notion of warmth as an essential attribute of older workers, hence they might be conceived of as a positive contribution to the psycho-social work environment of the workplace.

Work content and its organisation may also impact on ageing workers' capabilities. Job tasks with little variation and few demands on decision making, promote development of cognitive rigidity, whereas variation and responsibility for decision making promote cognitive flexibility (Schooler, Malatu, & Oates, 1999). Workers with a high mental workload have less risk for age-related cognitive impairment than workers with low mental demands in their job (Bosma, et al., 2003). Moreover it is found that complex work tasks improve intellectual skills (Schooler, Malatu, & Oates, 1999). It might be argued that older workers should be offered complex tasks at work, which in turn might sustain their work ability. Work with high cognitive demands mitigates rather than accelerates this deterioration (Baltes, Staudinger, & Lindenberger, 2002; Vaillant, 2002). Moreover, when compared with unemployment, work may be conducive to good health (Waddel & Burton, 2006). Work may provide purpose, challenge and meaning to life, and is an important arena for social involvement, social connectedness, bonding and friendships. It constitutes opportunities for learning, creativity, and personal and professional growth, as well as being an arena for exposing one's expertise and developing skills in order to experience success and achievement (Csikszentmihalyi, 1997). This applies to older workers as well (Vaillant, 1993, 2002). Social contact, respect and esteem from others, personal feeling of pride and self-worth, income and health benefits from work, and generativity - the opportunity to pass on one's knowledge and skills to others - were examples of the basic needs among older workers that were identified by Mor-Barak (1995). Noteworthy, an 11-year follow-up study of a large random sample from the Finnish workforce showed that shifting the focus from sickness prevention to health promotion in the workplace, combined with improvements in work organization, physical and psychosocial work environment, and improving leadership, contributed to better health and work ability, higher work quality, a better quality of life and a greater level of well-being, as well as a more active and meaningful retirement(Ilmarinen, Tuomi, & Klockars, 1997; Tuomi, Ilmainen, Martikainen, & Klockars, 1997).

TOWARDS THE STATEMENT OF THE RESEARCH PROBLEM

As can be concluded from the studies reviewed above, ageing may imply both a reduction and growth of individual capacities. Workforce capabilities are complex issues that are affected by several features including biological ageing, health, and working conditions. Each individual has his own ageing process where these aspects will be of different importance. According to Ilmarinen, Tuomi and Klockars (1997), heterogeneity increases with increasing age, and this is reflected in the individual's functional capacity and work ability. This diversity and complexity may harden the persistence of stereotypes of older workers, due to the dynamics inherent in the stereotyping as a psychological process, at least when the observer is remote to the in-group of the older workers at the workplace. This is also the departure for the research questions driving the present study. The respondents of the present study, the workplace managers, are increasingly dependent on older workers for the attainment of their organisations' goals, hence their perceptions of age and ageing might be less influenced by the general stereotypes and closer to the more nuanced characteristics of the older workers observed in research on ageing at work. The research questions addressed here were threefold: 1) How do managers perceive workers' age-related changes in characteristics related to work, and to what extent are these perceptions reflecting established stereotypes more than research findings with regards to the characteristics of the older workers? 2) To what extent are managers' perceptions general across workplaces, and do workplace differences in such characteristics apply? 3) What are the statistical characteristics of the scale used by Lyng (1997) when applied across three samples of managers?

The present research was inspired by Lyng (1999, 2007) who surveyed Norwegian employees' individual perceptions of age-related changes in workers' characteristics. By means of factor analysis he categorised the findings regarding age-related individual changes along six dimensions, respectively: social competence, problem competence, maturity, productivity, basic abilities and adaptive abilities. Among these, social competence, problem-solving skills and maturity are perceived to increase with age, while there are no perceived changes in productivity, and basic abilities and adaptive abilities are perceived to decline with age. Furthermore, a decline in basic abilities is perceived to affect work performance to a slight degree, while a decline in adaptive abilities is more often perceived to affect work performance. Lyng's (1999) study was based on a small Swedish study by Hallsten (1993). To our knowledge, no similar study has yet been undertaken on managers.

METHODOLOGY

This study analyses data from 1138 managers who were asked to rate their perceptions of 30 capabilities related to human development and working life, and how these capabilities develop with age (Lyng, 1999). These work-related capabilities include: independence, problem-solving skills, assessment ability, knowledge of human nature, conflict-handling skills, responsibility, work ethics, stability, loyalty, understanding of work, management skills, patience, consumer handling skills, communication skills, interpersonal skills, accuracy, stress handling capacities, stamina, memory, adaptability, speed, hearing, physical strength, sickness leave, creativity, efficiency, and vision. Managers were asked to rate how the 30 capabilities develop with age. 1= negative development, 2= no development, 3= positive development.

Data were collected from manager respondents in three different studies. These include A) one study in the public sector (n=672) (response rate = 42.3), B) one study in a public hospital (n=114) (response rate = 60.3), and C) one study in an energy company (n=352) (response rate = 49.1). In the analyses data are treated as a total sample containing three sub-samples. The sub-samples are referred to as sub-sample A, B, and C. Data are analysed by frequency (mean and standard deviation) and factor analyses (Varimax rotation, Maximal Likelihood, excluding loading below .35). Sum-scores were calculated based on the factor structure of the total sample, and tested for reliability (Cronbach's Alpha) for the total sample and sub-samples. Sum-score mean values were used to compare sub-samples to the total sample.

The presentation of results focuses on the following two aspects of the data, 1) how these thirty work-related capabilities are perceived to develop with age, in the total dataset and across three sub-samples, 2) what are the factor structures found in the total data set and across sub-samples, and what are the scale qualities as measured by alpha coefficients across the entire sample and for sub-samples? The discussion will centre around how the factors in this study compare to stereotypes of older workers found in research literature reviewed above.

RESULTS

Frequencies

Analyses of mean values showed that for the total sample, 17 out of 30 work-related capabilities were perceived to develop in a positive direction with increasing age (table 1). Sub-samples A and C showed the same pattern as the total sample for the changes in positive directions. However, for sub-sample B only 6 of these 17 capabilities showed changes in positive directions, and the remaining 10 were perceived to develop in a negative direction.

Thirteen of the capabilities were perceived to develop in a negative direction with increasing age. This tendency was supported in sub-sample A, and also partly in sub-sample C. In sub-sample B, however, only five of the thirteen capabilities showed changes in a negative direction, whereas the remaining eight capabilities were perceived to develop in the opposite direction of the total sample.

Across samples respondents in the sub-samples agreed that six capabilities (in bold, table 1) develop in a positive direction. These were knowledge of human nature, conflict-handling skills, assessment ability, problem-solving skills, patience, and communication skills. Five capabilities showed a decline across the sub-samples, namely, creativity, memory, hearing, physical strength, and vision. Although these data show some patterns, they also illustrate that respondents did not fully agree on how these workforce capabilities develop with age, across sub-samples. In particular, sub-sample B showed different perceptions.

Table 1. Mean values and standard deviations for perceived workforce capabilities, total sample (n=1138) and sub-samples A, B, and C.

	Work-related Capabilities	Total Sample		A		B		C	
	n =	1138		672		114		352	
		Mean	Std	Mean	Std	Mean	St.d	Mean	Std
Positive change in total sample	Knowledge of human nature	**2.80**	**.41**	**2.80**	**.41**	**2.65**	**.52**	**2.84**	**.37**
	Conflict-handling skills	**2.52**	**.59**	**2.47**	**.61**	**2.31**	**.64**	**2.68**	**.48**
	Responsibility	2.41	.59	2.49	.53	*1.57*	.52	2.55	.51
	Assessment ability	**2.52**	**.59**	**2.45**	**.60**	**2.31**	**.63**	**2.71**	**.49**
	Independence	2.34	.60	2.40	.56	*1.57*	.60	2.47	.51
	Work ethics	2.30	.55	2.39	51	*1.62*	.53	2.36	.49
	Stability	2.34	.64	2.36	.62	*1.58*	.60	2.52	.52
	Loyalty	2.30	.55	2.35	.50	*1.63*	.52	2.40	.50
	Understanding of work	2.26	.58	2.34	.54	*1.65*	.57	2.30	.54
	Problem-solving skills	**2.32**	**.60**	**2.35**	**.54**	**2.21**	**.61**	**2.35**	**.53**
	Management skills	2.34	.58	2.32	.57	*1.84*	.57	2.52	.51
	Patience	**2.32**	**.63**	**2.31**	**.62**	**2.44**	**.61**	**2.52**	**.52**
	Consumer handling skills	2.20	.56	2.26	.57	*1.79*	.51	2.23	.49
	Communication skills	**2.31**	**.56**	**2.22**	**.58**	**2.33**	**.58**	**2.44**	**.53**
	Interpersonal skills	2.21	.56	2.21	.53	*1.82*	.55	2.32	55
	Low accident risk and low fault proposition	2.24	.60	2.15	.59	*1.83*	.57	2.51	.51
	Accuracy	2.08	.46	2.11	.49	*1.81*	.52	2.11	.43
Negative change in total sample	Sickness leave	1.91	.49	1.93	.67	*2.03*	.70	1.82	.62
	Creativity	**1.89**	**.51**	**1.89**	**.54**	**1.85**	**.50**	**1.89**	**.45**
	Efficiency	1.90	.58	1.71	.58	*2.16*	.53	*2.51*	.44
	Stress handling capacity	1.94	.77	1.69	.74	*2.21*	.75	*2.11*	.65
	Computer skills	1.68	.61	1.55	.57	*2.49*	.50	1.66	.53
	Learning capacity	1.62	.60	1.53	.58	*2.28*	.55	1.58	.53
	Stamina	1.73	.70	1.49	.63	*2.44*	.65	1.94	.65
	Memory	**1.50**	**.52**	**1.46**	**.52**	**1.66**	**.55**	**1.52**	**.51**
	Adaptability	1.56	.62	1.36	.52	*2.40*	.61	1.67	.53
	Speed	1.50	.66	1.30	.51	*2.70*	.51	1.48	.53
	Hearing	**1.22**	**.41**	**1.23**	**.42**	**1.25**	**.43**	**1.20**	**.40**
	Physical strength	**1.22**	**.42**	**1.22**	**.43**	**1.26**	**.43**	**1.20**	**.40**
	Vision	**1.19**	**.39**	**1.20**	**.40**	**1.14**	**.35**	**1.17**	**.38**

Factor Analysis

The factor analysis produced five factors with Eigenvalues > 1, accounting for 41.2 percent of the total variance. Nine items did not produce loadings above .35, hence were excluded from further analyses. Figure 2 illustrates how the capabilities grouped together in five factors. Factor-based sum-scores were calculated. For the total sample all factor-based sum-scores showed satisfactory reliability levels, tested with Cronbach's Alpha. For the sub-samples factors could not be consistently reproduced, but Cronbach's Alpha showed values higher than .60 for all but two of the calculated factor-based sumscores (see table 2). The five factors are described below:

Interpersonal management skills (α= .83) consisted of the following eight items: management skills, interpersonal skills, responsibility, independence, stability, understanding of work, low accident risk, and consumer handling skills. In the total sample, all these items were perceived to develop in a positive direction with age. Factor loadings ranged from .52 to .69. This factor explained 19 percent of the total variance.

Learning and coping skills (α= .80) consisted of the items adaptability, learning capacity, speed, and stress handling capacity. In the total sample, all four items were perceived to decline with age. Factor loadings ranged from .45 to .76. This factor explained 11.8 percent of the total variance.

Creative problem-solving skills (α= .73) consisted of problem solving, assessment ability, knowledge of human nature, communication skills, and creativity. Across all sub-samples, all items except creativity were perceived to develop in a positive direction with age. Factor loadings ranged from .36 to .73. This factor explained 5.8 percent of the total variance.

Basic abilities (α= .75) consisted of the two items vision and hearing. Across all sub-samples, both items were perceived to decline with age. Factor loadings were .74 to .81. This factor explained 2.6 percent of the total variance.

Work moral (α= .85) consisted of work ethics and loyalty. In the total sample, both items were perceived to develop in a positive direction with age. Factor loadings were .61 to .70. This factor explained 2 percent of the total variance.

Figure 2. Factor loadings and scales, 21 items.

For each of the five sum-score variables, mean values were calculated (table 2). These mean values made it possible to compare sum-score means from the total sample with sum-score means from the sub-samples. The values were indicated on a scale from 1 to 3, where 1 indicated a negative change, 2 is neutral, and 3 indicated a positive change in the ability with age. The main pattern was that interpersonal & management skills, creative problem-solving skills, and work moral were perceived to develop in a positive direction with age. Learning & coping skills and basic abilities were perceived to develop in a negative direction with increasing age. This pattern could be found in sub-sample B.

Table 2. Sum-score variables, Cronbach's Alpha and mean values for total sample and sub-samples.

Scales (Sum score variables)	Total sample		A n=672		B n=114		C n=352	
	α	m	α	m	α	m	α	m
Interpersonal & management skills	.83	2.3	.77	2.3	.86	1.7	.74	2.4
Learning & coping skills	.80	1.7	.61	1.5	.60	2.4	.58	1.7
Creative problem-solving skills	.73	2.4	.64	2.3	.75	2.3	.64	2.4
Basic abilities	.75	1.2	.81	1.2	.36	1.2	.71	1.1
Work moral	.85	2.3	.82	2.4	.88	1.6	.77	2.4

Differences in factor mean scores within samples were tested for significance (95% confidence interval) with Error Bars. For the total sample, the mean for creative problem solving was significantly higher than all other factors. Interpersonal & management skills and work moral were also rated to develop positively but the mean scores were not significantly different from each other. The factors learning& coping and basic abilities, rated in that order, were significantly different and lower than the other factor means.

For sub-sample A, interpersonal & management skills, creative problem solving, and work moral were perceived to develop in a positive direction, but the mean scores were not significantly different from each other. However, they were significantly different from learning& coping, and basic abilities, which were significantly different from each other.

For sub-sample B, learning& coping, and problem-solving skills were perceived to develop in a positive direction, but the mean values were not significantly different from each other. Interpersonal & management skills, basic abilities and work moral were perceived to decline. Basic abilities were rated significantly lower than the other two.

For sub-sample C, all the positive factors were not significantly different from each other; however, they were significantly different from learning& coping, and basic abilities, which also shared significantly different mean scores.

As illustrated in figure 3, sub-samples A and C follow the same pattern as the total sample, whereas sub-sample B has a different pattern. The differences between the total sample and sub-sample B, showed opposite scores for interpersonal & management skills, learning& coping, and work moral are tested with T-test, and found to be significantly different.

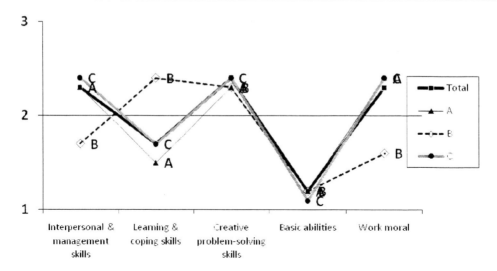

Figure 3. Perceived change in skills and capabilities with age, sum-score means for total sample and sub-samples A, B, and C.

DISCUSSION AND CONCLUSIONS

In this survey of managers' perception of how workforce capabilities change with age, seventeen out of thirty capabilities were perceived to develop in a positive direction with age, and thirteen capabilities were perceived to decline with age. In a factor analysis, the variables grouped in five factors. The five factors derived from the data were: interpersonal & management skills, learning& coping skills, creative problem-solving skills, basic abilities, and work moral. Three of these factors, interpersonal & management skills, creative problem-solving and work moral, were constituted of dimensions that were perceived to improve with age.

These findings are partly at variance with previous studies on stereotypes but more in line with research on behaviour and perceptions of age-related changes. With regards to the first of these factors (interpersonal & management skills), Lyng (1999) found social competence to be perceived by the workforce as increasing with age, and also Cuddy et al. (2003) pointed out warmth as a basic characteristic that often is attributed to the elderly stereotype. Research on behaviour indicates that safety focus increases with age, older workers engage less in counterproductive behaviour; demonstrate better emotional control and less aggression, thus supporting the improvement in interpersonal and managerial skills (Ng & Feldman, 2008). However, to the extent that this first factor may be claimed to represent competence, the present findings are at variance with the stereotypes of low competence for older people proposed by Cuddy et al. (2005).

As for the second of the factors representing positive age-related changes, creative problem-solving skills, support is mainly found in the research of Lyng (1999) who found problem-solving competence to increase with age, and Furunes & Mykletun (2005) who found that older workers gain from experience when solving problems. Due to experience older workers often have a different way of approaching a job task that helps them solve problems more effectively. Regarding behaviour, Levy and Langer (1999) argue that creativity is stable across life-span, although in the present study the creativity item, which loaded on the creative problem-solving factor, actually showed a tendency of minor decline with age. Regarding performance and age, findings are inconsistent, and most researchers conclude that age is not an important predictor of performance level at work (Davies, et al., 1991; Davies, et al., 1992; Griffiths, 1997; McEvoy & Blahna, 2001; Salthouse & Maurer, 1996; Warr, 1994, 1996). As problem solving capabilities may be claimed to be part of the competence structures needed for effective work performance, also these findings are mainly at variance with the stereotype of low competence proposed by Cuddy et al. (2005), and partly also those discussed by Keater (1995).

Regarding the third of the factors representing positive age-related changes, the work moral, Lyng (1999) refers to the concept of maturity as an attribute of older workers. Furunes & Mykletun (2005) found older workers to be more loyal, and suggest that the loyalty dimension is different for younger generations, as employees seem to have greater loyalty to their team than to their manager or organization. These findings are also supported by Ng and Feldman (2008), who found that older workers demonstrate higher levels of citizenship, as well as less on-the-job substance use, tardiness and voluntary absence. Also vigor (Van den Broeck, et al., 2008), positive work-related attitudes increase with age (Rhodes, 1983) as does engagement in work (De Lange, De Witte, & Notelaers, 2008; W. Schaufeli, pers. com), while job boredom declines(Birdi, et al., 1995). This factor does not lend itself so easily to comparisons with the stereotypes of older people stated by Cuddy et al. (2005) as it represents third dimension not touched upon by their research. Future research on stereotyping older workers may reveal how this dimension is generally conceived of and integrated into the stereotyping of the elderly.

Compared to previous findings, this study generally conveys more positive and more nuanced profiling of older workers' capabilities as is contained in previous studies of stereotypes. The perceptions reported by the managers are closer to research findings about older work-related capabilities than to revealed stereotypes of older people. Hence these findings confirm Furunes & Mykletun's (2007) assumptions regarding the variety of existing perceptions, and probably also stereotypes of older workers. This does not eliminate the occurrence of negative findings, as two of the factors derived here were constituted of dimensions that were perceived to decline with age. These two factors were learning& coping skills, and basic abilities. With regard to learning & coping, the findings are in line with previous research on stereotypes (Cuddy et al, 2005; Davies et al, 1991; Keater, 1995; Levy & Langer, 1999). It agrees with Lyng's (1999) findings that older workers have lower ability to adapt; cannot learn new things (Kaeter, 1995), and have greater resistance to change (Davies et al. 1991). These findings are also supported by Warr (1994) who found that older people may be slower in acquiring new skills and knowledge, and shortage of training offered to the older workers may strengthen this problem. Moreover, it may also be an effect of the ways in which job tasks and work is organized; as lack of variation and few job demands are detrimental to, whereas variation, responsibility, and complexity are constitutive to cognitive flexibility and improved cognitive skills (Schooler et al., 1999). Furunes and Mykletun (2005) found that although older workers are perceived to be slower than their younger colleagues, this is not perceived to influence performance, as older workers in general were perceived to be more thorough and cope in different ways compared to their younger colleagues.

Regarding the perceived decline in basic abilities, the current findings are in accordance with previous research on stereotypes (Kaeter, 1995); perceived capabilities (Lyng, 1999), as well as research on physical changes with age (Griffiths, 2007; Ilmarinen et al., 1997). However, decline in hearing and vision only to a little degree is perceived to affect work performance (Lyng, 1999).

Among the 30 items used to measure managers' perceptions of older workers capabilities, 21 items formed five interpretable factors. Five factor-based sum-scores demonstrated good reliability as tested with alpha coefficients. However, the factors were difficult to reproduce as identical structures across samples, and the alpha coefficients were insufficient in two out of 15 instances when the factor-based sum-scores were applied across samples. Hence this scale may be applied for future research and development projects, provided observation of the internal consistency of the scale.

The perceptions of work ability observed in the present study are not totally stable across organisations. This may have several implications. First, these findings indicate that workplace or organisational factors, e.g. culture or the developments of actual capabilities influence how managers perceive the older workers. Second and related to this, these perceptions may either not be conceived of as stereotypes, or the stereotypes of older workers are not as persistent and general as proposed by Cuddy et al. (2005). As the number of organisations is low in the present study it takes further research to provide evidence for this view, however this limited sample is sufficient to contradict the established view that the stereotypes of older workers are totally stable. On the contrary, which is the third implication, it is more likely that managers working with older workers will develop conceptualisations of this part of the workforce that are closer to the characteristics demonstrated by research on actual behaviour. Further studies should address this dilemma more in depth, addressing the relationships between stereotypes, actual performance and behaviour, and managers perceptions in relation to age at the workplace.

REFERENCES

Aronson, E., Wilson, T. D., & Akert, R. (2007). *Cram 101 Textbook Outlines to accompany Social Psychology (5th ed.)*: AIPI

Baltes, P. B., Staudinger, U. M., & Lindenberger, U. (1999). *Lifespan psychology: Theory and application to intellectual functioning.* Annual Review of Psychology, 50, 471-507.

Baltes, P. B., Staudinger, U. M., & Lindenberger, U. (2002). *Lifespan Psychology: Theory and Application to Intellectual Functioning.* In D. L. Infeld (Ed.), Disciplinary Approaches to Aging (Vol. 2, pp. 31-68). New York: Routledge.

Banaji, M. R., & Hardin, C. D. (1996). *Automatic Stereotyping.* Psychological Science, 7(3), 136-141.

Bargh, J. A., Chen, M., & Burrows, L. (1996). *Automaticity of Social Behaviour: Direct Effects of Trait Construct and Stereotype Activation on Action.* Journal of Personality and Social Psychology, 71(2), 230-244.

Birdi, K., Pennington, J., & Zapf, D. (1997). *Ageing and errors in computer-based work: An observational field study.* Journal of Occupational and Organizational Psychology, 70, 35-47.

Birdi, K., Warr, P., & Oswald, A. (1995). *Age Differences in three Components of Employee Well-being. Applied Psychology*: An International Review, 44(4), 345-373.

Blanchflower, D. G., & Oswald, A. J. (2004). *Well-being over time in Britain and the USA.* Journal of Public Economics, 88, 1359-1386.

Blanchflower, D. G., & Oswald, A. J. (2008). *Is well-being u-shaped over the life cycle?* Social Science and Medicine, 66, 1733-1749.

Bosma, H., Van Boxtel, M. P. J., Ponds, R. W. H. W., Houx, P. J., Burdorf, A., & Jolles, J. (2003). *Mental Work Demands Protect Against Cognitive Impairment: MAAS Prospective Cohort Study.* Experimental Aging Research, 29, 33-45.

Brush, D. H., Moch, M. K., & Pooyan, A. (1987). *Individual demographic differences and job satisfaction.* Journal of Occupational Behaviour, 8, 139-155.

Butler, R. N. (1969). *Age-Ism: Another Form of Bigotry.* The Gerontologist, 9, 243-246.

Chiu, W. C. K., Chan, A. W., Snape, E., & Redman, T. (2001). *Age stereotypes and discriminatory attitudes towards older workers: An East-West comparison.* Human Relations, 54(5), 629-661.

Csikszentmihalyi, M. (1997). *Living well: The psychology of everyday life.* London: Weidenfeld & Nicholson.

Cuddy, A. J. C., Norton, M. I., & Fiske, S. T. (2005). *This Old Stereotype: The Pervasiveness and Persistence of the Elderly Stereotype.* Journal of Social Issues, 61(2), 267-285.

Davies, D. R., Matthews, G., & Wong, C. S. K. (1991). *Ageing and Work.* In C. L. Cooper & I. T. Robertson (Eds.), International Review of Industrial and Organizational Psychology (Vol. 6, pp. 149-211): John Wiley & Sons Ltd.

Davies, D. R., Taylor, A., & Dorn, L. (1992). *Aging and Human Performance.* In D. M. J. a. A. P. Smith (Ed.), Handbook of Human Performance (Vol. 3, pp. 25-63). London: Academic Press.

De Lange, A. H., De Witte, H., & Notelaers, G. (2008). *Should I stay or should I go?* Work and Stress, 22(3), 201-223.

Doering, M., Rhodes, S. R., & Schuster, M. (1983). *The Aging Worker.* Bevery Hills: CA: Sage.

Furunes, T., & Mykletun, R. J. (2005). *Age management in Norwegian hospitality businesses.* Scandinavian Journal of Hospitality and Tourism, 5(2), 116-134.

Furunes, T., & Mykletun, R. J. (2007). *Why diversity management fails: Metaphor analyses unveil manager attitudes. [research article].* International Journal of Hospitality Management, 26(4), 974-990.

Furunes, T., & Mykletun, R. J. (2010). *Age discrimination in the workplace: Validation of the Nordic Age Discrimination Scale (NADS). [Research].* Scandinavian Journal of Psychology, 51(1), 23-30.

Griffiths, A. (1997). *Aging, health and productivity: A challenge for the new millennium.* Work & Stress, 11(3), 197-214.

Griffiths, A. (2007). *Healthy work for older workers: work design and management factors.* In W. Loretto, S. Vickerstaff & P. White (Eds.), The future for older workers: New perspectives (Vol. 1, pp. 121-138). Bristol: The Policy Press.

Hallsten, L. (1993). *Arbete och subjectiva förändringar under vuxenlivet.* [Vitenskapelig skriftserie]. Arbete och Hälsa(31), 1-35.

Hansen, T., Slagsvold, B., & Moum, T. (2008). *Financial satisfaction in old age: A satisfaction paradox or a result of accumulated wealth.* Social Science Indicators, 89, 323-347.

Hansson, R. O., DeKoekkoek, P. D., Neece, W. M., & Patterson, D. W. (1997). *Successful Aging at Work: Annual Review, 1992-1996: The Older Worker and Transitions to Retirement. [review]*. Journal of Vocational Behavior, 51, 202-233.

Hogg, M. A. (2006). *Intergroup Relations*. In J. Delamater (Ed.), Handbook of Social Psychology (pp. 479-501). Wisconsin: Springer.

Ilmainen, J. (2009). *Work ability—a comprehensive concept for occupational health research and prevention [Editorial]*. Scandinavian Journal of Work Environment & Health, 35(1), 1-5.

Ilmarinen, J. (2001). *Aging Workers*. Occupational & Environmental Medicine, 58(8), 546-552.

Ilmarinen, J., & Rantanen, J. (1999). *Promotion of Work Ability during Aging. [short]*. American Journal of Industrial Medicine Supplement, 1, 21-23.

Ilmarinen, J., Tuomi, K., & Klockars, M. (1997). *Changes in the work ability of active employees over an 11-year period*. Scandinavian Journal of Work Environment and Health, 23(1), 49-57.

Kaeter, M. (1995). *Age-Old Myths*. Training, 32(1), 61-66.

Kite, M. E., Stockdale, G. D., Whitley, B. E. J., & Johnson, B. T. (2005). *Attitudes Toward Younger and Older Adults: An Updated Meta-Analytic Review. [meta analytic review]*. Journal of Social Issues, 61(2), 241-266.

Levy, B. R. (1996). *Improving memory in old age by implicit self-stereotyping*. Journal of Personality and Social Psychology, 71, 1092-1107.

Levy, B. R. (2000). *Handwriting as a Reflection of Aging Self-stereotypes*. Journal of Gereatric Psychiatry, 33, 81 – 94.

Levy, B. R., Ashman, O., & Dior, I. (1999). *Be or Not to Be. The Effects of Ageing Stereotypes on the Will to Live*. Omega: Journal of Death and Dying, 40, 409 - 420.

Levy, B. R., & Banaji, M. R. (2002). *Implicit ageism. In T. D. Nelson (Ed.), Ageism*. Stereotyping and prejudice against older persons (pp. 49-75). Bradford: Cambridge.

Levy, B. R., & Langer, E. (1999). *Aging Encyclopaedia of Creativity (Vol. 1, pp. 45-52)*: Academic Press.

Lyng, K. (1999). *Oppfatninger av eldre arbeidstakeres yrkeskompetanse og omstillingsevne [Perceptions of older workers' competence and ability to change] (No. NOVA report 10/99)*. Oslo: Norwegian Social Research NOVA.

Lyng, K. (2007, August 3-5,2007). *The AAC User as an Older Worker. Paper presented at the Biennial Pittsburgh Employment Conference for Augmented Communicators*, Pittsburg, Pensylvania, USA.

Madon, S., Guyll, M., Hilbert, S. J., Kyriakatos, E., & Vogel, D. L. (2006). *Stereotyping the Stereotypic: When Individuals Match Social Stereotypes. [research]*. Journal of Applied Social Psychology, 36(1), 178-205.

Magd, H. (2003). *Management attitudes and perceptions of older employees in hospitality management*. International Journal of Contemporary Hospitality Management, 15(7), 393-401.

McCann, R. M., & Giles, H. (2002). *Ageism and the workplace: A communication perspective*. In T. D. Nelson (Ed.), Ageism (pp. 163-199). Cambridge, MA: MIT Press.

McEvoy, G. M., & Blahna, M. J. (2001). *Engagement or Disengagement? Older Workers and the Looming Labor Shortage.[exploratory study research article]*. Business Horizons, September-October, 46-52.

McEvoy, G. M., & Cascio, W. (1989). *Cumulative evidence of the relationship between employee age and job performance. [review]*. Journal of Applied Psychology, February, 11-17.

Merton, R. K. (1957). *Social theory and social structure*. Glencoe, Ill: Free Press.

Mor-Barak, M. E. (1995). *The meaning of work for older adults seeking employment. The generativity factor*. International Journal of Aging and Human Development, 41, 325-344.

Mortensen, E. L. (2007). *Det aldrende intellekt*. In L. Larsen (Ed.), Gerontopsykologi: Det aldrende menneskets psykologi. Århus: Århus University Press.

Ng, T. W. H., & Feldman, D. C. (2008). *The relationship of age to ten dimensions of job performance*. Journal of Applied Psychology, 93, 392-423.

OECD (2007). *OECD employment outlook 2007*.

Orpen, C. (1995). *The effects of Perceived Age Discrimination on Employee Job Satisfaction, Organisational Commitment, and Job Involvement*. Psychology: A Quaterly Journal of Human Behavior, 32(3-4), 55-56.

Perdue, C. W., & Gurtman, M. B. (1990). *Evidence for the automaticity of ageism*. Journal of Experimental Social Psychology, 26(3), 199-216.

Rhodes, S. R. (1983). *Age-Related Differences in Work Attitudes and Behavior: A Review and a Conceptual Analysis*. Psychological Bulletin, 93, 283-367.

Rodes, S. R. (1983). *Age-Related Differences in Work Attitudes and Behavior. A Review and a Conceptual Analysis*. Psychological Bulletin, 93, 282-367.

Rupp, D. E., Vodanovich, S. J., & Credé, M. (2006). *Age Bias in the Workplace: The Impact of Ageism and Causal Attributions. [research]*. Journal of Applied Social Psychology, 36(6), 1337-1364.

Salthouse, T. A. (1997, 22-25 September). *Implications of adult age differences in cognition for work performance*. Paper presented at the Work after 45? , Stockholm.

Salthouse, T. A., Hambrick, D. Z., Lukas, K. E., & Dell, T. C. (1996). *Determinants of Adult Age Differences on Synthtic Work Performance*. Journal of Experimental Psychology: Applied, 2(4), 305-329.

Salthouse, T. A., & Maurer, T. J. (1996). *Aging, job performance and career development*. In J. B. K. Schaie (Ed.), handbook of the psychology of aging (pp. 353-364). San Diego, CA: Academic Press.

Schaie, K. W. (2005). *Developmental influences on adult intelligence*. The Seattle Longitudinal Study. New York: Oxford University Press.

Schalk, R., van Veldhoven, M., de Lange, A. H., De Witte, H., Kraus, K., Stamov-Rossnagel, C., et al. (2010). *Moving European reserach on work and ageing forward: Overview and agenda*. European Journal of Work and Organizational Psychology, 19(1), 76-101.

Schooler, C., Malatu, M. S., & Oates, G. (1999). *The Continuing Effects of Substantively Complex Work on the Intellectual Functioning of Older Workers*. Psychology and Aging, 14(3), 483-506.

Smith, R., Parrott, W. G., Ozer, D., & Moniz, A. (1994). *Subjective injustice and Inferiority as Predictors of Hostile and Depressive Feelings in Envy*. [Research]. Personality and Social Psychology Bulletin, 20(6), 705-711.

Spector, P. E. (2007). *Job satisfaction*. Application, assessment, causes and consequences. London: SAGE.

Tuomi, K., Ilmainen, J., Martikainen, R., & Klockars, M. (1997). *Aging, work, life-style and Work Ability among Finnish municipality workers in 1981 - 1992.* Scandinavian Journal of Work, Environment and Health, 23, 58-65.

Vaillant, G. E. (1993). *Avoiding negative life outcomes: Evidence from a forty-five year study.* In B. Baltes (Ed.), Successful Aging: Perspectives from the behavioral sciences (pp. 332-358). Canada: Cambridge University Press.

Vaillant, G. E. (2002). *Aging Well.* New York: Little Brown.

Van den Broeck, A., Vansteenkiste, M., De Witte, H., & Lens, W. (2008).*Explaining the Relationship Between Job Characteristics, Burnout, and Engagement: The Role of Basic Psychological Need Satisfaction.* Work and Stress, 22(3), 277 - 294.

Waddel, G., & Burton, A. K. (2006). *Is Work Good for Your Health and Well-Being?* The Stationery Office.

Waldman, D. A., & Avolio, B. J. (1986). *A Meta-analysis of Age Differences in Job Performance.* Journal of Applied Psychology, 71, 33-38.

Warr, P. (1994). *Age and job performance. In J. Snel & R. Cremer, R. (Eds.), Work and aging.* An European perspective (pp. 309-322). London: Taylor & Francis.

Warr, P. (1996). *Younger and Older Workers.* In P. Warr (Ed.), Psychology at Work (4th Edition ed., pp. 308-333). London: The Penguin Group.

Willis, S. L., & Schaie, K. W. (1999). *Intellectual functioning in midlife.* In S. H. W. a. J. D. Reid (Ed.), Life in the middle: psychological and sociological development in middle age (pp. 233-248). San Diego, CA: Academic Press.

Wright, J. D., & Hamilton, R. F. (1978). *Work Satisfaction and Age: Some Evidence for the 'Job Change' Hypothesis.* Social Forces, 56(4), 1140-1158.

In: Psychology of Stereotypes
Editor: Eleanor L. Simon

ISBN: 978-1-61761-463-7
©2011 Nova Science Publishers, Inc.

Chapter 8

ADS AND SPORTS: STEREOTYPICAL SCENES

Stephane Heas, D. Bodin, L. Robene and J. Blumrodt
European University of Britain, France

EXECUTIVE SUMMARY

Purpose

The advertisementsof sportsare far from being able to reflect the changing realities of sports or physical activities in a country such as France. The purpose is to test the proposition that the gender relationships portrayed in specific sport advertisements perpetuate traditional and sexist stereotypes, are far from egalitarian shared social representations, and far from egalitarian social and professional activities[1].

Design/Methodology/Approach

There were 700 advertisements of sports in several French magazines analyzed during a twenty-two-year period (1986-2008) constituting the support of content analysis, using specific spreadsheet software(Sphinx®). Specifically, four men's readerships magazines and four women's magazinesare strongly represented here because of their large national diffusion. There are 25 encodings used to analyze this corpus, and they distinguish the people displayed, setting of Advertisements (nature, area's sport, and undetermined places), situations of equality or domination between male/female and *vice versa*, domination between male/male, domination between female/female, and the colours used, the appearance of physical movement, skin colour, the presence of hair and hairs, etc.

---

[1] Research conducted with the support of ANR-08-VULN-001-PRAS-GEVU, universities of Lyon, Rennes, France.

Findings

In sports advertisements and which use sports, males are over-represented: 57.4% are present, *versus* 18.5% females present. Women in sports are generally in situations of inequality or subordination: face to face, males dominating the females (11.9% of all ads, 28.5% of face to face ads). On the contrary, females rarely dominate the males: these amounts to occur five times less often (2.1% of all advertisements' situations, and 5.2% of face to face ads respectively).Men in sports seem to be more dynamic individuals: males move more often than their female counterparts (50.1% *versus* 36% respectively). Especially, a man's physical movements are more frequent when several men are represented in the magazine ads. Females are represented with fewer activities, often seen as spectators of male sporting events, and even nowadays are over-sexualised. However, on average, sports ads promote the entire female body (48.3% for women *vs* 42.7% for men):this frequency rejects the arguments of militant feminists who think that women are more often "cut" from advertisements. The male characters, strangely, are more often photographed in portrait style (9.2% for men *vs* 5.6% for women).The women are over-sexualized in the ads for sports: their breasts, legs and calves are more frequently seen in the advertisements. These body parts are over-represented more often than that of their male counterparts: 22.4% *vs* 14.2% respectively. These averages confirm stereotypes, and reinforce the previous sociological studies' results(Goffman, 1976; Wolin, 2003; Cortese, 2007; Grau et *al.*, 2007). Gender imbalance is reinforced by such adjuncts such as 1) colour utilisation, for instance, blue (31.3%) *versus* one percent for pink, 2) outdoor background which reinforces sociological link between males and outside activities, and 3) type of physical activities portrayed (traditional masculine sports in Europe like football-soccer, rugby or motorsports).

By and large, sports ads remain to be created from a classical masculine point of view rather than a gender reversal. Different shocking visuals are easier to remember by the public but are drowned in all ads of sports. On average, the advertisements of sports maintain an andrological point of view.

Research Limitations/Implications

Extensions of the present study, and future research, could increase both the breadth and depth of the investigation, and thereby contribute significantly to the wealth of knowledge pertaining to gender in advertising. During some periods of the year, advertisements can be less "gender'stereotypical". For example, in 1996 and 1997, in France there were some ads which had reversed the gender domination (Perret, 2003). In the long term, the ads of sports are always portraying the masculine point of view. Female athletes are often always devalued.

Practical Implications

There is still some way to go before sports advertisements reflect the real world, *a fortiori* an ideal world where equality is normal, and improves gender's innovations into advertising in the future. For instance, to propose gender egalitarian ads, (without women's degradations into visuals, or through sexists or demeaning slogans- not analysed here), to reinforce advertisement agencies' social responsibility or sports enterprises' social responsibility, to boost egalitarian relations between males and females, all done by extensions between different ethnic, sexual, generational, religious, etc., groups.

Originality/Value

This study examines a widespread social phenomenon in a specific and national context upon a large corpus (seven hundred ads of sports) and not only on provoking ads, nor during a period of time with most egalitarian ads.

KeyWords: Advertising, gender stereotypes, sport and exercise, France magazines, sociology

1. INTRODUCTION

Sports are a set of cultural practices in their own right ([1] [2] [3]). As Elias and Dunning [4] convincingly argued, sports have steadily added to the understanding of a worldwide social phenomenon. Sporting activities can thus become a lens through which to cast light on more cultural issues and social problems. In our study, we examine gendered relationships in sport-themed advertising campaignsin more than eight French magazines (1986-2008[2]). We do not spill over into a radical critique [5] and we do not develop arguments about different approaches, given the number of different conceptualisations of this phenomenon present[6].

The analysis of advertisements is very important. The analysis and the deconstruction of advertisements "are not trivial activities, especially in the sports world truly"colonized "by them"[7]. Sports are indicative of the dominant values (performance, dynamism, youthful, etc.).Sports are important today, through their economic and symbolic dimensions. The modern sport puts value primarily towards the men. The advertising images are sometimes shocking and they may cause adverse effects to some populations. Our analyses do notconcern these offensive advertisements in particular, but all others in magazines, week after week in France. We show that the subordination and the sexualization of women are maintained by ordinary advertising and not only by the most provocative advertisements. The degradation of women "is mobilized by their low participation in sports advertisements, and their cantonment in the roles of inaction, supporters of spectators, in short to second-athletes " [7].

Advertising functions as a technique of persuasion (or even seduction) in several ways. First, it informs potential consumers about the existence of a product. In developed societies, everyone is exposed to an abundant amount of advertisements, retaining certain images in their mind rather than others. Each of us is exposed to ads: some hundreds, even thousands, per day. This daily exposure to ads belongs to contemporary education by the media and new information technologies. The ads are describing and defining a product or service for the sports industry. The images in advertisements succeed in differentiating one offering from

---

[2] Some Ads have been edited before 1986 (N = 15). They don't take place here into our analyses.

another. Further, ads can arouse latent needs, to sell, and possibly to precipitate unpremeditated purchases. In its very complexity, the advertising seems efficient. In fact, it is a complex discourse with the consumer, not just a source of much information. Ads can transmit some powerful semiotic signifiers [8]. Today, ads are furthermore an indicator of main norms and values around us.

Sport and Exercise, here, embraces not only the major competitive sports in any society but also the many other forms of personal or collective physical activity that attract less media coverage and are therefore less familiar to society.

Our frame of reference for this study grew out of a gendered standpoint that analyzes the relations between the social sexes, and evaluates the concepts of masculinity and of femininity in today's world as processes. We ask ourselves whether this changing shape of the social representation of men and women is detectable into contemporary sport-themed advertising campaigns. We suspect that ads still perpetuate gender stereotypes that present males as active 'doers' and females as admiring onlookers. These stereotypes reinforce the conflict between the strength and hardness of the masculine world and the beauty and softness of feminine world [9]. These oppositions recall the fundamental's anthropological dichotomies, which are described and decried by Héritier [10], and are based on assumed differences between the male and the female roles. In the process of deconstructing French advertising for sport-related products and services, we were alert to evidence that the clothing of female figures – or, rather, the lack there of – might support assertions of the French feminist Movement Against Sexist Advertising, for which the woman is still a sex object in advertisements.

Our main research proposition is thus that masculine and feminine roles in advertisements of sports are still containing stereotypes, despite the noticeable evolution of sports themselves and of the societies in which the sport developed [11]. The analysis of advertising campaigns featuring images of sport and exercise can contribute to improve the understanding of such social processes as identification with sportsmen and women, or even the process of mythologization of sportsmen: reinforced by significant media attention [12]. We can assert confidently that the identity of male is shaped by the presence of celebrated male sports on screen and in the press [13], whether in advertising campaigns or during retransmitted live broadcasts. Men's sports seem evidently prized as models for lines of clothing or ranges of toiletries and cosmetics. The lesser frequencies - of female sports personalities in these roles -are unarguable. These trends limit the possibility for women's sports to influence her self-identity, to influence their small place in the real world of sports.Nowadays, in France, the cultural universe and the consumption practices are diverse and dynamic; tastes are now more 'dissonant' than they were before [14]. As 'cultural consumers', we can all accumulate life experiences. It seems in fact that cultural wealth is characterised by the ability to treat different ranges of cultural or "registers of culture" in a positive way [15]. Consumers and media audiences in general do not act and do not think unilaterally. One message can be interpreted differently even by individuals from very similar socio-economic levels, a fact that complicates targeting strategies for marketing professionals [16]. Moreover, studies of the reception of messages have shown that theses variations in interpretation are brought about by such mediatisation factors, not only because of social class effects but also because of ethnicity and gender [17] [18]. With their own results, surveys cannot explain the complex processes by which a particular signification is allocated to a given message [19].

Undoubtedly, this conceptual complexity and these recurring debates explain the absence of a consensus among the various specialist analysts of advertising as a social process. In fact, like most phenomena closely enmeshed with modern daily life, advertising ignites passions and thereby provides a fertile ground for the flowering of valuable judgments. Beneficial for some and harmful for others, the advertisements have several enthusiasts as well as detractors. Far from being resolved, these arguments draw attention to the complexity of a phenomenon that only continues to be developed, and thereby to confirm the relevance of making a contribution to the debate, however minor.

2. LITERATURE REVIEW

2.1 Sports in Society

The introduction has noted that the sociology of sport has been seen as a microcosm of general sociology. Violence in sports, for instance, is only one element of social relationships, whether personal and interpersonal, generally directed towards public and private goods According to researchers [20] [21] [22], analyses are not only in terms of power relationships among social and professional groups, but also between genders.

Such analyses are sometimes critical, and apparently entirely negative. For instance, a book with the strongly explicit title *Sport Against the People* argues that "sport succeeds to fix into the collective psyche only insignificant and empties stereotypes" (p. 47)[23]. Thus, professional sports appear like a distorted mirror. Professional sports reduce sportsmen to collaborators in a system in which profit is the key word [24] [25]. Sports are transforming those who enjoy watching them live or on television without playing the sport themselves, as mass groups which are hypnotized. This process fixed their daily life [26].

2.2 Sport as a Theme in Advertising

The French public is exposed to around "12,000 television spots and tens of thousands of press advertisements and posters in a year", according to an expert in a study [27]. This heavy saturation has attracted the interest of many researchers in the social sciences over the years, such as Goffman [28], [29], [30], [31], [32]. The formal analysis of advertisements is built into some academic syllabuses in the United Kingdom, in Canada and in Australia, as an aspect of the study of propaganda and persuasion[33]. The courses of Media studies are widespread. They are often incorporated with a strong advertising component. Media studies courses have been popular in France in recent years, according to Grésy [27]. In Canada, the bilingual Media Awareness Network or the Networks Media Education (*Réseau Éducation Médias*) pursues the goal to encourage media and information literacy for young people through a variety of teaching materials and events.

Media advertising has long been recognised as a safeguard against the loss of the independence of the press and freedom of speech. This is done by virtue of the revenue flowing for the media owners [34] and its broader impact on society is often subject to virulent criticism[35][36]. Advertisements are seen as the vehicle for the potential manipulation of opinions [37] and even the manipulation of minds [38]. New Marxist Frankfurt School, as a critical social theory, had seen advertising as having an alienating effect of the technical-scientific rationalisation, in its creation of false needs [39]. Such other perspectives of political economics have accused advertisements of creating "a standardized social image" [38] and fostering "the American dream" [40].

Recently, those who view advertising messages as a form of interactive symbolic communication, with less far-reaching consequences have called these critiques into question. Our own study is consistent with this conceptual framework, in treating them at once as creators of added value for products and services, thanks to their adaptability to ideologies, and also to some extent, as symbolic reflections of the social context in which they are transmitted and 'offered' to various publics. As Maigret [41] states: "the grand effect of advertising – indirectly – is to make products available in an imaginary world... so that they lend themselves to a game of personal tastes and social distinctions" (p.61).

2.3 Gender Relationships in Advertisements

The constant flood of information delivered through advertising campaigns reflects the dominant social imagery of today, and very probably reinforces this imagery. Featuring social relationships, the advertisements effectively present a gendered scenario to the audience [28]. Specifically, our study aims for a clearer understanding of the position of the human body in representations of sport and exercise, when humans are both actors in the advertisements and targets for the advertisement in question. Whether or not it is in the context of sports, a lot of informationreinforces the presence of male dominance[42], [43],[44], [45], [46],by means of what we call a gendered relationship segmented, as stated by Putrevu[32].

As the twentieth century approached its closing years, [47], [48], [49], different authors have asserted that male identity would be in trouble[50], in the new millennium. Men will encounter difficulties in walks of life progressively infiltrated by women, such as the hitherto male preserves of higher education and the professions. Indeed, there is some evidence that sport and exercise are gradually made more feminine despite many remaining obstacles to female participation.

In the media, however, the male figure remains dominant. Eveno [51] asserts that men monopolise the most valued occupations and the most respected positions, with only rare exceptions. Publishing, journalism, broadcasting and the new information media are all male dominated worlds. The advertising business in France is scarcely less so, according to the Creative Director of the Paris branch of the multinational agency Young and Rubicam, who told a researcher that "it's four women to twenty men in our office"[27].We do not categorically confirm this gender imbalance in the media, but it is reflected in the androcentric content of the magazine advertisements analyzed in detail for this study [52].It is furthermore the implicit circular rationale for the disproportionate media coverage of male sport and exercise[44],[53].

The sporting exploits of women through sports are almost always reported by the news media in male terms. For example, a French yachtswoman was dubbed "the little *fiancée* of the Atlantic" when she can be seen abandoning the *Rhum's Road* transatlantic race, but on the day that she won it by the headline in *Le Parisien*: "Flo, you're a real guy!". Similarly,

Reuters indicated: "Who is this guy?" when Amélie Mauresmo won the Australian Tennis Open in 1999 [54](p.109). The French first names of star women involved in sports are routinely masculinised: 'Flo' for Florence Artaud, the yachtswoman; and 'Marie Jo' for Marie José Pérec, the first female runner to win the 200 and 400 metres at the Olympic Games. These contractions of female-given names are frequently seen throughout the English-speaking world. Because this practice is so common, no one ever pauses to think that the shortened versions of the names are the same as those used for men's given names. Thus Sam is short for Samantha or Samuel, and Chris is short for Christine or Christopher. 'Jackie' is short for Jacqueline, and only rarely for John, which is usually shortened to 'Jack'. These familiarisations are the signals of the intimacy claimed by journalists, financial backers, coaches and, of course, the sport's public [55],[56]. It can even be seen as a process of trivialisation, which makes the athletes behave like children (process of infantilisation), and have been since at least the mid 1970s, when Goffman published his classic studies into the Anthropology of Visual Communication.Thus, we have a spectrum of stereotypes: at one pole, the male sporting environment in which strength and performance are valued; and at the other pole, we have the female world, in which the aesthetic and the sensual are emphasised. The analytical studies of these comments have mostly found that such gender distinctions are indeed made [57]. In short, media coverage seems to reinforce the stereotypes rather than oppose them. We ask ourselves if the same process is at work on the case of the magazines and posters advertising, which can be conceived of as alternatives for discourse and imagery.

2.4 Advertising Images as a Social 'Prescription'

The review of literature on advertising is particularly ambivalent when it comes to whether they are more or less stereotypical than in the past times. It also indicates that consumer advertisements always differ in the reactions people may have [58]. The gender is still an essential element to take into account when looking at the marketing strategies of segmentation, for example. For Wolin, gender is readily identifiable. Indeed, the media for men's viewers/readers offer a greater division between gender stereotypes.For many years now, historical and sociological analyses of advertising have regularly underlined its own prescriptive character. This 'normative order'(p. 271) [29] is seldom overturned. Today, however, a great interaction and a symbolic *modus operandi*of these implicit behavioural norms are emphasized, rather than constrained or coercive. The commercial referred requires " Without obey the rules, the qualification of the characters draws on the reserve of social stereotypes available and understood by many (...) The statistics predominance of gender roles are still differentiated in some areas of social reality. It also expresses the logic of communication for most advertisers, hoping for a favourable reception of their messages from the widest possible audience. They are naturally inclined to focus on messages with a smooth image and conventional social relationships " [11] (p. 166).

The representation of sport and physical exercise in magazine advertisements in France presents the audience an imaginary world with immaculate images or personas, far from the realities of physical exertion in the gym or sports clubs [46]. Notably, the rare exceptions to this rule occur in advertisements featuring males in sports, rather than the females in sports. Otherwise, ads are the links to a picture of a civilized, healthy, innocent activity, which is promoted as an ideal image to the world at large.The advertisements thus become the shopping window for a social conformism: to be active physically, sweat-free, stain-free and, above all, odour-free.

3. METHODOLOGY

3.1 Selection of Advertisements

The research sample is comprised of only advertisements which refer to sports and any type of physical activity. A few decades ago, sports were not seen as a valued activity. They were so rare in advertisements that they were not distinguished from other "products" such as cars or products for animals. This encoding would aggregate in sports to be in the same category as "other"[59].

Nowadays, if a magazine does no specialize in sports, the magazine presents very little advertising on sports. This explains why many years, there is, ultimately, little advertising available and made present about sports. Women's magazines had often none of these ads for weeks at a time. On the contrary, the specialized magazines for sports offer many ads about sports in each issue. We choose to work on with both the specialized magazines and magazines with no specialization.We had 700 advertisements collected from French magazines during the twenty-two-year period from 1996 to 2008, half of the magazines which have a predominantly male subscription (for instance, *Le Nouvel Observateur, L'Equipe Magazine, Science et Vie* and *L'Automobile magazine*) and the other half are read mainly by women (*Elle, Notre Temps, Santé Magazine,* and *Femme Actuelle*). The magazines with television programs have been added to this gender distribution because they are important in terms of national diffusion in France. In 2003, they occupied the seven first places in rankings of read weekly magazines(from four million to 1.6 million copies). The eighth place was occupied by *Femme Actuelle* with 1.3 million copies, then *Notre Temps* with 1 million copies[3].

The number of sources was large enough to generate a credible database and permit the identification of significant trends, which can be confirmed or refined by re-examination in future's research studies.

The advertisements collected can belong to one campaign extending over several weeks, but we made no attempt to assess the effect of this repetition. Nor did we try to control differences in the advertisers' brand importance (Nike "against" Asics, for instance) or levels of recognition and impact in the marketplace (the retailer Decathlon "against" Go Sport, for example: both are French, but there's a trading respectively in three European countries versus seven or eight around the world). We have not analyzed advertising agencies and the marketing strategies of sponsors.

---

[3] In 2007 : Le Nouvel Observateur (509 000 copies), L'Equipe Magazine (354 000), Science et Vie (278 000), L'Automobile magazine (140 000).

3.2 Data Analysis

Data analysis is done continuously and systematically over the period of data collection. The analytical strategy combines two methods. We first followed the well-established qualitative interpretative method set by such researchers such as Barthes [60], [61] [29], all of whom were interested in advertising as sociological phenomenon. We then used a more quantitative methodology. The software chosen to implement this second phase of the analysis is the Sphinx Lexica® software, an advanced spreadsheet application. For input, advertisements were formally coded by reference to:

> ➤ the presence or absence of human characters in the advertisement;
> ➤ the use of recognisable sports figures as implied endorsers of the product or service, or on the contrary, unknown people;
> ➤ the proxemics[4] of the relationships into the group (distance between protagonists, stature of participants, superior and inferior positions, foregrounding, posture, body language, etc.);
> ➤ the visual setting (a sports field, an urban scene, nature scene (sea, mountain, desert, etc.);
> ➤ the product (clothing, accessories, backpacks, equipment, toiletries, cosmetics, services, etc.);
> ➤ slogans or headlines.

This coding scheme, by specifying the spatial relations among the persons portrayed in the advertisements, minimizes the scope for subjective or partisan interpretations. The encodings are added gradually to allow for further specific issues such as the visible presence of hair, different skin colours, etc. We have 25 different encodings. Each one is validate into university courses. When a coding collects a near unanimous agreement by the majority of students (4/5), it is considered reliable.

In analysing the relationships between all elements within ads, we were trying to establish whether the people who featured in an advertisement were equivalent or not, and whether the relationship between them was dominant or submissive. For human relations, we adopted encoding from Ahlstrand [62]. Imagine an advertisement that depicts cyclists pulling ahead of another cyclist who is having obvious difficulties. If both are male, the situation is coded: 'male inequality', the coding is male > male; if it is a female cyclist who has fallen behind a male, the coding is male >female, the arrowhead symbolising the direction of the power relationship. The opposite situation, extremely unlikely even in advertisements in magazines with a female readership, would therefore be coded female >male.

With particular reference to the iconography of gender, we refined the coding scheme as shown above by recording such attributes as colours of clothing, length and style of hair, and so forth.The result was a 25 point coding frame.

The software compares this data as the titles and dates of the magazines in which the advertisements had appeared. It calculates mean values and frequencies, and tests each variable. This process of deconstruction allowed us to maintain an intellectual distance from material that, by definition, had been deliberately designed to excite attention. It permitted us to maintain objectivity with the ads. The outcome presented us with the fundamental building

---

[4] Cf. E. T. Hall, The hidden dimension, 1966.

blocks intended (implicitly if not explicitly) to attract readers, and convert them to customers. Our research protocol thus successfully delivers a more objective analysis.

4.FINDINGS

4.1 People and Objects Featured

This software-driven content analysis indicates that most common advertisements present different inanimate objects, in the foreground or background (Table 1). Objects are more prevalent in corpus (25.6% in the foreground, 35% of all ads elements) than anything else. These objects are included regardless of their relation to sports.

Table 1. The elements presented in Ads

The Items	Nb. cit. (rank 1)	Fréq.	Nb. cit. (rank 2)	Fréq.	Nb. cit. (rank 3)	Fréq.	Nb. cit. (rank 4)	Fréq.	Nb. cit. (sum)	Fréq.
Male	112	16,0%	41	7,5%	8	4,5%	2	5,4%	163	11,1%
Female	17	2,4%	22	4,0%	6	3,4%	1	2,7%	46	3,1%
Children	37	5,3%	39	7,1%	10	5,6%	0	0,0%	86	5,9%
Animals	8	1,1%	25	4,6%	10	5,6%	7	18,9%	50	3,4%
Objects	179	25,6%	294	53,6%	35	19,7%	3	8,1%	511	35,0%
Landscapes	16	2,3%	58	10,6%	102	57,3%	22	59,5%	198	13,5%
Couple Heterosexual	69	9,9%	13	2,4%	4	2,2%	0	0,0%	86	5,9%
Male Alone	193	27,6%	45	8,2%	0	0,0%	1	2,7%	239	16,3%
Femme Alone	68	9,7%	11	2,0%	3	1,7%	1	2,7%	83	5,7%
TOTAL CITATIONS	699		548		178		37		1462	100%

Note: One Advertisement is not informed.
The question is 4 ordered multiple responses.
The staffing table for each row and for the money.
The difference with the distribution of reference is very significant. chi2 = 269.70, df = 6, 1-p => 99.99%.
The Chi2 is calculated with the theoretical distribution follows: men (14.0%), women (14.0%), children (14.0%), heterosexual couples (14.0%), single men (14.0%), single women (14.0%)
The table is built on 700 observations.
The percentages are calculated with reference to the number of citations.

More often to sell sport, running shoes for instance, ads show no athlete, celebrity one or not. In ads, merchandises are 52% exclusively sports-related and 39.7% include sports along with non sport related objects.
For example, one advertisement shows a male tennis player, dressed in sports attire, with his racket, near a car (which is the purpose of the ad). In cases like these, we have

classifiedtheseadvertisementsunder the item:"tools of sport and others tools". In this case, there is a sporting character, sports equipment, and sports clothing, but the purpose of advertisement is to sell a non-racing car.Only 11.2% of ads use tools, landscapes, and places that are unrelated to the sport.These objects still play a strong role in their respective sports ads. This finding confirms the importance and relevanceof material sports related and non-related objects in sports today.

When humansare shown (for the purposes of statistical analysiswe exclude landscapes, animals and objects items in the following tables), men are undeniably the figureheads, far in front of women (Table 2). Sports advertisements with humans show a single male 34% of the time and male groups 23.2% of the time. Men are featured in more a half (57.2%) of the advertisements with sports as a theme (*versus* 18.3% for the females presence). Single males in the foreground are present in more than a third (38.9%) of the whole sample (*versus* 13.7% to single females).

Table 2. Presence of human characters.

Human characters	Nb.cit. (rank 1)	Fréq.	Nb. cit. (rank 2)	Fréq.	Nb. cit. (rank 3)	Fréq.	Nb. cit. (rank 4)	Fréq.	Nb. cit. (sum)	Fréq.
Males	112	22,6%	41	24,0%	8	25,8%	2	40,0%	163	23,2%
Females	17	3,4%	22	12,9%	6	19,4%	1	20,0%	46	6,5%
Children	37	7,5%	39	22,8%	10	32,3%	0	0,0%	86	12,2%
Couple Heterosexual	69	13,9%	13	7,6%	4	12,9%	0	0,0%	86	12,2%
Single Male	193	38,9%	45	26,3%	0	0,0%	1	20,0%	239	34,0%
Single Female	68	13,7%	11	6,4%	3	9,7%	1	20,0%	83	11,8%
TOTAL CITATIONS	496		171		31		5		703	100%

The question is 4 ordered multiple responses.

The staffing table for each row and for the money.

The difference with the distribution of reference is very significant. chi2 = 269.70, df = 6, 1-p => 99.99%.

The Chi2 is calculated with the theoretical distribution follows:men (14.0%), women (14.0%), children (14.0%), heterosexual couples (14.0%), single men (14.0%), single women (14.0%) .

The table is built on 700 observations.

The percentages are calculated with reference to the number of citations.

On average, men are omnipresent, three more time than women. Men are often more aged than women, 28.3 years old and 23.1 years respectively. When a man is near a woman, they are all both relatively more aged (29.3 years old). Men are more utilised in ads for traditional male interests: cars (45%), media (59%), technology (62%). Men are also present in advertising for cosmetical products(74% for after shave or cologne). Women tend to be present in health advertisements such as food supplements like magnesium, anti cholesterol oils, or margarine (31%[5]).

---

[5] This occurrence is very important.

4.2 Gender Balance

Almost one out of seventeen advertisements(5.9% of all ads) features males and females together (9.9% in the foreground). This frequency is more important when we analyze ads that exclusively include humans. Males and females are present in 13.5% of ads in the foreground, and constitute 9.5% of all ads with human people. Once every ten times, the ads can be seen as an authentic scenario of gender relations because they are visualized as the explicit model of heterosexual couples. The sportswomen are generally in situations of inequality or subordination: face to face, males dominating females (11.9% of all ads, and 28.5% of face to face ads, Table 3). In contrast, females rarely dominate males; in fact, four or five times less often (2.1% of all advertisement situations, and 5.2% of face to face ads). In sports where confrontation or struggle against an opponent or an opposing team is a norm, men in sports advertisements are not often presented as dominating other men (3.7% of all ads, 8.9% of face to face ads). Female characters are almost never shown in opposition to each other (0.7%). In the ads, opposition between people is rare, and opposition among women is non-existent.

Table 3. Relationship between the sexes.

RELATIONSHIP BETWEEN THE SEXES	Nb. cit.	Fréq.
Male > Female	83	28,5%
Female > Male	15	5,2%
Male = Female	47	16,2%
Male = Male	105	36,1%
Male > Male	26	8,9%
Female = Female	13	4,5%
Female > Female	2	0,7%
TOTAL CITATIONS	291	100%

The difference with the distribution of reference is very significant. chi2 = 220.23, df = 6, 1-p => 99.99%.

The Chi2 is calculated with the theoretical distribution follows: Ho> Fe (14.0%), Fe> Ho (14.0%), Ho = Fe (14.0%), Ho-Ho (14.0%), Ho> Ho (14.0%), Fe-Fe (14.0%), Fe> Fe (14.0%).

The table is built on 700 observations.

The percentages are calculated with reference to the number of citations

Differences between males and female are shown by others characteristics (movement[6], presence of hair, etc.) The sportsmen seem to be more dynamics: males move more often than their female counterparts (50.1% *versus* 36%). Male physical movement is especially more frequent when several men are present in the magazine ads.

Hair seems to both reveal and crystallise differences between males and females in sports advertisement (Table 4). When the ads present heterosexual couples, females have long hair (38.4%), and male have short hair (60.5%). However, on average, sports ads promote the entire female body (48.3% *vs* 42.7% for men).

---

[6] In the visual advertisements studied, the movement is suggested by the use of blurred images, of motor actions (spanning, running, jumping), non-smooth hair, etc.

Table 4. Hairiness presence and main elements in advertising by order of visual importance?

HAIRINESS PRESENSE AND MAIN ELEMENTS	Men	Women	Children	Hetersexula couple	Single man	Single Woman	TOTAL
Free long hair female	6,7% (11)	28,3% (13)	30,2% (26)	38,4% (33)	1,3% (3)	28,9% (24)	11,4% (110)
Hair Shaved Male	6,7% (11)	0,0% (0)	2,3% (2)	1,2% (1)	8,8% (21)	0,0% (0)	4,7% (35)
Others hairs	8,6% (14)	4,3% (2)	4,7% (4)	8,1% (7)	16,3% (39)	0,0% (0)	8,6% (66)
Invisible hairs	28,2% (46)	28,3% (13)	23,3% (20)	24,4% (21)	43,9% (105)	56,6% (47)	34,0% (252)
Tackles Hairs	9,8% (16)	6,5% (3)	4,7% (4)	5,8% (5)	11,7% (28)	13,3% (11)	8,3% (67)
Short Hair Male	52,8% (86)	37,0% (17)	55,8% (48)	60,5% (52)	32,6% (78)	7,2% (6)	33,0% (287)
Masculine Long Hairs	9,2% (15)	4,3% (2)	4,7% (4)	5,8% (5)	9,2% (22)	0,0% (0)	6,0% (48)
Feminine Long Tied Hairs	8,0% (13)	30,4% (14)	27,9% (24)	32,6% (28)	1,3% (3)	31,3% (26)	10,4% (108)
Helmeted Head	46,6% (76)	45,7% (21)	30,2% (26)	26,7% (23)	28,0% (67)	14,5% (12)	26,7% (225)
Feminine Short Hairs	2,5% (4)	6,5% (3)	7,0% (6)	11,6% (10)	0,8% (2)	16,9% (14)	4,3% (39)
TOTAL	100% (292)	100% (88)	100% (164)	100% (185)	100% (368)	100% (140)	100% (1237)

The dependence is very significant. chi2 = 352.83, df = 45, 1-p => 99.99%.

The framed boxes in blue (pink) are those for which the actual number is much higher (lower) than the theoretical strength.

The chi2 is calculated on the table of citations (marginal effective equal to the sum of actual rows / columns).

The values in table are column percentages based on 700 observations.

This frequency rejects the arguments of feminists who think that women are more often cut in advertisements (Table 5). Males are more often photographed in portrait form (9.2% *vs.* 5.6%). Women are over-sexualized in sports ads as well: their breasts, legs and calves are shown more frequently. These body parts are over represented in females relativeto their male counterparts: 22.4% *vs.* 14.2%. The ads were sometimes mixed into unusual situations in the real world of sport and exercise. However, in some cases, gender is ambiguous, because of the unclear image (11% of all ads) due to indistinguishable faces or silhouettes (8%). There are many sports that require helmets. For this reason, it is difficult to distinguish the presence of a sportsman or a sportswoman. Sometimes, intuition and experience helps to infer that this is a male. For example, there are no women drivers in Formula 1, thus those individuals must be males.

Table 5. What are the genders and body parts represented?

Gender and Body parts	Men	Women	Both genders	implicitly male	implicitly female	TOTAL
Whole Body	42,7% (144)	48,3% (43)	40,3% (58)	13,3% (12)	0,0% (0)	37,1% (257)
Legs Only	0,6% (2)	1,1% (1)	1,4% (2)	1,1% (1)	25,0% (1)	1,0% (7)
Single Head	9,2% (31)	5,6% (5)	9,7% (14)	0,0% (0)	0,0% (0)	7,4% (50)
Arms Only	1,5% (5)	2,2% (2)	0,7% (1)	1,1% (1)	0,0% (0)	1,3% (9)
Without Feet	15,7% (53)	14,6% (13)	11,8% (17)	2,2% (2)	0,0% (0)	12,1% (85)
Only Feet	3,6% (12)	0,0% (0)	2,1% (3)	6,7% (6)	0,0% (0)	3,1% (21)
Bust	13,6% (46)	21,3% (19)	20,1% (29)	0,0% (0)	25,0% (1)	14,1% (95)
Others Parts	0,3% (1)	1,1% (1)	0,0% (0)	2,2% (2)	0,0% (0)	0,6% (4)
TOTAL	100% (294)	100% (84)	100% (124)	100% (24)	100% (2)	100% (528)

The situations coded as depicting equality between males – when the protagonists are in competition on a game field – were much more frequent than into situations with women (15% versus 1.9%). The representations of movement and action are more frequent in situations of male domination than female (49.4% versus 33%). The equation between masculinity, the movement and the activity, seems to confirm a form of gender stereotyping. In advertisements of sport, men are expected to be 'active'.

Indeed our findings support the manly stereotype in ads: equality in mixed-sex situations was not wholly absent (6.7% of the sample), but inequality was the norm. Men dominated women significantly more often than the reverse (11.9% *versus* 2.1%). Only two advertisements on 700 reveal inequality between female, as against 26 (3.7%) that place men in relatively inferior positions to other men. This gender imbalance is shown in various ways. The emphasis on movement already noted was prominent in advertisements that showed domination of the female by the male (49.4% of cases *versus* 33.3%). Less predictable, women's faces, traditionally use to express beauty, are given less frequent than men's faces (9.2% of cases versus 5.6%).

4.3 Discussion

4.3.1 Male Presence

The omnipresence of men is confirmed. This result emphasizes what we can name the "innate androcentrism" into advertising campaigns that use sport and physical exercise, to frame both message content and targeting strategy. Sell a product or a service related to sport in France today evidently demands a male presence – without any formal explicit rules, of course. The advertising of sport thus acts as a 'masculine vector', a veritable keystone in the structure of adolescent identification with sport and physical exercise. Men are been more utilised in ads for traditional male sectors: cars, Medias, high technologies. Men are also present into cosmetically products(after shaving, toilet water)! Women are present in Advertisements of health (foods complement like magnesium, anti cholesterol oils or margarine, etc.). These differences are still important and maintain gender categorisations. The strong male attraction for sports is therefore unsurprising.These averages confirm stereotypes, and reinforce the previous sociological studies results[7][13][28][58].

According to Perret [11], in television commercials between 1996 and 1999 (N = 425 films), the majority of Advertisements mobilize a gender classical division (3/4 of ads), next alternatives' advertisings with more mixed gender (15%), and a minority is show power by women (10%) "(p. 164). The exchange of roles is therefore almost exclusively to male to female: it is rewarding for a woman to adopt a male attitude, but the reverse is still false. From this point of view, these images reflect the permanence of some symbolic male domination. In addition, the most common role for men is this one of characters in "ridiculous situations"(p. 164). Perret analyses this trend like a dominant privilege (because otherwise, to mock a woman involves the risk of criticism sexist). This risk is coupled with criticism of the treatment traditional manhood in the years 1996 and 1997 in France, where men are portrayed in advertisements as "heroes in the second degree" (p. 165).In the very large majority of the cases, the advertisements offer the audience a universe of heterosexual normalization, reaffirming the anthropological constant noted by Héritier [10].

Like themore recent researches, men are often more aged than women, respectively 28.3 years old and 23.1 years. As into research of Ahlstrand (p. 26), in France "women are more often portrayed as young, while men are portrayed as middle age".This can reinforce differences between genders. Men can be seen with more experimental in sport than women, with much power. Others researches indicate this power of the age (*gerontocraty*) into contemporary sports [63] (p. 523). The hair, use of colours, etc., confirm these ads as so much construction between genders. When sportive female are alone, their hairs are more often linked or shorted [64]; as if near man, a woman has to have long hair, symbol of beauty and seduction. These models of body are continuing long since. Side by side,ads permit to confirm this trend[7]. This is a real staging ads with men one side and women on the other side. The sport, as major form of male physical exercise, shows a real historical heritage, and therefore unsurprisingly sets man against man more often than man against woman or woman against woman. Indeed, gender cohabitation is always rare in major sports nowadays into Olympics Games, and in amateur sports [65]. So it's not surprising to observe this trend in ads of sports too. The comparisons are a good tool. The comparisons of ads, side by side, allow us to reveal the different constructions of advertisements. For the same product, the difference is obvious: the car is presented with a man, dressed in costume-tie. Advertising with a woman for the same car shows close his leg with fishnet. Side by side, Advertisements present an ordinary shoe of the man, close to a shoe heel of the woman (woman as a sexual vampire?). The ads for sport's shoes show women as calm persons, and show men in full effort. Another Advertisement for running shoes shows a naked woman from face ("open" to our eyes), and the same advertisement shows only a profile's naked man, etc.

Female equality, rare (N=12), is not related to particular forms of sport or physical exercise. However, third of advertisements analysed is about recreational swimming (4). The conventional sport and exercise places – stadiums, gyms and sports centres – was predominant, with unknown personalities.

Are the small frequencies of gender ambiguous are an indication of the hard-and-fast male-female distinctions made by the advertisers themselves and by the advertising agencies planning and executing the campaigns? This sexual (gender) ambiguity seems to be unacceptable, or at least looks too bad to sell goods or services...

Our findings demonstrate the general sexual and gender conformism of advertising and the token nature of innovations, on the evidence of this large number of advertisements and

[7]The Gender Ads Project. Created by Scott A. Lukas, Ph.D.. Created in 2002, South Lake Tahoe, California. <http://www.genderads.com>Accessed on: [2008 January].

bearing in mind that we did not deliberately underlined Advertisements with provocative or degrading situations.

4.3.2 The Role of Iconic Figures

Sports stars and champions are known to be used as "advocats" in sport-related advertising. Yet, in our corpus into magazine advertising, almost 68.3% of the characters featured were 'ordinary', unknown, persons: that is, unidentifiable by the mass audience. The stars represent only 18.8% (17.1% in sports, and 1.7% in others activities). This result is more important yet consistent with similar research. Dyson and Turco found that 11% of the ads feature celebrities (1998[8]). This would seem to suggest that the stars and celebrities of the sports do not play a significant role in press advertising in magazines, even if they are sought after for sponsorship contracts.

When taking a first glance at all the advertisements in their preliminary phase, however, we thought that celebrities would manage to arouse attention. To achieve this result, building the creative strategy around them would not necessarily be effective or successful, because their image and symbolic value would vary depending on the season of the sport and depending on their current performance in their sport [66]. The elite players of sport are also potentially damaged by personal scandals, usually being due to accusations of doping, a decrease in performance, or an abrupt end of career due of injuries.

These inherent risks are not the only possible explanations for this finding. The sport's superstars are characterized, de facto, by spectacular prowess that verges on a superhuman condition. We suggest that the advertisers of sport-related products or services in our survey chose to base their campaigns on unidentifiable players because it is expected that the target audience with more easily be able to identify themselves with the sport player in the advertisement. The unattainable nature of superstars' exploits can be counterproductive. Inescapably, the sport's player performances can separate prospective customers from their sport heroes.

CONCLUSION

Gender bias is still a widespread topic when discussing the advertisements of sport and physical exercise in France. The advertisements in magazines reflect this pronounced tendency between men and women. Men are more present, more active people, in the advertisements for high technologies, cars, etc. Women are less active people in ads; they are presented to sell health products. The innovative and creative strategy is a rarity in France's context. Some sport advertisers are innovative, for example, by emphasizing environmental attention, as in the case of one sportswear and accessories manufacturer in Patagonia, or the involvement in sustainable development. The markets for sports (products or services) slowly attract women. Only few examples are still found without sexual bias or gender bias. For instance, colours used as hooks to attract potential new customers remain largely stereotypical: the pink or pastels are indicators of traditional kinds of colours to make the

---

[8] The State of Celebrity Endorsement in Sport, Cyber Journal of sport Marketing. http://fulltext.ausport.gov.au/fulltext/1998/cjsm/v2n1/dyson.htm.

advertisement more appealing to women. This is the case for alternative's sports and recreations, as Loret [67] has been able to show, with regards into surfing and snowboarding.

In our survey, blue was the most common colour (30%) used. This is not surprising, given the focus of sport as a historically male activity. This predominance of male image is evident, and the fact that blue is the favourite colour among Westerners, confirms this trend [68]. The brand imagery in the context of sport and physical exercise is not a trivial activity. A study of the packaging of dairy products, found a transition from blue-and-white to a broader palette containing such symbolic colours as green or even pink.

The commercial imperatives demand more than simple experiments, of course, but the persistence is amazing of such strikingly traditional characteristics in advertisements of sports in France. If sport and physical exercise seem to be a paradigm of progress and innovation, the advertising of sports paradoxically deals with stereotyped representations of society, rather than adopting new and innovative perspectives. Shall we see the beginning of a truly alternative approach to sport-related communication, especially where gender is concerned?

REFERENCES

[1]   Pociello, C. (1995).*Les cultures sportives*. Paris, PUF

[2]   Leonard, W.M. II (1998*). A Sociological Perspective on Sport*. Boston: Allyn and Bacon.

[3]   Coakley, J. J. (2008). *Sports in Society: Issues and Controversies*. Mosby College Pub., for 1982 edition.

[4]   Elias, N. and Dunning, E.G. (1986), *Sport et civilisation*. La violence maîtrisée, Paris: Fayard. (French translation, 1994).

[5]   Delphy, C. (2001). *L'ennemi principal II*. Penser le genre. Paris : Syllepse.

[6]   Guionnet, C. and Neveu E. (2005). *Féminins/Masculins, sociologie du genre*. Paris: Armand Colin.

[7]   Cortese, A. J. P., (2007). *Provocateur: Images of Women and Minorities in Advertising*, Plymouth, Rowman & Littlefield (3rd edition).

[8]   Soulages, J-C. (2004*). Le genre en publicité, ou le culte des apparences*, in J. Bouchard and P. Froissart, Sexe et Communication. Paris: 'Harmattan, pp. 51-59.

[9]   Messner, M. A. (2002*). Taking the Field. Women, Men and Sports*. Minneapolis, USA: University of Minnesota Press.

[10]   Héritier, F. (2002). *Masculin/Féminin II. Dissoudre la hiérarchie*, Paris: O. Jacob.

[11]   Perret, J. B., (2003*). L'approche française du genre en publicité*. Bilan critique et pistes de renouvellement, Réseaux, Vol. 4, n° 120, pp. 147 à 173.

[12]   Duret, P. (1993). *L'héroïsme sportif*, Paris, Presses Universitaires de France.

[13]   Grau S. L., Roselli G., Taylor C. R. (2007). Where's Tamika Catchings? A Content Analysis of Female Athlete Endorsers in Magazine Advertisements, *Journal of Current Issues and Research in Advertising*, Volume 29, Number 1, Spring, pp. 55-65.

[14]   Lahire, B. (2004). *La culture des individus*. Dissonances culturelles et distinction de soi. Paris: La Découverte.

[15]   Michaud, Y. (2003). *L'Art à l'état gazeux*. Essai sur le triomphe de l'esthétique. Paris, Stock.

[16] Weil, P. (1993). *A quoi rêvent les années 1990 ?*. Paris: Editions du Seuil.

[17] Messner, M. A., Dunbar, M. and Hunt, D. (2004). *"The Televised Sports Manhood Formula"* in D. Rowe (Ed.). Critical Readings: Sport, Culture and the Media, London: Open University Press, pp: 229-245.

[18] Messner, M.A., Dunbar, M. and Hunt, D (2002). *The Televised Sports Manhood Formula*. Journal of Sport and Social Issues, 24, p. 380-394.

[19] Hall, Stuart (2003). *Representation: Cultural Representations and Signifying Practices.* London: Sage Publications.

[20] Cahn, S.K. (1995). *Coming on Strong; Gender and Sexuality in Twentieth-Century Women's Sport.* London: The Free Press.

[21] Jefferson Lenskyj, H. (1998*). "Inside Sport" or "On the Margins"? Australian Women and the Sport Media".* International Review for the Sociology of Sport, Vol. 33 No. 1, pp. 19-32.

[22] Bodin, D., Robène, L. and Héas, S. (2004). *Sports et violences en Europe*. Strasbourg: Editions du Conseil de l'Europe, Septembre. Available in English.

[23] Redeker, R. (2002).*Le sport contre les peuples*. Paris: Berg International.

[24] Bourg, J.F. and Gouguet, J.J. (2001). *Economie du sport*. Paris: La Découverte.

[25] Simonot, P. (1988). *Homo sportivus*. Paris: Gallimard.

[26] Brohm, J.M. (1997). *Les shootés du stade*. Paris: Paris Méditerranée.

[27] Grésy, B. (Ed.). (2002). *L'image des femmes dans la publicité : Rapport à la secrétaire d'Etat aux Droits des femmes et à la Formation professionnelle.* Paris: La Documentation française.

[28] Goffman, E. (1976). *"Gender Advertisements". Studies in the Anthropology of Visual Communication, Vol. 3, No. 2, p.69-154.*

[29] Leiss, W., Kline, S. and Jhally, S. (1990). *Social Communication in Advertising: Persons, Products and Images of Well-being.* London: Routledge.

[30] Smith, G. (1996). *"Gender Advertisements Revisited : A Visual Sociology Classic".* Electronic Journal of Sociology, Salford, UK: University of Salford

[31] Geuens, M. and De Pelsmacker, P. (1998). *"Feelings Evoked by Warm, Erotic, Humorous or Non-Emotional Print Advertisements for Alcoholic Beverages",* Academy of Marketing Science Review (online): http://www.amreview.org/articles/geuens01-1998.pdf

[32] Putrevu, S. (2001). *"Exploring the Origins and Information Processing Differences between Men and Women : Implications for Advertisers".* Academy of Marketing Science Review (online), http://www.amreview.org/articles/putrevu10-2001.pdf

[33] Hobbs, R. (2004). *"Does Media Literacy Work? An Empirical Study of Learning How to Analyze Advertisements".* Advertising & Society Review, Vol. 5 No. 4.

[34] Cathelat, B. (1968, 1992). *Publicité et société*. Paris, Petite Bibliothèque Payot.

[35] Jeudy, H.P. (1994). *La communication sans objet*. Paris: La Lettre volée.

[36] Darsy, S. (2005). *Le Temps de l'antipub : l'emprise de la publicité et ceux qui la combattent.* Paris: Actes Sud.

[37] Barnouw, E. (1978). *The Sponsor: Notes on a Modern Potentate,*.New York: Oxford University Press.

[38] Ewen, S. (1977). *Captains of Consciousness: Advertising and the Social Roots of the Consumer Culture*, New York, NY: McGraw-Hill.

[39] Marcuse, H. (1968). *L'homme unidimensionnel*. Essai sur l'idéologie de la société industrielle avancée, Paris: Editions de Minuit.

[40] Martin, M. (1991). *Communication et médias de masse : culture, domination et opposition*. Ste-Foy, Canada: Presses de l'Université du Québec.

[41] Maigret, E. (2003), *Sociologie de la communication et des médias*, Paris: Armand Colin.

[42] Bourdieu, P., (1998).*La Domination masculine*, Paris, Seuil.

[43] Burstyn, V. (1999). *The Rites of Men*. Toronto: University of Toronto Press.

[44] Koivula, N. (1999). *"Gender stereotyping in televised media sport coverage"*.Sex Roles, Vol. 41 Nos. 7/8, pp 589-604.

[45] Weil, P. (2001). *L'image des femmes dans la publicité*. Paris: Publicis.

[46] Héas, S., Bodin, D. and Forsyth, L. (2003). *"Sports and Advertisements like 'Hygienic'Vectors?"*. Proceedings of the 2nd World Congress of Sociology of Sport, Cologne: German Sport University, June.

[47] Welzer-Lang, D. (Ed.). (1998). *Nouvelles Approches des hommes et du masculin*. Toulouse: PU du Mirail.

[48] Duret, P. (1999). *Les jeunes et l'identité masculine*, Paris: PUF.

[49] Rauch, A. (2000). *Le premier sexe : mutations et crise de l'identité masculine*.Paris: Hachette-Littératures

[50] Faludi, S., (1999*). Stiffed: The Betrayal of the American Man*. New York, William Morrow & Company.

[51] Eveno, P. (2003). *"Les médias sont-ils sexués ? Eléments pour une gender history des médias français"*. Le Temps des médias, No 1, pp. 162-173.

[52] Héas, S. and Bodin, D. (2004). « *Sports et publicités. Normes et représentations corporelles : exemple des publicités imprimées dans les magazines en France* ». In L'individu social : autres réalités, autre sociologie ?, XVIIth Congress of Association Internationale des Sociologues de Langue Française, July.

[53] Urquhart, J. and Crossman J. (1999). *"The Globe and Mail Coverage of the Winter Olympic Games: A Cold Place for Women Athletes"?*. Journal of Sport and Social Issues, Vol. 23, pp. 193-202.

[54] Miller, T. (2001). *Sportsex*. Philadelphia, PA: Temple University Press.

[55] Duncan, M. C. and Messner, M.A. (1998). *'The media image of sport and gender'*. In L.A. Wenner (ed.), MediaSport. New York, NY: Routledge.

[56] Messner, M., Hunt D. and Dunbar M. (1999). *Boys to Men: Sports Media Messages about Masculinity*. Oakland, CA: Children Now.

[57] Brocard, C., (2000). « *Performances sportives et différenciation sexuelle dans les commentaires journalistiques, l'exemple des championnats du monde d'athlétisme* ». In C. De Montlibert, Sur le sport, Strasbourg: Regards sociologiques, pp. 127-142

[58] Wolin L. D., (2003). *Gender Issues in Advertising. An Over Synthesis of Research: 1970-2002*. Journal of Advertising Research, pp. 111-129.

[59] Mc Arthur, L., Resko, B. G., (1975). *The portrayal of men and women in American television commercials*. The Journal of Social Psychology, 97, pp. 209-220.

[60] Barthes, R. (1964, 2002). « *Rhétoriques de l'image* », Communications, Novembre. Reprinted in Œuvres complètes, Vol. 2. Paris: Editions du Seuil.

[61] Leymore, V. (1975). *Hidden Myth*. Structure and Symbolism in Advertising. London: Heinmann.

[62] Ahlstrand, M. (2007). *Gender Stereotyping in Television in Advertisement*. A case of Austrian State Television, Lulea tekniska universitete, Industriell ekonomi och samhällsvetenskap. http://epubl.luth.se/1402-1773/2007/236/LTU-CUPP-07236-SE.pdf

[63] Shaw S. M., (2006). *Scratching the Back of "Mr X" : Analysing Gendered Social Processes in Sport Organizations.* Journal of Sport Management, N°20, 510-534

[64] Héas S., Bodin D., Robène L., Misery L., (2007). *« La représentation des poils dans les publicités magazines en France ».* Annales de Dermatologie et de Vénéréologie, n°134, octobre, pp. 752-756.

[65] Bodin D., Héas S., (2002). *Introduction à la sociologie des sports*. Paris, Edition Chiron, janvier, 252 pages.

[66] Duret P. and Trabal P., (2001). *Le sport et ses affaires*. Paris : Métailié.

[67] Loret, A. (1995). *Génération glisse ; dans l'eau, l'air, la neige. La révolution du sport des années fun*. Paris: Autrement, Mutations collection, pp. 155-156.

[68] Pastoureau, M. (2000). *Bleu*. Histoire d'une couleur. Paris: Editions du Seuil.

In: Psychology of Stereotypes
Editor: Eleanor L. Simon

Chapter 9

PSYCHOLOGICAL IMPLICATIONS OF STEREOTYPING AMERICAN INDIANSTHROUGH THE USE OF NATIVE-THEMED MASCOTS, NICKNAMES, AND LOGOS

*Jesse A. Steinfeldt[*1], Paul Hagan[1] and M. Clint Steinfeldt[2]*

Department of Educational Psychology, Indiana University, Bloomington, Indiana, USA[1]
Department of Athletics, Fort Lewis College, USA[2]

ABSTRACT

The use of American Indian culture and imagery as mascots, nicknames, and logos in sport is a common societal practice that has been met with opposition from psychological research and from those interested in social justice and advocacy. Native-themed mascots, nicknames, and logos are considered harmful to American Indian communities because they misuse cultural symbols and sacred practices (e.g., eagle feathers, drums), perpetuate stereotypes of American Indians (e.g., noble savage, bloodthirsty savage, a historic race that only exists in past-tense status), and deny American Indians control over societal definitions of themselves. Additionally, this practice creates a racially hostile educational environment, and an estimated 115 organizations (e.g., American Psychological Association, American Counseling Association, Society of Indian Psychologists, National Association for the Advancement of Colored People) have produced resolutions calling for the immediate retirement of Native-themed mascots, nicknames, and logos. Because American Indians do not have control of these images, this process of racialized mascotery allows mainstream America to stereotype, undermine, and appropriate American Indian culture while systematically teaching the ideology of White supremacy. This manuscript describes ways that these stereotypic representations affect the psychological functioning of American Indians, and how this practice is harmful to both American Indian communities and to members of the mainstream culture. In sum, this manuscript provides an overview of psychological research and theory, discusses educational interventions and legislation aimed at curtailing this practice, and provides perspectives for the reader to have a greater understanding of the hegemonic and deleterious nature of racialized mascotery.

---

[*] Correspondence should be directed to Jesse A. Steinfeldt, Ph.D., Department of Educational Psychology, Indiana University, 201 N. Rose Avenue, Bloomington, IN, 47403; 812 856-8331 (phone); 812 856 8333 (fax); jesstein@indiana.edu

Psychological Implications of Stereotyping American Indiansthrough the use of Native-Themed Mascots, Nicknames, and Logos

The misuse and appropriation of American Indian culture and imagery is a widespread societal practice with a lengthy history that still occurs today. Stereotypes of American Indians have a pervasive and long standing foothold in American society (Graham,1993). The roots of this practice began weaving themselves into American popular culture over a century ago in a period where the native rebellion of colonization had withered from the public eye (Merskin, 2001; King, 2002; Davis, 1993; King & Springwood, 2001a, 2001b; Staurowsky, 1998). American Indian imagery permeated Western movies, tobacco products, beer, butter, children's games, toys, collectables, songs, stories, and art (Bird, 1996; Coombe, 1998; Deloria, 1998; King, 2002). Playing *Cowboys and Indians,* or singing songs like *Ten Little Indians* were common practices (Merskin, 2001). These practices became so entrenched within our culture, and were taught and learned so prevalently, that they became hegemonic norms: society's critical eye glazed over them, and found them to be unremarkable and beneath notice (Merskin, 2001; King, 2002; Kates & Shaw-Garlock, 1999; Green,1988; Pewewardy, 2001; Spindel, 2000). As a result, American society has become inundated by products, items, and sports teams that appropriate American Indian culture, usually without consent from or compensation to American Indian tribes. The following quote (Merskin, 2001, p. 167) provides examples that illustrate this point:

> "Apache helicopter,…Apache rib doormats, Red Man Tobacco, Kleek-O the Eskimo (Cliquot Club ginger ale), Dodge Dakota, Pontiac, the Cleveland Indians, Mutual of Omaha, Calumet Baking Powder, Mohawk Carpet Mills, American Spirit cigarettes, Eskimo pies, Tomahawk mulcher, Winnebago Motor Homes, Indian Motorcycles, Tomahawk missiles, many high school sports teams,…And the list goes on."

These racial images have been so hegemonically woven into the fabric of society that they largely exist without being questioned (Merskin, 2001). The widespread use and omnipresence of these images in society contribute to the pubic belief that the use of American Indian imagery in this regard must be acceptable (King, Davis-Delano, Staurowsky, & Baca, 2006; King, Staurowsky, Baca, Davis, Pewewardy, 2002). Furthermore, for many non-Indians, these images are the only exposure they have to American Indians (Merskin, 1998), which serves to perpetuate existing societal stereotypes of American Indians. Some early cinematic representations of American Indians revolved around the stereotypic *bloodthirsty savage* and *noble savage* iconography that framed American Indians as the enemy of progress (Strickland, 1998; Mihesuah, 1996). "These stereotypical representations of American Indians denies that they are human beings, and presents them as existing only in the past and as single, monolithic Indians" (Merskin,2001, p.167). The mechanisms used to perpetuate these stereotypic images reside under the control of a predominantly White industry, and this imagery is neither controlled nor sustained by American Indian communities. "White Americans developed the stereotypes; White Americans produced the collectibles; and White American manufacturers and advertisers disseminated both the images and the objects to a White audience" (Goings, 1994, as cited in Merskin, 2001, p. 161).

These practices (e.g., brands, logos, representations) contribute to an environment in which many non-Native Americans freely appropriate American Indian culture for their own use (King, 2002; King, 2001; Staurowsky, 2007; Grounds, 2001; Deloria, 1998; Spindel, 2000). For example, kids are taught from a young age to *play Indian* by dressing up in construction paper feathers next to the faux pilgrims for Thanksgiving Day plays. There are plenty of *Indian* Halloween costumes down the aisles of department stores.King (2002) reported that within various normative childhood institutions (e.g. YMCA, Boy Scouts, Summer Camp), the idea of pretending to be *Indian* gets reinforced ad nausea by allowing participants to become*Indian Princesses,* bygetting *Indian names,* and by performing *Indian rituals.* This process continues into adulthood with 'back to nature' and new age groups learning*Indian* ways and *Indian* rituals (King, 2002; Deloria, 1998; Mihesuah, 1996; Slapin & Seale, 1998). In addition to the societal pervasiveness of this practice, Native American communities face difficulties in effectively advocating for removing these stereotypic representations because American Indians represent less than 1% of the population, with nearly a fourth living below the poverty line, twice the rate found in the overall population (Merskin, 2001; U.S. Census Bureau, 2006). This lack of numbers and resources makes it difficult for American Indians to have the privilege and power of representation that other groups have benefitted from in order to advocate for cessation of images such as *Li'l Black Sambo* and the *Frito Bandito* (Merskin, 2001; Westerman, 1989). Subsequently, it is interesting to note that although it is socially acceptable to *play Indian*, it would be unacceptable in American culture if someone was *playing Black* or *playing Jewish*, particularly if it were done in such an organized, advertised, and sanctioned manner (King, 2002).

According to Staurowsky (2007), White privilege and power drive themainstream American appropriation and consumption of American Indian culture that is based on their own definitions of what they perceive to be *Indian*. Doing so affords White Americans the power to act *Indian* for their own social and economic gain (Staurowsky, 2007). By appropriating American Indian culture for their own use, mainstream America can effectively "exclude contemporary Native Americans from full citizenship by treating them as signs rather than as speakers, as caricatures rather than as players and consumers, as commodities rather than citizens" (Strong, 2004, p. 83). This process forces American Indians to remain on the sidelines of the discourse because contemporary American Indians are rendered invisible and replaced by stereotypic representations perpetuated by static societal portrayals of *Indians*.

In addition to perpetuating stereotypes and appropriating American Indian culture, these practices have historically served to dehumanize American Indians and to justify genocidal practices against them (King, 2002). American Indians are portrayed as morally inferior and prone to a host of undesirable attributes (e.g., violence, promiscuity, drunkenness). These stereotypes and perceptions have also been used to validate and inform the U.S. government's policies of American Indian assimilation that have resulted in cultural genocide, historic grief, and soul wound (Duran, 2006; Tafoya, & Del Vecchio, 1996). These policies of cultural genocide have included banning Native religious practices and ceremonies, placing American Indians into boarding schools away from their families, dividing land allotments individually despite Native's communal culture, and physically relocating American Indians into urban areas (King, 2002). These policies and practices have contributed to the difficulty for American Indian communities to actively combat the perpetuation of stereotypes that have been consistent and pervasive in U.S. culture. Thus, these stereotypes continue to exist and exude their influence today.

As an example, this practice of misappropriation and stereotyping of American Indian culture has recently come into mainstream consciousness with the death of three individuals during a sweat lodge in Arizona (McNeel, 2009). This event was conducted by the non-Native self-help expert James Arthur Ray as part of a "Spirit Warrior" program. According to an article in Indian Country Today, these individuals were charged up to $9,000 to participate in a seminar and ceremony. The Coeur d'Alene Tribal Council put out an official statement condemning the actions of Ray and others who would sell and exploit Native culture (McNeel, 2009). It is all too common in *new age* stores, magazines, and websites to see non-American Indians selling goods and services that are marketed as *native spiritual healing*. These examples represent modern practices that utilize the stereotype of American Indians as deeply spiritual, innocent, and at one with nature. These stereotypes result in American Indian communities continuing to be exploited and marginalized by the dominant American culture (King, 2002).

STEREOTYPING OF AMERICAN INDIANS WITHIN AMERICAN SPORT CULTURE

One of the most prominent mechanisms for perpetuating stereotypes of American Indians in society is the use of American Indian culture and imagery in sporting events (King et al., 2006).Scholars from a variety of disciplines have written at great length about the deleterious effects of these Native-themed sports mascots, nicknames, and logos (Baca, 2004; Fenelon, 1999; King, Staurowsky, Baca, Davis, & Pewewardy, 2002; King, 2004; Pewewardy, 1991; Russel, 2003; Staurowsky, 2000; Staurowsky, 2007; Vanderford, 1996; Williams, 2007). The common thread across these writings suggests that Native-themed mascots, nicknames, and logos (e.g., *Redskins, Indians, Braves, Seminoles*) should be immediately retired because they misuse cultural symbols and sacred practices (e.g., eagle feathers, drums, chanting); they perpetuate stereotypes of American Indians (e.g., noble savage, bloodthirsty savage, a historic race that only exists in past-tense status); and they deny American Indians control over societal definitions of themselves (King et al., 2002; Russel, 2003; Staurowsky, 2004; Staurowsky, 2007). Because American Indians cannot control the use of these images, this practice allows mainstream America to appropriate American Indian culture while systematically teaching the ideology of White supremacy (Pewewardy, 1991).

King et al. (2002) purport that in addition to perpetuating the ideology of White supremacy, the use of American Indian names and symbols as mascots serves to undermine the histories, perspectives, and realities of American Indians. Part of the allure of this stereotypic sport imagery is that some people view this process as being positive, respectful, and honorable (e.g., strong warriors, noble people; Steinfeldt et al., 2010). This sentiment is communicated by mainstream Americans who claim that they are honoring American Indians with this imagery (King, 2002; Staurowsky, 2007; Steinfeldt et al., 2010). However, mainstream America is honoring American Indians on their terms, not on the terms of

American Indians. The ultimate power is the ability to define reality for another (Sue, 2005). Accordingly, because sports fans have afforded themselves the power to play *Indian* without the consent of American Indians, relations between both groups are negatively affected (King et al., 2006; Staurowsky 2007; Williams 2006; Williams 2007). By using American Indians as sports mascots, nicknames, and logos, the "scripted form of White people "becoming" Indian renders invisible the ignominious history of American Indian genocide by the U.S. government, replacing it with a culturally comfortable and comforting myth of the 'American Indian warrior'" (Staurowsky, 2007, p. 62). Thus, majority culture participants can remove themselves from historic and ongoing marginalization of American Indians. Instead, a false sense of unity is forged between American Indians and White Americans, based on the assumption that American Indians feel honored and respected by being used as a mascot, nickname, or logo for sporting events (Black, 2002).

Through this process, members of society—both American Indians and White Americans—are prevented from obtaining an accurate picture of the heritage, legacies, and significance of American Indians (King et al., 2002). The effects of this imagery are not only harmful because of the influence on mainstream culture, but also because of the impact on American Indians. The dominant cultural transmission of these stereotypes is readily conveyed to American Indian children, which can have a deleterious developmental impact. The misinformation within these omnipresent images can lead to internalized representations of American Indians as lazy, alcoholic, and violent (Merskin, 2001). The pressure for acculturation and assimilation—as well as economic gain—on many American Indians has also influenced some American Indians to accept and even perpetuate Native stereotypes by endorsing Native-themed mascots, adopting a *Hollywood Indian* persona, which may entail selling arts/crafts, working at tourist locations, and selling spirituality to non-American Indians (King, 2002).

In order to better understand this process of internalizing negative stereotypes, it is necessary to discuss one of the largest mechanisms that perpetuate these images: Schools provide some of the greatest opportunities for students to be exposed to Native-themed mascots, nicknames, and logos. According to Baca (2004), the use of Native-themed mascots, nicknames, and logos contributes to a racially hostile environment for all students. American Indian students at schools with Native-themed mascots (or those who play against schools with Native-themed mascots) are subjected to a variety of racial microaggressions and overt racial hostilities (King, 2002). Baca (2004) envisioned how this imagery can pervasively manifest itself throughout the average school day of a student. The student may get off the bus in the morning to be greeted by a looming half naked American Indian 'warrior' statue in the front of the school, then pass the massive mural logo depicting a cartoon beak-nosed *Native* with a pot belly and a single bent feather painted in the main entrance hall. The student may carry this faux image around on a school issued book cover or calendar on the way to a game in the gymnasium where a giant logo in the middle of the floor gets pranced over by a White student who is painted and dressed in an *Indian* costume, performing fake rituals that they associate with Native culture. The American Indian student attending this school receives the message on a daily basis that it is acceptable for others to mock and caricature their race and cultural practices. Thus, American Indian students are likely to internalize that their race is inferior to other races that are not subjected to mockery and caricature in a state-sanctioned institution (i.e., public school; Baca, 2004). On the other hand, non-Native students attending this school receive the message that their race and culture are not subjected to this process. Thus, their race is superior to this culture (Baca, 2004; King et al., 2002). These subtle messages can influence a student's ability to differentiate stereotypes from reality in regard to the lived experience of members of other racial groups. These images also impact a student's ability to concentrate, academically achieve, and develop an efficacious sense of self.

THEORETICAL PERSPECTIVES AND PSYCHOLOGICAL RESEARCH

While it is important to discuss perspectives that can help people better understand the complexity and nuances of this issue, it is essential to ground these perspectives in theory and research, particularly research that addresses psychological implications of using American Indian culture and imagery in sporting events. A variety of theories have been used to explain this phenomenon (see Fryberg, Markus, Oyserman, & Stone, 2008), but one of the more prominent theoretical orientations is social representations theory (Moscovici, 1998). Social representations are ideas and meanings that are considered essential for social functioning because they lend organization and structure to the social world. By transforming abstract concepts into concrete forms, social representations provide meaning and definition to the object depicted. For example, social representations provide viewers of Native-themed mascots with a code to define and identify American Indians. Images used by mascots (e.g., tomahawk chop, feathers, faux dancing) concretely define the abstract construct of American Indian that exists in the minds of the viewers. In the absence of direct contact with contemporary American Indians, having mascots, nicknames, and logos serve as a default representative of a culture is dangerous because, "if representations are neither negotiated nor re-negotiated in social interactions, then they are likely to remain static" (Fryberg, 2003, p. 7). Social representations that remain static are likely to perpetuate stereotypes and negatively impact the psychological functioning of the group being (mis)represented.

Fryberg et al. (2008) examined the impact of Native-themed sports mascots on the psychological well-being of American Indian and European American students. The results indicate that, when exposed to Native-themed sports mascots, American Indian high school and college students reported significantly depressed state self-esteem and levels of community worth, along with fewer achievement related possible selves. These detrimental effects were found to be consistent for students who viewed the mascot as negative *and* those who had positive associationswith the imagery. Even the students that disbelieved the stereotype were negatively impacted by the dehumanizing effects of reducing people to stereotypes through this imagery. The authors suggest that these stereotypic images remind American Indians of the narrow view society has of them, which threatens their psychological functioning and limits the possibilities they see for themselves (Fryberg et al., 2008). On the other hand, White American students in the study reported higher levels of self-esteem after viewing images of Native-themed mascots, indicating a potentially insidious level of privilege enjoyed by majority culture participants whose culture is not subjected to the marginalizing process of racialized mascotery.

In another manuscript describing two related studies, Kim-Prieto, Goldstein, Okazaki, and Kirschner (2010) exploredthe capability of adverse effects of stereotyping to generalize to other marginalized groups—specifically, groups that were not directly targeted by the stereotypic imagery. They evaluated the effects of American Indian sports mascots (e.g. American Indians as savage warriors) as primers to determine if these imagesincreased stereotyping of Asian Americans (e.g., Asian Americans as socially inept). Their results demonstrated that those participants who were exposed to American Indian imagery endorsed significantly more stereotypes of Asian Americans than the control group. The results were consistent across two studies with the first having an unobtrusive prime, and the second a more engaged exposure. These findings suggest that exposure to stereotypes of one group increases the tendencyof people to endorse stereotypes of other groups, even when the stereotypes are different. Kim-Prieto et. al. (2010) suggested that the studies further support the evidence indicating that American Indian mascots create a racially hostile environment, not only for American Indians but for everyone exposed to this insidious practice.

In another study, Steinfeldt and Wong (2010) examined the relationship between color-blind racial attitudes and the awareness of the offensiveness of Native-themed mascots among a group of counseling graduate students. The rationale of the study was the observation of the similarity between rationales of mainstream American society for maintaining racialized mascots and the beliefs underlying color-blind racial attitudes (Neville, Lilly, Duran, Lee, & Browne, 2000). Conceptualized as the denial, distortion, or minimization of race and racism (Neville, Spanierman, & Doan, 2006), the adoption of color-blind racial attitudes among White Americans reflects an attempt to reduce the dissonance associated with a sincere desire to believe in racial equality (Neville, Worthington, & Spanierman, 2001). While this contemporary ideology appears egalitarian on the surface, colorblindness ignores the role of power in society, it invalidates the experience with multiple forms of racism (e.g., aversive racism, explicit individual racism, institutional racism, cultural racism, racial microaggressions) that racial/ethnic minority group members endure, and it serves to maintain the societal status quo wherein members of racial/ethnic minority groups have inequitable access to societal resources. To this point, significant relationships have been demonstrated between colorblindness and a wide range of social attitude indexes, including negative attitudes toward affirmative action (Awad, Cokley, & Ratvich, 2005), increased racial prejudice (Neville et al., 2000), and lower multicultural counseling competencies (Neville et al., 2006).

In support of their hypothesis, Steinfeldt and Wong (2010) reported thatresults demonstrated that awareness of the offensiveness of Native-themed mascots was significantly inversely related to color-blind racial attitudesThat is, the more a person indicated that Native-themed mascots were offensive, the less likely (s)he was to endorse color-blind racial ideologies. Individuals with color-blind racial attitudes endorse the belief that "race should not and does not matter" (Neville et al., 2000, p. 60), and supporters of Native-themed mascots, nicknames, and logos suggest that tradition and honor—and not race—are the primary reasons for supporting this practice (King et al., 2002; Russel, 2003; Staurowsky, 2007). Thus, both color blindness and supporting Native-themed mascots, nicknames, and logos serve to minimize and/or remove race from the discussion. The results of Steinfeldt and Wong's (2010) study indicate that the more a person acknowledges the offensiveness of Native-themed mascots, the more likely (s)he is to acknowledge that race is an important aspect of society. Furthermore, the belief that mascots honor American Indians may serve as an ego defense that helps preserve the individual's sense of egalitarianism, while simultaneously masking the destructive and genocidal acts of European Americans toward American Indian communities, both in past and contemporary times (Grounds, 2001). In short, the use of Native-themed mascots forges a false sense of unity between American Indians and White Americans (Black, 2002). Steinfeldt and Wong (2010) concluded that colorblind racial attitudes may serve as the glue that binds this false union.

Lastly, Steinfeldt et al. (2010) examined racial attitudes about American Indians that are electronically expressed in newspaper online forums by examining the University of North Dakota's (UND) *Fighting Sioux* nickname and logo used for their athletic teams. The authors analyzed 1699 online forum comments, and found that the majority of comments expressed negative attitudes toward American Indians. The authors coded the comments, and reported that online forum comments were organized within the themes of:(a) surprise about how the nickname/logo could be construed as negative; (b) power and privilege exerted in defending the nickname/logo; (c) trivialization of issues salient to American Indians; and (d) denigration and vilification of American Indian communities. The results indicated that American Indians are subjected to not only continued societal ignorance and misinformation about their culture, they are also being actively excluded from the process of prioritizing which issues they need to address. Results also indicated that a critical mass of online forum comments represented ignorance about American Indian culture and even disdain toward American Indians by providing misinformation, perpetuating stereotypes, and expressing overtly racist attitudes toward American Indians. While some online forum comments examined in the study contained the words *honor* and *respect*, the authors indicated that the sentiment underlying and surrounding these comments did not reflect a genuine sense of honor or respect (Steinfeldt et al., 2010). Rather, these comments expressed entitlement, privilege, power, and even subjugation and oppression.

Steinfeldt et al. (2010) interpreted their findings within the tenets of Two-Faced Racism theory (Picca & Feagin, 2007). According to this theory, boundaries for the expression of racial attitudes exist within shifting social contexts. Subsequently, racial ideologies--particularly those about societal out-group members (e.g., African Americans)—exist, but the expression of these ideologies take place in private (i.e., backstage) settings rather than public (i.e., frontstage) settings. Because public opinion has shifted to condemn blatant racist attitudes and behaviors in public settings (Picca & Feagin, 2007), explicit expressions of racist attitudes have begun to find a home in electronic communication formats (Bargh & McKenna, 2004; Melican & Dixon, 2008). As it relates to this study, the relative anonymity afforded to participants of online forums provides the privacy experienced in traditional backstage settings without the negative social consequences that these attitudes might receive in physical frontstage settings. For example, an online forum commenter might more readily call an American Indian a derogatory name in an online forum comment, but it is likely that (s)he might not say the same thing aloud at a social gathering for fear of social repercussions. Subsequently, with the omnipresence and power of the internet, the presence of a Native-themed nickname and logo can facilitate the posting of virulent racist rhetoric in online forums. And because these types of racist messages are able to electronically spread out with greater ease to a larger audience, simply reading the paper can subject anAmerican Indian to content that can negatively impact his/her psychological well-being.

EDUCATIONAL INTERVENTIONS TO ADDRESS THE ISSUE OF STEREOTYPING OF AMERICAN INDIANS

The emerging research on Native-themed mascots, nicknames, and logos indicates that this practice can have deleterious psychological effects on not only American Indian communities, but also on members of the dominant American culture (Fryberg et al., 2008; LaRocque, 2004). Subsequently, over 115 professional organizations (e.g., American Psychological Association, American Counseling Association, National Association for the Advancement of Colored People, Society of Indian Psychologists) have put forward resolutions condemning the practice and calling for immediate retirement of Native-themed mascots, nicknames, and logos (AISTM, 2010).However, despite this widespread support among professional organizations, there is resistance among members of the dominant American culture to retire these mascots, nicknames, and logos.

However, despite these difficulties, it is important to utilize research that can inform practice in an effort to effectuate change. A recent training intervention (Steinfeldt & Steinfeldt, 2010) was created to increase counseling students' multicultural awareness, knowledge, and skills related to American Indian issues. Trainings such as these are crucial steps to empower students with the ability to critically examine and articulate reasons why Native-themed mascots are considered problematic, and to facilitate the process for students to serve as advocates for change at multiple systemic levels (i.e., professional, organizational, societal; Sue, 2001). Davis (2002) pointed out that if mainstream America fails to comprehend the problem of American Indian mascots, then understanding sovereignty or other issues affecting American Indian quality of lifewould be that much farther out of reach. In one of many recent resolutions, the ACA (2001) charged counseling programs to be committed to training students (and themselves) to advance efforts for the eradication of American Indian stereotypic imageryin their own institutions and beyond. Counselors need to foster their own sense of awarenessfor societal forms of oppression against American Indians because societal stereotypes of American Indians permeate counselor's daily clinical work (Duran, 2006). As demonstrated by Steinfeldt and Wong (2010), after receiving this training intervention, students registered lower levels of color blind racial attitudes, increased awareness of the way that Native-themed mascots stereotype American Indians, and increased awareness of racism in society (Neville, Lilly, Duran, Lee, & Browne, 2000; Steinfeldt & Steinfeldt, 2010).

In a group-based educational intervention, Steinfeldt and Stockton (2010) employed social justice principles within a liberatory framework (Steele, 2008; Duran, Firehammer, & Gonzalez, 2008) to create a psychoeducational group to address the systemic marginalization of American Indians. This group format, intended for use with middle-school children but readily adaptable for use with other ages, provides educators the opportunity to take a direct role in confronting these issues. Doing so can allow counselors, teachers, parents, and students to become active agents of change, rather than being complicit in the problem by standing idly by while societal mechanisms institutionally continue to perpetuate a racially hostile environment for American Indian students (Steinfeldt & Stockton, 2010). The psychoeducational group experience can facilitate dialog about societal issues and racism among students that opens up the process for the next generation to become empowered advocates for change (Steinfeldt & Stockton, 2010; Portman & Portman, 2002).

Familiarizing themselves with internalized stereotypical messages of American Indians is a key component of consciousness-raising to enable the students to become more critical consumers of their own experience. In Steinfeldt and Stockton's (2010) group intervention, part of this process can take place by having students look in their history books to see how the terms *savage* and *civilized*are used in reference to American Indians and Whites respectively. Loewen points out that American Indians are consistently referred to as savages (and Whites as civilized), despite anthropologic discoveries of the civilized nature (e.g., government, religion, agriculture) of many Native pre-Columbian societies (Loewen, 2008). Steinfeldt and Stockton (2010) also stressed the need for an applying the knowledge in an active experiential learning manner. One phase of the group intervention asks students to take part in a social justice project of their own creationthat will allow them to gain actual experience of social justice advocacy (see Steinfeldt&Stockton, 2010, for specific examples of social justice activities). Information and experiences of individuals within the group are then shared with other members of the group so that members can mutually benefit from the social justice learning processwhile creating a space for dialog and reactions about the experience. Knowledge gained from this experience can cultivate sustained commitment to advocacy efforts by encouraging individuals to reflect on their current experiences and contemplate plans for future social justice projects.

LEGISLATIVE INTERVENTIONS TO ADDRESS THE ISSUE OF STEREOTYPING OF AMERICAN INDIANS

In addition to educational interventions, there is a need for legislative efforts that can facilitate the retirement of this practice. For example, the National Collegiate Athletic Association (NCAA, 2005) enacted a policy that precludes member institutions from hosting NCAA championships if they utilize American Indian imagery, mascots or nicknames in their athletic program. The NCAA policy (2005) states:

> A human dignity issue, racial stereotyping dehumanizes and results in a perpetuation of institutional racism and negative treatment. With this in mind, after four years of careful review, the NCAA Executive Committee enacted a policy that aligns the organization's core principles of cultural diversity, civility, respect and nondiscrimination with the practice of creating a non-hostile and educational environment for its championships (para. 2).

The NCAA identified nineteen colleges with American Indian imagery that needed to comply with the policy (Staurowsky, 2007). Most of these institutions changed their names, although one institution (i.e., North Dakota *Fighting Sioux*) recently settled a contentious five year lawsuit and settlement process by agreeing to retire their nickname/logo, while three schools received permission from a tribe (i.e., Utah Utes, Florida State Seminoles, Central Michigan Chippewas) to keep using their mascot, nickname, and/or logo. However, although permission was granted in a few select instances, this still remains a complex, nuanced, and contentious issue that requires critical inquiry. For example, the Seminole Nation of Florida consented to the use of their Seminole name, but the Seminole Nation of Oklahoma has produced a resolution condemning the use of Native-themed mascots, nicknames, and logos (AISTM, 2010).

At the state legislative level, the state of Wisconsin recently passed legislation that would provide a more defined mechanism for schools to assess whether Native-themed mascots, nicknames, and logos promote discrimination, pupil harassment, or stereotyping. Under this law, if a member of a school district objects to a race-based mascot, nickname, or logo, then the Department of Public Instruction (and **not** the local school district) will hold a hearing to determine if the practice promotes discrimination, pupil harassment, **or** stereotyping. If the hearing determines that the use of the race-based mascot, nickname, or logo promotes any of these three practices, then the school has up to one year to change, or face fines up to $1,000 per day. It is important to note that this law does not ban Native-themed mascots, nicknames, or logos; rather this law puts the onus of responsibility onto the school district, and effectively empowers members of American Indian communities to no longer bear the burden of proof in these matters of racial discrimination and educational disenfranchisement. Currently (without this legislation), if an American Indian community member objected to the use of a Native-themed mascot, nickname, or logo, then that person would need to convince the local school board to meet and discuss the matter. Even if the person brings an armory of evidence, the school board could still refuse to acknowledge that the practice promotes discrimination. In most cases, the school board refuses to even acknowledge the issue or the validity of the complaint, readily dismissing and minimizing the experience of the person (H. Gunderson, personal communication, November, 2009). Currently, because of the state of Wisconsin's ground-breaking legislation, this dynamic will change. Perhaps other states can be encouraged to follow the legislative lead to assist in ending this discriminatory and racist practice of using American Indian imagery and culture in a stereotypic manner in sporting events. While education is important, legislation often provides a more expedient solution to the problem.

CHAPTER SUMMARY

In sum, research indicates that the stereotypic use of American Indian culture and imagery for sports-related purposes has negative psychological effects on both American Indians and majority culture participants. This practice does so by perpetuating negative stereotypes of American Indians (e.g., bloodthirsty savage, noble savage, historical society that exists only in past-tense status), misusing sacred spiritual and cultural symbols and practices (e.g., eagle feathers, drums, chanting), and denying American Indian communities the ability to present accurate and respectful societal portrayals of their people and their culture (Baca, 2004; Fenelon, 1999; King, Staurowsky, Baca, Davis, & Pewewardy, 2002; King, 2004; Pewewardy, 1991; Russel, 2003; Staurowsky, 2000; Staurowsky, 2007; Steinfeldt et al., 2010; Vanderford, 1996; Williams, 2007). Additionally, this practice creates a racially hostile educational environment (Baca, 2004; King et al., 2002) and may represent a violation of the civil rights of American Indians (APA, 2005). With all the emerging evidence mounting to support these claims, it is reasonable to ask this question: In 30 years, how will we look back at this period of history, and how will we judge our continued engagement in this racist practice of appropriating another culture for use as sports mascots, nicknames, and logos? As a parallel process, it seems so obviously objectionable to use hindsight to reflect back on the period in history when Blacks were not allowed to drink from the same drinking fountain as Whites. However, at the time, that too was a practice that was seen by the majority of people as part of the normal order of society.

This chapter presented perspectives on appropriating and stereotyping American Indian culture, followed by theory and research that helps explain the psychological impact of this practice, and concluded with educational interventions that can be utilized in order to enlighten people about the nature, nuances, and severity of this issue. Using education—in combination with legislative endeavors—to encourage people to engage in social justice activism can help ensure that the practice of appropriating and marginalizing another race through the use Native-themed mascots, nicknames, and logos becomes a historical footnote about stereotypes and civil rights violations, rather than an ongoing practice of stereotyping and violating the civil rights of a living group of people that exist in contemporary times.

REFERENCES

American Counseling Association (2001, November 30). *Resolution: Opposition to use of stereotypic Native American images as sports symbols and mascots*. Retrieved from http://aistm.org/fr.sitemap.htm

American Indian Sports Team Mascots (AISTM; 2010). *List of organizations endorsing retirement of "Indian" sports team tokens*. Retrieved from http://aistm.org/fr.groups.htm

American Psychological Association. (2005, October 18). *APA resolution recommending the immediate retirement of American Indian mascots, symbols, images, and personalities by schools, colleges, universities, athletic teams, and organizations*. Retrievedfrom http://www.apa.org/pi/oema/resources/policy/indian-mascots.pdf

Awad, G. H., Cokley, K., & Ratvich, J. (2005). *Attitudes toward affirmative action: A comparison of color-blind versus modern racist attitudes*. Journal of Applied Social Psychology, 35, 1384–1399.

Baca, L. R. (2004). *Native images in schools and the racially hostile environment*. Journal of Sport and Social Issues, 28, 71-78.

Bargh, J. A., & McKenna, K.Y.A. (2004*). The Internet and social life.*Annual Review of Psychology, 55, 573-590.

Bird, S. E. (Ed.). (1996). *Dressing in feathers: The construction of the Indian in American popular culture*. Boulder , CO: Westview.

Black, J. E. (2002). *The "mascotting" of Native America*. American Indian Quarterly, 26, 605–622.

Coombe, R. J. (1998). *Embodied trademarks: Mimesis and alterity on American commercial frontiers.*Cultural Anthropology, 11, 202-224.

Davis, L. R. (1993). *Protest against the use of Native American mascots: A challenge to traditional American identity*. Journal of Sport & Social Issues, 17, 9-22.

Davis, L. R. (2002). *The problem with Native American mascots.*Multicultural Education, 9, 11-14.

Deloria, P. J. (1998). *Playing Indian*. New Haven, CT: Yale University Press.

Duran, E. (2006). *Healing the soul wound: Counseling with American Indians and other native peoples*. Multicultural foundations of psychology and counseling series. New York, NY: Teachers College Press.

Duran, E., Firehammer, J., & Gonzalez, J. (2008). *Liberation psychology as the path toward healing cultural soul wounds*.Journal of Counseling and Development, 86, 288-295.

Fenelon, J.V. (1999). *Indian icons in the world series of racism: Institutionalization of the racial symbols of wahoos and Indians*. Research in Politics and Society, 6, 25-45.

Fryberg, S. A. (2003). *Really? You don't look like an American Indian: Social representations and social group identities*.Dissertation Abstracts International, 64(1549), 3B.

Fryberg, S. A., Markus, H. R., Oyserman, D., & Stone, J. M. (2008*). Of warrior chiefs and Indian princesses: The psychological consequences of American Indian mascots*. Basic and Applied Social Psychology, 30, 208–218.

Goings, K. W. (1994). *Mammy and Uncle Mose: Black collectibles and American stereotyping*.Bloomington, IN: Indiana University Press.

Graham, R. (1993, 6 January*). Symbol or stereotype: One consumer's tradition is another's racial slur*.The Boston Globe, p. 35.

Green, R. (1988). *The tribe called wannabee: Playing Indian in America and Europe*. Folklore, 99, 30-55.

Grounds, R. (2001). *Tallahassee, Osceola, and the hermeneutics of American place-names*.Journal of the American Academy of Religion, 69, 287–322.

Kates, S. M., & Shaw-Garlock, G. (1999). *The ever-entangling web: A study of ideologies and discourses in advertising to women*.Journal of Advertising 28, 33-49.

Kim-Prieto, C., Goldstein, L. A., Okazaki, S., & Kirschner, B. (2010). *Effect of exposure to an American Indian mascot on the tendency to stereotype a different minority group*.Journal of Applied Social Psychology, 40, 534-553.

King,C.R.(2001).*Uneasy Indians: Creating and contesting Native American mascots at Marquette University*.In C.R.King &C.F.Springwood (Eds.),Team spirits: The Native American mascot controversy (pp.281-303).Lincoln: University ofNebraska Press.

King, C.R.(2002*).Defensive dialogues: Native American mascots, Anti-Indianism, and educational institutions*.SIMILE: Studies in Media and Information Literacy Education, 2(1). DOI: 10.3138/sim.2.1.001

King, C. R. (2004). *This is Not an Indian: Situating claims about Indianness in sporting worlds*.Journal of Sport and Social Issues, 28, 3-10.

King, C.R., Davis-Delano, L., Staurowsky, E., & Baca, L. (2006). *Sports mascots and the media*. In A. A. Raney & J. Bryant (Eds.), Handbook of Sports and Media(pp. 559-575). Mahwah, NJ: L. Erlbaum and Associates.

King, C. R., & Springwood, C. F. (2001a). *Beyond the cheers: Race as spectacle in college sports*. Albany: State University of New York Press.

King, C. R., & Springwood, C. F. (Eds .). (2001b). *Team spirits: The Native American mascot controversy*. Lincoln: University of Nebraska Press.

King, C. R., Staurowsky, E. J., Baca, L., Davis, L. R., Pewewardy, C. (2002). *Of polls and raceprejudice: Sports Illustrated's errant "Indian Wars"*.Journal of Sport and Social Issues 26, 381-402.

LaRocque, A. R., McDonald, J. D., Ferraro, F. R., Abe, S. (2004). *Indian sports mascots: Affective difference between American Indian and non-Indian college students*.Unpublished doctoral dissertation, University of North Dakota, Grand Forks.

Loewen, J. (2008*). Lies my teacher told me: Everything your American history textbook got wrong (2nd ed.)*. W. W. Norton & Company: New York.

McNeel, J. (2009). *Council resolutioncondemns exploiters of sweatlodges.*Indian Country Today. Retrieved from http://www.indiancountrytoday.com/archive/70621312.html

Melican, D. B., & Dixon, T. L. (2008*). News on the net: Credibility, selective exposure, and racial prejudice.*Communication Research, 35, 151-168.

Merskin, D. (1998). *Sending up signals: A survey of American Indian media use and representation in the mass media.*The Howard Journal of Communications, 9, 333-345.

Merskin, D. (2001*). Winnebagos, Cherokees, Apaches, and Dakotas: The persistence of stereotyping of American Indians in American a*dvertising b*rands.* The Howard Journal of Communications, 12, 159-169

Mihesuah, D. A. (1996). *American Indians: Stereotypes and realities.* Atlanta, GA: Clarity Press.

Moscovici, S. (1998). The history and actuality of social representations. In U. Flick (Ed.), The psychology of the social (pp. 209-247). Cambridge, England: Cambridge University Press.

National Collegiate Athletic Association (2005). *Native American mascots.* Retrieved from http://www.ncaa.org/wps/portal/ncaahome?WCM_GLOBAL_CONTEXT=/wps/wcm/co nnect/ncaa/NCAA/Media%20and%20Events/Press%20Room/Current%20Issues/General %20Information/native_american_mascots.html

Neville, H. A., Lilly, R. L., Duran, G., Lee, R. M., & Browne, L. (2000). *Construction and initial validation of the Color-Blind Racial Attitudes Scale (CoBRAS).*Journal of Counseling Psychology, 47, 59–70.

Neville, H., Spanierman, L., & Doan, B. (2006). *Exploring the association between color blind racial ideology and multicultural counseling competencies.*Cultural Diversity & Ethnic Minority Psychology, 12, 275–290.

Neville, H. A., Worthington, R. L., & Spanierman, L. B. (2001). *Race, power, and multicultural counseling psychology: Understanding White privilege and color-blind racial attitudes.* In J. G. Ponterotto, J. M. Casas, L. A. Suzuki, & C. M. Alexander (Eds.), Handbook of multicultural counseling (2nd ed., pp. 257–288). Newbury Park, CA: Sage.

Pewewardy, C. D. (1991). *Native American mascots and imagery: The struggle of unlearning stereotypes.*Journal of Navajo Education, 9, 19-23.

Pewewardy, C. D. (2001). *Educators and mascots: Challenging contradictions.* In C. R. King & C. F. Springwood (Eds.), Team spirits: The Native American mascot controversy (pp. 257-278). Lincoln: University of Nebraska Press.

Picca; L.H., & Feagin, J.R. (2007). *Two-faced racism: Whites in the backstage and frontstage.* New York, NY: Routledge/Taylor & Francis Group.

Portman, T. A. A., & Portman, G. L. (2002). *Empowering students for social justice: A structured group approach.*Journal for Specialists in Group Work, 27, 16-31.

Russel, S. (2003). *Ethics, alterity, incommensurability, honor.*Ayaangwaamizin: The International Journal of Indigenous Philosophy, 3, 31–54.

Slapin, B., & Seale, D. (1998). *Through Indian eyes: The native experience in books for children.* Berkeley, CA: Oyate.

Spindel, C. (2000). *Dancing at halftime: Sports and the controversy over American Indian mascots.* New York: New York University Press.

Staurowsky, E. J. (1998). *An act of honor or exploitation? The Cleveland Indians' use of the Louis Francis Sockalexis story.*Sociology of Sport Journal, 15, 299-316.

Staurowsky, E. J. (2000). *The "Cleveland Indians": A case study of American Indian cultural dispossession.*Sociology of Sport Journal, 17, 307-330.

Staurowsky, E. J. (2004). *Privilege at play: On the legal and social fictions that sustain American Indian sport imagery.*Journal of Sport and Social Issues, 28, 11-29.

Staurowsky, E. J. (2007). *"You know, we are all Indian": Exploring White power and privilege in reactions to the NCAA Native American mascot policy.* Journal of Sport & Social Issues, 31, 61–76.

Steele, J. M. (2008). *Preparing counselors to advocate for social justice: A liberation model.*Counselor Education and Supervision, 48, 74-85.

Steinfeldt, J. A., Foltz, B. D., Kaladow, J. K., Carlson, T., Pagano, L., Benton, E., & Steinfeldt, M. C. (2010). *Racism in the electronic age: Role of online forums in expressing racial attitudes about American Indians.*Cultural Diversity and Ethnic Minority Psychology, 16, 362-371.

Steinfeldt, J. A. &Stockton, R. (2010). *Social justice in group counseling: Addressing American Indian marginalization.*Manuscript under review.

Steinfeldt, J. A. &Steinfeldt, M. C. (2010). *Multicultural trainingintervention to address American Indian stereotypes.*Manuscript under review.

Steinfeldt, J. A. & Wong, Y. J. (2010). *Multicultural training on American Indian issues: Testing the effectiveness of an intervention to change attitudes toward Native-themed mascots.*Cultural Diversity and Ethnic Minority Psychology, 16, 110–115.

Strickland, R. (1998).The celluloid Indian. Oregon Quarterly (Summer), 9-10.

Strong, P. T. (2004). *The mascot slot: Cultural citizenship, political correctness, and pseudo-Indian sports symbols.*Journal of Sport and Social Issues, 28, 79–87.

Sue, D. W. (2001). *Multidimensional facets of cultural competence.* The Counseling Psychologist, 29, 790–821.

Sue, D. W. (2005). *Racism and the conspiracy of silence: Presidential address.*The Counseling Psychologist, 33, 100-114.

Tafoya, N. & Del Vecchio, A. (1996*). Back to the future: An examination of the Native American holocaust experience.*In M. McGoldrick & J. Giordano (Eds.), Ethnicity and family therapy (2nd Ed., pp. 45-54). NY: Guilford Press.

U.S. Census Bureau. (2006). *We the people: American Indians and Alaska American Indians in the United States.* Washington, DC: Retrievedfrom http://www.census.gov/prod/2006pubs/censr-28.pdf

Vanderford, H. (1996). *What's in a name? Heritage or hatred: The school mascot controversy.*Journal of Law and Education, 25, 381-388.

Westerman, M. (1989, March). *Death of the Frito bandito: Marketing to ethnic groups.*American Demographics, 11, 28-32.

Williams, D. M. (2006). *Patriarchy and the 'Fighting Sioux': A gendered look at racial college sports nicknames.* Race, Ethnicity, & Education, 9, 325-340.

Williams, D. M. (2007). *Where's the honor? Attitudes toward the "Fighting Sioux" nickname and logo.*Sociology of Sport Journal, 24, 437-456.

In: Psychology of Stereotypes
Editor: Eleanor L. Simon

ISBN: 978-1-61761-463-7
©2011 Nova Science Publishers, Inc.

Chapter 10

THE COMPLEX ROLE OF MOTIVATION IN STEREOTYPING AND STEREOTYPE THREAT EFFECTS

Lisa R. Grimm and Julie Milligan Hughes*

The College of New Jersey, Ewing, New Jersey, USA

We examine the role of human motivation on stereotyping. People are motivated to carve the world into comprehensible segments (i.e., engage in categorization) that allow them to predict characteristics of new things or people. Categorization is a basic cognitive process that helps us structure our mental world to represent the physical world and relies on the similarity of unknown objects or people to previously created and stored categories. Objects can be grouped based on characteristics (e.g., red objects) or relational information (e.g., student). Our ability to classify new objects or people into known categories allows us to infer unknown features or behaviors and provides us with a known set of guidelines to use during interactions. For example, knowing someone is a student may lead us to ask about the individual's current classes. With objects, imperfect classification could lead to errors in prediction and interactions. Similarly, human stereotypes develop from this fundamental motivational drive for order, but can have deleterious consequences. We discuss the development of stereotypes and their application by children and adults. Even young children spontaneously categorize individuals on the basis of gender and ethnicity, and use group membership to infer individual possession of stereotypic traits. As children get older, their awareness of stereotypes includes an awareness of collectively endorsed stereotypes (McKown & Weinstein, 2003), and children use this stereotype knowledge to make sense of their social world as well.

Furthermore, our research suggests motivation plays a critical role beyond the generation and use of stereotypic information in the classification of others. Simply, motivation explains how merely mentally representing negative stereotypic information about one's groups can result in performance decrements. When a negative-group stereotype is associated with a group an individual belongs to, he or she can experience a decline in performance, or a *stereotype threat effect*. For example, a woman who knows of the stereotype that "women are

---

* Please address all correspondence to:Lisa R. Grimm, Department of Psychology, The College of New Jersey, P.O. Box 7718, Ewing, NJ 08628-0718, grimm@tcnj.edu

bad at math" will experience a decline in her performance when taking a math test. We argue that a motivational framework can account for stereotype threat effects. Negative stereotypes induce a motivational state that is associated with avoidance and vigilance, while positive stereotypes induce a motivational state associated with approach. We use this framework to explain stereotype threat effects and offer solutions for improving the performance of stereotyped groups using evidence from mathematical problem solving, learning classification rules, and motor performance, specifically golf putting.

DEFINING MOTIVATION

Motivation is a complex construct that takes many forms and influences many cognitive and social processes. Human motives are assumed to drive people toward actions that lead to a fulfillment of needs (Carver & Scheier, 1998). These needs can be physical needs, like the need to eat or drink, or psychological needs, like the desire to belong. Researchers have demonstrated that active needs influence behavior and other cognitive processes, such as preferences and choice. For example, Brendl, Markman, & Messner (2003) tested chronic cigarette smokers who had been deprived of a cigarette. This population of individuals has a high need to smoke. Half of the participants were allowed to smoke a cigarette eliminating their need to smoke, while the other half remained with a high need. Brendl et al. demonstrated that the group with a low need was more likely to purchase raffle tickets to win money over raffle tickets to win an equally-valued carton of cigarettes, while the group with a high need chose to purchase more tickets to win cigarettes. Thus, motivational states may powerfully influence the degree to which we value different outcomes (e.g., winning money v. winning cigarettes).

We make two basic assumptions about the motivational system. First, we assume that our physical or psychological needs are mentally represented as goal structures. These goal structures are representations that contain information about the need and are connected to other representations that can lead to goal fulfillment (Kruglanski et al., 2002). Furthermore, the goal structures can represent end states that are desirable or undesirable (Carver & Scheier, 1990). For example, a job applicant may desire to have a *good* job interview (an approach or desirable end state) or may desire to *not* have a *bad* job interview (an avoidance or undesirable end state). It is important to notice that successfully obtaining a good interview or successfully avoiding a bad interview leads to the same outcome (i.e., a good job interview). When a particular goal becomes active, the activation spreads to connected structures highlighting objects that could lead to goal fulfillment. This spreading of activation privileges objects that are related to the goal (e.g., valuation) and devalues objects that are unrelated to the goal (Markman, Brendl, & Kim, 2007). This valuation and devaluation can be measured using preferences for objects. For example, Markman et al. demonstrated that a need to eat in the morning increased preferences for breakfast foods, but decreased preferences for dinner foods and non-foods (like a car stereo). Goal-objects with greater valuation will receive more attention relative to other objects because they best fulfill active goals, thereby increasing the likelihood of goal fulfillment.

Second, we assume that there are multiple methods of goal pursuit. Higgins (1987, 1997) proposed that there are two main methods of goal pursuit: approach and avoidance. These mechanisms focus individuals on different aspects of their environment and are self-regulatory strategies that increase the likelihood of goal fulfillment. Higgins and colleagues argue that goal end states can be classified into nurturance needs or security needs (Higgins, 1997; Shah & Higgins, 1997; Shah, Higgins, & Friedman, 1998). An approach strategy is used in the service of fulfilling nurturance needs, while an avoidance strategy is used for security needs. The active self-regulatory strategy influences attention to different aspects of the environment. An active approach strategy increases attention to potential gains or non-gains in the environment, while an active avoidance strategy increases attention to potential losses or non-losses in the environment. For example, in a job interview setting, an individual who is more attentive to potential gains/non-gains may be especially aware of positive feedback from the interviewer, like smiles and head nods. An individual who is more attentive to potential losses/non-losses in the same context may be especially likely to monitor the interview for potential problems, like scowls or "oh" responses from the interviewer. The specific attentional focus can be chronic or temporary and is known as a *regulatory focus* (Higgins, 1987, 1997). Higgins refers to individuals with a focus on gains and non-gains as having a *promotion focus* and individuals with a focus on losses and non-losses as having a *prevention focus.*

While the motivational system influences a vast array of processes and behaviors, in this chapter, we will consider two influences of the motivational system that relate to stereotypes. First, we will discuss how our basic drive to categorize and understand the world influences the creation and use of stereotypes. In this section, we describe developmental work that demonstrates how even young children represent stereotypic information and use this information to make sense of their world. Second, we will show how different regulatory focus states become activated in the presence of stereotypic information. Specifically, positive stereotypes activate promotion foci and negative stereotypes activate prevention foci. Furthermore, we will show how this activation of regulatory focus states can be used to reinterpret the occurrence of stereotype threat effects (i.e., the performance decrements that appear when individuals are faced with the possibility of confirming a negative stereotype associated with their group). Lastly, we conclude with a discussion of how our motivational account can be used to reduce stereotype threat effects.

MOTIVATION TO CATEGORIZE THE WORLD

Stereotypes as Categories and Concepts

Before describing the formation and use of stereotypes, it is important to understand stereotypes in context. We recognize that stereotypes can have deleterious consequences for groups and individual members of groups when those stereotypes are negative (and possibly also when those stereotypes are positive). That said, stereotypes are categories of human groups, and as such, basic cognitive processes generate and act on stereotype representations. Therefore, before describing stereotype formation and use, we first provide a very brief review of the extant literature on concepts and categories.

There have historically been many different ways of describing the relationship between category members and the category, and why people use categories. In the classical view of categories, it was assumed that categories were represented as definitions. Therefore, category members were incorporated into a category only if they met the definitional requirement of the category (Murphy, 2002). For example, an individual is a member of the category women if two X chromosomes are present in the individual's DNA. Although the classical view of concepts was rejected due to failures in accounting for typicality effects (i.e., doves are seen as more typical of the group "birds" than ostriches), a number of models attempted to revise this view. A representative model from this revision comes from Smith, Shoben and Rips (1974) in which categories were made up of features that were either defining or characteristic.

After the fall of the classical view of categories, other researchers focused on different ways to account for typicality effects using different category structures. For example, one of the researchers to fill the void left by the classical view was Eleanor Rosch. Rosch and colleagues argued that categories are represented by sets of attributes. An exemplar (or item) would be a member of the category if it has a strong family resemblance structure with the category, that is, it has attribute overlap with category members and few attributes in common with members of another category (Rosch & Mervis, 1975). Items that are more similar to one another are classified as being in the same category. For example, the category "apple" might be represented by the following attributes: red, fruit, sweet, round, nutritious, and shiny. For person categories (like object categories), the set of attributes represented for a category will be commonly occurring in members of the category. Using male and female categories, the category "male" might include the attributes, tall, short hair, and likes football, while the category "female" might include the attributes, short, long hair, and likes ballet. Using these representations, an individual who is tall, has short hair, and likes ballet will likely be classified as male because the attributes more closely match those represented in the category "male" than the category "female". We learn category attributes through exposure to the covariation of features in the world or by purposefully adding features to our category representations.

We acknowledge that readers may already be feeling uncomfortable thinking about how person categories are represented, despite not having any reaction to our example using the category apple. In both examples, we have relied on stereotypic information. That is, not all men are tall, have short hair, or like football, but also not all apples are red. Generally, people are uncomfortable with using stereotypic information with person categories but not with other categories, such as object categories. Fox (1992) argued elegantly that stereotypic thinking and generalizations have become synonymous with prejudice, and the field of social psychology therefore strove to eliminate stereotypes. He makes clear that by reducing the complexity of person representations (by forming person categories) stereotypes are performing a useful function.

There are many other functions of categories. As noted by Anderson (1991), people form categories in order to attach a linguistic label to the category, in order to distinguish objects that have a large overlap of features, and in order to distinguish objects that serve a similar function. Furthermore, people form categories to gain the benefits of inference (e.g., being able to infer the presence of a feature because an exemplar is a member of a category (Anderson, 1991; Markman & Ross, 2003)). That is, available information is used to predict the presence of another feature (Markman & Ross, 2003). For example, classifying an unknown person as a woman allows the perceiver to make inferences about how to behave with the person and about the kind of attributes that likely are present. The perceiver might decide not to tell a sexist joke or might infer that the person likes romantic comedies and so suggest a particular movie to watch. While these inferences rely on stereotypic information, the stereotypes reduce the complexity of the situation. They limit the amount of information that needs to be considered when deciding how to act. Simply, stereotypes are providing a cognitive constraint and limiting the information processed, which makes thinking and deciding and acting easier –although clearly not necessarily better.

Stereotype Formation and Use

Several theories of the development of gender and racial attitudes propose that cognitive processes, beginning with categorization, are at the heart of children's stereotype formation. For example, gender schema theory (Martin, Ruble, & Szkrybalo, 2002; Martin & Halverson, 1981), developmental intergroup theory (Bigler & Liben, 2006, 2007), social identity developmental theory (Nesdale& Flesser, 2001), and Aboud's (1988) application of cognitive developmental theory to children's racial attitudes all assume that in order for children to develop group stereotypes they must (1) reliably categorize others on the basis of gender or race, and (2) recognize that they are members of a gender or racial category.

The formation of social categories (e.g., male, African American) begins with infants' early sensitivity to the perceptual distinctiveness of category members. For example, infants as young as nine months can differentiate among images of male and female faces (Leinbach & Fagot, 1993; Walker-Andrews, Bahrick, Raglioni, & Diaz, 1991). The categorization of individuals into gender groups appears to happen for auditory as well as visual stimuli. By six months of age, infants treat different female voices as similar but distinguish between a female voice and a male voice (Miller, 1983). Infants in the first year of life also differentiate between perceptually distinct racial categories (Kelly et al., 2005; Levy, 2003), and this differentiation becomes remarkably more consistent over the next few years such that most 4-year-old children can reliably sort individuals according to racial background (Aboud, 1988).

The early categorization of people into gender and race categories may be a manifestation of infants' general mechanisms of category development (Arterberry & Bornstein, 2002; Cohen & Cashon, 2006; Quinn, 2002). By the end of the first year infants appear sensitive to the overlap of features among category members, and to the relative lack of feature overlap among non-category members (Younger & Cohen, 1986). This sensitivity in feature overlap and its role in forming categories also may explain infants' readiness to form categories along gender and racial lines. For example, in order to recognize the distinction between female and male faces infants may notice that the feminine facial markers of a relatively pointed jaw and smooth forehead tend to co-occur, and the masculine features of a square jaw and relatively protrusive forehead also tend to co-occur. The detection of these correlations among features may give rise to the formation of perception-based gender categories by the age of 12 months.

Infants' perception-based categories for gender, and possibly for race, quickly gain category attributes early in development.In one experiment, Serbin et al. (2001) tested whether 18- and 24-month-old infants associated gender-typed toys with one gender or another. In this study, infants saw a picture of a gender-typed toy (e.g., a doll for a girl-typed toy) followed by a picture of a girl and a picture of a boy. After viewing gender-typed toys, infants looked significantly longer at the stereotypically associated gender. By 18 months of age infants have apparently begun to associate gender categories with gender-stereotyped toys.Infants also appear ready to form associations between racial group membership and other attributes. For example, Levy (2003) showed 10-month-old infants pictures of the faces of White and African American women, and beside each face a household object appeared as well. These objects were race-specific, so that some appeared only beside a White woman's face, and others appeared only beside an African American woman's face. After habituating to these face-object pairings, during test trials infants looked significantly longer at face-object pairs that had violated the pairings presented during the habituation trials.

Developmental theories concerning the origins of gender and racial stereotyping generally agree that children's social stereotypes accumulate prolifically after children are able to categorize themselves consistently into their gender or racial ingroups (e.g., Aboud, 1988; Martin & Halverson, 1981). When children categorize themselves into gender or racial categories, these categories gain salience and lead children to organize their world along racial and gender lines, noticing which attributes or roles tend to be associated with different categories. In line with this theorizing, empirical work indicates that children's ascription of stereotypical attributes to various gender and racial categories accelerates during the preschool years, when children recognize that they are members of their racial or gender ingroup. By the time children reach grade school, they consistently endorse gender-based occupational stereotypes (Liben& Bigler, 2002) and exhibit preference for same-gender play groups (see Maccoby, 1988). By the early elementary school years children also assign different attributes to members of their own and other racial groups (Aboud & Doyle, 1995; Hughes, Bigler, & Levy, 2007).

According to developmental intergroup theory (Bigler & Liben, 2006), a number of environmental features contribute to the psychological salience of gender and race to children's social cognitions, and it is this salience of group membership that fuels the acquisition of stereotypical knowledge. The environmental features that contribute to the psychological salience of race and gender include the perceptual salience of group membership along both racial and gender dimensions, the implicit and explicit organization of the environment by group membership (e.g., prevalent racial segregation of neighborhoods, use of separate bathrooms for males and females), and the use of labels for group membership. All of these environmental features lead children to attend to race and gender as important dimensions of human variation. Because the environment has drawn children's attention to race and gender category membership, they construct an understanding of their social world along racial and gender lines and use their knowledge of gender and racial groups to predict the roles, attributes, and preferences of other individuals.

The cognitive feature of essentialist thinking also facilitates children's development of gender and racial stereotypes. Essentialist thinkers assume that category members share an underlying essence, and this essence has important implications for the shared features of those category members (Gelman, 2000, 2003; Medin & Ortony, 1989; see also Bloom, 2000). This often applies to young children's understanding of living categories (Gelman & Wellman, 1991). For example, children might reason that a dog belongs to the category of dogs due to an unseen and permanent "essence," and even if painted to resemble a skunk the dog will remain (essentially) a dog. Children also apply essentialist thinking to categories of people. Before children understand the biological or cultural features that differentiate men from women or that lead to distinctions among racial groups, children believe that members of these groups share unseen, permanent qualities that differentiate them from other groups (Hirschfeld, 1995). Importantly, these unseen essences that children believe are responsible for membership in one group or another are also assumed to lead to shared characteristics of group members (Gelman & Wellman, 1991; Hirschfeld, 1993, 1995). Children often judge individuals to be similar to each other if they share gender or racial group membership (Bigler, Lobliner, & Milligan, 2003), and such assumptions of interpersonal similarity based on shared group membership are tantamount to stereotyping.

In middle childhood and adolescence, children typically become more flexible in their application of gender and racial stereotypes, and view stereotyping as a socially unacceptable practice (see Killen, Lee-Kim, McGlothlin, & Stangor, 2002; Nesdale & Flesser, 2001). Nonetheless, children remain knowledgeable about racial and gender stereotypes, and they draw on these stereotypes to explain their social environments. For example, Bigler, Arthur, Hughes, and Patterson (2008) interviewed grade-school children to determine how they explained the historical lack of female, African American, and Latino U.S. presidents. Although the majority of children in the study reasoned that people should be able to be president regardless of race or gender, the most popular explanation for the lack of non-White or female presidents among older children in the study was that voters discriminated against candidates on the basis of their race or gender (e.g., "People think girls can't be good rulers," Bigler et al., 2008, p. 11). Thus, even if elementary school-aged children are less likely to apply their stereotypical knowledge explicitly to other individuals, they remain aware of collectively held racial and gender stereotypes and of the impacts these stereotypes may have on the behaviors of others.

MOTIVATIONAL SYSTEM INFLUENCES ON STEREOTYPE THREAT EFFECTS

Stereotype Threat Effects

We have presented evidence that children form and use gender and racial stereotypes to judge the similarity of one person to another, and also to make judgments about potential occupations. Based on the omnipresence of stereotypes by adulthood, there is a substantial body of research documenting the deleterious consequences of negative group stereotypes for members of those groups. Most commonly researchers demonstrate that there are performance decrements in domains associated with the negative stereotype, and have called these declines in performance a *stereotype threat effect* (Steele & Aronson, 1995). For example, the category "woman" includes the stereotypic belief that women are bad at math. To be clear, individuals may not believe this to be true, but will still have mentally represented this belief and associated it with their concept of woman because it is a commonly held cultural belief (see Devine, 1989). As a result of this negative stereotype associated with her group, a woman might underperform on a math test, but not underperform on a verbal test.

Stereotype threat effects have been documented in a range of domains and by a range of gender and ethnic groups (Aronson et al., 1999; Spencer, Steele, & Quinn, 1999; Steele,

1997; Stone, Lynch, Sjomeling, & Darley, 1999). In the classic study, Steele and Aronson (1995) framed an intellectual test as diagnostic of ability, not diagnostic, or challenging. They demonstrated that Black participants underperformed relative to White participants on the verbal GRE only in the diagnostic condition. Based on these results, Steele and Aronson (1995) argued that Black participants had underperformed because of the possibility of confirming the negative stereotype associated with their group. Similar results have been demonstrated for women in math testing situations (Spencer et al., 1999).

These effects also translate to non-academic testing situations. In Stone et al. (1999), they examined performance decrements for Black and White participants using a golf putting task. Black participants underperformed when they believed the golf task was diagnostic of sports intelligence while White participants underperformed when they believed the task was diagnostic of natural athletic ability. Interestingly, stereotype threat effects can even be found in groups who are not typically stigmatized. Aronson et al. (1999) demonstrated performance decrements for White men on a math test when they believed that their performance was being compared to Asian participants.

THE MOTIVATIONAL SYSTEM AND STEREOTYPE THREAT

There have been many explanations for stereotype threat effects and many attempts to remove or eliminate the effects. Several of these explanations are motivational in character. For example, researchers have hypothesized that stereotype threat effects may occur because stigmatized groups expect to perform worse and therefore have lowperformance confidence or expend too much or too little effort on the task (Cadinu, Maass, Frigerio, Impagliazzo, & Latinotti, 2003; Smith, 2004). In addition, Fein, von Higgel, and Spencer (1999) and Sinclair and Kunda (1999) argue that stereotype threat effects occur as a result of the specific stereotypes associated with active goals. As discussed above, goals are representational structures that once active spread activation to associated content. If a woman has a goal to perform well on a math test, content associated with math and performance expectancies will also become activated and therefore influence performance.

In our work, we reinterpreted the stereotype threat literature using a motivational framework that highlights the importance of the means of goal pursuit. As discussed above, there are two main strategies for pursuing active goals –an approach strategy and an avoidance strategy. Avoidance strategies increase vigilance and attention to losses and non-losses in the environment, while approach strategies are associated with increased attention to gains and non-gains in the environment. Individuals can vary in their attentional focus (e.g., a prevention focus produces sensitivity to losses/non-losses and a promotion focus produces sensitivity to gains/non-gains). Seibt and Forster (2004) argued that when individuals encounter a negative stereotype a prevention focus is activated, but when a positive stereotype is encountered a promotion focus is activated. Therefore, stereotypes differentially induce motivational states.

This important observation by Seibt and Forster suggested to us that stereotype threat effects may be understood as motivational effects and could be eliminated using a method from the motivational literature on regulatory focus (Grimm, Markman, Maddox, & Baldwin, 2009). Our prior work on promotion and prevention foci examined the influence of placing participants in a task environment that they were motivationally prepared to handle (Grimm, Markman, Maddox, & Baldwin, 2008). Individuals in a prevention focus are prepared to deal with losses and as such we hypothesized that they would perform better in a task environment that requires a focus on losses (i.e., minimizing points lost during the task) as compared to a task environment that requires a focus on gains (i.e., maximizing points gained during the task). The opposite is true for individuals with a promotion focus. These individuals are prepared to deal with gains, and so we hypothesized that they would perform better on a task that requires a focus on gains as compared to a focus on losses. Our results were consistent with our hypotheses.

In Grimm et al. (2009), we argue that the prior demonstrations of stereotype threat effects mostly occurred in task environments with a gain/non-gains focus. Research participants were likely trying to complete a research requirement to gain course credit or to receive money for performance, were trying to get answers correct as a result of task instructions, or were explicitly focusing on points earned. As such, participants who were members of a negatively stereotyped group, and therefore who had a prevention focus, would be completing a task in a gains environment –an environment that mismatches their sensitivity. As a result, we refer to this situation as a *stereotype mismatch* because there is a mismatch between the task environment and the motivational state of the individual which has been induced by the stereotype. In contrast, we hypothesized that placing individuals with a negative stereotype in a task context they are more sensitive to –a losses environment –would improve their performance on the task. We refer to this situation as a *stereotype fit*.

In a series of experiments in Grimm et al. (2009), we manipulated the active stereotype and the structure of the environment. In Experiment 1, we had men and women take a section of the math GRE. Based on the known stereotype that women are bad at math, we assumed that the negative stereotype for women would induce a prevention motivational state, while men have a more positive stereotype associated with math and so they would experience a promotion motivational state. In addition, half of each gender took the GRE in a gains environment. For each correct answer, they gained 2 points, while for each incorrect answer they gained 0 points. Participants were told to try to maximize their points on the test. The other half of each gender took the test in a losses environment. For each correct answer, they lost 1 point, while for each incorrect answer they lost 3 points. Participants were told to try to minimize their losses on the test. A point meter displayed on the computer screen updated after every problem and increased or decreased based on the participant's answer and experimental condition.

First, we replicated the classic stereotype threat effect. In the gains condition, women performed worse than men on the GRE math test. This was predicted because the negative stereotype for women induced a prevention focus, which mismatched with the gains environment, while the positive stereotype for men induced a promotion focus, which fit with the gains environment. Importantly, we demonstrated that placing women in a losses environment drastically improved their performance relative to the gains environment. They performed 12.38% better and furthermore performed at the same level as men in the gains condition. For men, we found a small performance advantage for the gains environment over the losses environment. This finding is nicely consistent with an argument in the literature that positive stereotypes can produce *stereotype lift effects* (Walton & Cohen, 2003).

In Experiments 2A and 2B, we created our own stereotypic expectancy using a category learning task. In this task, participants learned to categorize lines that varied in the length, orientation, and position on the screen into two categories. The correct classification rule required that all lines that were both long and steeply oriented to be categorized into one group and all of the other lines into the other group. Of course, participants are not told this rule prior to the categorization task but rather rely on trial-and-error to learn the correct rule. While learning this correct rule, typically participants start by using simple rules, such as lines on the right are in one category and lines on the left are in the other category, and then progress to testing more complicated rules or classification strategies until they find the correct rule.

In Experiment 2A we told participants that women tended to perform better than men on the task and in Experiment 2B we told participants that men tended to perform better. As in Experiment 1, half of the participants gained more points for correct classifications and half lost fewer points for correct classifications. We found results consistent with our stereotype fit approach. In Experiment 2A, women performed better in the gains task relative to the losses task and those in gains were more likely to find and use the correct classification strategy, while men performed better in losses than gains and those in losses were more likely to find and use the correct strategy. When we switched the performance expectancies in Experiment 2B, we reversed our results. This makes clear that it is not the negative or the positive stereotype that matters, but whether the participant is experiencing a stereotype fit or a stereotype mismatch.

Recently, we have been investigating our stereotype fit effects in a non-academic domain, golf putting (Grimm, Maddox, & Markman, 2010). As discussed above, Stone et al. (1999) demonstrated stereotype threat effects for Black and White participants. We used their manipulation of stereotype threat and told White participants that we were either studying sports intelligence or natural athletic ability. We assume that the sports intelligence framing primes a positive stereotype that induces a promotion focus and the natural athletic ability framing primes a negative stereotype that induces a prevention focus. All participants took a series of golf putts on an indoor putting surface toward a target. To create stereotype fit and mismatch states, half of our participants gained points based on the distance to the target and half lost points. For the gains group, they gained more points for better putts, while the losses group lost fewer points for better putts. Data shows that the stereotype fit groups (sports intelligence group in gains and natural athletic ability group in losses) performed better on the putting task than stereotype mismatch groups (sports intelligence group in losses and natural athletic ability group in gains).

CONCLUSION

Our research suggests that motivational factors influence stereotype formation and use, and can account for stereotype threat effects. We agree with Fox (1992) that stereotypes, as category structures, perform a useful function by reducing the complexity of person categories, while recognizing that stereotypes are harmful when related to prejudice and discrimination. To support this view, we presented research demonstrating that children use racial and gender information to categorize individuals into groups and that this reliance on salient features is not unlike the processes applied to non-person categories. Moreover, children seem to increase stereotype formation and use after developing racial or gender ingroup identities, which according to developmental intergroup theory (Bigler & Liben, 2006) stems from the salience of racial or gender group membership.

Beyond being motivated to carve the social world into useful categories, motivational factors influence stereotype threat effects. As we argue, negative stereotypes are associated with an avoidance strategy as a means of goal pursuit, while positive stereotypes are associated with an approach strategy. Our research demonstrates that stereotype threat effects likely occur because individuals, with negative stereotypes associated with their groups, are performing tasks in environments that they are not motivationally prepared to manage. That is, individuals with a negative stereotype are performing in environments that emphasize potential gains. We show that placing individuals with a negative stereotype in an environment that emphasizes potential losses dramatically improves performance because the motivational state induced by the presence of a negative stereotype matches the losses environment. As such, our work is compatible with the body of work on stereotype threat that focuses on improving the performance of stigmatized groups (e.g., Brown & Josephs, 1999; Cohen,Garcia, Apfel, & Master, 2006; Johns, Schmader, & Martens, 2005).

REFERENCES

Aboud, F. E. (1988). *Children and prejudice*. New York: Blackwell.

Aboud, F. E., & Doyle, A. B. (1995). *The development of in-group pride in Black Canadians*.Journal of Cross-Cultural Psychology, 26, 243-254.

Anderson, J. R. (1991). *The adaptive nature of human categorization*. Psychological Review, 98, 409-429.

Aronson, J., Lustina, M. J., Good, C., Keough, K., & Steele, C. M. (1999). *When white men can't do math: Necessary and sufficient factors in stereotype threat*. Journal of Experimental Social Psychology, 35, 29-46.

Arterberry, M., & Bornstein, M. H. (2002). *Infant perceptual and conceptual categorization: The roles of static and dynamic stimulus attributes*. Cognition, 86, 1-24.

Bigler, R. S., Arthur, A., Hughes, J. M., & Patterson, M. P. (2008). *The politics of race and gender: Children's perceptions of discrimination and the U.S. presidency*. Analyses of Social Issues and Public Policy, 8, 1-30.

Bigler, R. S., & Liben, L. S. (2006). *A developmental intergroup theory of social stereotypes and prejudice*. In R. V. Kail (Ed.), Advances in child development and behavior, Vol. 34 (pp. 39-89). San Diego, CA: Elsevier.

Bigler, R. S., & Liben, L. S. (2007). *Developmental intergroup theory: Explaining and reducing children's social stereotyping and prejudice*. Current Directions in Psychological Science, 16, 162-166.

Bigler, R. S., Lobliner, D., & Milligan, J. K. (2003, August*). Children's use of individuating information in making social judgments*. Paper presented at the 111th annual meeting of the American Psychological Association, Toronto, Canada.

Bloom, P. (2000). *How children learn the meanings of words*. Cambridge, MA: MIT Press.

Brendl, C.M., Markman, A.B., & Messner, C. (2003). *Devaluation of goal-unrelated choice options*. Journal of Consumer Research, 29, 463-473.

Cadinu, M., Maass, A., Frigerio, S., Impagliazzo, L., & Latinotti, S. (2003). *Stereotype threat: The effect of expectancy on performance.* European Journal of Social Psychology, 33, 267-285.

Carver, C. S., & Scheier, M. F. (1990). *Origins and functions of positive and negative affect:* A control-process view. Psychological Review, 97, 19-35.

Carver, C. S., & Scheier, M. F. (1998). *On the self-regulation of behavior.* New York: Cambridge University Press.

Cohen, L. B., & Cashon, C. H. (2006*). Infant cognition.* In D. Kuhn, R. S. Siegler, W. Damon, & R. M. Lerner (Eds.), Handbook of child psychology: Vol 2, Cognition, perception, and language (6th ed.) (pp. 214-251). Hoboken, NJ: Wiley.

Devine, P. G. (1989). *Stereotypes and prejudice: Their automatic and controlled components.* Journal of Personality and Social Psychology, 56, 5-18.

Fein, S., von Hippel, W., & Spencer, S. J. (1999). *To stereotype or not to stereotype: Motivation and stereotype activation, application, and inhibition.* Psychological Inquiry, 10, 49-54.

Fox, R. (1992). *Prejudice and the unfinished mind: A new look at an old failing.* Psychological Inquiry, 3, 137-152.

Gelman, S. A. (2000*). The role of essentialism in children's concepts.* In H. W. Reese (Ed.), Advances in child development and behavior, Vol. 27 (pp. 55-98). San Diego, CA: Academic Press.

Gelman, S. A., & Wellman, H. M. (1991). *Insides and essence: Early understandings of the non-obvious.* Cognition, 38, 213-244.

Grimm, L.R., Maddox, W.T., & Markman, A.B. (2010). *Regulatory fit from stereotypes is advantageous for golf putting novices.* Poster presented at the 10th Annual Meeting of the Society for Personality and Social Psychology, Las Vegas, NV.

Grimm, L.R., Markman, A.B., Maddox, W.T., & Baldwin, G.C. (2008). *Differential effects of regulatory fit on classification learning.* Journal of Experimental Social Psychology, 44,920-927.

Grimm, L.R., Markman, A.B., Maddox, W.T., & Baldwin, G.C. (2009). *Stereotype threat reinterpreted as a regulatory mismatch.* Journal of Personality and Social Psychology, 96, 288-304.

Higgins, E. T. (1987). *Self-discrepancy:* A theory relating self and affect. Psychological Review, 94, 319-340.

Higgins, E. T. (1997). *Beyond pleasure and pain.* American Psychologist, 52, 1280-1300.

Hirschfeld, L. A. (1993). *Discovering social difference: The role of appearance in the development of racial awareness.* Cognitive Psychology, 25, 317-350.

Hirschfeld, L. A. (1995). *The inheritability of identity: Children's understanding of the cultural biology of race.* Child Development, 66, 1418-1437.

Hughes, J. M., Bigler, R. S., & Levy, S. R. (2007). *Consequences of learning about historical racism among European American and African American children.* Child Development, 78, 1689-1705.

Kelly, D. J., Quinn, P. C., Slater, A. M., Lee, K., Gibson, A., Smith, M., et al. (2005). *Three-month-olds, but not newborns, prefer own-race faces.*Developmental Science, 8, F31-F36.

Killen, M., Lee-Kim, J., McGlothlin, H., & Stangor, C. (2002). *How children and adolescents evaluate gender and racial exclusion.* Monographs of the Society for Research in Child Development, 67, vii-119.

Kruglanski, A. W., Shah, J. Y., Fishbach, A., Friedman, R., Chun, W. Y., & Sleeth-Keppler, D. (2002*). A theory of goal systems.* Advances in Experimental Social Psychology, 34, 331–378.

Leinbach, M. D., & Fagot, B. I. (1993). *Categorical habituation to male and female faces: Gender schematic processing in infancy.* Infant Behavior & Development, 16, 317-332.

Levy, G. D. (2003). *Perception of correlated attributes involving African-American and White females' faces by 10-month old infants.* Infant and Child Development, 12, 197-203.

Liben, L. S., & Bigler, R. S. (2002). *The developmental course of gender differentiation: Conceptualizing, measuring, and evaluating constructs and pathways.* Monographs of the Society for Research in Child Development, 67, vii-147.

Maccoby, E. E. (1988). *Gender as a social category.* Developmental Psychology, 24(6), 755-765.

Markman, A.B., Brendl, C.M., & Kim, K. (2007). *Preference and the specificity of goals.*Emotion, 7(3), 680-684.

Markman, A.B., & Ross, B.H. (2003). *Category use and category learning..* Psychological Bulletin, 129, 592-615.

Martin, C. L., & Halverson, C. F. (1981). *A schematic processing model of sex typing and stereotyping in children.* Child Development, 52, 1119-1134.

Martin, C. L., Ruble, D. N., & Szkrybalo, J. (2002). *Cognitive theories of early gender development.* Psychological Bulletin, 128, 903-933.

McKown, C., & Weinstein, R. S. (2003). *The development and consequences of stereotype consciousness in middle childhood.* Child Development, 74, 498-515.

Medin, D. L., & Ortony, A. (1989*). Psychological essentialism.* In S. Vosniadou & A. Ortony (Eds.), Similarity and analogical reasoning (pp. 179-195). New York, NY: Cambridge University Press.

Miller, C. L. (1983). *Developmental changes in male/female voice classification by infants.* Infant Behavior & Development, 6, 313-330.

Murphy, G. L. (2002). *The big book of concepts.* Cambridge, MA: MIT Press.

Nesdale, D., & Flesser, D. (2001). *Social identity and the development of children's group attitudes.*Child Development, 72, 506-517.

Quinn, P. C. (2002). *Category representation in young infants.* Current Directions in Psychological Science, 11, 66-70.

Rosch, E. & Mervis, C. B. (1975). *Family resemblances: Studies in the internal structure of categories.*Cognitive Psychology, 7, 573-605.

Seibt, B., & Forster, J. (2004). *Stereotype threat and performance: How self-stereotypes influence processing by inducing regulatory foci.* Journal of Personality and Social Psychology, 87, 38-56.

Serbin, L. A., Poulin-Dubois, D., Colburne, K. A., Sen, M. G., & Eichstedt, J. A. (2001). *Gender stereotyping in infancy: Visual preferences for and knowledge of gender-stereotyped toys in the second year.* International Journal of Behavioral Development, 25, 7-15.

Shah, J., & Higgins, E. T. (1997). *Expectancy x value effects: Regulatory focus as determinant of magnitude and direction.* Journal of Personality and Social Psychology, 73, 447-458.

Shah, J., Higgins, E. T., & Friedman, R. S. (1998). *Performance incentives and means: How regulatory focus influences goal attainment.* Journal of Personality and Social Psychology, 74, 285-293.

Sinclair, L., & Kunda, Z. (1999). *Reactions to a black professional: Motivated inhibition and activation of conflicting stereotypes.* Journal of Personality and Social Psychology, 77, 885-904.

Smith, E. E., Shoben, E. J. & Rips, L. J. (1974). *Structure and process in semantic memory: A featural model for semantic decisions.* Psychological Review, 1, 214-241.

Smith, J. L. (2004). *Understanding the process of stereotype threat: A review of mediational variables and new performance goal directions.* Educational Psychology Review, 16, 177-206.

Spencer, S. J., Steele, C. M., & Quinn, D. M. (1999). *Stereotype threat and women's math performance.* Journal of Experimental Social Psychology, 35, 4-28.

Steele, C. M. (1997). *A threat in the air: How stereotypes shape intellectual identity and performance.* American Psychologist, 52, 613-629.

Steele, C. M., & Aronson, J. (1995). *Stereotype threat and the intellectual test-performance of African Americans.* Journal of Personality and Social Psychology, 69, 797-811.

Stone, J., Lynch, C. I., Sjomeling, M., & Darley, J. M. (1999). *Stereotype threat effects on Black and White athletic performance.* Journal of Personality and Social Psychology, 77, 1213-1227.

Walker-Andrews, A. S., Bahrick, L. E., Raglioni, S. S., & Diaz, I. (1991*). Infants' bimodal perception of gender.* Ecological Psychology, 3, 55-75.

Walton, G. M., & Cohen, G. L. (2003*). Stereotype Lift.* Journal of Experimental Social Psychology, 39, 456-467.

Younger, B. A., & Cohen, L. B. (1986). *Developmental change in infants' perception of correlations among attributes.* Child Development, 57, 803-815.

In: Psychology of Stereotypes
Editor: Eleanor L. Simon

Chapter 11

AMBIVALENCE IN STEREOTYPES AND ATTITUDES: THE IMPLICATIONS OF POSSESSING POSITIVE AND NEGATIVE PERCEPTIONS

Kimberley A. Clow[a] and Rosemary Ricciardelli[b]
[a]University of Ontario Institute of Technology
[b]York University

The content of most stereotypes are not uniformly negative. African Americans are stereotyped as loud and aggressive, but also as musical and athletic. Asian Americans are stereotyped as being cold and aloof, but also as high in intelligence. People express more respect for men than women, but more liking for women than men. Thus, rather than uniform negativity, many stereotypes appear to be ambivalent, containing both positive and negative elements simultaneously. Ambivalent sexism and the stereotype content model have emerged to explain the ambivalence that is prevalent in intergroup attitudes. This chapter will review these theories and key findings in the field, as well as present applied data investigating stereotypes of men in nursing and stigma toward the wrongly convicted to illustrate how the ambivalence of intergroup attitudes can suggest support for stigmatized groups, while at the same time discriminating against them.

Prejudice has traditionally been thought of as holding negative attitudes toward someone due to their group membership (e.g., Allport, 1954; Dion, 2003). Eagly (2004) challenged this definition, as women are often viewed more positively than men and yet are still the targets of discrimination. From the gender literature, ambivalent sexism emerged (and later ambivalence toward men), embracing the positive and negative components of gender attitudes to more fully understand sexism (e.g., Glick & Fiske, 1996, 1999). This conception of ambivalence, that intergroup attitudes hold both positive and negative dimensions, has been generalized beyond gender in the stereotype content model (e.g., Fiske, Cuddy, Glick, & Xu, 2002).Thismodel, in particular, emphasized the connections between stereotype ambivalence and prejudice. This chapter reviews the literature on ambivalence and argues that (1) stereotype content is often ambivalent and (2) stereotypes must be understood in the context of ambivalent attitudes. The implications of ambivalence for resistance to change and justification of the status quo are discussed.

STEREOTYPE CONTENT MODEL

The most influential paradigm for examining stereotype content in recent years has been the stereotype content model (e.g., Eckes, 2002; Fiskeet al., 2002). Differing prejudices and behaviours, based on social status and competition between groups, are associated with differing combinations of competency and warmth in social group stereotypes (Fiske et al., 2002; Fiske, Cuddy, & Glick, 2007). Paternalistic prejudice results when people feel warmth toward a social group, but consider the group low in competency. These stereotypes are driven by perceptions of particular outgroups as low in status and not competing with the ingroup for power and resources (Caprariello, Cuddy, & Fiske, 2009). Paternalistic prejudice is associated with feelings of pity and sympathy for outgroup members (e.g., Fiske et al., 2002). In contrast, outgroups that are perceived as highly competent can be viewed as possible competitors for resources, social status, or power. Groups that are viewed as competitors are stereotyped as lower in warmth (Carariello et al., 2009; Russell & Fiske, 2008). If these groups are also high in status or perceived as highly competent, this leads to envious prejudice: respecting a social outgroup (high competence) but not liking them (low warmth). As the name suggests, envious prejudice leads to feelings of envy and jealousy toward outgroup members (Fiske et al., 2002). Both paternalistic and envious prejudices are ambivalent, containing both seemingly positive and negative aspects (high warmth but low competency or low warmth but high competency). Stereotypes of most groups are assumed to fall into these two ambivalent categories (although the model also proposed contemptuous prejudice (low warmth and low competence) and admiration (high warmth and high competence) as well).

The stereotype content model has been successfully used to investigate the stereotype content of a number of diverse social groups (e.g., Clausell & Fiske, 2005; Eckes, 2002; Fiske et al., 2002). Across cultures and nations, the content of stereotypes has generally been found to be ambivalent, specifically in regards to ratings of warmth and competence (e.g., Asbrock, 2010; Cuddy et al., 2009; Glick et al., 2006). Across 12 different countries, stereotypes of Americans and the U.S. government were very similar, with participants reporting ambivalent stereotypes higher in competence than warmth (Glick et al., 2006). Many diverse stereotypes of West Germany participants are also captured by the stereotype content model's proposed combinations of warmth and competence (Asbrock, 2010). In an examination of stereotypes of 33 different immigrant groups, Lee and Fiske (2006) found that stereotypes toward all but four of these groups were ambivalent (i.e., participants rated the group as significantly more warm than competent or significantly more competent than warm).

The stereotype content model has provided insight into the impact of self-threat on the derogation of outgroups (Collange, Fiske, & Sanitioso, 2009), how stereotypes of biracial individuals compare to stereotypes of Whites and visible minorities (Sanchez & Bonam, 2009), and how women in different subgroups are stereotyped and discriminated against in the work place (Cuddy, Fiske, & Glick, 2004; Masser, Grass, & Nesic, 2007). Harris and Fiske (2006) scanned participants' brains while they were viewing social group stimuli and suggested that our medial prefrontal cortex responds differently when we are viewing targets of contemptuous prejudice (low competency and low warmth) than the targets of paternalistic prejudice, envious prejudice, or admired outgroups. Thus, there is considerable research evidence to support the stereotype content model and ambivalence in social group stereotypes.

Stereotypes of Blacks. Devine (1989) demonstrated that high and low prejudiced White participants were equally aware of the cultural stereotype of African Americans as poor, aggressive, criminal, low intelligence, uneducated, lazy, sexually perverse, athletic, rhythmic, and ostentatious. In addition, considerable research has focused on the close association between stereotypes of African Americans and crime (e.g., Blair, Judd, & Chapleua, 2004; Correll, Park, Wittenbrink, & Judd, 2002; Eberhardt, Goff, Purdie, & Davies, 2004; Payne, 2001). Although the overall tone of the Black stereotype is negative, there appears to be a positive component as well (e.g., Devine, 1989; Devine & Elliot, 1995; Madon et al., 2001; Wittenbrink, Judd, & Park, 1997). Czopp and Monteith (2006) proposed that people possess complimentary stereotypes of African Americans, which revolve around athleticism, music, being "cool," and sexual/social competence. Unfortunately, complementary stereotypes positively correlated with prejudice, such that participants who endorsed more complementary stereotypes toward Blacks also endorsed more prejudice toward Blacks. Therefore, even though complementary stereotypes may seem positive to the person possessing the stereotypes, these stereotypes still have negative consequences for the individual or group stereotyped. Interestingly, Devine and Elliot (1995) found that high and low prejudiced participants differed in their personal endorsement of negative stereotypes (e.g., lazy, ignorant, loud) but not positive stereotypes (e.g., musical, athletic, loyal to family). This suggests that people may not perceive positive stereotypes as inappropriate or damaging. However, positive stereotypes are still a form of stereotype and perpetuate stereotypical thinking, prejudice, and the status quo.

Considering these different research findings together, stereotypes of African Americans are ambivalent, containing negative as well as positive content. This ambivalence is found even within stereotypes of speech styles (e.g., Popp, Donovan, Crawford, Marsh, & Peele, 2003). Popp et al. (2003) found that White participants stereotyped Black targets' speech styles as more direct (e.g., talks mostly about facts, talks mostly about important things, articulate), more emotional (e.g., exaggerated gestures, talkative, emotional), less socially appropriate (e.g., offensive, impolite, inappropriate), and less playful (e.g., less humorous, less seductive) than White targets' speech styles. While the directness factor appears positive and the lower scores on the social appropriateness and playful factors appear negative, the emotional factor is more ambiguous, containing some seemingly positive (e.g., sensitive, talkative) as well as some seemingly negative components (e.g., demanding, loud). These findings underscore the ambivalent nature of stereotypes of African Americans.

Based on the stereotype literature, Fiske et al. (2002) used stereotypes of African Americans as an example of paternalistic prejudice (high warmth, low competence). Their preliminary analyses, however, found that stereotypes of Blacks fell around the midpoint on both competence and warmth scales. As they felt that stereotypes of different subgroups may be contributing to this finding (e.g., welfare recipients and criminals vs. Black professionals), they chose to investigate stereotypes of poor Blacks and Black professionals specifically in additional studies. Instead of paternalistic prejudice, participants expressed contemptuous prejudice (low warmth, low competence) toward poor Blacks (along with poor Whites and welfare recipients) and envious prejudice (low warmth, high competence) toward Black professionals (along with Northerners, business women, Jews, Asians, feminists, and the rich).

Using Fiske et al.'s (2002) items (1 = Not at All; 5 = Extremely), we investigated stereotypes of six different social groups (Blacks, Aboriginals, Chinese, criminals, doctors, and leaders) using a Canadian sample. As Fiske et al. (2002) reported, we also found that participants rated Blacks around the midpoint in both competence ($M = 2.78$, $SD = 0.72$) and warmth ($M = 2.79$, $SD = 0.77$). In fact, in a factor analysis, all of the warmth and competence items loaded on the same factor. Compared to the other social groups investigated in the study, participants rated Blacks as significantly less competent than Chinese, leaders, and doctors and significantly less warm than leaders and doctors. Ratings of Aboriginals and Blacks did not significantly differ. Although Blacks were rated as less warm and less competent than doctors and leaders, average scores are not below the midpoint of the scales, so it is not the case that participants were expressing contemptuous prejudice toward Blacks. Perhaps, as Fiske et al. (2002) suggested, there are extreme Black subgroup stereotypes that result in a neutral midpoint when averaged together.

Surprisingly, participants did not stereotype Blacks similar to criminals. Even though the items specify (as Fiske et al., 2002 did) that participants rate the groups as they are viewed by society and not according to their personal beliefs (the items actually start "As viewed by society, how _____ are members of this group?"), participants rated Blacks and criminals differently. This corresponds to past research using Canadian samples that has found the content of stereotypes of Blacks and criminals to be very distinct (Clow & Esses, 2007). Unlike Blacks, criminals were viewed with contemptuous prejudice (low competence, low warmth). Out of these 6 groups, criminals were rated significantly lower in both competence and warmth in comparison to every other group and were the only group to receive average ratings on the negative side of the scales. Also unlike ratings of Blacks, criminals were rated significantly higher in competence than warmth.

Within our data there was one group that was stereotyped in accordance with paternalistic prejudice:Aboriginals. Aboriginals were rated significantly higher in warmth than competence. These findings correspond with past research that has found attitudes toward First Nations peoples to be ambivalent (e.g., Bell & Esses, 1997; 2002; Donakowski & Esses, 1996; Maio, Esses, & Bell, 2000). These findings also correspond to unpublished data Clow and Esses collected in Canada using an open-ended stereotype measure, where participants ascribed many positive elements to Aboriginal peoples (e.g., cultural, spiritual, friendly, nature-loving) but considerable negativity as well (e.g., alcoholics/drug addicts, violent, uneducated, parasites). The overall stereotype was ambivalent and seemed to express more warmth than competence. The negative aspects of these Canadian participants' stereotypes of Aboriginals (drug use, violence, uneducated) share similarities to the negative component of Americans' stereotypes of Blacks.Perhaps this similarity arises because the African-American versus Caucasian-American struggle is the United States' most enduring racial conflict, whereas Canada's most enduring racial conflict is between immigrant Canadians (i.e., non-natives) and First Nations peoples.

Stereotypes of Asians. Comparatively, stereotypes of Asian Americans have been studied less extensively (Chu & Kwan, 2007). In the United States, the stereotype of Asian Americans seems to revolve around the idea of the "model minority" (e.g., Oyserman & Sakamoto, 1997; Wong & Halgin, 2006; Wong, Lai, Nagasawa, & Lin, 1998; Ying et al.,

2001).This model minority stereotype may at first appear positive, as it ascribes high academic achievement, intelligence, career success, hardworking, loyalty to family, and mental health to Asian Americans (e.g., Wong et al., 1998). The consequences of this stereotype, however, are negative. For example, researchers have argued that the model minority stereotype leads to the development of envious prejudice (e.g., Lin, Kwan, Cheung, & Fiske, 2005), feelings of threat and negativity (e.g., Maddux, Galinsky, Cuddy, & Polifroni, 2008), downplaying the mental health of Asian Americans (e.g., Sue, 1994), decreases assistance toward Asian Americans (e.g., Chao, Chiu, & Lee, 2010), and lowers life functioning among Asian Americans (e.g., Wong & Halgin, 2006). In addition, researchers have argued that the model minority stereotype is the seemingly positive aspect of ambivalent attitudes toward Asian Americans and is inherently tied to the negative "yellow peril" stereotype—the stereotypic belief that the mass migration of immigrants from Asian countries would threaten the standard of living of White Americans (e.g., Kawai, 2005).

Oyserman and Sakamoto (1997) asked Asian Americans how they were stereotyped by non-Asians. Over 20% of participants mentioned high achieving (e.g., intelligent, competitive, nerdy, don't have fun), physical characteristics or mannerisms (e.g., short, wear glasses, can't communicate), sticking together and denigrating others (e.g., tend to hang out in groups, racist, confined to own race) and personality characteristics (e.g., submissive, quiet, sly, devious). Chu and Kwan (2007) found that Asian Americans rated themselves as less individualistic and less sociable than did European Americans. Similar stereotypes of Asian Americans are held by non-Asian Americans as well (e.g., Ho & Jackson, 2001; Lin et al., 2005; Maddux et al., 2008; Wong et al., 1998).

Based on past research findings, Fiske et al. (2002) used Asians as one of their examples of envious prejudice and their data supported that categorization (see also Lin, Kwan, Cheung, & Fiske, 2005). Overall, Asians were perceived as high in competence but low in warmth (along with Black professionals, Northerners, business women, Jews, feminists, and the rich). In our own research, envious prejudice was expressed toward the Chinese, leaders, and doctors. The Chinese continue to be one of the largest minority ethnic groups in Canada (census data reveal that they were the largest ethnic minority group in Canada for many years and have only recently been surpassed by East Indians). Therefore, it was not surprising that Canadian participants rated the Chinese significantly higher in competence than warmth, similar to American data on Asian Americans (e.g., Fiske et al., 2002). In our research, the Chinese were rated significantly higher in competence than were Blacks, Aboriginals, and criminals. Of our six groups, only doctors were rated as more competent than Chinese people (ratings of leaders' competence did not significantly differ from ratings of competence for Chinese). In contrast, the Chinese were only rated significantly higher in warmth than criminals. Both leaders and doctors—who are not generally stereotyped for their warmth— were rated as significantly higher in warmth than the Chinese. These findings corroborate past research on the more general stereotype of Asian Americans, where Asians have been stereotyped as very industrious and competent but lacking in warmth and social skills (e.g., Ho & Jackson, 2001; Lin et al., 2005; Maddux et al., 2008; Oyserman & Sakamoto, 1997; Wong et al., 1998).

Gender. Parsons and Bales (1955) first referred to psychological traits that are stereotypically associated with each gender as instrumental and expressive. Instrumental characteristics include traits that are stereotypically associated with masculinity, such as assertiveness, competitiveness, and aggressiveness, whereas expressive characteristics include traits that are stereotypically associated with femininity, such as caring, sensitivity, anxiety, and tenderness (Eagly, 1995). These psychological dimensions map onto the stereotype content model's factors of competence (instrumental or agentic) and warmth (expressiveness or emotive).

Bem (1974) developed conceptualizations of stereotypically masculine and feminine traits in her research on gender androgyny. Masculine and feminine traits are traits that anyone can develop, as traits are not biologically based on sex. Spence and Buckner (2000) suggested that societal changes have affected current gender stereotypes, as women and men currently differ more dramatically on ratings of expressive traits than instrumental traits. Eagly and Mladinic (1989) found that participants evaluated women more favorably than men, whereas Jackson, Esses, and Burris (2001) found that participants respect men more than women and that hiring decisions are influenced by these differences in respect.

Looking at university professors in Spain, Fernandez et al. (2007) examined the link between instrumental/expressive traits and sexist attitudes. Not surprising, the data revealed that professors have less sexist attitudes than the general population, yet males have more sexist attitudes in comparison to females. Although male and female professors were equally instrumental, female professors were found to show more expressive traits than male professors. In the United States, Krefting (2003) argued that gender stereotypes are ideological and prescriptive rather than merely descriptive. For example, women earn almost half of all doctoral degrees in the United States yet only hold one third of all faculty positions and take longer to become tenured and promoted. Cikara and Fiske (2009) comment that rarely are successful women perceived as both competent and kind.

Studying White middle class students in Germany, Eckes (2002) found that many gender subgroups are perceived as ambivalent. Among subgroups of women, he found that participants perceived a number of subgroups paternalistically, rating them high in warmth but low in competence (housewife, wallflower, secretary, typical woman). Other subgroups were perceived enviously, rating them high in competence but low in warmth (vamp, intellectual, feminist, hippy, punk, women's libber, career woman). Eckes (2002) also investigated male subgroups and found evidence of ambivalent stereotypes corresponding to paternalistic (softy, senior citizen, radical, hippy) and envious prejudices (typical man, manager, social climber, Mr. Joe Cool, yuppie, egoist, career man). Overall, 65% of the female subgroups and 54% of the male subgroups consisted of ambivalent stereotypes (rated significantly higher on warmth than competence or significantly higher on competence than warmth). Cuddy, Fiske, and Glick (2004) found that when working women became mothers, they were stereotyped as warmer but less competent—but that fathers simply gained in warmth without the corresponding cost to their competence. Wade and Brewer (2006) agreed that warmth and competence are important aspects in stereotype content and that many subgroup stereotypes are ambivalent, but they suggested that the valence associated with a specific subgroup is important as well. DeWall, Altermatt, and Thompson (2005) suggested that moral virtue and power add to distinctions in female subgroups above and beyond the contributions of warmth and competence.

AMBIVALENT ATTITUDES

The realization that there are seemingly positive and negative components within intergroup attitudes is not new. Allport (1954) believed that most prejudice involved compunction (i.e., remorse), where differing values and attitudes conflicted. He provided excerpts from student papers on their experiences with, and attitudes toward, minorities in America and the examples demonstrated clear conflict between opposing views and values. Students often reported believing one thing and yet feeling another. For example, one student reported that "every rational voice within me says the Negro is as good, as decent, sincere, and manly as the white, but I cannot help noticing a split between my reason and prejudice," (p. 327).

Crandall and Eshleman (2003) proposed a Justification—Suppression Model of prejudice that incorporated three different kinds of ambivalence: suppression ambivalence, affective ambivalence, and equilibrium ambivalence. Suppression ambivalence is an attempt to suppress or inhibit prejudices that one feels one should not have or should not express. The ambivalence does not come from conflicting positive and negative views toward a social group, but between holding emotions that are not acceptable to the self (or society) and the efforts to suppress those thoughts. Affective ambivalence, in contrast, is conflict between genuinely positive and genuinely negative emotions toward the same social group, which is the type of ambivalence other researchers have talked about (e.g., Glick & Fiske, 1996; Katz & Hass, 1988). Equilibrium ambivalence was explained as a stable set of beliefs that alternated between prejudice suppression and expression, such that prejudices were usually suppressed but were able to be expressed when situations arose that were perceived as justified. This was viewed as a later and more developed stage of ambivalence, where cycles of suppression and justification hide and reveal existing prejudices in an organized manner, leading to greater stability and self-assuredness.

The idea of intergroup ambivalence has surfaced in a number of different theories of prejudice as well, such as aversive racism, symbolic racism, modern racism, and racial ambivalence (e.g., Dovidio & Gaertner, 1986; Katz & Hass, 1988; McConahay, 1986; Sears, 1988). For example, in aversive racism, ambivalence arises in Whites from an internalized egalitarian value system and unacknowledged antipathy toward African-Americans (e.g., Dovidio & Gaertner, 1986), whereas in racial ambivalence, conflict arises from large amounts of both pro-Black (supporting a push for greater equality and understanding of the experiences of Black Americans) and anti-Black sentiments (e.g.,Hass, Katz, Rizzo, Bailey, & Moore, 1992). Markus (2008) went so far as to claim that White Americans' approach to race and ethnicity—and psychologists' approach in particular—was ambivalent.

These ambivalent prejudices, however, are tied to stereotypes. Dovidio and Gaertner (1986) found that participants rationalized negativity toward high ability Black supervisors by perceiving the high ability as relative to other Blacks (stereotyping Blacks as low in competence) and lower in comparison to the self, whereas they perceived high ability White supervisors as high in ability when compared to the self. Katz and Hass (1988) created pro-Black and anti-Black scales to assess racial ambivalence and many of their items tap into underlying stereotypes. For example, items such as "On the whole, Black people don't stress education and training," "Blacks don't seem to use opportunities to own and operate little shops and businesses," and "Most Blacks have the drive and determination to get ahead" (reverse scored) capture stereotypes of poor education, low intelligence, and lazy.

Considering negative stereotypes in isolation of their positive attitudinal counterparts loses the context in which intergroup attitudes are experienced. Situating stereotypes within their attitudinal context increases our ability to predict under what circumstances prejudicial behavior will and will not be expressed. In addition, attitudinal ambivalence may, in itself, prevent individuals from acknowledging their own prejudices. Possibly, holding genuine positive beliefs and attitudes about a social group makes it possible to deny, even to the self, that the negative beliefs and attitudes exist. The positive component of ambivalent stereotypes and attitudes may actually work against individuals recognizing their own prejudices. As people can honestly report positive attitudes toward outgroups, they may convince themselves that they do not hold prejudicial attitudes. One could even rationalize that the positive aspects of one's attitude balance off the negative aspects, comprising a more realistic overall evaluation of the group. Logical as that may sound, it is not the case. As research investigating the seemingly positive aspects of `stereotypes of African Americans and Asian Americans has demonstrated, what appears positive to the perceiver can have detrimental consequences for individuals targeted by these supposedly positive stereotypes (e.g., Czopp & Monteith, 2006; Lin et al., 2005; Maddux et al., 2008). To more fully understand how seemingly positive attitudes can have serious negative consequences, a review of research on Ambivalent Sexism is warranted.

Ambivalent sexism. Glick and Fiske (1996) developed the concept Ambivalent Sexism to explain prejudice toward women, which was not uniformly negative but was instead ambivalent, where both negative and positive feelings coexisted. Hostile sexism refers to the subjectively negative aspect of gender attitudes involving domination and hostility, whereas benevolent sexism is defined as the subjectively positive, yet sexist, attitudes of protection and idealization. These forms of sexism emerge from paternalism (power differences), gender differentiation (stereotypes and roles), and heterosexual relations. Paternalism refers to attitudes of male superiority, dominance, and protection over women (Fiske & Glick, 1995). Gender differentiation is the desire to make distinctions between men and women, where men are viewed as superior to women, but women are simultaneously viewed favourably as mothers and homemakers (Eagly & Mladinic, 1993). Heterosexuality refers to intimate relationships between men and women, where sexual attraction can be positive and intimate or dominating and harassing (Fiske & Glick, 1995). In summary, hostile sexism is composed of dominative paternalism, competitive gender differentiation, and hostile heterosexuality whereas benevolent sexism is comprised of protective paternalism, complementary gender differentiation, and heterosexual intimacy motives. Thus, benevolent and hostile sexism both reinforce traditional gender barriers while preserving patriarchal social structures. Although each type of sexism is expressed differently, the basic idea remains that women are viewed as the weaker of the sexes (Glick & Fiske, 1996; 2001). More than 15,000 men and women, in at least 19 nations, have completed the Ambivalent Sexism Inventory and demonstrated that hostile and benevolent sexism exist cross-culturally (Cikara et al., 2009; Glick & Fiske, 2001a; Glick & Fiske, 2001b).

Ambivalent sexism has been applied to understanding the private sphere of life (e.g., marriage, mate selection, duties at home, etc.). Within the private sphere, women and men are often perceived in stereotypical gender-specific roles (e.g., women as care taker, man as provider/labourer) (Cikara, Lee, Fiske, & Glick, 2009). Sexist attitudes, in accordance with complementary gender ideologies, work to justify the gendered social hierarchy, where women are subordinate to men (Cikara et al., 2009; Glick, 2006; Glick & Fiske, 2001a; Thomas & Esses, 2004). Along these lines, ambivalent sexism influences men's perceptions of women (Sibley & Wilson, 2004) and women's experiences of body dissatisfaction (Forbes, Collinsworth, Jobe, Braun, and Wise, 2005), different environments (Fischer, 2006), and perceived threats (Takabayashi, 2007). Researchers have found that hostile sexism is related to less favorable evaluations of women in non-traditional roles (e.g., career-oriented women, women with a promiscuous sexual character), and benevolent sexism is related to positive evaluations of women in traditional roles (e.g., homemakers, women chaste in sexual character) (Glick et al., 1997; Sibley & Wilson, 2004; Takabayshi, 2007). In addition, Fischer (2006) found that women in hostile environments may respond with benevolent sexist attitudes as a means of self-protection.

Benevolent sexism, in particular,is implicated in mate selection and dating behaviours (Chen, Fiske,& Lee, 2009; Tendayi, Abrams & Hutchison, 2003), whereas hostile sexismis related to marriage norms (Chen et al., 2009). Those higher in ambivalent sexism were more likely to minimize the seriousness of domestic violence and rape and to blameand have less positive attitudes toward victimsof these crimes (Sakalli-AYurlu, Sila YalASin, & Glick, 2007; Yamawaki, Darby, & Querioz, 2007; Yamawaki, Ostenson,& Brown, 2009). Both hostile and benevolent sexism appear to play a role in legitimizing and justifying domestic violence (Glick, Sakalli-Ugurly, Ferreira, de Souza, 2002).Moreover, these attitudes and stereotypes are transmitted through communication mediums, such as jokes and rap music (Cobb & Boettcher, 2007; LaFrance & Woodzicka, 1998; Thomas & Esses, 2004). For example, Thomas and Esses (2004) found that men higher in hostile sexism were more likely to repeat female disparaging jokes and found such jokes more amusing than men lower in hostile sexism. Overall, hostile and benevolent sexist attitudes appear to shape men and women's interactions is the private sphere (Cikara et al., 2009; Glick, Diebold, Bailey-Werner & Zhu, 1997).

Ambivalent sexism has been examined in the public sphere as well (e.g., work, politics, etc.). Benevolent and hostile attitudes toward women serve to maintain gender inequality (e.g., Glick & Fiske, 1996). As such, ambivalent sexism is at the root of system justification—where stereotypical perceptions of women prevent women from being able to excel in the work place (Cikara et al., 2009; Feather & Boeckmann, 2007), as these perceptions influences how job applicants and female employees are viewed (Good & Rudman, 2009; Masser & Abrams, 2004; Salvaggi, Streich & Hopper 2009), and lead to discrimination and sexual harassment in the workplace(O'Connor, Gutek, Stockdale, Geer & Melancon, 2004, Russell & Trigg, 2004, Wiener & Hurt, 2000). For example, Masser & Abrams (2004) found that hostile sexism was associated with more negative evaluations of a female candidate applying for a masculine type position, lower recommendations that the woman be hired for a managerial position, and higher recommendations that a male applicant be employed as a manager.In terms of sexual harassment, although gender correlates with tolerance and labeling of behavior as sexual harassment, this relationship is highly influenced by hostile sexism as well (O'Connor et al., 2004, Russell & Trigg, 2004, Wiener & Hurt, 2000). Women—especially those high in Right-Wing Authoritarianism—have been found to direct hostile forms of sexism toward other women (Andrew & Mull, 2006; Sibley, Overall & Duckitt, 2007; Sibley, Wilson & Duckitt, 2007). Research has also found social dominance, the Protestant work ethic, and Catholic religiosity to correlate with benevolent sexism and prejudice toward different social groups (Andrew & Mull, 2006; Sibley, Ovreall, et al., 2007; Sibley, Wilson, et al., 2007). The main factor that research has found to have a diminishing effect on sexist beliefs is education (Glick et al., 2007). Overall, research tends to suggest that ambivalent sexism, and its associated stereotypes, result in negative attitudes toward women who have the potential to threaten men's status in the work place and community (Masser & Abrams, 2004; Salvaggi et al., 2009).

Ambivalence toward men. Later, the Ambivalence Toward Men Inventory (Glick & Fiske, 1999) was created to assess attitudes toward men in terms of hostility and benevolence. Theoretically, the underlying hypothesis behind ambivalent sexismtoward men is that, for women, male dominance leads to the hostile resentment of men because women are dependent on men as both their providers and protectors,but women also experience benevolence toward men who serve as these providers and protectors (Glick & Fiske, 1999).Ambivalence toward men is derived from the same structural forces that underlie ambivalence toward women—men's institutionalized and structured power and the interdependenceof the sexes. Hostility toward men is comprised of attitudes that presume men will always be superior to, and have power over, women.Hostility toward men is also broken down into the three subcategories of paternalism (e.g., show antipathy towards paternalism), gender differentiation (e.g., disdain for men's domestic abilities), and heterosexuality (e.g., men as sexual predators). Benevolence toward men includes attitudes that positively evaluate gender roles and power relations. Benvolence toward men includes the three subcategories of maternalism (e.g., domestically women take care of men in exchange for men acting as protectors and providers), complementary gender differentiation (e.g., men are positively viewed as protectors and providers, perhaps perceived as heroic or brave), and heterosexual intimacy (e.g., a romantic male partner completes a woman).

The Ambivalence Toward Men Inventory looks at how sexism toward men serves to justify the existing social hierarchy (Fiske, 2001). Fernandez, Castro, and Lorenzo (2004) examined the evolution of ambivalence toward men and found that men and women shared benevolent attitudes toward men but not hostile attitudes. In addition, generational, cultural, and historical changes play a role in the development of ambivalent sexist attitudes toward men. Across sixteen nations, Glick et al. (2004) found that benevolent and hostile attitudes toward men support gender inequality. Moreover, men were stereotyped as having more valuable traits than women and viewed as being "designed for dominance" (Glick et al., 2004, p. 1939). A couple of surprising findings include that feminists are lower in hostility toward men than non-feminists (Anderson, Kanner,& Elsayegh, 2009) and that benevolent sexism toward men, but not hostile sexism, correlates with rape myth acceptance (Chapleau, Oswald & Russell, 2007).

Clow and Ricciardelli (2010) applied ambivalent sexism toward men and women to perceptions of men and women in the field of nursing. Nursing is predominantly a female dominated career, to the extent that many people automatically associate femininity with nursing (e.g., Nelson, Acker, & Manis, 1996; Oakhill, Granham, & Reynolds, 2005). In addition, men encounter a number of barriers when trying to pursue a career in nursing, such as limited role models, the use of sexist language in lectures and texts, negative stereotypes, and the absence of material acknowledging the historical accomplishments of men in nursing (e.g., O'Lynn, 2004; Sherrod, Sherrod, & Rasch, 2006; Whittock & Leonard, 2003). Clow and Ricciardelli (2010) found that hostile sexism toward men negatively predicted the favorability of male nurse stereotypes, such that participants higher in sexism reported more negative stereotypes of men in nursing. The favorability of stereotypes about female nurses, however, was negatively predicted by hostile sexism toward women and positively predicted by benevolent sexism toward women. Thus, participants who were high in hostile sexism or low in benevolent sexism reported more negative stereotypes of women in nursing. These findings demonstrate that ambivalent attitudes are important even in examinations of female dominated careers.

BEYOND GENDER AND RACE

The original paper presenting the stereotype content model explored over 20 different social groups (Fiske et al., 2002). Although gender and racial groups (and subgroups) were included, many other stereotypes were investigated as well. For example, stereotype content model research has found paternalistic prejudice, expressed in ambivalent stereotypes that are high in warmth but low in competence, toward a number of diverse social groups, including housewives, house cleaners, elderly, Irish immigrants, Italian immigrants, as well as the blind, retarded, and disabled (e.g., Fiske, 2004; Fiske et al., 2002). Research has documented envious prejudice, expressed through ambivalent stereotypes of high competence but low warmth, toward a number of diverse social groups as well, including Black professionals, northerners, business women, Jews, Asians, feminists, rich, men, Japanese immigrants, Chinese immigrants, Korean immigrants, educated, professionals, tech-industry immigrants, and Americans (e.g., Fiske, 2004; Fiske et al., 2002, Glick et al., 2006; Lee & Fiske, 2006). Although gender and racial groups are present in these analyses, research has demonstrated ambivalence in many social group stereotypes that are not based on gender or race as well.

Söder (1990) reviewed the literature on attitudes toward persons with disabilities and concluded that the research evidence suggested ambivalence. For example, if people are asked to choose individuals or dolls to interact with, people preferentially select those without disabilities. Nonetheless, people express sympathy toward individuals with disabilities and are more likely to support government spending to assist persons with disabilities than other social groups (e.g., Blacks). This is consistent with findings from the stereotype content model, which has found paternalistic prejudice—ambivalent stereotypes of high warmth but low competence—toward individuals with disabilities (e.g., Fiske et al., 2002). Although Söder argued that attitudes toward persons with disabilities were ambivalent rather than prejudiced, more current research suggests that prejudice is more than uniform negativity and that ambivalent paternalistic attitudes are in fact a form of prejudice (e.g., Eagly, 2004; Fiske et al., 2002).

Attitudes regarding wrongful conviction seem ambivalent as well. With over 250 DNA exonerations in the United States alone (Innocence Project, 2010), wrongful conviction seems to be gaining public attention. Interviews with individuals who have been wrongly convicted reveal considerable stigma, prejudice, and discrimination toward exonerees (e.g., Campbell & Denov, 2004; Westervelt & Cook, 2008). For example, exonerees have lost jobs when they are recognized. Kirk Bloodsworth, the first man exonerated post-conviction by DNA evidence, has found "child killer" written in the dirt on his truck. Clow and Leach (2010) compared perceptions of individuals who have been wrongly convicted to perceptions of actual offenders and people in general. They found that participants stigmatized individuals who had been wrongly convicted in comparison to people in general (e.g., desiring greater social distance, stereotyping them with more negative characteristics) and that people perceived the wrongly convicted more similar to actual offenders.

In contrast, research investigating social support for policies regarding wrongful conviction has found more positive results. For example, the Angus Reid Group (1995) polled 7000 Canadians and found that approximately 90% of participants reported that it was the government's responsibility to compensate individuals who had been wrongly convicted and 65% of participants felt that the government needed to increase efforts in the area of wrongful conviction. Ricciardelli, Bell, and Clow (2009) found that most participants felt that the ratio of wrongful convictions to correct convictions should be very low (less than 1 in 1000); half of all participants reported that there should not be any wrongful convictions at all. Overall, these findings suggest attitudinal ambivalence toward individuals who are wrongly convicted, as the public is generally supportive of government policies to assist the wrongly convicted (e.g., compensation for exonerees) but exonerees are still the targets of stigma, prejudice, and discrimination.

Although the majority of ambivalence research has examined attitudes or stereotypes toward outgroups, research has identified ambivalence within ingroup attitudes and stereotypes as well (e.g., Costarelli & Callà, 2007; Jost & Burgess, 2000; Mucchi-Faina, Costarelli, & Romoli, 2002). Costarelli and Callà (2007) found that participants who highly identified with the ingroup (people from their own country) were more likely to report ambivalent stereotypes (negative affect but positive cognitions) of the ingroup when in an intragroup context than an intergroup context. Jost and Burgess (2000) manipulated whether participants thought their ingroup (their university) was high status or low status. This simple manipulation resulted in greater ingroup ambivalence for low status versus high status groups. Thus, even ingroup stereotypes can be ambivalent.

The stereotype content model offers one way to examine attitudinal ambivalence, focusing specifically on closed-ended scales of warmth versus competence. Open ended measures offer another viable approach (e.g., Bell, Esses, & Maio, 1996). Open-ended measures allow participants the freedom to express the full content of the stereotypes they perceive, rather than limiting them to an experimenter generated list. Participants do not refrain from reporting negative stereotype content on open-ended measures (e.g., Bell et al., 1996) and, if anything, more negative content seems to emerge from open-ended stereotype measures than closed-ended stereotype measures (e.g., Clow & Esses, 2000).

CONCLUDING REMARKS

In looking at stereotypes in isolation, stereotypes of women and Asians seem rather positive and stereotypes of African-Americans seem rather negative. Without taking into account the relationship of stereotypes to group attitudes, people might incorrectly assume that women and Asians are not discriminated against and attitudes toward African-Americans have not changed over the decades. Situating stereotypes within the context of ambivalent intergroup attitudes, such as ambivalent sexism and the stereotype content model, allows us to understand how even seemingly positive stereotypes can lead to very negative consequences (e.g., domestic violence, hiring discrimination, prejudice). Research supports that ambivalent attitudes are system justifying and maintain current power structures. In addition, investigating the positive and negative components of stereotypes themselves can lend insight into how otherwise liberal minded individuals may be able to convince themselves that they are not prejudiced.

REFERENCES

Allport, G.W.(1954). *The nature of prejudice*.NY:Doubleday Anchor Books.

Anderson, K.J., Kannner, M., & Elsayegh, N. (2009). Are feminists man haters? Feminists' and non-feminists' attitudes toward men. *Psychology of Women Quarterly*, 33(2), 216-224. doi: 10.1111/j.1471-6402.2009.01491.x

Andrew, C.N., & Mull, M.S. (2006). Conservative ideology and ambivalent sexism. *Psychology of Women Quarterly*, 30(2), p. 223-230. doi: 10.1111/j.1471-6402.2006.00284.x

Asbrock, F. (2010). Stereotypes of social groups in Germany in terms of warmth and competence. *Social Psychology, 41*(2), 76-81. doi: 10.1027/1864-9335/a000011

Bell, D.W., & Esses, V. M. (1997). Ambivalence and response amplification toward Native peoples. *Journal of Applied Social Psychology, 27*(12), 1063-1084. doi: 10.1111/j.1559-1816.1997.tb00287.x

Bell, D.W., & Esses, V.E. (2002). Ambivalence and response amplification: A motivational perspective. *Personality and Social Psychology Bulletin, 28*(8), 1143-1152. doi: 10.1177/01461672022811012

Bell, D.W., Esses, V.E., & Maoi, G.R. (1996). The utility of open-ended measures to assess intergroup ambivalence. *Canadian Journal of Behavioural Science, 28*(1), 12-18. doi:10.1037/0008-400X.28.1.12

Bem, S.L. (1974). The measurement of psychological androgyny. *Journal of Consulting and Clinical Psychology, 42*, 155–162. doi:10.1037/h0036215

Blair, I.V., Judd, C.M., & Chapleau, K.M. (2004). The influence of Afrocentric facial features in criminal sentencing. *Psychological Science, 15*(10), 674–679. doi:10.1111/j.0956-7976.2004.00739.x

Campbell, K., & Denov, M. (2004). The burden of innocence: Coping with a wrongful imprisonment. *Canadian Journal of Criminology and Criminal Justice, 46*(2), 139-163.

Caprariello, P.a., Cuddy, A.J.C., & Fiske, S.T. (2009). Social structure shapes cultural stereotypes and emotions: A causal test of the stereotype content model. *Group Processes & Intergroup Relations, 12*(2), 147-155. doi:10.1177/1368430208101053

Chao, M.M., Chiu, C-y, Lee. J.S. (2010). Asians as the model minority: Implications for US government's policies. *Asian Journal of Social Psychology, 13*(1), 44-52. doi: 10.1111/j.1467-839X.2010.01299.x

Chapleau, K.M., Oswald, D.L., & Russell, B.L. (2007). How ambivalent sexism toward women and men supports rape myth acceptance. *Sex Roles*, 57(1-2), p. 131-136. Doi: 10.1007/s11199-007-9196-2

Chen, Z., Fiske, S.T., & Lee, T.L. (2009). Ambivalent sexism and power-related gender-role ideology in marriage. *Sex Roles*, 60(11-12), p, 765-778. doi: 0.1007/s11199-009-9585-9

Chu, T., & Kwan, V.S.Y. (2006). Effect of collectivistic cultural imperatives on Asian American meta-stereotypes. *Asian Journal of Social Psychology, 10*(4), 270-276. doi: 10.1111/j.1467-839X.2007.00236.x

Cikara, M., & Fiske, S.T. (2009). Warmth, competence, and ambivalent sexism: Vertical assault and collateral damage. In M. Barreto, M.K. Ryan, & M.T. Schmitt (Eds.) *The glass ceiling in the 21st century: Understanding barriers to gender equality. Psychology of women book series.* (pp. 73-96). Washington, DC: American Psychological Association.

Cikara, M., Lee, T.L., Fiske, S.T., & Glick, P. (2009). Social and psychological bases of ideology and system justification. In Jost, J.T., Kay, A.C., & H. Thorisdottir (Eds).*Social and psychological bases of ideology and system justification. Series in political psychology.* (pp. 444-462). New York, NY, US: Oxford University Press. Xvii, 529.

Clausell, E., & Fiske, S.T. (2005). When do subgroup parts add up to the stereotypic whole? Mixed stereotype content for gay male subgroups explains overall ratings. *Social Cognition, 23*(2), 161-181. doi:10.1521/soco.23.2.161.65626

Clow, K.A., & Esses, V.M. (2007). Expectancy effects in social stereotyping: Automatic and controlled processing in the Neely paradigm. *Canadian Journal of Behavioural Science, 39*(3), 161-173. doi: 10.1037/cjbs20070013

Clow, K.A., & Esses, V.M. (2000, July). A qualitative and quantitative approach to stereotype content. Paper presented at the annual meeting of the Canadian Psychological Association, Ottawa, Ontario.

Clow, K.A., & Leach, A.-M. (2010). *After innocence: Perceptions of the wrongly convicted.* Manuscript submitted for publication.

Clow, K.A., & Ricciardelli, R. (2010). *Student perceptions of male and female nurses: The effects of nursing major, gender, and ambivalent sexism.* Manuscript submitted for publication.

Cobb, M.D. & Boettcher, W.A. (2007). Ambivalent sexism and misogynistic rap music: Does exposure to Eminem increase sexism? *Journal of Applied Social Psychology, 37*(12), 3025-3042. doi: 10.1111/j.1559-1816.2007.00292.x

Collange, J., Fiske, S.T., & Sanitioso, R. (2009). Maintaining a positive self-image by stereotyping others: Self-threat and the stereotype content model. *Social Cognition, 27*(1), 138-149. doi:10.1521/soco.2009.27.1.138

Correll, J., Park, B., Wittenbrink, B., & Judd, C.M. (2002). The police officer's dilemma: Using ethnicity to disambiguate potentially threatening individuals. *Journal of Personality and Social Psychology, 89*(6), 1314-1329. doi:10.1037/0022-3514.83.6.1314

Costarelli, S., & Callà, R.M. (2007). Cross-dimension-ambivalent in-group stereotypes: The moderating roles of social context of stereotype endorsement and in-group identification. *The Journal of Social Psychology, 147*(5), 543-554. doi:10.3200/SOCP.147.5.543-555

Crandall, C.S., & Eshleman, A. (2003). A justification—suppression model of the expression and experience of prejudice. *Psychological Bulletin, 129*(3), 414-446. doi: 10.1037/0033-2909.129.3.414

Cuddy, A.J.C., Fiske, S.T., & Glick, P. (2004). When professionals become mothers, warmth doesn't cut the ice. *Journal of Social Issues, 60*(4), 701-718. doi:10.1111/j.0022-4537.2004.00381.x

Cuddy, A.J.C., Fiske, S.T., Kwan, V.S.Y., Glick, P., Demoulin, S., Leyens, J-P, ... & Ziegler, R. (2009). Stereotype content model across cultures: Towards universal similarities and some differences. *British Journal of Social Psychology, 48*(1), 1-33. doi: 10.1348/014466608X314935

Czopp, A.M., & Monteith, M.J. (2006). Thinking well of African Americans: Measuring complimentary stereotypes and negative prejudice. *Basic and Applied Social Psychology, 28*(3), 233-250. doi: 10.1207/s15324834basp2803_3

Devine, P.G. (1989). Stereotypes and prejudice: Their automatic and controlled components. *Journal of Personality and Social Psychology, 56*(1), 5–18. doi: 10.1037/0022-3514.56.1.5

Devine, P.G., & Elliot, A.J. (1995). Are racial stereotypes really fading? The Princeton trilogy revisited. *Personality and Social Psychology Bulletin, 21*(11), 1139-1150. doi: 10.1177/01461672952111002

DeWall, C.N., Altermatt, T.W., & Thompson, H. (2005). Understanding the structure of stereotypes of women: Virtue and agency as dimensions distinguishing female subgroups. *Psychology of Women Quarterly, 29*(4), 396-405. doi:10.1111/j.1471-6402.2005.00239.x

Dion, K. L. (2003). Prejudice, racism, and discrimination. In T. Millon & M. J. Lerner (Eds.), *Personality and social psychology*. Vol. 5 of the Comprehensive handbook of psychology (Chap. 21, pp. 507-536). Editor in Chief: I. B. Weiner. New York: John Wiley & Sons.

Donakowski, D.W., & Esses, V.M. (1996). Native Canadians, First Nations, or Aboriginals: The effect of labels on attitudes toward native peoples. *Canadian Journal of Behavioural Science, 28*(2), 86-91. doi: 10.1037/0008-400X.28.2.86

Dovidio, J. F., & Gaertner, S. L. (1986). Prejudice, discrimination, and racism: Historical trends and contemporary approaches. In J. F. Dovidio & S. L. Gaertner (Eds.), *Prejudice, discrimination, and racism* (pp. 1–34). New York, NY: Academic Press.

Eagly, A. H. (1995). The science and politics of comparing women and men. American Psychologist, 50(3), 145-158. doi:10.1037/0003-066X.50.3.145

Eagly, A. H. (2004). Prejudice: Toward a more inclusive understanding. In A. Eagly, R. M. Baron, & V. L. Hamilton (Eds.), *The social psychology of group identity and social conflict: Theory, application, and practice* (pp. 45-64). Washington, DC: APA Books.

Eagly, A. H., & Mladinic, A. (1989). Gender stereotypes and attitudes toward women and men. *Personality and Social Psychology Bulletin, 15*(4), 543-558. doi: 10.1177/0146167289154008

Eagly, A. H., & Mladinic, A. (1993). Are people prejudiced against women? Some answers from research on attitudes, gender stereotypes and judgments of competence. In W. Stroebe & M. Hewstone (Eds.), *European review of social psychology*(Vol. 5, pp. 1–35). New York: Wiley.

Eberhardt, J.L., Goff, P.A., Purdie, V.J., & Davies, P.G. (2004). Seeing Black: Race, crime, and visual processing. *Journal of Personality and Social Psychology, 87*(6), 876-893. doi: 10.1037/0022-3514.87.6.876

Eckes, T. (2002). Paternalistic and envious gender stereotypes: Testing predictions from the stereotype content model. *Sex Roles, 47*(3-4), 99-114. doi: 10.1023/A:1021020920715

Feather, N.T. & Boeckmann, R.J. (2007). Beliefs about gender discrimination in the workplace in the context of affirmative action: Effects of gender and ambivalent attitudes in an Australian sample. *Personality and Psychology Bulletin, 57* (1-2), 31-42. doi: 10.1007/s11199-007-9226-0

Fernandez, M.L., Castro, Y., & Lorenzo, M.G. (2004). Evolution of hostile sexism and benevolent sexism in a Spanish sample. *Social Indicators Research*, 66(3), pp. 197-211. doi: 10.1023/B:SOCI.0000003553.30419.fl

Fischer, A.R. (2006). Women's benevolent sexism as reaction to hostility. *Psychology of Women Quarterly*, 30(4), pp. 410-416. doi: 10.1111/j/1471-6402.2006.00316.x.

Fiske, S.T. (2001). Effects of power on bias: Power explains and maintains individual, group, and societal disparities. In Lee-Chai, A.Y., & J.A. Bargh (Eds). *The use and abuse of power: Multiple perspectives on causes of corruption.* (pp. 181-193). New York, NY: Psychology Press. Xiv, 312 pp.

Fiske, S.T. (2004). What's in a category? Responsibility, intent, and the avoidability of bias against outgroups. In A. G. Miller (Ed.), *The social psychology of good and evil* (pp. 127-140). New York: Guilford.

Fiske, S.T., Cuddy, A.J.C., & Glick, P. (2007). Universal dimensions of social cognition: Warmth and competence. *Trends in Cognitive Sciences, 11*(2), 77-83. doi: 10.1016/j.tics.2006.11.005

Fiske, S.T., Cuddy, A.J.C., Glick, P., & Xu, J. (2002). A model of (often mixed) stereotype content: Competence and warmth respectively follow from perceived status and competition. *Journal of Personality and Social Psychology, 82*(6), 878-902. doi: 10.1037/0022-3514.82.6.878

Fiske, S.T., & Glick, P. (1995). Ambivalence and stereotypes cause sexual harassment: A theory with implications for organizational change. *Journal of Social Issues*, 51(1), pp. 97-115.

Forbes, G.B., Collinsworth, L.L., Jobe, R.L., Braun, K.D., Wise, L.M. (2005). Sexism, hostility toward women, and endorsement of beauty ideals and practices: Are beauty ideals associated with oppressive beliefs? *Sex Roles*, 56(5-6), pp. 265-273. doi: 10.1007/s11199-006-91-61-5

Franzoi, S.L. (2001). Is female body esteem shaped by benevolent sexism? *Sex Roles*, 44(3-4), pp. 177-188. doi: 10.1023/A:1919903003521

Glick, P. (2006). Ambivalent sexism, power distance, and gender inequality across cultures. In S. Guimond. *Social comparison and social psychology: Understanding cognition, intergroup relations, and culture.* (pp. 283-302). New York, NY: Cambridge University Press. Xii, 354 pp.

Glick, P., Diebold, J., Bailey-Werner, B., & Zhu, L. (1997). The two faces of Adam: Ambivalent sexism and polarized attitudes toward women. *Personality and Social Psychology Bulletin*, 23(12), pp. 1323-1334. doi: 10.1177/01461672972312009

Glick, P., & Fiske, S. T. (1996). The Ambivalent Sexism Inventory: Differentiating hostile and benevolent sexism. *Journal of Personality and Social Psychology, 70*(3), 491–512. doi: 10.1037/0022-3514 .70.3.491

Glick, P., & Fiske, S. T. (1997). Hostile and benevolent sexism: Measuring ambivalent sexist attitudes toward women. *Psychology of Women Quarterly*, 21(1), pp. 119-135. doi: 10.1111/j.1471-6402.1997.tb00104.x.

Glick, P., & Fiske, S. T. (1999). The Ambivalence Toward Men Inventory: Differentiating hostile and benevolent beliefs about men. *Psychology of Women Quarterly, 23*(3), 519–536. doi: 10.1111/j.1471-6402.1999.tb00379.x

Glick, P., & Fiske, S.T. (2001)a. An ambivalent alliance: Hostile and benevolent sexism as complement justifications for gender inequality. *American Psychologist*, 56(2), pp. 109-118. doi: 10.1037/0003-066X.56.2.109

Glick, P., & Fiske, S.T. (2001)b. Ambivalent sexism. In Zanna, Mark P. *Advances in experimental social psychology*, Vol. 33.(pp. 115-188).San Diego, CA: Academic Press. ix, 325 pp.

Glick, P., Fiske, S.T., Abrahms, D., Dardenne, B., Ferreira, M.C., Gonzalez, R., ... Yzerbyt, V. (2006). Anti-American sentiment and America's perceived intent to dominate: An 11-nation study. *Basic and Applied Social Psychology, 28*(4), 363-373. doi:10.1207/s15324834basp2804_10

Glick, P., Lameiras, M., & Castro, Y.R. (2002). Education and Caholic religiousity as predictors of hostile and benevolent sexism toward women and men. *Sex Roles*, 47(9-10), 433-441. doi: 10.1023/A:1021696209949

Glick, P., Lameiras, M., Fiske, S.T., Eckes, T., Masser, B., Volpato, C.,... Wells, R. (2004). Bad but bold: Ambivalent attitudes toward men predict gender inequality in 16 nations. *Journal of Personality and Social Psychology*, 86(5), pp. 713-728.

Glick, P., Sakalli-Ugurly, N., Ferreira, M.C., & de Souza, M.A. (2002). Ambivalent sexism and attitudes toward wife abuse in Turkey and Brazil. *Psychology of Women Quarterly*, 26(4), pp. 292-297. doi: 10.1111/1471-6402.t01-1-00068.

Glick, P., Gangl, C., Gibb, S., Klumpner, S., and Weinberg, E. (2007). Defensive reactions to masculinity threat: More negative affect toward effeminate (but not masculine) gay men. *Sex Roles*, 57(1-2), pp. 55-59. doi: 10.1007/s11199-007-9195-3

Good, J.J., & Rudman, L.A. (2010). When female applicants meet sexist interviewers: The costs of being a target of benevolent sexism. *Sex Roles*, 62, 481-491. Doi:10.1007/s11199-009-9685-6

Harris, L.T., & Fiske, S.T. (2006). Dehumanizing the lowest of the low: Neuroimaging responses to extreme out-groups. *Psychological Science, 17*(10), 847-853. doi:10.1111/j.1467-9280.2006.01793.x

Hass, R. G., Katz, I., Rizzo, N., Bailey, J., & Moore, L. (1992). When racial ambivalence evokes negative affect, using a disguised measure of mood. *Personality and Social Psychology Bulletin, 18*(6), 786-797. doi: 10.1177/0146167292186015

Ho, C., & Jackson, J. W. (2001). Attitudes towards Asian Americans: Theory and measurement. *Journal of Applied Social Psychology, 31*(8), 1553-1581. doi: 10.1111/j.1559-1816.2001.tb02742.x

Innocence Project. (2010). Retrieved from http://www.innocenceproject.org/

Jackson, L.M., Esses, V.M., & Burris, C.T. (2001). Contemporary sexism and discrimination: The importance of respect for men and women. *Personality and Social Psychology Bulletin, 27*(1), 48-61.

Jost, J.T., & Burgess, D. (2000). Attitudinal ambivalence and the conflict between group and system justification motives in low status groups. *Personality and Social Psychology Bulletin, 26*(3), 293-305. doi: 10.1177/0146167200265003

Katz, I., & Hass, G. (1988). Racial ambivalence and American value conflict: Correlational and priming studies of dual cognitive structures. *Journal of Personality and Social Psychology, 55*(6), 893-905. doi: 10.1037/0022-3514.55.6.893

Kawai, Y. (2005). Stereotyping Asian Americans: The dialectic of the model minority and the yellow peril. *The Howard Journal of Communications, 16*(2), 109-130. doi: 10.1080/10646170590948974

Krefting, L.A. (2003). Intertwined discourses of merit and gender: Evidence from academic employment in the USA. *Gender, Work & Organization*, 10(2), pp. 260-278. doi: 10.1111/1468-0432.t01-1-00014.

LaFrance, M. & Woodzicka, J.A. (1998). No laughing matter: Women's verbal and nonverbal reactions to sexist humor. In Swim, J.K.,& C. Stangor. *Prejudice: The target's perspective.* (pp. 61-80). San Diego, CA: Academic Press. Xiv, 332 pp.

Lee, T.L., & Fiske, S.T. (2006). Not an outgroup, not yet an ingroup: Immigrants in the stereotype content model. *International Journal of Intercultural Relations, 30*, 751-768. doi:10.1016/j.ijintrel.2006.06.005

Lin, M.H., Kwan, V.S.Y., Cheung, A., & Fiske, S.T. (2005). Stereotype content model explains prejudice for an envied outgroup: Scale of anti-Asian American stereotypes. *Society for Personality and Social Psychology, 31*(1), 34-47. doi: 10.1177/0146167204271320

Maddux, W.W., Galinsky, A.D., Cuddy, A.J.C., & Polifroni, M. (2008). When being a model minority is good ... and bad: Realistic threat explains negativity toward Asian Americans. *Personality and Social Psychology Bulletin, 34*(1), 74-89. doi: 10.1177/0146167207309195

Masser, B., Grass, K., & Nesic, M. 'We like you, but we don't want you'—The impact of pregnancy in the workplace. *Sex Roles, 57*(9-10), 703-712. doi:10.1007/s11199-007-9305-2

Maio, G.R., Esses, V.M., & Bell, D.W. (2000). Examining conflict between components of attitudes: Ambivalence and inconsistency are distinct constructs. *Canadian Journal of Behavioural Science, 32*(2), 71-83. doi: 10.1037/h0087102

Madon, S., Guyll, M., Aboufadel, K., Montiel, E., Smith, A., Palumbo, P., & Jussim, L (2001). Ethnic and national stereotypes: The Princeton trilogy revisited and revised. *Personality and Social Psychology Bulletin, 27*(8), 996-1010. doi: 10.1177/0146167201278007

Markus, H.R. (2008). Pride, prejudice, and ambivalence: Toward a unified theory of race and ethnicity. *American Psychologist, 63*(8), 651-670. doi: 10.1037/0003-066X.63.8.651

Masser, B., & Abrams, D. (2004). Contemporary sexism: The relationship among hostility, benevolence and neosexism. *Psychology of Women Quarterly*, 23(3), pp. 503-517. doi: 10.1111/j.1472-6402.1999.tb00378.x

McConahay, J.B. (1986). Modern racism, ambivalence, and the modern racism scale. In J.F. Dovidio & S.L. Gaertner (Eds.), *Prejudice, discrimination, and racism* (pp. 91-125). New York, NY: Academic Press.

Mucchi-Faina, A., Costarelli, S., & Romoli, C. (2002). The effects of intergroup context of evaluation on ambivalence toward the ingroup and the outgroup. *European Journal of Social Psychology, 32*(2), 247-259. doi:10.1002/ejsp.71

Nelson, T.E., Acker, M., & Manis, M. (1996). Irrepressible stereotypes. *Journal of Experimental Social Psychology, 32*, 13-38. doi:10.1006/jesp.1996.0002

Oakhill, J., Garnham, A., & Reynolds, D. (2005). Immediate activation of stereotypical gender information. *Memory & Cognition, 33*, 972-983.

O'Connor, M., Gutek, B.A., Stockdale, M., Geer, T.M., & Melancon, R. (2004). Explaining sexual harassment judgments: Looking beyond gender of the rater. *Law and Human Behavior, 28*(1), pp. 69-95. doi: 10.1023/B:LAHU.000001504.39462.6e

O'Lynn, C.E. (2004).Gender-based barriers for male students in nursing education programs:Prevalence and perceived importance.*Journal of Nursing Education, 43*, 229-237.

Oyserman, D., & Sakamoto, I. (1997). Being Asian American: Identity, cultural constructs, and stereotype perception. *Journal of Applied Behavioral Science, 33*(4), 435-453. doi:10.1177/0021886397334002

Payne, B. K. (2001). Prejudice and perception: The role of automatic and controlled processes in misperceiving a weapon. *Journal of Personality and Social Psychology, 81*(2), 1–12. doi:10.I037//0O22-3514.81.2.181

Parsons, T., & Bales, R.F. (1955). *Family, Socialization, and Interaction Process.* New York: Free Press.

Popp, D., Donovan, R.A., Crawford, M., Marsh, K.L., & Peele, M. (2003). Gender, race, and speech style stereotypes. *Sex Roles, 48*(7/8), 317-325. doi: 10.1023/A:1022986429748

Ricciardelli, R., Bell, J.G., & Clow, K.A. (2009). Student attitudes toward wrongful conviction. *Canadian Journal of Criminology and Criminal Justice, 51*(3), 411-430. doi:10.3138/cjccj.51.3.411

Russell, A.M., & Fiske, S.T. (2008). It's all relative: Competition and status drive interpersonal perception. *European Journal of Social Psychology, 38*(7), 1193-1201. doi:10.1002/ejsp.539

Russell, B.L., & Trigg, K.Y. (2004). Tolerance of Sexual Harassment: An Examination of Gender Differences, Ambivalent Sexism, Social Dominance, and Gender Roles. *Sex Roles, 50*(7-8), pp. 565-573. doi: 10.1023/B.SERS.0000023075.32252.fd

Sakalli-AYurlu, N.,Sila YalASin, Z., & Glick, P. (2007). Ambivalent Sexism, belief in a just world, and empathy as predictors of Turkish students' attitudes toward rape victims. *Sex Roles, 57*(11-12), pp. 889-895. doi: 10.1007/s11199-007-9313-2

Salvaggio, A.N., Streich, M., & Hopper, J.E. (2009). Ambivalent sexism and applicant evaluations: Effects on ambiguous applicants. *Sex Roles*, 61(9-10), pp. 621-633. doi: 10.1007/s11199-009-9640-6.

Sanchez, D.T., & Bonam, C.M. (2009). To disclose or not to disclose biracial identity: The effect of biracial disclosure on perceiver evaluations and target responses. *Journal of Social Issues, 65*(1), 129-149.

Sears, D.O. (1988). Symbolic racism. In P.A. Katz & D.A. Taylor (Eds.), *Eliminating racism* (pp. 53-84). New York, NY: Plenum.

Sherrod, B., Sherrod, D., & Rasch, R. (2006).From the bedside to the boardroom, nursing needs to increase the number of men in its ranks.*Men in Nursing, 1*, 34-39.

Sibley, C.G., & Wilson, M.S. (2004). Differentiating hostile and benevolent sexist attitudes toward positive and negative sexual female subtypes. *Sex Roles*, 51(11-12), pp. 687-696. doi: 10.1007/s11199-004-0718-x

Sibely, C.G., Overall, N.C. & Duckitt, J. (2007). When women become more hostilely sexist toward their gender: The system-justifying effects of benevolent sexism. *Sex Roles*, 57(9-10), pp. 743-754.doi: 10.1007/s11199-007-9306-1

Sibley, C.G., Wilson, M.S., & Duckitt, J. (2007). Antecedents of Men's Hostile and Benevolent Sexism: The Dual Roles of Social Dominance Orientation and Right-Wing

Authoritarianism. *Personality and Social Psychology Bulletin*, 33(2), pp. 160-172. doi: 10.1177/0146167206294745

Söder, M. (1990). Prejudice or ambivalence? Attitudes toward persons with disabilities. *Disability, Handicap & Society*, 5(3), 227-241. doi:10.1080/02674649066780241

Spence, J.T., & Buckner, C.E. (2000). Instrumental and expressive traits, trait stereotypes, and sexist attitudes. *Psychology of Women Quarterly*, 24(1), 44-62. doi:10.1111/j.1471-6402.2000.tb01021.x

Sue, D.W. (1994). Asian-American mental health and help-seeking behaviour: Comment on Solberg et al. (1994), Tata and Leong (1994), and Lin (1994). *Journal of Counseling Psychology*, 41(3), 292-295. doi: 10.1037/0022-0167.41.3.292

Takabayashi, K. (2007). The effect of threat to self on prejudice toward women: An examination from the perspective of ambivalent sexism theory. *The Journal of Social Psychology*, 23(2), pp. 119-129.

Tendayi, V., Abrams, D., & Hutchison, P. (2003). The "True" Romantic: Benevolent Sexism and Paternalistic Chivalry. *Sex Roles*, 49(9-10), pp. 533-537.

Thomas, C.A., & Esses, V.M. (2004). Individual differences in Reactions to Sexist Humor. *Group Processes & Intergroup Relations*, 7(1), pp. 89-100. doi: 10.1177/1368430204039975

Wade, M.L., & Brewer, M.B. (2006). The structure of female subgroups: An exploration of ambivalent stereotypes. *Sex Roles*, 54(11-12), 753-765. doi:10.1007/s11199-006-9043-x

Westervelt, S.D., & Cook, K.J. (2008). Coping with innocence after death row. *Contexts*, 7(4), 32-37. doi: 10.1525/ctx.2008.7.4.32

Wiener, R.L., & Hurt, L.E. (2000). How do people evaluate social sexual conduct at work?: A psycholegal model. *Journal of Applied Psychology*, 85(1), pp. 75-85. doi: 10.1037/0021-9010.85.1.75

Wittenbrink, B., Judd, C.M., & Park, B. (1997). Evidence for racial prejudice at the implicit level and its relationship with questionnaire measures. *Journal of Personality and Social Psychology*, 72(2), 262-274. doi: 10.1037/0022-3514.72.2.262

Whittock, M., & Leonard, L. (2003). Stepping outside the stereotype. A pilot study of the motivations and experiences of males in the nursing profession. *Journal of Nursing Management*, 11, 242-249. doi:10.1046/j.1365-2834.2003.00379.x

Wong, F., & Halgin, R. (2006). The "model minority": Bane or blessing for Asian Americans? *Journal of Multicultural Counseling and Development*, 34(1), 38-49.

Wong, P., Lai, C. F., Nagasawa, R., & Lin, T. (1998). Asian Americans as a model minority: Self-perceptions and perception by other racial groups. *Sociological Perspectives*, 41(1), 95-118.

Yamawaki, N., Darby, R., & Querioz, A. (2007). The moderating role of ambivalent sexism: The influence of power status on perception of rape victim and rapist. *The Journal of social Psychology*, 147(1), pp. 41-56. doi: 10.3200/SOCP.147.1.41-56

Yamawaki, N., Ostenson, J., & Brown, C.R. (2009). The functions of gender role traditionality, ambivalent sexism, injury, and frequency of assault on domestic violence perception: A study between Japanese and American college students. *Violence against Women*, 15(9), pp. 1126-1142. doi: 10.1177/077801209340758

Ying, Y., Lee, P.A., Tsai, J.L., Hung, Y, Lin, M., & Wan, C.T. (2001). Asian American college students as model minorities: An examination of their overall competence. *Cultural Diversity and Ethnic Minority Psychology, 7*(1), 59-74. doi:10.1037//1099-9809.7.1.59

In: Psychology of Stereotypes
Editor: Eleanor L. Simon

ISBN: 978-1-61761-463-7
©2011 Nova Science Publishers, Inc.

Chapter 12

EPILEPSY: MYTHS, STEREOTYPES AND STIGMA

Jane McCagh

Liverpool Hope University, Hope Park, Liverpool, United Kingdom

ABSTRACT

This chapter will discuss how epilepsy has been perceived throughout history and across different cultures. The chapter will highlight how historical conceptions of epilepsy and misrepresentation in the media have perpetuated current stereotypical perceptions of the disorder. Consequently, misconceptionsabout epilepsy serve to propagate discrimination and stigmatoward people with the condition. The myths that surround epilepsy will be explored emphasising how misconception, discrimination and stigma affect the quality of life of people with the condition. Myths, stigma and stereotypes can result in multiple interrelated psychosocial outcomes which can impede the cohesive integration of people with epilepsy in society. The impact of these factors on important psychosocial outcomes such as self esteem, depression, anxiety, employability, opportunities for social interaction and interpersonal relationships will be discussed.The chapter will explore these outcomes highlighting how society can be effective in engendering positive attitudes towards people with epilepsy. To conclude, educational interventions aimed at people with epilepsy, their families, employers, teachers and society at large will be considered along with future research suggestions with a view to reduce the impact of stigma and improve the social functioning of people with epilepsy.

WHAT IS EPILEPSY?

Epilepsy is the most prevalent serious neurological disorder in the world (Brodie & Schachter, 2001).In the region of 50 million people have epilepsy worldwide. Eighty percent of people with epilepsy live in developing countries with little if any access to treatment (Brodie & Schachter, 2001; de Boer, Mula & Sander, 2008). This is primarily due to differences in cultural beliefs where many developing countries view the condition to be a disorder of the soul that cannot be treated by modern medicine.

Epilepsy is an umbrella term which incorporates a constellation of different seizures and syndromes. It is evident by recurrent, typically unprovoked epileptic seizures (Guberman and Bruni, 1999). Seizures are transient episodes 'of neurological dysfunction brought about by abnormal, synchronous and excessive discharges of cerebral neurons' (Oxbury, Polkey, and Duchowny, 2000, p.11). Many definitions of epilepsy focus on the unprovoked and recurrent nature of seizures. This is significant because not everyone who has a seizure is considered to have epilepsy. Some individuals are more sensitive and have a lower threshold to electrical discharges in the brain. Consequently there are individual differences in how susceptible people are to having a seizure. Seizures caused as a consequence of systemic disturbances such as a rise in body temperature (febrile seizures), a lack of blood supply (anoxic seizures) as a consequence of illness, trauma or injury, or single isolated seizures do not necessitate a diagnosis of epilepsy (Baker and Jacoby, 2001). Epilepsy can be caused by almost any form of cerebral pathology such as birth trauma, head injury, infection, tumours, congenital defects, exposure to toxic agents, degenerative disorders and cerebrovascular disease.

HISTORICAL BACKGROUND

Epilepsy has been regularly documented since antiquity, in different parts of the world and in different cultures (International League Against Epilepsy (ILAE, 2003a). The word epilepsy comes from the Greek verb 'epilambanein', which meansto be seized or taken by surprise (ILAE, 2003a). Historically, all diseases were regarded as a form of punishment, curses from the gods or evil spirits and epilepsy was seen as a means of retribution for sin. Depending on the common popular belief at the time, people with 'the sacred disease' were believed to be possessed by demons, to be insane or their condition was associated with the divine and supernatural. Such misconceptions have meant that epilepsy has been surrounded by stigma, superstition and prejudice.

Many religions have regarded the epileptic as being possessed. The New Testament (Mark 14-29) clearly describes a young boy who has a tonic-clonic seizure and refers to the seizure as a 'deaf and dumb spirit' that possesses the boy. In the 2nd and 3rd centuries physicians and philosophers associated epilepsy with the lunar phases and this bred the misunderstanding that epilepsy was a form of lunacy (Chadwick, 1997). The belief that epilepsy was contagious goes back to Roman times when epileptics were spat on to ward away demons and avoid infection. This idea was still prevalent during the 13th century when Berthold of Regensburg wrote that the infection was contagious through the patient's 'evil' breath (ILAE, 2003a). The idea that epilepsy was infectious still prevailed in the 18th century (De Boer, 1995).

Throughout history many laws have discriminated against people with epilepsy. The Code of Hammurabi, dated 1780 B.C, declared that a person with epilepsy was not allowed to marry and could not be a member of a jury or a witness in court (ILAE, 2003a). Despite advances in clinical research and treatment, legislation which stigmatises people with epilepsy still exists in some countries or has only recently been revoked. Stemming from the eugenics movement, prohibiting marriage was seen as a way of preventing procreation and often sterilisation of people with epilepsy was encouraged. Until 1956 People with epilepsy in the United States were prohibited from marriage in 17 states and 18 states provided for sterilisation (Epilepsy Foundation of America, 1992). In the United Kingdom a similar law on the prohibition of marriage existed until 1970 (ILAE, 2003a).

Contrary to previous superstitious explanations, the Hippocratic collection of medical writings (400 BC) was the first attempt at a scientific explanation of epilepsy (Chadwick, 1997).These writings suggested that epilepsy was an organic disorder caused by an excess of phlegm and could be treated with diet and drugs as opposed to magic. It was during the 18th century when the idea of epilepsy as a physical disorder as opposed to a disorder of the soul began to gain credence. In the 19th Century the first asylums were built to accommodate both psychiatric and epileptic patients (Masia & Devinky, 2000). Ironically this created opportunities for patients with epilepsy to be closely studied and enhanced people's understanding of the disorder. In 1875 John Hughlings Jackson was the first neurologist to acknowledge that epilepsy was an organic disorder where disruption to electrical activity was responsible for causing a seizure (Brodie & Schachter, 2001).

Historical representations of epilepsy have been plagued with negativity and misconception, which has lead to fear and condemnation of the disorder within society. Negative attitudes towards epilepsy have meant that families have tried to hide the disorder by isolating the individual with epilepsy to reduce the associated social stigma (Devinsky, 2007). Knowledge of the disorder within the family was also thought to obstruct the prospect of marriage (Devinsky, 2007). Despite advances in education, myths and misconceptions about epilepsy still dominate today's society (Baxendale & O'Toole, 2007). How these misconceptions contribute towards the experience of stigma and psychosocial difficulties in people with epilepsy will be discussed in more detail throughout the chapter.

EPILEPSY AND SOCIAL FUNCTIONING

Intractable (difficult to manage) epilepsy is prevalent in 20-40% of people diagnosed with epilepsy despite the use of appropriate drug therapy (Oxbury, 2000).

A recurrent difficulty reported by people with intractable epilepsy is that they experience a number of difficulties in relation to social functioning. Such difficulties have been reflected in the wider epilepsy population where people with epilepsy often report difficulties in social settings, such as problems in forming friendships, stigmatisation, educational underachievement, low self-esteem and restricted opportunities for social activities (Austin & de Boer, 1997; Baker, Brooks, Buck, & Jacoby, 1999; Collings, 1990; Fisher et al, 2000; Jacoby, Baker, Steen, Potts &Chadwick, 1996; Mittan, 1986). Exactly why this clinical group experience problems in social situationsis unclear but likely to be a consequence of a number of complex interrelated psychosocial factors that impact upon the person with epilepsy. Such factors include the experience of stigma, unemployment or underemployment, anxiety and depression, cognitive dysfunction, poor self esteem, social isolation and difficulties in interpersonal relationships (Austin & de Boer, 1997; Corcoran & Thompson, 1993; Collings, 1990; De Souza & Salgado, 2006; Fisher et al, 2000; Grabowska-Grzyb, Jędrzejczak, Nagańska & Fiszer, 2006; McCagh, Fisk & Baker, 2009; Mensah, Beavis, Thapar & Kerr, 2007; Morrell, 2002; Suurmeijer, Reuvekamp & Aldenkamp, 2001; Thompson & Corcoran, 1992).

EPILEPSY, STIGMA AND DISCRIMINATION

People with epilepsypresent with more social difficulties than people with other chronic disorders (Aper et al., 1991; Austin, Smith, Risinger, McNelis, 1994;; Matthews, Barabas, Ferrari, 1982) and the general population (Austin & de Boer, 1997).

One important factor that has been linked with increased social difficulties in people with epilepsy is the negative attitudes of society towards the condition (Austin & de Boer, 1997). Discrimination and misconceptions about the condition lead to increased feelings of stigma and fear. This has been reflected in the difficulty that people with epilepsy have in finding employment and developing relationships.

The nature of epilepsy renders the individual with increased vulnerability in social situations where they may have a seizure without warning. Losing consciousness in public leaves individuals at the mercy of those around them. Living with the uncertainty of when and where a seizure may occur or whether their condition will ever be controllable can encourage people to withdraw from society which in turn reduces the opportunity for social interaction and leads to increased feelings of social isolation. Fisher et al. (2000) found that the fear of having a seizure and the uncertainty associated with epilepsy were reported as the most problematic features of having the condition.

Living with the social stigma of having epilepsy has detrimental consequences on quality of life. 'The stigma of epilepsy still is often more disabling than it's neurological effects' (Devinsky, 2007 p.304). The experience of stigma in people with epilepsy is very pronounced and can often lead to people trying to conceal their disorder (Morrell, 2002). Baker, Brooks, Buck & Jacoby (1999) found that over half of 5000 people who were surveyed with epilepsy in a large cross cultural European study reported that they felt stigmatised by the disorder. The impact of stigma and the resulting discrimination it causes has far reaching consequences and has been found to adversely affect finding and maintaining employment(Smeets, van Lierop, Vanhoutvin, Aldenkamp & Nijhuis, 2007). Jacoby and Jacoby (2005) also found that over a third of people with epilepsy who applied for one or more different types of insurance in the UK were declined. This discrimination interferes with the ability of the person with epilepsy to protect themselves and their loved ones in the event of a problem.

The effect of stigma is apparent cross culturally, in sub-Saharan Africa prejudice against those with epilepsy is common and even speaking the word 'epilepsy' is considered to be taboo (Carod-Artal & Vazquez-Cabrera, 2007). People with epilepsy in tribal communities in Central America are considered to be witches and there is still the myth that epilepsy is contagious in many African cultures (Carod-Artal & Vazquez-Cabrera, 2007). Contagion beliefs contribute towards the discrimination experienced by people with epilepsy in these countries. In a recent study in the Cameroon people with epilepsy expressed how their condition meant that they were often excluded from taking part in traditional social roles (Allotey, 2007). This exclusion has been reflected in a number of other African countries such as Ethiopia and Kenya where people with epilepsy have experienced social isolation, as well as difficulties in finding employment and in maintaining intimate and family relationships.Reduced quality of lifehas been reported in Canada and lower school attendance and performancehas been highlighted in the Netherlands. In Chinapeople with epilepsy have encountered difficulties in finding a partner due to negative family attitudes about having the disorder (ILAE/IBE/WHO, 1999; Wiebe, Bellhouse, Fallahy & Eliasziw, 1999).

MYTHS AND STEREOTYPES

Myths, stereotypesand stigma surrounding epilepsyare perpetuated by how epilepsy has been represented and recorded throughout history.Myths and misunderstandings about the disorder are still evident in society and are more pronounced in people who do not know someone with the disorder (Baxendale & O'Toole, 2007). This is compounded by inaccurate portrayals of epilepsy within the media. Baxendale and O'Toole (2007) investigated how epilepsy was represented on television and in the cinema and concluded that characters with epilepsy were stereotypically portrayed to propagate many of the ancient myths surrounding the disorder. Such representations include the person with epilepsy foaming at the mouth, being possessed, violent and in need of urgent medical intervention. Krauss et al. (2000) also found that nearly a third of all print media portrayed inaccurate representations of epilepsy. These inaccuracies reinforce stereotypical and historical views of epilepsy as being associated with possession and the divine.

One common myth is the idea that putting something in the mouth of a person experiencing a seizure will stop them from swallowing their tongue. This misconception may in fact endanger a person with epilepsy if they have a seizure. Baxendale & O'Toole (2007) found that a third of people in their study would attempt this and Long, Reeves, Moore, Roach & Pickering (2000) found as many as 41%of their sample would also take this action.

PSYCHOSOCIAL PROBLEMS

People with epilepsy present with a range of psychosocial difficulties. People with epilepsy report social isolation, loneliness, perception of stigma, adjustment and coping and psychological distress as having the most influence on their quality of life (Suurmeijer et al., 2001). De Souza and Salgado (2006) found that nearly half of their sample (N= 60) reported that epilepsy was stressful and had consequences for their quality of life, they reported problems in employment, school, leisure and in interpersonal and intimate relationships.

INTERPERSONAL AND FAMILY RELATIONSHIPS

Evidence that epilepsy can adversely affect intimate relationships comes from a study by Jacoby et al. (1996). This study found that the more seizures someone had the less likely they were to be married and the more likely they were to not be in a relationship or to be divorced or separated. These findings have been reflected in other studies which highlight disparities in marital status in people with epilepsy in relation to control groups (Arnston, Drodge, Norton & Murray, 1986; Collings, 1990).

Jacoby et al. (1996) also found that age of onset of epilepsy was an influential in explaining marital status where people who were younger at the onset of epilepsy were less likely to marry. The authors suggest that parental over protectiveness and social isolation in this population when they were younger as a consequence of having epilepsy may account for these findings. Social isolation may well be a consequence of a number of factors such as the fear of having a seizurein public, less chance of interaction with others because of difficulties in gaining and maintaining employment, parental over protectiveness or because their may be less chance of developing friendships and intimate relationships (McCagh et al., 2009).

'The attitudes and experiences of family members will greatly influence a person's coping ability' (Thompson, 2000, p.412). Morrell (2002) argues that parental beliefs and behaviour have a crucial impact on children's perception of stigma and what it means to have epilepsy. Parental beliefs may be self fulfilling, one study found that parents who believe their child will experience stigma and experience limitations reported more behavioural problems in their children than parents who did not hold such beliefs (Carlton-Ford, Miller, Nealeigh and Sanchez, 1997). This study also found that children with epilepsy who report their parents as over controlling had more behavioural problems than children with epilepsy who did not. The authors concluded that seizure type and frequency did not predict behavioural problems but parents perceived stigma, perceived limitations and extent of control did. Parental over protectiveness can also contribute to making the child less confident and independent (Austin & de Boer, 1997).

Thompson (2000) reports that in a survey of young people with intractable epilepsy the biggest area of dissatisfaction was social isolation and particularly in forming friendships and participating in social activities outside of the family home. Social networks and friendship are important sources for social support and will have a great impact on the individual's ability to cope with having epilepsy and being part of society.

EMPLOYMENT AND EDUCATION

People with epilepsy and those who have a history of epilepsy are prohibited by law from a variety of occupations (Jacoby & Baker, 2000). Practices that discriminate against people with the condition are another major contributing factor to unemployment. This is apparent in the difference between the availability of suitable employment and howreluctant employers are to hire people with epilepsy (Cooper, 1995; Hauser & Hedorffer, 1990).

The disparities between employment in the general population and people with epilepsy have been well documented and are prevalent across the world (Bahrs, 1990; Chaplin, Wester & Tomson, 1998; Elwes, Marshall, Beattie & Newman, 1991;Hauser and Hesdorffer, 1990; ILAE, 2003a, ILAE, 2003b; Reuvekamp et al., 1999). People with epilepsy are also often underemployed relevant to their skills and qualifications, this prohibits them from being able to achieve their full potential in the job market (Chaplin, et al., 1998).

Clarke, Upton and Castellanos (2006) make a validpoint with regards to familial attitudes in relation to employment. They suggest that people with epilepsy may lack autonomy in adulthood and parents may be over protective where fear of personal injury or injury to others of having a seizure at work may deter people with epilepsy to seek employment. This fear of work related accidents is also reflected in employer's attitudes towards employing people with epilepsy (Jacoby, Gorry & Baker, 2005).

Elwes et al. (1991) suggest that difficulties in finding employment may be a consequence of poor academic achievement as school leavers with epilepsy have less chance of gaining qualifications or securing apprenticeships. One quarter to one half of children with epilepsy have educational difficulties at school (ILAE, 2003 d). These difficulties may arise as a consequence of a number of factors. Drug therapy and post ictal confusion after a seizuremay slow cognitive functioning and impact on the child's capacity to learn. Children who experience absence seizures in class can often be mistaken for daydreaming, consequently they may not take in all the material taught to them or their attentiveness and behaviour in class may be misinterpreted by the teacher and result in adverse consequences. Children who experience more severe seizure types may miss time off school and may also be more prone to stigma if they have a seizure in class.

Clarke, et al. (2006) conducted a study investigating internal work beliefs in employed and unemployed people with epilepsy. They found that internal work beliefs were a very important factor in the successful inclusion of people with epilepsy into the workplace. Self perceptions of worth, worry about safety at work, perceptions of the likelihood of injury in relation to self and others at work and attitudes of family were primary factors in work status. Factors that deterred unemployed people with epilepsy from working were getting to work on time, transport (individuals would be relying on public transport), adherence to drug therapy and possible loss of pension benefits. Providing transport services to people with epilepsy may help overcome transport difficulties that impact on employability (Morrell, 2002).

The IBE Employment Commission (cited in Chaplin, 2005) conducted a cross cultural study investigating factors that contributed to unemployment in people with epilepsy. Professionals from a wide sphere of occupational settings were asked their views on what they felt contributed to the difficulties in finding work after school and how these barriers might be overcome. The most prevalent solutions cited were to increase awareness of employers, schools and employment providers and to provide more effective career guidance. Alternatively people with epilepsy attribute their employment difficulties to; employers having stigmatised views, lack of self worth, missing school and training, the uncertainty of whether epilepsy will cause a problem in the workplace and not getting the job they want. They felt that laws against discrimination, vocational assessment and epilepsy associations working together with employers would help solve the problem (Chaplin, 2005).As well as the financial gain from being employed it gives people a sense of identity, self worth, and provides a structure to their day whilst reflecting that the person is a valued member of society (Chaplin, 2005; Thompson, 2000).

People with epilepsy report that they are very concerned about disclosing their condition when applying for jobs (Bishop, 2002). Bishop (2004) suggests that role play maybe useful in increasing the confidence of a person with epilepsy in being able to disclose their condition and in being able to explain to employers and colleagues what might happen during a seizure and what they should do in the event of a seizure. This may have another added benefit by increasing feelings of control and sense of mastery in people with epilepsy and by encouraging positive coping strategies. Another strategy to improve employability in people with epilepsy is to make vocational training available to people with epilepsy (ILAE, 2003c).

PSYCHOPATHOLOGY, SELF ESTEEM AND SENSE OF MASTERY

Having epilepsy renders the individual at a much greater risk of mental health problems such as anxiety, depression and suicide than the general population (Brodie & Schachter, 2001; Pompili, Giradi, Rupeto, & Tatarelli, 2005; Pompili, Giradi & Tatarelli, 2006). Anxiety and depression are often co morbid features of having the condition and anxiety is the most commonly reported mental health problem (Jacoby et al., 1996). Anxiety may occur before or during a seizure, it can be triggered by the fear and uncertainty of having a seizure, by low self esteem or more generally by the stigma of having epilepsy (Vasquez & Devinsky, 2003). The uncertainty associated with epilepsy leads to a reduced sense of mastery in the individual and in turn can trigger anxiety, depression, agoraphobia, social phobia, an increased likelihood of committing suicide and reduced self esteem (Arnston et al., 1986; Baker, Smith, Dewey, Jacoby & Chadwick, 1993; Brier, Fuchs & Brookshire, 1998; Hermann & Wyler, 1989; Matthews and Barabas, 1981; Salgado & Souza, 2001; Thompson, 2000). Parental over protectiveness has also been highlighted as one factor that can mediate psychopathology in children with epilepsy (Ferrari, Matthews & Barabas, 1983).

One way to reduce the likelihood of psychopathology is via educational interventions. Educating people with the condition has shown significant gains in enhancing quality of life and increasing self esteem(Snead et al., 2004). Baker, Spector, McGrath and Soteriou. (2005) found that the more knowledge a person has about their disorder the less likely they were to experience social anxiety.Smith et al., (1991) also found that people who had greater knowledge about their condition had higher levels of self esteem.

CONCLUSION

The psychosocial effects of epilepsy are complex and interconnected. To a great extent a number of these psychosocial outcomes are determined by other people's attitudes and reactions towards people with epilepsy. In order to improve these attitudes educational interventions need to target family, employers, teachers and society at large to reduce stigma and discrimination and thereby improve the quality of life of people living with the condition (McCagh et al., 2009). Media representation need to be monitored so that they do not disseminate inaccurate information and reinforce myths and negative stereotypes about the condition. Educational, vocational and therapeutic interventions aimed at increasing knowledge, improving coping strategies and fostering more positive attitudes have also been successful in helping people manage and accept their condition and improve their social functioning.

FURTHER RESEARCH

Surgery is a consideration in the treatment of the disorder for those with intractable epilepsy where an identifiable focus for seizure activity can be established. Presurgical neuropsychological evaluation plays a major role in determining potential outcomes and treatment intervention after surgery. Pre surgical assessment for the treatment of epilepsy currently focuses on cognitive sequelae in determining the likelihood of successful surgical outcomes. One area of research which has started to gain momentum in the field of epilepsy is the investigation of social reasoning (socio cognitive functioning).Recent research has demonstrated that people with epilepsy have impaired socio cognitive functioning (Farrant et al., 2005; Fournier, Claverley, Wagner, Poock & Crossley, 2008; Schacher et al., 2006; Schillbach, Koubeissi, David, Vogeley & Ritzl, 2007; Walpole et al., 2008). In light of this neuropsychological assessment of people with epilepsy should incorporate measures of social reasoning. These tests may provide objective measures of social functioning for the clinician and may indicate people with epilepsy who are at risk of psychosocial difficulties. Such people could then be targeted for treatment intervention to improve their functioning within society. Pre and post surgical assessment will also indicate whether surgical intervention can remediate social reasoning deficits in people with epilepsy and thereby improve quality of life. Future investigations should assess the efficacy of such interventions in epilepsy.Such assessments should be complemented by an effective measure of the actual social difficulties that people with epilepsy experience in everyday life. A number of authors criticise current measures of social functioning used on people with epilepsy, currently these measures do not fully explore the impact that surgery has on interpersonal relationships or social competence (Kirsch, 2006; Schilbach et al.,2007). Therefore development of more appropriate measures is needed. Socio-cognitive skills may be particularly relevant to being able to identify and resolve psychosocial difficulties, thereby reducing the impact of epilepsy on the quality of life of people with epilepsy.

REFERENCES

Allotey, P. (2007). *Epilepsy, culture, identity and well-being: A study of social, cultural and environmental context of epilepsy in Cameroon*. Journal of Health Psychology, 12, 431-443.

Aper, A., Aviv, A., Kaminer, Y., Weizman, A., Lerman, P., Tyano, S. (1991). *Behavioral profile and social competence in temporal lobe epilepsy of adolescence*. Journal of the American Academy of Child &*Adolescent* Psychiatry, 30, (6), 887-892.

Arnston, P., Drodge, D., Norton, R. and Murray, E. (1986). *The perceived psychosocial consequences of having epilepsy*. In: S. Whitman and B.P. Hermann, (Eds.). Psychopathology in epilepsy: social dimensions. New York: Oxford University Press.

Austin, K., Smith, M.S., Risinger, M.W., McNelis, A.M. (1994). *Childhood epilepsy and asthma: comparison of quality of life*. Epilepsia, 35 (3), 608-615.

Austin, K. and deBoer, H. (1997). *Disruptions in social functioning and services facilitating adjustment for the child and adult*. In: Engel Jr. J., Pedley, T.A. (Eds.). Epilepsy: A Comprehensive Textbook (pp. 2191–2201). Philadelphia: Lippincott-Raven.

Bahrs, O. (1990). *Epilepsie und Arbeitswelt: Zusammenfassende Darstellung eine empirisschen Untersuchung unter besonderer Berücksichtigung von Wirklichkeit und Möglichkeit berüflicher.*Rehabilitation, 29, 100–11.

Baker, G.A., Smith, D.F., Dewey, M., Jacoby, A., Chadwick, D.W. (1993). *The initial development of a health-related quality of life model as an outcome measure in epilepsy*. Epilepsy Research, 16, 65-81.

Baker, G.A., Brooks, J., Buck, D., Jacoby, A. (1999). *The stigma of epilepsy: a European perspective*. Epilepsia, 41, 98–104.

Baker, G.A. and Jacoby, A. (2001). *Epilepsy*. In Johnston, D.W, Johnston, M., Bellack, A.S., Hersen, M. (Eds.). Health psychology, vol 8, comprehensive clinical psychology (pp 487-503). Amsterdam: Elsevier Science Publishers.

Baker, G.A., Spector, S., McGrath, Y., Soteriou, H. (2005). *Impact of epilepsy in adolescence : A UK controlled study.* Epilepsy & Behavior, 6(4), 556-62.

Baxendale, S. and O'Toole, A. (2007). *Epilepsy myths: alive and foaming in the 21st century.* Epilepsy and Behavior, 11, 192-196.

Bishop, M. (2002). *Barriers to employment among people with epilepsy: Report of a focus group.* Journal of Vocational Rehabilitation, 17, 281-286.

Bishop, M. (2004*). Determinants of employment status among a community-based sample of people with epilepsy: implications for rehabilitation interventions.* Rehabilitation Counselling Bulletin, 47, 112-120.

Brier, J.I., Fuchs, K.L., Brookshire, B.L. (1998). *Quality of life perception in patients with intractable epilepsy or pseudoseizures.* Archives of Neurology, 55, 660-5.

Brodie, M.J. and Schachter, S.C. (2001). *Epilepsy, (2nd ed.).* Oxford: Health Press.

Callaghan, N., Crowley, M., Goggin, T. (1992). *Epilepsy and employment, marital, education and social status.* Irish Medical Journal, 85, 17-19.

Carlton-Ford, S., Miller, R., Nealeigh, N., Sanchez, N. (1997). *The effects of perceived stigma and psychological over-control on the behavioural problems of children with epilepsy.* Seizure, 6, 383-391.

Carod-Artal, Vazquez-Carbrera (2007). *An anthropological study about epilepsy in native tribes from Central and South America.* Epilepsia, 48, 886-993.

Chadwick, D.W. (Ed.). (1997). *The illustrated encyclopaedia of epilepsy.* Merseyside: Roby Education Limited.

Chaplin, J.E., Wester, A., Tomson, T. (1998). *Factors associated with the employment problems of people with established epilepsy.* Seizure, 7, 299–303.

Chaplin. J. (2005). *Vocational assessment and intervention for people with epilepsy.* Epilepsia, 46 (suppl. 1), 55–6.

Clarke, B.B., Upton, A.R.M., Castellanos, C. (2006). *Work beliefs and works status in epilepsy.* Epilepsy & Behavior, 119-125.

Collings, J. A. (1990). *Psychosocial well-being and epilepsy: an empirical study.* Epilepsia 31, 418-426.

Cooper, M. (1995). *Epilepsy and employment: employer's attitudes.* Seizure, 4, 193-9.

Corcoran, R., Thompson, P. (1993). *Epilepsy and poor memory. Who complains and what do they mean?* British Journal of Clinical Psychology, 32, 199-208.

deBoer, H.M. (1995*). Epilepsy and society.* Epilepsia, 36: S8-11.

de Boer, H.M., Mula, M., Sander, J.W. (2008). *The global burden and stigma of epilepsy.* Epilepsy & Behavior, 12, 540-546.

de Souza, .E.A.P. and Salgado, P.C.B. (2006). *A psychosocial view of anxiety and depression in epilepsy.* Epilepsy & Behavior, 8, 232-8.

Devinsky, J (2007). A diary of epilepsy in the early 1800s. *Epilepsy & Behavior*, 10, 304-310.

Elwes, R.D., Marshall, J., Beattie, A., Newman, P.K. (1991). *Epilepsy and employment. A community based survey in an area of high unemployment.* Journal of Neurology, Neurosurgery and Psychiatry, 54, 200-203.

Epilepsy Foundation of America. (1992). *The legal rights of persons with epilepsy, (6th ed).* Landover, MD.

Farrant, A., Morris, R.G., Russell, T., Elwes, R., Akanuma, N., Alarcon, G., et al. (2005). *Social cognition in frontal lobe epilepsy.* Epilepsy & Behavior, 7, 506–516.

Ferrari, M., Matthews, W.S., and Barabas, G. (1983). *The family and child with epilepsy.* Family Process 22, 53-59.

Fisher, R.S., Vickrey, B.G., Gibson, P., Hermann., B., Penovich, P., Scherer, A. et al. (2000). *The impact of epilepsy from the patient's perspective II: Views about therapy and health care.* Epilepsy Research, 41, 53–61.

Fournier, N.M., Claverley, K.L., Wagner, J.P., Poock, J.L., Crossley, M. (2008*). Impaired social cognition 30 years after hemispherectomy for intractable epilepsy: the importance of the right hemisphere in complex social functioning.* Epilepsy & Behavior, 12, 460-471.

Grabowska-Grzyb, A., Jędrzejczak, J., Nagańska , E., Fiszer, U. (2006). *Risk factors for depression in patients with epilepsy.* Epilepsy & Behavior, 8, 411-417.

Guberman, A.H. and Bruni, J. (1999). *Essentials of clinical epilepsy (2nd ed).*Boston: Butterworth Heinemann.

Hauser, W.A. and Hesdorffer, D.C. (1990). *Epilepsy: frequency, causes and consequences.* New York: Landover, MD, *Epilepsy* Foundation of America.

Hermann, B.P. and Wyler, A.R. (1989). *Depression, locus of control, and the effects of epilepsy surgery.* Epilepsia, 30, 332-8.

International League Against Epilepsy. (2003a). *The history and stigma of epilepsy. Epilepsia, 44, (suppl. 6): 12-14.*

International League Against Epilepsy. (2003b). *Pharmacological treatment.* Epilepsia, 44 (suppl 6), 33-34.

International League Against Epilepsy. (2003c). *Living with epilepsy: Epilepsy education within statutory school system.* Epilepsia, 44, (suppl. 6): 45-48.

International League Against Epilepsy. (2003d). *Living with epilepsy: Employment.* Epilepsia, 44, (suppl. 6): 49-50.

ILAE/IBE/WHO. (1999*). "Out of the shadows": global campaign against epilepsy.* Annual Report. Geneva: WHO.

Jacoby, A., Baker, G.A., Steen, N., Potts, P., Chadwick, D.W. (1996). *The clinical course of epilepsy and its psychosocial correlates: findings from a U.K. community study.* Epilepsia, 37 ,148–61.

Jacoby, A. and Baker, G.A. (2000). *Psychosocial handicaps associated with the epilepsies.* In: Vinken, P.J. and Bruyn, G.W. (Eds.). Handbook of Clinical Neurology. Amsterdam, Elsevier Press.

Jacoby, K., and Jacoby, A. (2005). *Epilepsy and insurance in the UK: an exploratory survey of the experiences of people with epilepsy.* Epilepsy & Behavior, 5, 884–94.

Jacoby, A., Gorry, J., Baker, G.A. (2005). *Employers' attitudes to employment of people with epilepsy: still the same old story?* Epilepsia, 46, 1978-1987.

Kirsch, H.E. (2006). *Social cognition and epilepsy surgery.*Epilepsy and Behavior, 8, 71–80.

Krauss, G.L., Gondek, S., Krumholz, A., Paul, S., Shen, F. (2000*). "The scarlet E": the presentation of epilepsy in the English-language print media.* Neurology, 54, 1894–8.

Long, L., Reeves, A.L., Moore, J.L., Roach, J, Pickering C.T. (2000). *An assessment of epilepsy patient's knowledge of their disorder.* Epilepsia, 41, 727–31.

Masia, S.L. and Devinsky, O. (2000). *Epilepsy and behavior: a brief history.* Epilepsy and Behavior, 1, 27–36.

Matthews, W.S. and Barabas, G. (1981). *Suicide and epilepsy: a review of the literature.*Psychosomatics, 22, 515–524.

Matthews, W.S., Barabas, G., Ferrari, M. (1982). *Emotional concomitants of childhood epilepsy*. Epilepsia, 23, 671-687.

McCagh, J., Fisk, J.E., Baker, G.A. (2009*). Epilepsy, psychosocial and cognitive functioning*. Epilepsy Research, 86, 1-14.

Mensah, S.A., Beavis, J.M., Thapar, A.K., Kerr, M.P. (2007). *A community study of the presence of anxiety order in people with epilepsy*. Epilepsy & Behavior, 7, 438–46.

Mittan. R.J. (1986). *Fear of Seizures*. In: Whitman, S. and Hermann, B. (Eds.). Psychopathology in Epilepsy: Social Dimensions. Oxford: Oxford University Press.

Morrell, M.J. (2002). *Stigma and epilepsy*. Epilepsy & Behaviour, 3, S21–5.

Oxbury, J. (2000). *Drug treatment in adults*. In J. Oxbury, C. Polkey, and M. Duchowny, Intractable Focal Epilepsy (pp.475-490). London: W.B. Saunders.

Oxbury, J., Polkey, C., Duchowny, M. (2000). *Intractable Focal Epilepsy*. London: W.B. Saunders.

Pompili, M., Girardi, P., Ruberto, A., Tatarelli, R. (2005). *Suicide in the epilepsies: a meta-analytic investigation of 29 cohorts*. Epilepsy & Behavior, 7, 305–10.

Pompili, M., Girardi, P., Tatarelli, R. (2006). *Death from suicide versus mortality from epilepsy in the epilepsies: A meta-analysis*. Epilepsy & Behavior, 9, 641-8.

Reuvekamp, M., deBoer, H.M., Bult, I. Overweg, J. (1999). *Employment of people with epilepsy: is there a problem?* 23rd Epilepsy Congress. Janssen-Cilag Medical, Scientific News, 6, 175-9.

Salgado, P.C.B. and Souza, E.A.P. (2001). *Qualidade de vida em epilepsia e percepcao de controle de crises*. Arq Neuropsiquiatria, 19, 537-40.

Schacher, M., Winkler, R., Grunwald, T., Kraemer, G., Kurthem, M., Reed, V. (2006). *Mesial temporal lobe epilepsy impairs advanced social cognition*. Epilepsia, 47, 2141–6.

Schilbach, L., Koubeissi, M.Z., David, N., Vogeley, K., Ritzl, E.K. (2007). *Being with virtual others: Studying social cognition in temporal lobe epilepsy*. Epilepsy & Behavior, 316-323.

Smeets. V.M.J., van Lierop, B.A.G., Vanhoutvin, J,P.G., Aldenkamp, A.P., Nijhuis, F.J.N. (2007). *Epilepsy and employment: Literature review*. Epilepsy & Behavior, 10, 354–362.

Smith, D.F., Baker, G.A., Dewey, M. Jacoby, A and Chadwick, D.W. (1991). *Seizure frequency, patient perceived seizure severity and the psychosocial consequences of intractable epilepsy*. Epilepsy Research, 9, 231-241.

Snead, K., Ackerson, J., Bailey, K., Schmitt, M.M., Madan-Swain, A., Martin, R.C. (2004). *Taking charge of epilepsy: the development of a structured psychoeducational group intervention for adolescents with epilepsy and their parents*. Epilepsy & Behavior, 5(4), 547-56

Suurmeijer, T.P., Reuvekamp, M.F, Aldenkamp, B.P. (2001). *Social functioning, psychological functioning and quality of life in epilepsy*. Epilepsia, 42, 1160–8.

Thompson, P.J. and Corcoran, R. (1992). *Everyday memory failures in people with epilepsy*. Epilepsia, 33 (suppl.6.), S18-S20.

Thompson, P.J. (2000). *Psychosocial aspects of epilepsy*. In: Duncan, J.S., Sisodiya, S.J.J., Smalls, J.E. (Eds.). Epilepsy 2000 from science to patient. I.L.A.E.

Vasquez, B. and Devinsky, O. (2003). *Epilepsy and anxiety. Epilepsy & Behavior*, 9, s20–5.

Walpole, P., Isaac, C.L., Reynders, H.J. (2008). *A comparison of emotional and cognitive intelligences in people with and without temporal lobe epilepsy*. Epilepsia, 49 (8), 1470-1474.

Wiebe, S., Bellhouse, D.R., Fallahay, C., Eliasziw. M. (1999). *Burden of epilepsy: the Ontario Health Survey*. Canadian Journal of Neurological Science, 26, 263–70.

In: Psychology of Stereotypes
Editor: Eleanor L. Simon

ISBN: 978-1-61761-463-7
©2011 Nova Science Publishers, Inc.

Chapter 13

STEREOTYPES TOWARD FOOD AND EATING BEHAVIOR

Atsushi Kimura[a], Yuji Wada[a] and Takashi Oka[b]*

Sensory and Cognitive Food Science Laboratory, National Food Research Institute, 2-1-12, Kannondai, Tsukuba, Ibaraki 305-8642, Japan[a]
Department of Psychology, NihonUniversity, 3-25-40, Sakurajosui, Setagaya, Tokyo 156-8550, Japan[b]

ABSTRACT

In the last few decades, several studies, mostly performed in Western countries, have started to reveal the existence of various food and eating stereotypes. Interestingly, these studies imply that many people are still influenced by unfounded nutritional beliefs and practices regardless of the growing amount of scientific knowledge on nutrition and health. The aim of this chapter is to provide a brief overview of empirical research on food-related beliefs and stereotypes.

Firstly, we illustrate that consumer food choice and evaluation are influenced by various stereotypical beliefs about food. For example, people tend to categorize foods based on subjective beliefs (e.g., high-fat/low-fat, local/imported, branded/unbranded) and those beliefs further influence a consumer's food selections and food product evaluations (for example, a belief that local food products are more expensive than imports may prevent consumers from buying local products). We also discuss the nature of magical beliefs about food and health.

Secondly, we review consumption stereotypes, which are stereotypes based on what and how much people eat. Specifically, we focus on gender-based consumption stereotypes, in which femininity and masculinity are primarily associated with specific patterns of consumption. We discuss the nature of gender-based consumption stereotypes among the younger population in relation to social appeal and/or pressure. Young women often experience social pressure based on gender-based consumption stereotypes and form psychological barriers against consuming masculine foods and drinks. There is fear that these stereotypical attitudes among females result in several pathological eating behaviors.

---
*Corresponding author: E-mail address yujiwd@affrc.go.jp, Fax: +81-(0)29-838-7319 Phone: +81-(0)29-838-7357

Finally, we discuss the feasibility of introducing implicit attitude measures for the study of food-related stereotypes, partly based on our recent studies.

Keywords: Consumption stereotype; Gender role; Magical belief; Cognitive response; Indirect attitude measure

1. INTRODUCTION

People use a variety of criteria to conceptualize their everyday food choices and eating behaviors. As a social event, food consumption is influenced by various social and cultural values, and at an individual level, one may often possess stereotypes about food and eating behavior. In the last few decades, several studies have started to reveal the existence of various food and eating stereotypes. The aim of this chapter is to provide a brief overview of empirical research on food-related beliefs and stereotypes.

2. STEREOTYPICAL BELIEFS ABOUT FOOD

2.1 Good/Bad Food Stereotypes

People have stereotypical beliefs about particular foods and eating behaviors. For example, people tend to categorize foods as good or bad. This was first described in people with eating disorders (Garner, Garfinkel, & Bemis, 1982): anorexia nervosa patients classify carbohydrates, sugar, and meat as "bad" foods based on mythical beliefs. Such tendencies were later generalized to include people in the general population (Rozin, 1986; Rozin, Ashmore, & Markwith, 1996).

In more recent years, the nature and functions of good/bad food stereotypes have been closely examined by Oakes and his collaborators. Oakes and Slotterback (2001a, 2001b) had participants rate the healthiness of food names and each food's nutrient descriptions and found that for most foods, there was a significant difference in the healthiness rating of the name and that of its description. For instance, the name "1 oz potato chips" was rated unhealthier than its nutrient description "8% RDA of calories, 15% RDA of fat, 7% RDA of sodium." These results were interpreted as the standpoint of good/bad food stereotypes: people labeled certain food names as "good" (healthier) or "bad" (unhealthier). They also found that levels of fat in a food best predicted whether the food would be considered good or bad. Oakes and Slotterback (2001a, 2001b) discussed that consumers believe foods to be extremely good or bad for health and that they use simplistic overgeneralizations when judging foods. Thus, some foods are considered wholesome, others unhealthful, and very few are judged to be moderate in health value.

Furthermore, this proclivity for considering certain foods as good and others as bad also appears to impact the perceived characteristics of foods. For example, bad foods are perceived as promoting greater weight gain than good foods. Oakes (2005a, 2005b) demonstrated that lower-calorie-disreputable snacks (e.g., a 47-calorie Snickers miniature) were perceived as promoting greater weight gain than higher-calorie-reputable snacks (e.g., a large 569-calorie snack consisting of a cup of cottage cheese, three carrots and three pears). Surprisingly, even when participants were provided information concerning calorie contents, lower-calorie bad foods were again judged to promote greater weight gain than higher-calorie good foods (Oakes & Slotterback, 2005; Oakes, Sullivan, & Slotterback, 2007). Oakes (2004, 2005c) also demonstrated that U.S. consumers tend to believe that foods perceived as bad are deficient in vitamins and minerals. For instance, the apple (a "good" food) was perceived to have an abundance of vitamins and minerals while a caramel apple (a "bad" food) was judged to have significantly fewer of these essential nutrients. These findings suggest that when people have a negative stereotype toward a food it is difficult for many of them to recognize any positive characteristics in the food. The bad/good stereotypical beliefs about foods further affect people's judgment: eaters of the good or bad foods are viewed by others in association with good or bad moral values based on what they eat (Stein & Nemeroff, 1995). These stereotypes toward eaters of certain foods are known as consumption stereotypes as we see later in this chapter.

2.2 Biased Beliefs about Foods

Stereotypes can also be associated with foods and eating habits in specific countries or regions. For example, children who live in the U.K. exhibit rejective responses to unfamiliar French meat dishes due to stereotypes such as, "the French eat frogs" (De Moura, 2007). Moreover, recent studies have begun to further reveal the impact of food stereotypes on consumers' interpretations and behaviors. Niva (2007) reported that consumers tend to think that functional foods are healthy but unsavory. Chambers, Lobb, Butler, Harvey, and Traill (2007) found that a stereotype among U.K. consumers that local food products are more expensive than imports may prevent them from buying local products. Hoogland, de Boer, and Boersema (2007) demonstrated that an organic logo on food packages provides consumers with a positive but expensive impression, producing only small net impacts on consumers' purchase intentions. Wansink, Payne, and North (2007) revealed that a wine with a favorable ("new from California") label, served complementarily with a fixed-price meal to adult diners caused a significant increase in meal intake than the same wine with an unfavorable ("new from North Dakota") label. These findings imply that biased beliefs about foods sometimes govern consumers' food selections and eating behaviors.

2.3 Magical Beliefs about Food and Health

Several ethnographical studies have shown the unchangeable beliefs are usually rooted in cultural and emotional areas. Particularly, food has long been regarded as the ideal medium for "bewitchment of poison." In South Africa, for instance, pregnant women are not allowed to eat tender chicken for fear of breeding epileptics or weaklings. Bone marrow is also forbidden as this is believed to cause perpetual running noses and head colds in her progeny (Galli, 1973).

Even today, many people are still influenced by unfounded nutritional beliefs and practices regardless of the growing amount of scientific knowledge on nutrition and health. These beliefs, based on non-scientific health and food instructions, are called "magical beliefs about food and health" (Lindeman, Keskivaara, & Roschier, 2000). Beliefs that are defined as magical follow either of the two laws of magical thinking: the law of contagion and the law of similarity. The law of contagion holds that things that have once been in contact with each other continue to act upon each other at a distance after the physical contact has been severed (Frazer, 1922/1963, see also Aarnio & Lindeman, 2004; Rozin & Nemeroff, 1990). The assumed contagion may be positive or negative. An example of a positive contagion is the belief that food prepared by a loved one is better for the health than that made by a stranger. More often, however, contagion is associated with its negative effects (i.e. contamination and pollution). For instance, people tend to believe that even brief contact with an infectious source may transmit a disease, despite sterilization (Rozin & Nemeroff, 1990). The law of similarity holds that superficial resemblance indicates, or causes, deep resemblance. It implies that an effect resembles its cause and that like produces like (Frazer, 1922/1963; see also Aarnio & Lindeman, 2004; Rozin & Nemeroff, 1990). For example, Megis (1984) reported that a tribe in New Guinea avoids eating any food that is red because the color is identified with menstrual blood.

Lindeman and her colleagues developed a 17-item scale for measuring magical beliefs about food and health (MFH; Lindeman et al., 2000), and assessed individual differences in the tendency to adopt eating and health claims which obey universal laws of contagion or similarity in the Finnish population (Aarnio & Lindeman, 2004). The scale consists of items on general magical beliefs (e.g., 'Since our bodies are 70 percent water, we should be eating a diet that has an approximate water content of 70 percent'), and items on animal products as contaminations of food or personality (e.g., 'Consumption of meat dulls thinking'), and also 5 filler items (e.g., 'Vegetable oils are healthier than animal fats'). The total score of magical belief for an individual is calculated by averaging all the items (see Aarnio & Lindeman, 2004; Lindeman et al., 2000).

Using the MFH scale, Aarnio and Lindeman (2004) found that the magical beliefs about food and health were positively associated with the female gender ($r = .17$), vegetarianism ($r = .38$), a positive attitude toward alternative medicine ($r = .44$), the degree of negative life experiences ($r = .11$), and intuitive thinking ($r = .26$), but did not correlate with age. Aarnio and Lindeman (2004) also found that one of the most important functions of MFH beliefs among believers was the value-expressive function, which reflects the connection between these beliefs and personal identity. These results suggest that food and health beliefs are adopted, and held not only in scientific information, but also in the realm of emotions, intuition, and the eater's values and identity.

3. STEREOTYPES TOWARD FOOD AND DRINK CONSUMPTION

3.1 You are What You Eat

Eating particular foods often provides personal information about an individual. As advocated by a classical study on the product personality by Wells, Andriuli, Goi, and Seader (1957), beliefs about foods could further affect the personality of the eater.

In food science, stereotypes toward eaters of certain foods are known as the "you are what you eat" hypothesis of food by Nemeroff and Rozin (1989). Nemeroff and Rozin (1989) examined whether people ascribe to individuals impressions of physical and personality characteristics that are directly associated with food consumption. In their study, U.S. university students were asked to read a description of an exotic culture including information about the social structure of the culture and the daily activities and dietary habits of its members, and then to make judgments about the characteristics of the people in that culture. In their first study, participants read that the group ate marine turtles or wild boars. In their second study, participants were informed that the group members were meat-eaters (elephant-eaters) or vegetarians. Overall, participants rated the turtle-eaters as more turtle-like than the boar-eaters (e.g., good swimmer, slow-moving, long-lived), and rated the elephant-eaters as more elephant-like than the vegetarians (e.g., big build).These results suggest that individuals attribute a wide array of personality traits to other people on the basis of their food intake; in other wards, people believe that you are what you eat even in modern Western society. Individuals assess others and form opinions about them based on their eating behavior. They also use food selections to manage how others view them and to portray themselves in a positive manner while seeking to appeal to others.

3.2 Gender Roles and Eating Behavior

Among stereotypes associated with eating, one of the most consistently observed is a gender-based consumption stereotype, in which femininity and masculinity are primarily associated with the consumption of specific foods. For example, U.S. college students categorized "toasted bagel with cream cheese" and "spaghetti with tomato sauce" as feminine foods, while "flapjacks with syrup" and "broiled sirloin" were classified as masculine foods (Moony & Lorenz, 1997; Table 1). In addition, certain foods enhance or diminish the feminine or masculine impression projected by the individuals who eat them: those individuals who are described as consuming feminine foods are evaluated as more feminine and less masculine than those described as consuming masculine foods, regardless of the gender of the evaluators (Moony & Lorenz, 1997).

In Western countries, the association of femininity and masculinity with specific foods is often correlated with their profiles such as health value, caloric content and fat content, and further with good/bad classifications that arise from these profiles (e.g., Barker, Tandy, & Stookey, 1999; Oakes, 2004; Stein & Nameroff, 1995). In addition to types of food, there are also gender stereotypes towards the total amount of food ingested (Vartanian et al., 2007 for review). Specifically, ingestion volume association with female targets is well studied, and many studies have reported that the ingestion of a small amount of food is significantly bound to femininity (Basow & Kobrynowicz, 1993; Chaiken & Pliner, 1987).

While most studies on gender-based food stereotypes have been conducted in Western countries, we recently examined gender-based consumption stereotypes among Japanese (Kimura et al., 2009; see also Kimura, Wada, & Dan, in press). We found that the feminine foods among young Japanese could be categorized as low-fat foods (e.g., salad), sweets (e.g., cake), and fruit, All of which are Western foods. On the other hand, most of the masculine foods among young Japanese could be categorized as high-fat foods (e.g., beef rice-bowl, breaded pork cutlet), which are modern traditional dishes. These results suggest that, consistent with studies based on Western subjects, there are, among young Japanese, robust gender-based stereotypes towards foods that high- and low-fat foods are associated with femininity and masculinity, respectively.

Table 1 List of feminine and masculine foods among U.S. students (Moony & Lorenz, 1997). Feminine/masculine foods are marked with italics.

Feminine diet	Masculine diet
Breakfast	
Toasted bagel, 1 oz. cream cheese	*Flapjacks, 1 oz. syrup*
1 banana	8 oz. glass orange juice
8 oz. glass orange juice	1 cup of coffee, cream
1 cup of coffee, cream	
Lunch	
Tuna on whole wheat, lettuce	*Tuna sub, lettuce*
1 cup of tomato soup	1 cup of tomato soup
8 oz. glass of water	*8 oz. glass of milk*
1 chocolate chip cookie	1 chocolate chip cookie
Dinner	
6 oz. spaghetti, tomato sauce	*6 oz. broiled sirloin*
Tossed salad, Italian dressing	Tossed salad, Italian
Hard roll with butter	*Baked potato with butter*
12 oz. water	*Bottle of beer*
Apple pie, small slice	Apple pie, small slice
Snacks	
1 can diet Coke	*1 can of Coke*
Popcorn (vending machine)	Popcorn (vending machine)
Handful of carrot sticks	*Handful of Tostitos Salsa*

3.3 Gender-Based Consumption Stereotypes as Mediators of Impression Management

The femininity and masculinity of foods are commonly used in impression management and serve as gender advertisement (Goffman, 1979). Individuals use food selections to manage how others view them and to portray themselves in a positive manner while seeking to appeal to others. For instance, Amiraian and Sobal (2009) explored how U.S. university students conceptualize foods that were either suitable or inappropriate to eat on a date. In their study, participants were asked to name date foods and foods non-date foods. Amiraian and Sobal found that while most of the foods named overlapped into both categories, women more frequently named feminine foods (e.g., salad or vegetables) as date foods than did men. Eating feminine foods creates a more attractive and feminine impression (Stein & Nemeroff, 1995; Vertanian et al., 2007), so women might choose to eat such foods to portray themselves as more attractive for their partners.

Social effects on food intake may be especially strong in young women engaged in impression management. In fact, it has been found that stereotypical thinking about the health value of foods appears to be more pronounced in young women compared to men and older women (Oakes, 2003; Oakes & Slotterback, 2001a, 2001b). More directly, Young, Mizzau, Mai, Sirisegaram, and Wilson (2009) investigated the influence of gender, group size, and gender composition of groups of eaters on food selection in university cafeterias. They found that women observed eating with a male companion chose foods of lower caloric contents than those observed eating with another woman in a dyad, whereas men's choices were not affected by their companion's gender. These results are discussed from the standpoint of social appeal based on gender-based consumption stereotypes. Several studies have revealed that women are deemed more attractive and more feminine when portrayed as eating fewer calories (e.g., Basow & Kobrynowicz, 1993; Chaiken & Pliner, 1987; Moony & Lorenz, 1997; see also Vartanian et al., 2007 for review). Women seem to adjust their eating to accord with consumption stereotypes, specifically that women who eat less are viewed more favorably.

Gender stereotypes also substantially mediate many gender differences in drinking and other related behaviors. Specifically, a high level of masculinity has been related to greater alcohol consumption while high identification with traits of femininity has typically been related to lower alcohol consumption (e.g., Huselid & Cooper, 1994; Williams & Ricciardelli, 1999). Ricciardelli, Conner, Williams, & Young (2001) examined whether gender stereotypes, restrained drinking, and self-efficacy for alcohol refusal could be differentiated in moderate and high-risk drinking among women and men from an Australian university population. They found that both female and male high-risk drinkers displayed a response conflict, typified by high scores on restrained drinking but low scores on self-efficacy (e.g., high risk drinkers believed that they could easily control their drinking. However, they also felt that they could not refuse to drink when their friends were drinking). Furthermore, positive feminine stereotypes (e.g., "nurturing," "loves children," etc.) could be differentiated in moderate and high-risk drinking among women. Specifically, high-risk drinkers scored poorly for positive-feminine-stereotyped traits. These results suggest that heavy drinking among women is incompatible with desirable, stereotypic attitudes and behaviors typically expected of women, and further that food selection by women is more strongly governed by social pressure based on gender stereotypes than that of men. Stereotype-based barriers among women against certain foods and beverages may sometimes lead to loss of health. Further research is necessary in order to make clear the factors determining development and maintenance of gender-based consumption stereotypes in relation to moderate social pressures on women.

4. MEASURING FOOD-RELATED STEREOTYPES

Traditionally, the measurement of stereotypical attitudes toward foods and eaters has been dependent on participants' responses in explicit-attitude studies (Mooney, De Tore, & Malloy, 1994). However, self-reported attitude measured in this way is at risk of reflecting a skewed attitude flawed by self-presentation or social-desirability biases (Greenwald et al., 2002). To circumvent such plausible risks, indirect attitude measures have gradually come into use as alternatives to direct measures. In this section, we review the two techniques for measuring consumer attitudes indirectly used in studies on attitudes and stereotypes toward food and eating behavior: the shopping list technique and the semantic (affective) priming task.

4.1 Shopping List Technique

One technique designed for measuring food-based impressions indirectly used in marketing research is the shopping list technique (Haire, 1950; see also Boddy, 2005 for review). In this technique, one or more products are embedded in a shopping list, and respondents are asked to describe or rate their impressions of the owner of the shopping list. The responses, recorded either by open-ended responses or attribute ratings, can be compared with those for an otherwise identical list that did not include the target food product. This technique allows controlled comparisons of impressions created by different types of food products (e.g., users of functional foods can be compared with users of similar conventional food items; Saher, Arvola, Lindeman, & Lähteenmäki, 2004).

This technique was first introduced into marketing research by Haire (1950). In Haire's study, two almost identical shopping lists, where one list included instant coffee and one included drip coffee were produced (Table 2). Fifty U.S. housewives participated in each of the two shopping list conditions. They were asked to describe the personalities and characters of the owners of the shopping list. Haire revealed that the housewife who was attributed the list containing the instant coffee was more commonly evaluated as lazy, whereas the housewife attributed the list containing the ground coffee beans was more often evaluated as thrifty and a good housewife.

Table 2 The two shopping lists used in the shopping list study (Haire, 1950). The target foods are in italics.

Shopping list I	Shopping list II
Pound and a half of hamburger	Pound and a half of hamburger
2 loaves Wonder bread	2 loaves Wonder bread
Bunch of carrots	Bunch of carrots
1 can Rumford's Baking Powder	1 can Rumford's Baking Powder
Nescafé instant coffee	*1 lb. Maxwell House Coffee (Drip Ground)*
2 cans Del Monte peaches	2 cans Del Monte peaches
5 lbs. potatoes	5 lbs. potatoes

Haire also demonstrated that housewives who projected negative personalities onto the owners of the instant coffee largely did not buy instant coffee themselves. The researcher concluded from these results that some motives, because they are socially unacceptable, exist below the level of verbalization, and that these motives can be assessed if approached indirectly. The shopping list technique was subsequently applied to explore what kinds of impressions are formed about people shopping for beer (Woodside, 1972), functional foods (Saher et al., 2004), and canned cat food (Reid & Buchanan, 1979).

4.2 Semantic Priming Task

In the area of social psychology, indirect attitude measures such as the affective priming paradigm (e.g., Fazio, Sanbonmatsu, Powell, & Kardes, 1986), the implicit association test (IAT; Greenwald, McGhee, & Schwaltz, 1998), and the extrinsic affective Simon task (EAST; De Houwer, 2003) are widely used as alternatives to direct measures. These indirect attitude measures are considered to infer cognitive processes indirectly based on performances on a reaction time task. The virtue of these techniques is that they are independent of a direct verbal report of the relevant topics being studied. Rather than asking participants directly about their attitudes on a certain topic, these techniques indirectly infer their attitudes by examining their response patterns (e.g., changes in response time and accuracy of response) towards stimuli related to the topic.

The affective priming task developed by Fazio et al. (1986) is one of the most widely applied techniques for investigating stereotypic attitudes. In this task, quickly presented affectively polarized prime words are followed by positive or negative target words and the subjects are required to evaluate the valence of the target as quickly and accurately as possible. The typically observed effect is the congruency or affective priming effect, qualified by a prime target valence interaction: facilitation is expected in case of valence congruence of prime and target (e.g., "love" + "friendship"), whereas valence incongruence (e.g., "disgust" + "happiness") results in longer response latencies compared with a baseline (i.e., a neutral prime). This technique is sometimes called a semantic priming task when semantic primes, rather than affective primes, are used (e.g., Macrae, Mitchell, & Pendry, 2002). Recently, affective/semantic priming paradigms have gradually come into use in studies on attitudes and preferences toward food and eating disorders (Czyzewska & Graham, 2008; Lamote, Hermans, Baeyens, & Eelen, 2004; Roef et al., 2005), but their application to food and eating stereotypes has yet to be explored.

Thus, we explored the feasibility of introducing indirect measures for the study of gender stereotypes towards food using a semantic priming paradigm (Kimura et al., 2009). In this study, 37 Japanese university students were primed with a food name and immediately after the priming, they were presented with a forename, as the target stimulus, and asked to decide whether the forename given was masculine or feminine (Fig. 1). As a result, the reaction time for the semantically congruent condition (i.e., a female forename presented after a feminine food prime, and a male forename presented after a masculine food prime; mean RT = 450 ms, SD = 47.6) was significantly shorter than that for the incongruent condition (i.e., a female forename presented after a masculine food prime, and a male forename presented after a feminine food prime; mean RT = 491 ms, SD = 65.3). These results suggest that reaction time in a semantic priming task provides a good reflection of the semantic association of masculinity or femininity with specific foods.

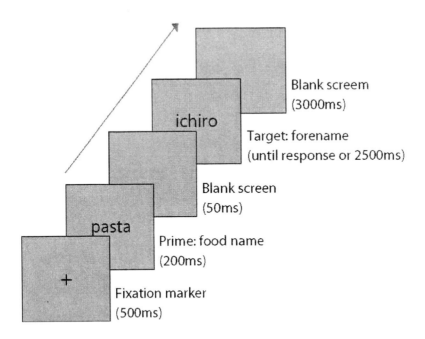

Figure 1. The time course of stimulus presentation in the semantic priming task. In this task, participants were primed with a food name (e.g., pasta) and immediately after the priming, they were presented with a forename (e.g., Ichiro) as the target stimulus, and asked to decide whether the forename given was feminine or masculine.

The research on stereotypes towards foods and eating has drawn growing interest, but is still in the developmental phase. To accelerate progress in this area, elaborated analysis on the social factors related to stereotypes towards foods and eating, such as culture, gender, and age is indispensable. Technical interventions for measuring such stereotypical attitudes towards foods and eating should be explored in the future. Indirect attitude measurements, as exemplified in the shopping list technique and the semantic priming tasks in this section provide effective tools in examining static and dynamic aspects of consumer stereotypes towards foods and eating.

5. CONCLUSION

In this chapter, we reviewed some brilliant findings on food-related stereotypes. These findings suggest that food-related stereotypes have a crucial impact on people's food selections and eating behaviors: People form biased beliefs about particular foods. These generalized beliefs about foods could further affect the personality and character of the eater, thus generating another facet of stereotype. Individuals assess and form opinions about others based on their eating behavior, and use food selections to manage how others view them. Understanding the social dynamics of food and eating could help us to better understand the social forces that influence people's eating behaviors.

ACKNOWLEDGMENTS

This work is supported in part by Grant-in-Aid for Scientific Research (B) from the Japan Society for Promotion of Science 21330148 awarded to T.O. and Y.W., 21330148 awarded to Y.W., and Grant-in-Aid for Young Scientists (B) from the Japan Society for Promotion of Science 22700775 awarded to A.K.

REFERENCES

Aarnio, K. & Lindeman, M. (2004). *Magical food and health beliefs: a portrait of believers and functions of the beliefs.* Appetite, 43, 65-74.

Amiraian, D. E., & Sobal, J. (2009). *Dating and eating. Beliefs about dating foods among university students.* Appetite, 53, 226-232.

Barker, M. E., Tandy, M., & Stookey, J. D. (1999). *How are consumers of low-fat and high-fat diets perceived by those with lower and higher fat intake?* Appetite, 33, 309-317.

Basow, S. A., & Kobrynowicz, D. (1993). *What is she eating? The effects of meal size on impressions of a female eater.* Sex Roles, 28, 335-344.

Boddy, C. (2005). *Projective techniques in market research: valueless subjectivity or insightful reality?* International Journal of Market Research, 47, 239-254.

Chaiken, S., & Pliner, P. (1987). *Women, but not men, are what they eat: The effect of meal size and gender on perceived femininity and masculinity.* Personality and Social Psychology Bulletin, 13, 166-176.

Chambers, S., Lobb, A., Butler, L., Harvey, K., & Traill, W. B. (2007). *Local, national and imported foods: A qualitative study.* Appetite, 49, 208-213.

Czyzewska, M., & Graham, R. (2008). *Implicit and explicit attitudes to high- an low-calorie food in females with different BMI status.* Eating Behaviors, 9, 303-312.

De Houwer, J. (2003). *The Extrinsic Affective Simon Task.* Experimental Psychology, 50, 77-85.

De Moura, S. L. (2007). *Determinants of food rejection amongst school children.* Appetite, 49, 716-719.

Fazio, R. H., Sanbonmatsu, D. M., Powell, M. C., & Kardes, F. R. (1986). *On the automatic activation of attitudes.* Journal of Personality and Social Psychology, 50, 229-238.

Frazer, J. G. (1922/1963). *The golden bough: A study in magic and religion.* New York: Maximillan.

Galli, E. (1973). *Some food customs and beliefs: in South Africa.* Nutrition and Food Science, 73, 5-7.

Garner, D. M., Garfinkel, P. E., & Bemis, K. M. (1982). *A multidimensional psychotherapy for anorexia nervosa. International* Journal of Eating Disorders, 1, 3–46.

Goffman, E. (1979). *Gender advertisements.* New York: Harper and Row.

Greenwald, A. G., Banaji, M. R., Rudman, L. A., Farnham, S. D., Nosek, B. A. & Mellott, D. S. (2002). *A unified theory of implicit attitudes, stereotypes, self-esteem, and self-concept.* Psychological Review, 109, 3-25.

Greenwald, A. G., McGhee, D. E., & Schwartz, J. L. K. (1998). *Measuring individual differences in implicit cognition: The Implicit Association Test.* Journal of Personality and Social Psychology, 74, 1464-1480.

Haire, M. (1950). *Projective techniques in marketing research.* The Journal of Marketing, 14, 649-656.

Hoogland, C. T., de Boer, J., & Boersema, J. J. (2007). *Food and sustainability: Do consumers recognize, understand and value on-package information on production standards?* Appetite, 49, 47-57.

Huselid, R.F., & Cooper, M..L. (1994). *Gender roles as mediators of sex differences in expressions of pathology.* Journal of Abnormal Psychology, 103, 595-603.

Kimura, A., Wada, Y., & Dan, I. (in press). *Gender-based food stereotypes among young Japanese. V. R. Preedy (Ed.) International Handbook of Behavior*, Diet and Nutrition. New York: Springer.

Kimura, A., Wada, Y., Goto, S., Tsuzuki, D., Cai, D., Oka, T., & Dan, I. (2009). *Implicit gender-based food stereotypes: Semantic priming experiments on young Japanese.* Appetite, **52**, 51-54.

Lamote, S., Hermans, D., Baeyens, F., & Eelen, P. (2004). *An exploration of affective priming as an indirect measure of food attitudes.* Appetite, 42, 279-286.

Lindeman, M., Keskivaara, P., & Roschier, M. (2000). *Assessment of magical beliefs about food and health.* Journal of Health Psychology, 5, 195-209.

Macrae, C. N., Mitchell, J. P., & Pendry, L. F. (2002). *What's in a forename? Cue familiarity and stereotypical thinking.* Journal of Experimental Social Psychology, 38, 186-193.

Megis, A. S. (1984). *Food, sex, and pollution. A New Guinea religion.* New Jersey: Rutgers University Press.

Mooney, K. M., De Tore, J., & Malloy, K. A. (1994). *Perceptions of women related to food choice.* Sex Roles, 31, 433-442.

Mooney, K. M. & Lorenz, E. (1997). *The effects of food and gender on interpersonal perceptions.* Sex Roles, 36, 639-653.

Nemeroff, C., & Rozin, P. (1989). *"You are what you eat": Applying the demand-free "impressions" technique to an unacknowledged belief.* Ethos, 17, 50-69.

Niva, M. (2007). *'All food affect health': Understandings of functional foods and healthy eating among health-oriented Finns.* Appetite, 48, 384-393.

Oakes, M. E. (2003). *Differences in judgments of food healthfulness by young and elderly women.* Food Quality and Preference, 14, 227-236.

Oakes, M. E. (2004). *Good foods gone bad: "infamous" nutrients diminish perceived vitamin and mineral content of food.* Appetite, 42, 273-278.

Oakes, M. E. (2005a). *Beauty or beast: Does stereotypical thinking about foods contribute to overeating?* Food Quality and Preference, 16, 447-454.

Oakes, M. E. (2005b). *Stereotypical thinking about foods and perceived capacity to promote weight gain.* Appetite, 44, 317-324.

Oakes, M. E. (2005c). *Bad company: the addition of sugar, fat, or salt reduces the perceived vitamin and mineral content of foods.* Food Quality and Preference, 16, 111-119.

Oakes, M. E., & Slotterback, C. S. (2001a). *What's in a name? A comparison of men's and women's judgements about food names and their nutrient contents.* Appetite, 36, 29-40.

Oakes, M. E., & Slotterback, C. S. (2001b). *Judgments of food healthfulness: food name stereotypes in adults over age 25.* Appetite, 37, 1-8.

Oakes, M. E., & Slotterback, C. S. (2005). *Too good to be true: does insensitivity and stereotypical thinking of foods' capacity to promote weight gain.* Food Quality and Preference, 16, 675-681.

Oakes, M. E., Sullivan K., & Slotterback, C. S. (2007). *A comparison of categorical beliefs about foods in children and young adults.* Food Quality and Preference, 18, 713-719.

Reid, L. N., & Buchanan, L. (1979). *A shopping list experiment of the impact of advertising on brand images.* Journal of Advertising, 8, 26-28.

Ricciardelli, L. A., Connor, J. P., Williams, R. J., & Young, R. M. (2001). *Gender stereotypes and high risk drinking among young women and men.* Drug and Alcohol Dependence, 61, 129-136.

Roef. A., Stapert, D., Isabella, L. A. S., Wolters, G., Wojciechowski, F., & Jansen, A. (2005). *Early associations with food in anorexia nervosa patients and obese people assessed in the affective priming paradigm.* Eating Behaviors, 6, 151-163.

Rozin, P. (1986). *Sweetness, sensuality, sin, safety, and socialization: some speculations.* In J. Dobbing (Ed.), Sweetness. New York: Springer-Verlag

Rozin, P., & Nemeroff, C. (1990). *The laws of sympathetic magic. A psychological analysis of similarity and contagion.* In J. W. Stiegler, R. A., Shweder, & G. Herdt (Eds.), Cultural Psychology. Essays on comparative human development. Cambridge: Cambridge University Press, pp.205-232.

Rozin, P., Ashmore, M., & Markwith, M. (1996). *Lay American conceptions of nutrition: does insensitivity, categorical thinking, contagion, and the monotonic mind.* Health Psychology, 15, 438-447.

Saher, M., Arvola, A., Lindeman, M., & Lähteenmäki, L. (2004). *Impressions of functional food consumers.* Appetite, 42, 79-89.

Stein, R. I., & Nemeroff, C. J. (1995). *Moral overtones of food: judgments of others based on what they eat.* Personality and Social Psychology Bulletin, 21, 480–490.

Vartanian, L. R., Herman, C. P., & Polivy, J. (2007). *Consumption stereotypes and impression management: How you are what to eat.* Appetite, 48, 265-277.

Wansink, B., Payne, C. R., & North, J. (2007). *Fine as North Dakota wine: Sensory expectations and intake of consumption food.* Physiology & Behavior, 90, 712-716.

Wells, W. D., Andriuli, F. J., Goi, F. J., & Seader, S. (1957). *An adjective check list for the study of "product personality".* Journal of Applied Psychology, 41, 317–319.

Williams, R. J. & Ricciardelli, L. A. (1999). *Gender congruence in confirmatory and compensatory drinking.* Journal of Psycholog, 133, 323-331.

Woodside, A. G. (1972). *A shopping list experiment of beer brand images.* Journal of Applied Psychology, 56, 512-513.

Young, M. E., Mizzau, M., Mai, N. T., Sirisegaram, A., & Wilson, M. (2009). *Food for thought. What you eat depends on your sex and eating companions.* Appetite, 53, 268-271.

In: Psychology of Stereotypes
Editor: Eleanor L. Simon
ISBN: 978-1-61761-463-7
©2011 Nova Science Publishers, Inc.

Chapter 14

GENDER STEREOTYPES AND MENTAL ROTATION: THE ROLE OF SELF-BELIEF

Angelica Moè

Department of General Psychology – University of Padua – Italy

ABSTRACT

A large body of evidence has shown male superiority in performance of a mental rotation task, notably the MRT proposed by Vandenberg and Kuse (1978). The difference is considerable, males scoring as much as one standard deviation higher than females. Many reasons have been put forward for this underscoring by females: biological, cultural, strategic and motivational. Males are favoured by lateral specialisation, early familiarisation with spatial tasks and toys, use of holistic strategies, and an incremental theory of spatial abilities. Recently, gender stereotyping has been considered to be one of the factors affecting test accuracy, particularly for females. As a result of widely held stereotyping, females are thought to be less able than males in spatial tasks such as mental rotation. Awareness of this stereotype can intimidate females and increase theirexpectation of performing poorly, this indeed having negative affect on performance. Research examining these male/female differences and the underlying causes is reviewed and suggestions made for channels of future research.

INTRODUCTION

The Mental Rotation Task

Imagine you have to mentally retain and rotate stimuli such as those shown in Figure 1.

What you are being asked to do is a typical mental rotation task: consider the target on the left and select the two correct rotations from the four shapes on the right. The test most commonly used to assess this ability is the Mental Rotation Test (MRT) developed by Vandenberg and Kuse (1978). This consists of viewing 20 target objects made up of assembled cubes, depicted as 3D objects in 2D space (the paper or computer screen), followed by four similar objects differing either in degree of rotation or as mirror images. In a set time (6 minutes), respondents are asked to identify the two figures that are identical to the target but rotated in space. In the example of Figure 1, the correct answer is '1' (first alternative) and '3' (third). Response '1' is easier given the smaller degree of rotation. One point is assigned if both answers are correct, otherwise score is zero (for no correct answers, just one correct, missing answer). Maximum score is thus 20.

Figure 1. Sample item from the MRT.

The ability to mentally rotate has very important implications in education. It predicts success in topics such as geometry, mathematics, chemistry and physics (e.g., Kirby & Boulter, 1999; Linn & Petersen, 1986). It can consequently affect career choice. Moreover, it helps in performance of everyday spatial activities, such as orienting in unfamiliar places or finding a route on a map.

Males Perform Better than Females: Why?

A vast body of research has documented male superiority in performing the MRT (Linn, & Petersen, 1985) with males scoring as much as one standard deviation higher than females (Voyer, Voyer & Bryden, 1995).

Many genetic explanations have been put forward, for instance hemispheric specialisation (Howard, Fenwick, Brown & Norton, 1992), prenatal brain organisation (e.g., Burton, Henninger & Hafetz, 2005) and hormonal factors (Driscoll, Hamilton, Yeo, Brooks & Sutherland, 2005). Use of fMRI has revealed gender differences in activation. With both verbal and spatial tasks females show bilateral activation, while males activate mainly the right-hand areas just for the spatial tasks (Jordan, Wuestenberg, Heinze, Peters & Jaencke, 2002).

However, alternative, less deterministic reasons have recently been put forward to fully explain the gender differences: strategies used, experience with spatial tasks, schooling, cultural factors, motivational aspects such as confidence or endorsed implicit theory, and socio-cognitive factors such as stereotyping. Males prefer strategies that are holistic (rotating the full stimuli) rather than analytic (counting cubes or rotating one segment at time); the former has proven best: time is reduced and accuracy raised (Pezaris & Casey, 1991). In fact, male advantage over females is even greater under time constraints, as a result of more guessing (Voyer, Rodgers & McCormick, 2004). Males tend to do more sport/play more games involving spatial processes than females, which helps them achieve better mental rotation scores (Quaiser-Pohl, Geiser, & Lehmann, 2006). The number of maths courses taken (generally higher for males) correlates with mental rotation abilities, and improvement in mental rotation ability is higher during the school year than after the summer break (Baenninger & Newcombe, 1995). From childhood, males play with toys and have preference for games involving spatial processing more than females (Baron-Cohen, 2003), which helps them perform better on tasks based on spatial processing. At least in western cultures, from a very young age, females are told they have low ability in tasks requiring spatial processing such as orienting or establishing distances (Devlin, 2001). This renders them less confident than males of being able to perform well on spatial tasks, this in turn having negative effects on MRT score (Cooke-Simpson & Voyer, 2007). Finally, an interactionist view has been proposed, according to which biology and experience are intertwined. One of the best known is that put forward by Casey (1996). There are females with a developmental tendency towards spatial tasks who seek experience with male toys, games, activities. The high practice level together with innate ability allows them toscore higher in mental rotation test than females, who from the outset showed no particular aptitudes where mental representation of space is involved (Casey, 1996).

EFFECTS DUE TO GENDER STEREOTYPES

The Stereotype Threat Explanation

Recently, a new suggestion based on fear of confirming a widely held stereotype has been put forward to explain the difficulties females have in mental rotation. This fear is termed stereotype threat and arises when a minority member is performing a task, aware of belonging to a group for which a negative stereotype is held: I am female, and males are considered to be better at the task in hand.

This stereotype threat has been studied chiefly in the realm of mathematics (e.g., Spencer, Steele & Quinn, 1999; Steele, 1997) and in investigations of gender and ethnicity as source of stigma. Asking for gender before performance of a test presented as diagnostic of maths ability is sufficient to raise the threat of demonstrating oneself as less able than the counterpart (male). Stating in the instructions that 'males do better than females on this kind of test' makes females afraid of confirming the stereotype. When it arises, this fear affects performance negatively through various different mechanisms: increased anxiety, intrusive thoughts, shift towards caution, evaluation apprehension, low performance expectations and disengagement (Maass & Cadinu, 2003; Steele & Aronson, 1995). Moreover, non-motivational factors such as disruptive mental load, measured through decrease in heart rate variability (Croizet, Després, Gauzins, Huguet, Leyens & Méot, 2004), and working memory depletion (Schmader & Johns, 2003) have been shown to contribute to explaining the decrease in performance under the threat. Increase in blood pressure (and index of fear and anger) has been observed as a psycho-physiological correlate of the stereotype threat (Blascovich, Spencer, Quinn & Steele, 2001). In fact, the stereotype threat induces negative affect that can interfere in performance of cognitively-demanding tasks.

For a female, simply being asked to perform a task in a stereotyped domain (maths test) together with two males, rather than two females is sufficient to activate the fear of confirming the stereotype, resulting in a fall in performance. The more males involved, the greater the effect. The same effect does not apply for males (Inzlicht & Ben-Zeev, 2000).

In this respect the stereotype threat concerns minority members such as females and the elderly. The problem is in their beliefs and the way they accept their influence. In other words, it is the environment that suggests certain stereotypes, but individuals can endorse these to different extents, depending on how far they identify as members of the target group.

Stereotype Threat and Mental Rotation: Bad and Good News

To what extent can the stereotype threat be a factor in explaining the gender differences in mental rotation? Below is a review of the few (just four) related studies carried out to date (based on MRT) – these are summarised in Table 1. A fifth study is included, although the authors (Massa, Mayer & Bohon, 2005) used the embedded figures test to measure spatial ability (rather than the MRT). Participants were required to find a simple shape concealed within a complex pattern. To do so they had to understand the relations of objects in space and manipulate them. Instructions consisted in presenting the test as measuring a skill either consistent (empathy) or inconsistent (spatial ability) with female gender role beliefs. Results showed that instructions consistent with the gender-role belief raised performance in the spatial ability test used. Females endorsing female gender roles performed better when receiving empathy instructions, females endorsing male gender roles doing better when receiving spatial instructions. The same effects were not found with males.

McGlone and Aronson (2006) explored effects due to gender or private school attendance identity, primed through questions asked before the MRT task: MRT performance was found to be higher for the groups focused on positive identity (private school for females and gender for males) suggesting high expectations. Thinking about their identity as attending a high-reputation school freed females from stereotype risk ('It does not matter if I am female; I have been selected to attend an important school'). This set of beliefs, linked to identity and aroused before taking the test, affected female performance until this reached that of males.

Wraga, Duncan, Jacobs, Helt and Church (2006) used an imagined self rotation task. Females were given this task on the basis of instructions that it measured perspective-taking, a task in which females outperform males (experimental condition), or were given neutral information (control group). Results showed that females in the experimental condition (positive stereotype) scored higher than females in control, but did not reach male performance levels when assessed in a preliminary phase of the research. The same paradigm was applied in a second experiment with males. Results showed a drop in performance for the group told that females do better on the task, because it measures a female ability. Performance of males receiving a stereotype message favouring females was the same as females having the same message. It seems that the 'experiential factors' (i.e., the instructions) really do affect performance and help minority members (females) perform as well as the majority.

Moè and Pazzaglia (2006) run two experiments with same-sex gender groups giving instructions confirming or disconfirming the widely held stereotype of men superiority in spatial tasks. First the female sample was considered. Results showed an increase with the instruction 'females are better at this task' and a decrease with the opposite instruction, 'males are better'. The male sample was then considered. Performance improved for the instruction 'males do better' and decreased with instructions stressing that 'females do better'. In addition, these authors assessed how far participants believe in stereotypes about spatial abilities, splitting the whole sample into two different sub-samples: those believing in male superiority in spatial tasks (e.g., finding a route on a map) vs. those believing there is no difference. Results showed that females believing there is no (or only a small) gender difference in spatial abilities were not negatively affected by instructions stressing male superiority in this type of task. In other words, beliefs *a priori* interacted with those suggested by instructions given.

Moè (2009a) added a further instruction to that of male/female superiority, namely task ease/difficulty. Comparison was made of six groups corresponding to the instructions: males are better-easy task, males are better-difficult task, females are better-easy task, females are better-difficult task, control condition-easy task, control condition-difficult task. Females were found to be unaffected by instructions on easiness or difficulty, performing as well as males when instructed that 'females are better at this task', but disadvantaged in the other conditions (males are better and control). Males improved performance when instructed that males are better, but only when expecting an easy task or in the control condition when expecting a difficult task.

Table 1. Stereotype threat and MRT.

Authors	Sample	Results
Massa, Mayer and Bohon (2005) *	237 female students (Exp 1a) 65 female students (Exp1b) 99 male students (Exp 2)	Improved performance when test presented as measuring a skill consistent with the gender role belief. In this condition, females perform as well as males. Performance on the spatial task correlates with motivation. Effects do not apply with males.
McGlone and Aronson (2006)	45 females, 45 males	Increase in performance when priming positive social identity: gender for males, private school attendance for females.
Wraga, Duncan, Jacobs, Helt and Church (2006)	30 females 20 males	A positive stereotype helps females perform better than a control group. Female performance is raised but does not reach that of males (note that participants imagined self-rotation around the shape, not 'classical' mental rotation). For males, fall in performance with the message 'females are better'. In this condition, females and males scores are equal.
Moè and Pazzaglia (2006)	107 females (Exp 1) 90 males (Exp 2)	Female MRT performance improves after instruction 'females are better' and falls after instruction 'males are better' (less for those not believing in male superiority in spatial tasks). The reverse is true for males. With the instruction 'females are better', females score as high as males.
Moè (2009a)	71 females, 81 males	Females improve MRT performance if instructed that 'females are better', up to male score levels. Males improve performance if instructed that 'males are better' and expecting an easy task, or in the control condition and expecting a difficult task.

* a spatial ability test other than MRT was used

Table 1 reveals a number of remarkable or even surprising findings.

Overall, stereotype threat effects can be observed, but, under certain conditions, a) females can improve performance or avoid a fall; b) males too can be affected by instructions inducing them to doubt their own ability to tackle the task.

Females improve when encouraged to believe they can perform better than males, when primed positively, or when engaging in tasks presented as belief-congruent. This 'lack of threat' leads to increase in performance up to male levels. Males show a drop in performance when explicitly told that 'females are better' and no further instruction is given. When instructions about characteristics of the task are given, together with those on gender, no significant drop in performance occurs.

One of the factors distinguishing males and females is 'difficulty' (Moè, 2009a). Is being told that a task is difficult beneficial or detrimental to performance? Data suggest that the answer depends on gender. Males are affected by instructions on test ease/difficulty, while females are unaffected. This finding is very interesting when considered together with a study carried out in a non-gender-stereotypical domain: recall of passage (Moè, 2009b). In this situation, there is no suggestion of associated stereotype, and women are affected by having received instruction on the ease or difficulty of the task they face.

Thus, in a neutral domain, task characteristics contribute to expectation, that, in turn, affects effort expended in attempting to do well. Instead, when there is perception of a threat to personal integrity (a possible definition of stereotype), only personal information ('you have the ability…' 'you can succeed…') is included in forming expectation and used to allocate resources or disengage from the task. It will be fruitful for future studies to address these postulated mechanisms, examining not just effects on performance but motivational aspects.

The 'bad' news is that if nothing is said in a task context, females are affected by the fear of confirming the stereotype according to which females are poorer than males at mental rotation.

The 'good' news is that priming a positive identity, presenting the test as evaluating a gender-congruent ability, or suggesting a positive stereotype, are all ways of raising female performance up to that reached by males.

Do Stereotypes Represent Reality? The Case of Mental Rotation

Stereotypes often assume that there are differences among groups, gender, ethnicity and so on that are thought to exist, but objectively do not. For instance in maths, there is evidence that males do not perform better than females. If a difficult maths test is presented with instructions stressing that it is not sensitive to gender differences, female performance equals that of males (Spencer et al., 1999). In fact, in maths females obtain higher marks than men, not the reverse (Kenney-Benson, Pomerantz, Ryan, & Patrick, 2006). However, they themselves think they lack ability in this field (Ruble, Greulich, Pomerantz, & Gochberg, 1993; Stipek & Gralinski, 1991), particularly in contexts outside school (e.g., objective tests, experiments) where the fear of not being able (i.e., the stereotype threat) gives disadvantage (Aronson, Quinn, & Spencer, 1998).

In this respect, mental rotation represents a particular situation. Females really do underscore if there is no "priming". The stereotype appears to reflect an objectively demonstrated reality. However, just reversing the situation, i.e., making females believe they are as good as males (or better), stressing a positive identity or priming congruent gender-beliefs, frees them and allows them to improve performance, even up to the level of males.

CONCLUSIONS

Theoretical Implications and Avenues for Future Research

Generally speaking, any test performance is affected by at least two broad categories of factors and their interactions:

i.   the participants' characteristics (these can be determined to some extent by biological constraints);
ii. the participants' interpretations of the situation and of the meaning the test has for them (demonstrating ability on the test, being successful, confirming a stereotype, etc.).

In this respect, others taking the test along with the participant, who is presenting the test, where it is performed, how it is presented, plus all the possible situational factors play a substantial role in explaining not only individual differences but also success.

Research in other domains has shown that even dominant groups such as white males can be affected by stereotype messages emphasising female abilities (e.g., Brown & Josephs, 1999; Leyens, Désert, Croizet, & Darcis, 2000). The same stereotype susceptibility has also been found with the MRT (typically male).This result is intriguing: effects depend not only on the specific task (considered masculine or feminine) or existence of objective data confirming the occurrence of gender gaps (e.g., MRT), but also on the messages (instructions) given. Males told that 'females do better' or 'females are better' show fall in performance. It may be that the underling mechanisms differ for males and females, as discussed earlier (Moè & Pazzaglia, 2006), but effects on performance are similar: a drop occurs when the out-group is presented as scoring higher or being more talented in the task they have to carry out.

In addition, it has been found with maths that amount of improvement in performance after a message stressing positive stereotype is about half the fall resulting from a similar but negative message, stressing negative stereotype (e.g., Cadinu, Maass, Frigerio, Impigliazzo & Latinozzi, 2002). It appears easier to undermine than to improve performance through messages reminding about common stereotypes. Results with the MRT are less clear-cut. There can be improvement (Moè & Pazzaglia, 2006) or simply no decrease (Moè, 2009a). This means that the variance is explained not only by the wording of the message, but by the meaning it can prompt in the belief system of people receiving it – indeed, it has been observed that instruction effects also depend on congruency with previously held beliefs (Massa, Mayer & Bohon 2005).

Summarising, genetic explanations of the female underperformance in mental rotation are not denied, but cultural-social-beliefs rooted factors also play a role in explaining the gender gap. The stereotype threat hypothesis is confirmed. The fear of failing and confirming the low achievement stigma affects the way females approach the MRT and consequently their performance, although this cannot be the only explanation. A combination of genetic and socialisation theories can explain at best the complex phenomena of gender differences (McGillicuddy-De Lisi & De Lisi, 2002).

In the absence of alternative arguments, there is a general tendency to explain gender differences in performancedue to genetic rather than experiential causes. When other explanations are put forward (e.g., cultural factors, stereotype threat) female performance improves (Dar-Nimrod and Heine, 2006). Future studies should therefore consider not only effects due to instructions given (females underscore, males underscore, no gender difference), but also those due to the explanations (given experimentally or held by the participants) of these gender differences (if any). As regards maths, it is probable that even for mental rotation, believing that the cause is genetic lowers performance. Instead, believing that the gender gap can be maintained (or otherwise) by experiential and above all controllable factors should give minority members more chance of improving.

Given that the stereotype threat contributes to the female disadvantage in mental rotation, any attempt at alleviating or even reversing (why not?) this disruptive belief is welcoming. The following section reviews strategies designed to tackle the stereotype threat (and hopefully win the battle).

Strategies for Overcoming the Stereotype Threat and having Success on Mental Rotation Tasks

To lighten the feeling of being "less talented" (or that others think so), a range of strategies or techniques can be employed: the best include teaching the stereotype, focusing on positively-evaluated identities, self-affirmation, and holding an incremental theory about target abilities. Each is presented in the following, along with empirical demonstration of effectiveness, mainly drawn from the realm of maths, but speculatively useful in all domains, including mental rotation.

First is teaching. One strategy – perhaps counterintuitive – for combating the stereotype threat is to 'teach about it'. Johns, Schmader and Martens (2005) explained to a mixed-sex group that anxiety arising in performing a math task was not due to lack of ability, but to a common stereotype positing that females perform worse than males in maths. They found that females in this 'teaching intervention' condition did as well as males. Instead, females in the control condition ('you are completing a standardised test for studying gender differences in maths performance') scored lower than males and lower than females in the teaching intervention condition. Knowing that stereotyping is the reason for underperformance is a way of externalising anxiety. In turn, externalising gives inner control that affects effort and engagement, and aids good performance. Prior knowledge of the effects of the stereotype can then mitigate its influence on performance.

The second way to combat the negative effects of the stereotype threat is to focus on a social identity (ascribed or achieved) for which there are positive expectations. As shown earlier in this chapter, this has been demonstrated by McGlone and Aronson (2006) for an achieved identity (attending a private school with strict selection criteria). Shih, Pittinsky and Ambady (1999) studied what happens in maths with the ascribed identity of Asians rather than females. Before taking a maths test, participants were asked some information that gave either gender or Asian identity relevance. Performance dropped when the female identity was stressed but was unaffected when there was a reminder about ethnicity. Keeping focus on positive identities reduces negative affect, in general, and anxiety, in particular (these hampering good performance in a stereotypical masculine domain).

However, a degree of caution should be exercised: even if a message suggesting a positive stereotype generally works, it can at times lead to a fall in performance by building concerns about confirming the high expectations. If focus is on self-confidence, as in the research of Shih, Pittinsky and Ambady (1999), a positive stereotype will favour performance. The effect is known as stereotype lift (Walton & Cohen, 2003) and has been observed in the studies reviewed in this chapter for females and males instructed that their own gender has been proven to perform better. Instead, if the focus is on how people demonstrate they perform, then there is increased likelihood of 'choking under pressure', and therefore concern at not being as good as others (not themselves) expect. Thus, perceiving (high) expectations from others can lead to a fall in performance (Cheryan, & Bodenhausen, 2000), while having personal expectations raises performance. Hence, social identity can be a vector for stereotype threat occurrence as well an antidote – performance actually depends on the specific identity and on how far a person really believes in it.

A third way of combating the stereotype threat is use of self-affirmation. Developed by Sherman, Nelson and Steele (2000), this technique requires participants to rank 11 'characteristics and values' such as creativity, social skills and physical attractiveness, and to write about an episode when the first characteristic proved important for them and explainwhy they ranked it top. In the 'no affirmation' condition, participants are asked to consider the 9th listed characteristic and again describe a situation, this time where it was found to be unimportant for self-identity, and to explain why they ranked it low as a value. Martens, Johns, Greenberg and Schimel (2006) found that using this way of maintaining self-integrity and sense of self-worth raised both motivation and performance: self-affirmation improved MRT performance of females under stereotype threat up to male levels. The stereotype threat acts negatively on the global sense of self-integrity, and self-affirmation contrasts this mechanism. Prior to taking a test, thinking about oneself as a person of value is sufficient to reduce anxiety and free up cognitive resources that can be used to perform the task in hand as well as possible.

Fourth, teaching an incremental theory, i.e., encouraging a view of intelligence (or at least of the ability tested) as malleable (Dweck, 1999), and believing that improvement is possible free from fear of failure, and alleviate negative effects due to stereotype threat. In a study of school achievement, participants instructed to conceive their abilities as developing skills gained higher grades and showed greater enjoyment than participants holding an entity view according to which abilities are entities that cannot be increased (Aronson, Fried & Good, 2002). In mental rotation, the more females believe in an incremental theory of male tasks the more they engage in seeking and adopting the best strategies to solve the MRT, gaining higher scores than females holding a less incremental view (Moè, Meneghetti & Cadinu, 2009).

Finally, exposure to positive role models (Marx& Roman, 2002; McIntyre, Paulson & Lord, 2003) and encouraging the expectation of succeeding by stressing in-group skills in specific tasks (Moè & Pazzaglia, 2006; Wraga et al., 2006) are further ways of transforming these 'positive thinking' modalities into 'positive results'.

Concluding Remarks

The mental rotation is a task where gender differences are undeniably a reality. Even so, positive effects of positive stereotyping have been found, notwithstanding all the biological, cultural and strategic constraints favouring high male performance. We can thus draw the optimistic conclusion that we are more than just inherited genes at work, expression of the culture we live in and were raised from, or demonstration that good strategies and hard work are the way to success. We are also what we believe in.

REFERENCES

Aronson, J., Fried, C. B., & Good, C. (2002). *Reducing the effects of stereotype threat on African American college students by shaping theories of intelligence.* Journal of Experimental Social Psychology, 38, 113–125.

Aronson, J., Quinn, D. M., & Spencer, S. J. (1998). *Stereotype threat and the academic underperformance of minorities and women.* In J. K. Swim & C. Stangor (Eds.), Prejudice: The target's perspective (pp. 83-103). San Diego, CA: Academic Press.

Baenninger, M., & Newcombe, N. (1995). *Environmental input to the development of sex-related differences in spatial and mathematical ability.* Learning and Individual Differences, 7, 363-379.

Baron-Cohen, S. (2003). *The essential difference. Men, women and the extreme male brain.* Allan Lane: Penguin Books.

Blascovich, J., Spencer, S. J., Quinn, D. M., & Steele, C. M. (2001). *African Americans and high blood pressure: The role of stereotype threat.* Psychological Science, 12, 225-229.

Brown, R. P., & Josephs, R. A. (1999). *A burden of proof: Stereotype relevance and gender differences in math performance.* Journal of Personality and Social Psychology, 76, 246-257.

Burton, L., Henninger, D., & Hafetz, J. (2005). *Gender differences in mental rotation, verbal fluency and SAT scores to finger length ratios as hormonal indexes.* Developmental Neuropsychology, 28, 493-505.

Cadinu, M., Maass, A., Frigerio, S., Impigliazzo, L., & Latinozzi, S. (2002). *Stereotype threat: The effect of expectancy on performance.* European Journal of Social Psychology, 33, 267–285.

Casey, M. B. (1996). *Understanding individual differences in spatial ability with females: A nature/nurture interactionist framework.* Developmental Review, 16, 241–260.

Cheryan, S., & Bodenhausen, G. V. (2000). *When positive stereotypes threaten intellectual performance: The psychological hazards of "model minority" status.* Psychological Science, 11(5), 399–402.

Cooke-Simpson, A., & Voyer, D. (2007). *Confidence and gender differences on the mental rotations test.* Learning and Individual Differences, 17, 181–186.

Croizet, J. C., Després, G., Gauzins, M. E., Huguet, P., Leyens, J. P., & Méot, A. (2004). *Stereotype threat undermines intellectual performance by triggering disruptive mental load.* Personality and Social Psychology Bulletin, 30(6), 721–731.

Dar-Nimrod, I., & Heine, S. J. (2006). *Exposure to scientific theories affects women's math performance*. Science, 314, 435.

Devlin, A. S. (2001). *Mind and maze. Spatial cognition and environmental behavior.*Westport, CT: Praeger Publishers.

Driscoll, I., Hamilton, D. E., Yeo, R. A., Brooks, W. M., & Sutherland, R. J. (2005). *Virtual navigation in humans: The impact of age, sex, and hormones on place learning.* Hormones and Behavior, 47, 326–335.

Dweck, C. S. (1999). *Self-theories: their role in motivation, personality, and development.* Ann Arbor, M. I.: Psychology Press.

Howard, R., Fenwick, P., Brown, D., & Norton, R. (1992). *Relationship between CNV asymmetries and individual differences in cognitive performance, personality and gender.* International Journal of Psychophysiology, 13, 191–197.

Inzlicht, M., & Ben-Zeev, T. (2000). *A threatening intellectual environment: Why females are susceptible to experiencing problem-solving deficits in the presence of males.* Psychological Science, 11, 365–371.

Johns, M., Schmader, T., & Martens, A. (2005). *Knowing is half the battle. Teaching stereotype threat as a means of improving women's math performance.* Psychological Science, 16, 175-179.

Jordan, K., Wuestenberg, T., Heinze, H. J., Peters, M., & Jaencke, L. (2002). *Women and men exhibit different cortical activation patterns during mental rotation tasks.* Neuropsychologia, 40, 2397–2408.

Kenney-Benson G. A., Pomerantz E. M., Ryan A. M., & Patrick H. (2006). *Sex differences in math performance: The role of children's approach to schoolwork.* Developmental Psychology, 42, 11-26.

Kirby, J. R., & Boulter, D. R. (1999). *Spatial ability and transformational geometry.* European Journal of Psychology of Education, 14, 283-294.

Leyens, J. P, Désert, M., Croizet, J. C., & Darcis, C. (2000). *Stereotype threat: Are lower status and history of stigmatization preconditions of stereotype threat ?* Personality and Social Psychology Bulletin, 26, 1189-1199.

Linn, M. C., & Petersen, A. C. (1985). *Emergence and characterization of sex differences in spatial ability: A meta-analysis.* Child Development, 56, 1479-1498.

Linn, M. C., & Petersen, A. C. (1986). *A meta-analysis of gender differences in spatial ability: Implications for mathematics and science achievement.* In S. Hyde & M.C. Linn (Eds.), The psychology of gender (pp. 67-101). Baltimore: Johns Hopkins Univ. Press.

Maass, A., & Cadinu, M. (2003). *Stereotype threat: When minority members underperform.* European Review of Social Psychology, 14, 243–275.

Martens, A., Johns, M., Greenberg, J., & Schimel, J. (2006). *Combating stereotype threat: The effect of self-affirmation on women's intellectual performance.* Journal of Experimental Social Psychology, 42, 236–243.

Marx, D. M., & Roman, J. S. (2002). *Female role models: Protecting women's math performance.* Personality and Social Psychology Bulletin, 28, 1183-1193.

Massa, L. J., Mayer, R. E., & Bohon, L. M. (2005). *Individual differences in gender role beliefs influence spatial ability test performance.* Learning and Individual Differences, 15, 99–111.

McGlone, M., & Aronson, J. (2006). *Stereotype threat, identity salience, and spatial reasoning.* Journal of Applied Developmental Psychology, 27, 486-493.

McGillicuddy-De Lisi, A. V., & De Lisi, R. (2002). *Biology, society, and behavior: The development of sex differences in cognition.* Greenwich, CT: Ablex/Greenwood.

McIntyre, R. B., Paulson, R. M., & Lord, C. G. (2003). *Alleviating women's mathematics stereotype threat through salience of group achievements.* Journal of Experimental Social Psychology, 39, 83–90.

Moè, A. (2009a). *Are males always better than females in mental rotation ? Exploring a gender belief explanation.* Learning and Individual Differences, 19(1), 21-27.

Moè, A. (2009b). *Expectations and recall of texts: The more able–more difficult effect.* Learning and Individual Differences, 19, 609-614.

Moè, A., Meneghetti, C., & Cadinu, M. (2009). *Women and mental rotation: Incremental theory and spatial strategy use enhance performance.* Personality and Individual Differences, 46(2), 187-191.

Moè, A., & Pazzaglia, F. (2006). *Following the instructions! Effects of gender beliefs in mental rotation.* Learning and Individual Differences, 16, 369–377.

Pezaris, E., & Casey, M. B. (1991). *Girls who use "masculine" problem-solving strategies on a spatial task: Proposed genetic and environmental factors.* Brain and Cognition, 17, 1–22.

Quaiser-Pohl, C., Geiser, C., & Lehmann, W. (2006). *The relationship between computer-game preference, gender, and mental rotation ability.* Personality and Individual Differences, 40, 609-619.

Ruble, D. N., Greulich, J., Pomerantz, E. M., & Gochberg, B. (1993). *The role of gender-related processes in the development of sex differences in self-evaluation and depression.* Journal of Affective Disorders, 29, 97-128.

Schmader, T., & Johns, M. (2003). *Converging evidence that stereotype threat reduces working memory capacity.* Journal of Personality and Social Psychology, 85, 440–452.

Sherman, D. A. K., Nelson, L. D., & Steele, C. M. (2000). *Do messages about health risks threaten the self ? Increasing the acceptance of threatening health messages via self-affirmation.* Personality and Social Psychology Bulletin, 26, 1046-1058.

Shih, M., Pittinsky, T. L., & Ambady, N. (1999). *Stereotype susceptibility: Identity salience and shifts in quantitative performance.* Psychological Science, 10(1), 80–83.

Spencer, S., Steele, C. M., & Quinn, D. (1999). *Stereotype threat and women's math performance.* Journal of Experimental Social Psychology, 35, 4–28.

Steele, C. M. (1997). *A threat in the air: How stereotypes shape intellectual identity and performance.* American Psychologist, 52, 613–629.

Steele, C. M., & Aronson, J. (1995). *Stereotype threat and the intellectual performance of African Americans.* Journal of Personality and Social Psychology, 69, 797–811.

Stipek, D. J., & Gralinski, J. H. (1991). *Gender differences in children's achievement related beliefs and emotional responses to success and failure in mathematics.* Journal of Educational Psychology, 83, 361–371.

Vandenberg, S. G., & Kuse, A. R. (1978*). Mental rotations: A group test of three-dimensional spatial visualization.* Perceptual & Motor Skills, 47, 599-604.

Voyer, D., Rodgers, M. A., & McCormick, P. A. (2004). *Timing conditions and the magnitude of gender differences on the mental rotations test.* Memory and Cognition, 32, 72–82.

Voyer, D., Voyer, S., & Bryden, M. P. (1995). *Magnitude of sex differences in spatial abilities: A meta-analysis and consideration of critical variables.* Psychological Bulletin, 117, 250-270.

Walton, G. M., & Cohen, G. L. (2003). *Stereotype lift.* Journal of Experimental Social Psychology, 39(5), 456–467.

Wraga, M., Duncan, L., Jacobs, E. C., Helt, M., & Church, J. (2006). *Stereotype susceptibility narrows the gender gap in imagined self-rotation performance.* Psychonomic Bulletin & Review, 13(5), 813-819.

In: Psychology of Stereotypes
Editor: Eleanor L. Simon

ISBN: 978-1-61761-463-7
©2011 Nova Science Publishers, Inc.

Chapter 15

WHEN STEREOTYPES BECOME LIFE THREATENING: KNOWLEDGE AND ATTITUDES ABOUT HIV/AIDS AMONG OLDER WOMEN AND THE HEALTH CARE PROVIDERS WHO TREAT THEM

Jennifer Hillman[*] and Molly Beiler
The Pennsylvania State University, Berks College, Reading Pennsylvania, USA

ABSTRACT

According to the Centers for Disease Control (2005), approximately 15 percent of all new HIV/AIDS cases are among those aged 50 and older. The greatest increase in infection appears among older Black and Latino women who contract the virus through heterosexual contact. With the rapid growth of the older adult population in the next decade, it becomes critical that stereotypes regarding elderly sexuality are examined and dispelled. Older women are often subject to ageism; many health care providers fail to ask appropriate questions regarding their sexual health and remain unaware of unique age and gender specific risk factors. Stereotypes to be examined include beliefs that older women are asexual and have no need for HIV/AIDS education. Additional barriers to prevention include older women's lack of experience with condoms, culture specific factors including machismo, and stigma and discrimination toward older adults living with HIV/AIDS. This chapter will focus on knowledge and attitudes about HIV/AIDS among elderly women and health care providers, and will provide relevant clinical and public policy recommendations.

INTRODUCTION

Imagine that older adults were facing an epidemic from a life threatening, but preventable, viral infection. Also imagine that this virus was increasingly infecting women,

---

[*] Please address correspondence to: Jennifer Hillman, Penn State Berks, PO Box 7009, Reading, PA or via e-mail at JLH35@psu.edu

including women of color, and that health care providers routinely failed to test these patients for the presence of the virus or educate them about ways to protect themselves. Unfortunately, this scenario represents the current state of affairs regarding HIV/AIDS among older women in the United States. Among older women, defined here as those aged 50 and older, based upon the Centers for Disease Control's (CDC) demographic criteria (2006), HIV/AIDS typically is contracted among older women primarily via heterosexual contact with HIV infected partners and through IV drug use. Various reports indicate that 11 to 15% of all new cases of HIV/AIDS are among adults over the age of 50, and half of all individuals with HIV/AIDS are African-American or Hispanic (CDC, 2005; 2007). Additional reports from the CDC indicate that women over the age of 50 are increasingly likely to become infected, and older African-American and Hispanic women are 12 and 5 times more likely, respectively, to become infected with HIV/AIDS than older White women (CDC, 2005). This increase in infection among women over 50, particularly among women of color, is staggering. A combination of ignorance and ageism among various health care professionals allows the virus to continue to spread in this typically ignored yet at risk population. Combating this problem is essential, as espoused by the Administration on Aging's *Older Adults and Mental Health: Issues and Opportunities* report (2001), in which a need is called for increased attention to prevention and intervention, interdisciplinary collaboration, and the special needs of older women and minority group members.

Common stereotypes older women face in our society that obscure their increased risk for HIV/AIDS infection include beliefs that older women are asexual and they do not need to use condoms due to menopause (i.e., their inability to become pregnant). Additional barriers to prevention and diagnosis include cultural specific factors and general fears among older adults that HIV can be spread by hugging or kissing. To complicate matters, public policy recommendations from the CDC mandate routine HIV testing, but only for adults up to the age of 64 (CDC, 2006). The present chapter is designed to review general epidemiology of HIV/AIDS among older adult women, focusing upon the stereotypes and stigma related to age, gender, and culture that must be addressed in order to reduce their increasing rate of infection.

ROLE OF STEREOTYPES

The presence of stereotypes and stigma is particularly relevant in relation to HIV/AIDS prevention and treatment among older women. Based upon the now classic work of Gordon Allport (1954), stereotypes represent static or rigid categorizations and beliefs that do not allow for individual variation or reality testing (Allport, 1954). Examples of a stereotype would include: "All Asian Americans are good at math and science" and "Old people don't use IV drugs." Such cognitive heuristics or assumptions are often employed in the presence of incomplete or contradictory information, and are more likely to be employed in decision making under conditions of time pressure, limited motivation, or stress (c.f., the Elaboration Likelihood Model; Petty & Cacioppo, 1986). Stigma, a negative social label ascribed to a individual or group, often arises as a behavioral manifestation of negative stereotypes. Current trends in U.S. culture indicate the presence of stereotypes in which older adults, and older women in particular, are viewed as too old, disinterested, unhealthy, and even unattractive to engage in sex. Such stereotypes also maintain that older men and women are highly unlikely to engage in high risk behavior for HIV, including participation in IV drug use (see Hillman & Stricker, 1998). Stigma persists toward individuals infected with HIV, particularly among older adults who may be infected (Emlet, 2006; 2008). When health care providers and older adults themselves sustain such inaccurate beliefs and negative attitudes, the results can be catastrophic.

EPIDEMIOLOGY AND UNIQUE RISKS

An examination of epidemiological data throughout the last decade reveals that older adults (again, defined here as adults over the age of 50) consistently represent between 10-20% of U.S. citizens infected with HIV or AIDS (CDC, 1997; Orel, Spence, & Steele, 2005). The CDC (2007) provides additional information that older Hispanic and African-American women are at increased risk for HIV infection, with their risk of infection ranging from 12 times higher among older African-American women and 4 times higher among older Hispanic women. In certain major metropolitan areas, including New York City, epidemiological data highlight that that significantly more older adults are affected or at risk. For example, a recent report from the New York State Department of Health AIDS Institute (Karpiak, Shippy, & Cantor, 2006) indicates that in New York City 35% of those living with HIV/AIDS are over the age of 50, and 74% of those living with HIV/AIDS are over the age of 40. Eighty percent of all new HIV/AIDS diagnoses in New York City 2007 were among older African-American and Latino women. It also is important to note that more than half (52%) of all deaths among people with HIV/AIDS in New York City were among those older adults than the age of 50. Despite these alarming statistics, no national public health messages or programs exist to address HIV/AIDS prevention or treatment among older adults (Oral, Wright, & Wagner, 2004).

Older women face unique risk factors for HIV infection in relation to both their age and their gender. With increased age, the body's immune system tends to decrease its level of functioning, making it more difficult to combat the HIV virus. Menopause itself can have a significant impact upon a woman's sexual health. With changes in estrogen production, the vaginal muscles receive less blood flow, become less elastic, and typically atrophy. Vaginal dryness may occur as there is a decrease in natural vaginal secretions. The vaginal wall also becomes thinner. All of these aforementioned factors can lead to an increase in both macro and microscopic tears in the vagina during intercourse, allowing the HIV virus increased access to the blood stream. A number of reports (e.g., Hillman, 2006; 2008; Zablotsky & Kennedy, 2003) indicate that, to complicate matters further, older women have significantly less experience with condoms when compared to their younger peers. In addition, older women and men tend to view condoms only as a means to block pregnancy, rather than as a need for HIV and STD protection. Among a sample of community living older adults, less than half believed correctly that condoms were "very effective" in preventing HIV infection. In addition, older women are less likely to ask their partner to use a condom than younger women. A variety of factors may account for this discrepancy, including an imbalance in perceived personal or power (i.e., the woman may defer emotionally to a man; the woman may be financially dependent upon her partner) and an older woman's fear of being viewed as dirty or a "hussy or loose woman" if she initiates the discussion.

Even though pervasive societal stereotypes insist that older adults are asexual, current research suggests that older adults do engage in sexual activity (Lindau, Schumm, Laumann, Levinson, O'Muircheataigh, & Waite, 2007), or wish to engage in sexual activity, with some regularity. A national study of women and men in their 70's (DeLamater & Sill, 2005) found that the majority of the older adults sampled reported moderate to high levels of interest in sexual activity. The study's findings also revealed that for those older than 70, more than half of the men and more than one fifth of the women engaged in intercourse within the past year, and nearly one fourth of those men and women reported having sex more than once a week. For older women, the presence of an available partner, not interest in sex, represents the primary predictor of sexual activity. With advancing age, the sexual response cycle and response to stimulation slows, but these typical, age-related changes do not prevent older adults from engaging in (or enjoying) sexual activity. Although older men and women report higher rates of sexual dysfunction than those in younger cohorts, most symptoms are associated with underlying health problems and medication side-effects rather than mental illness or a lack of desire (APA, 2004).

Older women also engage in high risk behaviors including IV drug use. Although older women are most likely to contract HIV via high risk heterosexual behavior, the second most commonly reported mode of transmission among members of this age group is IV drug use (Chiao, Ries, & Sande, 1999). Although the use of alcohol and non-injectable recreational drug use may not lead to immediate exposure to HIV infection, such substance use typically lowers one's inhibitions and may prevent the use of condoms in subsequent sexual activity. Consistent with this notion, research suggests that older IV drug users may engage in less risky injection practices (e.g., they may clean their needles or "works" with bleach) than their younger counterparts, they appear to engage in similar rates of high risk sexual behaviors (Kwiatkowski & Booth, 2003). Information from a recent AIDS Community Research Initiative of America study reveals that among older adults living with HIV/AIDS in New York City, 54% were in recovery from either drug or alcohol abuse, 39% reported the use of substances including alcohol and pain killers, and 16% reported that they engaged in high risk sexual behavior within the last three months (Karpiak et al, 2006). At a large HIV primary care clinic in Miami, researchers also reported that among HIV positive older adults, 20% of their sexually active participants failed to use condoms appropriately and 33% engaged in sexual activity with multiple partners (Illa et al., 2008). In other words, even among those already infected, a significant proportion of older adults can be expected to engage in various high risk activities.

HEALTH POLICY AND PROVIDERS

Stereotypes even can be inferred from our current U.S. public health policy. The newly revised CDC guidelines for routine HIV testing dictate that "all adults *up to the age of 64* should be routine tested for HIV" [italics added for emphasis]. In response, the CDC has been criticized by various individuals and groups for not mandating routine HIV testing for all older adults (Emlet, 2006; 2008; Hillman, 2008). Although not specific for HIV/AIDS testingor treatment, professional organizations in related fields (e.g., Psychology; APA, 2004) indicate that practitioners typically require specialized knowledge and skills to work effectively with older adult patients, and that advocacy may serve a particularly valuable role in the prevention and treatment of a variety of disorders affecting older adults. Tending to the unique needs of older adult minority group members also remains essential (APA, Committee on Aging, 2009) particularly in relation to the burgeoning rate of infection among older women of African-American and Hispanic descent.

Although the empirical research available is limited, it appears that health care providers possess relatively neutral attitudes toward older adults (e.g., Stewart, Eleazer, Boland, & Wieland, 2007), but remain generally unaware of the unique, increased risk factors associated with HIV/AIDS infection among older adult women. A number of reports indicate that health care providers are significantly less likely to talk to older adults with HIV/AIDS than younger adults (e.g., Skiest & Keiser, 1997). Additional biases exist in which health care providers appear significantly less likely to talk to their older female, as compared to their older male, patients about their sexual history, risk factors, and potential HIV testing (e.g., Hillman, 2008). This bias, in which health care providers fail to discuss HIV testing and risk factors with their older female patients, is particularly problematic as additional research suggests that among older adults who tested positive for HIV after the age of 50, encouragement and directives from their health care providers preceded their testing (Lekas, Schrimshaw, & Siegel, 2005).

When queried about their age and gender specific HIV/AIDS knowledge, a sample of health care providers professed limited or incorrect information. For example, only 1 in 4 knew that an older woman was at increased risk for contracting HIV (per exposure to the virus through vaginal intercourse) due to thinning of the vaginal wall and decreased vaginal secretions. Because the majority of the providers in this sample reported that they had specialized training in HIV, sexuality, or aging, it appears that the typical curriculum is devoid of age and gender specific HIV/AIDS risk factors (Hillman & Broderick, 2002). In short, older women at risk for HIV remain overlooked and ignored, within both general society and within the context of health care.

Additional barriers exist for the diagnosis of HIV among older women (as well as older men). Many of the early symptoms of HIV infection in older adults include cognitive changes (i.e., AIDS related dementia), which are often misdiagnosed as Alzheimer's Disease or "typical" aging. Additional early symptoms including fatigue and weight loss also are commonly attributed to aging (Hillman & Stricker, 1998; Whipple & Scura, 1996). Once older women receive appropriate antiviral medication, they are more likely to experience side-effects than younger women due to age-related declines in liver and immune system functioning, as well as interactions with other medications the older adult may be taking for additional concurrent or chronic medical conditions. Sadly, older adults diagnosed with HIV infection suffer increased mortality when compared to their younger peers, and are more likely to be diagnosed at a later stage of infection when HIV-related disease is already present (Skiest et al., 1996).

CULTURE SPECIFIC FACTORS

A number of culture specific factors are related to why older women are experiencing an increase in contracting HIV/AIDS. By using proper protection while engaging in sexual intercourse, individuals can decrease their chances of contracting HIV/AIDS. One popular method of protection is condoms. Although a study done by Manji, Pena, and Dubrow (2007) on adolescents in Latin America found that religious beliefs did not have an influence on one's condom use, it is possible this finding would not be generalized for the population of older women. Because of generational differences, it is more likely that the older women who are at an increased risk for contracting HIV/AIDS have been exposed to the idea that methods of birth control should not be used for religious reasons. Catholicism is one religion which discourages condom use. Unfortunately, there is a lack of data on this generation and no significant findings to support this hypothesis.

Within the population of older women, Latino older women are diagnosed with HIV/AIDS at an alarming rate. As of 2002, six percent of all Latinos with HIV/AIDS were women aged 55 or older (Beaulaurier, Craig, & Rosa, 2009). Older women of Latino cultures are often viewed as having very traditional ideas of gender roles and religion. In the realm of gender roles, Latino women are seen as dependent on male figures. A woman of this culture does not question a male, especially in relation to sexual activities. Latino women are often called promiscuous if they ask a partner to use a condom (2009). Also, gender roles inhibit Latino women of gaining education, which limits their knowledge of health and sexual education. Lack of education contributes to the notion that older Latino women often have inaccurate knowledge of HIV/AIDS (Gonzalez, Hendriksen, Collins, Duran, & Safren, 2009; Hillman, 2008). A study done by Hillman (2008) found that half of its Latino participants were unaware that HIV could be passed through vaginal, anal, and oral sex. Results from this study also found that older women are unaware that they are at a greater risk for contract HIV/AIDS (2008).

Another specific culture factor which can contribute to increased transmission of HIV/AIDS is machismo, a male trait in Latino cultures. Machismo is used to define a man who possesses certain traits, good and bad. Examples of machismo include being a provider, strength, dominance, and engaging in frequent sexual activity. Latino men, even those who are married, are likely to have more than one partner at a time (Beaulaurier, Craig, & Rosa, 2009); Gonzalez, Hendriksen, Collins, Duran, & Safren, 2009). When a male Latino is seen as macho, his partner is more likely to be fearful of asking him to wear a condom (Rios-Ellis, Frates, D'Anna, Dwyer, Lopez-Zetina, & Ugarte, 2008). A study done by the chapter's first author found that nearly half of the participants stated that the presence of machismo was a "barrier to condom use" and that requesting for a man to use a condom "would damage the relationship: (Hillman, 2008, p.251). In addition to the male gender role of machismo, the Latino culture also has a female gender role called marianismo. Marianismo is defined by female submission, dependence, and lack of freedom (Rios-Ellis, Frates, D'Anna, Dwyer, Lopez-Zetina, & Ugarte, 2008). Coupled with machismo, marianismo also contributes to older women's lack of condom use because this gender role does discourages questioning of the opposite sex, especially in relation to sexual activity.

African Americans and Latinos are the two ethnic groups with the highest proportion of older women diagnosed with HIV/AIDS. Over half of all women over 50 who have

HIV/AIDS are African American (Sormanti & Shibusawa, 2007). This increased incidence is thought to be because these older women are from a lower socioeconomic status, have poorer health, have poorer access to health care have higher rates of sexually transmitted infections, are more likely to underestimate their risk, and have more misinformation regarding HIV/AIDS transmission. Simply by being part of a large ethnic group with health disparities seems to increase an older women's risk of contracting HIV/AIDS.

PREVALENCE OF STIGMA

Although stigmas are present in everyday life, an older woman with HIV/AIDS will ultimately face multiple stigmas. Women are subjected to stigmas of gender, older women are often faced with sexual stigmas which claim them to be asexual, and ethnic women are additionally faced with racial stereotypes and stigmas (Collins, Unger, & Armbrister, 2008).Older women infected with HIV/AIDS are often subjected to two types of stigma: one relating to HIV and one relating to age. A study by Emlet (2006) that examined stigma felt by older adults who were HIV positive found that 68 percent of participants experience ageism and HIV stigma. Many older women are still under the assumption that homosexuals, prostitutes, and drug users are the most common individuals who pass on HIV/AIDS (Rios-Ellis, Frates, D'Anna, Dwyer, Lopez-Zetina, & Ugarte, 2008). These false beliefs cause much of the infected individual's family and friends to reject the individual with HIV/AIDS. One study found that the majority of their HIV positive participants had less social support, especially from family members (2008). Specifically, one participant stated, "They're afraid I will infect them. When they invited me for Christmas dinner, they served my food on paper plates with plastic utensils. I felt terrible" (p.454).

Stigmas in any form cause adverse effects. Stigmas related to HIV/AIDS can produce feelings of shame, guilt, fear, anger, depression, and self-loathing (Emlet, 2005). Emlet used the HIV Stigma Scale, consisting of 13 items, to measure the differences in stigma of younger and older adults. This study found that older adults scored higher on the Blaming subscale, suggesting that older adults feel blamed by others for their illness and are ashamed of having HIV/AIDS (2005). It is important for professionals in psychology to understand what effects HIV/AIDS stigmas have on older women so they can address their specific issues properly.

Race can also increase the amount of stigma an older woman with HIV/AIDS is subjected to. Emlet (2008) found that, although gender did not have a significant impact on HIV stigma, race did have a significant impact. Specifically, African Americans had higher scores than whites on all of the stigma subscales including those which measured consequences of others knowing one's HIV status, disclosure, negative self-image, and public attitudes.

RECOMMENDATIONS

Understanding the specific stereotypes older women face is the first step in conquering the growing number of older women infected with HIV/AIDS. Older women are not asexual, and on the contrary, often engage in risk-taking behaviors related to sexual activity well into late adulthood. Older women also are less experienced with condoms and have a number of culture-specific factors which account for their sexual behaviors. It is of the utmost importance that healthcare providers begin to realize the error of their previous ways. Education which teaches healthcare providers about older women's increased risk for contracting HIV/AIDS and about older women's sexuality is critical.

Upon intake, healthcare professionals must become more comfortable asking about clients' sexual health and risky behaviors. Professionals need ask about an older woman's current sexual behavior, sexual history, change in sexual desire, and prevalence of sexual problems. Lindau, Leitsch, Lundberg, and Jerome (2006) explored older women's sexual activity and found that only a little over half of their participants' physicians discussed sex with them after turning 60. Additionally, healthcare providers must begin testing older adults, especially older women, for HIV/AIDS. Studies have found that only a mere 25 percent of older adults between 55 and 64 have been tested for HIV/AIDS (Beaulaurier, Craig, & Rosa, 2009). Also, it is important for older women to be asked about any use of recreational drugs, blood products, and any history of care giving for others with HIV/AIDS. By covering the many facets of older women's health and sexuality, healthcare professionals will be able to test and treat older women with HIV/AIDS more effectively.

There are many barriers to assessing older adults' sexual health. Often, physicians do not have the knowledge of the sexuality of older adults, are ageist to the older population, and respond negatively to exploring the sexuality of older adults (Hillman & Stricker, 1998). Professionals should create a safe environment by explaining to older women the issues of confidentiality and normalizing the experience. Wording questions in a positive manner that suggests others have engaged in the same behaviors (e.g. stating "Other women often do not feel that it is necessary to wear condoms during sexual activity because they can no longer get pregnant. Could you tell me about your experience with condoms during sex?). The PLISSIT model has been identified as a useful tool in sex therapy and can be used to assess older adults' sexual health (Stahmann, 1997). The PLISSIT model works in four steps: 'P' allows the professional to obtain permission for the client; 'LI' provides limited information to the client related to his or her sexual functioning; 'SS' gives specific suggestions related to the sexual problem; and 'IT' provides intensive therapy surrounding issues of sexual counseling. By using parts, or all, of this model, physicians and therapists can become more comfortable when asking an older client about her sexual activity. Stahmann also suggests providing a beginning step of 'EX,' or providing an expectation about the therapy (1997).

Older women with HIV/AIDS can be greatly helped through psychotherapy. The diagnosis of HIV/AIDS is one that does not provide an individual with any hope for recovery, especially if this individual is an older woman. When treating older women with HIV/AIDS, therapists should be aware of the connection between depression and HIV (Gonzalez, Hendriksen, Collins, Duran, & Safren, 2009). Treating this depression could have very positive effects for older women's health. Cognitive-behavioral therapy, medication, and interpersonal therapy have been shown to be effective for HIV/AIDS patients, specifically in older Latino women (2009). Also, although the research is limited, there is support for the efficacy of cognitive-behavioral stress management in the treatment of HIV positive men and women.

In order to reverse the trend older women are facing in being diagnosed with HIV/AIDS, public policy changes must occur. The Center for Disease Control should make it policy for adults over age 64 to continue to be routinely tested for HIV. Physicians need to take a strong role in coaching and encouraging older women to get tested for HIV/AIDS. Although we have discussed the Latino and African American populations at length, future research and information should be gathered on older women of other minority populations such as Asian and Native American women. Additionally, national media campaigns should be created which present information related to older women and their risk for contracting HIV/AIDS. Such media campaigns should include illustrations of older women and should be available where older women may receive them privately, such as in restrooms or exam rooms. Additionally, these campaigns should be tailored to various cultures. Information should be presented in non-English languages and should display older women of various ethnic backgrounds. With rates of elderly women contracting HIV/AIDS climbing at an alarming rate, this has very much become an issue of life and death. We as a society have a lot to lose if we continue to adhere to these stereotypes of older women and their sexuality, including their participation in high risk behaviors.

REFERENCES

Administration on Aging. (2001). *Older adults and mental health: Issues and opportunities.* Department of Health and Human Services: Author.

Allport, G. (1954). *The nature of prejudice.* Cambridge, MA: Addison-Wesley.

American Psychological Association. (2004). *Guidelines for Psychological practice with older adults.* American Psychologist, 59, 236-260.

American Psychological Association, Committee on Aging. (2009). *Multicultural competency in Geropsychology.* Washington, DC: American Psychological Association.

Beaulaurier, R.L., Craig, S.L., & Mario, D.L.R. (2009). *Older Latina women and HIV/AIDS: An examination of sexuality and culture as they relate to risk and protective factors.* Journal of Gerontological Social Work, 52, 48-63.

Centers for Disease Control. (1997). *HIV/AIDS surveillance report.* 8, 15.

Centers for Disease Control (2006). *Revised recommendations for HIV testing of adults, adolescents, and pregnant women in health care.* Morbidity and Mortality Weekly Report, 55(RR-14), 1-17.

Centers for Disease Control (2007). *HIV/AIDS surveillance report,* 2005, 17, 1-54.

Centers for Disease Control (2007). *Racial/ethnic disparities in diagnosis of HIV/AIDS—33 states, 2001-2005.* Morbidity and Mortality Weekly Report, 56, 183-193.

Chiao, E. Y., Ries, K. M., & Sande, M. A. (1999). *AIDS and the elderly.* Clinical Infectious Diseases, 28, 740-745.

Collins, P. Y., Unger, von. H., Armbrister, A. (2008). *Church ladies, good girls, and locas: Stigma and the intersection of gender, ethnicity, mental illness, and sexuality in relation to HIV risk.* Social Science and Medicine, 67, 389-397.

DeLamater, J. D., & Sill, M. (2005). *Sexual desire in later life.* Journal of Sex Research, 42, 138-149.

Emlet, C.A. (2005). *Measuring stigma in older and younger adults with HIV/AIDS: An analysis of an HIV stigma scale and initial exploration for subscales.* Research on Social Work Practice, 15, 291-300.

Emlet, C.A. (2006). *"You're awfully old to have this disease": Experiences of stigma and ageism in adults 50 years and older living with HIV/AIDS.* The Gerontologist, 46, 781-790.

Emlet, C.A. (2008). *Experiences of stigma in older adults living with HIV/AIDS: A mixed-method analysis.* AIDS Patient Care and STDs, 21, 740-752.

Gonzalez, J.S., Hendriksen, E.S., Collins, E.M., Duran, R.E., & Safren, S.A. (2009). *Latinos and HIV/AIDS: Examining factors related to disparity and identifying opportunities for psychosocial intervention research.* AIDS Behavior, 13, 582-602.

Hillman, J. (2007). *Knowledge and attitudes about HIV/AIDS among community-living older women: Reexaming issues of age and gender.* Journal of Women & Aging, 19, 53-67.

Hillman, J. (2008). *Knowledge, attitudes, and experience regarding HIV/AIDS among older adult inner-city Latinos.* International Journal of Aging and Human Development, 66, 243-257.

Hillman, J., & Broderick, K. (2002). *HIV among elderly women: Ignored and overlooked by health are providers and public policy makers.* In L. H. Collins, M. R. Dunlap, & J. C. Chrisler (Eds.) Charting a new course for feminist psychology (pp. 193-215). New York, NY: Praeger.

Hillman, J.L., & Stricker, G. (1998). *Some issues in the assessment of HIV among older adult patients.* Psychotherapy, 35, 483-489.

Illa, L., Brickman, A., Saint-Jean, G., Echenique, M., Metsch, L., Eisdorfer, C., Bustamante-Avellaneda, V., & Sanchez-Martinex, M. (2008). *Sexual risk behaviors in late middle age and older HIV seropositive adults.* AIDS and Behavior, 12, 935-942.

Karpiak, S. E., Shippy, R. A., & Cantor, M. H. (2006). *Research on older adults with HIV.* New York: AIDS Community Research Initiative of America.

Kwiatkowski, C. F., & Booth, R. E. (2003). *HIV risk behaviors among older American drug users.* Journal of Acquired Immune Deficiency Syndromes, 33, S68-S75.

Lekas, H, Schrimshaw, E. W., & Siegel, K. (2005*). Pathways to HIV testing among adults aged fifty and older with HIV/AIDS.* AIDS Care, 17, 674-687.

Lindau, S.T., Leitsch, S.A., Lundberg, K.L., & Jerome, J. (2006*). Older women's attitudes, behavior, and communication about sex and HIV: A community-based study.* Journal of Women's Health, 15, 747-753.

Lindau, S. T., Schumm, L. P., Laumann, E. O., Levinson, W., O'Muircheataigh, C.A., & Waite, L. J. (2007). *A study of sexuality and health among older adults in the United States.* New England Journal of Medicine, 357, 762-764.

Manji, A., Pena, R., & Dubrow, R. (2007). *Sex, condoms, gender roles, and HIV transmission knowledge among adolescents in Leon, Nicaragua: Implications for HIV prevention.* AIDS Care, 19, 989-995.

Orel, N. A., Spence, M., & Steele, J. (2005). *Getting the message out to older adults: Effective health education risk reduction publications.* Journal of Applied Gerontology, 24, 490-508.

Orel, N. A., Wright, J. M., & Wagner, J. (2004). *Scarcity of HIV/AIDS risk education materials targeting the needs of older adults among state departments of public health.* The Gerontologist, 44, 693-696.

Petty, R. E., & Cacioppo, J. T. (1986). *Attitudes and persuasion: Classic and contemporary approaches.* Dubuque, IA: Brown.

Rios-Ellis, B., Frates, J., D'Anna, L.H., Dwyer, M., Lopez-Zetina, J., & Ugarte, C. (2008). *Addressing the need for access to culturally and linguistically appropriate HIV/AIDS prevention for Latinos.* Journal of Immigrant Minority Health, 10, 445-460.

Skiest, D. J., & Keiser, P. (1997). *Human immunodeficiency virus infection in patients older than 50 years. A survey of primary care physicians' beliefs, practices, and knowledge.* Archives of Family Medicine, 6, 289-294.

Skiest, D. J., Rubinstien, E., Carley, N., Gioiella, L, & Lyons, R. (1996). *The importance of comorbidity in HIV-infected patients over 55: A retrospective case-control study.* American Journal of Medicine, 101, 605-611.

Sormanti, M. & Shibusawa, T. (2007). *Predictors of condom use and HIV testing among midlife and older women seeking medical services.* Journal of Aging and Health, 19, 705-719.

Stahmann, R.F. (1997). *Therapists must be EXPLISSIT.* Journal of Family Psychotherapy, 8, 67-70.

Stewart, T. J., Eleazer, G. P., Boland, R., & Wieland, G. D. (2007). *The middle of the road: Results from the Aging Semantic Differential with four cohorts of medical students.* Journal of the American Geriatric Society, 55, 1275-1280.

Whipple, B., & Scura, K. W. (1996). *The overlooked epidemic: HIV in older adults.* American Journal of Nursing, 96, 22-28.

Zablotsky, D., & Kennedy, M. (2003). *Risk factors and HIV transmission to midlife and older women: Knowledge, options, and the initiation of safer sexual practices.* Journal of Acquired Immune Deficiency Syndrome, 33, S122-130.

In: Psychology of Stereotypes
Editor: Eleanor L. Simon

ISBN: 978-1-61761-463-7
©2011 Nova Science Publishers, Inc.

Chapter 16

AN ANALYSIS OF RESPONSE TIME CHARACTERISTICS WITH STRENGTH AND REVERSIBILITY OF STEREOTYPES FOR DETERMINING OPTIMUM CONTROL POSITION ON A HORIZONTAL DISPLAY

Alan H.S. Chan[*]

City University of Hong Kong, China

ABSTRACT

In this paper, the effects of few design parameters on human performancefor a common horizontal display/rotary control arrangement wereexamined. The results showed that the knob position, pointer type, and scale side and in particular the control position x scale side interaction significantly affectedhuman response time. Response time was found to decrease with increasing values of stereotype proportion and index of stereotype reversibility, andthe extents of decrease were different for the top and bottom controls. Based on the consideration of response time and stereotype characteristics, the optimum location for positioning a rotary control on a horizontal scale was found.

Keywords: human machine interaction, man-machine interface, compatibility

I. INTRODUCTION

The relationship between a control movement and its effect most expected by a population is known as a population stereotype, and such a relationship is said to be compatible. Design of a control and display configuration should conform to the expectations of relevant user population for reduction of human error and response time required. The

---

[*] Phone: 2788 8439; E-mail: alan.chan@cityu.edu.hk.

central concept in human factors practice is 'compatibility'. It was suggested that even after extensive practice with a noncompatible relationship it is unlikely that someone will achieve the performancelevel which is achieved with a compatible arrangement.Also there may be a tendency to regress to the compatible relationship especially under stressful circumstances.

Good display/control compatibility is usually reflected by a strong stereotype strength and short response time.The strength of a stereotype has been measured in terms of the majority proportion of responses ($\geq$ 50%) for a test condition; a value of 50% indicates no choice preference while a value of 100% indicates a perfect stereotype. Apart from stereotype strength, reversibility of stereotypes is another important factor in interface design for consideration for improved human performance [1]. A 'reversible stereotype' is one where, for example, if turning a rotary knob clockwise is expected to move a circular display pointer clockwise (CC responses), then turning the knob anticlockwise is expected to move the pointer anticlockwise (AA responses). Stereotypes are not always reversible and an index of reversibility (IR) has been calculated from the sum of the product of the proportions of AA and CC responses, and the product of the proportions of AC (anticlockwise response for clockwise instruction) and CA (clockwise response for anticlockwise instruction) responses [2]. The index may range from zero for absolute non-reversibility, to one for perfect reversibility where the response for clockwise pointer movement is opposite to the response anticlockwise pointer movement.It is noted that a person's expectation is 'reversible' cannot be safely assumed. The existence of stereotype reversibility is obviously very important when considering population stereotypes and designers of man machine interfaces should use stereotype with reasonable degree of reversibility to reduce confusion and enhance efficiency and safety in industrial systems.

Recently, directions of motion stereotypes for different arrangements of control and display have been extensively studied. In the studies of stereotypes for linear display with rotary control, four major principles have been proposed and verified. They are the 'clockwise-for-right (CR)' principle, 'clockwise-for-increase (CI)' principle [3], Warrick's principle [4], and the scale-side principle [5]. The Warrick's principle states that the pointer on a linear display will move in the same direction as that side of the control which is nearest to it. Obviously this principle only applies when the rotary control is positioned on the sides of the display and it does not apply when the control is located at the ends of the display.

For a configuration of rotary control and horizontal display, Chan et al.[6] analysed the validity of the above four principles and examinedthe effects and interactions of design factors like control position, scale-side, and pointer type on the stereotype strength, stereotype reversibility, and human response time. It was done for investigating the relationships amongst the human response measures and their implications on compatibility between individual control positions and the display. They had examined the relationship of different types of stereotypes with response time. But the variation patterns of the stereotype characteristics across different positions were not shown, and the interaction effects of scale side and control position were not well illustrated. In this paper, the data of the study was reanalyzed to establish the quantitative relationship between the response time and stereotype strength and stereotype reversibility,which will be separately done for different groupings of control positions. Graphical illustration of scale side and control positionwill also be prepared for exploring. All these should be helpful in confirming the validity of determination of optimum control position for the rotary knob and horizontal display configuration.

II. DESIGN OF EXPERIMENT

Two pointer types (directional and neutral), two scale sides (top and bottom) and eight control knob locations were examined in the study (Figure 1). A three-factor general factorial design with 32 runs was used to examine the effects and interactions of these three factors on response preference and speed. Each run of conditions was tested two times for each subject. For each test, a pointer was shown in the middle position of the linear scale. The destination position was 10 mm to the left or right of the pointer. Subjects were required to turn the rotary control either clockwise or counterclockwise to move the central pointer to the target position immediately after the target position was shown.

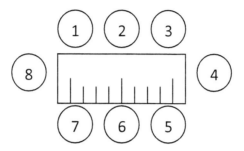

Figure 1. Different control knob positions tested in the study.

III. METHOD AND PROCEDURE

Forty-two Chinese right-handers of ages ranging from 19 to 29 participated in the experiment. All subjects were volunteer engineering students and they were all right-handed and manipulated the controls with their right hands. The display was always shown directly in front of subjects in the frontal plane. There were eight different control knobs located in different positions of the control panel for testing. The response preferences and response times of the subjects towards the instructions were collected for analysis. A comprehensive set of instructions and a two-minute practice were given to the subjects before the test of each stimulus condition. They were told that there were no definite answers and they just had to rotate the control in the anticlockwise or clockwise direction to move the pointer to the destination mark in response to the instructed direction of movement of the pointer. The pointer on the display always moved to the target direction independent of subjects' choice of knob movement. The subjects initiated and paced presentations themselves. The time between the showing of the instruction of pointer movement direction and subject's triggering the control was recorded as the response time.

IV. RESULTS

A. Response Time

The results showed that responses for the bottom scale and directional pointer were shorter. Amongst the three two-way interactions, only the scale side x control position interaction was significant ($p < 0.0001$) (Figure 2).

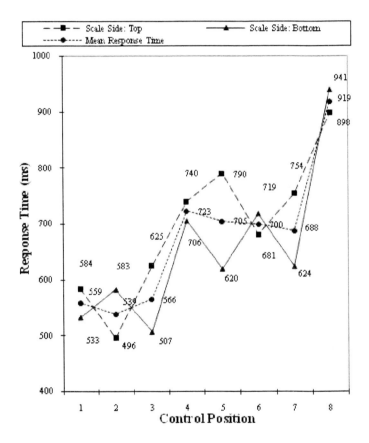

Figure 2. The interaction plot of scale side × control position on mean response time.

B. Response Preference

The majority of responses ($\geq 50\%$) for a testing condition is a traditional measure of the strength of stereotype. In this study, for quantifying the stereotype of subjects' responses towards the two instructions of moving the pointer rightwards and leftwards, two stereotype strength values, viz. S_{CW-R} (stereotype strength of clockwise response for right) and S_{CC-L} (stereotype strength of counterclockwise response for left) were defined. S_{CW-R} is the ratio of the difference of proportion of clockwise response for right and the no choice preference (0.5) to the no choice preference, while S_{CC-L} is the ratio of the difference of the proportion of counterclockwise response for left and the no choice preference to the no choice preference. With these definitions, a strength value of zero indicates chance selection of response direction and hence a lack of a movement stereotype, while a strong stereotyped response is reflected by a strength value approaching unity. The S_{CW-R} and S_{CC-L} values were calculated for all test runs. The stereotype strength was found ranging from 0% to 80%, with a mean of 43%, and the standard deviation was 30%.An analysis of variance performed on the strength values unveiled significance of the main factors of direction of instruction ($p< 0.0001$), but the control position was not significant ($p> 0.05$).

C. Index of Reversibility

For investigating the reversibility of stereotypes, the values of IR values were computed from the sum of two cross products in this study. One product was derived from the proportion of counterclockwise response for towards left instruction and the proportion of clockwise response for towards right instruction. The other product was derived from the proportion of clockwise response for towards left instruction and the proportion of counterclockwise response for towards right instruction. It was found that the *IR* values increased from the left end control position, bottom left corner, top right corner, middle positions, top left corner, bottom right corner, to the right end position of the display, giving a minimum and maximum value of 50.84% and 55.91% at positions 8 and 4, respectively. The average IR for all the eight control positions was low at 53.88%. The patterns of increase of stereotype strength and reversibility amongst the eight control positions are illustrated in Figure 3-4. They were found to exhibit similar trends of increase along the control positions.

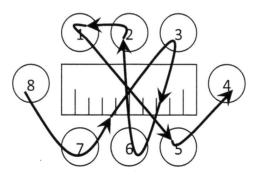

Figure 3. Path of increasing values of index of reversibility.

An analysis of variance on the IR values was conducted and the results were similar to those for the response times that all the main factors of pointer type, scale side, and control position, and the scale side x control position interaction were significant.

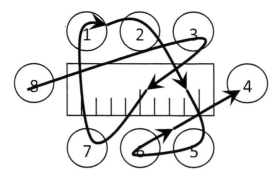

Figure 4. Path of increasing values of overall strength of stereotype.

V. DISCUSSION

The results showed that shorter response times were obtained when a bottom scale was used. The subjects also performed faster for both scale sides with a directional pointer. A directional pointer is thus more desirable for shorter response time and shows robustness towards scale side effect. Amongst the eight control positions, the shortest response time was obtained at the top middle position 2 and the longest one at the left end position 8. The results of Duncan's test for pairwise comparisonsof the response times of the eight control positions showed that the top three control positions formed the shortest response time group and the left end position formed the longest response time group, while the others formed the group with medium response times.

For more detailed understanding of the effects of pointer type and scale side, the interactions of pointer type x control position and scale side x control position were examined. The results indicated that the mean response times for the top and bottom scale sides were different at different control positions. Duncan's test showed that in general there was no significant difference in response times for the two scale sides ($p > 0.05$) amongst all control positions, but the mean response times were significantly smaller ($p < 0.05$) for bottom scale side at control positions 3, 5, and 7. Therefore, as far as response time is concerned, bottom scale side is preferable at control positions 3, 5, 7, and consideration of scale side is trivial if the control is located at other positions.

Although the pointer type x control position interaction was non-significant, Duncan's test detected significant difference in mean response time between the two pointer types at positions 5, 7 and 8 ($p < 0.05$) while the two types of pointers gave statistically equal response times at all other positions. Therefore, a directional pointer and bottom scale side are preferable for all control positions for faster response.

Figure 3 unveils a parallel between the stereotype strength and index of reversibility across the control positions. It shows that control positions with higher strength of stereotype also gave higher reversibility. In fact, the IR is composed of the two stereotype strengths mentioned earlier, S_{CW-R} and S_{CC-L} by the expression:

$$IR = \frac{1 + S_{CW-R} \times S_{CC-L}}{2} \qquad \text{whereas} \qquad 0.5 \leq IR \leq 1 \qquad (1)$$

The results showed that stronger S_{CW-R} over S_{CC-L} was found for all control positions. Duncan's test further confirmed that the paired differences between S_{CC-L} and S_{CW-R} were all significant ($p < 0.05$) at all control knob positions. Testing with controls at the two ends of a horizontal display with no scales, Loveless [10] had shown that a clockwise movement of the control drove the pointer rightwards but no test on counterclockwise movement for left pointer movement was conducted. A pairwise comparison of the mean IR values for the eight control positions was then performed with the Duncan's test. Significant difference was identified only between the pairs of (4,8) and (5,8), suggesting that based on the magnitudes of IR, it was noted that the reversibility of the 'clockwise-for-right' and 'counterclockwise-for-left' response stereotypes was enhanced at control positions 4 and 5 and they are more preferable than other control positions. With the additional consideration of the response time effects, position 4 offers the flexibility of using either scale side and pointer type for optimized response time and stereotype reversibility. However, control position 5 is more preferable for faster response due to the compatibility between the Warrick's principle and the CR principle. If control position 5 is chosen, a directional pointer with scale at the bottom should always be chosen for optimum overall human performance.

The eight positions could be divided into two groups according to their conformance with the clockwise for right and Warrick's principle. One group includes the bottom positions at which the two principles are compatible with each other. The other group include the top three positions and the two end positions, at which the two principles are non-compatible or non applicable. The S_{CW-R} values and corresponding response times for various control positions are shown in Figure 5(a). For these two groups of positions, the response time was found to have no relationship with S_{CW-R} at compatible positions on line ① but decrease with S_{CW-R} at non-compatible positions on line ②. This suggested that the CR principle is not the dominating factor affecting response time at positions where the Warrick's principle is also valid. When the Warrick's principle conflicts with the CR principle, S_{CW-R} influences human responses and reduces response time. The S_{CC-L} values and corresponding response times are shown in Figure 5(b). Interestingly, response time was also found significantly related with S_{CC-L} for bottom control positions as shown by the regression line (③). The negative slope of line ③ showed that higher S_{CC-L} values resulted in shorter response time at compatible positions. That is, response time decreased not only with the strength of S_{CC-R} at non-compatible positions, but also with the strength of S_{CC-L} at bottom positions on which the S_{CC-L} agrees with the Warrick's principle.

A comparison of the two regression lines (② and ④) of Figure 5 (a) and (b) for the top and end positions indicated that response time decreased with both S_{CW-R} and S_{CC-L}, but the reducing effect (slope) of S_{CW-R} on response time was about 3.3 times of that of S_{CC-L}. Therefore, the influence of S_{CW-R} on response time was stronger than that of S_{CC-L}. A comparison of the slopes of the lines ③ and ④ showed that at the non-compatible positions, the reducing effect of S_{CC-L} was 1.4 times of that at compatible positions. The precise analysis of S_{CC-L} and S_{CW-R} on response time with horizontal display of this kind was not done in previous studies[7-9] in which only the S_{CW-R} was considered. Moreover, it was noted that the effect of S_{CC-L} increased starting from left end position, through the middle positions, and reached its maximum at right end position in a way similar to the overall strength of stereotype shown in Figure 4. For the index of reversibility, it was found that response time generally decreased with increasing value of IR (Figure 6).

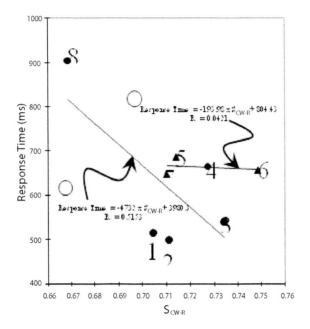

Figure 5(a). S_{CW-R} and corresponding response time at various control positions; line ① (▲) for compatible positions, and line ② (●) for non-compatible positions.

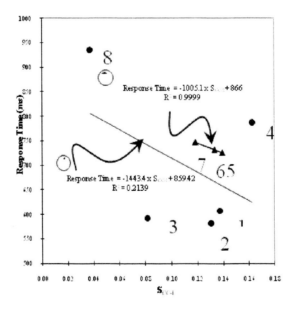

Figure 5(b). S_{CC-L} and corresponding response time at various control positions; line ③ (▲) for compatible positions, and line ④ (●)for non-compatible positions.

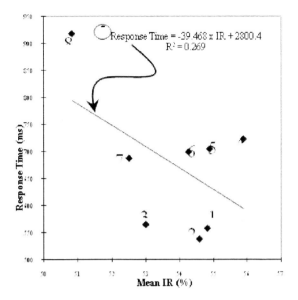

Figure 6. Relationship between response time and IR atvarious control positions.

VI. CONCLUSION

The linear display with rotary control type is commonly used in human machine interfaces. The effect of few selected design features of scale side, indicator type, and control knob position on the strength of stereotype, index of reversibility, and response time for a horizontal display/rotary control arrangement was examined in this study. Based on the consideration of response time, stereotype strength, and stereotype reversibility, the results of this study established the optimum location for positioning a rotary control on a horizontal scale. The results should help industrial designers to develop effective interfaces and improve overall system design and performance.

ACKNOWLEDGMENTS

The work described in this paper was fully supported by a grant from the Research Grants Council of the Hong Kong Special Administrative Region, China (Project No. CityU 110306).

REFERENCES

[1]   Chan, A.H.S. and Courtney, A.J., *Testing Reversibility of Population Stereotypes, Proceedings of 1999* International Symposium on Ergonomics and Conference of Ergonomics Society of Korea, p.387-393 (1999).

[2]   Chan, A.H.S. and Chan, W.H., *Movement compatibility for rotary control and circular display-computer simulated test and real hardware test*, Applied Ergonomics,**34**, p.61–67 (2003).

[3]   Loveless, N.E., *The effect of the relative position of control and display upon their direction-of-motion relationship,* Ergonomics, 2, p.381–385 (1959).

[4]   Warrick, M.J., *Direction of movement in the use of control knobs to position visual indicators*, USAF AMC Report No. 694-4C. (1947).

[5]   Petropoulos, H. and Brebner, J., *Stereotypes for direction-of-movement of rotary controls associated with linear displays: the effects of scale presence and position, of pointer direction, and distances between the control and the display*, Ergonomics, 24, p.143-151 (1981).

[6]   Chan, A.H.S., Shum, V.W.Y., Law, H.W. and Hui, I.K., *Precise effects of control position, indicator type, and scale side on human performance*, International Journal of Advanced Manufacturing Technology, 22, p.380-386 (2003).

[7]   Courtney, A.J.,*Hong Kong Chinese direction-of-motion stereotypes*, Ergonomics, 37(3), p.417-426 (1994a).

[8]   Courtney, A.J., *The effect of scale-side, indicator type, and control plane on direction-of-turn stereotypes for Hong Kong Chinese subjects*, Ergonomics, 37(5), p.865–877 (1994b).

[9]   Hoffmann, E., *Strength of component principles determining direction–of–turn stereotypes – linear displays with rotary controls*, Ergonomics, 40(2), p.199–222 (1997).

[10] Loveless, N.E., *Direction of motion stereotypes: A review*, Ergonomics, 5, p.357–383 (1962).

In: Psychology of Stereotypes
Editor: Eleanor L. Simon

ISBN: 978-1-61761-463-7
©2011 Nova Science Publishers, Inc.

Chapter 17

A FRENCHMAN, AN ENGLISHMAN, AND A GERMAN…STEREOTYPES IN HUMOROUS TEXTS

Arthur Asa Berger

118 Peralta Avenue, Mill Valley, CA94941, USA, Tel: (415) 383-2999, E-mail
arthurasaberger@gmail.com

Stereotypes are conventionally understood to be generalizations about the behavior and characteristics of some group of people--based on race, nationality, ethnicity, religion, occupation, gender, and so on. Stereotypes can be negative, neutral, positive, or mixed. Some common stereotypes are that women are lousy drivers, Jews are cheap, Scots are thrifty, British people are snobs, and that Japanese are honest. The negative stereotype of the Japanese is that are also robotic and a bit fanatic. Stereotypes generally involve people characterizing some group on the basis of a limited experience with a relatively small number of representatives of that group. But in many cases, stereotypes are learned, from exposure to stereotypes found in the media and carried in jokes and other forms of humor.

Statistically speaking, stereotypes are overgeneralizations based on sampling errors— assuming that all members of some group are like some of the members of the group—the one that has been "sampled" either in person or carried in the media. From a semiotic perspective, stereotypes involve a process known as synecdoche, which can be defined as "a part that stands for the whole" or vice versa. Thus, the Pentagon "stands for" the United States military establishment and Uncle Sam "stands for "America." Synecdoche is a weak for of metonymy, which involves communication by association. Metonymy, along with metaphor, pervades our use of language and is often found in advertising, where associations are quick ways of providing people exposed to the advertising with reference points and information they already have that can be used to sell products and service.

Stereotypes are often used in formulaic genres that rely on stereotypes to suggest character types and personalities. These stereotypes or "stock types" enable audiences of these texts (the term used in academic jargon for works of all kinds, and in this case, riddles, jokes and other kinds of humor) to quickly come to conclusions about various characters and means that the writers of these texts do not have to spend time in these texts developing and establishing their characters. Thus, if a script writer needs a gangster, making that character an Italian, to tie in with all the news in the media about the mafia in Italy, is an understandable choice. What we are dealing with is "types" of people. Henri Bergson wrote that "every comic character is a *type.* Inversely, every resemblance to a type has something comic in it." (Quoted in Sypher, 1956.) These types often have fixations that drive their behavior, as we seen in plays such as Moliere's *The Misanthrope* and *The Miser.*

In my work on humor, I developed a typology that focuses on the techniques in humorous texts that generate everything from smiles to mirthful laughter. Most theories of humor attempt to explain why we laugh. The most important theories are Freud's notion that humor is based on unconscious or masked aggression, Aristotle's belief (and Hobbes) that humor is based on a sense of superiority, and Schopenhauer's belief that all humor is based on incongruity. There are many writers and humor theorists who support one of these three why theories. My work on humor doesn't' attempt to deal with why we laugh but what makes us laugh.I made an analysis of many forms of humor, such as jokes, theatrical comedies, and cartoons from texts in many different periods and came up with 45 different techniques that, I argue, inform all humor. This list is shown in the table that follows:

Table 1. The 45 Techniques of Humor.

LANGUAGE	LOGIC	IDENTITY	ACTION
Allusion	Absurdity	Before/After	Chase
Bombast	Accident	Burlesque	Slapstick
Definition	Analogy	Caricature	Speed
Exaggeration	Catalogue	Eccentricity	
Facetiousness	Coincidence	Embarrassment	
Insults	Comparison	Exposure	
Infantilism	Disappointment Grotesque		
Irony	Ignorance	Imitation	
Misunderstanding	Mistakes	Impersonation	
Over literalness	Repetition	Mimicry	
Puns/Wordplay	Reversal Parody		
Repartee	Rigidity Scale		
Ridicule	Theme/Variation	Stereotype	
Sarcasm	Unmasking		
Satire			

When I identified these techniques I had no notion that I could classify them in an interesting way, but after looking at my list of techniques, I saw that they could all fit nicely in four different categories: techniques based on language, logic, identity and action. Stereotypes are humor that involves identity. I believe that humorists use stereotypes because they provide an easy way to ridicule and make fun of or attack various kinds of targets such as politicians, professors, lawyers, doctors, women, gays (and other so-called "deviant" groups), Catholics, Jews, Muslims…you name them and there are stereotypes about them. Many of these stereotypes are extremely hostile and can have a negative affect on the members of the group being stereotyped.

We must realize that a humorous text that makes use of stereotypes also uses other techniques, so, for example, a joke using stereotypes may also have allusions, insults, and repetition in it. Let's consider some jokes, defined as short tales with punch lines that are meant to generate mirthful laughter, and other kinds of humorous texts that involve stereotypes. I will start with a classic joke about nationalities.

> The United Nations asked a number of different nationalities and ethnic groups to write books about elephants. They receive the following books. The French write a book titled "The Love Life of Elephants." The English write a book "The Elephant and English Social Classes." The Germans write a five-volume book titled "A Short Introduction to the History of the Elephant." The Italians write a book "The Elephant and the Renaissance." The Americans write a book "How to Raise Bigger and Better Elephants." And the Israelis write a book "Elephants and the Jewish Question."

This joke deals with popular stereotypes about the French (love, romance), the English (social classes), the Germans (methodological), the Italians (fixated on their history and the Renaissance), The Americans (with their passion for outdoing others), and Jews (fixated on the Jewish question). There are, I might add, many variations on this joke that include people from other countries.

A book by Alan Dundes, *Cracking Jokes: Studies of Sick Humor Cycles and Stereotypes,* offers some other examples involving nationalities. His book is one of the most sustained studies of stereotypes in humor and is full of wonderful jokes and other kinds of humor. Here are some jokes on nationalities from his book.

> Two men and a woman are shipwrecked on a desert island. If they are Spanish, the men will fight a duel and the survivor gets the girl. If French, one man becomes the husband, and the other the lover. If English, nothing will happen because no one is there to introduce them so they won't speak. If Italian, they will play cards to decide who will have the girl. If Greek, they will start fighting over politics and forget the girl. If Turks, one will have the front way and the other the back passage.

The next joke involves Germans and Russians.

> A ship goes down in the Pacific. Nobody survives except two men and a woman. They save themselves on a small island. What happens if the two men are Italian? The one murders the other in order to possess the woman for himself. If they are Frenchmen, they live peacefully a *trois*. If they are English or Germans, then the men move to another island and leave the woman alone. If they are Russians, the set a bottle afloat for Moscow for further instructions.

Dundes comments that (1987:100) "Although the basic structure of a joke may remain constant, the specific content may reveal definite character traits. These culture –specific traits are what form the essence of international slurs."

Cycles of ethnic riddles occur every once in a while that are based on stereotypes. For example, there were riddles about Polish people (dumb), Italians (lovers not fighters), and Jews (materialistic) that were popular a number of years back.

- Q. What has an IQ of 375?
- A. Poland.

- Q. Did you hear about the Polish fish?
- A. It drowned.

- Q. How do you break a Pole's finger?
- A. Punch him in the nose.

- Q. What is the gear makeup of Italian tanks?
- A. Four reverses and one forward, in case they are attacked from the rear.

- Q. How does a JAP (Jewish American Princess) get exercise?
- A. "Waitress!" (frantically waving her arms).

- Q. How does a JAP commit suicide?
- A. She piles all her clothes on top of her beds, climbs on top of them and jumps.

Freud's notion that humor involves masked aggression helps explain why these ethnic riddles and other kinds of stereotyping humor appeal to so many people and my work on techniques helps explain how these texts generate mirthful (and in some cases, not so mirthful) laughter in people. Because they are often so silly and absurd, people can tell these jokes without feeling any anxiety; the id/aggressive aspects of stereotyped humor are masked and disarm the superego/conscience elements in our psyches, which enables us to take pleasure in telling stereotyped jokes and asking riddles based on stereotypes.

We also have to recognize that there are differences in power (whether perceived or real) between those who tell the jokes with stereotyping in them and the groups that are being stereotyped. Those who tell jokes with stereotyping in them generally feel superior to those they are stereotyping, since so many stereotyped jokes and other forms involve insults and ridicule. Aristotle argued that humor involved "an imitation of men worse than average" and Hobbes wrote, in *The Leviathan,* that "The passion of laughter is nothing else but sudden glory arising from a sudden conception of some eminency in ourselves by comparison with the infirmity of others, or with our own formerly." Ethnic riddles also can be explained by incongruity theorists in that the answers to the riddle are always unexpected and incongruous. The problem with all these "why we laugh" theories about humor is that they are so broad and at such a high level of abstraction and generality that they do not provide us with an understanding of what is going on in a particular humorous text that generates humor. The proponents of humor theories also argue among themselves, generally suggesting that the other theories are actually examples of their theory. Thus, incongruity theorists argue that superiority theories and aggression theories are, in reality, kinds of incongruity.

Let me conclude with a joke about two types of stock characters: professors and farmers.

A farmer and a professor shared a seat on a train. They found it hard to converseso, to while away the time, the professor suggested they play a game of riddles for a dollar a game. "That's not fair," said the farmer. "I'll play you a dollar against your fifty cents, then," said the professor. "Okay," said the farmer. "You go first," said the professor. "What animal has three legs when it walks and two when it flies?" asked the farmer. The professor thought for a moment and then said "I give up." He handed the farmer a dollar. "What's the answer?" asked the professor. "I don't know," said the farmer, handing the professor fifty cents.

The humor in this joke comes from the stereotypes of professors as intellectual and unworldly (given, perhaps, to writing abstruse articles on humor) and farmers as shrewd and clever. In this joke, the egalitarian nature of American society affirms itself as the farmer outwits his more educated opponent, the professor. To the extent that humor involves relationships between different types of characters, we can say that stereotyping—either overtly or covertly—informs a great deal of our humor, and that it plays a major role in both spreading and reinforcing stereotypes.

REFERENCES

Berger, Arthur Asa. (1993) *An Anatomy of Humor.* New Brunswick, NJ: Transaction Publishers.

Berger, Arthur Asa. (1995) *Blind Men and Elephants: Perspectives on Humor.* New Brunswick, NJ: Transaction Publishers.

Dundes, Alan. (1984) *Cracking Jokes: Studies of Sick Humor Cycles and Stereotypes.* Berkeley, CA: Ten Speed Press.

Sypher, Wylie. ed. (1956). *Comedy.* New York: Doubleday Anchor Books.

INDEX

D

O

P